THE PERSPECTIVE
OF MORALITY

THE
PERSPECTIVE
OF
MORALITY

Philosophical Foundations of
Thomistic Virtue Ethics

Martin Rhonheimer | Translated by Gerald Malsbary

The Catholic University of America Press
Washington, DC

The original edition was published under the title
Die Perspektive der Moral: Philosophische Grundlagen der Tugendethik
© 2001 by Akademie Verlag GmbH, Berlin

Library of Congress Cataloging-in-Publication Data
Rhonheimer, Martin, 1950–
[Perspektive der Moral. English]
The perspective of morality : philosophical foundations of Thomistic virtue
ethics / Martin Rhonheimer ; translated by Gerald Malsbary.
p. cm.
Includes bibliographical references (p.   ) and indexes.
ISBN 978-0-8132-1799-4 (pbk. : alk. paper)
1. Ethics.   2. Virtue.   3. Thomas, Aquinas, Saint, 1225?–1274.   I. Title.
BJ1521.R4 2010
171'.2092—dc22
                    2010035468

Contents

Preface to the English Edition

This book was originally written in 1989. At that time, no German-language publisher was interested in the manuscript, so I used it as a basis for lectures, but also shared it with friends and some other interested groups. The first edition finally appeared in 1994—immediately after the appearance of the encyclical *Veritatis splendor*—in an Italian version entitled *La prospettiva della morale*. A slightly enlarged Spanish translation appeared in 2000. At last, in 2001, a German edition (considerably enlarged, by that time) was published by the Berlin publisher Akademie Verlag, under the original title *Die Perspektive der Moral. Philosophische Grundlagen der Tugendethik.*

The English translation now in hand is a translation of the text of this German edition, which had been significantly expanded and updated from its predecessors. This accounts especially for numerous critical exchanges with discourse-ethics as well as a more profound and detailed criticism of Kantian ethics and of utilitarian ethics, the latter representing the specific counterposition to the position represented here, that of classic virtue ethics in the tradition of Aristotle and Saint Thomas. At the same time, the German edition also includes replies to the criticisms of my own position made especially by German-speaking authors with reference to my other books *Natural Law and Practical Reason* (original German ed. *Natur als Grundlage der Moral*, 1987; English ed. 2000) and *Praktische Vernunft und Vernünftigkeit der Praxis* (1994). This English edition, which corresponds, as I said, with the German 2001 edition, has now been updated once again, although I could not take account of all the discussions and literature of the intervening years.

A few remarks about the content and the character of this book may be necessary here, especially for English-speaking readers. In contrast with other works primarily addressed to a smaller specialized audience, this book offers a systematically planned exposition of philosophical ethics in the tradition of Aristotle and Thomas Aquinas—my ethical theory, so to speak. It is, in fact, a virtue ethics. As explained in more detail in the introduction, while the book does indeed claim to be a self-standing exposition of an ethical theory, it is also intended to serve as a textbook and guide precisely because of this systematization; in this sense it has been conceived as an introduction to the study of philosophical ethics. The previous editions have already been put to much good use in this respect. This explains the occurrence of repeated passages typical of academic textbooks.

The Perspective of Morality presents, as it were, my *background theory* of ethics, on the basis of which the individual aspects of many other English language publications of mine can be better understood (especially the essays included in *The Perspective of the Acting Person: Essays in the Renewal of Thomistic Moral Philosophy,* ed. with an introduction by William F. Murphy [Washington, D.C.: The Catholic University of America Press, 2008]).

In recent years the interest not only in Aristotelian ethics but also in Thomas Aquinas and his moral theory has dramatically increased, especially in the English-speaking world. This book, purely philosophical in its method and contents, intends to contribute to this philosophical discussion, above all. I am convinced, however, that a "classically" oriented philosophical ethics like this might also be helpful for moral theologians—at least that has been my experience. And this is the case to no small degree because *The Perspective of Morality* presents, in a certain sense, an attempt to refute systematically the utilitarian, consequentialist, and proportionalist moral theories that have increasingly invaded moral theology in recent decades (a development which, as is well known, the encyclical *Veritatis splendor* sought to oppose). In relation to such theories, this book strives to elaborate the *specifically moral perspective* that such theories fundamentally lack, and which is decisive in my view not only for a criticism of those theories but also for an understanding of classical virtue ethics.

On the other hand, contemporary moral theology—and by that I mean specifically Catholic moral theology—is still in large part committed to certain modes of argumentation whose plausibility is sustained by forgetfulness of the tradition of classical virtue ethics, a tradition that was still fully present to Thomas Aquinas. Classical or, as I also like to call it, "rational" virtue ethics belongs fully to the kind of ethical theory called *ethical realism* by some Thomistic writers today. "Ethical realism" actually denominates a *meta-ethical* doctrine that holds that moral judgments can be true, that is, correspond to something real and objective in the real world, "outside" the subject. "Ethical realism" thus claims the existence of facts of value that are independent from pure conventions or subjective preferences (as, in contrast, utilitarian ethics claims). Thomists who claim to be "ethical realists" mean something similar, even though more basic (they also do not normally have "meta-ethical" concerns): they simply want to stress the dependency of morality upon ontology, of the moral order upon the order of nature, that is, of value-laden facts of being.

This is why, as I said, classical, or "rational," virtue ethics actually is a kind of "moral realism." This is because classical virtue ethics is founded on a metaphysical view of man, is embedded in an ontologically grounded anthropology, and thrives on the awareness that the human intellect, and thus the practical intellect, is capable of grasping a truth that does not depend on subjective preferences but is rooted in value-laden being. At the same time, classical virtue ethics avoids the error of certain varieties of current Thomistic "ethical realism": the error of considering the realistic character of morality to be sufficiently established through the assertion of an ontological foundation and the demonstration of morally relevant natural teleologies, and then identifying the morally good with the ontological good or deriving it immediately therefrom. I have long been concerned to point out that just such a narrow conception—sometimes called "physicalism" or "naturalism"—actually shares the blame for the emergence within Catholic moral theology of revisionistic ethical theories such as so-called proportionalism. In their concern to locate the foundation of the moral good in the being of man and his nature, the, as it were, "naturalistic school of ethical realism" misses the truth that is so essential for classical metaphysics that both "being" and "good" are spoken of with different meanings.

Let me comment on this briefly because it is crucial for correctly understanding the way the order of being and the moral order are connected and how this connection can be *known* and moral norms be derived from this knowledge: whereas *in God* essential being and its corresponding goodness (on the one hand) and moral perfection and its corresponding goodness (on the other) are identical, *in man* this is not the case: as Thomas explains in the famous fifth article of the twenty-first question of *De Veritate*, man in his essential being or in his nature is good only in an accidental sense; substantial moral goodness in the case of man is a perfection that is *added* to this essence. Even an immoral, say, an unjust man, is "good" insofar as he exists, but this goodness is not moral goodness, but only that which he has simply because he is a human being (i.e., on the basis of his essence, his being, his nature). Being *morally* good, by contrast, is something that comes in addition to the essential being, and transcends the ontological being of nature. Only the "good" that we call *moral* good is good simply and, as Aquinas puts it, in an "absolute" sense. The substantial being of man, however—the good, that is, that corresponds to his substantial or natural being—is only "good" in an unspecific and accidental sense. The moral good, the good in the real, "absolute" sense, is, as Thomas says, "added to being through the virtues."

Consequently the moral good cannot simply be reduced to, or be identified with, the ontological good—that can only happen in the case of God. That being and good are convertible, that every form of the good is also a form of being (and vice versa), does not in any way necessitate the reduction of the *moral* being and the *moral* good of man to *ontological* structures and *natural* teleologies, nor does it call for an attempt simply to derive good from being, *without any further mediation on the part of reason*. For Aquinas, reason is the principle of order and the measure of *moral* teleology and goodness: it is precisely the mediation by reason—and the argumentative reconstruction of such mediation in ethical discourse—that forms the theme of an ethical theory based on the normative relevance of nature in the way of classical virtue ethics. To a large extent, this is also the subject matter of *The Perspective of Morality*.

According to classical—rational—virtue ethics as I try to retrieve it in the present book, moral virtue is the unfolding and perfection of nature, and thereby really "human nature" in the fullest sense of the word. This unfolding is essentially a work of reason and the reason-informed will. The virtuous, Aristotle says, live *kata logon*, "according to reason." Moral virtue can therefore not simply be derived from mere nature; instead, human nature can only be recognized in the light of its completion, or virtue. And virtue cannot be known unless we come to know the order of reason, which, in addition and in a higher perspective, is an order of love (because moral goodness is essentially a property of the will and every kind of willing is a kind of loving). That we have to come to understand nature on the basis of its perfection, and not the other way round, corresponds to a general principle of classical epistemology and is perhaps one of the most fundamental Thomistic principles: we know of powers or faculties from their operations—the perfections of these powers—and not vice versa. We cannot derive acts from the potencies they actualize; rather, we understand the nature of a potency through its corresponding act or perfection. Therefore a virtue ethics needs both an anthropological-metaphysical *and* an epistemological foundation: a theory of practical reason, that is, that points out for us the way to knowing the "good for man" and thus for what is natural to him. The two elements go hand-in-hand and are mutually complementary. Ethics and anthropology are inseparably connected. This leads at one and the same time to a consistent and morally relevant view of human nature and to the principles of an ethical action and decision theory. This is exactly the service that philosophy can render to moral theology, a service requested by Pope John Paul II in the following words of *Fides et ratio:* "moral theology requires a sound philosophical vision of human nature and society, as well as of the general principles of ethical decision-making" (68).

Unfortunately there are proponents of "ethical realism" who make an appeal to human nature but are scarcely (or not at all) aware of the necessity for the contextualization of ethical realism and its *ontological* claims within an equally realistic ethical *epistemology*. At the same time, they sometimes happen to attack those who do concern themselves with such questions, and accuse them of neglecting the fundamental convertibility of good with being, of betraying ethical realism, and even of being infected with the virus of Kantianism. Such—I regret to say—epistemologically uninformed and, as it were, methodologically deficient ethical realists fail to recognize the fundamental intention of an ethical epistemology that is in fact anthropologically grounded. They especially criticize the doctrine (which I maintain) that moral good (and its opposite) are *originally* and *in a fundamental sense* the object—*qua* principles—of practical and not theoretical reason (as Thomas Aquinas himself also clearly states not only in his *Summa Theologiae* but also in other, less known writings as, e.g., *De virtutibus in communi*, q. un., a. 8), and they disregard that it is in fact these *practical* principles—the principles of natural law—that open up to us the way to a deeper knowledge of human nature and to an adequate anthropology. This genuinely Thomistic doctrine is reformulated by its critics in a distorted or hair-splitting way, and then pilloried in this disguised appearance as "Kantian." I hope that this book can contribute to the dissipation of such misunderstandings and misinterpretations by reconciling those who are trying to defend Thomistic orthodoxy and by suggesting a broader path and a more up-to-date basis for the many efforts being made today on behalf of a true ethical realism in the Aristotelian and Thomistic tradition. I am convinced that for the modern Thomist it is not enough simply to limit oneself to recovering what Thomas taught; he should also attempt to philosophize *with* him and in his spirit, and when necessary go beyond him. It seems only right and just that the principle that Thomas himself honored should be applied to our approach to him—and I refer here to what he famously wrote in his Commentary on the Aristotelian *De Caelo et Mundo* (lib. 1, lectio 22, nr. 8): "the study of philosophy is not meant for discovering what people think, but for discovering what is true."[1] We honor Aquinas and the truth-containing character of his moral theory—and show ourselves to be real Thomists—precisely when we not only engage in a historically correct exegesis of what he actually said, but also when we try to develop the implications of his doctrine in a broader and more up-to-date perspective.

Before closing, brief mention must be made of some important philosophical works that appeared subsequent to the German edition of *The Perspective of Morality,* and could not be taken into account as fully as they deserve in

---

1. *Studium philosophiae non est ad hoc quod sciatur quid homines senserint, sed qualiter se habeat veritas rerum.*

the English translation. First, Steven J. Jensen's *Good and Evil Actions* (2010) is most valuable for its awareness of the importance of reason in the moral specification of human acts. Contemporary Thomistic ethicists frequently overlook this important feature of Thomas's treatment of the morality of human acts, a feature central to my own understanding of Thomistic virtue ethics. Apart from some important details, Jensen's views and my own are much more complementary than in disagreement, and I hope that *The Perspective of Morality* will help to remove much of that disagreement. Similarly, I could only include a very few references to Joseph Pilsner's *The Specification of Human Actions in St. Thomas Aquinas* (2006). This book is unique for its thoughtful consideration of a large amount of textual evidence, and shows the richness and complexity of Aquinas's moral thinking, as well as the frequent ambiguity of his terminology. While Pilsner's analysis and interpretation offers a very useful account of the single elements of Thomas's theory, it still lacks a general picture, a lack that appears to me to be due to a neglect of Aquinas's "background theory" of practical reason and especially of natural law. This theory, I want to show, is grounded in an Aristotelian conception of ethics. Steven A. Long's succinct treatise *The Teleological Grammar of the Moral Act* (2007) deserves a more detailed critical treatment than can be offered here. Long's approach is not complementary to mine, but different: intelligent and sophisticated, but nevertheless centered in what I would consider a questionable interpretation of some texts of Aquinas. Lacking here, too, unfortunately, is a background theory of practical reason, especially of natural law (which contains the principles of practical reason). To make morality exclusively dependent on natural teleology, as Long suggests, seems to me to be an idea alien to Aquinas, who so constantly emphasizes the importance of reason as the measure and rule of morality. Finally, Kevin L. Flannery's important book *Acts amid Precepts* which appeared in the same year (2001) as the German version of *The Perspective of Morality* (for which Flannery wrote an extended review in the journal *Gregorianum* 83 [2002]: 591–94), seems to me to support several key points of my own reading of Aquinas and Aristotle: the parallelism of theoretical and practical reason; the autonomous intelligibility of ethics as practical science (i.e., its nonderivability from metaphysics); the doctrine that the will never operates independently of the intellect, and therefore that a person cannot will something without previously understanding what he or she is objectively doing; and finally the crucial idea that freedom is intrinsically linked to, and rooted in, rationality. The reader will easily recognize the sections of *The Perspective of Morality* to which these key insights of Flannery's book are relevant, and might serve both to deepen and correct. On the other hand, because Flannery has offered some critical objections to my views in his above-mentioned review of the German edition of *The Perspective of Morality*, I have tried to respond to these in chapter 8 of my *The Perspective of the Acting Person*.

It only remains for me to express my heartfelt thanks above all to Gerald Malsbary for his sensitive and congenial translation of the German original. His work is admirable—especially in its concern for technical details. I would also like to thank him for some stimulating suggestions concerning content that have helped improve the text. Thanks are extended as well to the Catholic University of America Press for its efforts in producing a quality edition. Finally, I would like to express my heartfelt thanks to the Knights of Columbus, without whose financial support this translation would never have been possible.

THE PERSPECTIVE
OF MORALITY

PHILOSOPHICAL ETHICS
AS VIRTUE ETHICS

1. Classical Ethics in the Tradition of Aristotle and Thomas Aquinas

Many introductory treatments of philosophical ethics are available; the present one pursues at once a theoretical and a didactic objective. It is not intended to provide a survey of various approaches or methods of argumentation or problematic issues in the field of ethics. Nor is it intended as a history of ethics. What this book offers instead is a methodical, closely argued, step-by-step presentation of a fundamental course in philosophical ethics, while developing a systematic ethical position—an ethical theory, in fact. More precisely, it is concerned with working out the fundamental elements of a *virtue ethics* in a consistent train of thought, and in conscious contrast to a form of ethics that primarily understands itself as a discourse of justification for "moral norms."

This is a virtue ethics of a "classical" type, which reaches back to ancient tradition[1] and builds upon Thomas Aquinas in a running debate with modern moral philosophy; it can therefore also be categorized, after a fashion, as "Aristotelian." But was not Thomas a theologian? He certainly was. And consequently a moral philosophy[2] that takes its inspiration from Thomas cannot limit itself to a mere repetition or compilation of what the Parisian Master wrote some seven hundred years ago. And this applies even more in the present case, which offers a *philosophical* ethics. Although the proof that a genuine philosophical ethics can be found in Thomas the *theologian* was produced

1. For a comprehensive orientation, cf. the outstanding study by J. Annas, *The Morality of Happiness* (Oxford: Oxford University Press, 1993).
2. The concept "moral philosophy" will be used here as synonymous with "philosophical ethics" and (in case it is not immediately obvious from the context) *not* in opposition to classical appetitive or virtue ethics. "Morality," on the other hand, denotes the subject matter of ethics or moral philosophy. Sometimes, in any case, I will use the adjectives "ethical" and "moral" as synonymous, in the classical meaning of the words.

some time ago, it still requires some special effort to extract the *philosophical* method and content from the theological synthesis, granted that for Thomas the "last word" is the theological word.[3]

But what still needs to be done is to actualize this content today—to refine, complete, and develop it through the asking of new questions, with a more differentiated sense of the issues. We cannot simply "go behind" Kant, J. S. Mill, G. E. Moore, or J.-P. Sartre. If we were to attempt such a thing, we would not only be deprived of many lines of inquiry and approaches to finding solutions, we would also not be able to inspect these philosophers' arguments carefully, and when appropriate, refute them. What is needed is not a "return to Thomas" or a "return to Aristotle," but *both,* and in this way retrieve for the present day the entire tradition that takes its beginning with the Platonic Socrates, in order to have it all before us once again, and relearn much that we have possibly forgotten. Despite all the fascination with modern and contemporary moral philosophy, which is generally only a reflex of a fascination with the modern as such, and despite all the complexity of newer problems and lines of inquiry, this book was written in the conviction that an ethics of a classical type that is especially indebted to the tradition of an Aristotelianism as developed by Thomas remains decisively superior to contemporary approaches at the fundamental ethical level. The reader, of course, will have to form his own judgment on this. Whether I have actually succeeded in handling the material as it deserves in the pages that follow is another question altogether. This too must be left to the reader's judgment.

As long as we understand "Aristotelian ethics" not simply as a certain instance of ethics from history, but rather as a *type* of ethics that, although taking shape in history, by being *true* nevertheless transcends the confines of the merely historical, then it seems to me that the position of Thomas Aquinas can be described as a kind of advanced Aristotelian ethics.[4] Its basic categories have an undeniable currency and fruitfulness. That Thomistic moral philosophy is fundamentally Aristotelian and despite other far-reaching influ-

---

3. W. Kluxen, *Philosophische Ethik bei Thomas von Aquin* (Mainz: Matthias Grünewald, 1964; cited here according to the second edition, Hamburg: Meiner, 1980), was a pioneer in this regard. My own contribution to the effort can be found especially in *Natural Law and Practical Reason: A Thomist View of Moral Autonomy* (New York: Fordham University Press, 2000); *Praktische Vernunft und Vernünftigkeit der Praxis: Handlungstheorie bei Thomas von Aquin in ihrer Entstehung aus dem Problemkontext der aristotelischen Ethik* (Berlin: Akademie Verlag, 1994). A criticism of this and other attempts to find a philosophical ethics in Thomas Aquinas has been most recently expressed by D. J. M. Bradley, *Aquinas on the Twofold Human Good: Reason and Happiness in Aquinas's Moral Science* (Washington, D.C.: The Catholic University of America Press, 1997).

4. On the double meaning of the concept "Aristotelian ethics," see my treatment of this matter in *Praktische Vernunft und Vernünftigkeit der Praxis* (see previous note), 6ff.

5. On this, see the classic work by M. Wittmann, *Die Ethik des Hl. Thomas von Aquin* (Munich: M. Hueber Verlag, 1933).

ences[5] can only be adequately understood from the Aristotelian perspective has been increasingly emphasized in recent years.[6] This "Thomistic Aristotelianism" makes possible—indeed, directly requires—an engagement with Thomas today not merely from historical interest, but rather in the sense of a productive and updated appropriation that would not neglect the demands of a historically exact hermeneutic and textual interpretation. In this way the moral theory of Aristotle as further studied and transposed into another cultural context proves to be an approach that contains unexpected answers to questions discussed today: questions, that is, that are especially capable of being fruitfully developed in the context of contemporary moral-theoretical problems. Certain aspects of moral thought of decisive import in connection with questions asked today can be found in Thomas, either in statements he makes in passing, or simply as something he presupposes. And this very fact makes the study of Thomas especially attractive. In this sense, much of what the "School Thomism" of the twentieth century had often as not concealed has been brought to light once again only in recent years. In any event, I would not like to make the claim that here at last can be found the "authentic" Thomas, unless we understand that the "authenticity" of a reception of earlier thought involves a development and an updating of the "received" philosophy in question. The question is not so much whether Aristotle or Thomas had really said this or that, but rather whether they *would* say it today, or whether we can or should say something *with them*. The present introductory presentation, consequently, is intended to develop the nonexplicit suppositions—especially ones that concern action-theory—of an Aristotelian virtue ethics as further developed by Thomas (above all, through his theory of the principles of practical reason) in hopes of contributing to the task of bringing a classical tradition to the level of reflection required today. This is a claim that reaches rather high, particularly in the framework of an introductory text, and is certainly not going to be fully accomplished by any single author.[7]

6. To name a few items: in works by R. McInerny, *The Philosophy of Thomas Aquinas* (Washington, D.C.: The Catholic University of America Press, 1992); C. Martin, *The Philosophy of Thomas Aquinas* (London: Routledge, 1988); A. J. Lisska, *Aquinas' Theory of Natural Law: An Analytic Reconstruction* (Oxford: Oxford University Press, 1996); D. Westberg, *Right Practical Reason: Aristotle, Action, and Prudence in Aquinas* (Oxford: Claranden Press, 1994); and Kevin L. Flannery, S.J., *Acts amid Precepts: The Aristotelian Logical Structure of Thomas Aquinas's Moral Theory* (Washington, D.C.: The Catholic University of America Press). Like McInerny, I have also expressed in detail in *Praktische Vernunft und Vernünftigkeit der Praxis* my disagreement with the reproach of R. A. Gauthier ("Introduction" to Aristotle, *L'Ethique a Nicomaque, Traduction et Commentaire,* with J. Y. Jolif, vol. 1 [Louvain: Publications universitaires, 1970]), that Thomas distorted Aristotle for theological reasons.

7. This kind of undertaking would thus be different from the rather restorative "neo-Aristotelian" tendency of Alasdair MacIntyre, *After Virtue: A Study in Moral Theory,* 2nd ed. (South Bend, Ind.: University of Notre Dame Press, 1984). In contrast with MacIntyre, my approach sees in modern moral philosophy not simply the results of a decline and a forgetfulness of tradition, but rather the specifically modern answer to unsolved problems and inadequacies of premodern ethics.

The so-called higher level of reflection of modernity is, of course, in part also a myth. The drive toward ever "higher" levels of reflection should not be automatically understood as progress. The "level of reflection" of the Ptolemaic astronomy was higher than that of the Copernican; geocentrism needed an ingenious mechanism to "save the phenomena," the need for which increasingly fell by the wayside with the Copernican revolution.

The impulse toward a constant expansion of the mechanism of reflection in philosophy is largely caused by the effort to overcome the problems that result from philosophical one-sidedness and reductionism. The philosophy of the modern era begins with *terribles simplificateurs* like Descartes, Locke, Hume, and then—to put it simply—with the antithesis between rationalism and empiricism. Kantianism both in its theoretical and its practical sides marks the definitive beginning of a still unfinished effort to bring under control the problems that result from such one-sidedness. In ethics, the lofty compound expression "meta-ethics" as distinguished from "normative ethics" (e.g., the question, what the word *good* is supposed to mean) should only with caution be taken as a sign of a "higher level of reflection" or of an advanced awareness of problems; it can also be understood as the expression of moral-philosophical crisis management, the consequence of a loss of reflective *content,* that must now be compensated by the "technique" of reflection. Meta-ethical problems appear mostly not to be problems *of* ethics at all, but rather problems that philosophers have *with* ethics. Now this is not to say that questions about the meaning of the word *good* are meaningless questions; it means only, that they are not questions *about* ethics, but must be answered in the course of undertaking ethical reflection itself, and this leads to an unavoidable "sinking" of the level of reflection.[8]

If someone is only a little acquainted with current approaches to ethics and the discussions that go along with them—whether this has to do with the question of "ultimate justification" or with questions of concrete ethical norms—there is no doubt that such a person can also catch a glimpse in Thomistic ethics (or in classical ethics in general) not only of the possibility of finding some decisive completions, but often also the crucial point of view—the "perspective of morality"—that really makes it possible to grasp the phenomenon of morality and moral action in an adequate way. Now, the representative of classical ethics today will have for rivals, besides the representative of discourse-ethics, two others as well: the moral philosophy of Kant and that

---

8. That ("meta-ethical") questions about the foundations of ethics are not to be distinguished from the questions of ethics itself, but are themselves part of ethics, is characteristic of the antique-classical ethical tradition; cf. J. Annas, *The Morality of Happiness* (note 1 above), 135. This does not explain away "meta-ethical" questions as meaningless, but suggests another approach to be taken to them.

of the utilitarians or consequentialists. Of course, an exhaustive confrontation with Kant cannot be provided here—a man whose genius, although trapped in so many prejudices of historical awareness, possessed nonetheless such a profundity and brilliance of thought that even his critics cannot withhold their admiration. Whether or not justice is done to Kant or his moral philosophy in these pages will, again, have to be left to the reader's judgment. One may even come to the conclusion that the confrontation with Kant contributes more to the understanding of my own viewpoints than to the understanding of Kant's. In any case, the development of my own position is the central concern, so that I can limit myself to making occasional references to essential, and thereby illuminating, differences from Kant. Less frequently, references to discourse-ethics (which is in the Kantian tradition) will be of some use now and then, even though discourse-ethics constitutes in many respects an outspoken "contrasting project" to an Aristotelian virtue ethics; discourse-ethics understands itself as arising straight out of a diagnosis that a classical ethics of the good life has been shown to be *impossible* within modern conditions, and gains no small part of its legitimacy from precisely this. But the largest space will be given to the confrontation with consequentialist utilitarianism, or so-called teleological ethics, because consequentialist moral rationality is the real *antipodes* to what is here understood as the "perspective of morality." This confrontation will run like a red thread throughout the entire book, to emerge, finally, in a thorough discussion in the penultimate section (on the "calculation of goods" and the "weighing of consequences").

2. The "Perspective of Morality"

The "perspective of morality" intended here is not identical with what may currently be known in the English-speaking world as "the moral point of view."[9] This "moral standpoint" would place value on the interests of others or the community, while reducing the pursuit of a person's own interests. As against the subject who pursues merely personal interests, morality would represent the standpoint of the community and of impartiality, of what is valid for all, and takes into account the interests of all concerned.

Of course, by no means will it be maintained in this work that the perspective of morality is *not* that of a "universal" or "higher" standpoint that corrects pure self-interest. To that extent the *moral point of view* is in fact the standpoint of morality. The only thing I dispute is the alleged opposition between

9. Cf. K. Baier, *The Moral Point of View: A Rational Basis of Ethics* (Ithaca, N.Y., and London: Cornell University Press, 1958).

"personal interest" and "morality," or a conception of morality as a restriction on what belongs to our personal interest.[10]

The "perspective of morality" as it is to be understood here is the standpoint of the human being as body-and-soul unity and *acting subject,* equipped with drives, affects, and emotions, weak in instinct but at the same time capable, through intellect and will, of moving out from his own center and transcending himself toward what is "other"; free, and at the same time constantly liable to the loss of his freedom, master of his own action and yet always in danger of becoming the slave of this very action and of his often unclear motivations; and from this perspective, the standpoint of the acting subject, who in his striving, willing, and acting seeks the "good for himself," and thereby, finally, heads toward something ultimate that is sought for its own sake and is capable of satisfying all desires, a fulfillment that we call "happiness." From this perspective, the dichotomy "self-interest" versus "morality" makes no sense. This is because here morality is placed right at the service of one's own interest in the good, namely, in the service of the *truth* of this good, and thereby serves an interest in the success of one's own existence, of the "good life." At the same time, however, the interest of the others or the community in *their* well-being and in the good for *them,* can be understood as one's own interest as well, since it seems impossible—at least, if we want to be consistent—to recognize and pursue "what is truly good for myself," if I do not also understand it as fundamentally "a good for others" as well, even to the extent of having a personal interest that others also partake of that good.

This fundamental orientation of practical reason not to an "ought" transcending merely subjective inclination, but to the "good" as presented to a rationally guided desiring, may not, of course, guarantee the harmony of self-interest with the interests of others, but on the other hand, it does ensure that one's own interest can also *include* the interests, and the well-being, of another, because it is an interest in the truly good. The relevance of morality and its truth-claims for the carrying out of my own personal interest guarantees the universalizability of such claims, the commonality of interests, and consequently a fundamental—and not necessarily flawless—*intertwining* of morality and self-interest. Of course, this does not mean that the moral demands of practical judgments are essentially universal or universalizable. On the contrary, they are particular judgments, situationally bound, and concrete;

---

10. In his *The Morality of Freedom* (Oxford: Oxford University Press, 1986), 313ff., J. Raz criticizes in exactly the same sense the opposition current in today's ethics between *morality* directed toward what is in the interests of others, and *prudence,* which follows one's own interests. H. Krämer, *Integrative Ethik* (Frankfurt am Main: Suhrkamp, 1992), on the other hand, offers what is really an apotheosis of this typical modern-contemporary opposition in an approach that he conceives of as "postmodern."

as Aristotle has it, they are "always capable of being otherwise." But just to the extent that practical judgments are judgments of particular actions, they are, in turn, not a theme of moral philosophy or ethics, but rather the subject of prudence as it guides action. Moral philosophy really concerns itself with the universal that underlies these judgments: the universal whereby concrete judgment and action themselves become "moral." This is also why in any case moral philosophy must be concerned with the boundaries of what is "morally possible," since nothing can be positively determined if it is not at the same time understood both in terms of what it includes and what it excludes. *To the extent* that ethics concerns itself with the boundaries of what is moral, to that extent also will it arrive at concrete assertions about what "may" or "may not" be done.

The true dichotomy that is proper to the perspective of morality is therefore the dichotomy between the merely subjective appearance of good and the truth of this "appearance of good" to the practical reason. "Morality" does not stand in the service of overcoming or suppressing subjectivity (not even empirical and sense subjectivity), but rather in the service of subjectivity's *truth,* and even—this is said with a critical glance at Kant—the truth of subjectivity as molded through our empirical and sensitive drives. The perspective of a morality that has to do with such a "truth of subjectivity" is always the perspective of the acting subject, of the "first person."[11] The standpoint is that of an acting human being, always and necessarily looking toward a good, and, because the acting subject does not want to be deceived in his movement toward the good, always looking for what is "truly good"—this is the standpoint that must come into view, as well as the ethical discourse that reflects it. Contemporary work on ethics, especially if it is understood primarily as a discourse for the establishment of "norms," often suffers from not getting this perspective right, despite all the valuable partial insights acquired. It suffers from the loss of the question about just what is ethical.[12] This is especially so when ethics only lays a claim to ground formal rules for the establishment of norms, but not the material content and values to which such norms are supposed to relate and which would be capable of providing some kind of practical orientation to the process. Such orientations become longer and longer with each attempt; it is not surprising that philosophical ethics is turning increasingly today to a discourse about content and values, which can perform the work of orientation.

But an ethics that confines itself to the establishment of formal procedures

11. See II.1.a, below.
12. Cf. also F. Ricken, "Kann die Moralphilosophie auf die Frage nach dem 'Ethischen' verzichten?" *Theologie und Philosophie* 59 (1984): 161–77.

for the justification of moral norms on the analogy of ethical-political and legal-political discourse appears to lose sight of just what is "moral" about these moral norms, even when fully concerned with the solution of "moral problems." Does the "basic question of morality" really consist in determining "how interpersonal relationships can be legitimately regulated"?[13] Is that not rather the basic question of all politics and the theme of political justice? Finally: where moral norms are understood in a Kantian manner (but still not going as far as Kant did) as "practical rules for the self-limitation of freedom for the sake of everyone's freedom," which essentially reflect the "mutual process of recognition within a lived context,"[14] then that also means that ethics corresponds to what Charles Taylor called the "Ethics of Inarticulacy,"[15] in which no hierarchies of value can be established, since the question about the superiority of some understandings of the good over other understandings is excluded from discussion at the outset. And yet authors like Joseph Raz and Charles Taylor have pointed out clearly that there cannot be *any* autonomy if the meaning of autonomy is not related to that good for which autonomy is good, which again requires criteria for the designation of morally valuable possibilities of action and forms of living;[16] the "authenticity" of the autonomous individual who seeks self-fulfillment is not possible if the horizon of meaning and significance prior to all autonomy is not first recognized: the horizon which makes possible, *independently* of what the autonomous subject in each case considers valuable and therefore chooses to value, that certain things are more important and more significant than other things.[17]

The often one-sided concentration on the question about the merely procedural conditions of the legitimate justification of moral norms is connected essentially with an opinion that has acquired canonical status (at least among professional philosophers) that such a thing as "truth" is not a theme for ethics; this holds for the philosophy of consciousness, for Kantian and post-Kantian critical philosophy, for Nietzschean metaphysics-criticism, and finally for the postmetaphysical epoch characterized by the *linguistic turn*. For similar reasons, the modern style is also very uncomfortable with posing the

13. J. Habermas, "Richtigkeit versus Wahrheit. Zum Sinn der Sollgeltung moralische Urteile und Normen," in Habermas, *Wahrheit und Rechtfertigung. Philosophische Ansätze* (Frankfurt am Main: Suhrkamp, 1999), 301.

14. A. Pieper, *Ethik und Moral. Eine Einführung in die praktische Philosophie* (Munich: C. H. Beck, 1985). Pieper defines here as "morality" what for Kant was merely subject matter of the "law doctrine" of the metaphysics of morals, which Kant nevertheless supplemented with a virtue ethics.

15. Charles Taylor, *Sources of the Self: The Making of the Modern Identity* (Cambridge, Mass.: Harvard University Press, 1989), 53ff.

16. J. Raz, *The Morality of Freedom* (see above, note 10), 400ff.

17. Charles Taylor, *The Ethics of Authenticity* (Cambridge, Mass., and London: Harvard University Press, 1991), 38f.

classical question that is still central for "common sense" and everyday reasoning: the question about "the good life."[18] Even the (pejoratively) so-called neo-Aristotelianism[19] that depends for its life on premodern sources is aware, of course, that in Aristotle too there is a difference between *practical* truth, and truth in the epistemic-theoretical sense. Consequently, ethical discourse in the modern manner (in case it does not, in "neo-Aristotelian" fashion, tie practical reason to the tradition of the community) replaces truth with validity, or rightness (of a utilitarian or pragmatic type), or purposefulness. Strategies of justification replace knowledge of the truth, even though one may be well aware that normal everyday use of reasoning is "realistic" and is thus oriented toward certainty and truth-claims.[20] It is nevertheless illuminating that in such a situation ethics can still only be understood as an activity for the establishment of norms, since programs of norm establishment can leave questions of truth aside in favor of strategies of mere justification.[21]

3. Norm-Ethics Approaches to Moral Philosophy and the "Perspective of Morality"

Serious norm-ethics approaches of a philosophical kind are current today above all in the form of utilitarianism and discourse-ethics. Kantian ethics, by contrast, is not so much a norm-ethics as a maxim-ethics.[22] Even so, it shares with utilitarianism and discourse-ethics the central characteristic of every norm-ethics, which is to judge actions from the point of view of an observer, from a standpoint *outside* that of the acting subject. Again, this is an expression of the typically modern opposition of morality to self-interest, which leads one to let morality begin where one's own interests are limited by the interests of another. Virtue ethics in the classical tradition, however, is eudaimonistic and (consequently) "first-person" ethics, which is to say, it begins with the fundamental ethical question, "What constitutes good for one who acts?" and it asks this question from the perspective of the person acting

---

18. Cf. U. Wolf, *Die Philosophie und die Frage nach dem guten Leben* (Reinbek bei Hamburg: Rowohlt, 1999); A. W. Müller, *Was taugt die Tugend? Elemente einer Ethik des guten Lebens* (Stuttgart: W. Kohlhammer, 1998), a splendid, engaging summary of a virtue ethics.

19. H. Schnädelbach, "Was ist Neoaristotelismus?" in W. Kuhlmann, *Moralität und Sittlichkeit. Das Problem Hegels und die Diskursethik* (Frankfurt am Main: Suhrkamp, 1986), 38–63.

20. Cf. J. Habermas, "Richtigkeit vs. Wahrheit" (see note 13 above), 288ff.

21. An exception can be made here for the "moral realism" that has planted a kind of colony in the territory of consequentialism; this position maintains, again in the "commonsense" tradition, the truth-capability of moral judgments, since this results from the "idea of the right moral answer" or the "right solutions to moral problems"; cf. P. Schaber, *Moralischer Realismus* (Freiburg and Munich: Alber, 1997), 34f. and 41f.

22. Cf. O. Höffe, *Immanuel Kant* (Munich: C. H. Beck, 1983), 186ff.

(which, as we have said, has nothing whatsoever to do with egotism, since in a correct interpretation of eudaimonism—i.e., one that does not mistakenly interpret it as mere hedonism—the good of the other person also belongs to the good of the person acting).[23] Nevertheless, for Kant, the subjective maxims remain central and they express wishes and interests of the acting person, but only on a premoral level. It is unthinkable for Kant that there is such a thing as a subjective interest in the good that could be moral to begin with, and not just "egotistical" in itself.

Utilitarianism and discourse-ethics (or combinations of the two, such as ethical contract theories that bear certain utilitarian and discourse-ethics traits) both fail in their own ways to capture what is here understood as the "perspective of morality," although they are both more consistent in this respect than Kantian ethics. As will be shown, thanks to its "eventistic" concept of praxis, utilitarianism (or consequentialism) excludes the acting person from consideration for the sake of optimizing the consequences and states of affairs that result from the person's actions. Consequentialists[24] proceed from the idea that the acting person is obliged in each case to perform that action by which he can predictibly optimize the consequences for all concerned. Not only do consequentialists assume it as obvious that one action with better consequences is to be preferred to another with less good consequences; according to them, this is also the single point of view from which the moral rectitude of actions can meaningfully be judged. This makes it very difficult for them to have any dealings with virtue ethics arguments, since for a consequentialist virtue is at most a name for the disposition to carry out in each case the right action, that is, the action with the best consequences. Consequentialists arrive at this position because they exclude from consideration that which is central for virtue ethics: namely, that the subject of action himself or his choice of actions has a privileged status with respect to the subjects affected by his actions. This makes judgments of the following kind possible: an action x (e.g., the killing of a man in an extreme situation, in order to prevent the death of many others) would probably have better consequences for *all* concerned than *not* doing the same action; nevertheless, *I* will not do it, because by doing it, I would commit an injustice, and would become an unjust person. From the consequentialist perspective, such judgments are not possible, since what is "just" can be determined only on the basis of the consequences of actions for all concerned, so that actions and omissions are ac-

23. On this, see below II.1.a, and III.1.a. Cf. "The Good Life and the Good Lives of Others," part III of J. Annas, *The Morality of Happiness*, 223ff., esp. 322ff.

24. For a precise definition of different forms of consequentialism, see J. Nida-Rümelin, *Kritik der Konsequentialismus*, 2nd ed. (Munich: Oldenbourg, 1995).

corded the same status. Virtue ethics criticisms of consequentialism will be circular precisely when they presuppose a consequentialist concept of "virtue."[25] Within the tradition of utilitarianism, consequentialism has the peculiarity of permitting to count as "moral" only what includes the interests of all possibly concerned persons. Consequentially established moral norms then necessarily reflect this intersubjective viewpoint.

By contrast, discourse-ethics approaches seem from the outset to discount (or treat as simply impossible to think about) the moral discourse of the individual subject, and aim instead for an intersubjectively attained consensus for the establishment of norms that would be acceptable for all concerned, in the context of the entire society. Discourse-ethics thereby presupposes, first of all, participants in the discussion who are already constituted as moral subjects (without offering any ethical theory for this, whether with Habermas, in the form of sociological evolutionary theories, or with Apel—and against Habermas—in a transcendental analysis of an a priori communicative praxis, understood as an ultimate grounding);[26] secondly, the doctrine also calls for a "discourse of application" [*Anwendungsdiskurs*] to complete the discourse-ethics norm establishment—somewhat akin to a prudential discourse[27]—in which fully consequentialist points of view can be drawn upon and—rather "too late" for discourse-ethics to have anything to add—the whole gamut of fundamental ethical issues can emerge.

Discourse-ethics reveals the symptoms of modern moral philosophy, insofar as it proceeds as a cognitive ethics from the starting point that, under the modern conditions of a "postmetaphysical" epoch, practical reason can no longer find an answer to the question of "What is good for me?," but rather can only be competent for an answer (ascertainable through consensus) to the intersubjective question, "What should *one* do?"[28] This leads, as to be expected, to the insight that a discourse-ethics is really only practicable as a

25. That is the case, e.g., with P. Schaber, *Moralischer Realismus* (see note 21 above), 309–14, and his criticism of P. Foot, "Utilitarianism and the Virtues," in S. Scheffer, ed., *Consequentialism and Its Critics* (Oxford: Oxford University Press, 1988), 224–42. Schaber's criticism is a *petitio principii*. Cf. also below, V.4.f.

26. K. O. Apel, "Das Apriori der Kommunikationsgemeinschaft und die Grundlagen der Ethik. Zum Problem einer rationalen Begründung der Ethik in Zeitalter der Wissenschaft" in Apel, *Transformation der Philosophie*, vol. 2: *Das Apriori der Kommunikationsgemeinschaft* (1973), (Frankfurt am Main: Suhrkamp, 1976), 358–435.

27. J. Habermas, "Diskursethik—Notizen zu einem Begründungsprogramm," in Habermas, *Moralbewusstsein und kommunikatives Handeln* (Frankfurt am Main: 1983), 114 (= *Moral Consciousness and Communicative Action*, trans. Christian Lenhardt and Shierry Weber Nicholsen [Cambridge: Cambridge University Press, 1990]), and also J. Habermas, "Treffen Hegels Einwände gegen Kant auch auf die Diskursethik zu?" in Habermas, *Erläuterungen zur Diskursethik* (Frankfurt am Main: Suhrkamp, 1991), 24.

28. Cf. J. Habermas, "Lawrence Kohlberg und der Neoaristotelismus," in Habermas, *Erläuterungen zur Diskursethik*, 77–99.

theory of legal and political discourse,[29] that the discourse principle is then no longer understood as a moral principle,[30] which has led in turn to the diagnosis of a "definitive collapse" of discourse-ethics.[31] But still, this shows that discourse-ethics is not a supplement to the practical reason of the individual, but at best a theory of how the social validity of moral norms—and ultimately, legal norms—is brought into being. This is how it becomes a political ethics—a tendency that goes to its very foundations from the outset, in its character of allowing only intersubjective reason, and the "communicative" actions that correspond to this, to be the criterion of rationality.[32]

Virtue ethics does not in principle need to enter into rivalry with discourse-ethics. To the extent that someone emphasizes the political-legal ethical logic of discourse-ethics and thereby its intersubjective basis of legitimacy in opposition to virtue ethics, then it really does not have to be considered an "alternative paradigm." From the perspective of classical virtue ethics, one would have to say that discourse-ethics simply lacks the really fundamental subject matter of ethics: the acting subject in his original striving for the good, his interest in the rectitude of this striving, and the corresponding practical truth of his concrete action. Discourse-ethical viewpoints are very suggestive for a political ethics, which is closer to an institutional and legal ethics than to a virtue ethics. Institutional and political-ethical discourses are essentially disposed toward the solution of conflicts. And that is exactly what discourse-ethics seeks (as opposed to utilitarian reasoning, which really "argues away" conflicts for the sake of a rationalized social technology). Discourse ethics relocates the classical theme (still dominant in Kant's thinking) of the conflict between false (ego-centered, irrational) interests and true interests—at once retranslating Kant back into Rousseau—onto the level of social discourse, in which an unforced consensus, acceptable to all, represents the reason of morality, which rejects all reasoning that is trapped in mere (or at least, unenlightened)

29. J. Habermas, "Vom pragmatischen, ethischen und moralischen Gebrauch der praktischen Vernunft," in *Erläuterungen zur Diskursethik*, 117. The program is in fact carried out in *Faktizität und Geltung. Beiträge zur Diskurstheorie des Rechts und des demokratischen Rechtsstaats* (Frankfurt am Main: Suhrkamp, 1992) (= *Between Facts and Norms: Contributions to a Discourse Theory of Law and Democracy*, trans. William Rehg (Cambridge, Mass.: Harvard University Press, 1996).

30. Ibid., 140.

31. K.-O. Apel, *Auseinandersetzung in Erprobung des transzendentalpragmatischen Ansatzes* (Frankfurt am Main: Suhrkamp, 1998), 733ff.

32. This tendency is only increased by Apel, by his addition of a realistic responsibility-ethics, the so-called completion principle or Part B of discourse-ethics, a (fully pragmatic/utilitarian) ethics, which is concerned with creating the social conditions that alone can make possible the ideal discourse. Cf. K.-O. Apel, *Diskurs und Verantwortung. Das Problem des Übergangs zur postkonventionellen Moral* (Frankfurt am Main: Suhrkamp, 1990), e.g., 453ff; also Apel, "Diskursethik vor der Problematik von Recht und Politik," in Apel and M. Kettner, eds., *Zur Anwendung der Diskursethik in Politik, Recht und Wissenschaft* (Frankfurt am Main: Suhrkamp, 1992), 29ff.

self-interest. The discourse-ethical requirements of uncoerced acceptability, reaching all those affected, of the foreseeable consequences of a generally valid norm, and the discursive and consensus-driven redemption of normative validity-claims in an ideal discussion, becomes thereby a moral principle that applies to everything, and includes the "application of a substantial, content-rich moral point of view."[33] It can readily be seen that such a viewpoint appears, at any rate, to be more relevant for the political-legal realm. This is because it does not ground any substantial comprehension of the good, but is rather a principle of political justice, according to which—in the sense, perhaps, of Rawls's "overlapping consensus"—conceptions of the good that are not generally accepted or acceptable are to be excluded from public validity.[34]

As virtue ethics, *The Perspective of Morality* is concerned directly with the space or region that lies in front of all possible intersubjective discourse and communication-oriented action. This region comprises a double aspect: first, the conditions under which discursive behavior, communicative praxis, is possible at all (such behavior only being possible among subjects who are already constituted as moral subjects with corresponding convictions and a moral language intelligible to all of them; although this is not developed as a distinct theme in discourse-ethics, it is never denied).[35] Secondly, it contains the basic contents of such ethical discourses: discourses without nonformal (i.e., substantial) criteria of rationality—primarily, but not exclusively, criteria of justice—are not possible, least of all in a political context. But then there is a third level, alongside and above every norm-related discourse, which surpasses as well the so-called discourse of application: that of the concrete action of the individual subject. That is why there is also a need for an ethics of particular judgments of actions (prudence). Here there is no longer any recourse to any intersubjective agreement, but only to personal responsibility. What is moral is not unconditionally that concerning which there has come into being some consensus, but rather, as Robert Spaemann emphasizes, in certain conditions, is what breaks free of all consensus, or even opposes it, and by that very fact makes a claim to be right.[36] An ethics which, like discourse-ethics, permits only an intersubjective understanding of the good must

33. J. Habermas, "Treffen Hegels Einwände gegen Kant auch auf die Diskursethik zu?" (see note 27 above), 21.

34. J. Rawls, *Political Liberalism* (New York: Columbia University Press, 1993), 133ff., now also in Rawls, *Collected Papers*, ed. S. Friedmann (Cambridge, Mass.: Harvard University Press, 1999), 421ff. ("The Idea of an Overlapping Consensus").

35. From a completely different perspective, E. Tugendhat, "Drei Vorlesungen über Probleme der Ethik," in Tugendhat, *Probleme der Ethik* (Stuttgart: Reclam, 1984), 118, has pointed out that "consensus-theory is useless as a general theory of justification."

36. R. Spaemann, *Happiness and Benevolence*, trans. J. Alberg (South Bend, Ind., and London: University of Notre Dame Press, 2000), 140.

finally omit this decisive level, or be blind to it. It would replace practical truth with consensus-created rectitude.[37]

In what follows, I am concerned to present an introduction to philosophical ethics, with a special emphasis on developing what has been called "the moral perspective" in contrast with the various forms of norm-ethics. This of course has nothing to do with "moralism" but rather with understanding that the answer to the question about the establishment of moral norms has already been decided at a place where it cannot yet be expressly stated: namely, at the level of insight into just what "human action" or "practical reason" is to begin with—in short, by insight into what an acting human being is. The conceptions that ethicists have about this are often silently presupposed or only brought to light afterward, once everything has already been treated. But these conceptions are ultimately what determine everything. And it is just for this purpose that decisive foundations of virtue ethics can be elaborated in the tradition that runs from Aristotle through Thomas Aquinas. A few distinctions and clarifications will be necessary.

4. Philosophical Ethics as Rational Virtue Ethics

Classical virtue ethics, the tradition to which the present text on the fundamentals of ethics claims to belong, differs from many contemporary forms of *virtue ethics,* especially those that have been elaborated in the English-speaking world and have become widespread in recent decades, in opposition to the dominant *moral philosophy.*[38] It begins with a now famous 1958 article by G. E. M. Anscombe[39] and the criticism made by her of the category of the "mor-

---

37. Cf. also A. Wellmer, *Ethik und Dialog. Elemente des moralischen Urteils bei Kant und in der Diskursethik* (Frankfurt am Main: Suhrkamp, 1986), 69ff., who, like Tugendhat, points out that the reasons why we take something for true or right are prior to every intersubjective communicative action and any consensus aimed at thereby: "The fact of consensus, even when it arises under ideal conditions, can be no reason for the truth of what is held to be true" (72; trans. G. Malsbary here). Habermas replies to this today with the replacement of "truth" by rightness: "A discursively sought agreement about norms or actions under ideal conditions has more than a merely authoritative power; it holds within itself the rightness of moral judgments. Ideally justified assertability is what we mean by moral validity" (J. Habermas, "Richtigkeit versus Wahrheit" (297; see note 13 above; trans. G. Malsbary here).

38. A few important classical contributions pro and contra virtue ethics and further bibliography can be found, e.g., in R. Crisp and M. Slote, eds., *Virtue Ethics* (Oxford: Oxford University Press, 1997); P. Rippe and P. Schaber, *Tugendethik* (Stuttgart: Reclam, 1998); cf. also in more detail M. Slote, *From Morality to Virtue* (Oxford: Oxford University Press, 1992). Important contributions are also to be found in P. A. French et al., eds., *Ethical Theory: Character and Virtue,* Midwest Studies in Philosophy 13 (South Bend, Ind.: University of Notre Dame Press, 1988). See further: Philippa Foot, "Virtues and Vices," in Crisp and Slote (see above), 163–77; A. W. Müller, *Was taugt die Tugend? Elemente einer Ethik des guten Lebens* (see note 18 above). A critical overview of modern virtue ethics and an analysis is offered by J. Schuster, *Moralisches Können. Studien zur Tugendethik* (Würzburg: Echter, 1997).

39. "Modern Moral Philosophy," *Philosophy* 33, no. 124 (1958): 1–19; also available in Crisp and

al ought" or "moral duty." According to Anscombe, this category should be replaced by a return to the paradigm of "moral virtue."[40] Explorations of virtue ethics received a definite impetus with the publication of Alasdair McIntyre's epoch-making *After Virtue* (1981). In its more extreme or "radical" forms,[41] this type of virtue ethics has a largely noncognitive character, that is to say, it maintains that the morality of an action and finally of the subject himself does not really originate from the recognizable rectitude of ways of acting—that is, from what is subsequently capable of being formulated as norms, principles, or rules—but much more from the current moral state or competency of the acting subject. "Rightness of acting" does not here define what the virtue of the subject is; rather, virtue, as the right disposition of the subject, defines and generates the "rectitude of action." What is most important, then, is not so much doing what is "right" (and certainly not on the basis of norms, principles, or rules) but rather feeling the right way, thinking the right way, having the right motives—in sum, to be a subjectively rightly disposed actor. From this follow right, morally worthy actions.

These are in fact characteristics of any virtue ethics, even of a classical virtue ethics. But modern virtue ethics theories tend to exalt these motivational aspects and separate them from the rationally cognitive aspects. Now, they are correct, it seems to me, to hold that the principal moral question is "What kind of a human being should I be?" and not "How should I behave?" but they have difficulties with posing the first question—the question about the good life—at least, with how to arrive at it, starting from the question about right actions. "Virtue" as the subjective disposition of the acting subject thereby becomes more or less sharply opposed to the awareness of and compliance with principles, moral norms, and rules of right action.[42] Right motivation through the virtuous disposition of the subject stands over against "duty" as expressed through principles, norms, and rules. While the (modern) moral philosopher places at the forefront the awareness of the rectitude of ways of acting, the corresponding principles, norms, or rules, and the moral duty that these create, and conceives of the virtues, by contrast, as merely derived factors, in the sense of a subjective disposition that is in *accordance with* the known prin

---

Slote (see note above), 26–44, and in *The Collected Papers of G. E. M. Anscombe* (Oxford: Oxford University Press, 1981), 3.26–42.

40. Cf. also the criticism of the concept of moral obligation and its central position in modern moral philosophy by Bernard Williams, *Ethics and the Limits of Philosophy* (Cambridge, Mass., and London: Harvard University Press, 1985), 174ff.

41. Cf. K. Baier, "Radical Virtue Ethics," in P. A. French et al., eds., *Ethical Theory: Character and Virtue* (see above, note 38), 126–35.

42. Cf. also here N. J. H. Dent, *The Moral Psychology of the Virtues* (Cambridge: Cambridge University Press, 1984), 31f.

ciples, norms, and rules, the (modern) virtue ethicist understands the moral virtues as the primary thing, and as the source of morality, while the rectitude of actions, by contrast, is something derived from the virtue of the subject, from the rightness of his disposition. In this way, "virtue" or right motivation is put in the place of moral duty: one carries out the morally right and good, not because one is fulfilling duties, rules, or norms, but rather because one is rightly disposed, a good person.

Contemporary virtue ethics, especially as pursued in the English-speaking world, justly criticizes some weak points of "modern moral philosophy" and thereby accentuates the essential concerns of classical virtue ethics. But the differences that remain are considerable. Contemporary virtue ethics is often one-sided and extremist, and consequently not seldom dismissed as a "shot in the dark," since ultimately virtues, too, can only be defined on the basis of the rightness of actions.[43] To be sure, today's exponents of virtue ethics do not absolutely deny this. Some of them recognize explicitly that the rectitude of actions is distinguishable from dispositions and is not completely derivable from the latter.[44] Nevertheless, the two aspects do not appear to be very satisfactorily reconciled in today's virtue ethics.

But classical virtue ethics, in any event, is *not* noncognitivist (i.e., it maintains that the rightness of a way of acting does not simply spring from positively valued motivations, and it understands virtue as intimately related to reason),[45] nor does it recognize an opposition between virtue and duty. Virtue in the classical sense likewise does not attempt simply to justify our given moral intuitions, nor is it (in neo-Aristotelian fashion) tied to the predominant ethos of any given time. As a rational category, virtue aims to clarify our moral intuitions as given to us through upbringing, custom, and character and, in given cases, improve on them. On the other hand, classical virtue ethics does not reduce the virtues, in the way modern moral philosophy does, to a merely habitual appropriation of principles, norms, and rules. On the contrary, it is an outspoken doctrine of happiness, conceiving the good, the right, and the obligatory always with a view to attaining what truly conduces to happiness—even if it is only a very imperfect happiness in certain circumstances. Classical virtue ethics in the Aristotelian tradition understands virtue as that emotional or affective disposition of the subject that is (1) grounded in rationally recognized principles and through which (2) what is right, duty, or the "ought" is only really adequately understood in the individual case, because moral vir-

---

43. F. Ricken, "Aristoteles und die moderne Tugendethik," in *Theologie und Philosophie* 74 (1999): 391–404.

44. This is maintained, e.g., by M. Slote, *From Morality to Virtue* (see note 38 above), 89.

45. Cf. J. Annas, *The Morality of Happiness*, 450.

tue disposes affectivity according to reason and thereby enables and confirms rationality in particular actions.

This second point is really the decisive characteristic of every genuine virtue ethics. According to a current misunderstanding, which degrades the concept of virtue to the point of triviality, virtues are simply positively valued character qualities[46] or, as already mentioned, dispositions to fulfill moral rules or norms—dispositions especially important in the case of children, who do not yet have the rational competence to understand moral rules or to have a discriminating engagement with them.[47] The salient point is really this: working with a concept of moral virtue that is not *trivial*, "virtue" does not consist in a disposition, an affective tendency or inclination to do "whatever is right," but rather in doing what is right *by affective inclination, that is, on the basis of an emotional disposition or inclination, to hit upon the right thing to do in each case.* If virtue were to be understood only in the trivial sense of "a disposition to do whatever is right," this would indeed mean that virtue in itself cannot really be a foundation for determining this "right thing," since the action that is according to virtue would be determined by the "right thing." But it is the other way around: the virtuous disposition first makes it possible even to recognize what is concretely right and effectively to carry it out, because practical reason effectively leads and confirms virtue. Moral virtue is not simply the mere affective disposition or inclination to do whatever is right (one's "duty"), but rather an inclination or affective disposition through which what is right—here and now—is adequately recognized as "good," and is effectively met with (and of that, of course, there can be no theory or universally normative assertion). Moral virtue is the empowering of rationality with respect to concrete actions.

Once virtue is understood in these terms, then it seems really out of place to speak of possible conflicts between single virtues as if they were collisions between various moral obligations, and then (on the grounds that this problem was not sufficiently addressed in Aristotle's virtue ethics) to promote a "ready power of judgment for virtue conflicts" as a "metavirtue."[48] This notion simply bypasses the classical and Aristotelian understanding of moral virtue which, to begin with, in its basic concept already provides room for the adequate understanding of what is to be done in particular cases, and second, insists that there could not even be such a thing as "single virtues" coming

---

46. Thus, e.g., J.-C. Wolf and P. Schaber, *Analytische Moralphilosophie* (Freiburg and Munich: Alber, 1998), 63.

47. B. Gert, *Morality: Its Nature and Justification* (New York and Oxford: Oxford University Press, 1998), 277ff. (= the third edition of B. Gert, *The Moral Rules: A New Rational Foundation for Morality*, 1970).

48. O. Höffe, "Aristoteles' universalistische Tugendethik," in Rippe and Schaber, eds., *Tugendethik* (see note 38 above), 42–66, 61.

into conflict with one another, since in the truly virtuous person all the virtues form an organic unity that in fact enables the virtuous person to do what is right in any concrete situation. "Real virtue has, so to speak, already resolved the conflict, before the conflict could impair the decision."[49]

Now this does *not* in any way entail that what is right in a particular situation cannot be rationally justified or be dependent on rationally transparent normative presuppositions, or could not appear before the conscience of the acting person as "duty." The virtuous person's judgment of action is always a judgment of reason, or to be precise, of prudence. The affectively guided practical understanding of the virtuous person is nevertheless a superior mode of practical knowing, especially distinguished by three features: (1) such knowing makes possible *a flexible approach* to the concrete situation, and does this through meeting the morally right that corresponds to the goal of the appropriate virtue; (2) it not only refines the understanding, but also leads to the effective *accomplishment* of the recognized good (in contrast with the *akratos,* or incontinent, weak-willed person, so thoroughly analyzed by Aristotle); and finally, (3) (in contrast this time with the *merely* continent person, who fulfills his recognized duty against his inclination) such a mode of knowing brings together motivation and the rationale of action to a full, and *subjectively satisfying, harmony.*[50] The affectively guided practical judgment of the virtuous person is still a rational judgment, and is in fact more rational than the practical judgment of an affectively misguided person. In the latter case, the judgment does not arise from a reason that has been empowered through well-ordered emotions, but from a reason that finds itself in the tow of affects and emotions that have been left to follow their own logic, and is thus less "rational" than the reason of the virtuous person.[51] In this way, moral virtue defines and confirms the conditions under which our striving toward happiness is accomplished on the tracks of reason, so that we are after an ultimate, or a good-for-its-own-sake, that can also be *reasonably* willed as an ultimate and highest good. Classical virtue ethics, as presented here, is *rational* virtue ethics.

This kind of virtue ethics, then, does not hold the rightness of actions to be derived, in a one-sided way, from favorably judged emotional attitudes and motives, but in fact links the latter to rational criteria, permitting a discourse about moral rules and norms, and firmly retaining a normative concept of the "good" that is preordained to a teleology of the subject's wishes, inclinations,

49. A. W. Müller, *Was taugt die Tugend?* 17 (trans. G. Malsbary here).

50. Cf. also M. Stocker, "The Schizophrenia of Modern Ethical Theories" (orig. *Journal of Philosophy* 73 [1976]: 453–66; also in Crisp and Slote, eds., *Virtue Ethics,* 66–78).

51. The anthropological implications and presuppositions of this assertion cannot be developed at this stage. But see below, III.4.

and striving. And just because of this, it has been maintained that neither Aristotle nor Thomas represented "pure virtue ethics."[52] But such a view is a misunderstanding and only makes sense to someone who is already starting with a radical concept of virtue ethics. A rational virtue ethics, as the one presented here, is a no less "pure" virtue ethics—just without the one-sidedness of the radical form of it sometimes encountered.

Nevertheless, in a rational virtue ethics fashioned after the classical model, principles, rules, and norms do have a different status than they have in modern moral philosophy. They are ultimately the expression of the goals of striving, which, since they are also linked anthropologically, are oriented toward the good-for-man and bring that good to expression on the foundational-universal level. "Moral virtue" here does not mean a disposition to satisfy laws, norms, or rules, but rather the complete kind of fulfillment of what comes to expression in laws, moral norms, or rules: not just the fulfillment of a norm, but the targeting, at once cognitive and affective, of the good that principles and their corresponding norms indicate. According to a deep-seated prejudice, the Aristotelianism of Thomas Aquinas succeeded in bringing nothing more than a conception of virtues as the "habits of obedience to laws."[53] We should say, rather, that for Thomas the (natural) law—the *lex naturalis*—made explicit the rationality of the virtues. Virtues do not help us fulfill a moral law that stands over against us or that is imposed upon us; as "natural law," the moral law is rather the fundamental cognitive principle that makes virtue possible at all. Virtues are not to be understood as "means" or dispositions to fulfill the moral law, but contrariwise, the moral law is a "means" or the principle with whose help we can acquire virtues. And as a "means," it is not something standing over against us or imposed upon us, but rather the structural principle of practical reason itself. The basic phenomenon is always the human person as a cognitive, appetitive being, and not norms, rules, or laws. Norms and rules are normative statements, derived linguistic universals, by which we are able to come to an understanding about the practical good. Practical principles, on the other hand, insofar as we *distinguish* them from norms and rules (as will be the case in what follows), are at the same time the intelligible moving causes of praxis—that is, principles of praxis as such, and not simply normative assertions *about* it—and are thereby the foundation as well of the entire intelligibility of the concrete good that a judgment of action has for its object at any given time. This means that the principles of practical reason are the principles both of actions and of morality.

52. J. Schuster, *Moralisches Können* (note 38 above), 52.

53. J. B. Schneewind, *The Invention of Autonomy: A History of Modern Moral Philosophy* (Cambridge: Cambridge University Press, 1998), 20.

Virtue ethics in this sense investigates the conditions under which an appetitive being is reasonable, or the conditions under which it strives for a good that alone is *reasonably* to be striven for. To do this, virtue ethics recurs in the greatest variety of ways to the "rational by nature" or the "naturally rational" [*das von Natur aus Vernünftige*]. It is common to all forms of classical virtue ethics that "natural" is not understood in a "naturalistic" sense, but rather as what is really and primarily good for man, as an ideal of successful human existence.[54] The "rational that comes from nature" is what grounds the moral competence of the acting subject and praxis as such—it is the original cognitive achievement of the practical reason, which broadens out into moral virtue, and which, as thus constituted, is interpreted as "natural law."

Virtue ethics understood in this way would have the same goal as all virtue ethics—namely, the rehabilitation of the moral competence of the acting subject—but will also link this competence to definite conditions. The concern is not with an ultimate justification of ethics, but rather with an identification of the unavoidable and ultimate moral "givens" that will not be logically derivable—in fact they are more like starting points or preliminary conditions for any moral discourse—but nevertheless, as stated before, are "naturally" open to every acting subject as an *individual*. Now this is not to be taken, of course, in the sense of a special "feeling" of value, in Max Scheler's or Nicolai Hartmann's sense: a kind of "organ" for understanding values that would be distinct from the practical reason. Rather, it is the very starting point of practical reason, and a component of practical reasoning as such. The view that ethical validity-claims can be made intelligible only through the medium of intersubjectivity would conflict with maintaining an immediately possible and inescapable givenness of what grounds all morality, or the entire sphere of the moral as such.[55] These givens are by no means controversial—that it is good for us to live, to survive, to live with other human beings in society, to behave rationally, to know the truth, to enjoy the deserved fruits of our labor, to join with the opposite sex, to have children, and so on—are normally not subject to dispute today. What is controversial, however, is not only the importance of these actions but above all the interpretation of them as "goods." One can, that is, explain them as mere "raw material" or material starting points for the not-yet-attained individual and social creation of values that is ever renewed in the historical process, and through which human identity and corresponding moral norms are formed, historically and socially conditioned at

54. Cf. J. Annas, *The Morality of Happiness*, 135ff.
55. For a criticism of the juncture of ultimate justification and intersubjectivity in discourse-ethics, cf. also V. Hösle, *Die Krise der Gegenwart und die Verantwortung der Philosophie* (Munich: C. H. Beck, 1997), 179ff.

every stage; alternatively, they can be understood as the unavoidable, "natural" presuppositions of practical reasonableness, upon which human identity and the creation of values depends. And this must not be understood naturalistically—no more so than in the tradition of natural rights that adopted the same approach. A virtue ethics in the classical tradition represents in any case a certain "naïve" interpretation of these givens as principles, as the unavoidable starting points of all practical reasonableness, which also requires an ethical clarification of these givens on the horizon of rationality[56]—in this sense, the approach is neither "naïve" nor naturalistic.

This means also that virtue ethics is the opposite of a "morality of the experts." It is essentially different from conceptions of ethics, which, like discourse-ethics, only proceed from intersubjective communication processes and only accept validity-claims as based on consensus, or, like utilitarian consequentialism, need to collect an abundance of consequences of all kinds, affecting as large as possible a circle of concerned parties, for its calculation of maximum utility. These procedures reflect the reasoning of "ethics committees" rather than the daily behavior of morally competent subjects (which does not mean that such subjects cannot be greatly assisted by ethics committees, or that such committees for decision making are not important within certain institutions such as hospitals). Virtue ethics does not reproduce the reasoning of philosophizing or scientifically enlightened subjects—although it can be suggestive, of course, even for these; rather, it considers the reasoning of the person as a moral subject *tout court,* that each one of us is: subjects who lead their lives and intend to live this life "well." What this "well" (and the "good") means, and what it contains, we call "morality," and ethics is the philosophy about it.

The moral givens that have just been mentioned ground the moral competence of the acting subject. In this presentation of a rational virtue ethics, such givens will be referred to as "the rational by nature" [*das von Natur aus Vernünftige*]. This is not an *ultimate* justification (that would not be possible)

---

56. U. Steinvorth, *Klassische und moderne Ethik. Grundlinien einer materialen Moraltheorie* (Reinbek von Hamburg: Rowohlt, 1990) maintains the view that an ethics is "modern" if it grounds moral obligation on the "binding nature of human interests, needs, and decisions," but "classical" if it bases its determination of moral bindingness on objective relationships, "which are constituted independently of human interests and desires" (56). This statement with its bald opposition between "subjective interests" and "objective relationships" must be questioned because classical virtue ethics proceeds precisely from the fact that our conceptions of goods and their bindingness *are* in fact based on our interests and wishes, especially our *true* interests and our *rational* wishes. The distinction of "objective" as opposed to "merely subjective" is not then one of "outer" versus "inner," but rather of "rational" versus "contra-rational." For classical virtue ethics, "the good" is only what we reasonably strive for. Only *then* is it also true that the morally binding is what is "good," independently of our actual wishes and interests (implying that the "good" is in fact the "rationally striven for").

but rather the indication of something "final" or "primary," depending on how we approach it.[57] These givens, the "rational by nature" and the corresponding practical principles, are not "grounded" or "derived" but are simply discovered.

But a price must be paid for the rehabilitation of the moral competence of the subject. This price consists, first of all, in no longer treating all the interests and preferences of such subjects as of the same weight. "Advantage" here is not utilitarian advantage, the fulfillment of preferences of the largest possible number of affected persons, and normative rectitude here is not, as in discourse-ethics, the unforced agreement of moral norms with the (subjective) interests of all discussion participants. Secondly, virtue ethics in the classical tradition maintains that moral competence has a connection with the moral disposition of the subject. Being morally good is itself, to a certain extent, held to be the condition for understanding what is good. "Moral virtue" is in fact that disposition of acting persons, in which the good in reality also really *appears* good to them. Contemporary virtue ethics in many respects is relativistic in its approach.[58] It differs in this way from the classical tradition, which although treating the good that corresponds to virtue as a good also "in relation to us," nevertheless keeps firmly, at least in its Aristotelian form, to a concept of the practical truth of this good. This kind of truth, however, does not consist in the correspondence of judgments to some state of affairs that exists outside of the subject. Instead, it consists in the correspondence of the concrete judgment made in each case about the practical good (and about the willing that goes with that) with right appetition. Of course the "right appetition" is itself a state of affairs, and the rectitude of this appetition [Ger. *Streben*, "striving," cf. Lat. *ad-petere*, to "seek toward"] implies a relationship to the "objective world," but it is the "objective world" that the acting subject itself is.[59] Even the intersubjectively created rectitude in Habermas's sense does not come without a "relationship to the objective world," and is in fact

57. Apel's transcendental/pragmatic "ultimate justification" appears to be not a *grounding* at all, but rather has the character of a *discovery* of something presupposed in every communication process. In any case, what is here discovered (the structure of mutual recognition that underlies every communication process) is much too "thin" from the virtue ethics perspective to serve as the foundation of an ethics.

58. M. C. Nussbaum disagrees with this somewhat: "Non-Relative Virtues: An Aristotelian Approach," in P. A. French, T. E. Uehling, and H. K. Wettstein, eds., *Ethical Theory: Character and Virtue* (South Bend, Ind.: University of Notre Dame Press, 1988), 32–53; slightly expanded in M. C. Nussbaum and A. Sen, eds., *The Quality of Life* (Oxford: Oxford University Press, 1997).

59. The statement of J. Habermas (in "Richtigkeit vs. Wahrheit" [note 13 above], 296) really misses the point of practical truth: "Moral validity claims lack the relationship to the world that is characteristic of a truth-claim. This deprives them of a transcendentally justifying point of reference" so that they can only be created through a "discursively targeted agreement." The substitution of consensually attained rectitude rests upon an initial narrowing of what "truth" can mean in the philosophy of praxis.

that ever-changing objective world *to which* I relate as a subject, a relationship in which mutual recognition is offered as to a member of a communicative community and as a discussion participant. The insistence on the underlying moral rectitude of such mutual recognition—and this doctrine is the soul of all discourse-ethics—consequently does possess the character of an assertion of truth about reality [*Wahrheitsbehauptung*].

The rectitude of appetition, or striving, arises fundamentally from these previously mentioned givens that are not chosen by the subject, but are discursively demonstrable as ultimate moral givens or principles; it forms the foundation of the "rightness" or practical truth of all judgments of action, but such rectitude still lags behind what is concretely to be done: what is to be done cannot be derived with rigid logic from the principles, since the principles are at the same time underdetermined with relation to the concrete direction of actions; what is concretely done and willed can still be critiqued as being in contradiction to the principle. Practical principles are consequently the foundation and limit of rectitude and as such are the ground of all practical truth. One of the decisive contributions of Thomas Aquinas to philosophical ethics lies in the supplementation of Aristotelian virtue ethics with just such a doctrine of principles.[60]

In this way, ethics keeps the profile that it typically held in antiquity, with the exception of the Cyrenaic school of hedonism. It is a doctrine of the "good life" in the sense that it compels us to think about our priorities and standards and to revise our mode of living as circumstances require. In any event, according to this viewpoint, ethics can only be practiced by subjects who are striving for an improvement of their way of life. Precisely thanks to its eudaimonistic character, classical virtue ethics seeks a rationally oriented revision of spontaneous and unreflective ideas of happiness. The motive to improve

---

60. This hermeneutical perspective of a completion of Aristotelian ethics through a Thomistic doctrine of principles, as developed in my work entitled *Praktische Vernunft und Vernünftigkeit der Praxis* [*Practical Reason and the Rationality of Praxis*; see note 3 above] has been opposed by D. J. Bradley, *Aquinas on the Twofold Human Good* [see note 3], 250ff. Bradley holds, first, that the Thomistic doctrine of principles cannot be united with the Aristotelian conception of the *phronimos* and the plurality of human goods maintained by Aristotle (on why such a unity is indeed possible in my view, see below, especially II.3.b and V.1.f.). Second, Bradley holds that Thomas is not filling in something that was missing in Aristotle, and consequently not solving an Aristotelian problem, but rather one that arises from the Christian-theological law perspective, especially from the moral commandments of the Decalogue. My response to this objection is that the thesis that Thomas is supplying what was lacking in Aristotle was not meant to imply that Thomas was solving a problem of the historical Aristotle; rather, that Thomas's expansion of Aristotelian virtue ethics through a doctrine of principles of the practical reason responds to an inner necessity of Aristotelian virtue ethics as a *type* of ethics, and the expansion begins exactly at the place where it would be both possible and natural to begin, if seen from an "Aristotelian" perspective it is possible for it to begin, and is required by the nature of things (on why, according to my view, such an expansion was needed, see below, IV.2.d and 3.c).

one's praxis of living still survives in Kantian ethics, but only in a rudimentary, anti-eudaimonistic form. Kant's ethical doctrine is not a program for the reform of "the inner man," but rather a program for the defeat of the amorality, evil, and selfishness of the inner man, under the demands of morality. Such motives are scarcely present any longer in utilitarianism and discourse-ethics. Instead, they aim in a rather more classical manner for the improvement of praxis and for "reform" in the widest sense—for the improvement of a *social* praxis that transcends the subject; without this, they would not be ethics at all. Utilitarianism thereby functionalizes the acting subject for the purpose of optimizing the world situation, while discourse-ethics would like to coordinate individual interests harmoniously and in a noncoercive manner toward what is best for all with a view to society as a whole, transposing in this way the essential motive of Kantian legal philosophy into ethics.

5. Philosophical Ethics and Religious Belief

As stated at the beginning, the presentation of virtue ethics in this book is inspired above all by Thomas Aquinas, but now a second point must be added to that statement: everyone who pursues ethics finds himself in his "own situation." This means that before he even begins to reflect on ethical problems and express his conclusions, he has already lived a substantial part of his life span. He has his own experiences, and writes from within a certain lived context. This cannot be more obvious in the case of the classical founders Socrates, Plato, and Aristotle, but it is no less valid for the Greek and Roman Stoics and Epicureans. None of them were philosophers in a vacuum. And of course the same goes for Thomas Aquinas as well as Kant, Hegel, Sartre, Rawls, or Habermas. There is no such thing as "philosophy in itself"; there are only philosophers, that is, philosophizing human subjects, and these subjects are acknowledged as philosophers when they attempt to ground their thinking rationally, without recourse to myths or the tenets of faith or majority opinion. Certainly, Aristotle's statements about friendship are conditioned by the fact that he knew what friendship was, since he had friends himself and understood how to be a friend to others. Someone who was not capable of that would scarcely have been in a position to say something reasonable about friendship. But this does not mean that Aristotle's analysis of friendship is "unscientific." Prescientific experience—"prejudging" or *prejudice* in a good sense—is always a factor, and whoever claims to be free of that, to represent "philosophy itself" and not simply a certain human being who philosophizes, deceives not only his readers, but himself.

As a philosopher, someone can be pagan, Muslim, Jew, or Christian, be-

liever or nonbeliever, man or woman, married or single, raised in the country or in the town; one has enjoyed a certain upbringing; one is molded by
relationships with others, by cultural prejudices, cognitive habits, a certain
level of education. Thinking is determined not only by what we know but also
by what we do not know. Everyone has a temperament, ideals, regrets. There
have been pagans who were outstanding philosophers and Christians who
were inferior philosophers. Aristotle was a great philosopher not just because
he was Greek but because he searched for the truth and knew how to think.
If someone is a Christian, that is still far from meaning that he will take upon
himself the effort of a rational search for the truth or that he can think; but
neither is the opposite true. Is there any reason why someone who is an unbe-
liever will be able to think better? If he can think well regardless, it is certainly
not *because* he lacks faith. True philosophy lives in the conviction that the
rational discourse we call philosophy is, so to speak, always possible *anyway,*
because it originates in an interest in truth.

What is the purpose of these remarks? Philosophical ethics under the conditions of the religious beliefs of one who practices it (and this pertains to the
author of the present work) and under the conditions of the religious faith of
those for whom it is written, is not free of problems: believing Christians in a
certain respect already "know too much" for philosophy. After all, are they not
already in possession of the most important answers? As Heidegger put it, is
philosophy under the conditions of faith not an oxymoron, "wooden iron," a
misunderstanding?[61] Is it meaningful, or even possible at all, for a Christian to
practice *philosophical* ethics? Can there be any "nonbelieving" knowledge as
such for a believing Christian? Can philosophy exist alongside theology?

The present work expresses the conviction that while it is not possible for a
human subject who is a "philosopher" simply to shut off his faith, even when
he philosophizes, just as little is it possible for one who philosophizes simply
to forget how much his horizons have been widened by the personal experience of wishing the good of someone else, or of loving or being attracted to
someone. It is still possible, and in fact indispensable, that the *philosophy* he
pursues does not *argue* on the basis of any truths of faith. In the case of ethics, a comparable kind of exclusion or bracketing should come into play: the
theme of philosophical ethics needs to be distinguished from moral theology.

How far such bracketing may succeed in each case is not, finally, the decisive question. The decisive question is whether the arguments that a philosopher uses are *philosophical* arguments that can be discussed within the
forum of reason as such. Arguments are philosophical when they rely neither

---

61. M. Heidegger, *Einführung in die Metaphysik,* 3rd ed. (Tübingen: M. Niemeyer, 1966), 6.

on authority nor on religious revelation, but arise from generally accessible experience and justifiable insight.

And this is a situation that *every* human being is in, not just the believer. Prescientific or nonscientific experience should never be simply shoved aside, and in fact nobody does this. Someone who has never felt the attraction of a man or a woman would not have much to say on the theme of love and sexuality. But if what someone is going to say is not going to be poetry but philosophy, it must be presented with justified arguments. If someone wanted to have knowledge or some ethnological information about the people of a newly discovered continent, he would first have to believe the people who told him of the existence of the continent in the first place. In order to acquire scientific knowledge, of course, he would have to go there himself. But he would never progress even as far as that if he had rejected mere traveler's reports as having nothing whatever to contribute to ethnology.

Faith is related to philosophy as hearing is to seeing.[62] Through the "hearing" of belief, one who philosophizes is able to grasp much that for a long time had remained outside his field of vision, but which he is now able to find by looking in the right direction. But what he *cannot see with his own eyes*— because it exceeds the power of his vision—that he must leave to the hearing of faith. And who would maintain that the believer can see with his own eyes—his reason—only as much, and no more than, the nonbeliever would, independently of the "hearing" of faith? All that is required is that the one who sees something be able to *make it visible to others too*—and that means (to abandon the metaphor) that he can rationally justify it.

But then a new question arises: Does the believer need philosophy at all? This question is definitely to be answered, "Yes." First, because faith does not take the place of natural knowing ability, but only supplements it, and raises it to a higher level. "Supplementation" and "elevation," however, are not possible unless there is something already there to be "supplemented" and "lifted up." And following from this is the second reason: faith does not tell us *all.* It is light *in* the human intellect and strengthening *in* the human will. This is why faith can never replace human, naturally reasoning insight, and in fact presupposes it in many respects.

Now the suspicion may arise that we are speaking here in favor of philosophy as the "handmaiden of theology" (*ancilla theologiae*). There are various ways of interpreting this. One could take it to mean that theology has need of philosophy, and that philosophy is not of service to theology, but *subservient*

---

62. This happy metaphor comes from J. Pieper, *In Defense of Philosophy* [*Verteidigungsrede für die Philosophie*], trans. L. Krauth (San Francisco: Ignatius Press, 1992), 118–20.

to it, even if that is not the original meaning of this very doubtful metaphor.[63] In any case, this would not be any downgrading of philosophy. Mathematics also "serves" the natural sciences, and this does not degrade mathematics or threaten its independence. On the contrary, if such a use were *not* being made of it, mathematics would be living a merely "academic" existence and would have a socially marginal status—just as philosophy does, now! But philosophy has in fact the highest value not only academically but socially, whenever faith flourishes and theology is considered important. This would apply not only to the Christian Middle Ages but also to the seventeenth century, arguably the most theological century of all time.

So, then, let philosophy be the *ancilla*. But she will not prove to be a useful servant unless she *really is* philosophy—and in this sense she is essentially *not* a "handmaid," but rather is that "opening up" to the whole of reality that is peculiar to the human being, arising (to use Kant's expression) from a "natural disposition" of man. She is the search for the whole *as* the whole, that is, the search for the understanding of reality on the basis of its ultimate and most deeply lying reasons and causes. As a human undertaking, such searching is essential for philosophy. More than possession of truth, she is the love of truth, because her wisdom must ever remain incomplete. Furthermore, this kind of knowledge is always bound up with one's own way of living. Knowledge and personal interest cannot be separated here. For this very reason, philosophy will always remain controversial in itself. This is no argument against it, only a sign that it is really concerned with the "whole." And this is also why as an academic discipline philosophy is always an "institutionalized crisis about fundamentals."[64] The crisis is not just about "issues" but more immediately the philosophizing human being in his existential understanding of himself. There comes to mind what Nicias says to Lysimachus in Plato's *Laches:* "You seem not to be aware that anyone who is close to Socrates and enters into conversation with him is liable to be drawn into an argument, and whatever subject he may start, he will be continually carried round and round by him, until at last he finds that he has to give an account both of his present and past life."[65]

63. For its origin, cf. the article "Ancilla Theologiae," in J. Ritter, ed., *Historisches Wörterbuch der Philosophie* (Basel: Schwabe, 1971), 1.249ff.

64. R. Spaemann, "Die kontroverse Natur der Philosophie," in Spaemann, *Philosophische Essays* (Stuttgart: Reclam, 1983), 104–29, esp. 117. In a similar way, MacIntyre diagnoses the insurmountably controversial nature of various versions of moral philosophy in Alasdair MacIntyre, *Three Rival Versions of Moral Enquiry: Encyclopedia, Genealogy, and Tradition* (South Bend, Ind.: University of Notre Dame Press, 1990).

65. Plato, *Laches* 187e–188a, trans. Jowett, in *The Collected Dialogues of Plato*, ed. E. Hamilton and H. Cairns (Princeton, N.J.: Princeton University Press, 1961), 131.

The believer has *his* knowledge interests. In the context of a believing life, philosophy will then truly be *philosophy* when she exclusively uses her own methods, without looking furtively to theology and the needs of theology, but also without falling victim to the error of thinking that she must arrive at the same exact place where the believing philosopher already is located. Philosophy must often exercise "heroic self-denial" for the sake of truth. The difficulty consists in the fact that we all live and philosophize in the context of a Christian ethos, in which moral values have a validity that is positively Christian and cannot really be justified *purely philosophically.* Such, for example, are the commandment to love one's enemies, the ethos of compassion, the beatitudes, and above all the "wisdom of the Cross" which must seem to the merely philosophical reason as foolishness. All attempts, such as the Kantian one, to justify the Christian ethos in purely philosophical terms ultimately lead to the destruction of that ethos. But just because Kantian ethics in its fundamental structure as a *philosophical* ethics is *too* Christian, it ceases to be Christian (and something similar can be said about the entire tradition of German idealism, especially Hegel). Philosophically, one must restrain oneself, by rendering unto Caesar what is Caesar's but to God what is God's. This does *not* mean that God has no place in philosophy. But it is not *the same place* in philosophy as in theology—this point will soon be clarified further.[66]

6. Moral Philosophy and Ultimate Theological Justification: What It Includes and What It Excludes

There is a temptation for the Christian to think with the presupposition, even in ethics, that nothing can happen without God. He might think that only a "theological ethics" is possible. In my view this would be a serious mistake. Certainly, without God, nothing exists or happens at all. And the philosopher would want to find reasons why that is so, even in ethics. But many contemporary moral theologians are less distant than might seem at first from the error of thinking that everything in ethics "hangs upon" God. Even though they may vouch for the autonomy of morality, still the whole must be ultimately grounded in God, to keep everything from falling into the void.

In reality, not even morality in its "ultimate justification" is "hanging upon" God. Like everything that exists—stars, planets, atoms, grass, flies, and elephants—so man and his action is constantly "in God" and "through God." God does not come into ethics only at the end, but is always present. The question is only *how* He is present, and how this presence becomes effective.

66. I will return to this topic in I.4, and in V.2.c.

At what point in human moral action God "appears," so to speak, is very hard to say. At the most it can be reconstructed. This is because we already know about God before we begin to analyze human behavior and practice ethics. The knowledge of God is not an achievement of practical reason. Rather, as a rule we have already taken our first steps as moral subjects on the basis of some form of insight into the existence of God and then we interpret the work of practical reason accordingly. Of course, the ideas of "practical reasoning" and "morality" lead to an awareness of God. Nevertheless, this is not a practical knowing but a form of *theoria* that discovers in the phenomenon of the moral the traces of that cause "which everyone calls God."[67] But the "hanging" of morality and human autonomy upon "God as ultimate justification" is thereby exposed as self-deception, and often only a convenient escape, in order to bring back at the end as an "ultimate justification" what one was not able to justify beforehand.[68]

But what is the place of philosophy in the context of that whole to which faith is directed and which forms the subject matter of moral theology? Many solutions to this have been offered in the past, and they are still very unsatisfying. Most of all, it was understood that philosophy was supposed to "limit itself" to the "natural goal" of man and what was required to reach this. Theology, finally, would then treat human existence insofar as it was ordered to a "supernatural goal." This made philosophical ethics into a kind of "narrow-gauge" moral theology, a moral theology with exclusions, an ethics at a lower level, or even a purely hypothetical discussion about a *natura pura,* a "mere nature" concerned with a kind of human being that does not exist in reality. This had the paradoxical consequence that in theological terms the "natural" would have to be relativized as a mere "leftover" concept [*Restbegriff*].[69]

New reflection is needed about the boundaries of philosophical ethics. My intention is to show that Thomas Aquinas gives us the decisive starting points for doing so. In any case, we will see that this defining must arise from the fundamental analysis of action-theory. Instead of beginning with the definition as such, we will justify it afterward, after we have already proceeded a certain way in our exposition. This may seem strange at first, but it will prove to be advantageous in due course.

Philosophical ethics, in the form presented here—a virtue ethics that is rational in its foundation—is understood as an ethics that can be constituted

67. This is the formula that concludes each proof of God's existence in Thomas Aquinas's *Summa Theologiae;* cf. Prima Pars, Quaestio 2, articulus 3 (hereafter = I, Q. 2, a. 3).

68. That is the tendency of numerous contributions in A. Hertz, W. Korff, T. Rendtorff, and H. Ringeling, eds., *Handbuch der Christlichen Ethik* (Feiburg im Breisgau: Herder, 1978); cf., e.g., 1.75 and 146.

69. So K. Rahner, "Über das Verhältnis von Natur und Gnade," in *Schriften zur Theologie* (Einsiedeln: Benziger, 1956), 1.323–45, esp. 340.

as *philosophical* even under the conditions of Christian faith. To this extent it is *not* a Christian ethics, even though it fully recognizes, and holds in due respect, the existence of a specifically Christian morality that is founded on revelation and already embraces the whole of life. Only in the latter sense is it a "Christian philosophy." But it is *not* a Christian philosophy when it comes to its methods and its contents. As philosophical ethics, it should be strictly adequate to the demands of a purely philosophical method, a method that can be recognized by believers as well as unbelievers. It understands itself as a free-standing discipline that *can* be integrated into moral theology, but also has a validity within its own realm, independently of theology: a validity that *moral theology too must respect and not limit or relativize.* If the "perspective of morality" as developed in a purely philosophical ethics does not comprehend the whole, it is still—even as an incomplete and partial view—an indispensable component of the truth of the whole.

In other words, I am writing in the conviction that philosophical ethics is something different from theological ethics or moral theology, even for the believing Christian. They are different—apart from the question of content—above all in their starting points and architecture, and in the structure of their arguments. In this matter I believe that I am suggesting some new paths in several respects. Consequently the overall structure of the book and the order of steps in the argument are of primary importance.

7. The Structural Peculiarities of Classical Virtue Ethics and the Order of the Argument in This Book

Julia Annas has very helpfully explained[70] that classical virtue ethics has several differences in methodology from modern moral philosophy. Annas tells us that according to a widespread current understanding, an ethical theory must have two characteristics: hierarchical structure and completeness. "Hierarchical" means that some concepts in an ethical theory are basic and all the others are understood to be derived from these or as reducible to them. Thus for consequentialism the basic element is the circumstances and states of affairs produced by the foreseeable consequences of actions, from which is derived that which we are obliged to do in our actions—namely, the production of the best possible circumstances and states of affairs. What it is to be a good or just human being or what would be called a "virtue" are questions that are answered by determining to what degree such a "virtue" can produce the optimal circumstances or states of affairs. In other words, "virtue" or "justice" are reduced to

---

70. *The Morality of Happiness,* 7ff. (see note 1 above).

the concept of a disposition to bring about actions that would have optimal consequences. If a theory is "complete," on the other hand, this would mean that its basic concepts and all the secondary concepts derived from them are capable of explaining the sum total of moral phenomena. A consequentialist would not allow for any judgment that would *not* be based on judging a disposition or an action on the basis of the consequences that follow from it. Accordingly, he would maintain that cowardice is to be judged as cowardice because bad consequences flow from it, which naturally leads to the position that it is the same thing to say that someone has done a misdeed from cowardice as from injustice. Both come to the same thing, since moral evaluation is made on the basis of the consequences that are produced by the action. Courage is then the disposition always to do the right thing (i.e., that which produces the best consequences), and the same goes for justice and temperance. Finally, all moral elements, especially the various concepts of the virtues, become so many different names for designating the same thing: namely, the consequentialist rationality of optimizing consequences. Such ethical theories are reductionist because they reduce everything to a single moral principle.

Classical virtue ethics is conceived neither as having a hierarchical structure nor as being "complete" in the sense just mentioned. The same can be said about a Thomas Aquinas–oriented rational virtue ethics belonging to the same tradition, with one qualification soon to be clarified. Classical virtue ethics does not begin with basic notions from which everything else is derived or to which everything is reduced. Instead, it begins with *primary* notions such as the ultimate goal of the acting person, the striving (or appetition) toward happiness (as an ultimate goal of appetition, willed for its own sake), and the concept of virtue itself (as an excellence of someone who attains what really is good in all his choosing and acting). The concept of "right" or "good" action is not derived from these notions, however, nor is reducible to them. Thus, for example, all classical virtue ethics from antiquity understand virtue as a disposition to do what is morally right; nevertheless the "morally right" is not defined as that which is suited for producing or favoring a virtuous disposition of the subject. Actions that are done virtuously do not have their moral value from being useful for the acquisition of virtues, but rather because they make it possible to choose what is morally right in each case; the virtues are the habitual disposition to do just that. The purpose of virtue is not to be a virtuous subject with good motivations, but to be a subject who acts rightly. The point of being a good, just, courageous, or temperate human being consists in being someone who likes what is just, courageous, or rightly measured, and also does it. For this very reason the question is quite important, what kind of a man or woman we make ourselves, when we choose or do this or that. A "just action" would therefore not be defined as an action through which someone becomes a just man (although naturally every virtue ethics holds that we become just persons through just actions). What is morally right must nevertheless be understood independently of this, because we become just men or women through the choosing and doing of just actions, that is, through choosing what is right according to the requirements of justice. Only in this way do we understand what makes a disposition to action or an affective state of the subject into a *virtue* at all: that is, into a *moral* disposition, which is a disposition of doing the morally right, and not just *any* disposition that someone could call admirable or excellent, but which may not have anything to do with morality.[71]

Classical virtue ethics does indeed have primary concepts like happiness or virtue, since there are primary and secondary things in our moral experience, but there is no hierarchical line of derivation from one to the other. Neither "happiness" nor "virtue" are moral principles. This becomes clear in the relationship between the concepts of "happiness," on the one hand, and "right" or "good" action, on the other. Even though the concept of happiness is the concept of the highest good, the right and good, through which we can reach that happiness, are not "derived" from that. The concept of the highest good or happiness is likewise not a standard on the basis of which actions can be evaluated (on this, see below, III.1). This is why a "hierarchical" structuring of ethics (in Annas's sense) is impossible. Now a lack of hierarchical structure leads to a lack of the "completeness" that would correspond to the hierarchy. Virtue ethics cannot explain everything in terms of virtue. This is why virtue ethics needs, for example, the supplementation of an institution ethics that is not reducible to virtue ethics concepts (whereas consequentialists do in fact ground institutional ethics statements with consequentialist logic). A virtue ethics also fully recognizes consequence-oriented arguments and can see a limited application for the discourse-ethics principle of consensus, especially when it widens into a political ethics. In general, virtue ethics is open in a pluralistic way to a whole variety of rational modes of argumentation. And this is an Aristotelian and fully non-Cartesian principle: the method must submit to the subject matter, and not the subject matter to the method. A virtue ethics likewise does not pretend to offer a solution for every case. "Borderline cases," "tricky moral problems," "quandaries," and "dilemmas" do not necessarily receive a clear "solution" (whereas for consequentialists there is always

---

71. J. Annas, *The Morality of Happiness*, 9. On this very point modern virtue ethics theories are problematic. M. Slote, *From Morality to Virtue* (see note 38 above), 90, holds that the "aretaic" qualities characteristic of virtues are not to be taken as *moral* qualities, but rather as "admirable" or "excellent" or "praiseworthy" characteristics. In Slote's virtue ethics, "virtue" is not a moral disposition.

a precise solution to be reached, namely, the one that brings the best foreseeable consequences). Nonetheless, the virtue ethics perspective can theoretically explain *why* such moral problems cannot be finally judged with absolute exactitude.

If someone is skeptical about virtue ethics, he often has come to this position by judging virtue ethics from the perspective of modern moral philosophy, through applying the typical requirements of hierarchical structure and completeness. As one critic has it, virtue ethics likewise "beginning with a root conception of the morally good person, proceeds to introduce a different set of secondary concepts which are defined in terms of their relationship to the primitive element."[72] In this way virtue ethics would only be another strategy for building a hierarchically structured and complete ethical system. This misunderstanding then leads directly to a discounting of the usefulness of the concept of virtue, since it is obvious that not much can be made out of a "core-concept of the morally good man" that must be defined as "the original element" in relation to everything else, and ultimately refers us back to a normative discourse that alone can ground what is meant as "good." Virtue ethics, then, so the criticism proceeds, is chaotic, unclear, and incapable of solving concrete moral problems or of giving an answer to casuistic questions. Now, in general, there is a certain amount of truth in this criticism. But it misses the really significant point. The criticism is justified when virtue ethicists make the concept of virtue into a fundamental concept out of which they derive everything else or to which they try to reduce everything else. Virtue, in this case, has become an all-determining concept, and virtue ethics is pursued in the spirit of modern moral philosophy. Such a modern "virtue ethics" which attempts to understand the rightness of actions through the motivations from which they arise naturally forgets the ancient wisdom that we can do what is right from poor motives and can also sometimes do what is wrong from good motives. In other words, we do not simply judge actions on the basis of the motives by which they are accomplished.

But we would not expect the virtue ethics represented by Thomas Aquinas to preserve the characteristics of classical virtue ethics as we have so far identified them. The conjunction of the classical and especially the Aristotelian tradition of ethics with the Christian law-ethics seems calculated to permit the concept of virtue to become a merely derivative concept, such as "a disposition to obey the moral law." If G.E.M. Anscombe was correct in her 1958 article (see note 39 above), then "virtue" and "moral law" are mutually exclu-

---

72. R.B.Louden, "On Some Vices of Virtue Ethics," *American Philosophical Quarterly* 21 (1984): 227–36; reprinted in Crisp and Slote, eds., *Virtue Ethics* (see note 38 above), 201–16, at 204.

sive ethical categories. But this is not necessarily so, and Thomas Aquinas is the proof that it is not. His interpretation of the "natural moral law" as a doctrine of principles supplementing a classical virtue ethics shows this, and also takes the classical tradition of Aristotelian virtue ethics to a level that is by no means un-Aristotelian, but can be called, as already mentioned, a kind of "broadened Aristotelian position."[73] A doctrine of principles of the practical reason is in fact a hierarchical element because it allows an actual discourse for the justification of norms. But it still remains faithful to the nonhierarchical logic of ancient/classical virtue ethics. This is because nothing concrete for praxis can be derived from the principles. Above all, practical principles are hierarchically structured only to the extent that some of them are higher and more important than others, but not in the sense that they are derivable from each other (for then they would not be principles). And because they are multiple, they rule out all claims to completeness in the sense discussed above.

But this means that there can really be an actual virtue-ethical discourse of justification as a display of practical principles. In this book, this will be done especially in chapter V, and it is significant that it is situated at the end and not at the beginning. The grounding of *ethics* as carried out in what follows is exactly for this reason not hierarchical in the sense we have indicated. However, the foundation of *morality* itself is "hierarchical" because the principles (in a sense not yet explained) are the "primary thing," grounding all morality and constituting the human being as a moral subject. But this "primary" of morality is not primary for ethics or moral philosophy. Like all philosophy and science, ethics does not arise from principles or causes, but is rather a way of *discovering* causes and principles. The ethical discourse about practical principles stands at the conclusion of the argument and is, in a way, its result—only then does it become a justification or foundation.

The following systematic exposition and "foundation" should not be misunderstood as a discourse of derivation.[74] This does not mean that the single chapters and sections do not follow a logical order. The opposite is true. But

73. I tried to show this in *Praktische Vernunft und Vernünftigkeit der Praxis* also against the opposite thesis, that Thomas created a Christian-theological reinterpretation and counterfeit of the essentially pagan-philosophical Aristotle. This position was maintained not only by R. A. Gauthier (see above) but also, and above all, by H. Jaffa, *Thomism and Aristotelianism: A Study of the Commentary by Thomas Aquinas on the Nicomachean Ethics* (Chicago: University of Chicago Press, 1952). Even though Jaffa's interpretation can today be held as definitively superseded, in many circles it still enjoys almost canonical authority.

74. In this way it is not liable to one of the three alternatives of H. Albert's "Münchhausen's Trilemma" which are valid for deductive methods of arguing. Cf. H. Albert, *Traktat über kritische Vernunft*, 5th ed. (Tübingen: Mohr, 1991), 13ff. In this sense, Aristotle was already aware that there can be no ultimate justification, since what is ultimate—which is at the same time the principle—cannot be established but can only be shown, precisely because it is the principle. And yet there is *a way to* the principles, and this is how principles acquire the function of an ultimate justification of what went before.

the reader will notice that every chapter, in a way, makes a fresh start. There will be reference to what has already been said, but also to other things, which will have to be introduced, but are still foundational. The argumentation is a kind of "circling around" the same subject matter: the human being as an acting, rational being that strives for fulfillment. The circling follows a certain logic of argumentation that can now be briefly sketched.

Chapter I. "Ethics in the Context of the Philosophical Disciplines"—this part treats preliminary clarifications about subject matter, method, and terminology.

Chapter II. "Human Action and the Question about Happiness"—this part clarifies, in terms of action theory, the origin of the basic question: the question about happiness and the really successful life. Two classical answers to the questions are sketched out and explained. These answers in both their Aristotelian and Thomistic versions are many-sided and rather like quandaries, but they still do help in leading to an abundance of fundamental action-theoretical insights. They also lead to a more precise delimitation of the various themes that are proper to a pure philosophical ethics.

Chapter III. "Moral Actions and Practical Reason"—this part works out the foundations in action theory and anthropology of philosophical ethics as a rational virtue ethics in which the concept of intentional action is especially developed. An understanding of the practical reason in its various anthropological dimensions is central here, since without it the intentional character of human action would remain incomprehensible.

Chapter IV. "The Moral Virtues"—this is a systematic treatment of the concept of moral virtue, built on the foregoing action-theoretical foundations. Although "virtue" is a primary concept, it must now be more precisely grasped in the context of the anthropological and action-theoretical analyses. The Thomistic reception of the Aristotelian definition of virtue will stand in the foreground, as well as the closely associated analysis of the dual (affective/cognitive) and anthropological function of the moral virtues, and the importance of the interconnectedness of the single virtues, making an "organism" of the virtues.

Chapter V. "Structures of Rationality"—this part contains what ethicists consider most important: the *normative* part of ethics in the proper sense. As explained, the questions about the moral norm or about the establishment of moral norms, the moral law, practical principles, and the like, are not left to this concluding position by chance. This is in fact the concluding discourse-of-justification for a eudaimonistic virtue ethics. Before this as a background, the last part ends with a critique of so-called teleological ethics (consequentialism, proportionalism). The reader may find it helpful to read part 4a of chapter V before anything else ("The Unity of the Practical Reason and the Perspective of Morality"). That section orients the overall course of argumentation and the position that results from it.

Finally, the epilogue, "From the Philosophical to the Christian Perspective of Morality," will show how in fact the inner *incompleteness* of the purely philosophical perspective justifies Christian morality, which again finally shows itself as a "rescue" and justification of philosophical reason, while at the same time staying true to the logic of a eudaimonistic virtue ethics.

Many themes that have received only an outline treatment on the following pages have been treated by the author at fuller length elsewhere, to which reference will be made at appropriate places in the footnotes and bibliography. In general, reference to scholarship has been limited to only the most essential. And yet it seems important to me to set forth my own thinking through precise historical references and the extensive support of primary texts. To this extent the book may also offer, as a kind of by-product, a certain stimulus for research in the history of philosophy. I believe that I have profited greatly from the debate with the exponents of analytical action-theory, and this applies particularly to the fundamental concept of intentional action. This explains the references, but also the critical stances, toward certain assertions of analytical philosophers.

This book attempts an introductory presentation, and—for the sake of completeness—cannot avoid, at times, the manner of a textbook. Many things must be treated with a view to comprehensiveness that cannot receive the development and differentiation they deserve. But for the most part, the book is designed to present an argument. It is not simply exposition, but also analysis, reflection, and the step-by-step, argumentative unfolding of a unified concept. I have striven for clarity and readability; the philosophical notion has constantly to be explicated through concrete illustration. The passages in smaller font comprise supplements and refinements of the main text, but at times they offer examples or short excurses. They form a part of the whole argument complex, but can be skipped over without any loss to the connection of thought.

It is my hope that this book will be useful not only as a self-standing contribution to philosophy, but at the same time as a philosophical preparatory course for moral theology. The latter purpose is responsible for certain emphases that result from my concern to develop specific and independently valid philosophical methods, lines of enquiry, and styles of argument for problems that have been posed with theological interests in view.

ETHICS IN THE CONTEXT OF
THE PHILOSOPHICAL DISCIPLINES

1. The Ought and the Good

Ethics is practical philosophy. That means that ethics reflects upon praxis—that is, human actions—and has praxis as its goal. Anyone who does ethics is an acting subject, and just because this subject knows itself as acting, there arise what we call ethical questions. These questions do not aim simply to know something. They are directed to praxis itself: to the *doing* of "good" or "right."

Now there are other ways of knowing that also aim toward doing something that is "good" or "right." Examples would be the knowledge of music theory or architecture. The Greeks called such knowing *technē,* and we call it art or technique. Certainly, art and technique have something to do with ethics. But *as such,* they ask only about how someone does some "definite thing" well, such as composing a musical piece or building a house. The really *practical* question aims at how to live as a human being. It aims at the whole of human life and of what it means to be human.

Kant, and essentially all the moral philosophy of the last two centuries, has maintained that the real ethical question is "What ought I to do?"[1] But this question does not reach far enough: it is not the first question. Previous to the question about "should" (or "ought") is the question about *good.* One "ought" to do what is "good," and do it just *because* it is good. The good is not good *because* one "ought" to do it, but vice versa—in fact, it *has* to be the other way round, since there has to be a reason for the "ought," and this is that which is reasonably to be aimed at, to be striven after. This is why Aristotle's *Nico-*

1. Immanuel Kant, *Logic,* trans. Hartman and Schwartz (Indianapolis: Bobbs-Merrill, 1974), 29. Cf. also *Critique of Pure Reason,* trans. J. M. D. Meiklejohn ["Great Books of the Western World" 42] (Chicago: University of Chicago Press, 1952), 236.

machean Ethics begins with the sentence: "Every art and every inquiry, and similarly every action and choice, is thought to aim at some good, and for this reason the good has rightly been declared to be that at which all things aim."[2] And the first principle of practical reason, then, founded on this, will be "one ought to do what is good, and avoid what is evil."[3] At the beginning of ethics, the question is about the good that we ought to do.

2. The Good and the Right

Can we distinguish the question about the (morally) good from the question about the (morally) right? It would indeed make sense to do so, since we often do what is not right with the best intention, and sometimes we do what is in itself right with a bad intention or poor attitude. And isn't it the important thing to do what is good, and not merely what is "right" or "correct"?

We are confronted here with an apparent problem only. Of course, it ultimately comes down to having a good will. But in ethics as in practical philosophy we are not searching for an answer to the question whether it is more important to act correctly or to act with a good intention. What we want to know is, what sort of actions *are* done with good intentions? That means, we want an answer to the question, *how* should we act, *what* ought we to do. It has to do with the question about the good that is realized in our *intentional, purposeful, freely chosen* actions and decisions not to act. Here, the good and the right are one and the same. Since it naturally happens that sometimes we do what is not right with the best intentions, this only means that even with the best intentions we sometimes do what we should not, and this happens because we *mistakenly think* that what we are doing is good.

The distinction between "good" and "right" or "correct" only makes sense in the realms of technology or technique. In these areas many things are done technically right that are nevertheless wrong in the moral sense. For example, we can say, "He should not have done this operation without her permission," even though he performed the operation flawlessly from a technical standpoint. The ethical question aims at enlightening us about the good that makes our action right with respect to life as a whole. And *this* "right" or "correct," as long as we move within the perspective of morality, we call the (moral) "good." And in this way, one could also say within the perspective of moral-

---

2. Aristotle, *Nicomachean Ethics* I, 1 1094a 1–3 (henceforth cited as *EN* [= *Ethica Nicomachea*], according to the Ross-Urmson translation in Jonathan Barnes, ed., *The Complete Works of Aristotle: The Revised Oxford Translation* (Princeton, N.J.: Princeton University, 1984), 2.1729–1867. This is the opening sentence of Aristotle's work.

3. Thomas Aquinas, *Summa Theologiae*, I-II, Q. 94, a. 2.

ity that "It wasn't right for him to perform this operation without her permission," even though we grant that he acted with good intention.

In the perspective of morality, the right is always the same as the good. This is because in the moral perspective we consider actions insofar as they are actions of a *human being* and not only the actions of a doctor, contractor, architect, and so on.[4]

3. Ethics Is Reflection On Praxis

Ethics reflects on praxis and aims at praxis. And we can now say more precisely that ethics reflects on the good that we ought to do, and has for its aim that we do the good. The point of departure for ethics is accordingly the good that—as we understand it—we have already done and are accustomed to do. This means the doing of what *appears* to us as good, of what we consider as good. We want to reflect on this doing, examine it, look into it, have reasons for it, improve on it. Through reflection on our action, we want to make sure of ourselves, in a way: to ensure that we are headed in the right direction, to ask ourselves whether our life "makes sense." Finally, we want to come to an understanding about all this with others. The ancient/classical virtue ethics, as teachings about the good and happy life, were in fact concerned with "revising priorities," and because they presupposed that *all* men in all their actions were striving for happiness, these ethical doctrines were always also concerned with acquiring some illumination about false or merely apparent expectations of happiness.[5]

Such questions are not uniquely asked by professional ethicists. Every person asks them, without practicing the science of ethics. Reflection upon praxis accompanies praxis incessantly. It is a special form of awareness, which we can call moral consciousness, or even conscience. Ethics practices this reflective knowledge in a systematic and methodical way.

This does not mean that ethics is concerned with the analysis of the formal *a priori* of moral behavior. There *are* ethical philosophies that do this—the philosophy of Kant, for example, and discourse-ethics that follows Kant's tradition in a certain sense. By the same token, ethics is not concerned with the analysis of our moral feelings. What is meant here, first of all, is merely that

---

4. Cf. below, III.3.c, as well as my full discussions in M. Rhonheimer, "Gut und Böse oder richtig und falsch—was unterscheidet das Sittliche?" in H. Thomas, ed., *Ethik der Leistung* (Herford: Busse Seewald, 1988), 47–75; for a slightly expanded version, see "Ethik—Handeln—Sittlichkeit. Zur sittlichen Dimension menschlichen Tuns," in J. Bonelli, ed., *Der Mensch als Mitte und Maßstab der Medizin* (Vienna and New York: Springer, 1992), 137–74.

5. J. Annas, *The Morality of Happiness*, 329ff.

ethics operates in the form of reflection and acquires its own subject matter through reflection. It arises from a lived ethos, from each person's practical experience, which is the experience of *actions,* and attempts to illuminate this experience. Ethics is not simply a derivative from other philosophical disciplines, such as metaphysics or anthropology, or even sociology. As a philosophical discipline ethics enjoys a point of departure specific to itself alone, which is the same point of departure that moral consciousness in general has: the self-experience of "myself" as acting (and passionately) striving—a subject that is sensitive to emotions, that wills, and that rationally judges and chooses. In this *methodological* sense, ethics is also autonomous: precisely on the basis of this irreducible starting point within the given experience of the self as a subject of actions.

> Of course moral consciousness has other sources as well. It does not come about in a kind of "free-floating" or solipsistic fashion. In fact, moral consciousness is always bound up with an ethos, with the sum total of existing norms already in place through cultural, social, and legal factors and put into practice by the processes of socialization.[6] But it is also such as to be not incapable of distancing itself at times from that ethos, or of behaving in a critical and revisionist way toward the currently valid norms—and to do this for moral reasons. On the other hand, it can also be said that the stability of an ethos would not be intelligible unless it rested upon givens that are present to the moral consciousness, and which, as morally relevant givens quite independent of sociocultural validation, make such validation intelligible in the first place.

Now the subjects that practice ethics are subjects that have, or can have, many other kinds of experience apart from their own practical experience, or experience of their own actions. And if we define ethics as the analysis of moral consciousness with a practical aim, we are implying that ethics is a special form of knowledge of a *human being.* It is a human being's knowledge insofar as this knowledge appears *in* moral consciousness. But we need to understand the content of this consciousness. How should we interpret it? Do we limit ourselves to the phenomena that are revealed in this consciousness? We know other things as well, we know about the reality of which the human being is a part. We possess insights about the structure of acting in general, which are not what we would call *practical* insights. These are insights that can be gathered from action-theory and metaphysical analysis. There are also insights of an anthropological nature that do not originally spring from the

---

6. Cf. also W. Kluxen, "Ethik und Ethos, bzw. Das Allgemeine und das Gemeinsame. Moralische Normen im konkreten Ethos," in Kluxen, *Moral-Vernunft-Natur. Beiträge zur Ethik,* ed. W. Korff and P. Mikat (Paderborn: Schöningh, 1997), 3–16 and 42–49; see also Kluxen, *Ethik des Ethos* (Freiberg and Munich: K. Alber, 1974).

moral consciousness, but lie deep at its foundations. We can even already *know* (and this means a rational knowing) that something exists "which all men call God."

But ethics also has the reverse function of completing anthropology. Ultimately, of course, everything is interconnected: reality does not form itself out of philosophical disciplines—it is not divided up into academic departments. The organization into distinct disciplines comes from the peculiar nature of our knowledge of reality and from the limitations of our knowledge. The *interconnected whole* must constantly be sought out and reflected upon.

In other words, granted that ethics is "autonomous" in this methodological sense by having a starting point peculiar to itself, this autonomy would not be such as to separate it off from other ways of knowing that can also tell us something about man, or about "reality" or being in general, which in fact make it possible to complete moral-practical consciousness and make it as intelligible as possible.

> Knowledge of the empirical human sciences (psychology, human biology, behavioral research, sociology, etc.) are not so much the primary "tool set" for a philosophical understanding of the human being, but rather make up that sum total of experience that is itself in need of a philosophical (anthropological and ethical) explanation and ordering (even apart from the fact that empirical/human scientific knowledge is never itself free of theoretical and philosophical presuppositions, and thus remains subject to the possibility of a philosophical critique and subordination to principles). A social-scientific version of ethics passes easily into a "morality of the experts," which ends up by devaluing practical reasoning and the moral autonomy of the individual. By contrast, what interests us here is ethics as reflection upon the moral consciousness that is available to each individual human subject. Regardless of the importance of empirical, social/human scientific knowledge, the real point of ethics is to order this empirical element in a normative fashion, to weigh its significance, and to overcome its factual pressures at the horizon of what one ought to do from a moral point of view. This is because the moral ought is not fundamentally confined to the level of the empirically given—let alone the "purely natural"—but is always passing beyond it toward what is truly good for man. In this sense, ethical reasoning is not simply to be reduced to some other, merely empirical given. But in order to keep this transcendence within realistic and practical bounds, knowledge of the human and social sciences can provide indispensable orientation.

In this way ethics presents a reasonable kind of interplay of practical experience, action-theory, metaphysics of action, and philosophical anthropology. Furthermore, we do not have to exclude knowledge about the being "that everyone calls God" because we are not required to accept the Kantian rejection of the proofs of God's existence (and this would be because we ourselves reject the proofs that Kant criticizes, and consequently can maintain that there *are* other ways of knowing about the existence of God that are not affected in the least by his criticism; besides this, we are likewise not compelled to accept the Kantian theory of the constitution of experience, there being good reasons to consider it as incorrect and finally unjustified).[7] If, then, we do not exclude such rational knowing of God, even though the reasoning for it does not belong to the subject matter of ethics, then that being "which everyone calls God" can and must play a role in ethics. This is *at least* as valid as Sartre's approach, which proceeds from the nonexistence of God—a position that equally lacks any justification from the viewpoint of ethics.[8] In fact, such a manner of proceeding is not even rationally justified, since no one can *prove* the nonexistence of God. The most one can do is try, as Kant did, to prove the impossibility of proving God's existence. But that means that one would have to prove the impossibility of *all possible* or *already existing* proofs of His existence, and Kant did not succeed in doing that, either. And until someone succeeds in this, it will always be more reasonable to assume that there *is* a God rather than there isn't. Kant would be the last to deny this.[9]

This is why an ethics that does not exclude at the outset any knowledge about God's existence is not an "unphilosophical" ethics, but simply a *different kind* of ethics than one that *does* make such an exclusion. If the presentation of ethics in this book is *different* from the Kantian or the Sartrean ones, that in itself should not be a compelling argument against it!

7. This is ultimately because it rests on an unproved thesis that has taken on the function of a constantly recurring argument (which Kant's *Critique of Pure Reason* turns into a systematic "begging of the question," or *petitio principii*), namely, the assertion that necessary and universal concepts can in no way arise from experience and must therefore be understood as an *a priori* of the cognitive structure of the human subject (see the "Introduction" to the *Critique of Pure Reason*). In response to this John McDowell would like to supplement Kant in an "Aristotelian" way, by pleading for the rediscovery of the conceptual content of experience, which would have for its effect, although McDowell does not say so, the collapse of the basic underpinning of Kantian transcendental philosophy. Cf. J. McDowell, *Mind and World* (Cambridge and London: Cambridge University Press, 1994). Cf. also the "Aristotelian" remark by U. Wolf that turns Kant's philosophy on its head (in *Die Philosophie und die Frage nach dem guten Leben* [see note 18 above], 180): "In a certain sense, everything naturally arises empirically at some time, even the so-called given *a priori* concepts."

8. Cf. J.-P. Sartre, "Existentialism and Humanism," trans. P. Mairet, in J.-P. Sartre, *Basic Writings*, ed. S. Priest (New York: Routledge, 2000), 25–46, esp. 28: "Atheistic existentialism, of which I am a representative, declares . . . that if God does not exist, there is at least one being whose existence comes before his essence, a being which exists before it can be defined by any conception of it . . . there is no human nature, because there is no God to have a conception of it . . . man simply is . . . what he wills."

9. Cf. also the debate in more recent times between Richard Swinburne (*The Coherence of Theism* [1977]; *The Existence of God* [1979]; *Faith and Reason* [1981]) and J. L. Mackie (*The Miracle of Theism* [1982]); cf. also F. Ricken, "Die Rationalität der Religion in der Analytischen Philosophie: Swinburne, Mackie, Wittgenstein," *Philosophisches Jahrbuch* 99 (1992): 287–306.

4. Philosophical Ethics and God

But I would not want to create the impression that this book will constantly be speaking about God. On the contrary: we actually "need" God less than Kantian ethics does. By this I mean the reference to the "idea of God," whereby Kant can speak of a "moral proof of God's existence" to be found in the heart. For Kant, the practical reason stands or falls by the postulate (not the knowledge) of God's existence. Kant supports a kind of "ethico-theology" by which moral action is not possible at all without the idea of God (and vice versa). Although the God that Kant speaks of is only postulated and hence not known, it nevertheless is a God on whom absolutely *everything* depends.[10] If the concept of ethics as developed here begins with a God who is known—just as Aristotle does in his *Ethics*—in a peculiar way, this has the opposite effect as in Kantian ethics: we will be in a position to explain the inner disposition of moral actions without having constantly to tie them back to the "idea of God."

In this ethics, "God" enters the picture as the original starting point [*Ursprung*], without which the human being, practical reasoning, and moral action cannot be explained, but not as a postulate, as with Kant; for Kant, making such a postulate is the condition for practical reason to become *practical* at all, and for it to lead to action.

> Kant writes, "Thus without a God, and without a world, invisible to us now, but hoped for, the glorious ideas of morality are, indeed, objects of approbation and of admiration, but cannot be the springs of purpose and action."[11] Even if the "moral laws" of reason are autonomously recognized, the presupposition of a "wise ruler of the universe" would be necessary "to give [those laws] effect."[12]

The inner moving force of Kantian practical reasoning consists in striving to make oneself worthy of happiness (*"Do that, which will render thee worthy of happiness"*)[13] through subordination to the pure "ought" (the rational imperative), without ever allowing the yearning for happiness to have any influence upon the practical reason. This is a heroic denial, the possibility for which stands or falls with postulating a God who in "another life" will provide

---

10. This becomes clear especially in the "Transcendental Method" section near the end of the *Critique of Pure Reason*, where Kant writes: "my belief in God and in another world is so interwoven with my moral nature" that one cannot exist without the other. But what about someone "who is entirely indifferent with regard to moral laws?" Kant answers that "even in this case enough may be left to make him *fear* the existence of God and a future life" (trans. Meiklejohn; see note 1 above), 242. This means that Kant holds that according to his theory, it would not be possible to *acquire* a moral sense without fearing a God whose existence is postulated.

11. *Critique of Pure Reason*, trans. Meiklejohn, 238.

12. Ibid., 240.

13. Ibid., 237.

the reward of happiness [*Glückseligkeit*] to such worthiness. Without such a belief, practical reason would not only not be practical, it would not even be *reasonable*. The Kantian practical reason is interested in the existence of God at every step, it must believe in Him and hope in Him (or fear Him), because otherwise as rationality it would dissolve into "nothing." Here, God operates despotically: one must neither recognize Him nor act lovingly toward Him, because otherwise morality would not be possible. But one must also believe in Him with all one's strength (i.e., *postulate* Him), because otherwise, it would be irrational to be moral.

> The problem of the "mainspring" or "incentive" [*Triebfeder*] has in any event two aspects, which Kant does not clearly distinguish from each other: (1) the question, how practical reason ever becomes practical, that is, how what is moral can ever become the "spring of purpose and action," and (2) the question about the moral principle itself, that is, the "formal ground" of our actions: when do I behave morally? Only then, when I do not attend to the reward of happiness, that is, when I act exclusively out of respect for the moral law (= the imperative of pure reason), with "reverence for duty" [*Ehrfurcht vor der Pflicht;* cf. *Critique of Practical Reason,* trans. M. Gregor, 70; see below: II.1.e, note 37]. But this only answers the question, *what kind* of incentive is a *moral* incentive, but not the first question, how in general do we arrive at *actually doing* what duty commands? How can the acknowledged duty become "the spring of purpose and action"? In contrast with the view expressed in the *Critique of Pure Reason,* in the *Groundwork of the Metaphysics of Morals* (trans. M. Gregor; see below, II.1.a, note 3), Kant speaks of the "impossibility of discovering and making comprehensible an interest which the human being can take in moral laws" (63) and notes that "it is impossible for us to explain, in other words, *how pure reason can be practical,* and all the pains and labor of seeking an explanation to it are lost" (65). Now this question is in fact never answered in the *Critique of Practical Reason* and its doctrine of the "respect for the law" (68). Thus it cannot be surprising, that later, in the *Metaphysics of Morals* (trans. M. Gregor; see below, IV.2.c, note 39) Kant says that "to have religion" is "a duty of the human being to himself," and that means, to assume an idea of God that "we ourselves make" (i.e., we postulate) "for the purpose of serving as the incentive in our conduct" (193). But this once again becomes the subject of a problem in the *Critique of Judgment:* the moral laws would also be recognized as binding by someone who maintains that "there is no God" (*Critique of Judgment,* trans. J. C. Meredith, "Great Books of the Western World 42," 596). Nevertheless, Kant becomes more exact on the point: since, for atheists, in the end all human beings will be hurled "back into the abyss of the aimless chaos of matter," and "one wide grave engulfs them all—just and unjust, there is no distinction" (ibid.), so the contentment and benevolence of the morally acting person cannot meaningfully motivate as the *ultimate purpose* of action.

"[The atheist] must assume the existence of a *moral* author of the world, that is, of a God. As this assumption at least involves nothing intrinsically self-contradictory he may quite readily make it from a practical point of view, that is to say, at least for the purpose of framing a conception of the possibility of the final end morally prescribed to him" (ibid.). And this means that even the atheist, in order effectively to *act* morally (and not just merely *acknowledge* the moral law) must postulate God, as a "reality that is subjectively practical" (ibid.). In this way, it seems to me, Kant has masked over rather than really solved the fundamental problem of his practical philosophy—how the reason can become *practical*.[14]

In contrast, the "known God" appears very differently in moral philosophy from the "postulated God." For God is present here as the moving *telos* of a reason, which would, indeed, in the same way fall into nothing without Him, but for all that, *in itself* and *by itself* is not only moral reason but also, and as such, *practical* reason as well. (This presupposes giving up the Kantian dichotomy of freedom or autonomy of the will versus "empirical" inclination, that is, it is a return to an appetitive ethics.) As practical, reason is neither believing nor hoping in the Kantian sense, but just *reasoning*, and reality disclosing, and only as such can it then open itself to that faith and hope which "surpasses all understanding."[15] If Kant's God is a God "within the limits of reason alone," so is Kant's reason—as practical reason—one that cannot be thought of as rational *without* God, and—as pure reason—one that cannot become practical, because no subjective interest is available to it, by which the consciousness of duty and the respect for law could really lead to *action*.

Kant wanted to ground the autonomy of the will, but the price that he had to pay for it was enormously high. For the price to be exacted was being forced to recognize another, and now truly problematic "heteronomy": the total dependence of practical reason on "faith and hope," and this involves the structural decomposition of reason as such. For a reason that fundamentally depends on "belief"—even if Kant calls it a "rational belief"—is, first of all, no longer reason, and secondly, can no longer open itself up to any further belief than the one from which it obtains its postulates. And that means that such reason can no longer even rationally believe, certainly not in that which "passes all understanding."

14. Cf. the analysis of N. Rotenstreich, *Practice and Realization: Studies in Kant's Moral Philosophy* (The Hague-Boston-London: Martinus Nijhoff, 1979), which clearly reveals the difficulty.
15. Cf. Philippians 4:7.

II

HUMAN ACTION AND
THE QUESTION OF HAPPINESS

1. Action Theory: Intentionality and Freedom in Human Action

a) The Perspective of the Acting Subject

We noticed that Aristotle's *Nicomachean Ethics* begins with a simple declaration of a fact of experience: "Every art and every inquiry, and similarly every action and pursuit, is thought to aim at some good; and for this reason the good has rightly been declared to be that at which all things aim." "Good" then, is what someone "aims for." The concept of the good is given through the experience that in everything we do—art, research, action, choice—we are going after something. This aim—"what we are looking for"—we call good. The concept of the good is therefore *identical* with the concept of "the goal of striving." Goods—and this means *practical* goods—are goals of striving, of appetition, of aiming at. And whatever we do, we strive after a good, we aim at something.[1]

> Some clarification is needed about the concept of "practical good." A car or a computer are "things." And as things they are "good" in several respects. But only to the extent that appetition or striving meets with these objects in a *practical* way (to want to get one, to want to steal one) does a car or a computer become a *practical* good. This kind of goodness is not founded in the thing-ness of these objects, but rather in their relationship toward a willing. The practical good in this case is no longer the car or the computer as such but rather their *possession.* The practical good is not "car" but "having a car." And the corresponding actions that can be formed within the perspective of such a practical good would be "buying a car" or "stealing a car." Something analogous holds

---

1. See also O. Höffe, "Kategorie Streben," in O. Höffe, *Ethik und Politik. Grundmodelle und -probleme der praktischen Philosophie* (Frankfurt am Main: Suhrkamp, 1979), 311–33.

for persons: they become practical goods insofar as they are objects of acts of appetition and actions (as, e.g., objects of goodwill, love, respect, contractual obligations, or even of actions such as "get information from someone," or "bribe someone," or "use someone for one's own purpose," etc.). As Kant expressed it, unlike things, persons have "worth," which means that any relationships to them as practical goods may never sacrifice the fact that they are "good" independently of such relationships, which means nothing other than that in the context of actions they should never be *merely* a means.

And so we find ourselves within the perspective of action. It does not make any difference that we are also including art in this. Art can be described as a kind of *praxis*. In the activities of artful production (technique in the broadest sense), we are "looking for something." And this "looking for" we call *intentionality* [Lat. *intendere*, to stretch toward, to aim at].

Already the first sentence of Aristotle's *Ethics* places us within a quite specific perspective. We can call this the perspective of praxis. We will never depart from this perspective in this book. It is the perspective of the "first person," the perspective of the acting subject. It is necessary to emphasize this because the entire tradition of modern ethics, and especially its major types— Kantian duty-ethics and utilitarianism—are ethics of the "third person."[2] As surprising as this may sound, these are ethics of absolute objectivity. As Kant puts it, "Practical good is . . . that which determines the will by means of representations of reason, hence not by subjective causes but objectively, that is, from grounds that are valid for every rational being as such."[3] The starting point for Kantian ethics is in fact just the exclusion of the perspective of the "interested" acting subject for the sake of the "disinterested" commands of reason. Only the universally valid can ever be morally valid. Only a maxim of action capable of being willed as a universal law is moral, but not what corresponds to the inclinations, appetition, or strivings of the acting subject. Duty is the command of reason, which comes into play *against* the good that is conditioned by inclinations. Again, Kantian-inspired discourse-ethics only recognizes intersubjectively communicative and consensus-oriented action as sufficient for moral significance; it concedes normative validity only to such

2. On the difference between an ethics of the "first person" and one of the "third person," cf. G. Abbà, *Felicità, vita buona, e virtù. Saggio di filosofia morale* (Rome: LAS, 1989), 97ff., and J. Finnis, *Fundamentals of Ethics* (Washington, D.C.: Georgetown University Press, 1983). On this theme, see also A. Rodriguez Luño, *Etica* (Pamplona: Universidad de Navarra, 1982). This difference largely corresponds to the difference between the perspective of the (neutral) observer and the perspective of the acting subject. Cf., e.g., B. M. Riedel, "Handlungstheorie als ethische Grunddisziplin," in H. Lenk, ed., *Handlungstheorien interdisziplinär*, Bd. 2, I (Munich: W. Fink, 1978), 142f. More recently H. Krämer, *Integrative Ethik* (Frankfurt am Main: Suhrkamp, 1992), 84, has recalled that classical appetitive ethics are ethics of the first person.

3. Immanuel Kant, *Groundwork of the Metaphysics of Morals*, trans. M. Gregor, 25.

claims of value as can be accepted without coercion by all concerned; it wants to subordinate merely subjective interest to the objectivity of a consensus that has been reached by discussion—and with certain qualifications this makes very good sense for ethics at a *political* level. Utilitarianism, too, in all its varieties, is an ethics of objectivity: in this case the objectivity of the "calculation" (or "weighing") of advantages, consequences, and goods. This theory treats the acting person, in a way, from the outside, as the disinterested producer of the best possible world situation. It approaches the person—to use the expression of an American philosopher, Thomas Nagel—by a "view from nowhere."[4] For example: even if it utterly repels me—on the basis, say, of my upbringing and the convictions and feelings I might have—to kill a human being, according to utilitarian standards I would nevertheless be obliged to do it if I could thereby save the lives of ten others, *to the extent that* by doing this, according to my estimation, the overall balance of consequences would optimize the world situation.[5]

But ethics, as said before, arises from a reflection upon practical experience which is an experience of acting subjects. If ethics is not going to distort the phenomenon of "human (moral) action," it can never depart from this perspective of action. If, within this perspective of action, we speak of "goods" and "ends," we always mean correlates of an *appetition,* and we treat human activity as a "seeking for the good." That is always what happens when we do something.

Therefore the good, as we also learn from Aristotle, is always something that "appears good" to an acting subject. "Appearance of good" does not mean in this case a *deceptive* appearance, but rather the good insofar as it shows it-

---

4. Cf. Nagel's book with the same title: *The View from Nowhere* (Oxford: Oxford University Press, 1986) and his critique of "overobjectification" (162ff.)

5. According to H. Krämer, *Integrative Ethik* (see note 2 above), 119, the classical, appetitive ethical perspective of the good life [*Glücksethik*] cannot be blended with the modern perspective of moral philosophy [*Sollensethik*] into a unified ethics; they form, rather, two complementary perspectives. The first is concerned with the success "of my own life" (here there is no "ought" [*sollen*], but only a more or less coherent "willing" [*wollen*]); the second is concerned with what we owe to others (here we experience the "ought," norms, duties, etc., that delimit our own willing). The ultimate reason why a "unified ethics" (even a Thomistic one) is impossible—an ethical theory that would combine into one the good life perspective with an obligation perspective, modern moral philosophy with appetitive ethics—appears to Krämer to lie in the fact that such a unity of the striving for happiness with the moral ought—making it necessary to present the concept of "right" as the "truly good" striving—would radically contradict the "self-determination" and "sovereignty of preference" of modern postteleological man. This historical characterization of the modern moral subject and his (apparently) inevitable understanding of himself that categorically relegates all attempts at a unified ethics to a "utopian nowhere," becomes an absolute principle for Krämer that cannot be questioned, but this does not make it any less doubtful as a premise. An important calling-into-question of Krämer's basic thesis can be found in J. Raz, *The Morality of Freedom* (Oxford: Oxford University Press, 1986), 313ff., esp. 315; Raz characterizes the opposition of personal interest (the "appetitive-ethics" aspect) and morality or moral rectitude (the "moral philosophical" aspect) as a misleading "popular and philosophically fashionable picture of human beings," which needs to be overcome.

self as such in the *judgment* made by the acting subject. In the perspective of praxis, good is just that which we *judge* to be good and which *appears* good.

That here the "judgment about the good" leads to an "appearance of good" is due to the fact that judgments about actions are judgments about appetitions [*Strebungen*]. It is a matter of affectively conditioned judgments and judgments about affects and appetitions. This is also why, as Aristotle remarks, "our whole inquiry must be about these; for to feel delight and pain rightly or wrongly has no small effect on our actions."[6] It is not because we always act from "desire," but because desire indicates the affect that is most capable of disorienting the reason, but at the same time, if operating "in the right way," is the most powerful support of the reason.[7]

The decisive question for praxis consists in making clear just what the conditions are that would make this "seeming," or judgment, meet truth as well, so that what "appears to be good" is also "good in reality." This is only going to occur when the striving or appetition itself (the emotions and the will) hits upon what truly is good. This is exactly what happens with the virtuous person. "The good man judges each class of things rightly, and in each the truth appears to him."[8]

Ethics is a doctrine of virtue. But this is to anticipate. Only so much should be taken as established: we are *not* looking for an "objectivity" of the "universal commands of reason" or for a "human nature" or an "optimal world situation" or even a noncoerced consensus of all participants in an ideal discourse. What we need, rather, are the criteria for determining a kind of objectivity that we might call *the truth of subjectivity:* the truth of the practical judgments made by acting subjects about the goods presented to their striving. Now this does not mean that praxis and ethics have nothing to do with "universal commandments of reason" or with "human nature" or with the "best condition of the world." It means only that ethical reflection cannot find its starting point in those areas.

It should be emphasized at the outset that the opposition "subjective-objective" distorts our perspective in ethics. The "morally good" (or "right") is neither an objectivity separated off from subjectivity, nor a subjectivity in the sense of a "subjective" relativism. In the perspective of morality—as shall be shown more fully later—"objectivity" is not a concept *opposed* to "subjectivity," but rather a certain "disposition" of subjectivity—namely, *truth.* The fundamental perspective of morality, nevertheless, is essentially always the perspective of subjectiv-

---

6. *EN* II, 2 (1105a 6–7).

7. Cf. F. Ricken, *Der Lustbegriff in der Nikomachischen Ethik des Aristotleles* (Göttingen: Vandenhoek & Ruprecht, 1976).

8. *EN* III, 6 (1113a 30–31).

ity, that is to say, the subjectivity of the striving *subject,* of the subject who acts on the basis of such striving.

In order to answer the question about *conditions for the truth of subjectivity,* several steps of exposition will be required. In fact ethics as a whole is nothing other than the answering of this question. This is also why—just like every other science—it has to do with truth.[9]

Accordingly, ethics begins with a fundamental analysis of action, which is in turn nothing other than a theory of the moral subject. The development of an ethics is the development of this analysis and theory of the acting human being. This is what we are interested in: understanding ourselves as beings who act.

Consequently, it is quite illuminating that Thomas Aquinas opens the moral-theoretical part of his systematic masterpiece [*Summa Theologiae,* Prima Secundae] with the question whether it is peculiar to man to act for the sake of an end.[10] The goal-directed nature of human action and the basic categories that can be derived from the analysis of this goal-directed nature will here serve as the starting point for everything else.

b) Goal-Directedness and the Concept of "Human Action"

The intentional character of human action, as briefly sketched above, means that action is always "targeted" to something. And we use the word "good" to indicate something we aim at.[11] This already includes the fact (as already explained) that the "good" that we aim for in action is that "seeming-good," which correlates to a judgment by the subject. If we were not to *judge* concerning the "end" or "good," and not continually act on the basis of such judgments, or abstain from acting (which is a form of action, namely, willing omission), a corresponding striving or doing would no longer interest us. It would

9. H. Krämer, *Integrative Ethik,* 52f., objects in general to the notion that "truth" would be a suitable category for the practical realm; only "validity" and "rightness" can function here. Krämer also maintains that even in classical appetitive ethics the "good as object of action" is essentially "synonymous with what is willed and striven-for" (79). It is correct to say that, in fact, a peculiarity of classical ethics is for the good to be treated essentially as something sought and willed; but that is only the starting point. The business of ethics then consists in answering the question, in what does the *truly good* consist, or how can one distinguish it from the *merely apparent* good—in other words, what someone *should* strive for and what one should not.

10. I-II, Q. 1, a. 1.

11. The problem that G. E. Moore raised in his *Principia Ethica* (Cambridge: Cambridge University Press, 1903) about the nonnatural meaning of the word "good" solves itself in this perspective. Obviously, "good," cannot be reduced, like "yellow," to any other natural property. "Good," in the sense of *"practical* good" is not at all a "natural quality" of something, but is rather the "something" itself, insofar as this something is a correlate of an appetition. Cf. also, from the perspective of analytic philosophy, B. Williams, *Morality: An Introduction to Ethics* (New York: Harper & Row, 1972).

then simply be a matter of some purely "spontaneous" or "natural" *happening*, the analysis of which would belong to a natural science (or a natural scientific psychology), but not to ethics.

One component of our practical experience is that our action is *free*, meaning that it is carried out on the basis of reasoned judgments, and that we always have control in some form over the striving that follows from such judgments. Freedom of action must not wait to be established in the process of developing ethics. It is a primordial experience, and without it there would be no such thing as ethics or practical philosophy at all. Practical philosophy is always reflection upon our experience of freedom in our actions. We do not need to postulate this freedom. It is not a postulate or "condition of the possibility" of praxis; it is rather the *occasion* and *subject matter* of the reflection that we call practical philosophy. An ethics that has to postulate freedom and that tries to establish its existence has already chosen a false starting point in some way, and has already missed its proper subject matter.

The freedom that has been referred to just now as a primordial experience is called *dominium* by Thomas, or mastery over one's own striving and doing. This mastery is peculiar to a certain kind of appetition: the kind that is based on *reason*, the kind that is called *willing*.[12]

This freedom has then a double root: it has its seat in willing, which is the kind of striving that proceeds on the basis of rational judgments. The will is the root of freedom insofar as it is the subject (the bearer, the seat) of freedom. Thomas calls *reason itself* the root of freedom because it is the *cause* of freedom: "The will is capable of directing itself freely to different objects, because the reason is capable of having various conceptions about what is good."[13]

The appetition of sensual desire, for example, rests upon the perceptions of the sense organs. Such perception depends upon conditions of the organs (the subject) and certain characteristics of the objects striven for. The relationship between the perceiving subject and the striven-for object is naturally determined in this case. The sense judgment takes place in one dimension: it is natural and spontaneous. When speaking about living things that are active on the basis of strivings based on sense perception, we would not call it "action" in the full sense: *non agunt sed aguntur* (they do not "act" but "are acted," are "put-into action"), as Thomas puts it in a Latin word play that cannot be translated.[14]

Reason, on the other hand, is capable of judging the good—including the good of sense appetition—and under various points of view, the reason can

---

12. On this, see esp. Thomas Aquinas, *De Veritate*, Q. 22, a. 4.
13. I-II, Q. 17, a. 1, ad 2.
14. *De Veritate*, ibid. (Thomas is quoting John Damascene, *De Fide Orthodoxa*, II, 2).

consider different aspects, can weigh "pro" and "con," and so forth. Reason is not determined through any particular good. For the appetition of sense perception, the good that is presented is good in every respect, and that is because the sense appetites only possess *one* aspect each. The reason grasps that what may be good "in every respect" for sense desire is not truly good "in every respect," because the reason is capable of judging with reference to a manifold of perspectives.

The human being only acts on the basis of an appetition or striving [*Streben*] that follows the judgment of reason. This too is a primordial experience. This appetition we call the "will." It has the openness and many-sidedness of the reason. And that means that it can even have itself for its own object. Because of the various points of view that can be taken, judgments of reason can in turn be judged by the same reason. And what can be striven-for (willed) on the basis of rational judgment, can itself become the object of a second-order desire.[15] Reason and will are reflexive. "Seeing" cannot see itself, "hearing" cannot hear itself, "touching" cannot touch itself: sense consciousness is never self-consciousness. But reason can operate rationally upon itself, can judge itself, and thus willed appetition can itself be willed or not willed over and over again.

Thanks to will and reason, our action is something that we have in our control. To be able to will means to possess mastery over one's own striving. Now, this does not mean that there is not also something in reason and will that is *not* in our power: there are judgments of the practical reason that we accomplish in a natural/spontaneous way. One such would be "Good is to be done, evil is to be avoided." There are also appetitions of the will, over which we are *not* masters in a certain respect, such as, for example, the striving toward self-preservation and above all the desire for happiness. But this will be taken up at a later stage (V).

An action over which we have mastery, and which we can carry out on the basis of such mastery, was called a "human action" *(actus humanus)* by the theologians of the Scholastic era. Such actions must be distinguished from the activities of human subjects that do not originate from reason and will, and even though they are "doings" or "actions of a man" *(actūs hominis),* they are not *human* actions, that is, actions that arise from what is specific to human

---

15. This reality—quite familiar to classical philosophical psychology, and self-evident, really—that the will can stand in relation to itself, can take up a position toward itself, thereby making its own willing into an object of its own willing or not willing on another level, has again been emphasized by, e.g., H. Frankfurt, "Freedom of the Will and the Concept of a Person," *Journal of Philosophy* 67 (1971): 5–20, and, with reference to Frankfurt, Charles Taylor, "What Is Human Agency?" in Taylor, *Human Agency and Language* (Cambridge: Cambridge University Press, 1985), 15–44, and "What's Wrong with Negative Liberty?" in *Philosophy and the Human Sciences* (Cambridge: Cambridge University Press, 1985), 211–29.

action. These other actions have the external appearance of human actions, perhaps, but not the "soul." In other words: they do not arise from *free will,* whereby "free will" signifies nothing other than "striving on the basis of rational judgments." "Free will" is not an undetermined or undeterminable will, but rather a will that can become determined no otherwise than through rational judgments about the good.

Analytical philosophers do not as a rule make any distinction between *actus humanus* and *actus hominis,* since this distinction naturally already presupposes a "strong" concept of action that includes will. This nondistinction then often leads to unnecessary complications and obscurities and finally results—as in the case of Donald Davidson—in the reduction of actions to corporeal movements. Actions are interpreted as happenings caused in a certain way: "We never do more than move our bodies: the rest is up to nature."[16] The following example adduced by Davidson is characteristic: "Tripping over a rug is normally not an action; but it is if done intentionally."[17] On the basis of the distinction between *actus hominis* (act of a human being) and *actus humanus* (human action), it becomes immediately clear that "to stumble" is not a "human action," although it is of course something that one somehow "does." In the case of someone doing it on purpose, that would not be an "intentional stumbling" (that would contradict the very concept of "stumbling"), but rather merely "acting (i.e., in a theatrical way) just as if one stumbled," and that is a (purposeful) simulation of an unintentional corporeal movement or event or happening (of stumbling).

Actions carried out in sleep are not "human actions." Nor, by the same token, are certain spontaneous or reflex actions. Young children that do not yet have the use of reason do not carry out "human actions." Nor do the mentally handicapped (to the extent that such actions are pathologically caused). Nor is it a "human action" when someone, hearing a sudden scream, pushes someone else in a reflex action. In all these cases, we can speak of "acts of human beings," since people asleep, small children, the mentally handicapped, and people acting by automatic reflex are all human beings. But the actions in question are not carried out on the basis of characteristics that are peculiar to these subjects as *human beings.* An action of ours is distinguished as *human* because it is voluntary, that is to say, it originates from rationally guided striving, and when we have the corresponding mastery over it: we know what we are doing and we know what the consequences of our action will be for others, and because we accept responsibility for these consequences, we can

16. D. Davidson, "Agency," in Davidson, *Essay on Actions and Events* (Oxford: Clarendon Press, 1980), 43–61, here 59.
17. Ibid., 44.

do something and not do something else.[18] Actions done by small children, the mentally handicapped, and the like, are not really carried-out actions at all; they approximate, rather, "natural events." In a certain respect they have more in common with earthquakes than they do with human actions. We would refer to an earthquake as being "responsible" or "to blame" for the existence of evils only in a metaphorical sense, and in the same way the actions in question are events that do not pertain to the categories of "responsibility," of "penalty and reward," or of "praise and blame." This is the sign that they are actions that are, and remain, irrelevant to ethics. And this is also why we said before that "human actions" are extensionally (comprehensively) identical with "moral actions." "Moral" in this connection is not the opposite of "immoral," but rather the opposite of "not morally assessable" or "morally irrelevant." A moral action is an action that someone can praise or blame.[19]

Ethics, therefore, is concerned with human action. Or to put it another way: moral action is the realm of those actions of human subjects that originate from rationally guided striving or appetition (= human action). Consequently, ethics is concerned with the doings of man that we can call "free," or "willed" and "responsible," and where we can praise or blame someone. The province of the moral has identical boundaries with the region where praise and blame arise.

c) Purposefulness and Rationality

We should now look more closely, and clarify the interconnection between rationality and the purposefulness of actions. Let's imagine a man who deposits money into a bank account. We could ask him "what" he is doing. And we have the answer to this question when we have information about the "why" or "what for" of this action: "I'm putting some money away." Or: "I'm saving some money." Or: "I'm engaged in laundering some dirty money." Or: "I'm paying a bill." And so on. This is *intentionality:* a relationship between a doing and a "why" or "what for" of this doing, where the "why" is what specifies "what" someone is *really* doing.

That in this case the "*why* someone does something" is actually the "*what* someone does" may also be illustrated another way. If we see someone lying on a bed in the middle of the day and ask him, "What are you doing?" and he

---

18. Cf. also R. Spaemann, *Happiness and Benevolence,* 145.

19. This is connected as well with "the excusable," whether it be someone's recognition of his own fault along with a request for forgiveness, or someone's excusing himself and justifying his action. In both cases, the very *possibility* of being able to give an excuse for one's own or another's action is a sign of the freedom and responsibility of the action. John L. Austin introduced this argument into the discussion from the perspective of linguistic analysis in "A Plea for Excuses," *Proceedings of the Aristotelian Society* 57 (1956–1957): 1–30.

answers us, "I'm lying on my bed," we would probably consider his answer evasive. What we really meant when we posed the question was, "Why are you lying on your bed?" The answer should then be something like, "I'm just resting" or "I'm doing yoga." This would mean: *What* I am doing is the following: I am lying on my bed *to get some rest*" or "I am lying here to *focus my attention*." This answer is a clarification of intention, or the expression of an intention. That is exactly what the questioner wanted when he asked his question.[20]

We are not yet including here intentions in the sense of purposes, like "to steal a car, *in order to* bring an injured person to a hospital," or "putting money away, *in order to* finance my children's education." We mean instead the intention that constitutes a definite action in the first place as a meaningful "human action," and therewith as an action that can be morally qualified. This is the intention that forms as it were the lowest threshold for even speaking about a human action. "To steal a car" is already an action that can be so defined. But not, however, "To open a car door with a wire," because in this case it is not at all clear *what* someone is doing (it could be my own car, because I have accidentally locked my keys in it, or it could simply be car theft). In order to know what action is going on, only an answer to the question "what for" will bring clarification: "He is stealing a car." This is the kind of intentionality that concerns us.

The expression "lowest threshold" can be explained as follows: "human actions" are always *chosen, willed* actions. For an action to be willed or chosen at all, it requires a fundamental or primary intentional structuring. "To lie on a bed" cannot be "willed" or carried out at all in this rudimentary (nonintentional) form. If someone *chooses* to lie on a bed, he does so "under a description," which is the description of a basic intention; for example, "to get some rest." We are speaking here of *basic intentional actions*, whose intentional content is identical with what is referred to as the "object" of an action.[21]

Intentionality implies *practical reason*. Birds, for example, do not have reason, and consequently do not know what they are doing when they bring together twigs and moss and such in order to build a nest. Intentionality characterizes that kind of appetition or striving that includes a twofold work of reason: knowledge of a goal and knowledge of the connection between "that which one does" (in the purely physical sense, e.g., "opening a car door" or "collecting twigs") and the goal of this, the "what for" ("stealing a car" or "building a nest"). Only both of these together forms what we can call a "hu-

---

20. This second example is taken from G. E. M. Anscombe, *Intention*, 2nd ed. (Oxford: Oxford University Press, 1963), sec. 22, p. 35. The English word "why" is in Anscombe's original text, which is correctly translated by *"Warum?"*; the "why" question is more comprehensive. But as long as we are referring to the intentionality, *"What for"* [German *wozu?*] appears more appropriate.

21. Cf. G. E. M. Anscombe, *Intention* (see note 20 above), sec. 35, p. 66. For further discussion of the concept of the basic intentional actions, see III.2.a below.

man action," and allows us to identify the real *content*, the *object*, that is to say, the "what" that is relevant to praxis. Such action is called *voluntary action*. Human action is therefore in essence (1) voluntary action, (2) intentional action, and (3) action based on practical reason. These are all coterminous.

From the perspective of an *observer*, of course, there is no recognizable difference between the action of a bird building a nest and an intentional human action. One would have to describe "action" in this case simply as the causal connection of observable bodily movements (and other "events") with the effects that arise as a result of those movements. Intentionality is not "observable," in contrast to the mere goal-directedness (teleology) of an action. "Intentionality" is, as it were, teleology as viewed from within: not only doing something, but doing something this way, because the goal is the *reason* for doing it. This, precisely, is intention. Now in this same context there is the debate, quite pronounced in analytical philosophy, between the so-called intentionalists and the causalists. The former understand reasons (intentions) as factors that clarify what someone is really doing, and are thus a *component* of action, but not (mental) causes of an action. The latter maintain that "reasons" are mental occurrences that *cause* the action (= certain bodily movements) in a strict sense. But this means that action is reduced to "bodily movement." It is not possible in the present context to address fully the extent to which this is only a pseudoproblem that grows out of a reductive concept of causality. It appears, in any event, that analytical philosophy has no theory of voluntary action, by which these dichotomies could be reconciled. Gilbert Ryle's critique of the dualism of will and bodily action (the mind-body problem) has also had a decisive effect on this discussion.[22] In what follows, a position will be developed in which intentions can be understood both as components and as causes of actions.[23]

For this reason, Thomas supplements Aristotle's discussion of the "voluntary" (*hekousion*) with a clarification that the voluntariness of an action requires two things: first, that the action arises out of one's own striving, and not from some external force (this would be equally true of the bird building the nest) and second, that the one who performs the action has knowledge and understanding of the goal.[24]

But this is still not enough, because the knowledge of a goal can be of two kinds: animals also need perceptions, or sense cognition, in order to do what

22. *The Concept of Mind* (New York: Barnes & Noble, 1949).

23. Texts relating to this debate can be found in A. Beckerman, ed., *Analytische Handlungstheorie*, Bd. 2 (Frankfurt am Main: Suhrkamp, 1985); see esp. the contributions by A. I. Melden, A. MacIntyre, and W. D. Gean. G. H. von Wright represents a more developed position on the matter in "Das menschliche Handeln im Lichte seiner Ursachen und Gründe," in H. Lenk, ed., *Handlungstheorien interdiziplinär*, Bd. 2, II (see note 2 above), 417–30. For the reconciliation of the conflict, see also W. Vossenkuhl, "Freiheit zu handeln," in H.-M. Baumgartner, ed., *Prinzip Freiheit* (Freiburg and Munich: Alber, 1979), 97–137.

24. I-II, Q. 6, a. 1. Cf. *EN* III, 1.

they do. The instinctual mechanism is triggered by perception, and that is a kind of knowing. But this form of goal knowledge is incomplete, because it grasps the goal only as a thing *(res quae est finis)*, but not what Thomas calls the *ratio finis*, the thing "under the aspect of an end." Only when this latter aspect is known is there real (or complete) voluntariness; only then is it possible to integrate the *relationship* between the goal and the action that leads to the goal. Only then is it possible to structure one's own action intentionally, to carry it out so to speak (or not carry it out, as the case may be) under one's own direction, that is, to consider, on the basis of goals, what should be done, and the *choosing* of what to do with a view to the goal being pursued, or the *directing* of what one is already doing anyway to a goal that would be suitable to these actions.[25] This is precisely what the practical reason accomplishes.

> A simple example would be the following: the human being not only possesses a drive for nourishment, but can also grasp "nourishment" as a goal of the acts of nourishment. Grasping the "purposes" of "nourishment" (self-preservation, health, well-being) with relation to concrete acts of consuming food and drink opens the possibility of choosing, structuring, modifying, restraining oneself (for the sake of health or self-preservation, and for other reasons as well).

This analysis of intentionality and practical reason, undertaken as a preliminary here, can be set aside now, and we shall return to it later (III.3). The discussion is aimed in another direction for the time being, and it has been hinted at: To what do we meaningfully orient our action, our human action? Does it even need such orientation? Does human life consist in a jumbled multiplicity of goals, or is there only one ultimate goal? If yes, is this ultimate itself an ordered multiplicity of goals, or one single goal only? Before we can pose this question properly, there are still a few points concerning the concept of moral action that need to be mentioned.

d) Moral Actions as "Immanent Activities"

So far, when we have been speaking of praxis, we have also been including making-actions (art and technology). This is because building houses or mak-

---

25. I-II, Q. 6, a. 2. Cf. also A. Kenny, "Thomas von Aquin über den Willen" in W. Kluxen, ed., *Thomas Aquinas im Philosophischen Gespräch* (1975), 101–31, esp. 119ff. Unlike Kenny, A. MacIntyre emphasizes that according to Thomas, animals also have "reasons for action"; see A. MacIntyre, *Dependent Rational Animals: Why Human Beings Need the Virtues* (Chicago and La Salle, Ind.: Open Court, 1999), 53ff. That would not contradict what is stated here, since "animal reasons" are in fact the content of animal (sense) perceptions. It is only from the (outside) "observer's perspective"—from which MacIntyre never departs—that there is no visible difference between this and human intentionality and voluntariness; MacIntyre refers to J. A. Barad, *Aquinas on the Nature and Treatment of Animals* (San Francisco: International Scholars Publications, 1995).

ing shoes are also a kind of praxis. The same can be said for the work of artists and medical doctors.

But now, in order to determine more exactly the concept of "moral action" as "human action," we must distinguish between praxis in the strict sense and the actions of making. This is the difference between *praxis* and *poiesis*, between "acting" and "producing."

The distinction does not mean that everything that we do is *either* action *or* production. Every production is always also an action, or praxis. But these very words "always also" justify the distinction. A doctor achieves the health of his patient, an architect builds houses, a shoemaker makes shoes. If the doctor, the architect, or the shoemaker dies, the product of their action—the patient's health, the houses, the shoes—are not affected. Production is therefore known as a "transitive" activity *(operatio transiens)*.[26] Transitive actions are actions whose effects remain "outside" the agents themselves and can consequently keep on existing apart from the agent.

Now, let's stay with the shoemaker, but not with his productions. What is the shoemaker really doing when he makes shoes? And what is meant here is, "What does he do, apart from the purely technical aspect of his actions?" Possible answers are: he is earning his living, he is serving his customers, he is fulfilling his creative urges, and so on. A "good" shoemaker is one who makes "good" shoes. But we could also say that a good shoemaker is one who earns his living by doing so, who takes care of his family, or serves his customers. We have spoken of "good shoemaker" twice, in two different senses. In the second case, "good" does not mean the result, the making of the product, but rather the result of the praxis that belongs to this production. This result of praxis is not a characteristic of the shoes that have been made, but of the shoemaker himself. It is the result that remains in the one who acts, because it is a part of the life lived by the agent. Praxis is then called *immanent* action *(operatio immanens)*, on the analogy of knowing, the result of which remains in the knower. Likewise, "seeing" remains in the sense of sight, and "feeling" in the one who feels.

When we treat "shoemaking" as praxis, we are not concerned with the goodness of the shoes produced, but rather with the good accomplishment of the action of "shoemaking." And this activity has not only the technical meaning of its orientation toward the finished product (a goal that is by no means irrelevant for praxis), but also a sense in which it remains immanent in the maker: the lived life. If we speak in *this* sense about the "good shoemaker," we mean that the good shoemaker is in some way good *as a human being*. We

26. In 1 Ethic. lect. 1.

are speaking not of the shoes that he makes, but of an aspect of the success of his life.

This means that we find ourselves again in the realm where we praise or blame. To be sure, we can praise a shoemaker just for his ability to make good shoes. But strictly speaking, we don't do this just because he makes excellent shoes (otherwise we could praise robots who do the same thing), but insofar as he is responsible for the work that he does himself and we treat "the making of excellent shoes" as a responsible fulfillment of human capabilities. We are then looking at "the making of excellent shoes" as a "human action," as praxis, and the achievement of the shoemaker not as of one who makes shoes, but rather as the achievement of a human being. If someone had an *inborn* capacity to produce excellent shoes, we would not *praise* him but would merely congratulate or perhaps envy him. And if we praise a robot, we are really praising the robot's maker. This makes it clear that to do something technically good also has a moral component, which nevertheless is not reducible to the technical component, and can still be distinguished from it.[27]

In every action, whether it be producing or another kind of action such as knowing, scientific research, political activity, raising children, teaching, eating, playing tennis, and so on we pursue something that is not simply "this action," but something that gives the action its practical meaning. We can describe such goals as "bringing human capacities to fulfillment," "learning the truth," "earning one's livelihood," "resting," "getting richer," "exercising power," "serving justice," and so on. Goals like these, which we can actually call *practical goals* and *practical goods,* have the peculiar characteristic that the result of their being attained *remains in the agent* because they are not a product or a condition outside of the one who acts, but instead fulfill (or degrade) the doer himself. In fact, even the mere striving as such changes the one who strives. This is precisely the perspective of praxis, and consequently the perspective of morality: "moral action" is not "one's attitude to objects" or "affecting something outside of ourselves," "producing," but rather, *the realization of what we can be, to realize one's own human nature.* Good action makes a person a good person; through just actions we become just men. In moral action we change first and foremost the little part of the world that we are.

For Kant, too, the perspective of morality is the perspective of the "good will." What counts is not what we finally attain to but the quality of our will—even if it is capable of accomplishing nothing without blame—"then, like a jewel,

---

27. Cf. also A. W. Müller, *Praktisches Folgern und Selbstgestaltung nach Aristoteles* (Freiburg and Munich: Alber, 1982), 209–30; also Müller, "Praktische und technische Teleologie. Ein Aristotelischer Beitrag zur Handlungstheorie," in H. Poser, ed., *Philosophische Probleme der Handlungstheorie* (Freiburg and Munich: Alber, 1982), 37–70.

it would still shine by itself, as something that has its full worth in itself."[28] Nothing is truer than this. But Kant's teaching on the good will remains ambiguous, nevertheless. For he is of the opinion that the will is and remains necessarily amoral, as a first mover: it is "good" only in its alignment with the law of reason. Consequently, Kant holds that the "perversity of the heart," the "evil heart" can "co-exist with a will which in general is good."[29] A "good will" is one that acts according to the right commands of reason, but not a will that is good *as* appetition.

This "realization of one's own human nature" we have been speaking of should not be taken as meaning mere self-realization in a conventional sense. Something much deeper is intended, but at the same time something more ordinary. What is meant is that what we do in any way at all—to the extent that what we are doing is a human action, a doing that comes from reason-directed will, from freedom—that in all such doing we are really doing something with ourselves. Action, *praxis*, always means that someone "becomes," and as a result, "is." It does not mean to optimize the world-situation or the world-process. We are often greatly responsible for the condition of the world, of course. But just how far our responsibility extends is something we can determine only if we understand what the stipulations are, for us not to become bad human beings through optimizing the world-situation.

Here it should be emphasized above all, that the perspective of praxis is a perspective that is concerned with the realization of the good *within* the acting subject. It is concerned with what the Greeks called "the good life." The good life is not the life of contentment nor a condition of society, but rather the lived life of acting subjects, through which these subjects "are "truly good"— [Gr. *alēthōs agathos*], as Aristotle expresses it with a reference to the poem of Simonides discussed in Plato's dialogue *Protagoras*[30]—even if it means giving up one's life. It has to do, using Platonic terms, with the "good of the soul." The Greeks had their own word for this specific form of the good *(agathon)*, which, as the "truly" moral, practical good, remains within the doer and makes him into a good human being: *to kalon,* the "morally beautiful." It is the "worthwhile" and the "advantageous" that does not itself need to be justified for something else because of its worth or advantageousness. Its advantage consists in being advantageous to man simply as man, as, for example, "being just."

This is how ethics stands revealed as a doctrine of the "good life." If we

---

28. I. Kant, *Groundwork of the Metaphysics of Morals*, trans. M. Gregor, 8.

29. I. Kant, *Religion within the Limits of Reason Alone,* trans. T. Greene and H. Hudson (New York: Harper, 1960), 32.

30. *EN* I, 11 (1100b22); Plato, *Protagoras* 339b.

consider the matter carefully, it should become clear that it really could not be concerned with anything else. Even when you blame someone for not having any concern for his fellow man, that he is antisocial or unjust, such criticism arises from the fact that you are convinced that such actions keep one from being a good human being. If someone next to me is hungry and I am *unable* to help him, the most you could do is lament the fact—you could not blame me. The evil in the moral sense here is not someone's death by starvation; rather, my failure to provide help *when I could* would be a moral evil, deserving of censure. We do not "blame" nature if an earthquake causes buildings to collapse and many people die as a result. At the most, we could blame people for not building earthquake-proof buildings if they could have, or if they had not taken care to evacuate people in time. They would then be considered irresponsible people, and it could emerge that by profit motives, carelessness, or culpable incompetence they neglected to do what was necessary. It is always a question of the *acting* person, with what he does by his action, and exactly to the extent that he bears *responsibility*. This is where fault and merit enter the picture. Fault and merit are qualities of acting persons, not of events.

Nevertheless, the question emerges, just *what* a good life is. That is, if we do everything we do for the sake of a goal—and that is what led us to the concept of the good life—then the question arises whether life in its totality has a goal. The question emerges for two reasons. First, because we need to know if the multiplicity of actions and practices that make up a human life have to be brought together into a unity, so that life as a whole can have meaning. Second, because the question leads us to ask whether everything we do and strive for, we always do and strive for the sake of some other thing, or whether it is not more reasonable that there is an ultimate end, that we do not seek for the sake of another thing, but simply for its own sake. This is a question that arises necessarily from the analysis of human action and the nature of practical reason.

e) The Ultimate End and Happiness

In regard to the first question: it is probably possible to live a life without a goal to unify it. But this would be a life without direction. We need to frame the answer more precisely: if it is indeed possible to lead this kind of directionless life—a life, that is to say, not permanently dominated by a single goal—it is certainly not possible *not* to follow some goal in a definite activity; even if this purpose changes with the change of activity, the purpose is always there, because otherwise no one would be able to decide on any action; or it might be a case of an action that is not a genuinely human one, an externally coerced action that in extreme cases could be pathological.

Nor need we maintain—Aristotle, for example, does not maintain it—that the multiplicity of all strivings and actions must necessarily end in some goal. The only thing that has to be said so far is that *every single* series of strivings necessarily ends in some ultimate goal.[31] Whoever goes to the office every morning certainly does this because of some ultimate purpose that he is striving for in doing this; but this last end does not have to be the same one that he strives for in his daily physical exercise. Every praxis has its own final goal: here, for example, "working" is one and "staying in good physical shape" is another. The question is only whether "working" and "keeping healthy" are both really striven for as ultimate ends. And that means something else is intended: namely, whether we strive for such goals for their own sakes, or if there is not something further for the sake of which we do them. At this level, it is really not possible to strive for "working" and "staying healthy" *at the same time* for their own sakes. That would result in inner conflicts and at times conflicts in external behavior as well. Here, it is no longer the directing of single activities toward an ultimate, but rather the self-orientation of the acting subject in general toward an ultimate, and that means the orientation of one's whole *life* to a final goal. If someone located this in "staying healthy," he would probably not go to work some days, even if he risked losing his job and becoming unemployed. If he considered his ultimate goal to consist *at the same time* in working, he would probably from time to time cancel his exercise program. The position would be self-contradictory, even impossible. If the same person modified his ultimate goal as situations changed, we would probably think he lacked character.

But do we ever will anything for its own sake? We should first clarify just what is meant by "seeking something for its own sake." To seek something for its own sake means to will something that someone can consider good from every conceivable perspective, without exceptions, so that there is no possibility of subordinating it to some other good. This would be a good that, once attained, would satisfy every desire: all striving would find its fulfillment there and come to a standstill. And since we are dealing with the realm of praxis, this good must be a practical good, meaning a good that can be in some form *the object or content of activity.* Consequently, we are speaking about an activity that will not be carried out for the sake of any other activity, but rather has its goal in itself. It is good, even though it is good for nothing else.

Now Aristotle tells us that if we had no such ultimate goal in our action, then "the process [of choosing] would go on to infinity, so that our desire

31. On this, cf. John Finnis, "Practical Reasoning, Human Goods and the End of Man," *New Blackfriars* 66 (1985): 438–51, esp. 439f.

would be empty and vain."[32] What does this mean? It means exactly what Thomas expresses with the sentence *omnes appetunt suam perfectionem adimpleri,*[33] which we could reasonably translate as "all strive to reach their own fulfillment." And yet we seem to have arrived at a perfect tautology: a striving that goes into infinity would be empty and vain, because a striving that tried to attain every good for the sake of another one to infinity would never reach the end, or its fulfillment.

But this is really no tautology, but rather the description of a basic state of affairs in anthropology (or action-psychology). It only means that we really always seek an ultimate—period. This is simply a fact of the psychology of action. There are some for whom the dominating goal of life is physical health, but there are others for whom the goal might be material prosperity, or public recognition, or sense pleasure, or having adventures. But what interests us at present is not *why* someone would pursue material prosperity as a life goal, for example. Rather, the question is *what* such a person is seeking when he seeks possessions as a life goal. We might say: he believes that he will find happiness there. And what we mean by *that* is that he believes that he will find there what we do not seek for any further reason, but just for its own sake. Since in fact we all will an ultimate end, as otherwise all willing would be empty and in vain (and that is a fact), so then we will what in each case we will as an ultimate (e.g., the possession of material goods) from the viewpoint of *fulfilling* our striving. And *fulfilled* striving is precisely what everyone calls happiness. We are speaking here of a "weak" concept of happiness, because this still does not determine in any way exactly what "happiness" consists of.

We are concerned here with what Aristotle called "self-sufficient good": "The self-sufficient (*autarkes)* we now define as that which when isolated makes life desirable and lacking in nothing; and such we think happiness to be."[34] We could add that every human being seeks with a natural necessity for something that makes life desirable for its own sake. Everyone wants his or her own life to turn out well *as a whole*. And that is precisely what we mean by happiness.[35]

What have we achieved so far? A lot—and yet rather little. It depends, first of all, on what we really understand by happiness. If we understand what Kant intended by it, when he spoke of the "purpose of happiness" that we have by a "natural necessity,"[36] we have not achieved much. Kant also holds

---

32. *EN* I, 11 (1100b22).   33. I-II, Q. 1, a. 7.
34. *EN* I, 5 (1097b 14–16).

35. R. Spaemann has introduced the expression *das Gelingen des Lebens* [translated into English by J. Alberg as "a life that turns out well"] as a more precise equivalent for *das Glück* [happiness]; cf. *Happiness and Benevolence,* 8ff.

36. I. Kant, *Groundwork of the Metaphysics of Morals,* trans. M. Gregor, 26.

that "to be happy, is necessarily the demand of every rational but finite being, and therefore an unavoidable determining ground of its faculty of desire."[37] And yet by "happiness" Kant means the same thing as well-being, a condition that is "not an ideal of reason, but of imagination, resting merely upon empirical grounds."[38] According to Kant, this natural drive for the attainment of a state of contentment actually distorts the view of what one *ought* to do according to the law of reason! To say that every man ultimately seeks happiness would tell us nothing at all. It is an empty formula, and a dangerous one, too, because it clouds the view of "what ought to be done" and leads us astray.

This explains how Ernst Tugendhat could criticize the classical concept of happiness for providing "no objective, generally valid rules for attaining happiness" because "true happiness can only determine happiness for itself" and "a definite concept of happiness cannot be grounded."[39]

Such criticism is based on a concept of "happiness" that is not the classical one.[40] This concept, and not the classical concept, understands happiness as a kind of psychological *condition* of *experiences* of contentment. Kant is even explicit about it: happiness is not an "ideal of reason," but rather the ideal of a condition of well-being, or of the avoidance of displeasure, a kind of pleasure-oriented self-love,[41] that moves on the *hedonistic* horizon of "well-being" and "ill-being": "Well being or ill-being always signifies only a reference to our state of agreeableness or disagreeableness, of gratification or pain; and if we desire or avoid an object on this account, we do so only insofar as it is referred to our sensibility and to the feeling of pleasure and displeasure it causes."[42] "Good or evil," however, would be determined through the law of reason, directly *counter* to the inclination to be happy (or, at least, independently of that inclination).

For Aristotle, and—apart from the Cyrenaic school—for ancient philosophy in general, such an understanding of happiness as a state of experienced contentment is unthinkable.[43] As J. Annas[44] has made clear, the ancient concept of happiness is bound up with the concept of virtue and subordinated to it. It is not held that the virtuous person is finally the happy person, rather, that true happiness, the fulfilled, successful, and "good" life, consists in vir-

37. I. Kant, *Critique of Practical Reason,* trans. M. Gregor, 23.

38. I. Kant, *Groundwork of the Metaphysics of Morals,* trans. M. Gregor, 29.

39. E. Tugendhat, "Antike und moderne Ethik," in E. Tugendhat, *Probleme der Ethik* (Stuttgart: Reclam, 1984), 46.

40. For the classical concept, see J. Annas, *The Morality of Happiness* (note 1 above).

41. *Critique of Practical Reason,* trans. M. Gregor, 23–24.

42. Ibid., 52.

43. See also U. Wolf, *Die Philosophie und die Frage nach dem guten Leben,* 48ff.

44. *The Morality of Happiness,* 329ff.

tue. For just this reason, ancient ethical doctrines often have explicit contrain-tuitive features, and in any case they compel us, in our pursuit of ethics, to reconsider our first intuitions about what happiness is: happiness cannot consist in the state of contentment, but rather in that fulfillment or success of life that can only be characterized by this life's goodness, and that, in turn, is the life lived according to virtue.

Of course—and here there seems to arise an unavoidable contradiction—happiness is a definite form of "contentment" or "fulfillment." Indeed, we just defined happiness as "fulfilled striving." And Thomas in another place says that "to strive for happiness" consists in nothing other than "striving that the will be satisfied."[45] Now the will is a *rational* striving. And that is exactly why the formula for happiness is neither empty nor disturbs our view of the "ought." The opposite is true: it shows us, to begin with, just what "ought" means at all. The Aristotelian formula, that we all strive toward happiness as an ultimate goal, includes, namely—and here again there is consensus in ancient ethics—that happiness is only to be found in what we all can *rationally* will for its own sake (we can will all sorts of things for their own sakes, of course, but not if we employ the standard of *reason*). Consequently, the Aristotelian formula of happiness leads us to an analysis of what *alone* can be willed for its own sake, wherein alone can be sought a rational fulfillment of striving, a rational satisfaction of the will. Since "striving for happiness" is not a psychologically empty formula for the description of a subjective state of experiences of contentment, but instead a formula for the ultimate goal of a *reason-guided striving*—that is, for an ultimate according to reason—just so, the determination of the content of happiness is in principle open to a rational grounding.

2. Metaphysics of Action, Anthropology, and the Determination of Human Happiness

a) Two Aspects of "Goal": The Goal "For the Sake of Which" and the Goal "Through Which"

It was said that happiness consists in what we *rationally* can strive after for its own sake. Therefore the question about being happy is a question that from the very beginning is subject to the demands of rational criteria. *How* can we become happy? *What* is the good whose attainment "in itself alone makes life worthwhile, so that it needs nothing further"? These are not questions of an empirical kind, or questions about the subjective experience of happiness;

45. I-II, Q. 5, a. 8.

they arise from rational consideration, carried out in ethics as an anthropological analysis of the metaphysics of actions.[46]

Thomas's way of treating the problem is complex.[47] First, because the philosophical perspective is embedded in a theological synthesis; second, because Thomas approaches the question from two different viewpoints, and the Aristotelian treatment of the theme corresponds almost exclusively to only one of these.

At first, one might think that everything would already be decided in an ethics that proceeds from an acknowledged God: the ultimate goal of man is God. How could it be otherwise? And in fact, this hasty conclusion is often encountered. But the situation is not quite so simple. That God is the ultimate goal of human action does not immediately follow from the existence of God, let alone from the existence of a *Creator* God.

This is because Thomas distinguishes (following an idea taken from Aristotle) between two aspects under which we can speak of "end" [Lat. *finis*]: an end can be "finis cuius" or "finis quo."[48] We could translate this as "a goal *for the sake of which*" and "a goal *through which*." The "goal *for the sake of* which

46. In addition to this, Aristotle also is familiar with handling the question in a dialectical way, "in the light of what is commonly said about it," and of course this would mean the opinions of the "best" (who according to what is commonly said, are considered the "best"). Aristotle himself says that the dialectical method is only a supplement to the systematic/conceptual analysis; see *EN* I, 8 (1098b 9–12).

47. Cf. also W. Kluxen, *Philosophische Ethik bei Thomas von Aquin* (Hamburg: Meiner, 1980), 108–65. My discussion here is significantly indebted to this work, and direct reference should be made to it for the details. Cf. further: W. Kluxen, "Glück und Glücksteilhabe. Zur Rezeption der aristotelischen Glückslehre bei Thomas von Aquin," in G. Bien, ed., *Die Frage nach dem Glück* (Stuttgart and Bad Canstatt: frommann-holzboog, 1978), 77–91; E. Schockenhoff, *Bonum Hominis. Die anthropologischen und theologischen Grundlagen der Tugendethik des Thomas von Aquin* (Mainz: Matthias Grünewald Verlag, 1987), 85–128; H. Kleber, *Glück als Lebensziel. Untersuchungen zur Philosophie des Glücks bei Thomas von Aquin* (Münster: Aschendorff, 1988); G. Abbà, *Felicità, vita buona e virtù* (see note 2 of this chapter), 32–75. For other philosophers as well as Thomas, see also M. Forschner, *Über das Glück des Menschen. Aristoteles, Epikur, Stoa, Thomas von Aquin, Kant* (Darmstadt: Wissenschaftliche Buchgesellschaft, 1993).

48. Cf., e.g., I-II, Q. 1, a. 8, corp.: "As the Philosopher says, 'end' [*finis*] is said in two ways, namely 'for the sake of which' [*cuius*] and 'by means of which' [*quo*]; that is, the thing itself in which the nature of good is found, and the use or *adeption* of that thing" [*ipsa res in qua ratio boni invenitur et usus sive adeptio illius rei*].—*Translator's note:* The second expression (Greek *to hou heneka hōi*) has been widely taken in modern language translations of the text of Aristotle's *De Anima* (415b 3 and 20) as "finis cui," whereby the ambiguous Greek form *hōi* is understood as a dative of interest ("end for whom" or "being in whose interest" or "beneficiary") rather than as a dative of instrument (Lat. "finis quo," "end through which, by way of which"): e.g., in the J. A. Smith trans. (1984): "That 'for the sake of which' has two senses, viz. the end to achieve which, or the being *in whose interest* anything is or is done." But the interpretation of the Greek *hōi* here as a dative of reference (= *finis cui* in Latin) is not in fact followed by Thomas in his commentary on the *De Anima*. *Quo* and not *cui* is provided in the accompanying Latin translation by William of Moerbeke, and Thomas's explication of the passage assumes an instrumental meaning (= *finis quo*, with ablative case in Latin): "by 'end' [is meant] not only what is principally intended, but also *the means to be employed* (= id quo illud adipiscimur, "That through which we acquire it"); cf. *De Anima, in the Version of William of Moerbeke and the Commentary of St. Thomas Aquinas*, trans. K. Foster and S. Humphries (New Haven, Conn.: Yale University Press, 1951), 215.

(finis cuius)" for a miser is *money*; the "goal *through* which *(finis quo)"* for a miser is *possessing* the money. The former is the "thing" that is the goal; the latter is the act or activity that reaches out to the "thing," the striving toward it, the getting of it. They are two aspects of a single situation.

Now it is clear to Thomas (and to Aristotle, too, but in a somewhat different way) that all being is oriented to God as to its ultimate goal. This is part of metaphysics—of physics, too, for Aristotle—and to this extent there is nothing more to be said. But the perspective of the *"finis cuius"* ("end for the sake of which") is not at all the perspective of practical philosophy. When we know that *all* creatures, thanks to their createdness, are related to God as to the ultimate goal of the entire creation (that "they glorify God")—and Aristotle says that animals and plants strive by nature "to partake in the eternal and the divine"[49]—we still are a long way from knowing the good *through which* man, as *practical* or *acting* subject, seeks what is ultimate, that is to say, what is the only good he can rationally seek and acquire for its own sake in his own *action,* and consequently, wherein lies his happiness, since that is the question that concerns us here. "It is not a question of the (given) metaphysical determination of man as a created being, but rather his own carrying out of the goal he sets for himself—*that* is the criterion for his practical behavior."[50] Now, what interests us is not the final end and good toward which man is oriented, as toward the *bonum commune* ("common good") of the created universe, insofar as he is a created and finite being (in the same way as all animals, plants, and nonliving bodies); what interests us instead is the ultimate goal of his *action.* In metaphysical terms, we know that man glorifies God—that is, he directs himself to God as to the common good of the created universe—exactly to the extent that he reaches the final goal peculiar to him (which we call happiness). The question is still open, then, precisely in what consists this ultimate goal, *through which* (= "finis quo") man "glorifies" God.

It is at least conceivable that the orientation of the human being toward God, in terms of the metaphysics of being, may in fact find expression, not in the way that God is an object of some human activity (e.g., knowing or loving), but rather in the way of some other activity, *through which,* or *by way of which* man glorifies God. Animals glorify God by reproducing their kind according to nature's regulation, as well as by carrying out the actions that are proper to their natures; but all this does not have anything specifically to "do" with God. If God were also the *finis quo* of man, meaning the goal *through which* for the human being, then what is specific to man would have to consist in the

49. *De Anima,* II, 4 415b1.
50. W. Kluxen, *Philosophische Ethik bei Thomas von Aquin* (see note 47 above), 116.

fact that God Himself could become the object of his activity! But there must be some *human activity* that relates to God. And it would have to be shown to be that very thing that alone can rationally be sought for its own sake. But this would first have to be demonstrated, and the activity in question would also need to be identified.

Thomas in fact accomplishes just such an identification, and he goes about it in two steps: first, the question is asked, "In what realm of goods in general is the final end of the human being—happiness—to be found?" Only at the second step does it emerge that happiness is an *activity*, and what kind of activity happiness consists in.

Aristotle is familiar with the first step in his analysis of the "ways of life" (*EN* I, 5). He lists them as follows: the life of pleasure, the political life (consisting in the pursuit of honor), and the life of contemplation. And in addition to these there is also the life directed to the acquisition of wealth. But his main emphasis lies on the second step. Consequently it is not easy to harmonize the argumentation of Thomas with that of Aristotle, also for other reasons that will be discussed later.

In both cases, however, we are concerned with the analysis of what the human being can *reasonably* seek as a last end, for its own sake. In other words, the question is, "not 'what should we do?' but 'what do we fundamentally and truly want?'"[51] This way of putting it only seems strange if we miss the fact that *willing* is an appetition, or striving, that is guided by *reason*. What we truly and fundamentally *will* is precisely that which we only *rationally* can strive for, because "to will" means nothing but "to seek with the guidance of reason." This means, then, that whoever does not seek for happiness where it can be found according to rational criteria is not simply someone who has a "different" lifestyle, different opinions, or different tastes; rather, such a person is—mistaken and irrational. And he will have no proper way to steer his actions and his life. But this is *not* because knowledge of what makes for the happiness of man also tells us what we are supposed to do *in particular*. What such knowledge gives us, instead, is insight into the *criterion* for determining what is good to do in particular.

51. R. Spaemann, *Basic Moral Concepts*, trans. T. J. Armstrong (London and New York: Routledge, 1989), 14. See also E. Tugendhat (note 39 above), 44: "Die Fragestellung der antiken Ethik war: was ist es, was ich für mich wahrhaft will"? ["The question posed by ancient ethics was: what is it that I *truly* want for myself?"] This truth aspect is filtered out from the ethics of appetition for H. Krämer, *Integrative Ethik*, 79, who holds that the "good as an object of action" for the acting person is "synonymous with what is willed or striven for." By contrast, a synthesis of morality and happiness ("well-being")—of truth-based ethics and subjective interests—which does not recognize an automatic identity of the "willed" with "what is truly good for me," can be found in J. Raz, *The Morality of Freedom* (see note 5 above), 315ff.

b) The Twofold Happiness of This Life and the Anthropology of Desire (Aristotle)

Once happiness has been formally defined as complete and self-sufficient good, the possession of which alone makes life worth desiring, and which—because it must be a good that can actually be attained—has to be a *human* good (a good *for* man and *within* man), then the content of this good is explicated as "activity of soul in conformity with excellence" and, since there is more than one excellence, "activity according to the best and most complete." But Aristotle has something else to say too: "But we must add, 'in a complete life.'"[52]

Reason is the distinguishing characteristic of the human being. It is peculiar to us, and distinguishes us from other kinds of living things. Accordingly, happiness must consist in an activity of the soul, namely, in that part of the soul that has reason, or in the activity of other parts of the soul but under the direction of reason. The train of thought may not be entirely satisfying at first, because it has not yet been made clear just why such activity is the only activity we can rationally pursue for its own sake. This is not clarified until the tenth book of the *Nicomachean Ethics*.

We read there that "those activities are desirable in themselves from which nothing is sought beyond the activity."[53] The virtues of the "political life"—existence in the human community—do not formulate activities that are sought for their own sake. They all strive toward something that is different from that life. What someone seeks for its own sake is an activity that is free from worry, from weariness, full of freedom and contemplation: an activity that satisfies without bringing satiety. Such an activity can only be the *contemplation of truth*, or *theoria*. It is an activity that provides nothing in itself, and yet provides everything, because it alone can be carried out just for its own sake. Seeing brings its own fulfillment. In the *Eudemian Ethics* Aristotle speaks even more clearly about the "consideration of God" as that ultimate goal wherein alone human striving and action comes to rest.[54]

This happiness, and this life of contemplation—Aristotle adds—appears to be more divine than human. Indeed, as in the twelfth book of the *Metaphysics,* God is pure intellect that contemplates itself. But man then should strive toward this divine nature, since the intellect *(nous)* is the best and most divine thing in us, and we should strive toward what is best.[55]

But the other virtues too—the moral virtues that we exercise in the areas

---

52. *EN* I, 6 (1098a 18).
53. *EN* X, 6 (1176b 7).
54. Cf. Aristotle, *Eudemian Ethics* VIII, 3. The formula used at 1249b21, "to cultivate and consider God" *(ton theon therapeuein kai theorein),* has become controversial, to be sure, since its exaggerated interpretation by W. Jaeger.
55. *EN* X, 7 (1177b33–34).

of human community life (the *polis*)—are activities in accordance with reason. At this point Aristotle draws the conclusion that has caused so much distress for the scholars of Aristotle: "But in a *secondary degree,* the life in accordance with the other kind of excellence [or virtue, Greek *aretē*] is happy."[56] It is a question here of a human kind of happiness that is not characterized by a *single* activity, but rather by an ordered multiplicity of activities in accordance with reason: a life according to all the moral virtues that is *also* an activity according to reason, the best and most divine thing in us.

The last word on the theme, then, is this: a human being is happy insofar as, and only insofar as, he somehow participates in *theoria*—insofar as, that is, his life is characterized by the activities of reason and intellect. Anything that makes us happy can only do so because it has something to do with rationality. In the first place, it is the seeing, the beholding of that which God Himself sees (and that is God Himself: since for Aristotle, God is *noesis noeseos,* pure knowing activity that discovers itself in the very act of knowing); in the second place, it is the development of emotions and actions in accordance with reason within the life of the human community (the *polis*).

What may surprise us here is that there can even be such a thing as a "second-rate" happiness. It seems to contradict the very concept of happiness as something complete and perfect. But the Aristotelian doctrine of *duplex felicitas* ("dual happiness") as it was later designated can only be made sense of in anthropological terms. And Aristotle himself supplies the key to its understanding.

What has not yet been mentioned is that the doctrine of happiness in the tenth book of the *Nicomachean Ethics* is an appendix to the treatment of *pleasure.* Furthermore, it really belongs to that discussion and forms its culmination. Aristotle means that happiness must be the most pleasurable and enjoyable thing there is. Fullness of pleasure is an indicator of the fullness of happiness. And then degrees of perfection can be found: "Whether, then, the complete and blessed man has one or more activities, the pleasures that complete these will be said in the strict sense to be pleasures proper to man, and the rest [the other kinds of pleasure] will be so in a secondary and fractional [or multiple] way, as are the activities."[57]

When pleasure and enjoyment are mentioned, we have touched upon something that is a peculiar property of what is "ultimate": the completion of activity,[58] the end of striving and its coming to rest. Pleasure is a "whole,"

---

56. Ibid., X, 8 (1178a 9–10). J. L. Ackrill discusses the various solutions proposed by more recent interpreters in "Aristotle on Eudaimonia," in A. O. Rorty, ed., *Essays on Aristotle's Ethics* (Berkeley-Los Angeles-London: University of California Press, 1980), 15–34.

57. *EN* X, 4 (1176a 26–29).   58. Ibid., X, 4 (1174b 23).

without duration, because it is timeless, without becoming. Aristotle compares pleasure with the sense of sight: "Seeing seems to be at any moment complete."[59] Each sense has its pleasure, but contemplation or *theoria* has its own peculiar kind of pleasure that we call joy: it is a special, spiritual kind of pleasure or enjoyment in the possession of what is beloved. But just because everywhere there is activity there is also pleasure, and because all pleasure has the characteristic of what is ultimate, the seeking of pleasure can disorient us. And of course there are spiritual joys and pleasures that can lead us astray. "Pleasure" is here taken in a wide sense, covering any kind of pleasure and enjoyment.

Is happiness then merely a state of having pleasurable experiences? Not exactly. To be sure, happiness is a very enjoyable state, or rather an enjoyable and pleasurable activity. But if happiness consisted essentially in the enjoyment, *how* we attained to the enjoyment would not matter at all. Then the desire for happiness would be the same thing as striving for pleasure or contentment.

> For example, suppose I am of the opinion that listening to Mozart's music is the best kind of musical enjoyment there is. But when I put on a Mozart CD, I am not doing this because I am looking for a certain kind of pleasure. If there was a machine that gave me the same kind of pleasure without the music, I still wouldn't use it. This is because I want to hear the music, and not just have the pleasure connected with the music. What we want is a certain *activity* (in this case, actually listening to Mozart's music). That this particular music promises to give us the highest pleasure, means that (for us) it is simply the best, that is, listening-to-this-music is simply the best, or (in this case) the most beautiful kind of listening-to-music. We would not be content merely to have the pleasure or "enjoyment" [*Vergnügen*], if that meant excluding the activity of taking in this music with our ears (i.e., receiving this beauty in this way is precisely the good attained through this activity). We would not be willing to have the pleasurable feeling and at the same time *not* possess the good of which the pleasure is the by-product.

Now this is precisely the point: whatever we strive for or desire is a practical good, an *activity* (e.g., listening to music), and not the pleasure that follows upon this activity. To seek happiness means to seek out that kind of activity that satisfies our longing, that pleases us and is *therefore* pleasurable in the highest degree. This is because our striving is not put to rest because we enjoy; we enjoy because our striving is put to rest. Consequently "wanting to be happy" is not "striving for pleasurable experiences" and then asking, "What kind of activities give me the most pleasure?" The question about happiness is rather the question about what kind of activity I can *reasonably* seek

59. Ibid., (1174a 15).

to do for its own sake, because I know that only what I reasonably seek for its own sake is also pleasurable in the highest sense, or *complete* pleasure. And this is so because only what we reasonably seek for its own sake, only what is really meaningful, makes sense and brings our seeking to an end, can satisfy us, since our striving and seeking—our "willing"—is a *rational* striving.

Now just because we look for activity, and not pleasure, the following comment of Aristotle's should strike us as rather illuminating: "No one would choose to live with the intellect of a child throughout his life, however much he were to be pleased at the things that children are pleased at, nor to get enjoyment by doing some most disgraceful deed, though he were never to feel any pain in consequence."[60]

Pleasure always leads us astray just when we intend it directly. The result is frustration and an inability to be joyful.[61] At the level of sensitive appetition this is already clear: the sense appetites are not stimulated by the concept of what such experiences can bring. No sense appetition *aims* for the experience of pleasure. The sense of sight is not actualized by the concept of enjoying pleasingly matching colors, but rather by colors and colored things and shapes. Pleasure as the object of an intention is already an indirect one, an *intentio obliqua*. This is why human beings and not animals can behave in a hedonistic way.

What we call "will" is the appetition or striving that follows reason. But reason does not have enjoyment as its object but rather goods, practical goods, in fact, and that means activities, definite behaviors *over which* one can experience joy. We can of course direct our intentions directly toward the enjoyable experiences. But we will certainly not find what we are seeking. It is the best way to miss out on real pleasure.

> We attain to pleasure often in a roundabout way, that is, only when we do what is good to do, without thinking about the pleasure. If the best action is the most pleasurable, it is so only under the concrete circumstances in which we carry it out or pursue it, which are often not the most pleasurable circumstances. This is because a sensitive displeasure (pain or anxiety) can momentarily dominate, and the pleasure only enters when we do what is good despite the displeasure. As Aristotle says: "There are many things we should be keen about even if they brought no pleasure, e.g., seeing, remembering, knowing, possessing the virtues. If pleasures necessarily do accompany these, that makes no difference; we

60. *EN* X, 2 (1174a 1–4). On this point, cf. also J. M. Finnis, *Fundamentals of Ethics* (Washington, D.C.: Georgetown University Press, 1984), 17–19.

61. This has been proven in psychotherapeutical terms; cf. V. Frankl, *On the Theory and Therapy of Mental Disorders: An Introduction to Logotherapy and Existential Analysis* ([1956] New York: Brunner-Routledge, 2004).

should choose these even if no pleasure resulted."[62] Even the hedonist J.S.Mill had to concede that it is better to be a dissatisfied human being than a satisfied pig, or a dissatisfied Socrates rather than a satisfied ignoramus.[63] The problem with Mill's theory is that it cannot explain what is meant by "better" in this situation.

There is no way to get around the question of the best kind of activity—provided we have a correct anthropology of pleasure at our disposal. When Aristotle places the inquiry into pleasure at the forefront, this does not make him a hedonist; it is only a way of showing that the accomplishment of each striving or action is what brings the enjoyment proper to it. This is not something to criticize—far the opposite. It is an anthropological fact. Aristotle does not hesitate to call pleasure and enjoyment something divine, since the gods, he says, have the most enjoyment. And in terms of creation-metaphysics we could say that the consummation of every action in the form of pleasure or, as in the case of spiritual activities, in the form of joy, is the participation of the creature in the divine perfection. The experience of joy is a sign of perfection. The human person is a being made for enjoyment. And this is precisely why the theory of pleasure is so especially important for ethics, as Aristotle recognized. But the fullness of pleasure, and thereby its goodness or badness, depends on the action from which it follows, and its suitability for the one who experiences it.

To know what kind of pleasure is good, we need to know what actions are good. And to know what the best pleasure is, we have to know what the best activity is, because then we will also know where happiness can be found. Happiness, the best activity, and the highest pleasure all coincide. And *just for this reason* pleasure-seeking, or being on the lookout for pleasurable experiences, cannot make us happy, but can only disorient us. To strive for contentment as a goal of action is the best way to miss out on happiness. What we need to know is what is the best activity for the human being. "For this reason, then," says Aristotle, "our whole enquiry must be about these [i.e., pleasure and pain]; for to feel delight and pain rightly or wrongly has no small effect on our actions."[64]

The best activity is that which the virtuous person delights in. To determine what this is, Aristotle's argument provides an anthropological key that is quite illuminating: "That which is proper to each thing is by nature best and most pleasant for each thing; for man, therefore, the life according to intellect [*ho kata ton noun bios*] is best and pleasantest, since intellect more than

62. *EN* X, 3 (1174a 4–8).
63. J.S.Mill, *Utilitarianism*, II [vol. 43 of "Great Books of the Western World"] (Chicago: University of Chicago Press, 1952).
64. *EN* II, 2 (1105a 5–7).

anything else *is* man. This life therefore is also the happiest."[65] At the highest level, this would be the life of *theoria,* or contemplation; at the next level, life according to the moral virtues, which is a life according to reason, consisting in the ordering of our human actions and emotions in our body-soul unity.

And yet somehow this answer is not entirely satisfying, and is "characterized by a deep ambiguity."[66] Aristotle is the last one who would try to deny this. The happiness of which Aristotle speaks is a highly precarious disposition. The "first rank" of happiness would be the life of philosophers, and very few are granted the opportunity to live a theoretical life, and even these few have to attend to the many other things that are a part of life. The second-rank happiness seems to be no less imperfect as the first-ranking kind. And furthermore, it depends very largely upon the possession of external goods and upon "luck" *(tyche).* Indeed, the Aristotelian position is "unstable,"[67] but this very thing strikes me as part of its truth (a matter to which we shall return in the epilogue of this book when we discuss the fragmentary character of all philosophical ethics). But by no means does this instability of the Aristotelian position signal the "collapse of eudaimonistic ethics," or that some other principle needs to replace the principle of happiness.[68] The truth of Aristotle's insight into happiness remains undisturbed, despite its problematic character. "We must, so far as we can, make ourselves immortal, and strain every nerve to live in accordance with the best thing in us; for even if it be small in bulk, much more does it in power and worth surpass everything."[69] And the best thing in us is "the divine in us": the intellect—or reason—which discloses a "dimension of truth, of goodness, of holiness, and of the absolute . . . a dimension which would disappear, if one understood reason as having merely a practical function in service of the preservation of the species."[70]

c) Thomas Aquinas on Complete Happiness and Incomplete Happiness

Thomas Aquinas handles the problem of determining what happiness is by looking at it in the light of the *metaphysics of action.* This leads at once to a full integration of the Aristotelian teaching, including its subordination to theology and its philosophical delimitation. From the outset, the enquiry pur-

65. *EN* X, 7 (1178a 5–8).

66. R. Spaemann, *Happiness and Benevolence,* 54.

67. J. Annas, *The Morality of Happiness,* 364ff.

68. Such is the view of O. Höffe, "Aristoteles' universalistische Tugendethik," in K. P. Rippe and P. Schaber, eds., *Tugendethik* (Stuttgart: Reclam, 1998), 42–66, 65ff.

69. *EN* X, 7 (1177b34–1178a2).

70. R. Spaemann, *Happiness and Benevolence,* 54.

sues what Thomas calls *beatitudo perfecta*, the "utmost capability of man."[71] The analysis is pursued until it is determined where human action ultimately aims, where human activity is directed in the utmost capacity of its being.

The possession of wealth, honor, good reputation, and power cannot be such an ultimate. And four reasons are given:[72] All these things can belong to good men as well as evil men. But happiness does not lack anything, and "to be evil" is a deficiency. Secondly, all these goods are compatible with the possibility that someone who has one of them may lack something else, such as wisdom or good health. Third, out of all these goods evil can come; and fourth, all these goods depend on external circumstances, luck, coincidence, and the like, and not from causes that exist within the human person; but the desire for happiness comes from within a person, and can only be satisfied by something within.

Does happiness consist in a good of the body?[73] In self-preservation? Or health? That is not possible. The captain of a ship is not ultimately concerned with the preservation of his vessel, but with arriving at his destination. Only someone who is himself the highest good, and who consequently does not have any further good to pursue—or someone who has already arrived at the ultimate goal—for such alone could "self-preservation" be an ultimate goal.[74] Secondly, the goods of the body are ordered to the goods of the soul. It is not possible for a corporeal good to be rationally sought as the ultimate goal.

Happiness can likewise not be found in pleasure,[75] because pleasure, even intellectual pleasure, only *follows from* the possession of a good, and this good is what we are concerned about. Happiness cannot consist in pleasure of the senses, because this is always finite and cannot provide the kind of satisfaction that we desire. The desire for happiness is a desire of the will—an intellective desire. Seeking happiness in sense pleasures leads to frustration, to an ever greater striving for ever smaller satisfactions.

Does happiness consist in a good of the soul?[76] If we treat the good that we seek as the *finis cuius*, or the "thing for the sake of which [*res ipsa cuius causa*]" our longing is satisfied, it cannot be a good of the soul. "Because human

---

71. To use an expression of W. Kluxen, *Philosophische Ethik bei Thomas v. Aquin* (see note 47 above).

72. I-II, Q. 2, a. 4.

73. Ibid., a. 5.

74. Self-preservation can become the most important thing in practice, when the doctrine of a *summum bonum* has been replaced by a doctrine of the *summum malum*, a doctrine about the worst evil to avoid. This is the case with the ethics of Thomas Hobbes, who recognizes only the dying of a violent death as the fundamental, normative evil. Cf. also M. Rhonheimer, *La Filosofia politica di Thomas Hobbes. Coerenza e contradizioni di un paradigma* (Rome: Armando, 1996).

75. Ibid., a. 6.

76. Ibid., a. 7. Cf. a. 8: "The end is said to be twofold, 'of which' and 'by which' [*cuius et quo*]: that is, the thing itself in which the nature of good [*ratio boni*] is found, and the use or adeption of that thing."

appetition, the will, is directed toward a universal good"—and that means something that is good from every possible point of view, from an infinite or indefinite number of points of view. Every good of the human soul, nevertheless, is particular and finite. But if we consider the ultimate goal of human life as the *finis quo,* or the "end through which" man attains the ultimate (i.e., a practical good), it must be said that it *does* consist in a good of the soul: it is a good that is *in the possession of* the powers of the soul, something that man reaches *through* and *in* the activities of the soul. And just such a good is what we are seeking when we speak of happiness from the perspective of *praxis.*

We still need to enquire what the cause of happiness is that lies outside the soul. Is this cause a created or an uncreated good?[77] Thomas repeats: "The object of the will—the specifically human striving—is the universal good, just as the object of the intellect is the universal truth. It follows from this that nothing can satisfy human willing except a universal good." But God is such a good: "Therefore only God can satisfy the human will" *(Unde solus Deus voluntatem hominis implere potest).*

Of course, this is the answer we were expecting. But, nevertheless, it is an answer that is justified and ascertained through an action-metaphysical analysis, and remains an overpowering answer. It is founded on an understanding of the nature of intellectuality. The human intellect is a cognitive power that cannot of course do everything *at once* (a mark of its finiteness), but it is nevertheless capable of taking in all of reality and can open itself to the infinite and to that which *is* through an infinite number of perspectives. The intellective soul is "in a way, all existing things,"[78] it is *quodammodo omnia.* And the appetitive power such as the will that directs itself according to the intellect is a striving that can never be satisfied at all unless it can share in a good that is good from an *infinite* perspective. This is exactly what St. Augustine's words mean: *fecisti nos ad te, et inquietum est cor nostrum, donec requiescat in te*[79] ("You made us for yourself, and our hearts find no peace until they rest in you").

Now, the point of the argument is the following: It is not because God is the Creator or "highest existence" that He alone can be the ultimate goal of man—for in that case, animals would also find their fulfillment in God—but rather because only He is that good which is capable of satisfying the human will. Because the human desire for happiness is characterized by intellect, it is *incapable* of being satisfied except through attaining the infinite. And now we need to clarify just what this attainment would be. After asking the question,

77. Ibid., a. 8.
78. Aristotle, *De Anima,* trans. Smith, III, 8 (431b21).
79. *Confessiones,* I, 1, trans. R. S. Pine-Coffin, p. 1.

"What is the good that can satisfy our longing?" we proceed to the next question: "What *is* happiness? How does this satisfaction occur?"[80]

Happiness is first considered as a *finis quo,* and this is what interests us here: happiness as a *created* good.[81] If there is such a thing as human happiness, then this would be "something created, and present in a human being," even if its cause might be something uncreated. It is "entirely a 'creatural' reality governed from within by our humanity; it is *not* something that descends overwhelmingly upon us from outside. That is, it is not only something that happens to us; we ourselves are intensely active participants in our own happiness."[82]

This is exactly why happiness must consist in a *doing.*[83] Doing, or activity, being-in-act, is the ultimate fulfillment of every being. And happiness is fulfillment, an *immanent* fulfillment, in fact; not only the highest form of "being able to do" (in the sense of a transitive making of something), but the highest form of praxis, and the living-out of life. And because the result of praxis remains within the doer, this means the highest possible form of being. In order for it not to break up into a multiplicity of "activities" but to have the character of a completely lived life, both "continuity and unity" must belong to it.[84]

This activity cannot be an act of sense perception: it is not possible on the basis of sense perception to come into connection with an uncreated, infinite good.[85] And how about the intellective part of the soul? Is happiness an activity of the will?[86] This is also not possible, for the reasons that we learn from Aristotle's analysis of pleasure: the resting of the will is *delectation,* spiritual enjoyment or joy, a type of pleasure. "Willing" is the desire for the good, the inclination toward it, moving toward it as a goal. But happiness cannot consist in that. When the will comes to rest, that is because the goal is now *present* to it, and the will is fulfilled. *Delectatio,* enjoyment, and joy are consequences of the presence or possession of the good. The will cannot be responsible for that, because then it has nothing more to will. To will or to be joyful is to "will *something,*" and "to be joyful *about something.*" The presence of what is willed is necessary for the will to come to a rest. All willing is either the anticipated presence of that which is sought, or resting in the possession of what was sought; but it is not what *brings about* this presence or this resting.[87] This operation is the work of cognition, making what is good become visible and

80. I-II, Q. 3.
81. Ibid., a. 1.
82. J. Pieper, *Happiness and Contemplation,* trans. R. Winston and C. Winston (Chicago: Henry Regnery, 1966), 52.
83. I-II, Q. 3, a. 2.   84. Ibid.
85. Ibid., a. 3.   86. Ibid., a. 4.
87. Cf. also E. Schockenhoff, *Bonum hominis,* 104f.

desirable to the will, making it capable of being experienced in the first place. This is why happiness can only consist in an act of the intellect.[88] And that means that happiness is the grasping of the truth, the apprehension of reality, the seeing of that which is. We have now arrived back at Aristotle, and also Augustine, who called happiness *gaudium de veritate* ("joy in the truth").[89] Happiness is the joy that comes through the will's satisfaction in knowing the truth.

But since the intellect is related in a variety of ways to the truth, our investigation is not finished yet, even though all the possibilities that still remain will only be aspects of what truly deserves to be called happiness.

If happiness essentially consists in an act of the intellect, then this would be the speculative (or theoretical) intellect rather than the practical; it consists more in the grasping of truth than in the rational ordering of actions and emotions.[90] But it is only a question of "more," of what is relatively greater. The Aristotelian *duplex felicitas* of a primary and a secondary level of happiness is not ruled out. Does happiness lie in the speculative activity of the theoretical sciences?[91] That cannot be: all speculative knowledge of the human being proceeds from the senses. At the most, we can reach the knowledge of the existence of God ("that" He exists), but not the knowledge "what" He is. The theoretical sciences are only a participation, a sharing in complete *beatitudo*.

Only at this point is the thought made precise and brought to a conclusion.[92] Man cannot be happy as long as there is something left over for him to seek. Since we know now that happiness is an act of the speculative intellect, it can only be satisfied in the achievement of the act in which the intellect finds its fulfillment. It is the nature of the intellect, however, to advance to the knowledge of what things are. Knowledge *that* something exists is not enough. And so, as long as someone only knows *that* God exists, his "will-to-know" is not satisfied: he remains in a state of wonder or amazement. But wonder pushes us on to a further "will-to-know." Only when we know *what* God is, that is, when His *essence* is somehow comprehended, can the intellect reach the ultimate, to which its nature is driving it. As long as this does not occur, the human being cannot be fully happy.

This "drivenness" of the intellect toward knowing "what," Thomas calls a "natural desire" *(naturale desiderium)* to grasp the "what" of causes. It is a natural longing that is set off by amazement at "what is," and drives on to further investigation. And this natural desire does not rest until the intellect has

88. I-II, Q. 3, a. 4.
90. I-II, Q. 3, a. 5.
92. Ibid., a. 8. In the present context we can pass over article 7, which covers the question whether happiness consists in the knowledge of the "separated substances," or angels.

89. *Confessiones,* X, 23.
91. Ibid., a. 6.

grasped the essence, or nature, of a cause. "Consequently, it belongs to complete happiness, for the intellect to understand the essence of the first cause. And thereby it reaches its perfection, in which it unites with God as the object of its intellection," because intellective understanding means uniting in the *act* of knowing with the object of knowing: in act, the knower and the known are the same.[93] Here also is found the vision of the divine essence *(visio divinae essentiae)*, which constitutes the ultimate goal of man as the utmost capability of his being. This "seeing" is the *visio beatifica*, "the vision that makes one happy *(cf.* Lat. *beatum facere,* "to make happy") in the fullest sense."

We may be inclined here to think that this may only be an ideal for a philosopher or theologian. "Knowing the nature of God" sounds a little . . . dry, perhaps. We can only interpret it in terms of what we normally experience when we "know something." But the "vision of God" is something essentially different—as different, in fact, as what is essentially infinite differs from what is finite. But knowing or seeing, whose highest and most comprehensive form is intellective seeing, means the same as being in possession of that which human striving longs for at its deepest level. To see God can only mean to share in the life of God, to take into oneself all truth, all beauty, harmony and splendor, to live in that and delight in that; it means to have fulfilled and satisfied any and all possible, conceivable, authentically human possibilities and needs, in an "endless moment" that is also the most intense activity.[94] To "know God" is more than just "knowing something." Exactly just *what* it is, we do not know. Even St. Paul could only say on this matter that "what no eye has seen or ear has heard, what has never come into the mind of man: such is the greatness that God has prepared for those who love Him" (1 Cor. 2:9). Thomas cites Boethius's classic formula: *beatitudo est status omnium bonorum congregatione perfectus* ("It is the perfection of all good things and contains in itself all that is good").[95]

But what does this say about man? It says that the human being is *capable* of seeing God on the basis of the nature he is provided with (the intellect). This means that the nature of the human intellect, and the human being as such, is *capax Dei,* "capable of God,"[96] capable of taking in God by knowing. "Capable" means that it is possible for this to happen without the nature of the intellect or human nature in general being coerced or altered in any way. Even though God as the object of knowing is related to man as the infinite to

93. Cf. Aristotle, *De Anima* III, 5 (430a 5).
94. According to the *Summa contra Gentiles,* III, cap. 63, to "see God" implies the satisfaction of the following human longings: the desire for knowledge of the truth, for a virtuous life, for glory, fame, wealth, pleasure (even sense pleasure), and for preservation in being.
95. Boethius, *De Consolatione Philosophiae,* III, prose ii, trans. V. Watts, p. 48.
96. Cf., e.g., I-II, Q. 5, a. 1. The formula is patristic in origin.

the finite, the man who looks on God is still man. *As a human being,* he is capable, despite his finitude, of having the infinite in his possession, of resting in it (satisfaction of the will) and of rejoicing in it, not as passively and forcibly subjected to something higher, but rather by virtue of the fact that this higher reality, the life of God Himself, has become his own life. What we are talking about is really an ultimate, most intense level of human subjectivity.

If we consider this carefully, such a statement is rather overwhelming. Aristotle's declaration that the intellect is something divine in us takes on a completely new coloring and immediacy within the dimension referred to by the Christian tradition as the divine *imago*-character of the human being. But this capability of seeing God means something quite definite, namely, "that it is *possible* for our soul to look in an intellective way upon the nature of God."[97] This "possibility" means: if the human soul shares in the sight of God, this happens as an actualization of some potentiality already present in the human soul, a disposition of its *intellectuality,* which thereby reaches its ultimate level as intellectuality, that to which its nature is oriented; this natural disposition is referred to in the expression *naturale desiderium* (natural desire).

But there is a corollary to this, and only here does Thomas's treatise on happiness finally reach its conclusion: "To see God in his essence exceeds the power not only of human nature, but the power of any created being whatsoever."[98] Even if man is *capax Dei,* that is, possesses within himself the power of looking on God with his intellect, he nevertheless cannot *attain to this* with his natural powers alone. First, all human knowing begins in the senses; the nature of God cannot be abstracted from any object of sense perception.[99] Second, while God is infinite, the human power of intellectual comprehension is finite. But to look upon God is to look upon the infinite. And that is not possible for the human intellect. With his own powers, then, man cannot reach the ultimate and perfect beatitude: he needs God's help and God's initiative—the elevating power of grace. The ability to look upon God is—as theologians would later formulate it—only a *potentia oboedientialis:* an ability to accommodate oneself to "being-elevated" to God's level. This "elevation" is made possible by the connaturality of man with God, through God's "uniting of himself by grace with the human intellect as an object of knowing."[100] Nevertheless, at the basis of this self-accommodation is a human ability, meaning, again, that such "being-elevated" *is appropriate for* the human intellect. The *elevatio* by way of grace *presupposes* nature and *perfects* it, brings to fulfillment the final possibility of what lies within it, brings it to its utmost capac-

97. *Summa contra Gentiles,* III, cap. 51.   98. I-II, Q. 5, a. 5.
99. Cf. I, Q. 12, articles 4, 11, 12.   100. Ibid., a. 4.

ity of being, *without altering or removing its humanity.* The concept of an ultimate capability of the human being does not necessarily imply an "utmost"
that the human being can reach by his own power. The concept resides in the
possibility of an existential capacity that brings what is naturally within human nature to its ultimate realization, even when the power of that-which-is-
brought-to-fulfillment is not sufficient to bring about the fulfillment. But even
so, this "utmost" is still the "utmost" of a *human being.* As long as man is not
looking upon God, the *naturale desiderium* of the intellect, and that means
something naturally seated in man, remains unfulfilled.[101] So, then, the result
is the apparent paradox that man is by nature suited for a happiness that he
is incapable of reaching by the powers of his own nature. Perfect happiness,
consequently, cannot be a practical good, until God intervenes with His grace
and makes it practicable. But the analysis that has led us to this point is purely philosophical in nature.

Anything more is a matter for theologians. Perfect blessedness, we know
as believers on the basis of revelation, has in fact been promised us by God.[102]
Thomas cites Aristotle and his somewhat resigned formulation, that we can
be happy in only an incomplete way, as mere human beings.[103] Only through
revelation, Thomas tells us, do we know that complete beatitude is actually
attainable and thereby the highest goal of all praxis, which we can nevertheless only reach through the help of grace. It is a final good of praxis through
vocation, on the horizon of faith, love, and hope.

This should make it clear how a philosophical ethics in the context of Christian revelation can have nothing to do with perfect happiness and the "ultimate
end." It will now be possible to define more closely just what the object of such
a philosophical ethics should be. We shall see that in substance it does not differ at all from the object that Aristotle defined for it. What does distinguish it is
nevertheless something essential: it knows that philosophical ethics is not the
last word, but rather a theory of praxis that can only provide us with a fragment,
a part of the whole. Of course, Aristotelian ethics is likewise incomplete. But
this is the case because in every "nonbelieving" ethics and anthropology, man
is considered incompletely. But even a philosophical ethics carried out within
the framework of faith is incomplete, because there is an awareness that this
fragmentary conception of the human being is not the last word on the truth of
being human. Such an ethics knows that what is incomplete is only a part of the
whole, not the whole itself.

For this reason, we would also have to acknowledge that a systematic, self-

101. Ibid., a. 1.   102. I-II, Q. 3, a. 2, ad 4.
103. *EN* I, 10 (1101a 20–21).

standing "philosophical ethics" in Christian terms, with a claim to comprehensiveness and inclusiveness, is unthinkable,[104] and in fact would have to be characterized as false from the perspective of faith. But this does not mean that *no* philosophical ethics is possible at all under such conditions. It is quite possible and in fact very much needed—it just accepts its own fragmentary character as one of its fundamental principles. In philosophical terms, this is actually not a disadvantage in comparison with nonbelieving ethics, but in fact an advantage, since a nonbelieving ethics must necessarily remain fragmentary if it is not going to overextend the possibilities of human intelligence. In any event, the *denial* of the fragmentary character of all investigation into human praxis is in fact dangerous for nonbelieving reason—a burden that can scarcely be sustained.

d) The Twofold Nature of Happiness in This Life

But what do we end up with, once we know that man cannot reach with his natural powers what he is fitted by nature to reach? Is a nontheological ethics even possible? And if so, would it still be of any interest for believers?

To begin with: what becomes of the Aristotelian doctrine of the *duplex felicitas*, the doctrine of two levels of happiness? Thomas provides an exact account of it: "In this way the *final and complete* happiness that we await in the future life consists entirely in contemplation. The *incomplete* kind, which we can attain to in this life, consists *primarily and before all else* in contemplation; *in second place,* however, it consists in the activity of the practical intellect, which puts human actions and emotions into order, as Aristotle maintains in the tenth book of the *Nicomachean Ethics*."[105] This gives us the following:

(1) *Complete* happiness *(beatitudo ultima et perfecta)*
    The vision of God in the next life
(2) *Incomplete* happiness *(duplex felicitas)*
    The happiness of life in this world
        a) in the first place: contemplation
        b) in the second place: active life according to reason.

How is it possible to refer to "incomplete happiness" as "happiness" at all? From Thomas's comprehensive theological viewpoint, this is naturally not a

---

104. In this sense, we must concede the point to Denis Bradley, who rejects the possibility of a philosophical ethics in the spirit of Thomas Aquinas; cf. D. J. M. Bradley, *Aquinas on the Twofold Human Good: Reason and Happiness in Aquinas' Moral Science* (Washington, D.C.: The Catholic University of America Press, 1997).

105. I-II, Q. 3, a. 5.

problem. It is a stage which, although still incomplete as the happiness of this life, leads into the complete happiness of the life to come; the latter is already present in the form of hope. There is no such thing as incomplete happiness *by itself.* But what if the perspective that includes complete happiness is absent, as in Aristotle's case? Even then, there is, so to speak, a reason to refer to this as incomplete happiness. This is because we designate as happiness only what we can *rationally* seek for its own sake. Having to limit ourselves to the best that is possible, as Aristotle does, is quite reasonable. It is reasonable to limit oneself to an *ethos* of the *conditio humana* as an answer to the human longing for happiness.

We do not pose the question about human happiness to discover how we can live most pleasurably. If we had posed the question for that purpose, we would have had to conclude that it is never possible for the human being to be happy in this life. A second-rate happiness is not really happiness at all, because it does not know how to satisfy all desire. The question that led us into this, however, was intended to give an orientation for our action: What is the only thing that we really can reasonably seek for its own sake? To what alone can we direct our lives in a truly reasonable way as to an end? Even if we end up with the answer that the ultimate existential capacity of the human being is finally unreachable, this is still a very important answer: for we know what *false* hopes would be. But we also know that there is a clear orientation and measure for "incomplete" happiness: life according to what is "best in us," a life according to reason.

This Aristotelian perspective is *not* left aside by Thomas, but rather justified and supported. For according to this understanding, *we know,* in fact, that complete happiness is possible and can be attained. To live "according to the best in us" will be at one and the same time the preparation and the precondition for that which will come after. This brings an increased theological motivation to the interest in understanding the incomplete happiness of this life and its conditions.

e) The Subject Matter of Philosophical Ethics

The doctrine of "twofold happiness" by no means leads us to conclude that a theological ethics of moral theology concerns itself with "perfect beatitude" *(beatitudo perfecta),* or the complete happiness of the next life, while philosophical ethics must content itself with the *duplex felicitas* of the present life. Such a "division of labor" is unthinkable. The theological way of proceeding considers the whole picture, but from an angle that is specific to theology: on the basis of revelation, from God's perspective so to speak, which is the perspective of the human being, as called to the life of grace. This life begins, of course, here on earth, and remains an earthly, imperfectly happy life, even under the conditions of grace. Even theologians know very little that they can say about the next life, and a practical science dedicated to the state of perfect happiness is not to be had. What can be said about it in theological terms is, again, really only applicable to life here: so that we know what we have to hope for.

Philosophical ethics, on the other hand, concerns itself with only a fragment or selection of the whole. To repeat: in terms of its subject matter, it is not in any way different from the philosophical ethics of a nonbeliever. But the nonbeliever must take the fragment as the whole, and this will tend to lead him toward considering man himself as fragmentary, or (alternatively) toward reinterpreting the fragment into a whole, and trying to make up the difference: the possibilities are then reductionism on the one side, and utopian ideology or an immanent doctrine of salvation on the other. Here is where philosophical ethics can come to the fore in critical opposition to nonbelieving philosophies that try to provide "ultimate answers" within the perspective of mere philosophy—even if such a final answer consists only in the dictum that something like happiness is not available in nature at all.[106]

> Two qualifications are called for here: (1) nonbelieving ethics does not imply atheistic ethics—Aristotelian ethics is a nonbelieving, but not an atheistic ethics; (2) even a nonbelieving ethics can speak of a life after death, and accordingly about complete happiness in a future life. An example would be Plato. But under the circumstances of faith, to speak about such things is still only relevant for theology.

The subject matter of philosophical ethics is the realm of happiness in this life, and to this extent the conditions for its exercise amount to what can be done with the means at the disposal of reason alone. But philosophical ethics does *not* concern itself with a so-called natural end of man, in contrast with a "supernatural end," which would be the concern of theology. A "two-level" theory like that would be rendered impossible by the Thomistic anthropology and action-metaphysics of the utmost existential capability of man.

This needs a little clarification. To speak of the coexistence of "natural" and "supernatural" ends of man would imply either that the human being has two different natures or would lead to the consequence that the philosophically knowable human nature is not the *real* human nature. The "nature of a

---

106. Cf. the 1928 letter of Sigmund Freud to Richard Dyer-Bennet in S. Freud, *Briefe, 1873–1939,* ed. E. Freud and L. Freud (Frankfurt am Main: Suhrkamp, 1960 [2nd ed.]), 398. On Freud's theory of the human being as "an inhibited hedonist," see also R. Spaemann, *Basic Moral Concepts,* trans. T. J. Armstrong (London and New York: Routledge, 1989), 18.

being" and the "end of a being" are in correlation with each other, and mutually affect one another. *One* nature can only have *one* end, and an end is always the end of a definite nature. If "elevation to grace" meant that the vision of God becomes the ultimate existential capability of man only through such elevation, it would mean that human nature becomes another nature through this elevation (the traditional account of the two levels of happiness tended to overlook this point). It would not then be possible to distinguish an "order of nature" from an "order of grace": the latter would simply be the "real" human nature, and the former—as a so-called *natura pura*—an "unreal construct" of philosophers. The concept "supernatural" would then be obsolete, since everything, even nature, would be "supernatural"—a consequence that some theologians have actually accepted.

But what Thomas is saying, is, in fact, that human *nature* is already disposed toward the possibility of such an elevation and that it is elevated *in the nature that it always has had*. In being elevated, the human being remains the same as he would be without the elevation. This is not a kind of external, new "second floor" added on top, but rather something that is already contained in nature: or to be more precise, already implicit in the intellect. Man does not only participate in the divine nature through the elevation of grace, he also fulfills thereby the utmost capacity of his being—his *human* being. It is just that he cannot *reach* this "utmost" by using the powers that he naturally possesses.

When we consider man as we do in philosophy, we abstract from the fact of this elevation. What remains is a human being who in anthropological terms possesses the same goal, the same ultimate capacity of being as the human being elevated to the life of grace. And "goal" here refers to the inner—teleological—structure of being of the human person: the natural desire of the intellect not to rest in its search for understanding until the "what is" has been grasped of everything that can be present to it as merely something "that is."

When theologians distinguish "supernatural" from "natural," they quite rightly do so, but that is something different. They are treating things from the perspective of biblical revelation, and they are concerning themselves with the "goal" that God has set before man, or the *calling* that goes out *from God* toward man. The distinction makes sense in this respect. It would then be correct to say that the philosopher treats the human being as if God had only set him a natural goal, and that means a goal that he could reach with the powers of his own nature. The theologian, however, starts on the basis of revelation, that God has determined the human being from the outset to a supernatural life, and has called him to it—that is, to that goal that he can only reach with the help of grace—but which is no less the goal to which human nature has already always been heading, as toward the ultimate capacity of its being.

So when the theologians distinguish a "natural" from a "supernatural" goal, they are right to do so, but they mean something specifically *theological* by it: the difference between what the human being can do on his own power, and what requires the help of grace. Such a distinction presupposes the theological perspective and method. That means that the distinction is irrelevant to the philosophical perspective, even for the believing philosopher. This is because philosophy *doesn't speak at all* about what man can only do with the help of grace. She speaks only about man, to the extent that he is knowable by reason. Now this human being (as we now know from our action-metaphysical analysis) has only *one* goal—namely, one that transcends his nature and which he is not able to reach with the powers of his own nature. The perspective of philosophical ethics is accordingly and from the outset the perspective of the incomplete happiness of a being that is not capable by its very nature of reaching the perfection—the ultimate, the utmost—of what it is built for. And this is also Aristotle's perspective.

> A philosophical ethics of a believing person does not need to *rule out* immortality and a life after death (which belongs to the subject matter of philosophical anthropology). It would be wrong to say that philosophical ethics concerns itself with this world and theological ethics with the next. Theological ethics, to the extent that it is a practical science, is concerned with the this-world life of someone who has been called by grace to the perfection of the beatific vision. The *philosophical* ethics of a believer cannot concern itself with the "natural happiness of the next life" simply because the believer, even as one who philosophizes, knows that there is no such thing. His view of what happens after death must limit itself to the philosophically demonstrable, anthropological foundations that *make possible* such a life after death. All else would be mere speculation without any basis in reality.

The philosophical perspective of incomplete happiness is nevertheless, as already mentioned, extremely precarious, and can only really be sustained, finally, with the presumption of faith. Faith directly supports philosophical reason in this, and protects it from resignation, on the one hand, and from the intoxicating ideology of earthly utopias, on the other. It does not add something additional to the possible theories of human happiness, but instead brings about a "Copernican revolution of eudaimonism."[107] This would ultimately consist (on the one hand) in not allowing that "essence of perfect happiness"—which we bear within ourselves but which we cannot adequately

---

107. R. Spaemann, *Happiness and Benevolence*, 61 (and cf. the entire chap. 6, entitled "The Antinomies of Happiness").

realize within the empirical conditions of human existence—to be simply *rejected* as chimerical, nor (on the other hand) trying to *force it to be realized* within our condition of finiteness (on this, see further the epilogue).[108]

But now an entirely different question arises: does the doctrine of a *desiderium naturale*—the doctrine of an inner, natural orientation of the human being to the vision of God as the ultimate capacity of that being—*require* an elevation to the life of grace? Do we not have to *derive* the elevation directly from this fact, so that the anthropology of *beatitudo perfecta* and of the utmost capacity of the human being leads directly and necessarily to theology? On the other side, is a purely "natural" man something that can reasonably and meaningfully exist? Or is it not bound to frustration?

f) *Desiderium Naturale* and the Conceptual Possibility of a Natural Human Being

The question that has just been posed is, again, a theological question, and as such does not need to be developed here. But one aspect of it deserves mention: Would it be theoretically possible to think of someone who has *not* been raised to the life of grace? This question, in itself theological, is philosophically relevant to the extent that an answer to it could provide some clarification over whether or not, *despite* the existence of a *desiderium naturale* that aims at what can be reached only by surpassing natural powers, we can still speak at all of a "human nature" that would be relevant in a purely philosophical sense—or whether this would not rather fall aside as a kind of purely hypothetical concept, a mere "remainder."[109] The question again is: Can philosophical ethics be justified under the conditions of faith?

In order to answer the question, we must make a theological hypothesis, and conceive of a human being whose *actual* (i.e., not naturally given or po-

---

108. Denis Bradley has objected to my attempt to delimit a philosophical ethics of the believer and its confrontation with the ethics of a nonbeliever, maintaining that such an ethics could not be considered philosophical; the delimitation as well as the confrontation could only be part of a *moral theological* position (cf. D. J. Bradley, *Aquinas and the Twofold Human Good*, 523; Bradley's argument is carried out on the basis of the original [1994] Italian language edition of this book). This objection does not appear compelling, since the fact that the necessity for such a delimitation would only be a necessity for a theologian and is to that extent a theological delimitation, does not imply that the *product* of such a delimitation, even if considered theologically or from the perspective of faith, is then itself theology as well. On the contrary, it can be a matter of a theologically grounded "liberation" of philosophical reason (allowing the philosopher to think philosophically *and* theologically without mixing the two). In any event, it must be granted that a liberation of philosophical reasoning on this basis would *not* be theologically indifferent (cf. Bradley, ibid.). In this sense, it would be "Christian philosophy," but still philosophy.

109. As it is for K. Rahner, "Über das Verhältnis von Natur und Gnade," in *Schriften zur Theologie* (Einsiedeln: Benziger, 1956), 1.340.

tential) ultimate capacity of being would *not* consist in the vision of God. This person's *desiderium naturale* of seeing God would remain never satisfied at all. Is this a possible, meaningful perspective?

To this extent, the question is unanswerable in theological terms, and probably meaningless, since theological investigation starts from the given that man proceeds from God's creative act and was raised from the very beginning to the level of grace in the moment of creation. This means that the theological answer would be: to begin with, God aimed in the very creation of man at his ultimate elevation to the beatific vision. And the nature given us is already made for this in its core, and experiences in this elevation the ultimate perfection that comes to its natural powers as a gift of grace.

Such an answer would only increase the difficulty for the philosopher. As correct as the theological answer is, it does not solve our problem. What we need, again, is a purely philosophical answer that does not take into account that man has in fact been raised by grace, but simply affirms that the human being possesses a nature whose inner orientation points beyond what can be reached by the powers of this nature. This is, it must be emphasized again, demonstrable in purely philosophical terms. And on the same basis, then, the question needs to be answered.

In a certain respect, Aristotle has already given us the answer. The intellect, he tells us, is something divine, the best that is in us: the life of contemplation would be more a divine than a human life. We have to be content with the human. It would be a mistake to want to be happy the way the gods are. We have something in common with them, of course, and therefore we should strive as far as possible to live according to this "best thing in us."[110] Therefore the life of the gods "which surpasses all others in blessedness, must be contemplative; and of human activities, therefore, that which is most akin to this must be most of the nature of happiness."[111] Of course, it does not occur in the least to Aristotle to speak of a humility that would allow one to be elevated by gift to the level of the gods, because he does not know of such elevation. "Humility" in the Aristotelian perspective would only mean recognizing one's own finiteness and the divine as "the totally other that is above us," and as far as possible to strive to win the favor of the gods.

> As Aristotle says: "Now he who exercises his intellect and cultivates it seems to be both in the best state of mind and most dear to the gods. For if the gods have any care for human affairs, as they are thought to have, it would be reasonable both that they should delight in that which was best and most akin

110. *EN* X, 7 (1177b35).
111. *EN* X, 8 (1178b21–23).

to them (i.e., intellect) and that they should reward those who love and honor this most, as caring for the things that are dear to them and acting both rightly and nobly. And that all these attributes belong most of all to the wise man is manifest. He, therefore, is the dearest to the gods. And he who is that will presumably be also the happiest; so that in this way too the wise man will more than any other be happy."[112]

This is a pagan perspective, but not at all an unreligious one. It is a possible perspective on the "natural man." It recognizes the natural longing and lives with it.

Is man then condemned to unhappiness, because, understood in this way, he would have a natural longing for something that he knows is not capable of being satisfied? That is not necessarily the case. This natural longing is a longing of "nature" but not a *practical* striving. A man in this state would be condemned to unhappiness only if, despite his awareness of his finiteness, he would seek, as goal of his actions, a practical good that is impossible and not attainable for him. The object of the natural desire can only *reasonably* become a practical goal of action—and thereby the object of practically relevant striving and behavior—on the basis of revelation, of an invitation, a calling, by God Himself.[113] Without the revelation of such a calling it would be impossible for man rationally to direct his free action toward receiving the gift of a "supernatural" blessedness; it would be frivolous. The frustrated person would be the one who lacks humility and therefore reason, the one who would refuse to accept the *conditio humana*. "Humility" then really only means recognizing the truth of one's own position and living according to this truth.[114]

But how does Thomas argue from the existence of the desire to the elevation as such? And add, as well, that such a natural desire could not be "in vain"? The difficulty can be solved along the following lines.[115] Thomas says that this desire would be in vain if there were no *possibility* of an elevation. But since it fact it has been granted—as we know because of revelation—this natural longing is the strongest rational argument for showing the rationality of the Christian revelation. Thomas is speaking here as a theologian, and also as an apologist: the natural longing for the vision of God would be "in vain" only if it were *not possible to be elevated* to the beatific vision, or, in other words, if it were not possible for God to elevate man to it without changing

112. *EN* X, 9 (1179a23–29).
113. This is the argument pursued by W. Kluxen, *Philosophische Ethik bei Thomas von Aquin*, 140.
114. Thus D. Bradley appears to go too far by maintaining that according to Thomas, human beings without the possibility of satisfying their natural longing would be "vain creatures whose natures promise only a restless pursuit of happiness" (D. J. M. Bradley, *Aquinas on the Twofold Human Good*, 525).
115. Cf. once more Kluxen (note 113 above), 141.

human nature. But it is not in vain, even if it exists, and in fact a man has not been raised to it. The longing would have had another function in human life. It would in its way have made clear to man his place as a finite creature. It would not be fruitless even then. For without the intellect, to the nature of which this longing really belongs, man would not be man. It would at least have for its point that the human being can be what he is: a human being. In this way the natural longing grounds two different ways for the human being to relate to the divine. In the case of revelation and the calling to the eleva- tion of grace, it leads to the humility of someone, who in a practically relevant way directs his or her free will to receive the gift without any deserving, know- ing that fulfillment can ultimately only be reached through grace, and not by one's own efforts. That is the Christian perspective of humility. In the other case—in the absence of such a calling—the natural longing leads to the humil- ity and self-modesty of someone who in a practically relevant way limits his or her free will to the search for such happiness as is available to the "human being," a finite being. This is precisely the "Aristotelian humility," such that Aristotle is able to tell us the truth about man that is also open to the nonbe- liever. And this truth is the object of philosophical ethics.

3. Philosophical Ethics as a Doctrine of Human Virtue

a) The Nonrelativity of the Human

The truth of the philosophical reason is for the believer, we have said, only one segment of the whole. But that does not make it any less valid. Even the theologian must continue to refer to it as undeniable philosophical truth. Even if the theologian considers *everything* from the perspective of revelation, he is not allowed simply to disregard the autonomy of everything that exists. "Natu- ral morality," as the morality of this life insofar as it is accessible to mere rea- son, is "not to be understood as a hypothetical complex of norms" that would not be able to provide any practical orientation without a theological comple- tion: "it is rather the real morality of real life—the life in which everyone, with or without the help of grace, finds himself,"[116] but even so, this is still but a part, a selection from the whole. This selection, however, is only accessible to a genuinely *philosophical* manner of knowing, and the theologian can neither "jump over" this phase nor relativize it, and thereby lose the "perspective of morality." For this perspective must first be *philosophically* demonstrated, in

---

116. W. Kluxen, ibid., 149. Kluxen is here rightly opposing Maritain's conception of an only hypo- thetical natural morality, that would not be able to provide any orientation for practical living without an integration into theology.

order for someone to be capable of understanding what it can mean for a human life to have the help of *grace*, which transcends natural powers.

Someone might ask whether this conception of a "natural morality" is not called into question all over again by the doctrine of original sin. And yet, when correctly understood, the doctrine of original sin does not change anything for the philosophical perspective, even for the philosophizing of a believer. For "original sin" designates the state that nature finds itself in through being deprived of the grace of elevation, or *natura sibi relicta,* nature "left to itself." For reason as such, man that has fallen as a result of the first sin is no other than the actually existing "natural" man.[117]

Philosophical ethics, therefore, is a doctrine of human virtue according to the Aristotelian concept of the twofold happiness. All virtue is a life lived according to reason, the divine and the best in us. In first place here, too, is contemplation; in second place is the life lived according to the moral virtues, which makes for happiness in this life. Life is desirable in itself exactly to the extent that it orchestrates itself according to reason.

b) The Human Reason: Measure and End

Reason is the shaping principle of praxis that is specific to the human being, and in reason human nature really comes to be *human.* This is the meaning of the much-discussed Aristotelian *ergon* argument: the peculiar "function" *(ergon)* of man that distinguishes him from other forms of life is, Aristotle says, "an activity of the soul in accordance with, or not without, rational principle." And this is why the good life for a human being consists in a life according to reason.[118] Now this does not at all mean that only the activity of the mind is the goal of human life, and not the activity of it by way of other inclinations and strivings. It is not necessary to object against the *ergon* argument that we are here concerned with *"integral* human fulfillment."[119] In fact, that *is* what Aristotle's argument is concerned with. When Aristotle says that what is "peculiar" to man is his rationality, this argument does not have the function of separating off from the multiplicity of goods that exist that which is specifically good for man; rather, it is to identify the principle of order according to which the entire complex of actions and appetites (even those that originally and in themselves are nonrational) become components of human excellence, or human virtue.[120]

117. Cf. further discussion of this in M. Rhonheimer, *Natural Law and Practical Reason,* 324–27.
118. *EN* I, 6 (1098a 5*ff.*)
119. As does J. Finnis, *Fundamentals of Ethics,* 122ff.
120. For my critique of Finnis on this point, see further M. Rhonheimer, *Praktische Vernunft und*

Reason is consequently *telos* (end) and standard in one. A distinction has been made between the *inclusive* goal and the *dominant* goal.[121] The inclusive goal consists of a multiplicity of goods, whose unity is founded on the unity of the common principle of order. Thus a human life according to reason is the whole, reason-ordered complex of the multiplicity of appetitions, inclinations, executed actions, and goods. A dominant goal, on the other hand, is what is ultimate in the dimension of the most valued activity in general, an ultimate that reveals wherein alone the ordering principle of human praxis can consist, and toward which this praxis is guided as to its highest possibility. This dominant goal is the contemplation of truth.

The teleological dominance of contemplation is the foundation, accordingly, for the concept of what we can call "integral human fulfillment." It does not lead us away from the practical, and does not allow the multiplicity of what belongs to the human being—even as a sensing being—to sink into irrelevancy, but rather lends it that specifically human dimension, which consists in the fact that the whole is always at risk in every single element of this manifold of human good: the orientation of the human being to reality as such, to the *truth* of the good.

All "success" of human life, all that is good and valuable, or that can succeed in being realized in a human life—human goodness, which is what action is concerned with—has something to do with truth, as that which can only be an object for the reason, or, more generally, intellective understanding. This is "practical truth," the truth of praxis, a truth that can only come into being through action. But it is a truth that concerns the deepest truth of man.

In all areas of human action there is a connection in some way with a truth such as can only be the object of reason. The human being is the only form of life in the visible world that can and must behave with relation to what is good for him, under the formal aspect of the truth of this good. Animals do not need something like this because they behave under the guidance of instinct. Man behaves willingly, that is, on the basis of reason, and as a consequence something can appear good to him which in truth is not so. The teleological dominance of the vision of truth, as the highest human possibility, is at the

---

Vernünftigkeit der Praxis, 53ff. See also the remarks of U. Steinvorth, *Klassische und moderne Ethik. Grundlagen einer materialen Moraltheorie* (Reinbek bei Hamburg: Rowohlt, 1990), 123ff.; and also B. M. Ashley, "What Is the End of the Human Person? The Vision of God and Integral Human Fulfillment," in L. Gormally, ed., *Moral Truth and Moral Tradition: Essays in Honour of Peter and Elizabeth Geach* (Dublin: Four Courts Press, 1994), 68–96 (Elizabeth Geach, wife of the logician Peter Geach, is also known as G. E. M. Anscombe).

121. Cf. A. Kenny, "Happiness," *Proceedings of the Aristotelian Society* 66 (1965–1966): 93–102; critical of this is J. L. Ackrill, *Aristotle on Eudaimonia* (see above, note 56). The distinction has been used very fruitfully by G. Abbà, *Felicità, vita buona e virtù* (see note 47 above), 61f.

same time the foundation of reason as the standard of truth for the human good, and thereby for happiness in life, as realized in the inclusive multiplicity of human possibilities.

Exactly to the degree that human life and action is guided by reason, it is also a form of participation in that *beatitudo perfecta,* identified above as the utmost existential capacity of the human being. And exactly to this extent does the perspective of the most perfect and ultimate remain ever present, even if this ultimate could never be realized and even though it remains outside of philosophical consideration. As Thomas emphasizes, even the imperfect happiness of this life is in fact a participation in that perfect blessedness and is a likeness of it—a participation to which the same *naturale desiderium* reaches out, in its longing for "a certain likeness and participation."[122]

> This imperfection of the happiness of this life is also essentially based, as Thomas stresses, on the fact that in this life activity in the area of human action (the "active life") can be only imperfectly united with contemplation.[123] The perfection of a "continuity and duration" of the act of contemplating is not to be had in this life. Thomas is not maintaining an opposition between the active and the contemplative life, but merely the imperfection of their coordination with each other in this life. And precisely *for this reason* can the happiness of this life be understood as a *participation in* complete happiness.[124]

According to Thomistic teaching, then, perfect blessedness always remains present as *telos,* even if the utmost capacity of human being that it speaks for cannot enter into the philosophical perspective as a practical good. It contains what is decisive in anthropological terms—and that also means in philosophical terms: namely, what the Christian tradition has identified as the *imago Dei* character of the human being, our being made in God's image. This is also a philosophical theme, known not only to Aristotle but also to his teacher Plato in a preliminary fashion.

The imperfect happiness of this life does not have the unity of the *beatitudo perfecta.* What actually shapes it is not God Himself, nor even some human action that would have God for its object, but rather the multiplicity of virtues in their unification through the reason. God is not the *finis quo* here, not a desired good that would somehow be the end of a human action. As Thomas points out, God can only be this in the order of the virtue of *caritas* which belongs to the elevation of grace; human virtue does not have God, but rather the *bonum humanum,* the human good, for its object. It is not simply

122. Cf. I-II, Q. 3, a. 6, ad 2.
123. Ibid., Q. 3, a. 2.
124. Cf. W. Kluxen, *Glück und Glückseligkeit,* 83f.

related to the ultimate end, but only to the order of human affairs according to right reason.[125]

"Happiness" is something that is going to be different for everyone, according to the multiplicity of the ways of living and of the situations in which lives are lived. Nevertheless, this plurality of the possibilities of happiness is unified by what makes a human being human: rationality. Every form of happiness is always subject to the demand of that which alone can *rationally* make life desirable in and of itself. And this very thing keeps the perspective of virtue ethics open, since virtue only implies the happiness that is available to man as a finite rational being subject to concrete empirical conditions.

Consequently, not God but reason (or intellect) is here the highest principle of order: a reason, to be sure, that is directed toward God, but does not have God as an object in the manner of the theological virtues faith, hope, and charity (or love). The "natural man's" relationship to God exists in the dimension of justice, to which the virtue of religion belongs: the recognition of God as Creator and Lord, and subordination to Him in the recognition of one's own finitude. Such a perspective still falls short of the Christian viewpoint of being a child of God, or a friend of God, even if it stays intact within that viewpoint—as does everything naturally human. Aristotle is quite right to say that the divide between man and God is too great for something like friendship![126] And just because this is correct, we can see something completely new and different in the elevation of grace: it establishes the basis for a friendship between God and man.[127] Keeping the two perspectives distinct—the "natural" and the Christian, and with that, the philosophical and the theological—may prove to be a not insignificant contribution of the foregoing remarks.

125. Cf. *De Virtutibus Cardinalibus*, Q. un., a. 2.

126. *EN* VIII, 9 (1159a5).

127. Cf. II-II, Q. 23, a. 1: *Caritas amicitia quaedam est hominis ad Deum* ("Love [i.e., supernatural, grace-given love] is a kind of friendship of man with God").

III

MORAL ACTIONS
AND PRACTICAL REASONING

1. Morality and the Urge for Happiness

a) The Urge for Happiness and the Motives of Action

The moral perspective, as it has been expounded so far, is the perspective of a *eudaimonistic* ethics. An ethics is eudaimonistic when it holds *striving for happiness* to be constitutive in the determination of what is good and right for man. A eudaimonistic ethics considers a rightly understood drive for happiness to be the key to a good and successful life, without simply deriving this solution from the merely empirical fact of the urge as such. More precisely, a eudaimonistic ethics of any variety will always maintain that good action and virtue coincide with happiness, that happiness in life consists in good actions, in *eupraxia*.

Now, acccording to a classical critique (most widely and persistently disseminated through Kant and Max Scheler), the urge for happiness endangers—destroys, in fact—any morality whatsoever. Morality here means the purity of the motives that suggest what we do in each instance. But does eudaimonism mean that someone chooses in order to become happy? If that were the case, then eudaimonism is just a form of egotism that would necessarily distort our view of what ought to be done.

In fact, the above formulation would rather fit the position known as "hedonism." If hedonism is a form of eudaimonism, it is but a counterfeit form. The deception that leads to hedonism is not merely the reduction of happiness to sensual pleasure: the *hedone* of the hedonist can also be intellectual enjoyment. The hedonist error lies elsewhere, namely, in the interpretation of happiness as a condition of contentment, and the conviction that what motivates our conduct is the intention of reaching such a condition. The urge to happiness, in other words, is interpreted as a fundamental motive of action.

We already argued against the hedonist conception of desire in the context of the Aristotlelian doctrine of happiness (see above, II.2.b).

What Kant understood as eudaimonism was in fact hedonism: Kantian ethics proceeds from the idea that all human beings by nature strive for happiness and are hedonists. Then he adds that this hedonistic motivation, which is natural to man, is immoral. Consequently, Kant rejects the use of a hedonistically conceived urge for happiness as a criterion of moral behavior, and develops instead a conception of morality that enables us to channel our egotistical nature within the confines of reason.

What is a motive of action? It is "for the sake of which" we choose and do something. It means everything that we referred to above as "intention" in the broadest sense. Let's take a familiar example. We find someone, X, lying on a bed. We ask him, "What are you doing?" Now X's answer—something that may be obvious—would be: "I'm getting some rest." This is really an answer to the question, "*Why* are you lying on that bed?" or "*Why* did you lie down on that bed?" When X *chose* "lying down on the bed," he did this with the intention of getting rest. "To get some rest" therefore, was X's motive of action.

> In general, I avoid distinguishing "motive" from "intention," since the difference appears rather pointless to me, and introduces an unnecessary complication.[1] There are of course motives that are not intentions at all, but all intentions are motives of action (something that will become clearer when we study the concept of "intention" more closely). What would these motives be that are not intentions? The question about the motive of action could be answered in other ways: "He did it for revenge," "Because of compassion," "Because of envy," and so on. Now such things—what are usually called "motives"—are not the "for the sake of which" or the "why" of an action but rather a general impulse that explains why something was done at all ("Why did he do that, anyway?"). But the real motive of action on the basis of which, for example, someone kills someone else by revenge can still be something like "to get even." And if someone lends someone else money "out of mere compassion," this happens always on account of a "why" of the action itself (e.g., to help him, to finance his education, etc.). What is of interest here are these actual motives of action, by which *this and no other* action is chosen. Nobody does anything concrete "out of compassion" without some reason for doing *this* rather than *that*.

But to return to our example: "to get some rest" definitely brings some satisfaction and pleasure along with it. We know that this is a component of happiness. The hedonist would have to say that the motive that led X to lie on

---

1. For the opposing view, cf. M. Konrad, *Werte versus Normen als Handlungsgründe* (Bern-Berlin-New York: Peter Lang, 2000), 98ff.

his bed was, for example, "to feel better" (as an aspect of being happy). Such a motive of action is conceivable of course, and possible. But this would not demonstrate that what one does to feel better, one does to be happy.

There is also the possibility that X wanted to take some rest in order to get back to work, refreshed. What he really intended, then, was "to be able to work again." Consequently, his ultimate motive of action was really not "to feel well," but "to be capable of finishing his work." The hedonist can object that even finishing one's own work is associated with satisfaction and pleasure. X lay down on the bed for the sake of "being happy about finishing his work." But that is even less likely. He possibly wanted to finish his work because he had been obliged to do it, and wanted to reach some *other* end, reach some definite result (discover something, learn something, earn money, etc.). We could keep going in this way until we reach the last thing that motivated the action, or that to which the action of X was directed. Can this last consist in being happy?

If that were the case—so comes the seemingly paradoxical conclusion—then X should not have done anything at all: neither worked nor rested—that is, he would perform his action without any practical orientation. Thus we observe that between "lying on the bed" and "refreshing oneself" exists a connection that is knowable to the reason in the sense of a means-end relationship. There is likewise such a relationship between "refreshing oneself" and "finishing a job," and once again between "finishing a job" and "earning money." These connections of an intentional kind make it possible to structure action and to carry it out through acts of choosing. It is on the basis of such means-end relationships that someone *chooses* and *acts*. They are the transparent intentional connections that constitute praxis as an intelligible and thereby meaningful complex.

But if "wanting to be happy" were the ultimate motive, and "wanting to earn money" the next-to-ultimate motive, would that really constitute an intelligible means-end relationship between "wanting to be happy" and "wanting to earn money"? In fact, there is really no connection here discoverable by reason that could become constitutive for praxis. Nothing at all can be derived for action from "wanting to be happy." On the basis of the desire for happiness not even the least can be inferred about what someone should reasonably strive for and do in order to become happy. The urge toward happiness cannot be a constitutive motive of action for the intentional structure of praxis.

> On the basis of what was said in the preceding section we can be more precise: when someone pursues the earning of money for the sake of becoming happy, he is not choosing the earning of money as a means to the end of happiness, but rather is aiming at the earning of money as that activity which alone can

rationally be sought after for its own sake. This means that he would think that "being happy" *is attained* by earning money. The ultimate motive for praxis would then be earning money, not being happy. "To want to be happy" is thus never the ultimate for the sake of which someone chooses, but rather a characteristic of what one intends as ultimate—earning money, for example. It is the characteristic of choosing something *as an ultimate.*

"Wanting to be happy" appears to be a motive of action only when we misinterpret the acting subject through the hedonist perspective. But this misinterpretation has already been sufficiently refuted. In reality, striving for happiness cannot be a practical motive of action.[2] What fundamentally moves us to action is the insight into the meaningfulness of actions in the context of a means-end relationship. The ultimate, as stated before, is therefore not happiness, but rather in each case an ultimate within a determined context of actions: "to earn one's keep," "to know the truth," "to promote justice in society," and so on. We are concerned here with what has been referred to in the classical sense as the goals of various virtues. Each virtue has its own peculiar ultimate goal. To ask "Wherein lies happiness?" is to ask about what alone we can rationally seek for its own sake, and that is to inquire into the *formal* characteristic of why we want something, to the extent that it is ultimate, that is, something that satisfies all seeking and is consequently the formal ground of motivation for choosing and doing anything at all. Therefore "happiness" is also not a *material* motive of action, that is, not a motive for why we choose and do *this* rather than *that.*[3]

Wanting to be happy, then, does not motivate human action as the motive for doing "this" or "that," but it does so as a motive for doing something *at all.* This is because, if we did not always intend an ultimate—on the basis of a natural desire for happiness—we would not act at all, nor strive for anything that could rationally be sought for its own sake.

b) Motives of Action and Objects of Action

Motives of action in the really practical sense are, accordingly, objects of action, and as such have to be grasped within the complexity (still to be analyzed) of "means" and "ends." An object of action is the good that is objectified to the choosing and intending will—and therefore always and already objectified to the practical reason. It is in each case what is recognized in a definite context as "good," and as such is striven after and realized in action.

2. Cf. also R. Spaemann, *Happiness and Benevolence*, 21ff.
3. T. Engberg-Pedersen shows this with regard to Aristotle in *Aristotle's Theory of Moral Insight* (Oxford: Oxford University Press, 1983); see esp. chap. 1 on "Eudaimonia and Praxis," 3–36.

As such, the object of an action is precisely its *content*, an aspect of the action itself.

Seeking happiness, however, is not seeking an action because "being happy" is not a type of action. Someone can indeed want to be happy, but still do nothing or strive after nothing practical, because he simply is not able to figure out what is good, or what can reasonably be done. This condition is called despair: someone can despair only because he wants to be happy. People whose life goes along without an orientation toward an ultimate are in despair to the extent that they experience their lives as meaningless—an experience that can be repressed under certain conditions and for a certain stretch of time.

That can be the case only to some degree, and one can still find a meaning in life. If somebody wants to be healthy, but sees no possibility of becoming so, it could be said that such a person despairs about his health. But even then he would only despair about his happiness—that is, about any meaning in life whatsoever—if he were to see in health the ultimate thing that someone can rationally seek for its own sake. The search for happiness, and where we look for happiness, determines very largely when we still hope and when we despair. This shows, again, that the search for happiness does not appear as a motive of action, but rather as that inner dynamic of our striving that leads us to want to do anything at all. *What* we then rationally can will to do (= what we ought to do) the striving for happiness can never decide, but only practical reasoning which directs itself to the practical good, to that which can be attained in action.

And so, what leads us to do *this* or *that*, or to want to do this or that, as a motive of action, is not the urge for happiness but judgments of reason concerning what is *good* to do. "Striving for happiness," on the other hand, means—to cite Thomas once again—nothing other than "striving, that the will be satisfied."[4] Seeking happiness is a kind of hunger or thirst of the will; what we will, we call the good. And this is what really motivates action.

The desire for happiness itself can motivate only as a by-product or secondarily—as a suggestive urge to do something, as when someone does something "only for envy" or "out of pure compassion" (as discussed above). And this occurs when we already know, for example, what is good, but for various reasons find it difficult to do, or are afraid to do it. But this connection between virtue and happiness never takes us any farther in determining what is good to do. If "wanting to be happy" was our motive of action, we could never actually be happy, since we would never know what the good consisted in, through which we become happy.

4. I-II, Q. 5, a. 8.

c) Being Happy and Being Good

Motives of action, then, as really *practical* motives and thereby as *moral* motives, are directed toward a good attainable in action. This would also be true for an ethics (such as theological ethics) in which God Himself is objectifiable as the ultimate practical for-the-sake-of-which (this would apply to the theological virtues: faith, hope, and love or charity). Here, God Himself is the object of action and the motive of action. But God cannot be the motive "insofar as He makes me happy." That would be the hedonist approach. Of course, it is quite possible to misinterpret Christian morality in a hedonist way! Fichte fought against such interpretations with his verdict: "Your God is the giver of all pleasure."[5] But Fichte did not reject this interpretation as a *mis*-interpretation; instead (in order, like Kant, to rescue morality, but going beyond him) he rejected in general the idea of an expectation of happiness and a God that had anything to do with that: "He who expects blessedness is but a fool, ignorant of himself and of his whole situation; there is no blessedness, no blessedness is possible; the expectation of this, and of a God who would provide it, are fairy tales. A God who is supposed to serve desires is a despicable God: he performs a service that itself repulses every responsible man. Such a God is an evil entity: He supports and immortalizes human failure, and the degradation of reason."[6]

But God as motivation is not conceived in hedonistic terms to the extent that He is recognized and loved as the highest *good,* in the way Augustine meant when he said, "Do not love God for a reward, He *is* himself the reward."[7] But that does not belong to philosophical ethics, but rather to the perspective of complete happiness, which is that of theology. The perspective of philosophical ethics remains on the plane of the good life, ordered by reason, but still incomplete.

> The foregoing considerations show, again, how Kant *finally* remains a hedonist. His postulated God must be postulated as "that which makes me happy (or blessed)," but not as a "good." The highest good, for Kant the thoroughgoing hedonist, is one's own happiness, but not the activity that alone can reasonably be sought for its own sake. Therefore, *because* Kant was, finally, a hedonist in his thinking and because he interpreted happiness in a hedonist way, in order to rescue morality he had to remove all striving for happiness from the ethics of this life, and reduce it to the perspective of duty.

Motives for action that pertain to one's own happiness are thus a betrayal of practical reason. They are structurally irrational, and indeed impractical in

5. J. G. Fichte, *Appellation an das Publikum gegen die Anklage des Atheismus* (1799), in *Werke,* ed. I. H. Fichte (Berlin: Walter de Gruyter, 1971), 5.218 (trans. here by G. Malsbary).
6. Ibid., 219.
7. St. Augustine, *Commentary on the Gospel of John,* 3.20.

the true sense of the word, because they can provide no rational orientation for our praxis. Someone who chooses to do *this* action rather than *that* one from the motive of becoming happy acts without orientation. His praxis and consequently his life possess no rational cohesion, and in the end he becomes the plaything of fleeting impulse and circumstance. He loses what is distinctive of human action: the *dominium,* or rationally ordered mastery over his own action.

Knowing about the connection between "happiness" and "good action" is, to be sure, something that comes incidentally and can often be an additional stimulus. But this is so because the urge for happiness naturally helps us be disposed to strive and to act. But one *rationally* seeks happiness, contentment, and pleasure only to the extent that someone seeks what is good. Doing good and being happy coincide, of course (if not always immediately); but "wanting to do good" is what alone provides orientation for praxis. Then a rightly understood urge for the good leads to the question, "In what does the goodness of actions consist?" That is precisely Socrates' strategy against Polos in the *Gorgias.* It is because the question "Is it worse to do injustice or to suffer it?" has finally to do, says Socrates, with "knowledge or ignorance of who is happy and who is not."[8] In order to answer that question, the question must first be answered, "Who is *just?*": "According to my opinion, Polos, the wicked man and the doer of evil is in any case unhappy . . . [because] I think it impossible . . . that a man who does evil and is unjust can also be happy."[9]

2. On the Structure of Intentional Actions

a) Intentions and Objects of Actions: The Concept of the Intentional Basic Action

The question about the goodness of actions emerges under various aspects.[10] It asks first of all: "What is a good action, as opposed to a bad action?" Or: what do we *mean* at all when we say "action," when we call an action "good" or "bad," "right" or "wrong" in a morally relevant sense? This question is a question about the *object of action [Handlungsgegenstand]*. This means we are asking, what is there in the content of the act that we morally judge, when we morally judge it? We also can call this objective content of actions the "object of the action" *[Handlungsobjekt]*, and the identity that an action has on the basis of this content would be the "objective meaning" of actions—whereby we always speak of "human actions" or of "moral actions."

The question about the object of action is always aiming toward getting an

8. Plato, *Gorgias* 472c.
9. Ibid.
10. Cf. W. Kluxen, "Thomas von Aquin: Zum Gutsein des Handelns," *Philosophisches Jahrbuch* 87 (1980): 327–39.

answer to the question, *"What* are we doing?" It was shown previously (II.1.c) that the question about "what one is doing" is always also a question about a "why?" or "to what end?" one is doing something. "What are you doing here?" means just the same as "Why are you lying in your bed?"[11] This intentional structure of human actions must now be reconsidered and analyzed more fully.

There is, as we have seen, a first and fundamental intentionality, a first and fundamental "To what end?" that is necessary before we can treat any concrete action at all as an *actus humanus* (human action)—that is, as a willed, rationally guided, and chooseable act—and not only as an event or happening that is describable in physical categories. For example, in "raising the arm" we have only described a bodily movement, and not yet an action.

However, before we attempt to describe "raising an arm" as an action, it might be helpful to begin by posing Wittgenstein's question: "What is left over if I subtract the fact that my arm goes up from the fact that I raise my arm?"[12] We would have to say that what is left over is, at least, my *wanting* to raise it. This does not in any case mean that an action is a mere "bodily movement" that is caused by a (foregoing) "willing," in the way one billiard ball hits another and sets it in motion. The willing that is "left over" in this case is rather a *component* of the action "raising the arm." This action itself, as a corporeal movement, *is* also an act of the will (in the phase of carrying out what is willed), so that, if we abstract the mere fact of the arm's rising, conceptually the *willing* of the raising-of-the-arm is left over. This willing was already present before the situation came about "that my arm rises" (as can also occur when someone only *attempts* to raise his arm: he does this, without the fact of "the rising of the arm" ever taking place). In any case, such a willing is always a "willing to raise my arm." The willing itself, as *this* willing and no other, cannot be described without relation to the raising of the arm. Therefore, the "willing" and the "raising of the arm" are identical in a certain sense.

> In the debate between the so-called causalists and intentionalists, both sides may well have a good share of the truth: "intentionalists" say that the "willing" that implies an intention is not distinguishable from the action itself: "willing" and "bodily movement" are not two separable events; rather, an ac-

11. This is the fundamental point of the so-called intentionalist, G. E. M. Anscombe. Cf. also A. I. Melden, *Free Action* (London: Routledge & Kegan Paul, 1961).

12. L. Wittgenstein, *Philosophical Investigations,* trans. G. E. M. Anscombe (Oxford: Basil Blackwell, 1958), no. 621. Just before the sentence here quoted, he writes: "Let us not forget this: when 'I raise my arm,' my arm goes up." This sentence contains a peculiar mix of the observing-perspective and the acting-perspective. The fact "my arm goes up" is an observation from outside; "I raise my arm," by contrast, is the *accomplishment* of an *action.* "I raise my arm" (= a human action), cannot be observed; what *can* be observed is "my arm rises" (= fact). Consequently, Wittgenstein's formula "the fact that I raise my arm" is not correct: "I raise my arm" is really not a "fact"—i.e., as a fact, it is always something *more* than a fact.

tion is only intelligible when it is understood as a *unity* of intent [*Absicht*] and bodily movement: the action *is* bodily movement "under a certain description" (i.e., a bodily movement carried out with a definite intention). But it cannot be concluded from this (as the intentionalists in fact do) that the will [*Absicht*, intention] does not *cause* the action, that there is no causal nexus between will and action. Nevertheless, this does not require us to take up the dualistic position (as G. Ryle's "ghost in the machine") of a "willing" that sets a certain bodily movement into action. It is enough to understand that actions themselves are a certain stage of the act of willing. In raising an arm, the will brings itself to the execution of a certain bodily movement, which *first* needs to be willed, in order for it to be carried out; but then in the stage of execution it again implies this same willing, without which it wouldn't have been reached at all. We thus have *two* acts of the will: (1) the will as a will *choosing* with an intention (the Aristotelian *prohairesis:* a decision to do something), and (2) in this case, the bodily movement of the raising of the arm, which is itself a completion of *willing:* the raising of the arm is in fact once again a "willing," but now only in the stage of carrying out of what was willed. This is the kind of act referred to as an *actus imperatus* in Scholastic philosophy (cf. below, III.5.d). And this also means that the raising of the arm is in fact identical with the *willing* of the raising of the arm, but *at the same time* something *more* than the "mere fact, that the arm is raised."[13]

Such a willing is related to the carrying out of the raising of an arm in the dimension of a "why" or a "to what end?"—to this extent even "raising an arm" is a human action. And consequently the action of raising an arm, viewed intentionally, is always *more* than the mere occurrence that an arm is raised: for example, "to give a starting signal" or "to greet someone." The same is true for the fundamentally intentional "what one does" when someone is lying on a bed, for example, "to get some rest." I would like to call this an *intentional basic action*. Such actions take place, as already mentioned (II.1.c), at a, so to speak, "lowest threshold" of intentional structuring.[14]

What this means, to repeat, is that it is not in fact possible to choose the action of "lying on the bed" *in this way,* that is, to make it the object of an ac-

---

13. Cf. in this connection the finely developed, and, as they appear to me, conciliatory expositions by A. MacIntyre, "The Antecedents of Action," in B. Williams and A. Montefiori, eds., *British Analytical Philosophy* (London: Routledge & Kegan Paul, 1966), 205–25. On Wittgenstein's example of raising the arm, see, from the Thomistic viewpoint, S. L. Brock, *Action and Conduct: Thomas Aquinas on the Theory of Action* (Edinburgh: T. & T. Clark, 1998), 174ff.

14. An "intentional basic action" is thus to be distinguished from what Arthur C. Danto calls a "basic action": the last physical elements of an action that cannot be composed of any further elements of action, for example, "to move an arm." These elements are themselves no longer actions. If this is correct—that actions cannot be described without intentional content—then Danto's concept of basic action is wrong. Cf. A. C. Danto, "Basic Actions," *American Philosophical Quarterly* 2 (1965): 141–48. A critique which in my view is largely correct is provided by R. Bubner, *Handlung, Sprache, und Vernunft. Grundbegriffe praktischer Philosophie* (Frankfurt am Main: Suhrkamp, 1982), 91–100.

tion. When we choose "to lie on the bed," we are always choosing "to get some rest," or "to relax" or "to do yoga," and so on. The description in relation to which we choose the physical action is the intentional content, the "why?" or "to what end?" of the action.

What is decisive here is that the concept of the action includes with it an act of the choosing will, determining that action. Actions can only be described as *chosen* actions and that means that they always already possess a basic intentional structure. "To get some rest for oneself" can be done in turn for some further purpose, some further "to what end?" For example, "getting some rest, in order to finish a job." In this way it would also be possible for someone lying on a bed to answer the question "What are you doing?" by saying, "Leave me alone. I'm trying to finish my dissertation." The answer may not be immediately intelligible to the person asking the question, but the answer would be correct. It provides the reason, the "to what end?" for the "lying on the bed." While "getting some rest" already adequately defines the "what" of an action that is intelligible in itself, the content of the "what" is further enriched by the added information: "to the end of finishing my dissertation."

Accordingly, we find the "to what end" or "why" that a "what" defines occurring on *at least* two levels: the first is the level at which a concrete human action as such is defined as a human action and thereby as an action that is chosen "to do," that is, an intentional basic action. We call this—that is, the basic intentional content of such an action—the *object of action* in the proper and stricter sense. The second level is that on which the *further* purpose is found, for the sake of which this concrete action is chosen. This "intention" [*Absicht*] we call "intention" in the proper and stricter sense.[15]

This is a terminological clarification that can help us avoid many misunderstandings. When speaking in action-theoretical terms, all objects of actions are always also intentions, which means that a willed "to what end" lies at their foundation. "To lie on a bed" is not yet an object of action. But "to get some rest" is. This is because the latter contains the "why" of "lying on the bed." And "to lie on the bed" can only be chosen at all "under the description of a purpose," in this logic of "why."

But in another respect, we must also say that it is important to distinguish intentional basic actions from further, additional intentionalities. And then we arrive at the difference between the objects of action and what was referred

15. Consequentialist ethicists are inclined to blur this distinction; on this point, see M. Rhonheimer, "'Intrinsically Evil Acts' and the Moral Viewpoint: Clarifying a Central Teaching of *Veritatis Splendor*," *The Thomist* 58, no. 1 (1994): 1–39, and "Intentional Actions and the Meaning of Object: A Reply to Richard McCormick" *The Thomist* 59, no. 2 (1995): 279–311; reprinted in J. A. Di Noia and R. Cessario, eds., *Veritatis Splendor and the Renewal of Moral Theology* (Princeton-Huntington-Chicago: Scepter/Our Sunday Visitor/Midwest Theological Forum, 1999), 241–68.

to above as intention in the narrower sense: everything further, to which we order a concrete, chosen action as going beyond itself, and that means not the "why we choose *what* we do" (in the way we choose to lie on the bed, in order to get some rest)—the "why" in this instance provides the *what* we intelligibly are doing as such, and constitutes the intentional basic action—rather, the *to what end* (or, for the sake of what) we "really do" what we do, why we choose to do this (thus we choose "to get rest" in order to "finish the dissertation," or in other words, we "lie on the bed to get some rest" and we do this, in turn, "in order to finish the work"). This further thing, for the sake of which we choose concrete human actions, we call in general the intention *with which* someone carries out an action (an action already describable in terms of intention).

But then we must also say that *this* intention also possesses the character of an *object* of action, and to this extent it too determines in a wider perspective "what" we are really doing. If we find someone lying on a bed in the middle of the day, we might at first be inclined to think him somewhat lazy, and—in case we don't know him—we may even guess he is acting from mere sloth, perhaps sleeping off a night of debauchery. But as soon as we learn that he is doing this in order to be in a better position to finish up a difficult project, we would probably start to have the contrary opinion of him.

> We read in Aristotle as follows: "If one man commits adultery for the sake of gain, and makes money by it, while another does so at the bidding of appetite though he loses money and is penalized for it, the latter would be held to be self-indulgent rather than grasping, but the former is unjust but not self-indulgent; evidently, therefore, he is unjust by reason of his making gain by his act."[16] "Adultery" here defines a moral species that is formed by an object of action which is identical in both cases and which in itself defines a human, choosable action with an intentional structure. A further "to what end" has been added to it—and that is the intention in the narrower sense.

The "what" that someone is really doing, and, along with that, the good that one seeks in action, is complex in structure. It is composed of what is referred to as "means" and "end."[17]

b) Means and Ends

When we speak of "means," we naturally think first of tools like hammer and nails, or financial means, medical measures, and so on. But in Aristotle we do

---

16. *EN* V, 2 (1130a24–27).
17. Cf. also the already cited (II.1.d, note 27) works of A. W. Müller, "Praktische und technische Teleologie," in H. Poser, ed., *Philosophische Probleme der Handlungstheorie*, 43ff., and *Praktisches Folgern und Selbstgestaltung nach Aristotleles*, 224.

not find any word that corresponds to "means." The Greek language only has the expression used so frequently by Aristotle: *ta pros to telos* ("what is toward the end").[18] The situation is the same with Thomas. The Greek expression is found in his writing as *ea quae sunt ad finem,* "that which is to the end," or perhaps a little more felicitously: "that which is headed toward an end," "what is ordered to an end." This "that which is ordered to a goal" is nothing other than a concrete, choosable, or chosen human action. "Means"—as we would like to use the expression—are *concrete actions* that are chosen and carried out in order to reach a certain goal. A means is also *at least* an intentional basic action, whereas means are *not* the ontic—physical—elements of intentional basic actions (such as bodily movements, tools, material objects, physical events).

Consequently, "to get some rest" is a means, and in fact a means to a certain goal, "finishing a work." The adultery Aristotle discusses is also a means, either for the goal of having a sexual encounter or for making money. "To lie on the bed," by contrast, is not a means *in this sense,* to reach the end of "getting rest." In other words, it is not a means in the sense that interests us here, because it does not define any human action (intentional basic action), or any practical good, but is only a means in a physical sense, in exactly the same way a certain kind of pill is a "means" to employ in fighting off a headache. But this is *not* what is meant here by "means."

If we designate a pill used to reduce one's headache as "X," then "swallowing X" is no more *intentional* a description of an action than "lifting one's arm," but merely a description of something that *happens;* but it does not furnish any information about what is being *done,* that is, what is being *chosen,* because the description of any "to what end" is missing. So then: *"what"* is someone who takes aspirin really doing? We cannot say at all if we don't know *to what end* he is doing it. We can only grant that the physical or ontic process of action for a three-year-old child is the same as it is for a grownup who *chooses* to "take aspirin" in an intentionally describable way, that is, in the horizon of a "to what end" or "why."

The action "swallowing X" in itself is not a practical good, nor an action that can be *meaningfully* chosen and carried out. As some good in the practical sense, this action is chosen and carried out only on the horizon of a "to

18. Cf. the extensive study by M. Ganter, *Mittel und Ziel in der praktischen Philosophie des Aristoteles* (Freiburg and Munich: Suhrkamp, 1974). M. C. Nussbaum, *The Fragility of Goodness* (Cambridge: Cambridge University Press, 1986), 297, points out that in a certain sense the *"pros to telos"* is not only "what is towards the end" but is also "what *pertains* to the end," and is thus not only the path to the goal, but also a certain component of the goal. This is correct, since the "means" anticipates and realizes the end, and is not simply an "instrument" (which would lose its meaning after the goal has been reached).

what end," which defines "swallowing X" as an intentional action. Only in this way does the action "swallow X" become the action "take a pill to relieve one's headache." This intentional action we can then designate as a means that is chosen for the sake of "relieving a headache" (a goal that someone could also try to reach through other means than taking a pill). The "to what end" that lies *in* the swallowing of X as such is what defines the action as human—as intentional basic action—and as such alone can it also be meaningfully chosen. And this is the sense of "means" that interests us here.

For this reason it would be wrong to say that someone chooses "to swallow X" in order to "to take a pill to relieve a headache." The "in order to" is here precisely the "to what end" which constitutes the action as an intentional action. A child who is nibbling on whatever he finds and swallows X is not carrying out the action "taking a pill to relieve a headache," even though X is still in this case a "means" to combat a headache. And someone could probably lie on a bed without performing the action of "getting some rest," even though it may look like that to any external observer.

Consequently even "raising one's arm" is not a means to the end of "greeting someone." Rather, "raising one's arm" is itself the intentional action of "greeting someone." But "to greet someone" can, nevertheless, in turn still be a means (for example) of expressing one's respect for the person one greets or to obtain that person's favor for something. In the same way, taking up the example of "adultery," it would not make sense to say that someone was seeking to have sexual intercourse with X as a "means" to the end of having a sexual relationship with X. Rather, someone seeks the sexual relationship with X *in* the act of sexual intercourse with X. Rather than choose the physical action "sexual intercourse," someone seeks the "to what end" of it as well, that is, "sexual intercourse with X." Likewise, in the sense that concerns us here, "depositing money in one's bank account" is not a "means" to the end of saving money. The "saving" itself is rather the "why," which constitutes the material action "depositing money" as a human (or intentional) basic action.

"Means" are therefore always intentionally defined human actions; actions that are chosen, and *insofar* that they are objects of choices—arising, that is, from reason-governed will (we are leaving to one side for the moment actions that result from so-called weakness of the will). To the extent that a concrete intentional action is guided toward some further goal and is chosen for the sake of it, it also possesses the character of a means (whereby a goal can become, in its turn, a means to a superordinate goal).

But we can look at the same thing in the opposite way, and treat it so to speak from the top down: when someone sets a goal for himself, he seeks means to accomplish that goal. If someone wants to become healthy, he looks for means of getting healthy. He decides, for example, to begin an exercise program. The example of health is one of Aristotle's favorite analogies, but it can be confusing because it involves something closer to the means-end relationship of art (such as, "take aspirin in order to reduce pain"). Nevertheless, "means" taken to improve one's health can often really be described as human actions (this would apply to an exercise program or some other form of athletic activity: when we see a jogger, we know "what" he is doing, in the sense of intentional action, even if we don't see a *further* "to what end," in the sense of an intention: to stay healthy, to live longer, to work more effectively, to enjoy being outdoors, etc.); in other cases, however, we do not know even "what" someone is doing (e.g., when someone "takes aspirin," or when we don't know what the athletic activity in question is—as when someone who watches a game of soccer without understanding what is going on would ask why these twenty-two people are chasing a ball around a field: he doesn't know "what" they are doing at all). Here the other example is less confusing: if someone is trying to finish his work and is exhausted, he looks for a means to finish the work. He chooses the means "to get some rest" (not "to lie down on a bed"). When someone wants to make sure that his son has a good education, he chooses the action "saving money," not "putting money into a bank account"; for, whether he puts money into an account or whether he keeps it at home in a safe, they are both only two different ways of *carrying out* or *executing* the intentional act of "saving money."

Viewed in this way, "means" (that is to say, the concrete actions that are chosen for the sake of a definite goal) are a kind of concretization of the intended goal *in* action, or an anticipation of the good of that goal *through* action. If someone is getting some rest in order to finish his work, he is already engaged in finishing that work. If someone saves money in order to make possible a quality education for his son, he is already making that education possible in the very act of saving money. "To get some rest" is here a component of the action-complex "finishing my work," and saving money is likewise a part of the action-complex "education of my son." In this way, human praxis organizes itself into meaningful wholes, into an intentionally ordered structure, into a whole life lived with purpose.

c) Choosing and Intending as Acts of the Will: Their Intentional Unity

Human actions are chosen for the sake of a definite goal. When someone chooses an action and carries it out, the intention is *in* the act of choosing and *in* the act of execution. Not only the choosing, but also the intending of the goal for the sake of which it is chosen, are acts of the will, and that means that they are reason-directed appetitive acts. In every instance of willing, no matter how complex, practical reason is always the guiding source of knowing. Practical reason holds a potentially infinite number of possibilities for organizing and structuring praxis.

The act of the will that aims toward the execution of a concrete action (means) we call the *choice of action* or simply "choice" (Aristotle's *prohairesis*, Thomas's *electio*) or also the "choosing act of the will" or "choosing will" *(voluntas eligens)*. The act of the will that in choosing and acting aims toward a further goal, we call the *intention of a goal* or simply "intention" (Thomas's *intention*), or "the intending act of the will" or the "intending will" *(voluntas intendens)*.[19]

The choice of action, as should have become clear from the foregoing discussion, is always directed toward a practical good that can be reached in a concrete action. It relates to what can be done by us, to what is means toward an end.[20] The choice of action is "a deliberate desire of things in our own power"[21] and which, in general, can be both the way it is and otherwise than it is. Intentions, on the other hand, relate to practical goods, which do not lie in the domain of immediate action and which therefore must be concretized or, so to speak, made present in action. If it is impossible for parents to afford a professional education for their children, but they still want to carry out that intention, they look for means whereby "financing the education of their children" becomes an object of action that they can carry out. The means would then be, for example, denying themselves certain things, spending less money, and so on. A choice of action (= choice of means) brings the goal down a level, to make it accessible to action and thus attainable. This is why Aristotle designates the (intentional) goal as the "beginning [or principle, Gr. *arche*] of action," because striving and practical deliberation *begin* with an intentional goal; practical reasoning succeeds in bringing this beginning of action, this "moving principle," back to the doer himself.[22] "To intend something" is then already a potentially practical way of willing something: intending leads to deliberating, to choosing, and to acting.

For this reason we must distinguish "intending" from "mere willing" or

19. Aristotle lacks a proper word for the concept of the intention, and this is probably one of the major deficits of his action-theory. Cf. G.E.M.Anscombe, "Thought and Action in Aristotle," in J.Barnes, M.Schofield, and R.Sorabji, eds., *Articles on Aristotle* (London: Duckworth, 1977), 2.61–71; and A.Kenny, *Will, Freedom and Power* (Oxford: Blackwell, 1975); cf. also the article by Kenny cited above in II.3.b. Of course, Aristotle also knew an act of "setting a goal" distinct from prohairesis. But he doesn't have an action-theoretical concept for it. For a fuller discussion, see M.Rhonheimer, *Praktische Vernunft und Vernünftigkeit der Praxis*, 229ff.

20. Cf. *EN* III, 3 (1112b 32–33). On the theme *electio*, see I-II, Q. 13, and *De Veritate*, Q. 22, a. 15.

21. *EN* III, 3 (1113a11).

22. *EN* III, 3 (1113a 6).

"wishing."[23] A wish is not an intention. What you only "wish for" does not lead to action, such as "I wish he were still alive . . ." or "I wish I had his wealth." Someone who is convinced that he is incurably ill still wishes to be healthy. But to the extent that he is certain that no means can bring it about and he no longer looks for any means, he also does not *intend* to get healthy again, so he remains in the state of "mere willing" or "wishing." To intend something always means at the same time seeking for means—actions—through which it will be possible to reach what was intended.

This shows that what someone is *really* or primarily doing when he chooses something and does something is not at all that which he does or chooses, but is instead what he *intends* with (or, rather *in*) this choosing or acting. A politician who during an election campaign shows commitment to charities to win public favor, is not ultimately aiming to benefit these charities; he wants to be admired and amass as many votes as he can. Ultimately, our intentions are decisive for the content (and also the worth) of our actions because they are finally what determine *what* we really want and *what* we really do.

As Plato wrote in the dialogue *Gorgias:*

Do you consider, then, that men will what on any occasion they are doing, or rather that for the sake of which they act as they do? For example, do you consider that those who drink medicine at the doctor's orders will what they are doing, namely the drinking of medicine with all its unpleasantness, or the health for the sake of which they drink?

Obviously, the health.

So too with those who sail the seas and engage in money-making in general—they do not will what they do on each occasion. For who desires to sail and suffer dangers and troubles? But they will, in my opinion, that for the sake of which they sail, namely wealth, for it is for wealth's sake that they sail.

Certainly.

And is this not a general truth? If a man acts with some purpose, he does not will the act, but the purpose of the act.[24]

Intentions are like the souls of chosen actions. And as the concrete action is "ensouled" by the choosing will, so the soul of the whole complex is the will that intends. Although "get some rest," "save money," or "rob a bank" are meaningful, *choose*-able, intentional human actions, we can ask the question, "What would such an action mean, if someone did not have a further intention in getting rest, saving money, or robbing a bank?"

23. On the theme of "intention," see I-II, Q. 12, and *De Veritate*, Q. 22, a. 13 and 14.
24. d, trans. Woodhead, in E. Hamilton and H. Cairns, eds., *Plato: The Collected Dialogues* (Princeton, N.J.: Princeton University Press, 1961).

For this reason, Thomas tells us that the object of the choice of action and the object of the intention really form a single object of action (or a single object of the will). The goal relates to the means as light relates to color: what stimulates the sense of sight to see something is light and color, but light makes it possible for the color to be seen at all. Just so, both the goal and the means toward it are objects of our striving, but the goal makes it possible for the means to be something "striven for" at all. The goal is the reason for the willing of the means. As light and color are both seen in one and the same act, so means and end are both willed in one and the same act of the will.[25]

The point Plato made in the *Gorgias*, that when someone does something for the sake of a purpose, he does not will the action itself, but the purpose for which he is doing the action—in other words that what we really will, when we will and choose something, is what we intend—needs clarification in two respects. First, this does not mean that the intention is always consciously present. Parents who care for their children every day and make many sacrifices for them do not choose with a conscious intention, "I now intend to care for my children." Intentionalities like that are *habitually* present in the will: they are founded on concretely realized acts of the will, which can nevertheless "dominate" and guide praxis over a long period of time, and in this way constitute a lifetime's accomplishment. Second, this primacy of the ultimate "reason why" of a willing in each case does not imply that the "morality of the means" is meaningless. In contrast with Plato, Aristotle brought this perspective of the morality of the means into the foreground: what is decisive is not only that the ultimately willed goal is right, but also the actions that lead to this goal. "Ultimately" good intentions are not enough to make our praxis good.[26]

d) Good Intention and Good Will

Now, if we were to allow the passage cited from Plato's *Gorgias* to stand without any correction, we would have to ask ourselves: "If someone who robs a bank does it to support the poor, is he not *really* doing something good on the basis of this intention, since what he really wants is to provide assistance to the poor?" That would be the case if human willing were a kind of game where you count up objects of concrete acts of choosing and set them off against ob-

25. I-II, Q. 12, a. 4; *De Veritate*, Q. 22, a. 14.
26. On this adjustment of perspective from Plato to Aristotle, cf. P. Aubenque, *La Prudence chez Aristote* (Paris: Presses Universitaires de France, 1963). Another extensive discussion is found in M. Rhonheimer, *Praktische Vernunft und Vernünftigkeit der Praxis*, 231ff. (and for some important reservations about Aubenque's thesis, see ibid., 344ff.).

jects of intentions—a kind of balancing process, whereby the intention of a bad action is so good that in the end an excess of intended good makes the balance positive.

To begin with a terminological clarification: when we speak of "intention" we can understand it in two ways: (1) as the *object* (or content) of an act of the will (the intended, aimed-at goal) and (2) as the *act of the will* itself, that directs itself toward its corresponding object (the *act of intending* a goal, the *act of aiming-at*).[27] We can distinguish objects of intentions, or "intentions" in sense (1), from objects of choice-acts. Nevertheless, as soon as we speak of "intention" in sense (2), we are talking about an act of the human will. But it is impossible to distinguish the intending and the choosing act of will as two different acts of the will. Instead, it is a matter of a single act of willing in which a means is chosen for the sake of an end, and this act of the will constitutes, accordingly, *a single intentional action*.

And so, to return to our example: if the bank robbery succeeds, the agent attains his goal of helping the poor. The problem to be solved, however, is not whether he reaches his goal or not; the problem is whether his will can still be good (and in this case, just) despite the fact that he is carrying out an unjust deed. This does not depend on whether he actually attains his goal of helping the poor. The actual accomplishment of this goal cannot be decisive for the goodness of his will. If we were content with such an answer, it would mean that we are understanding the means-end relationship as purely instrumental, and thereby lose the moral perspective. This is because—in an ethically relevant action-theory perspective—the goal is not simply reached "through" the means, but really "in" it. An action that is undertaken for the sake of justice must already "be just" as an action (i.e., as a means).

For what alone determines the goodness of the intention "helping the poor" is whether this intention suits *justice* and real *good will*. Consequently the chosen means is an action through which someone intends the goal of "justice" or "good will." Only for that reason would the intention "helping the poor" be good at all, and only for that reason can the means—insofar as it really is a *means*—be good. Now since "choosing a means for the sake of a goal" is a single act of the will that constitutes a single intentional action, the answer can only be as follows: even when the goal of "helping the poor" is in fact successfully attained through an (in itself, unjust) action of bank robbery, nevertheless, by these means, the goal of "justice" cannot be attained, which

27. In an analogous way we use the word *faith* to convey the act of faith as well as its content or object. In the former meaning, it is used in the expression, "He has a strong faith" or "with her faith she could move mountains," while in the latter sense one would speak of Jewish, Christian, or Islamic faith or of belief in an angel, or life after death, and so on.

was the aspect of the goal on the basis of which "helping the needy" was *good* in the first place. Indeed, it is contradictory to want to reach the goal of "justice" through an act of injustice. (The only thing one could accomplish would be assistance for the poor, which in itself, to be sure, would be a promotion of justice, but *as an action* it could not be described as *just.*) The action of bank robbery could only be justified under the assumption that the intended goal is not good through any correspondence with "justice" or "good will." But in that case it would no longer be clear *why* someone should help the poor at all, or why the intention "to help the poor" is even good to begin with.

This context will become still clearer if we recall that moral actions are immanent activities. Through actions, that is to say, through the choosing of actions and the intending of goals of our action, we change ourselves, we become better or worse human beings. Man is not what he produces and what he accomplishes in his environment. Man is what he wills. Through willing, the acting subject becomes a human being of a certain kind or other. And willing includes not just intention, but also choosing.

For a human being to act, which means standing in practical-appetitive relation to the kinds of goods that are accessible to action, and for a human being to choose and intend, he moves, as it were, in the direction of what he is striving for. If someone is moving in the direction of justice, he becomes a just person. This moving-oneself-toward-something is only a metaphor, of course. But it expresses how the acting person *above all* changes himself. What matters is not only the state of affairs that we create through our action, but also what kind of people we are who have produced that state. Whether the people are good or bad is something that is also part of the state of affairs.

That in everything we choose and do as a means, we ultimately will the end for the sake of which we have chosen a concrete action, has the following significance: after we have brought, through our consideration, an originally goal-directed willing to the level of praxis, so that we are choosing a concrete action as a "means toward an end," so we now, in a way, really will the goal *in* this means: that is, the willing of the goal runs right through the willing of the means. What we really want is the end; but we really will this by way of our willing of the means.

Consequently if someone robs a bank in order to help the poor, that person is someone who wants to rob a bank, and *thereby* intends his act of good will or his act of justice. Only the intention in sense (1), as the object of the intending will, is good; not, however, the goal-intending *act* of the will; because this is really the same as the act of the will that wills the bank robbery.

If the intention in sense (1) is good, this will is perhaps "more understandable" and less bad than the will of one who robs a bank in order to support terrorists. But it is still an unjust will and the doer of the action is an unjust person. The will of the agent is accordingly *either* a good *or* a bad will; it cannot be partly good and partly bad, but only more or less good or (alternatively) more or less bad. This is what is meant by the classical dictum that good requires a cause that is without any flaw, but for evil any single defect is enough: *bonum ex integra causa, malum ex quocumque defectu.*[28]

Hence there is a real connection between what someone *chooses* to do and that which someone *intends* with this doing. There is such a thing as "moral competence": someone is morally *in*competent when he seeks to attain justice by way of means that are themselves unjust. And for this very reason, a good purpose cannot make a bad means wholesome. Now, the utilitarian/consequentialist interpretation of the statement "The end justifies the means" is still immune to this argument, and at this stage has not yet been refuted: a consequentialist ethicist would consider all I have been saying here as merely pointless (for reasons that will later be presented and discussed; cf. below, V.4.c and f).

The argument just now presented, that the acting person changes himself above all, may sound very egotistical. The concern is apparently only with one's own perfection: to behave any way, so to say, as long as one's own hands are clean. And to this possible objection, at present I will not say more than this: if the commandment to "love your neighbor as yourself" is in fact a fundamental principle of interpersonal behavior and morality (something we can safely assume from its obviousness), then we must *first* know what it means "to love oneself." For to do just that is here presented as the standard for loving one's neighbor. And this kind of "self-love" is manifestly not egotism. An egotistic self-love could never be a standard for loving one's neighbor.[29]

What is meant, rather, is this: Everyone is a friend to himself in the first place. A friend is someone who wants what is good for the person to whom he is a friend. "To love oneself" or "to love one's friend" means to open oneself to what is really good for a human being. And this can only happen when someone always wills what is good, and that always also means choosing to do good.

If we are not in a position to want what is good for ourselves and consequently *be* good, we cannot will the good for our fellow man. For in that case

---

28. The dictum goes back to Pseudo-Dionysius the Areopagite, *De Divinis Nominibus* IV, 30. Cf. Thomas's commentary, In IV Div. Nom., lectio 22. Dionysius's original Greek was translated into Latin in Thomas's commentary as follows: *"Bonum ex una et tota est causa; malum autem ex multis et particularibus defectibus."*

29. On Thomas's viewpoint here, cf. D. M. Gallagher, "Thomas Aquinas on Self-Love as the Basis for Love of Others," *Acta Philosophica* 8 (1999): 23–44.

we wouldn't know what good is at all. Thus Aristotle rightly remarks, "it is from this relation [i.e., a man's attitude toward himself] that all the characteristics of friendship have extended to others."[30] True, and truly useful, friendship (love of neighbor) is only present where there is virtue: true self-love is love of virtue, love for what is in truth good, for the "honorable cause [Gr. *ta kallista kai malist' agatha,* 'the noblest and best things'].[31] "If *all* were to strive towards what is noble and strain every nerve to do the noblest deeds, everything would be as it should be for the common good, and everyone would secure for himself the goods that are greatest, since excellence [i.e., virtue] is the greatest of goods. Therefore the good man should be a lover of self (for he will both himself profit by doing noble acts, and will benefit his fellows)."[32] In a society where each person only intended justice for the other without paying any attention to *doing* justice himself (i.e., choosing it), any conception of what justice actually is would be lost, so that nobody could even so much as *intend* justice for anyone else. It is impossible for good intentions to spring from a bad will ("a wicked heart"). And, as I have tried to show, the will is "good" or "bad" not only on the basis of what someone intends, but also on the basis of what one concretely *chooses*. When someone is accustomed to choosing and acting unjustly, he becomes incapable of intending justice, of having intentions that are directed to justice. Someone who robs a bank today to help the needy will be capable tomorrow of robbing the people he just helped the day before, even to accomplish some further good deed. And the people who have been helped by him will perhaps be persuaded by his example that injustice is the best way to accomplish things.

3. Practical Reason and the Constitution of Good and Evil

a) What Is Practical about Practical Reason?

It was said that the practical good is in correlation to an appetition (II.1.a). Human action is a phenomenon of appetition (i.e., of "seeking," or "striving," *Streben*): action is *willing* activity, or activity *insofar as* it is willing. "To will" means to strive on the basis of reason, on the basis of reasoning that springs from judgments of reason. As we went through the analysis of the intentional character of human action and willing, we already encountered the practical reason at several points, if indirectly. "Intentional action" and "practical reason" really are only two sides of a single coin: *practical reason is the reasoning that cognitively directs intentional action.*

---

30. *EN* IX, 8 (1168b 5–6).   31. *EN* IX, 8 (1168b 25–30).
32. *EN* IX, 8 (1169a 8–14).

When the word "reason" is used here, it refers to a rather complex phenomenon: reason (Ger. *Vernunft*, Gr. *logos/dianoia*, Lat. *ratio*) is strictly speaking only part of a whole: the intellect or understanding (Lat. *intellectus*, Gr. *nous*). The human intellect is a spiritual cognitive power, whose action, beginning with the grasping of immediate first knowables or principles, takes these and works them out further through the conclusions of reasoning, and then brings back what has been thus discovered to the first principles, the content of which then becomes more explicit thanks to the movement of reason. In the present context it should suffice to point out that when we speak of reason here, it is the whole that is meant: the human intellect, which is characterized not only by an ability to grasp in an intellective manner, but also to consider discursively ("rationally"). A human being's intellectual cognition is always intellection mediated by reason. It is always an incomplete intellection. "Reason" will then be the word for that kind of intellection.[33] In addition, sense perception is also present at each stage of an intellective act. Without sense perception neither reason nor intellection is possible.

It was said that intellect is a cognitive power, a power of knowing. Is there then a *theoretical* and a *practical* intellect in the sense of two different *powers?* It is not at all necessary to assume such a thing to be able to establish a distinction between theoretical and practical *judgments.* The intellect, which is naturally oriented to the apprehension or "grasping" of what exists, and is thus called "speculative," becomes "practical" through a certain kind of "widening" *(extensio)* of its act.[34] This is an extension of its action to doing, and it is an extension of its knowing *power.* It does *not* mean that practical *judgments* are an extension or application of theoretical *judgments.* The singleness of the intellective power and the fact that practical reason becomes practical through its extension to the realm of actions does not imply that practical *judgments* are merely extensions or derivations of theoretical judgments. It makes much more sense to say that the intellect's practical judgments have their own peculiar point of departure. Only theoretical conclusions can come from theoretical judgments. But practical judgments are ones whose final conclusion is *practical,* and that means they are judgments that cause a "movement," since action is a form of "movement."[35] The last conclusion of practical reasoning is the *choice* of an action, or the action itself. Such a movement could not be accounted for without the "practical" already being present at

33. A more detailed account of the "inner structure" of intellect and reason can be found in M. Rhonheimer, *Natural Law and Practical Reason,* 267–74.

34. Cf. I, Q. 79, a. 11: on the whole subject, see M. Rhonheimer, *Natural Law and Practical Reason,* 24ff.

35. *Eudemian Ethics* II, 3 (1220b 27) and 6 (1222b 30); cf. also *EN* VI, 2 (1139a 32).

the origin of the practical judgment. It could not be accounted for on the basis of a purely theoretical act of the intellect.

From two theoretical judgments only a theoretical conclusion follows (a *statement* "about something") and no *action*, nor anything that leads to action by extension.

From the theoretical judgment

(1) *for all A, p is true*   (p is an action of some kind)

and from the particular fact

(2) *X is A*   (X is a concrete individual)

we cannot derive

X does p   (i.e., the action p is chosen and carried out)

but only

(3) *For X, p is true.*   (i.e., a statement about X)

If we take A to stand for "living creatures," and p to stand for "stay alive by taking in nourishment," and X stands for myself, we then have:

1) For all living creatures it is true that they stay alive by taking in nourishment
2) I am a living creature
3) I stay alive by taking in nourishment

But I don't *do* anything here that concerns taking in nourishment: 3) is not an action of the kind "to take in nourishment," but only a (theoretical) statement about myself. In order for an action to follow from the reasoning, a practical premise is needed, such as:

1a) I want to stay alive (I am striving for it, I move toward it)

This premise is not a theoretical judgment, but a judged, considered act of appetition, which we can formulate as follows:

(1a) *It is good (for me) to keep myself alive*

A second premise could then be:

(2a) *Taking in nourishment keeps me alive*

The conclusion would then be:

(3a) *I want to take in nourishment*

or

(3a) *It is good (for me) to take in nourishment*

The second premise (2a) is a statement based on experience and as such is not a practical judgment, but only a statement about a practically relevant state of affairs (i.e., a theoretical judgment or a simple sense perception); it mediates between the practical premise (1a) and the conclusion, which is also practical.

To counter a widespread misunderstanding: to affirm as I have that the practical reason possesses its own point of departure and that practical judgments are not to be understood as derivations from theoretical judgments in no way should be taken to mean that practical reason somehow constructs the good for man or is totally free of all the reality that supplies theoretical reasoning with its object, or free of "pure fact" or states of affairs.[36] Practical reason is not, as Kant sees it, essentially a reason that "has causality with respect to its objects,"[37] which produces its object itself; it is, rather, speaking in an Aristotelian way, essentially a moving reason (and of course to this extent does produce something). But practical reasoning must not be understood fundamentally as constructive reasoning, and this is for at least two reasons. First, because acts of reason that lead to practical judgments always need a mediation through judgments about states of affairs (such, e.g., as "taking in nourishment keeps one alive") which have a thoroughly "theoretical" character, and second (this is the main reason), reason is only practical by being embedded in the natural inclinations of the human person, which by simply being there have, in turn, the peculiarity of being an unavoidable natural presupposition for the knowledge of objects, or of the "good" (more discussion on this point can be found in V).

The structure of reasoning that we have just analyzed in schematic fashion corresponds to what was known to Aristotle as the *practical syllogism*.[38] This does not mean that we "think" in this way before we do something. Rather, the practical syllogism is the thinking involved in doing. The practical syllogism is not a customary process of deriving a conclusion, not a process by

---

36. Such objections on the part of Thomists originate especially from Ralph McInerny; cf. his critique of John Finnis in R. McInerny, *Aquinas on Human Action: A Theory of Practice* (Washington, D.C.: The Catholic University of America Press, 1992), 184ff., where he misinterprets Finnis's assertion of the original underivability of practical from theoretical reason—a fundamentally sound assertion, to my view—as the assertion that practical reasoning is completely independent of the knowledge of "brute facts," of states of affairs, such as that only human beings have language, and so on (188), and that practical knowing is independent of "nature." It appears to me that nothing of the kind is to be found in Finnis: in fact he shows how the original acts of practical reasoning provide the way for us to understand human nature (see J. Finnis, *Fundamentals of Ethics*, 10ff.). I do agree with McInerny, however, in his critique of Finnis's deconstruction of Aristotle's *ergon* argument (cf. ibid., 15ff.; my own objections to Finnis's argument are found in *Praktische Vernunft und Vernünftigkeit der Praxis*, 53ff.).

37. *Groundwork of the Metaphysics of Morals*, trans. M. Gregor, 54.

38. Cf. above all *De Motu Animalium* 7. In the *EN* the practical syllogism appears in various contexts, esp. in books VI and VII. The term "practical syllogism" *(syllogismoi tōn praktōn)* in *EN* VI, 13 (1144a 32) is disputed in any event. This point of Aristotelian doctrine was made fruitful once again for action theory by G. E. M. Anscombe (cf. *Intention*, sect. 33ff., p. 57ff.).

which some truths are derived from other truths. The practical syllogism is itself a component of praxis, and belongs with the phenomena of "striving" and "acting." It makes explicit a kind of process in the soul, focusing on the cognitive structure of that process. And just as for Aristotle, praxis in general is a kind of movement, so does the practical syllogism lead to a movement. "That the action is the conclusion is clear,"[39] and not only a *statement* about an action, but rather what someone "straightaway does."[40]

What Aristotle described as the practical syllogism is consequently the adequate expression of practical reason as a type of reasoning which has appetition as its starting point, is embedded in appetition and cognitively guides it, and has for its final judgments (or conclusions) not statements of a theoretical kind, but choices of actions or actions themselves. We can clearly recognize in this syllogism the intentional structure of action: the relation between ends and means, between the goals of an intention and the choice of actions.

The example of the practical syllogism above has not, of course, been completely formulated. "To nourish oneself" is still not a performable action. The process of practical reason will go further, so that the conclusion (3a) will now become the first premise of a new "syllogism," in something like the following way:

> (1b) *I want to nourish myself*

or

> (1b) *It is good (for me) to nourish myself*
> (2b) *This piece of bread is a suitable means of nourishment*
> (3b) *I want to eat this bread*

or

> (3b) *It is good for me to eat this bread*

The conclusion (3b) is now in fact the choice of an action or its actual accomplishment. The result of the syllogism is a concrete action: the eating of this piece of bread, or more precisely, a last practical judgment that immediately triggers action, which we could also formulate like this:

> (3b) *What I have to do now is eat this piece of bread*

Of course, this is all only an attempt to formulate the process in words, at the level of reflection upon it; the process itself does not need to be carried out in any linguistic form. And in reality the processes of practical reasoning are often much more complex (e.g., the minor proposition [2b] may only take shape

---

39. *De Motu Animalium*, trans. Farquharson, 7 (701a 24).
40. Ibid., (701a 22).

on the foundation of a consideration of possible alternatives and a selection of the best among them). But that is not at issue now. The Aristotelian doctrine of the practical syllogism is really only a means for making obvious *how* practical reasoning processes are structured. It provides a "formal representation of the practical conclusion" in which the decisive moment of the appetition or willing cannot be formulated along with it.[41]

It seems rather important to emphasize that in this process we have been describing there is no one supreme and theoretical statement, such as a metaphysical or anthropological proposition about the nature of man, nor any such statement expressing moral duties. It is much more likely that such statements only arise after reflection upon the process of practical reason and interpretation of it. *Because* we know that we *strive* toward survival or self-preservation, and that we therefore also *will* to eat—because the practical judgment is familiar to us from our own experience, that "it is good for us" to keep ourselves alive, and because we know what we normally do in order to get nourishment— for this reason also we understand a little more about the nature of the human being and what our duties are and can make theoretical formulations like: "Man is a living creature that strives to preserve itself" or "Self-preservation is a fundamental human good."

Practical reason thus has its *own* and *original* point of departure. Theoretical knowing about the nature of man can in turn become relevant to praxis, but that knowledge is still not practical as such; in order for it to become practical, it must be a component of a practical syllogism. And to do this it always needs a first *practical* premise: a striving or a judgment of the practical reason *embedded* in striving: "I want p," that is, "p is good for me," which in turn means "p must be done" (whereby p stands for some human action).

The point of departure of a practical syllogism, which is a process of striving under the guidance of practical reason, is something striven after, something willed.[42] And the whole subsequent process of practical reason is car-

---

41. G. E. M. Anscombe, "Thought and Action in Aristotle" (see note 19 above), 65. Another account— insufficient, as it seems to me—is offered by A. MacIntyre, *Whose Justice? Which Rationality?* (South Bend, Ind.: University of Notre Dame Press, 1988), where on 130 we read: "But the premise itself says nothing about desire." MacIntyre reduces the phenomenon of the "practical syllogism" to a mere structure of *judging* and *considering* without observing that a practical syllogism is in fact not just a syllogism but the judging and considering *involved* in the appetitive process. Here we can also join in with the viewpoint of M. C. Nussbaum ("Practical Syllogisms and Practical Science," in M. C. Nussbaum, *Aristotle's "De Motu Animalium." Text with Translation, Commentary, and Interpretive Essays* [Princeton, N.J.: Princeton University Press, 1978], Essay 4, 165–220): the practical syllogism, she says, is a "model for explanation." In any case, Nussbaum sees here an opposition between Aristotelian action theory and what she would call an ethics of deductive principles, in which there are fixed moral rules, under which action would be "syllogistically" subsumed. But such an opposition is not at all necessary: see below, V.1.f).

42. Cf. Aristotle, *De Anima*, III, 10, and the precisely paraphrasing commentary of Thomas Aquinas: in III *De Anima*, lectio 15: "the appetible [= what is capable of being striven for, *das Erstrebbare*] is the principle of the practical intellect, the *primum consideratum ab intellectu practico*."

ried out within this logic of willing, although, as already explained, this logic of willing in the practical syllogism is not really formulated along with it as a formal representation of the process. But practical reason always has its starting point in an appetition, and this is why it *moves* to action: "That which is last (in the process of thinking) is the beginning of the action."[43] Practical reason is, as it were, the intellective "eye" of appetition that becomes determined to the point of concrete action through intending and choosing, and unleashes this action. And this is why, according to Aristotle, the practical intellect differs from the theoretical "in the character of its end,"[44] which is "something striven for," "something willed," or "something intended," and thus already practical in nature.

This "willed" something, or point of departure and first object of the practical reason, is not mere feeling or affect, that is, something irrational, but rather a reason-guided striving. At its basis lie the phenomena known as drives, desires, and inclinations. To be sure, "in the beginning" of the process of practical reason there are necessary cognitive acts which themselves are not practical in nature, but simply grasp reality, or what is. In order for a drive or inclination to have "something" to aim at or for the will to have "something" to will, "something" must be seen, felt, or known. Praxis cannot begin without drive, inclination, or striving toward "something." And we don't have to decide about this first. Drive and inclinations are always already there. And it is in these inclinations, or more precisely, in judging them, that practical reason has its starting point (for more detail on this and its crucial importance in Aquinas's doctrine of natural law, see below, V.1).

G. E. M. Anscombe likewise pointed out that a practical syllogism—and that means practical reason *as such*—has nothing at all to do with "morality," and Aristotle himself treats the practical syllogism and other things in a work that bears the title *On the Movement of Animals*. Animals too are practical beings in a limited (or analogous) sense: they carry out actions on the basis of *phantasia,* sense perception, "sense-judgments" about what is desired, in the sense of "p is good for me." And on the basis of perceptions (the second premise, or minor term) they arrive at action (the conclusion), like *automata*.[45] In the human being this process is steered by reason; it is a *voluntary* or *willing,* reason-guided appetitive process that is open to many alternatives. And according as the good that is striven for in this way is morally relevant—that is, concerns the human being *qua* human being—the practical syllogism is also a process of moral reasoning.

Nevertheless, the practical syllogism is not moral simply because expres-

---

43. *De Anima* III, 10 (433a 17).   44. Ibid., (433a 15).
45. *De Motu Animalium* 701b 1.

sions such as "p is to be done" are present, which can also be formulated as "I *should* do p" or "I *must* do p" (in the sense, "it is necessary to do p"). If Aristotle occasionally designates the first premise and the conclusion with expressions like "one should" or "it is necessary" or "I must" (using Gr. *dei* or the equivalent of the Lat. gerundive construction),[46] this has nothing to do with a reference to a "moral norm." The word "ought" for the most part simply indicates the fact that practical judgments are correlated to appetitions and lead to action. "Ought" and "should" are ways of *speaking* about practical judgments, that is to say, they express in linguistic form that which is practical in such judgments about the good—the imperative of the practical reason. "I *should* do p," "it is necessary to do p," is the linguistic formalization of the specifically practical, imperative component of the judgment "p is good," which in this form could really be confused with a mere statement about p. What we experience within ourselves, for instance, with natural spontaneity, when we want to stay alive (which implies the judgment that it is good for one to stay alive), we express linguistically with the categorical imperative, "I should stay alive." And what we draw as practical conclusions from such an appetition, such as "I will now eat this piece of bread" (because here and now this is recognized as "good for me"), we express with the hypothetical imperative "I should eat this piece of bread" (in order to nourish myself, in order to stay alive). This has nothing to do with morality as such. "Ought" or "should" are here simply the imperative of the practical reason, "this is good for me," or "this should be done now" or "do this, here and now."

The "ought" of the categorical and hypothetical imperatives are thus not derived from a "being," but arise *originally* in the process of the practical reason and constitute *practical experience,* on the basis of which "being" is then interpreted (for a more detailed account of this, see below, III.5.e and V.1 and 2). From the above cited proposition "I am a being, for whom it is true that it stays alive by being nourished" the proposition "I *should* stay alive by nourishing myself" cannot be derived. Why then "should I" at all? Simply because I "should" stay alive. But how does one arrive at this "should"? Ultimately, only because of the fact that behind all practical imperatives lies a fundamental "*will*-to-stay-alive," whereby this "willing" is a *reason-guided* appetition and thus implies the practical judgment "it is good for me to stay alive."

46. Cf. *De Motu Animalium* 7, 701a 13–14: here, the first premise, or major, is described in this way: "One thinks that every man ought to walk [*badistéon* = Lat. *ambulandum est*]"; second premise, or minor: "and [one thinks that] one is a man himself"; conclusion: "straightaway he walks." This is a description from outside as it were, a reconstruction. Cf. *EN* VII, 5 (1147a 29–31): "'If everything sweet ought to be tasted' and 'this is sweet,' in the sense of being one of the particular sweet things, the man who can act and is not restrained must at the same time actually act accordingly."

Critics of the idea here being defended—the concept of practical reason as possessing an original, self-standing origin, not derivable from theoretical reason—may object at this point that (theoretical) knowledge of the connection between nourishment and survival is sufficient to reach the practical judgments and actions in question; this shows that practical reason is only an application of "knowledge of reality." But this objection lacks the telling point. Of course, the insight into the state of affairs consisting in the aforesaid connection is constitutive for the *content* of practical judgments, but it alone cannot produce what is *practical* in such a judgment. Even someone (for example) who is deeply depressed and decides to end his own life through starvation certainly "knows of" this connection between nourishment and survival, and still chooses not to take nourishment because the appropriate, rationally guided appetition is lacking (while at the same time the intentional starvation is itself based on a practical judgment).

> The classical verdict first formulated by David Hume about the "naturalistic fallacy," the behest not to derive "an ought from an is,"[47] is based, to the contrary, on the assumption that reason can only ever make *statements about facts* (and also about our own feelings), but cannot move to action. Here there is no longer any practical reason at all. Hume says that the reason is "perfectly inert" and "inactive"; it has only "true" and "false" for its object, and never "good" or "evil." Actions can only be "praiseworthy" or "blameworthy," but never "reasonable" or "unreasonable."[48] What each person does depends above all on his feelings or emotions, and the task of reason is limited to showing to feeling what its object is, and—on the basis of recognizing cause-and-effect relationships—to show the path to the satisfaction of emotional needs.[49] It is clear that Hume would wonder how someone could arrive at a word like "ought." Hume's position still possesses today a kind of canonical status for many philosophers in the English-speaking world.[50]

If the "ought" in itself has nothing to do with morality, there still does exist a specifically moral "ought." We have it in view, as soon as we are aware, for example, that "to want to stay alive" really belongs to the fundamental strivings that constitute what we call "morality." Because here there is a practical good of man *as* man. Here we are concerned in a fundamental way with human life as a whole. And when such is the case, then a practical syllogism is also an expression of the process of moral judgments. And "to stay alive" or "self-preservation" becomes recognizable as a *moral* good.

---

47. Cf. David Hume, *A Treatise on Human Nature*, ed. D. F. Norton and M. J. Norton (Oxford: Oxford University Press, 2007), III, 1, sect. 1, 302.

48. Ibid., 294f.   49. Ibid., 295.

50. Cf. also J. Finnis's excellent critique of Hume in his *Fundamentals of Ethics*, 26ff.

b) Good and Evil in the Perspective of Morality

The perspective of morality is always the perspective of practical reason. And that is the perspective of a relationship of the subject to reality: a relationship characterized by appetition (willing), by intending and choosing.[51]

No one would confuse "a piece of bread" in the above example with a "moral good." Neither bread, nor a hammer, nor a piece of wood, a car, or even the life of a human being are moral goods. They are all "good" insofar as they exist, and insofar as they each are a definite "something." But that is not what we understand by "moral good." Moral good is the consequence of activity, a perfection that is added to mere existence or "being something."[52]

Now, choosing to eat a piece of bread as a way to nourish oneself or as a means of survival is something quite different from simply "a piece of bread": namely, it is an *act of self-preservation*. The specific action could be called "to eat a piece of bread." And this action, as object of an act of willing, is what one could call a practical good—and in some cases—also a moral good.

Practical goods as such are not all also moral goods. They are moral goods to the extent that they are concerned with action of the human being *qua* human being. If, in the midst of a heart operation, a doctor makes the judgment: "I need instrument X," then X, or the use of X (in the context of the rationality of a heart operation) is a practical good; but we would scarcely consider the action "using X" *as such* to be a moral act. But "using X" (in the context of medical practice as a life-saving activity) can also be understood as a lifesaving measure. Considered this way, the judgment "I need X now" is also something more than a merely surgical measure: if the doctor by reason of a culpable incompetence or neglect or laziness did not use X, and the patient were to die, we would say that the doctor acted "badly" or "poorly" not only as the performer of heart surgery, but as a human being. He is to blame in a moral sense on the basis of his incompetence or neglectfulness. This is because in the case of a heart surgeon, competent medical practice belongs not only to his being "a good surgeon" but also to his being "a good human being."

We could, for example, find a judgment of the following kind meaningful: "Doctor X is not very intelligent, of course, but he is a good human being" (perhaps he is thoroughly conscientious, if not brilliant as a doctor, and he really can't do anything about not being particularly brilliant). But we would

---

51. On what follows, cf. also M. Rhonheimer, "Gut und böse oder richtig und falsch—was unterscheidet das Sittliche?" in H. Thomas, ed., *Ethik der Leistung* (Herford: Busse Seewald, 1988), 47–75; or, in a slightly changed and expanded form, "Ethik—Handeln—Sittlichkeit. Zur sittlichen Dimension menschlichen Tuns," in J. Bonelli, ed., *Der Mensch als Mitte und Maßstab der Medizin* (Vienna and New York: Springer Verlag, 1992), 137–74.

52. Cf. *De Veritate*, Q. 21, a. 5.

not consider meaningful this statement: "Doctor Y is a wretched doctor; he is incompetent, neglectful, and his methods are antiquated; but he is a good person." We would probably consider that as what somebody would say to poke fun at this so-called good person. Doctor Y is a laughable individual just *because* someone could say this about him! In any case it is certain that if Doctor Y were competent, conscientious, and up to date in his methods, we would also think him a *better* human being in a moral sense.

The concept "morally good" refers to human *action*, and therefore always includes *types of action* insofar as they are objects of appetitive acts, that is, acts of intending or choosing, and insofar as we consider such actions not only as the actions of a surgeon, cook, or mortician, but as actions of these persons as human beings. "Morally good" is therefore a characteristic of *intentional actions*, but not only on the narrow horizon of professional efficiency and functional correctness, but rather from that perspective in which an action determines whether someone is also a good human being. We could acknowledge that a bank robber has done a "good" job, even though we would not want to call his action "good" in the moral sense.

"Human life" is not in itself *morally* good to a higher degree than a piece of bread. Both are what we could call a "physical good": on the basis of their *physis* or nature, on the basis of what they *are*. To this extent, of course, human life is a great deal more than a piece of bread: it has a much higher degree of perfection in being. But that does not make any difference to what we are calling a *moral* good.

If an earthquake kills ten persons, this is not the destruction of *moral* goods, and thus no moral evil, but a natural occurrence. A physical (nonmoral) event produces another physical event. The causality in question here is natural causality. The same distinction applies to spontaneous abortions. Nothing happens in such cases to deserve moral censure. If we say that the earthquake is "responsible" for the deaths of ten people, this would only be meant metaphorically, since we are speaking about an earthquake as if it were a subject of human action; we are anthropomorphically describing natural causality as if it were moral causality.

"Good" and "evil" in the moral sense appear exclusively as objects of the will of acting subjects. "Good" and "evil" in the moral sense are correlates of intentions and acts of choosing; and correlates of intentions and acts of choosing are *actions:* the "death of X" is not a moral evil, but rather *intending* or *choosing* the "death of X," that is, "killing X." This means the same thing as "to *will* the death of X."

To maintain that the objects of intentions are also *actions* may be surprising at first. Are not objects of intentions "values" such as justice, goodwill, truthfulness, and the like and actions only the objects of choices, which consist in the choosing of actions that realize these "values"? But if we say—in the perspective of praxis—that "justice" is the object of an intention, this can only mean that by "justice" here we mean "*doing* what is just" or "*acting* rightly" (e.g., to intend to always give to each one his due, or not to "do unto others" what we would not have them "do unto us," etc.). Of course, the word "justice" can always be used in a different meaning: for example, in the sense of "the justice of the tax laws is a condition for social peace." Here, however, "justice" does not mean something practical, or any object of the intention of an acting subject. For example, such would be: "to create a just tax law," that is, an action that in any case (since it is in fact an intention) can not immediately be carried out, but must be brought down by the practical reason to the level of concretely chosen actions. That can mean, for example, "To become a candidate for the parliament, in order to establish a just tax law," and to do this, in turn, for the "sake of ensuring social harmony."

In the practical perspective, in the case when someone *wants* to eat a piece of bread, even "to eat a piece of bread" can be a *moral* good, namely, insofar as an act of self-preservation is in question. But it can also be an immoderate act, or I can want to do it for the purpose of making someone angry. Moral goods and evils are recognizable as such when we treat "something" as the content of an *action*, and thereby as an object of the will: of intention or choice.

"Moral good," then, is a predication that we make of a *will* that is related to an action, to a will that is "incarnate" in action, and *to that extent* it is also a predication made of actions themselves. By contrast, an operation of craftsmanship or technique as such can be called "very good" or even "perfect" without the will of the one performing the action having to be good. What decides is the goodness of the *intentional* action in each case, which is something that can always *also* be considered *in addition* in the case of something that has been produced. This is because here we are concerned with the will and with the realization and fulfillment of one's *humanity*. "As long as someone is acquiring scientific knowledge, he is a good scientist. If someone produces something, he will have the skill and will be excellent in doing that. But if the will is good, then the man as a whole is good, because the will is the universal power of aiming at goals, of bringing in its path everything that is in man, and amid all strivings it is the 'first mover' because of its universality, to which everything is referred—not in its technical determinateness, but as human realization—whatever is realized in man. To consider action as human— as action as such—means to consider it, finally, from the point of view of the ultimate good to be achieved."[53]

---

53. Cf. Wolfgang Kluxen, "Thomas von Aquin: Zum Gutsein des Handelns" (see note 10 above), 333.

c) Two Distinctions: Moral/Nonmoral Goods and Right/Good Actions

Those who practice "teleological" or "consequentialist" utilitarianism claim that it is essential for an ethical theory to distinguish "moral" from "nonmoral" goods and, in the evaluation of actions, to keep "right" and "good" separate from "wrong" and "bad." What is to be said for these distinctions?

1) *The distinction between "moral" and "nonmoral"* (physical, ontic, non- or premoral) *goods and evils.* The distinction rests on the following train of thought: human action relates to goods such as life, health, physical wholeness, procreation, and property, or to evils such as damage to wholeness, pain, sickness, death, loss of property, and deception: none of this can be termed *moral* good or *moral* evil. A moral good could only be "a human being as person or subject, insofar and to the extent that he is completely responsible in free self-determination,"[54] and the characteristics of persons such as justice, responsibility, integrity, and so on. Moral evils would be the corresponding disvalues of persons as free subjects (e.g., injustice, anger, irresponsibility, etc.), and actions that mistreat human beings in their characteristic of being free subjects, such as compromising the freedom of someone's conscience.

This distinction throws a sudden light on matters. It differentiates a realm of physical, ontic, states of affairs from that area of life in which alone the moral can appear: the human free will. Thus arose the traditional distinction between the *malum physicum* and the *malum morale:* a between "defective condition" (blindness, death, suffering) and a defect in the free will of man (fault, blame).

This distinction between moral and nonmoral goods and evils is quite significant and necessary. It reflects the difference between the sphere of being and the sphere of action; between the perspective, on the one hand, of what simply is, what simply happens, what is the case, or what occurs, and, on the other hand, the perspective of morality: free, rationally guided, willing action.

The difference between moral and nonmoral goods as a difference between the sphere of events and the sphere of actions goes back to the Stoics: "Life, health, pleasure, beauty, strength, wealth, fame, noble birth, and their opposites: death, disease, pain, ugliness, weakness, poverty, obscurity, low birth."[55] All these are *adiaphora* (Lat. *indifferentia*): "indifferent things"—indifferent when compared with what really matters: virtue. Only virtue is truly

54. This formulation stems from B. Schüller, *Die Begründung sittlicher Urteile*, 2nd ed. (Düsseldorf: Patmos, 1980). Schüller is a prominent Catholic moral theologian who advocates utilitarianism and consequentialism ("teleological ethics"). The following critique of the moral/nonmoral and the right/good dichotomies is also directed against the moral theological methodology of Schüller (and of other consequentialists and proportionalists) which was very influential in the years after the Second Vatican Council.

55. This catalogue is reported by Diogenes Laertius, *Life and Opinions of the Famous Philosophers*, trans. Hicks (London: Loeb Library/ Heinemann, 1950), VII, p. 102.

good and beautiful, and only vice is really evil. Virtue for the Stoics is the right attitude toward the *adiaphora* and this attitude is called *apatheia,* lack of emotion. Real, moral goods—virtue and virtuous actions—are goods of the *soul.*[56]

> Kant well describes the self-knowledge of the Stoics as follows: "one may always laugh at the Stoic who in the most intense pains of gout cried out, 'Pain, however you torment me I will still never admit that you are something evil *(kakon, malum)*!' Nevertheless he was correct. He felt that the pain did not in the least diminish the worth of his person but only the worth of his condition. A single lie of which he had been aware would have had to strike down his pride [*Mut*], but the pain served only as an occasion to raise it when he was aware that he had not incurred it by any wrongful action and thereby made himself deserving of punishment."[57]

The Stoics drew the conclusion from this that an action is morally right *(katorthoma)* only on the basis of an insight into the indifference of those things that "conduced neither to happiness nor unhappiness"[58] and the removal of the emotion based on them, but not on the basis of this or that kind of performance of an action. For the Stoics, the very condition of the world was also an *adiaphoron,* and to their understanding morality was not supposed to change the course of the world. Nevertheless, the attractiveness of the Stoic teaching on the *adiaphora* remains certain: that conditions and events like death or life, health or sickness, wealth or poverty, glory or shame do not decide whether or not we are good as free subjects in the moral sense.[59]

The Stoic *adiaphora* doctrine distinguishes, then, between a moral sphere of *actions* and a nonmoral sphere of *conditions* in which the acting person finds himself. But the distinction we are here examining (a distinction often used by contemporary consequentialists and proportionalists) maintains something quite different: a difference between "moral good" and "nonmoral good" *within* the sphere of human action itself. The distinction does not serve (as it did for the Stoics) to make the realm of the nonmoral indifferent for praxis, but divides up the sphere of praxis itself into a nonmoral realm of actions not yet decisive for the goodness of the person and a moral realm. Those who adopt this view are not in the least convinced that the point is for the acting person to be freed from emotion about the conditions in which he finds himself, such that the peculiar nature of these conditions doesn't even matter; instead, they say that moral action has to do with taking serious responsibility for these conditions and for the developing state of affairs of the world, and to optimize both. Now

56. Ibid., 95.
57. *Critique of Practical Reason,* trans. M. Gregor, 52–53.
58. Diogenes Laertius, *Life and Opinions of the Famous Philosophers,* VII, p. 104.
59. Cf. also M. Forschner, *Die Stoische Ethik* (Stuttgart: Klett-Cotta, 1981).

since, for instance, "life" or "death" is only a nonmoral good or evil, causing the death of a human being, when considered in itself, is characterized as only a destruction of a nonmoral good or the production of a nonmoral evil. But whether or not a *moral* good or evil arises in the will of the one who causes this *adiaphoron*—that is, praise or blame—still remains an open question.

In any event, everything depends on just what this means. If what is meant, for example, is that only the *intentional* basic action "kill X," or the corresponding basic intentionality of this action could be designated as morally evil, but not the *state of affairs* that X is dead, one would have to agree. But something else is meant, namely, choosing to "kill X" cannot yet be judged morally *at all* and therefore also determines nothing as yet concerning the morality of the will of the one who performs the action. To "kill X" only means to cause a nonmoral evil. If someone does this for unjustified reasons, then such an action would at worst be *wrong* (see below). We would speak of a *moral* evil, however, only if the one who brought about the death of X did so out of negligence, irresponsibility, or for self-satisfaction, or the like—in other words, with some kind of wicked attitude.

Now a rather weighty objection could be raised against this position: for it would mean that action types such as "to kill a human being" are not being treated as *human actions* but just as if they were natural occurrences—not as the willed killing of X but as a merely physical "causing of the death of X." One would object as follows: whether X is alive or dead is indeed an *adiaphoron,* a nonmoral value, although very meaningful for any weighing of values. But then the problem is this: Are you saying that the question, whether or not it is right to kill X under such and such circumstances, is the same as the question, whether it is good under such and such circumstances for X to die in an earthquake? "Yes" (they answer) "it would be 'good' as long as we are convinced that the state of affairs of the world would be better as a result!" Now it is conceivable that someone may have good reasons to sleep more soundly after someone else's death. But there is a fundamental difference between a human action and an earthquake.

> Under certain circumstances, it can be quite justifiable that we have wishes like "I hope that X dies soon," because, for example, X is terminally ill, cannot be communicated with, is in extreme pain, and it would be for him and for everyone who knows him a relief if he were to die. We can hope for this, because the actual *state of affairs* "X being dead" would be better. But where, we might ask, would be the difference between "wishing that X were dead" and "wanting to do something, so that X be dead"—that is, an *action* that would bring about the desired state of affairs? A wish that someone soon die is not an intention: for an intention is related to the *doing* of something in order to bring

about the situation "X is dead." The relationship of the *will* to the life of X is therefore a different one. And this relationship of the will constitutes a practical and therefore moral good or evil.[60]

This makes it clear: the category "morally good" is only grounded in the perspective of action. Types of action and concrete actions are always intended, chosen, or willed doing. Kant also rightly recognized this: "What we are to call good, must be an object of the faculty of desire in the judgment of every reasonable being."[61] "States of affairs" [*Zustände*], even if they are *adiaphora* (in the Stoic sense) in themselves, as the effects of human actions are not "physically" caused but "morally" caused: on the basis of the will of the acting subjects, resulting from inner attitudes or intentions, by freedom and by "free self-determination." Once detached from types of actions there are no intentions, attitudes, or the like: whoever intends something, whoever wants or has an attitude to something, intends, wants, and has an attitude toward some *doing*. If the distinction between "moral" and "nonmoral" good is introduced into the sphere of praxis, it means implicitly that "to do something" is not an intentional action at all, is not to be judged in any way other than as an event. The judgment of actions and of their moral rectitude thereby becomes reduced to a judgment of the states of affairs caused by those actions.

The separation of morally good intentions or attitudes from the nonmoral goods to which concrete actions are thought to be related presupposes a human being whose moral intentions and attitudes are formed in a kind of vacuum. In reality, man as acting subject lives in a world of other human beings, things, circumstantial relationships, and so on, in relation to which his attitudes, intentions, choices of action, and the like are formed. Stoicism wanted to abstract from all this, and in this way the matter remains harmless. But it is not harmless when we are not abstracting from it. For then out of the *adiaphora* doctrine arise literally murderous consequences. For then someone can think that we can and must decide between the lives of persons and prefer the one to the other, depending on the consequences that are foreseen to result from the one death as opposed to the other. To kill someone only means to cause a nonmoral evil. What someone is doing in a morally relevant sense

60. Jean-Claude Wolf, a utilitarian moral philosopher in the analytic tradition, maintains that the wish to kill is insignificant, because intentions do not form any "independent normative factors." The only decisive thing is the "assessment of the goal," that is, the evaluation of the states of affairs and the conditions that would be caused by the action. Only after that has been done can an evaluation of intentions be undertaken. Wolf's consistently consequentialist position considers "action" as the causation of events, situations, and states of affairs, and he rejects all corresponding rival positions as mistaken, irrational, and narrow-minded. Cf. J. C. Wolf, "Der intendierte Tod," in A. Holderegger, ed., *Das medizinisch assistierte Sterben. Zur Sterbehilfe aus medizinischer, ethischer, juristischer und theologischer Sicht* (Freiburg, Switzerland-Freiburg-Vienna: Freiburger Universitätsverlag, 1999), 76–97.

61. *Critique of Practical Reason*, trans. M. Gregor, 53.

is only bringing about an optimal balancing, allowing an optimal state of affairs to come about. An attitude that showed itself as fulfilling its own purpose would then be called "morally good."[62]

The distinction I am critiquing here seems to miss in a fundamental way the theme of ethics as the perspective of morality: *freely willed behavior,* the attitudes and conscience that are related to this and formed by this, and the goodness of the human being as a free subject *through* his action. The realm of moral intentions, purposes, attitudes is exactly coterminous with the realm that comprises what is morally good or bad *to do.*[63] It is clear that *within the perspective of praxis* the terms "*morally* good" and "*morally* bad" are really redundant terms, because here we are speaking of the goodness and badness of *actions,* and these can never be "nonmorally" good or bad.

2) *The difference between "right" and "good" and "wrong" and "bad"* (with relation to actions or persons). This difference is closely related to the foregoing.[64] According to it, an action is "right" or "wrong" depending on whether the best possible consequences are foreseen to result from it, these consequences referring to a state of affairs characterized by the existence or nonexistence of nonmoral goods/evils (e.g., it would be *right* to kill a man if thereby, and only thereby, ten others could be saved: "life" would then be a nonmoral good). Whether an action and thereby the acting person is morally *good,* in this view, depends on the attitude or good intention or even, for example, on whether or not, in acting, one respects the intentions of another. For many writers on ethics therefore, in general, actions are right or wrong, but doers of actions, or persons, are good or bad (evil).

> Thus we read in W. K. Frankena, for example: "In some of our moral judgments, we say that a certain action or kind of action is morally right, wrong, obligatory, a duty, or ought or ought not to be done. In others, we talk not about actions, or kinds of action, but about persons, motives, intentions, traits of character, and the like, and we say of them that they are morally good, bad, virtuous, responsible, blameworthy, saintly, despicable, and so on."[65]

---

62. For a confrontation of this consequentialist position, see below V.4.f., as well as M. Rhonheimer, "Intentional Actions and the Meaning of Object: A Reply to Richard McCormick," *The Thomist* 59, no. 2 (1995): 279–311; reprinted in my *The Perspective of the Acting Person: Essays in the Renewal of Thomistic Moral Philosophy,* ed. with an introduction by W. F. Murphy Jr. (Washington, D.C.: The Catholic University of America Press, 2008). Here can be found, among other things, an engagement with an article by J. Fuchs, "Der Absolutheitscharakter sittlicher Handlungsnormen," in H. Wolter, ed., *Testimonium Veritati* (Frankfurt am Main: J. Knecht, 1971), 211–40, esp. 230–33, where the position here criticized is represented.

63. A. Donagan also correctly reached this conclusion in *The Theory of Morality* (Chicago and London: University of Chicago Press, 1977) 127.

64. It was introduced by W. D. Ross, *The Right and the Good* (Oxford: Clarendon Press, 1930) and has achieved virtually canonical status among English-speaking philosophers.

65. W. K. Frankena, *Ethics* (Englewood Cliffs, N.J.: Prentice-Hall, 1963), 8.

What this means, finally, is that "rightness" or "wrongness" are predicates for judgments of the "factual" moral appropriateness of types of actions or behavior. "Good" or "evil," by contrast, we use to evaluate persons or actions but only insofar as we treat them as a kind of embodiment of inner attitudes, bringing the goods of persons to expression.

The accompanying diagram may serve to illustrate clearly how the consequentialist or teleological analysis and moral evaluation of human action characteristically bifurcates into an intentional level and a behavioral level (see table 3-1).

Of course, this distinction is liable to the same criticism discussed before: it detaches "action" from the context of praxis, and treats it not as the object of a willing, but rather as an event that produces other events, which bring about certain results (consequences, states of affairs in the environment, world, society, of persons affected by the action), or as a happening that can be judged with reference to "commandments" or "obligations" and whether it satisfies these or not.[66] The generally recognized context that speaks *in favor* of this schema is the possibility of saying that a "wrong" action can be a "morally good" action and that a "right action" can nevertheless be a "morally bad" action—that it is possible, in other words, to act wrongly and still be a good person.

In case this distinction means that a technically, functionally correct or efficiently carried out action can nevertheless be morally bad, the point would not have any further significance. In such a case we could say that the technically right thing is morally wrong, as when a properly executed operation is still murder, or when a crime is carried out with technical perfection. Instead of the word "right" we could even use the word "good" in its narrower meaning that differs from the specifically moral meaning (see above at 4.b): in the moral meaning of "good" we do not refer to the cook's ability to cook but to his action as a human being. And if we speak of this moral dimension of an act, it is indifferent whether we call it (morally) good or (morally) right. If it is presupposed that we are speaking of an action in its moral dimension, the predicate "moral" is superfluous.

In the perspective of moral action the "right" is a concretization of moral values *in* action. Consequently the right is always also the concretely moral good, and similarly, the functional, technical correctness of an action—implying the competence of the doer—is really constitutive for the moral goodness of an action. For otherwise, someone could at the most *intend* a good, but nev-

---

66. This conception of action, which forms the basis of "teleological ethics" or consequentialism, will be discussed further below at V.3.c and V.4.f.

Table 3-1. The Consequentialist Splitting of Actions

Level of intentions (proposals, fundamental attitudes)	The action/ acting person is: morally good/bad	Through: intending moral values*	Result: good/bad will
Level of concrete behavior (doing, acting)	The action is/ the person acts: morally right/wrong	Through: Optimization of nonmoral values (weighing of goods)	Result: States of affairs in the world

* A moral value of this kind, the intending of which makes a person good, is really the effort exerted toward the rightness of the concrete action or behavior (lower level), independent of whether the right thing is actually accomplished. It is not whether we actually act rightly that decides the goodness of our will, but whether we generally strive for the rightness of our actions in each case.

er *do* it. The practical good is not floating around in a "heaven of values" but lies in concrete human actions and conduct. For example, it is not the "idea" of solidarity or some fundamental "solidarian" attitude that is good in praxis, but rather a concrete *act* of solidarity. It arises from a "solidarian consciousness" and brings about such a consciousness at the same time, as a firm inner disposition or virtue. Such acts of solidarity and the corresponding consciousness can be conceptually conveyed in the idea of solidarity.

The kernel of truth in the differentiation between "right" and "good" can be justified more easily by way of the action-theoretical distinction, as treated previously, between intentions and acts of choice as related to concrete ways of acting (means): bad actions can be chosen and carried out with good intentions, and good actions can be chosen and carried out with bad intentions. Something considered in itself as a good action, can—depending on the intention—become a bad action, although without considering whether the intention is *in itself* good, or "right."[67]

The inverse situation is also conceivable: someone does what is wrong with good intention. Here again there are two possibilities: first, the person in question acts wrongly in a certain way (though with good intention and conscience) which we can designate as "bad" without further consideration. Now this applies when the person is responsible for the wrongness of his own action, that is, when his wrong action originates from a lack of moral integrity. This is the case, for example, when someone, overwhelmed by the influence of affects, emotions, and passions, acts anxiously and with too little con-

67. This is exactly P. Geach's argument against W. D. Ross in "Good and Evil," *Analysis* 17 (1956): 33–42. It has been reprinted in Philippa Foot, ed., *Theories of Ethics* (London: Oxford University Press, 1967), 64–73, esp. 72.

sistency. The injustice of his act derives finally from a lack of prudence. But someone who does wrong because of imprudence is acting in a morally bad way (on "prudence," see below, IV.3.c).

Only in another case of the combination "good intention + bad act" can we really say that someone "was wrong, but acted well morally": only when the wrongness of an action comes from an error for which the doer was not responsible.

For example: A would like to do a good deed and give B a gift, without knowing that B is a drug dealer. That is naturally a "wrong" action, so long as we believe that it is wrong to support drug dealing. But because A believed that he was supporting a socially beneficial cause, his action is certainly a morally good action. It was a justified, well-intentioned, and generous act, and consequently we can judge A as being a just, well-intentioned, and generous person. But if A had known that B was a drug dealer, then "giving B a gift" would not only be wrong but also morally bad. This is because if we have the view that it is wrong to support drug dealing, it would also be morally bad to *do* this by supporting drug dealers.

The difference between "right" and "good" here is simply founded upon the fact that A did not know at all what he was doing and that he *couldn't* have known—that he had no responsibility for his ignorance.[68] If he had acted in good faith, but carelessly, then "to give B a gift" is not only wrong, but also bad, that is, imprudent (even if for a different reason—negligence or irresponsibility). To *distinguish* the rightness of an action from its goodness can only be meaningful in cases where there is a reason to judge an action *independently* of the intentional conditions under which actions are normally judged. And that only makes sense when the doer in reality did not do (or choose) what he had intended to do (or choose).

But there is something more to notice here. The distinction between "good" and "right," as developed above, only emerges in the perspective of someone who judges the action either of some other person or of that person himself, but after it has already been accomplished: and this is the "third-person" per-

---

68. This kind of ignorance has traditionally been named *ignorantia facti,* or ignorance about a mere particular fact related to action, in contrast with an *ignorantia iuris,* which is ignorance in relation to a moral justification, whether or not it is good to perform some action (ignorance of the moral norm). This question—whether it is possible on the basis of this second kind of ignorance to act wrongly, but still, so far as one is following one's conscience, to be morally good and to act well morally—will be taken up briefly below, in connection with the discussion on the conscience (V.2). This also involves the question (to be dealt with later on) whether someone who is convinced that it is right to be racist, to practice sexual promiscuity, to practice politics by terrorism, or, as in our example, to support drug dealers—whether in doing so he may be acting wrongly (through ignorance of the moral norm), but insofar as he is following his conscience is nevertheless carrying out "morally good" actions and is therefore also a good human being.

spective. The distinction can never reflect the standpoint of practical judgment implicit in the act of choosing that leads to action. For in this latter perspective, the perspective of the "first person," what "appears good here and now" is necessarily always chosen, in the conviction that it is in fact what is *right* to do, here and now, and for this reason alone is error possible, which leads to the separation of "right" from "good" in action.

> This distinction corresponds to the traditional differentiation of "formal" and "material" sin. A material sin is a way of acting that is wrong (bad) in itself, but which is chosen without any subjective possibility of an understanding of this wrongness. The acting person therefore acts wrongly, performing an action that is (materially) evil but still (morally) good. A sin is "formal" when the wrong thing is done with an understanding of its wrongness or when it is done out of a blameworthy ignorance. Only "formal sin" is (morally) evil and thus a blameworthy action, that is, a moral evil for the doer.

These considerations show that an ethics for which the distinction between "right" and "good" is constitutive—that is, important, and in a misplaced way—is an ethics that does not treat actions under the normal conditions, in which they are constituted as human, that is, intentional, actions. It is an ethics of the "third person" that misses the perspective of the acting person—and thereby the perspective of morality—at the outset. An ethics of this kind brackets the fact that actions are incarnations of acts of will and are not mere events—that they are willed, are chosen, such that each accomplished human action implies an intentional "why" shaping the will of the doer. Such an ethics would also exclude the fact that the human being through his very action, that is, through his choice of concrete actions and attitudes, changes into a good or bad person: the goodness of the person—his characteristic of being a benevolent, just, generous person—is determined precisely by what kind of concrete doing the choosing will is directed toward as its good. Moreover, in the distinction between (morally) right and good it is overlooked how intentions, purposes, and attitudes are always related to ways of behaving, and that stupidity, blameworthy incompetence, and ignorance are not compatible with moral virtue—that is, with the goodness of the person. "Doing wrong" can only be a good action when someone can simply do nothing about mistaking what is wrong for what is right, and in that case ignorance is not stupidity but only a mere happening, and in relation to its consequences we stand in the same way as we stand with respect to the consequences of an earthquake: not with blame but with sorrow and compassion.[69]

---

69. The contradictions that arise from the moral theoretical disjuncture (at the level of principles) between "good" and "right" have led revisionist moral theologians such as J. F. Keenan to the conclu-

Of course it is also conceivable that someone can act morally well, but without any joy in the good when doing so, but with a sense of duty, with reluctance, or only to avoid some disadvantage. There is no bad intention there, to be sure, but the person's attitude is not perfect. Although such actions can be called good, they still do not have the characteristic we are concerned with when we say that an action is virtuous. They measure up to what virtue requires—and in this sense such actions are right also—but they do not measure up to the *manner* in which the virtuous person does what is right: by an affective inclination to the good (see below, IV). Nevertheless, this right is also the (moral) good, if not in the manner of its highest fulfillment.

To sum up: the "rightness of an action" is an element that has been analytically, and erroneously, separated out of the original phenomenon, "good action." The concept of the rightness of an action in distinction to its goodness rests upon an abstraction that disregards the intentional structure of human action. Consequently, presupposing a moral perspective, *the distinction between "the right" and "the good" is not a relevant distinction.* What is important is the distinction between the *perspectives* through which we speak about actions at one time or another: we can look at actions "from the outside" as events and causes of states of affairs, or we can look at them as intentional accomplishments, and again, they can be either a special, technically delimited category or "human actions," that is, the intentional actions of a subject insofar as the subject is a human being. *Within* each of these perspectives we can still use "good" and "right" in each case as synonymous: if we say it is *good* for someone to do something, we can also say that it is *right* for him or her to do so. A technically *right* heart operation is also a technically *good* heart operation. And a morally *good* action is likewise a *right* one (except for cases of non-culpable error), or in other words, what is right in the moral sense, *because it is right,* also means an increase in the moral goodness of the person (under the assumption, of course, that the action was not done with an evil intention). The different shades of meaning between the synonyms "good"/"right" result in each case exclusively from the perspectives (eventistic, technically limited, or moral), on the basis of which we are speaking about the actions.

The predicate "good," in any event, has a wider range of meaning available to it in popular language than does the predicate "right" or "correct." Manfred

<hr />

sion—not without grave consequences—that even the rectitude of appetition on the level of moral virtue still says nothing at all about the goodness of the person. In this way, the entire field of human ethics is intelligible only through the categories of "right" and "wrong." Keenan—a theologian—concludes that only through *caritas* infused by grace does man become "morally good" (independently, then, of whether he is "right" on the human level). Cf. J. F. Keenan, "Die erworbenen Tugenden als richtige (nicht gute) Lebensführung: ein genauerer Ausdruck ethischer Beschreibung," in F. Furger, ed., *Ethische Theorie praktisch* (Münster: Aschendorff, 1991), 19–35; see also Keenan, *Goodness and Rightness in Thomas Aquinas's "Summa Theologiae"* (Washington, D.C.: Georgetown University Press, 1992).

Riedel is on target when he says: "If we orient ourselves once more to collo-quial language, and the interpretative 'pre-understanding' of action concepts, then we may affirm that actions are "praised" and "blamed," but effects and events are not. For example, we are saddened or consoled about mistakes or betrayals, or, on the other hand, our successes are either wished for or envied. The rules of usage for value-predications are similarly differentiated. While we can say of events, as we can of actions, that they are "good" or "bad," events cannot be said to be "right" or "wrong." We can only speak intelligibly of ac-tions that they are either "right" or "wrong.""[70] Of course, it is also true to say that whether "good" and "bad" possess a *moral* connotation, depends on the perspective in which one uses these predicates. "Good" and "bad" as predi-cates of *actions* are at one with the predicates "right" and "wrong."

Ethicists who hold that the distinction between "right" and "good" is rel-evant *within* the moral perspective are depending on an understanding of con-crete actions that does not ultimately take them as intentional accomplish-ments, but only as analogous to events that alter states of affairs in some way (we will return to this theme in V.3 and 4).[71] They must consequently move the intentional aspect of action to the level of attitudes, sensitivities, funda-mental options, and confine it there. "Actions" then become a kind of hybrid mixture of (good) intentions and (right) "interventions into the realm of non-moral goods." The paradigm behind this concept of action is technological in nature.

What appears to be at work here, more than anything else, is a *method-ological* mistake. On the level of the concrete execution of actions, actions are referred to from the "observer's" perspective: actions appear analogous to events. Only on the level of the "whole person"—that is, the level of inten-tions, attitudes, sensitivities, and the like—are actions recognized in the actual perspective of actions as the (personal) accomplishment of free subjects tak-ing a voluntary stance toward good and evil. But this bifurcation into what is often referred to as a "categorical" level and a "transcendental" level is just as unfounded as is the simultaneous use, and mixture, of the two perspectives.

The distinction between "right" and "good" will always keep its plausibility for ethicists who take the phenomenon of "moral norm" or "moral duty" as their

---

70. M. Riedel, "Handlungstheorie als ethische Grunddiziplin" (see above, II, note 2), 146.

71. Clearly, there is here an implicit, involuntary omission of the intentional character of actions. Even those authors whom I criticized in the above-referenced article, "Intentional Actions and the Meaning of Object: A Reply to Richard McCormick," are of course trying to describe actions intentional-ly. But they reduce the intentional element of actions to the level of the attitudes with which actions are accomplished: they do not describe the concrete accomplishment of the action itself as an intentional act. In reality, therefore, they do not reach the concept of "intentional action," but only to a mere plac-ing together of physical elements (concrete actions) with intentions (the purposes, *with which* someone carries out these actions).

point of departure. In this way ethics is split into a so-called normative ethics which gives us information about how to arrive at judgments about "what one is supposed to do," or what one is obliged to do ("right" action), in order to *add to this* something else, namely, that a right action is also morally good (the expression of the action of a "good person") only when the intention, the attitude, and so on is good: when, for example, someone acts "out of pure duty" or "with a good intention," or "from a responsible conscience." It appears that ethics is being developed here from the wrong direction (and the discipline of "meta-ethics" has to be called in to solve the problem, answering questions like "What is a moral norm?" or "What is duty?" or "What is virtue?" or "What does the word *good* mean?"). But we proceed in the reverse direction (with "meta-ethical" questions being taken care of as we go along, meaning that they are no longer "*meta*-ethical" questions). Beginning with the analysis of human action and its goodness, it is only at the conclusion that we determine a moral norm, or what our duty is. The approach I have been criticizing, however—which is typical of positions referred to as utilitarian, consequentialist, proportionalist, and "teleological"—begins with a fragmentation of the phenomenon of morality into moral norms, on one side, and the virtues, attitudes, inner dispositions with which norms are followed, on the other, in order to attempt to create a unity of both elements at some later stage. But this still does not seem possible, because we cannot establish a moral norm or duty if we don't know beforehand what really makes a good human action into such a norm, that is, if we don't know what virtue is. If we miss that, what is morally normative becomes a social-psychological phenomenon, or something that is politically, socially, economically, technologically, or biologically useful, or practicable and expected. But that *by itself* has nothing to do with ethics or morality, and is rather a substitute for ethics and morality (even if it deals with political ethics and morality; discourse-ethics tends in this direction, but appears to allow only a discourse on politics and law to be ethical discourse).

The foregoing critical considerations point us toward a deeper analysis of what is meant by "morally good," and what "good" means in the perspective of morality. "Morally good," we could say at this stage, is an attribute of *human actions,* and thereby, of course, also an attribute of acting *persons.* We identify as "morally good," then, what we have named as practical objects, that is, objects of reason-guided striving or appetition (will) and, consequently, practical reason.

d) The Moral Difference

Human praxis has to do with other human beings and things, but also with natural strivings, inclinations, and drives *within* the human acting subjects themselves (we have said only a little about this so far). *To the extent* that all this occurs within the realm of human praxis, that is, to the extent that it involves the whole region of striving, willing, intending, aiming, choosing (i.e., a willed "putting-of-oneself-in-relation-to"), and *to the extent* that actions can be formed in relation to this, it appears to the acting subject as a good, and because of this, to cite Aristotle once again, "the good has rightly been declared to be that at which all things aim."[72]

A practical judgment of the type "p is good," we noted, is not a statement of a judgment about x, y, . . . z (persons, things, drives, etc.), but rather a judgment about the relationship between *my will* in each case and x, y, . . . z (really, it is implicit in this willing, the judgment that *informs* this willing). In a practical judgment, "p is good" means not to will x or y (e.g., "Peter" or "a car"), but to will "something in relation to x, y, . . . z," because to will something means to have judged it as good. "P is good," accordingly, means, for example, "to want to buy x," or "to want to eat y," or "to want to kill z." To be in practical relation with x, y, . . . z, means just the same as intending or choosing "p in relation to x," or "q in relation to y." The judgment "p is good" means, for instance, "I want to buy x" or "take x," or the like. The content and effect of such a judgment is an *action*.

Actions, then, are realized intentions and choices of action in relation to x, y, . . . z. Such judgments can be formulated as "it is good to buy x" (= "p is good"); "it is good to use y." Insofar as we decide "to do" something, we always judge it as *good*. We don't do anything on the basis of the judgment "it is bad to buy x" (= "p is bad"), since this last judgment means nothing other than "p should not be done." Practical judgments that lead to actions—in this latter instance, the *choice of action* (*iudicium electionis*)—are also always judgments of the type "p is *good*." Classically, this would be expressed in the following sentence: *quidquid appetitur, appetitur sub ratione boni*, "everything sought for, is sought for, insofar as it is a good," is sought, that is, *under the aspect of "good"*—and only for this reason can such a striving lead to action (since the practical predicate "bad" is really the correlative of avoiding, fleeing, abstaining from an action).[73]

---

72. *EN* I, 1 (1094a2).

73. Cf. Kant's criticism of this principle in the *Critique of Practical Reason*, trans. M. Gregor, 51–52. He understands it, at any rate, in his own way, namely, as hedonistic, on the one hand (in the sense that he rejects), that we supposedly strive for our "well-being and woe" in everything we seek—our pleasure or our avoidance of displeasure; on the other hand (in a way that he can agree with), insofar as it means that we seek for all the good that is contained in it according to the recommendation of reason, or avoid all the bad, as the case may be. However, both of these senses miss the meaning of the classical dictum. But it is not by chance that Kant misses the point here. The principle is formal in nature and can be confirmed in both of Kant's possible scenarios. The principle, to be sure, tells us nothing at all about the nature of the "good," but only about the nature of the appetition or willing. The principle is constitutive for a eudaimonistic ethics which is centered upon the analysis of acts of striving and appetition.

One can also, of course, do something by the willed nonperformance of something, and to a degree, that, too, is action. But still, one doesn't always do something when one abstains from an action. If A purposely does not rescue a drowning man B whom he could have rescued, A is committing murder by his abstention. The judgment that leads to the abstention would be "p is good," where "p" means "letting B drown." The letting B drown is here *chosen* as a "good" (under the description "so that B dies"). But if it were impossible for A to rescue B (e.g., because A can't swim and cannot get any help), even though he wanted to, the nonperformance of the rescue would not be the consequence of a choice with respect to "letting B drown" but as the consequence of a choice with respect to "rescuing B." This latter is *not* chosen, and such not-choosing occurs on the basis of a judgment of the type "p is not good," where "p" means "rescue B" (or "leap into the water to rescue B"). In this kind of nonperformance, it is not that something has been done, but rather that something has simply *not* been done, that is, no action was carried out.

Nevertheless, not only do we say "p is good," we also say "q is bad," and we treat *both* judgments as practically relevant judgments. On the basis of this kind of judgment we do not immediately do something, but we first of all judge a particular doing (not yet accomplished, or already accomplished) as something "to do" or "not to do." While in the first sense "good" means "p is to be done" (and accordingly "bad" means "q is not to be done" or "is to be avoided"), and this already means that I now immediately *want* to do "p," and choose it (or avoid "q," choose not to do "q"), just so, "good" and "bad" in the second sense means "doing p is good," but "doing q is bad" (it is also possible to say "*not doing* p is good" or "*not doing* p is bad"). This second kind of judgment *can* then lead to a judgment of the first kind, to a choosing-judgment (after the exclusion of possible alternatives): "because doing p is good, so p is now to be done," that is, "p is good" in the first sense of a choosing-judgment that effectively triggers the action "p" (this is because "p is good" means that same thing as "I now *want* to do p"). On the basis of the judgment "doing p is bad," on the other hand, in certain circumstances p is *not* done. The second kind of judgments do not, however, necessarily lead to an action: from "doing p is good" can also result: "Still, I won't do p," that is, I find (for other reasons) that "doing p is bad." And from "doing q is bad" can follow: "Even so, I will do q anyway," namely, for some other reason leading to the choosing-judgment "q is good."

What does this mean? It means that *before* we reach a concrete judgment of action ("p is good" or "p is to be done"), we judge whether it is "good" or "bad" to do p. In the earlier presentation of the practical syllogism, before the conclusion ("p is good" or "p is to be done," "I want to do p"), an act of judgment had to take place, about whether "doing p" or "not doing p" is good or bad.

This formulation, to be sure, is rather oversimplified. The practical judgment that precedes the actual choice to act emerges from practical reasoning with respect to the means to be chosen. Within this reasoning there can be found a variety of viewpoints, such as functional (or technical) correctness, appropriateness, consideration of consequences or unforeseen consequences (all the aspects of the goodness of an action), but also the question whether the action that is being weighed is even "permitted," that is, whether it is not, perhaps, bad under all circumstances; this can also be a question about the objective identity of the action (which itself can also be determined in part by circumstances and consequences). The act of the conscience plays a role here as well. We cannot at this stage weigh or justify these elements (e.g., whether there are such actions that are evil under all circumstances). This will be the task of chapter V.

This second kind of judgment of actions is *not* a judgment whether or not Peter, for example, is a good doctor, or whether a Mercedes is a good car or not, nor is it about whether and in what respect men or doctors in general, and Peter in particular, is good, or whether cars as such are "good." Instead, the concern is with whether it is good to give Peter a loan, or whether it is good to buy this Mercedes, or to steal this Mercedes. That the Mercedes is a good car does not say anything decisive about whether it is good to buy it. That Peter is a good doctor does not adequately move us to the practical judgment that it is good (and that I choose) to give him a loan (he may not even need one and it would be presumptuous of me or "excessive" for me to do it). The difference of "good" and "bad" that we find in actions (or rather, in the judgments we make about them) is not founded as such in the goodness of the Mercedes or in Peter's "being a good doctor." *Practically* we can stand in a good or bad (right or wrong) relationship toward what is "good" in this sense. Depending on the circumstances, it can be (practically) good to buy a bad (or not an especially good) car, or to give Peter a loan, even though he is not a very good doctor. And although the drive for self-preservation and the sex drive are good, we can be in a good or bad way with respect to them. This difference between "good" and "bad," as encountered in practical judgments (judgments about actions p . . . q), and which does *not* coincide with the ontic or physical (natural) difference between "a good x" or "a bad x," we can call the *moral difference*.[74]

The moral difference designates an "opposition of absolute, irreducible, and unconditional meaning"[75] which only appears within the perspective of praxis. As soon as we move about within the field of human praxis, we are

74. I have taken this term from W. Kluxen, *Ethik des Ethos* (Freiburg and Munich: K. Alber, 1974), 17f.
75. Ibid., 17.

also moving in the field of the *moral* difference of "good" and "bad," of "good" and "bad" actions.[76] "In this merely formal meaning, empty with regard to content, the moral difference is a *datum*, a 'given' that is met with in all human action that is specifically human. It is not, consequently, in need of being established by ethics, since it is presupposed by ethical reflection. But what ethics will do is assign single actions to one side or the other."[77]

Clearly, then, the difference as such in its formal disjunctive power is not in need of justification. What *is* to be established, however, is how this difference comes into play in human actions. What is in need of justification is the assignment of actions to one side or the other of the division: that is, the criterion to be used for such assignment.

What is the criterion, then, for distinguishing a (morally) good from a (morally) bad action? On the basis of the foregoing analysis and criticism (made just above) of the distinction between "moral goods" and "nonmoral" goods, or between "morally good" and "morally right" actions, this criterion cannot consist in the intention, the inner attitude, the consciousness, and so on, but rather something *within* the actions themselves, whereby intentions, attitudes, consciousness are first formed. The good and the bad of a certain way of acting depends on its *content,* and this means, again, its object [*Gegenstand*]—which, as we have already explained, cannot be thought of or described independently of a certain basic intentionality.

> If the action "doing p," for example, means "killing x," the object or "content" of "doing p" is not "x" but "killing x." To "do p" would be "doing the killing of x." If I *choose* an action of the kind p, I do not choose x (e.g., Peter), but I choose "to kill x." And if I do not do, or abstain from p, I do not abstain from x, rather I abstain from "killing x." The object of an action, as paradoxical as it may sound, is this action itself. Objects of actions are the *contents* of actions, just as the content of the action "playing Beethoven's 'Moonlight Sonata'" is not the "Moonlight Sonata" but "*playing* the 'Moonlight Sonata'" (or "playing the piano," "performing music"). If the "Moonlight Sonata" were itself the object, the content and object of *playing* it would be identical with *composing* it, and there would be no objective difference between performing music and composing it: they would be objectively identical actions, the same type of intentional action.

We know, of course, that the intention is also the object of an action. But the intention "with which someone acts" does not say everything about the

---

76. Kluxen, ibid., refers to the moral difference as "good" and "evil." The word "evil" has the advantage that it connotes perhaps more clearly the *moral* significance of "bad." In its true significance, an "evil" action is a "bad" action that is carried out with a bad intention. To act "evilly" is thus an intensified form of acting "badly." One can act morally badly, without acting evilly. But finally this becomes a quibble about words.

77. Ibid., 18.

objective meaning and thereby about the goodness or badness of an action. If one speculates in the stock market in order to earn one's daily bread, if "earning one's daily bread" is a good thing, nothing has yet been said about whether it is good or bad to speculate on the stock market.

We need to clarify more profoundly just what an object of action is and how it is constituted. Since human action is *willed* action, it is action that is guided by judgments of *reason*. Therefore, as in the well-known statement of Thomas Aquinas, "through the reason, the good is represented to the will as object *(repraesentatur voluntati ut obiectum)* and insofar as it falls within the order of reason *(sub ordine rationis)* it pertains to the realm of the moral *(genus moris)* and causes moral goodness in an act of the will. For reason is the principle of human and moral actions."[78] To act well morally means just so much as acting rationally or according to reason—but what does it mean to act rationally, to act according to reason?

4. The Objective Meaning of Human Actions and Its Determination through the Reason

a) Intentional Actions and Objects of Action. The Concept of Action-Types

By way of a concept introduced at an earlier stage (III.2.a)—namely, the "intentional basic action"—we grasped an action at the most basic level, that is, an action wherein "what someone does" only becomes intelligible when the information "why someone does it" is provided. This means the following: so long as the answer to the question "why" remains unknown, we cannot understand such an action *as* human, meaningful, chosen action. "To lie on the bed" is *not yet* an intentional basic action, since we still do not know by any information given to us about the state of affairs, just what the person is really *doing* (even if this state of affairs must not necessarily be a part of a context of actions; it is presupposed, for now, that it is). But "lying on the bed, in order to get some rest" or "getting some rest," or "doing a yoga exercise" or "taking it easy" are in fact basic intentional actions. "To get some rest, in order to be able to finish writing a paper" is already *more* than a basic intentional action; because in this case, when we know that someone is lying on the bed, we know what he is doing. We can then ask further *why* he is doing what he is doing.

Intentional basic actions accordingly already possess *in themselves* an in-

---

78. I-II, Q. 19, a. 1 ad 3. *Dicendum quod bonum per rationem repraesentatur voluntati ut obiectum, et inquantum cadit sub ordine rationis, pertinet ad genus moris et causat bonitatem moralem in actu voluntatis. Ratio enim principium est humanorum et moralium actuum.*

tentional identity, which is the object [*Gegenstand*] or content [*Inhalt*] of acts of choosing. Actions with such an identity are in themselves meaningful, intelligible, accomplishable actions. This "primary" (because fundamental) intelligible *basic* meaning-content we call the *object* of an action (e.g., "to get some rest") which stands before the practical reason either as a good to be pursued or an evil to be avoided, and corresponds to an (intentional) description of action, under which the action is chosen.

The objective-intentional structuring of actions is the work of the reason. Through it, certain types of actions are constituted, such as "get some rest," "work," "steal," "get a divorce," "murder somebody," "eat a meal," and so on. None of these actions are merely natural events, physical states of affairs, or bodily movements; they are human actions. Sometimes particular actions such as these make up a type of actions or a *species* of action. To be more precise: (1) they belong (in themselves) on the side of *good* actions, or on the side of *bad* actions, or they can be *indifferent;* (2) as good or bad actions, they all belong further to a *species of action* such as just/unjust or moderate/immoderate.

> Actions that are "indifferent" according to their species are intentional actions whose identity or object cannot yet be objectified for the reason as good or evil. Thomas Aquinas gives the examples "picking up a stick from the ground" and "taking a walk outside."[79] "Getting some rest" could also be designated as an indifferent action. Such actions do have a practical meaning-content, of course—they are intentional actions—but from that alone one cannot yet say that their content is something good or something evil. The qualification "indifferent" is, even so, related exclusively to the basic intentionality of these actions (the object that constitutes them in their species). As *accomplished,* concrete human actions, they fall on one side or the other of the moral difference, by reason of added intentional content. One cannot *carry out* an indifferent action.[80]

This is why "killing someone" is either *at one and the same time* bad and unjust or *at one and the same time* good and just. The moral category of good actions is consequently divided into just, temperate, and the like actions; bad actions can be differentiated into unjust, intemperate, and so on; unjust actions can once again be differentiated into "stealing," "robbing," "being unfaithful to one's spouse," "lying," "overcharging someone," and the like; just actions, on the other hand, would be "staying faithful to one's spouse," "speaking the truth," "paying the right price," "returning what was owed,"

---

79. I-II, Q. 18, a. 8.
80. Ibid., a. 9.; This does not apply to acts that do not arise from the free will at all (e.g., reflex actions); they are not human actions and they are referred to as indifferent because by definition they simply do not belong to the category of moral actions (ibid.).

"keeping a promise," and so forth. In this way we arrive at actual *types of action* that can be assigned to one side or the other of the moral difference.

It is of course true in an analytical sense, or tautological, that an *unjust* action is also a *bad* action. It is similarly analytic to say that "shoplifting is bad, because shoplifting is unjust." But that is not significant at present. Here, we are concerned above all only with the fact that the moral difference good/bad is further subdivided all the way down to the most specific types (species), which we can in turn identify as basic intentional actions. Practical good and bad does not exist "in itself," but rather in various *kinds of behavior.* This was already Aristotle's point in objection to the Platonic idea of the Good.[81]

Once we have reached actual kinds of actions, we cannot go any "further down": these are the basic intentional actions. "Stealing" cannot be divided any further into "stealing a car" or "stealing a horse" because these are not two different types of action, but only two different *instances* of the same type: both are thefts ("Taking what rightfully belongs to another"). The *moral* object (i.e., the object morally considered) of these actions is the same, even if "horse" and "car" are, in another sense, different "objects" to which a theft might relate. If it is wrong to steal a car from someone, it is also wrong to steal a horse from him, it being assumed that both car and horse are rightfully possessed by the person (otherwise, in certain circumstances, it would not be theft). Neither does it make any sense to subdivide the action "stealing a horse" into two types such as "ride away on the horse" or "take the horse away in a trailer." For these, again, are not two types of action (there is no difference of "why" between the two cases), nor two cases of the same type of action, but two different *ways* of carrying out one of the two cases of the action-type "stealing," namely, "horse thievery." Both ways of carrying out horse thievery *are* the action "horse thievery": to classify these as "riding away on a horse" and "driving away with a horse" does not add anything to the intentional specification that was not already contained in the action "stealing a horse" (it being assumed that you are not also stealing the vehicle you would be using in the latter case; for even then, the species would not be different but only intensified, being a theft twice over). On the other hand, we do not mean to imply that "riding away on a horse" or "driving away with a horse" are necessarily thefts at all.

In the same way it makes no difference if I am getting some rest whether I do so by lying on my bed or by sitting in my chair. "Lying on the bed" and "sitting in the chair" both belong to the same type of action: they are the same type of basic intentional action and thus have the same object of action (let's

81. Cf. *EN* I, 4 (1095a20–26).

say, e.g., that for some reason you had no right to sit in the chair: this would be a circumstance relevant to modifying the objective structure of the action; on this see below, V.4.d).

And so we discover again that there is a *lowest threshold* here: it is the level at which the moral difference is first constituted. If "making off with a car" is an unjust action, this is not because it is unjust to steal a *car* (as opposed to a horse), but rather because it is unjust to make off with (= "steal") someone else's (rightful) possession. But what does "stealing" mean, as opposed to "stealing a car (and not a horse)"? If it is a good idea for you to get some rest by lying on the bed, it is not because "lying on the bed (as opposed to sitting in the easy chair)" is a good idea, but because "getting some rest" is a good idea. But how does "getting some rest" differ from "lying on a bed" or "sitting in a chair"? If it is unjust or inappropriate for A (who is married) to have sex with B (who is not his wife), but this is not unjust and inappropriate because A does it with B precisely (and not with C, who is likewise not his wife), but simply because he has done so with a woman who is not his wife, so then one may ask, "Wherein lies the difference between 'having sex with one's wife' and 'having sex with a woman who is not one's wife'?" The evil of stealing did not consist in either the car or the horse; neither in "riding away on the horse" nor in "transporting the horse away." The good idea in getting some rest consisted neither in "lying on the bed" nor in "sitting on the easy chair," and the evil of "having sex with a woman other than one's wife" consisted neither in the other woman nor in "having sex with a woman." How does this moral difference of basic intentional actions ever become established? And what about all further morally relevant specification?

b) The Establishment of the Moral Difference and the Species of Action through the Reason

Thomas Aquinas's answer is both short and categorical: the species of human actions and the difference between good and evil in them is established through the *reason*. For man, according to his substantial form—that is, *insofar as he is man*—is a rational living being. And what is good or bad for a being is determined according to what corresponds to that being's substantial form.[82] This is an (easily recognized) variant and adaptation of Aristotle's *ergon* argument (see above, II.3.b), for which Thomas in any case normally calls in the authority of Pseudo-Dionysius.[83]

In the context of practical philosophy, such metaphysical argumentation

---

82. Cf., e.g., I-II, Q. 18, a. 5, and Q. 71, a. 2.
83. *De Divinis Nominibus*, IV, 32; cf. In IV De Div. Nom. lect. 22, n. 592.

might appear somewhat abstract and less than convincing. We will return to a few of its implications later (III.5.e). Nevertheless, the argument does prove its worth on the basis of the practical experiential content at its foundation, which it puts into order at the level of the metaphysics of actions. We are already acquainted with this experiential content: to the extent that a human being acts, he acts on the basis of a reason-led striving. This is how he has mastery over his action and takes responsibility for it. Reason is the root of freedom, since it is the cause of freedom. So when a human being does something specifically human, that is, on the basis of reason and will, so it can only be the task of reason to formulate what is good. Reason is the measure of good and evil in human actions, and that implies as well that it is the *measure* of just and unjust, moderate and immoderate; and thereby, too, is reason the measure for the difference between (for example) stealing and rightfully taking possession, between fraudulent and fair contracts, and so on.

The saying that "reason is the measure *(mensura, regula)* of good and evil in human actions" sounds like an empty formula or perhaps somewhat exaggerated. Consequently there have always been attempts to fill it in, to provide it with more content, to fortify it, or alternatively—in case it seems exaggerated—to soften it, tone it down, and relativize it, or to reduce it to a merely structural formula without any content at all. Many argue that when Thomas says that reason "measures" or "regulates," that he only means "*right* reason." That is (so they say), the reason which regulates rightly, the reason which is directed toward the good, meaning, finally, that that reason is the measure that *applies* the right measure: the reason which judges according to the moral norm. But now the question about the measure of good and evil has only been sidestepped: reason itself only retains the mere functionality of a kind of expression-tool for the application of moral norms, for bringing oneself "into line with the moral law," for "following nature," and so on.

But that is not what Thomas means. And it cannot have been, because at the level of human actions, and independently of revelation, he recognizes nothing that could be referred to as a "moral law" or "moral norm" as distinct from reason.[84] Thomas means that in fact the reason is *itself* the measure; that it is itself the "norm" for everything that is not already rational in itself. For Thomas, the reason, *insofar as it really is reason,* is always "right reason." It does not merely "apply" any and all moral measures of good and bad to actions; rather, it establishes from the outset the very difference between good and evil. *It is itself the measure.*

This cannot be otherwise because in fact the intentional structuring of an

---

84. Not even the "natural law" *(lex naturalis)* could be named here, because this in fact arises from reason—as Thomas says, it is a "work of the reason"—but this will be treated later.

action is essentially and necessarily a work of the reason. Let's consider for an example the action of "stealing a horse." This includes a horse, an owner of the horse, and a legal relationship between the owner and the horse; then there is a concrete physical action, as, for example, "loading the horse onto a horse trailer and driving away with it." Then there is also a "why" of this action. We could refer to this "why" as "taking the horse for oneself" (because the whole affair could also have come about because someone is playing a joke on a friend, or perhaps because someone is taking a sick horse to a veterinarian against the will of a neglectful owner). In the action "stealing a horse," then, we find a multiplicity of elements: things, actions, relations between things, circumstances, and a "why." Only the reason can bring this complex— which is, indeed, an action—into a meaningful whole. Only the reason can perform the task of distinguishing this complex from the action of "repossessing a stolen horse and returning it to its rightful owner" or "playing a trick on a friend," because considered purely externally, all these actions would be identical. The object of action, consequently, can in no way be reduced to "only what happened" or "the mere facts," that is, to the mere "matter" of the action, which is traditionally called the *materia circa quam,* the "matter concerning which" some action is carried out (in distinction from the *materia ex qua,* the "matter out of which" some thing is constituted). The matter of action is not yet the object of an action; the *form* of the action still has to be considered.[85]

This terminology comes from metaphysics. By "matter" is meant that component of an action in each case that is still open to many interpretations, and that can be further determined, can take on form (further specification), which at the same time is limited by the matter. In classical metaphysics "matter" signifies the potential, still indeterminate foundation of a structured whole, while "form" designates the actuality of the matter, through which it is structured or informed, that is, becomes a structured whole of this or that kind (analogous to the form, say, of "Venus" by which the unformed block of marble becomes a statue of Venus). The composite form-matter is to be understood structurally or functionally: a matter can itself already be structured, and a structured whole can itself in turn become the matter for a structured whole of a higher order (and in this way also "end" is related formally to "means," or in other words the object of the intention is formally related to the object of the choice of means). "Material" does not necessarily have to with something "physically material," but rather designates what is "still further to be determined," "ca-

85. For some interesting reflections on the differentiation of formal and material aspects of the objects of action from the viewpoint of linguistic analysis, see A. Kenny, *Action, Emotion, and Will* (London: Routledge & Kegan Paul, 1963), 187ff.

pable of being actualized," "informable"—and thus standing *in potency* to further informing. The classical example is the soul as the form of the body.

Now since the object of action is not the "horse," nor even "somebody else's horse," but rather the content of the intentional action "make off with someone else's horse," such an object can only be the object of reason, which means it can only be *formed*—formally determined—by the reason. There "exist," of course, horses, and people who own horses, and even the actions "riding away on a horse" or "driving away with a horse" can be reduced to the physical components of bodily movements. But the action "steal a horse" cannot be reduced in the same way: in the complexity of its various elements it is the exclusive object of a power that is capable of setting the various items of this kind into relationship, that is, of creating *order* in the midst of the multiplicity of elements. Such a power can only be the reason, and through its act the object of action attains its *form* within the region of a certain matter.

This is why Thomas says, "as the species of natural things is constituted through natural forms, so the species of moral actions is constituted from forms that are conceived by the reason": *species moralium actuum constituuntur ex formis prout sunt a ratione conceptae.*[86] And correspondingly, as he says

---

86. I-II, Q. 18, a. 10. Though this article explicitly refers only to the *species* of a human act, it necessarily must also refer to the very object which determines the moral species of an action. The parallelism between the constitution of the moral species of a human act and its moral object can be substantiated by referring to Aquinas's further teaching that the moral object is a *bonum apprehensum et ordinatum per rationem* (I-II, Q. 20, a. 1, ad 1). For a detailed analysis of this, see my "The Perspective of the Acting Person and the Nature of Practical Reason: The 'Object of the Human Act' in Thomistic Anthropology of Action," in *Nova et Vetera* (English ed.) 2, no. 2 (2004): 461–516; reprinted as chap. 8 in my *The Perspective of the Acting Person.* See also incidental remarks like this: "species sumitur ab obiecto, quod est materia actus" (II-II, Q. 154, a. 1). Most of the relevant texts for this question and a useful discussion of them can be found in J. Pilsner, *The Specification of Human Actions in St. Thomas Aquinas* (Oxford: Oxford University Press, 2006). Critical toward my view is S. Brock, "Veritatis Splendor §78, St. Thomas, and (Not Merely) Physical Objects of Moral Acts," in *Nova et Vetera* (English ed.) 6, no. 1 (2008): 1–62; and in the same issue, 63–112: L. Dewan, "St. Thomas, Rhonheimer, and the Object of the Human Act." (These are responses to my article quoted above: "The Perspective of the Acting Person and the Nature of Practical Reason: The 'Object of the Human Act' in Thomistic Anthropology of Action"). Dewan's criticism, I believe, neglects precisely the "perspective of morality" and thus misses the point of moral philosophy. He attributes moral goodness to things or states of affairs and affirms that the moral goodness of a human act derives from, and is specified by, the goodness of things they refer to (e.g., on page 83: "the operation of possession gets its species as a good operation from the goodness of the thing that is its object"); and he attributes such a view to Aquinas. This may be true metaphysically, but—as I am trying to point out in this book—from a moral point of view it is simply erroneous: one might ask, is the operation of possessing *morally* good (e.g., just) simply because the thing possessed is "good"? Moreover, Dewan interprets several texts of Aquinas, which seem to me to speak in my favor, in what I consider to be a prejudiced and partial reading; he also misrepresents several of my arguments and ignores others. Finally, Dewan reproaches me with rejecting the key doctrine of I-II, q. 18, a. 2 (concerning the first and basic moral specification of human acts by the object), though I only mentioned some difficulties of interpretation and apparent inconsistencies of this article. A detailed answer to both Brock and Dewan must be postponed, however, to another occasion. (Unfortunately, I was not allowed by *Nova et Vetera* to respond to Dewan's and Brock's articles in a subsequent issue of

in another passage, the "good" of an action is constituted on the basis of a certain "measuring" *(commensuratio)* of the act in relation to the circumstances and the end, a measuring that the reason brings about: *quam ratio facit*[87]—because it is the task of reason to *order.* "Act," "circumstances," "goal" are formed into an object of action by the reason, which constitutes a species of action.

It is crucial to understand that not only the species itself is a form "conceived by reason," but also that the so-called moral object which gives to a human act its first and basic moral species (e.g., "theft") is something conceived by reason and as such presented to the will; as Aquinas says, the object of the so-called interior act of the will which specifies a human act morally is "a good, understood and ordered by reason."[88] Thus, as we saw above, objects of human acts are not "things" (as in *res aliena,* "a thing which belongs to another person"), but the whole so-called exterior act (e.g., *subtrahere rem alienam,* "taking away something which belongs to another person") as it is conceived and understood by reason and presented to the will as an object of its choosing or intending act. Objects that specify human acts morally, by putting them into the (moral) species of "good" or "evil," "just" or "unjust" (e.g., "theft," "adultery," "lying") are thus *practical goods* for the agent. The moral good or evil is not in the things, but—provided "things" are concerned at all—in how reason and consequently the will practically *refer to* things.[89] The view that the morally specifying "object" of a human act is properly the "exterior act" as understood (or conceived) and ordered by reason and that the exterior act by itself has no additional morally specifying object,[90] as well as my denial that the object that morally specifies a human act is the "thing" to which an action refers, has been challenged by those who see no basis for such a view in Aquinas.[91] Ralph McInerny, however, has put it rightly: "The object of the ac-

---

that journal). Some remarks on Dewan's article can be found in the following excursus below and in my *Vital Conflicts in Medical Ethics: A Virtue Approach to Craniotomy and Tubal Pregnancies* (Washington, D.C.: The Catholic University of America Press, 2009), 54 (note 40), 140 (note 59), and 145 (note 64).

87. In II Sent. D. 39, Q. 2, a. 1.

88. See I-II, Q. 20, a. 1, ad 1. *Bonum apprehensum et ordinatum per rationem.*

89. See for this and the following in more detail my "The Perspective of the Acting Person and the Nature of Practical Reason: The 'Object of the Human Act' in Thomistic Anthropology of Action" (reprinted in my *The Perspective of the Acting Person* as chapter 8, esp. 198–217). See also W. F. Murphy, "Aquinas on the Object and Evaluation of the Moral Act: Rhonheimer's Approach and Some Recent Interlocutors," *Josephinum Journal of Theology* 15, no. 2 (2008): 205–42; D. Sousa-Lara, "Aquinas on the Object of the Human Act: A Reading in Light of the Texts and Commentators," *Josephinum Journal of Theology* 15, no. 2 (2008): 243–76; esp. 249–50; and from the same author in the same issue of the *Josephinum Journal of Theology,* "Aquinas on Interior and Exterior Acts: Clarifying a Key Aspect of His Action Theory," 277–316.

90. Of course it can have an object which physically specifies an act, e.g., as an act of "car washing" (instead of an act of "bicycle washing").

91. See the two articles by L. Dewan and S. Brock referred to in the preceding note. Surprisingly Steven J. Jensen has also recently subscribed to this criticism in his thoughtful book *Good and Evil Actions. A Journey through Saint Thomas Aquinas* (Washington, D.C.: The Catholic University of America

tion is that which the agent sets out to do, to effect."[92] Although it is true that Aquinas sometimes seems to speak about "things" as "objects" of human acts, I think that these critics have overlooked why Aquinas does so: not because he holds that the moral species of a human act derives from the things to which it refers, but because sometimes a "thing"—for example, a human being—can be a *circumstance* which turns out to be a "principal condition of the object that is repugnant to reason"[93] or an "essential objective difference"[94] (see more about this in V.3.d). Hence such a circumstance, which in fact ceases to be a circumstance in the strict sense, gives to a human act the moral species (e.g., a simple theft, because of the circumstance of the thing stolen is sacred, turns out to be a sacrilege by its object).[95] Thus, in a way one also may talk as if the morally specifying object of "theft" were the *res aliena,* because the circumstance of its being *aliena* ("belonging to someone else") is precisely determinative for specifying an act of "taking away" as "theft" und therefore as *unjust.* But that does not mean that the object of the human act "theft" is the "thing belonging to someone else" (the *res aliena*); the morally specifying object is the exterior act *tollere rem alienam* ("to take away something which belongs to another person"), whereby the "taking away" is not only the *physically* taking it, but includes the basic intentional content, shaped by reason, of *appropriating* it for one's own use (which is not the case for the police officer, who takes away—that is, confiscates—a *res aliena* from a thief to return it to its legitimate owner). This is why Aquinas does not properly speak of a morally specifying *object* of the exterior act; he rather holds that the first moral goodness (or evil) of the exterior act derives from its "matter" and "circumstances," which must be configured and understood by reason. This seems to accord with Aquinas's statement: "The goodness or malice which the exterior act has of itself, on account of its being about due matter and its being attended by due circumstances, is not derived from the will, but rather from reason,"[96] that is, it is not itself derived from a morally specifying "object" *previous* to reason and its ordering act—"due matter" and "due circumstances" not being the object, but the conditions for an object (the exterior act conceived by reason) to be morally good.

Now with this, to be sure, we have not yet made it clear how reason is the "measure" or "rule" of the goodness or badness of an action. But we have clar-

---

Press), 117. I say "surprisingly" because Jensen's awareness throughout his book of the central role of reason in Aquinas moral theory, in my view, should have taught him otherwise.

92. R. McInerny, *Aquinas on Human Action: A Theory of Practice,* 81.

93. "principalis conditio obiecti rationi repugnans" (I-II, Q. 18, a. 10).

94. "circumstantia quandoque sumitur ut differentia essentialis obiecti, secundum quod ad rationem comparatur: et tunc potest dare speciem actui morali" (I-II, Q. 18, a. 5, ad 4).

95. See on this also W. F. Murphy, "Aquinas on the Object and Evaluation of the Moral Act: Rhonheimer's Approach and Some Recent Interlocutors," 222, note 52; and J. Pilsner, *The Specification of Human Actions in St. Thomas Aquinas,* 86–91, and 193–97.

96. "Bonitas autem vel malitia quam habet actus exterior secundum se, propter debitam materiam et debitas circumstantias, non derivatur a voluntate, sed magis a ratione" (I-II, Q. 20. a. 1).

ified what must really be judged first and foremost as "good" or "bad": neither the horse, nor the possessor, nor the actions of riding or transporting away, or even the "taking," but rather the object of action that is "stealing what rightfully belongs to someone else." And it has been shown that, like the species of an action corresponding to a determinate moral object, the very objects of action are also a work of reason, *formae a ratione conceptae*, "forms conceived by the reason," or "determinations of a certain kind formed by the reason."

c) Natural and Moral-Intentional Identity of the Objects of Action

When we characterize the content of an action as the object through which the action obtains its intentional identity as a human action, it should become clear that the "things" to which actions relate cannot become the "objects" of action. Because it is through their *objects* that actions *differ* in their moral-intentional identity. Horses and the contents of bank vaults do not differentiate different kinds of actions, but at most only furnish different "cases" of the same kind of action, for instance, various kinds of "theft." And horses can appear as "things" in quite various types of actions, not only in thefts.

Even an additional determination of the "thing" is not enough to distinguish intentional actions objectively, if information about "why" is lacking. If we said "someone else's property" were the object of a theft (i.e., the "thing" that belongs to someone else), a theft and a repossession of stolen property by the police (for the purpose of restoring it to the rightful owner) would not differ with respect to their object, and then "repossession of a stolen horse" and "repossession of a stolen car" would be two objectively different kinds of actions, which would naturally make no sense.

Likewise, the natural purposes of drives or inclinations that do not arise from the reason *as such* are not objects of human actions. Each drive or inclination possesses, of course, its natural act and its natural object. An example would be the sexual inclination. The act and the object of the act that belong to this drive are *as such* not objects of action. This is because human actions are willing, reason-guided acts. What someone does *exclusively* on the basis of the sex drive is by definition not a human action at all. For it to be one, it needs at least a judgment of the reason that it is "good" to follow the drive and to carry out the act that goes along with it ("p is good"), and the agreement of the will that has been formed by this judgment. In this way, the corresponding action obtains an object, and yet this is an object that has been formed through the reason.

However, as soon as the act of the sex drive becomes an object of the reason, this act is something more than an act of the sex drive, namely, it is a practical good conceived by the reason; and within this object-space of the reason is found not only the natural action of the drive—for example, the "object" that sets off the dynamic of the drive (say, the body of some other person)—but rather an entire complex of elements that are circumstantially related to the natural drive. The "why" of the intentional human action known as the "sexual act" is more than the mere "why" of the drive itself: it is a "why" of the reason, even if the stimulus that originally sets off the action depends on a sensual inclination.

In this way—to keep the same example—objectively different types of the human actions known as "sexual activity" are formed: "married sexual intercourse" and "adulterous sexual intercourse." Thomas clarifies this as follows: "Insofar as we treat married sex and adulterous sex as objects of reason, they differ in type *(specie)* and have effects that are different in type, because one of them deserves praise and reward, while the other deserves reprehension and punishment. But insofar as we treat them with regard to the procreative power, they do not differ in type at all, and have one and the same effect."[97] This is an example of the difference between the so-called *genus naturae* of an act (its "natural species" or "natural identity") and its *genus moris* (its "moral species" or "moral identity"). We can treat and describe every accomplished human action either on the level of its natural (ontic, physical, empirical, etc.) structuring—and then there is no difference between actions of sexual intercourse: where, when, and with whom not making any difference, adulterous and conjugal acts being identical actions at this level of the matter of the action. And at this natural, ontic, or "physical" level there is also no difference between intentionally different (and thus formally different) acts of "taking a horse away" or "lying on a bed" (and that is why in each case we must ask "What is *really* going on here?"). But as soon as we consider such actions as the objects of a willing, acting subject, that is, as soon as we treat them *formally,* they have a "measuring" that can only come from the reason. This is treating the action in question at the level of its *genus moris.* The action then belongs to an identifiable species of moral actions and is then either good or bad (or, as the case may be, indifferent), "getting some rest" or "doing a yoga exercise" or "just being lazy"; "theft" or "repossession of stolen goods"; a conjugal act or an act of adultery; and so on. And insofar as an act is the object of reason, it also becomes an object of the will, and is carried out as a human action.

Acts of the will also have their *genus naturae* (or *species naturae,* natural species), which is, so to say, their natural identity. But this is now identical with the *genus moris* (or moral species), its moral identity. Since the will is reason-guided appetition and consequently its object is the good that is presented to the reason, the *bonum rationis*, there is no difference between the natural and the moral identity of its act. What the will naturally strives for is always the good in the moral dimension. The difference between natural and moral identity immediately appears when an act is objectified as *not* being the object of a (choosing or intending) will.

Since human actions are willed (chosen) actions; and since, secondly, the will always strives for something "good" only on the basis of judgments of reason, we can say that an act—as a human act—is never willed or chosen on the basis of its *genus naturae*. For that would be impossible: *we either choose it on the basis of a judgment of the reason or it is not a human action at all, and thus cannot be morally evaluated.* The object of a human action is necessarily always subject to the moral difference, because it is the object of a reason-guided appetition of the will.

This does not affect the fact that there also exist objectively indifferent actions. The objective indifference of a basic intentional action is not the same as the indifference that characterizes the natural identity of an act. The latter is the indifference of what is not yet within the sphere of the judgment according to reason, that is, it is detached from the total context of "human action" and is treated "formlessly." The objective indifference of a basic intentional action, by contrast, is an actual indifference *for the reason* and *in the judgment of reason*. It is a determination of the form. To designate an action as objectively indifferent means proposing a *moral* evaluation. It is very important to distinguish these two kinds of "indifference."[98]

Apparently the theory criticized above (at III.3.c), which holds that our action only concerns itself with "nonmoral" goods or evils and that only the attitude with which we act can be morally evaluated, arises precisely from a confusion in action theory about the two kinds of indifference. The mistake originates, as we have seen, from not treating actions as human actions, but rather as if they were natural events or processes that bring forth desirable states of affairs, and as if these were the object of the choosing will, and the actions themselves were merely causes of these states of affairs, somehow "produced" by the doer. In reality, however, actions as *accomplished actions* are objects of the practical reason and a choosing will (otherwise we couldn't "act"). The position criticized above (at III.3.c) is therefore a radical "physicalism" that excludes the perspective of morality at the critical point. It treats all actions in their objective basic content as *indifferent*, while taking "indifference" to be the same as the "natural identity" of an act. As is well known, the first one to commit this

98. Cf. on this also M. Rhonheimer, *Natural Law and Practical Reason,* 87ff.

error and build a comprehensive moral theory on it was the medieval philosopher Peter Abelard (1079–1142).

Another example that Thomas uses to illustrate the difference between the natural identity *(genus naturae)* and moral identity *(genus moris)* of an action is the action "killing a man." On the ontic level this action is similar to any occurrence that causes someone to die (for a more exact description, see below, at V.3.d). Thomas adds the following: "It is possible, however, that acts that are identical with regard to their natural species, are ordered to two different ends of the will: as the act which is 'killing a man' is always the same according to its natural species, but can be ordered to the ends 'preservation of justice' on the one hand, or to 'satisfaction of anger' on the other. And on the basis of this ordering there will be two different acts according to the moral species: one will be an act of justice, the other will be an act of vice." And then he adds a clarification: "Moral ends are something added to a natural reality *(fines morales accidunt rei naturali)*, and conversely, the natural finality of an act is something added to a moral end *(ratio naturalis finis accidit morali)*. And therefore nothing prevents actions that are the same with respect to their natural species from being different with regard to their moral species, and vice versa."[99] Thomas thus distinguishes here between "the death penalty" and "murder" as two "objectively" and thereby morally different actions.

> It must be pointed out that this distinction is separate from the question whether the death penalty can be justified today. Even if we were not of this opinion (a matter not to be discussed here), nevertheless the two actions are still objectively different, and this is of great importance for the formulation of the corresponding moral norms (cf. below, at V.3.d).

If Thomas speaks here of "two different ends of the will," this shows that he is of the opinion that the moral species of human actions comes into play because concrete acts are objects of the will and thereby of practical reasoning. That is why, in such an action, the formal "why" of the reason is found, which constitutes the basic intentional action in its objective content. What we can call the *ethical* context of an action is only an object to the reason.

The case is similar with the action "lying." It is an injury to the human communication community. The act of "false speaking" (a statement wherein the linguistic signifiers do not correspond to the thinking of the speaker) can only be a lie, that is, an untruth, insofar as a context is present in which speech is understood as a medium of communication and in fact has this function in a determinate interpersonal context (cf. below, V.3.d.).

99. I-II, Q. 1, a. 3, ad 3.

A further example is the action "contracepting." In its natural identity, this act is, for example, "taking an ovulation-hindering drug," or, more generally, "making the generative power unfruitful." But this alone does not yet characterize the human action of "contracepting." We still are missing information about the "why." We could describe the *intentional* action "contracepting" as "hindering the procreative consequences of one's own act of sexual intercourse." This means that contraception is an action that is intended to hinder the procreative consequences of one's sex act (that is its "why"). One can see instantly that for an athlete to take a drug that hinders her ovulation for the purpose of preventing her menstruation during the Olympic Games is an act that is identical in its *genus naturae;* but the moral identity and therewith the object of the action is completely different (there is no intentional relationship to sexual activity or to its procreative consequences, and the "why" is different, but at the level of the *genus naturae* exactly the same thing is done). In the same way, we would consider the same action done to prevent the possible procreative consequences of a foreseeable rape as an act of self-defense and not as the human action "contracepting." The latter is a determinate form of behavior in relation to the procreative consequences of one's own, freely chosen sexual behavior: prevention of these consequences instead of avoiding them by modifying one's behavior through acts of self-restraint. A moral judgment can only relate to this intentional action, but not to the physical act of "hindering ovulation" or "intervening in natural processes."[100]

In order to answer such questions in a normative way, we must first speak of moral virtue and practical principles. Here we are only concerned with determining the object-structure of human action.

One may now ask, wherein, then, lies the difference between this position and the one, typical for consequentialism and proportionalism, that always considers nonmoral goods and evils as the objects of actions, or actions in their natural identity? The difference is this: the position represented here maintains that the objects of such actions possess something more than their natural identity: they have an ethical context, a measuring of circumstances and a "why," all of which is the work of the reason. Actions are always chosen and carried out at least as basic intentional actions. When we said that acts can only be chosen *within* the moral difference, and thereby as either good or bad (or at times indifferent) actions, we did *not* mean to say that the moral identity of these actions, or the assigning of them to the one or the other side of the difference, was to be decided through the sum total of the intentions of the doer, or the weighing of the foreseeable consequences of an action. The

---

100. See the full argument in my *Ethics of Procreation and the Defense of Human Life: Contraception, Artificial Fertilization, and Abortion* (Washington, D.C.: The Catholic University of America Press, 2010), 33–150, esp. 65–69.

underlying moral identity of the concrete accomplished action is rather a *datum* that is objectified to the reason, a fundamental given that underlies all *further* intentions. If someone takes a horse away from a neighbor, which the neighbor rightfully owns, this action objectively *is*—that is, regardless of further consequences or intentions—either a theft or not a theft; one cannot say that taking away what belongs to another is a nonmoral evil that must still be weighed off against the nonmoral goods that are foreseen to result from the action, after which it would become clear whether the action is just or unjust. The various elements of the matter of the action are, in any case, contingent givens, which must be *grasped* by the reason. The commensuration carried out by the reason is therefore very much an act of knowing, and very much a work accomplished by the acting subject. The taking over of the rightfully owned property of another is an injury to justice that is presented as an object only to the reason. *That* it is such, or *whether* it is such, the doer can only *recognize*, but cannot *decide*, or, in other words, redefine each time on the basis of further intentions or foreseeable consequences.

> A "theft of a horse" means: A takes a horse from B that rightfully belongs to B, to make it his own. Even if A would have in mind *not* to steal a horse but to carry out an act of benevolence toward C, and thus took the horse not to have it for himself but to give it to C, and even if B would not notice that a horse was stolen from him, because he owns so many, and C would have been helped in this way to get out of poverty, nevertheless the action of A remains *objectively* the intentional action described at the outset, namely, the theft of a horse, and therefore, it being granted that stealing is *objectively* unjust, it is an unjust act. Thomas Aquinas would say in this case that the *matter* of the action (of the chosen means to the goal of "benefiting C") is a *materia indebita*, inappropriate matter.

If a private person takes the life of another, objectively it either *is* murder (an injustice) or it is not; if a criminal who has been convicted according to law is executed, it objectively *is* either an act of restoration of justice or an inappropriate and therefore unjust punishment (but not murder). If someone makes a false statement to someone else who shares in the same communicative community, it objectively *is* either an unjust action or it is not—and always regardless of further consequences or purposes. Our analysis has of course still not reached the point where we can say whether and why the acts just mentioned should be assigned to one side or the other of the moral difference. We need in addition a concept of moral virtue (see IV) and practical principles (see V). Here we have been exclusively concerned with the analysis of the structure and constitution of the objects of actions and their moral species. If we had started with the theory of nonmoral goods, any talk about the objective identity of concrete actions and their being assigned to one or the other side of the moral difference would have been impossible and unmanageable, because this identity and this assigning would have only been possible in the context of the sum total of the actual consequences and intentions.[101]

d) The Reason as Measure of the Moral Evaluation of Objects of Action

Once we have understood *what* an object of action is and *how* it comes into being (on the basis of a *commensuratio* by the reason), then the question can also be answered, *why*, after all, the reason is the "measure" of good and evil in human actions. We already recognize that the question is not rightly framed in this way. This is because we do not have to justify that, or why, the *reason* (and not something else) is the measure. The justification runs exactly in the other direction. This is because we have proceeded from the idea that the human being is a being who acts on the basis of mastery over his own striving, that he is a creature who acts freely. And we saw also that he will only be in a position to do this because, and to the extent that, he can make judgments about good and bad, about what to do and what not to do. Consequently, the question that really arises is, based on *what* notion of "good" and "bad" does a human being act? We have already answered this question, at any rate, because the answer has already been given in the concept of human action: the human being acts on the basis of judgments of *reason*, that is, on the basis of what the reason or intellect formulates as good. But is that good as measured or judged by the reason also that which we call "moral good"?

The answer to this question is also "yes," and the corresponding justification has already been sufficiently made: the moral good is not a good toward which attitudes, feelings, and intentions (in contrast to actions) are aimed, since attitudes, feelings, and intentions are "action-projects" that are themselves formulated by the reason, so that the stated distinction would end in a circle. What we call "good" or "bad" is in fact the good or evil that lies *in* the actions, as intentional actions. A just human being is not only someone who wants or intends what is just, but rather someone who wants to *act* justly,

---

101. The difference between the actual object of the action and further intentions for the sake of which the action is willed is thereby nullified. The identity of the action is therefore determined only on the basis of what R. A. McCormick calls the *expanded notion of object*, according to which all relevant premoral elements must be counted as the object. This means, finally, that also all the intentions belong as well to the definition of the concrete action. In order, for instance, to define, in a concrete case of an act of killing in a certain situation, what kind of action is really being done, the intentions must also be considered, for the sake of which the (physical) act of killing was carried out (thus the killing of X for the purpose of saving the life of other human beings can be described as "an act of rescue"). For a critique of the concept of *expanded object*, cf. again M. Rhonheimer, "Intentional Actions and the Meaning of Object: A Reply to Richard McCormick" (see note 62 above).

and, so far as is possible for him, actually *acts* that way. To follow "justice" as a purpose or intention means wanting to *do* what is just, that is, understanding that what one actually chooses to do and also does is "just action," and *not* simply to will the existence of certain states of affairs which correspond (as states of affairs) to the criteria of justice *as intended* by the actions through which these states are brought into being (cf. below, V.4.f). This (moral) good (e.g., that which is just) is formulated by the reason, and it only *can* be formulated by the reason. Good and bad in human actions is measured according to the good, in the way only it—the good—*can* be an object for the practical reason.

Thus we must not ask *whether* the "moral good" is formulated through the reason and *whether* the reason or intellect is the criterion for this good. It is the other way around: what we *first* know is that the human being acts on the basis of judgments of reason (insofar as he accomplishes "human actions"). The good that is formulated by such judgments is precisely that good to which we give the name "moral good." The word "moral" is actually superfluous here: it is enough to say that it is the good that man pursues when he acts *as man,* and that means willingly, on the basis of reason-guided appetition. We call this good "moral" good simply because we use the expression "moral action" for the whole phenomenon of "human action." "Moral" (not as opposed to "immoral" but as opposed to "nonmoral") is what we call the kind of doing that emerges from reason-guided striving—which is willed action, in other words—action for which a person bears responsibility, which brings reward or guilt with it and earns praise or blame. The real heart of what is moral, or of morality, is nothing other than a name for the characteristics of human conduct just mentioned. And these characteristics are not phenomena that need to be established or justified, because they are rather the starting point of every discourse about the constitution of what we call ethics. In other words, granted our concept of "human (moral) action," it is absolutely evident that reason is the measure of morality. It really involves nothing more than grasping the immediate implication of the concept "human action."

> Here again we are justifying anew what was said above (III.3.c): we need the expression "moral good" not to distinguish the moral good from nonmoral aspects *in* human actions, but rather to distinguish the sphere of human actions from the sphere of merely natural occurrences. Within the sphere of ethics constituted by the practical or moral perspective, the expression "moral good" is redundant and pleonastic.[102]

---

102. G. E. M. Anscombe pointed this out rather provocatively in her 1958 essay, "Modern Moral Philosophy," already referred to in the introduction (also available in R. Crisp and M. Slote, eds., *Virtue Ethics,* 26–44, esp. p. 43).

Without having yet clarified how the reason can distinguish the "moral" from the "immoral," the "good" from the "bad," or the "truly good" from the "apparent good," we have, to begin with, the following action-theoretical context: *Because* the human being, insofar as he acts humanly, acts on the basis of reason and will, the good of his action is also determined according to reason. If the moral difference were not constituted on the basis of reason and if reason were not its measure, we could not say that man acts on the basis of reason. That means, we could not say he acts on the basis of judgments like "p is good"; we would have to say, rather, that he acts on the basis of judgments like "p is prescribed" or "p is a moral norm," or "I must do p" or "it is required of me that I do p," and so on.

> Of course, one could act rationally on the basis of "p is prescribed." But the practical judgment that leads to action cannot be "p is prescribed"; the judgment of action is formulated as follows: (1) "it is prescribed to do p," (2) "this prescription is good," or "it is good to follow this prescription," and (3) "it is good to do p." The judgment (2) that "it is good to follow this prescription" does not necessarily ever have to be based on an insight into the goodness of what is contained in the prescription; it is enough, for example, to trust in the person, or respect the authority of the person, who has given the prescription. Consequently even in this case when there is no judgment of the doer about the goodness of p, the person in question still acts on the basis of a judgment, "it is good to do p." And this judgment is the measure of the goodness of the action of trust or obedience. The final judgment about the goodness of the action can never be a prescription, commandment, or moral norm, but always only the reason of the one acting—otherwise it would not be a human action. Even obedience, insofar as it is not submission to mere coercion and is then not really "obedience" at all, is always an act of freedom and reason.

Only the reason can be the measure of good and bad in human actions. This function of the reason, normative in the true sense of the word, coincides with the determination of human action as *free* and in this sense *autonomous* action.[103] "Freedom" means just the same as possessing "mastery over one's own striving," that is, the capacity to act on one's own initiative and to direct oneself to the good. And this good is always a *bonum rationis,* a "good of the reason," which means a good as settled on by the reason. The reason, we saw before, is the *root* of freedom, because it is the *cause* of freedom. It can be this because it can have "various conceptions of the good";[104] it is not determined to some one thing.[105] As Kant rightly saw, the concept of "human dignity" can

---

103. For the concept of autonomy, see my longer discussions in *Natural Law and Practical Reason,* 179ff.

104. I-II, Q. 17, a. 1, ad 2.   105. Ibid.

only be derived from the concept of autonomy.[106] We have been speaking here, in any case, of an autonomy of *action,* founded in the dependence of the will on reason, that is, in a *cognitive autonomy.* This is the conception defended in this book. Kant, however, speaks of the autonomy of the *will* as self-legislation, and its freedom as an independence from all materially objective or natural determination, a position whose problematic nature I am concerned to show. Kant's reason, then, is a reason that is formal and independent from "nature." Instead of a defense of reason or of reason's intrinsic cognitive autonomy, his position amounts, rather, to a (questionable) defense of the freedom of the will. As a legislator independent from any conception of the good springing from nature, reason, according to Kant, commands the will, both conserving and morally orientating its "transcendental freedom" through categorical imperatives; this freedom would be lost by any determination springing from nature, even if the goods it chose were understood and ordered by reason. The deep divide between Aquinas's conception of cognitive autonomy (ultimately grounded in his theology of creation and a corresponding anthropology), and Kant's constructivist conception of the autonomy of the will (in which "practical reason" becomes in fact another name for the will), cannot be discussed here more extensively (for further details concerning their difference, see III.5.c, V.1.a, V.2).

This is why Thomas Aquinas says: "He is free, who is cause of himself *(qui est causa sui);* the slave stands beneath the disposing-power of his master: whoever acts on his own, acts freely; he, on the other hand, who acts being moved by another, does not act freely. And so the one who avoids what is evil not because it is evil but because God commands it, is not free; but he who avoids evil because it is evil, is free."[107] The same goes for what is good. Only the *insight* into the good, and an action that springs from this insight, is truly free action. But, of course, an action that is based on the rational insight that it is good to follow the advice of another is also free action; that too is a form of insight into the goodness of the action, even if someone does not know *why* the action in question is itself good as such. The action would not be free, if it were accomplished only because someone commanded it (through sheer subjugation).

Now, does this mean that what any human being's reason considers to be "good" is also good for that person? If this is taken to mean that what each person's reason judges as good is the measure of what he actually *will* do, that is correct. This is because we always act on the basis of judgments of the kind "p is good." But if it is taken to mean that this is the *measure* of what *is* good in reality, of what, therefore, is (morally) good in distinction from what is (mor-

106. I. Kant, *Groundwork of the Metaphysics of Morals,* trans. M. Gregor, 37.
107. *Super secundam Epistolam ad Corinthios Lectura,* cap. III, lect. 3.

ally) bad, that is not correct. But we have not discussed this second distinction as yet. To be sure, we have approached it more closely. Because *if* it is a question of a difference between what is "truly good" and what "only seems good," or between "objectively moral good" and "objectively moral bad," then this difference must in some way be equivalent to the difference between "rational" and "irrational," in the sense, "what corresponds to reason" and "what does not correspond to reason." In reality, an *anthropological* statement is hidden behind this formulation: an anthropology of moral action that merely illuminates what it means to say that the reason is the measure of good and bad in human actions. It is just such an anthropology of human action that underlies the phenomenon "moral virtue."

5. The Anthropology of Moral Action

a) The Anthropological Primacy of the Reason

In support of his position that the reason is the measure of good and evil in actions, Thomas, as we saw, employs the following concise justification: what is good for every being is what corresponds to its substantial form, and to the specificity of its being. The human being, as a body informed by a spiritual soul, is distinguished precisely by rationality. Consequently, it is something *natural* for man to determine what is good for him, *in relation to* the reason, and *through* the reason. Accordingly, "good" and "bad" with regard to the objects of action must in each case be that which corresponds to reason and intellect or (alternatively) what does not so correspond.[108]

Aristotle had already said the same thing in essence with his *ergon* argument: virtue is an action that directs itself to "the part of the soul" that is rational. The condition for good action is that a human being's reason is in control, that it assumes leadership, so to speak, and that the nonrational urges of the human being are ordered according to reason.[109]

In order to clarify this, we need to be reminded again that action is a phenomenon of appetition. We act because, and to the extent that, we are seeking something. And what we seek or strive *for*—the correlate or object of the striving—we call "good." There is a good for sense appetition and for the variety

108. I-II, Q. 19, a. 5, and Q. 71, a. 2: In II Ethic., lect. 2. On possible mistaken interpretations of this passage, cf. M.Rhonheimer, *Natural Law and Practical Reason*, 39–42. See on this subject also the classic book by L.Léhu, *La raison, règle de la moralité d'après Saint Thomas* (Paris: J.Gabalda et Fils, 1930) who already in his time had to defend Aquinas's doctrine against influential misinterpretations (e.g., by P.Elter and O.Lottin). I am much indebted to Léhu for my understanding of the role of reason in Thomistic ethics.

109. Cf. *EN* I, 13.

of drives that we collect under the comprehensive concept of "sensitive appetition." Every desire formulates a good on the level specific to itself. And on this natural level of sense perception there are also things that the desire flees from, that are objectified as evils or that stir up the opposite of pleasure.

Because man is still man on the basis of his intellectuality or rationality, and because he acts on the basis of reason, that is to say, because the judgments "p is good" that he acts on are judgments of *reason* and not judgments of the senses (these latter, as such, only being able to direct sense desire), so can the good that is good for him as man only be a good formulated by the reason, a *bonum rationis*, a "good of the reason": that is to say, good as it appears good to the judgment of the reason. "But the good of the reason is that which is moderated and ordered by the reason."[110]

The reason appears here no longer as a mere power to make judgments, but rather, according to Aristotelian terminology, as the "part of the soul" that provides a standard. As Aristotle teaches, there is a hierarchy of parts of the soul, and reason is the highest part, destined to mastery. In fact, our free responsible action is grounded in the reason. The other parts of the soul that are not rational in themselves, must be subordinated to the reason. Sense appetite is not in itself rational and does not seek its objects rationally, but can be brought to strive rationally when the subject directs his striving to the good, as only it can be an object for the reason. If my neighbor's horse or wife appears good (worthy of being desired) to the corresponding sense perception, the reason can judge: "But it is not good to desire this," and it can consequently moderate and put into order the sensitive appetition. A judgment of action "p is good" would then be a judgment with relation to this sense desire: a judgment to follow it or not to follow it, and this takes place in fact within the "order of reason."

Since a human being is a human being because his body possesses an intellective or rational form, so the actions of a human being are "human actions" insofar as they are carried out on the basis of reason and rational striving (the will). And accordingly, human actions are "good" or "bad" on the basis of their agreement or nonagreement with the reason.

As shown above (II.3.b), the reason does not isolate the realm of the good for man, but is rather the principle of order according to which the manifold of what belongs to being human is pursued. Accordingly, not only are the acts and operations peculiar to reason good for man, but also the correlatives of nonrational (sense) appetition, and these as *according* to the reason, that is, ordered through the reason as *bonum rationis*.

110. I-II, Q. 59, a. 4.

But it seems that we have not made any forward progress here, and that we only have a purely formal criterion of the good: rationality. But the doctrine that Thomas has taken over from Aristotle does in fact take us farther, as soon as we think more precisely about the *nature of reason:* to the extent, namely, that the reason is not hindered by some kind of "external" influence on its own action of judging, and thereby on the rationality that corresponds to its nature, it will unerringly reach the good. The rational or reasonable is also always what is *truly* good for man. If the reason fails to attain this, the fault is not in the reason, but in a *lack* of reason brought in by other influences. "False reason" or "irrationality" means the same as "too *little* rationality." The unreasonable is the nonrational.[111]

This thesis may cause surprise at first. But it becomes more understandable on closer inspection. The sense desire also meets the sense-perceived good unerringly in its own way, that is, the *adequate* object for the sense in question—its organ, that is—and every sense cognition possesses a physiological-organic set of conditions, which in one way or another can be compromised in its ability to function. There is such a thing as color blindness, and there are some people who are sexually unresponsive. But this is caused, at least in part, by pathological disturbances of the physiological-organic foundations of sense desires or affectivity.

The adequate object of reason is the intelligible. Pathological disturbances of the reason *as* reason are not possible, since the act of the reason *as* reason is not dependent on any bodily organs. The proof of this statement does not belong to ethics. But its foundation can be indicated: both reason and will are powers that are capable of reflection. When a power can reflect upon itself, it means that it is capable of making its own acts apparent to itself. The eye cannot see itself (except in a non-self-reflective way, as in a mirror); a sense desire cannot be in a desiring relation to itself, and cannot nondesire its own act of desiring (this is why animals do not have freedom). The intellect or reason can itself recognize its own actions and make judgments over its own judgments, and the will can make willing again an object of the will, or not will it. Reflexivity indicates independence of corporeal organs, and that means spirituality.[112] The reason cannot be "sick" or be deceived, like the senses; it can only be "hindered," "distorted," and so forth, and this happens because the human reason is the reason of a creature with sense organs; strictly speaking, it is not the reason that knows but the human being as body-soul unity that knows.

111. We should recall that here the term "reason" (or "intellect") is being used to signify the human intellective power as a whole; cf. the remarks in small print at III.3.a. More detailed exposition of the matters now to be presented can be found in M. Rhonheimer, *Praktische Vernunft und Vernünftigkeit der Praxis,* 117–72.
112. On this, see again *De Veritate,* Q. 22, a. 4.

What does this imply? That the reason (or intellect) is *naturally* ordered (like any faculty) to knowing the object that is adequate to it. "Now intellect," Aristotle explains, "is always right; but appetite and imagination may be either right or wrong."[113] "Wrong," that is, with respect to the demands of reason, and consequently they must be ordered according to what has been recognized by reason as right.

What we call the "truly good" is really nothing other than the natural object of the reason. This means that *true* knowing, even in the realm of praxis, is what we call the knowledge that is achieved by reason. We do not need to enquire any further, "How can we guarantee that what the reason knows *as reason* is 'true'?" The question is superfluous because of the following consideration: as long as the reason can carry out its peculiar task without hindrance, this action is "knowing of the knowable" carried out under the conditions of its own nature, just as the corresponding act of the sense of sight is "seeing of the visible" and as the sense of touch is "feeling what can be touched." And reaching that which is knowable for the intellect is what we call *true* knowing. Otherwise, we could not meaningfully speak about a difference between true and false knowledge.

But now something of decisive importance must be noted: reason or intellect reaches what is true without fail, or what is truly good is what the *reason* judges as good, but it must be kept in mind that this is a statement about *the reason of the human being* (i.e., about the faculty as such), and not a statement about *the human being who makes rational judgments*. A human being is not only reason. And actions are carried out, not by single faculties, but always by the whole person in his body-soul complexity *by means of* the faculty.[114] Judgments of reason of a human being coexist in interaction and in a certain conditioned relationship with the acts of sense perception and sensitive appetition. If someone judges with his reason that "p is good," there is no guarantee that this judgment is rational or even "true." It is rational, that is, it meets with the truly good, to the extent that in this judgment the demands of reason are really given their due, and not other demands that compete with it.

This may sound "rationalistic" or "stoic," but it does not have to be taken in that way. And it cannot be gotten around, as we move ahead in our analysis. In due time matters will become clearer.

---

113. *De Anima* III, 10 (433a27–28). Smith's translation of *nous* as "thought" has been corrected here to "intellect."

114. "Actus sunt suppositorum" is the classical principle for this: acts are not carried out by the single powers, but by a concretely existing individual, the *suppositum* or person, in his or her totality. My hand does not form a fist to strike someone, but *I* do it, with my hand.

The "unerringness" of the reason or intellect we have been speaking of does not mean that man cannot make mistakes. What is meant is only that the error does not result by reason of a defect of the intellective faculty, but by way of other influences. The intellect abstracts intelligible content from sense perception.[115] Here of course, inborn talent, psychological disposition, exercise, and so on play a large role. Moreover, and this applies especially to the practical intellect, the affective dispositions influence the judgment of reason. More will be said on this below. In the meantime it should be noted here that for these reasons, the intellect needs a habitual orientation to its own act. This takes place through the so-called dianoetic or "intellectual" virtues to be discussed in what follows.

We can conclude as follows: the reason possesses in the "true" or the "intelligible" the object that is adequate for it, and to which it is naturally orientated, but from which it can still be diverted. The reason *as* reason meets with what is its peculiar good, and this good is the criterion for the goodness of human actions. Therefore it is really self-evident that the reason is the *measure* for good and bad in human actions. For anthropological reasons, any other measure is simply unconceivable. Secondly, we can say: the reason judges everything else, that is, what does not originally arise from the reason, with relation to itself— "in its own interest," as it were—and orders it and subordinates it to its own way of knowing. This interest of the reason is double: to preserve itself as reason, and to order everything else according to goods objectifiable to the reason. Accordingly—Thomas teaches—for the nonrational appetites, that situation is really the "naturally right" one, through which "the act of the reason and the good of the reason is not disturbed, but rather supported." In the contrary case, there is a situation that is "by nature a sin" *(naturaliter peccatum)*. So, for example, acts of intemperance "through which the reason is hindered in its act" and generally "to be subordinated to the emotions, which do not leave the judgment of the reason to exist in freedom: all this is naturally bad."[116]

---

115. This is founded on a theory of knowledge—we can call it "methodical realism" with E. Gilson—which remains unaffected by the Kantian and post-Kantian epistemology as well as later "linguistic turn" theories. That no intelligible content can arise from sense perception is an unproven presupposition of Kantian epistemology taken from Hume, which, as I have already said, takes on the function, for Kant, of an argument that makes his critique of knowledge circular. Kant took over the presuppositions of his argumentation from the rationalism of the Cartesians (for whom all that is intelligible comes from or is produced by the intellect) and from empiricism (for whom "intelligibility" is understood only as a combination of sense data and never goes beyond that). He constructed his theory of knowledge out of these as a combination of sense data plus the *a priori* of the understanding. The alternative would be to return to the doctrine—stemming from Aristotle and in accordance with common sense, but in Kant's day practically forgotten—of the ability of the intellect to abstract intelligible structures from sense data. The doctrine of abstraction was practically forgotten in the eighteenth century by nearly everybody but Thomas Reid; cf. T. Reid, *Essays on the Intellectual Powers* ("Essay Five: Of Abstraction"), in Reid, *Inquiry and Essays*, eds. R. E. Beanblossom and K. Lehrer (Indianapolis, Ind.: Bobbs-Merrill, 1983), 234ff.

116. *Summa contra Gentiles*, III, cap. 129: *Est igitur naturaliter rectum quod sic procuretur ab homine*

This demand for "freedom of the reason" rests on the principle that reason is what guarantees an encounter with the good for man *qua* man. A "depraved" reason is not a "wrongly used" reason. The reason itself cannot in the true sense be misused, but it can find itself in the tow of the nonrational appetites—to which group, as we shall see, even the will can belong—"wrong" or "depraved" reason is *really not reason at all: "ratio corrupta non est ratio."*[117]

More than an "organ" that can be used for this or that purpose, the act of reason and intellect as a whole can be described with the metaphor of *light.* Light cannot be used to darken anything. So long as it is light, it lightens, brightens, makes visible, brings what is hidden into the open. Light can be weaker or more intense, its rays can meet with obstacles, can be dimmed, filtered, or diverted. The intellective faculty is comparable to a light source, its act to a beam of light. Everything that falsifies its act does not come from it, but comes from elsewhere as an obstacle to its own activity. Intellection is the specific power that belongs to man for access to reality, and to what is relevant for him as a whole, in the fullness of its meaning. A "life according to reason" means: living in the truth, in what, and in accord with what, is *worthy* of a human being and fits him in the deepest and truest sense. Again: it does not make any sense to ask how we can know what is rational. First we have to realize that "good" for a human being is what is a "good" object to the reason, and is in this sense "rational." Only then can we ask *under what conditions,* then, are we rational, and do, in fact, live according to reason? Under what circumstances or conditions do we rationally strive for the good, and seek as an ultimate what alone can rationally be striven for as an ultimate? That is the theme of the tradition of ethics that was inaugurated by Socrates, Plato, and Aristotle, but also by the Stoics and Epicureans, only much later to be subjected to a profound reworking by Kant, coming thereby in a certain way to an end, because at that point the question at the center of ethics was no longer about the conditions of rationality, but rather—in the philosophy of subjectivity—about the conditions of the autonomy of the *will.* Nevertheless both traditions are still at one in considering human freedom as existing only on the condition of rationality.[118]

The question about the conditions of rationality is at least in part identical

---

corpus, et etiam inferiores vires animae, quod ex hoc actus rationis et bonum ipsius minime impediatur, magis autem iuvetur: si autem secus acciderit, erit naturaliter peccatum (It is naturally right, therefore, that the body be taken care of by the human being, as well as the lower powers of the soul, so that the act of reason and the good [of the reason] be least interfered with, and helped all the more. When it happens otherwise, it is naturally sinful).

117. In II Sent. D. 24, Q. 3, a. 3, ad 3.

118. In any case, classical virtue ethics is not simply a doctrine about the right affective dispositions, motivations, attitudes, or character qualities, but rather always an ethics of "right reason" *(orthos logos).*

with the following question: What can "disturb" the reason, divert it from the good that is presented to it in the proper way, and thereby provoke "irrationality"? There are two factors to mention here: the emotions (or passions) and the will. And in another respect, there can also be lack of imaginative power *(phantasia)*, and of another inner sense (responsible for organizing sense perceptions), and finally false opinions (erring judgments) or ignorance.

At the same time, it should be emphasized that the emotions and the will, as human givens, are not only that which can "hinder" the reason. They are also the drives through which alone reason can become *practical* and human action can become *good action*. This is not a defense of a rational morality in the sense of a "morality exempt from emotions." On the contrary, the moral ideal of a virtue ethics consists in doing the good—that is, what is according to reason—passionately, or in other words, to act rationally *with* the emotions, or to follow sense appetitions and the dynamic of the will *with* the reason. But what are these "passions" or emotions? And how are we to understand the relationship between reason and will?

b) Passions (Affects, Emotions, and Similar Drives) and Their Influence

Human action is an appetitive phenomenon. Actions springs from practical reason, which is, in turn, a reasoning embedded within striving (appetition) and cognitively guiding this striving. This appetition that is dependent on reason, or *will*, we have already analyzed under various aspects, and in its double dimension as intention and choice of means. Now human appetition is not only "willing." There are also sensitive appetites or sense-powers in the human being, which are immediately connected to the human body and have their origin in it, and in their own way exercise an influence on reason and will.

The phenomenon of reason and will being affected by the actions of these sense powers is known as "passion." Passions, abstractly considered, are drives of the senses, and yet they are also actions that have an effect on reason and will. Reason and will experience this as a *passio,* or "suffering" [Lat. *pati/passus,* "to suffer, experience"], which explains the term "passion."

More exactly: passions are acts or movements of our sense inclinations that are directed toward objects grasped in sense perception. These sense-objects are the particular correlatives of the good (or evil) for each of these inclinations or feelings. There are feelings of attraction or repulsion. We also use the terms "emotions" or "affects." They all have a sensed content and are in some way connected with bodily organs and corporeal contexts, and they reveal themselves mostly through immediate psychological effects. Such passions, to name just a few, are anger, grief, fear, joy, and so on.

Classical anthropology distinguishes two different faculties (corresponding to two basic types of sense-drives) that are responsible for sense appetition, or for such inclinations that bring about passions, affects, emotions, and feelings: *desiring* (the "concupiscible" appetitive power) and the *spirited* (or "irascible") appetitive power (understanding the latter not as a virtuous characteristic but as an appetitive power or "disposition").[119]

As the will is the appetition that depends on the reason—and thus strives for a good that is grasped and judged by the reason—sense appetition of the concupiscible and irascible kinds depend on sense perception. To a sensed object, the concupiscible or "desiring" faculty responds with *love* [*amor*]— here, the emotion—that is, "being-attracted-to," the desiring of an object not yet possessed; or with *joy* [*gaudium*] that is, "enjoyment" of a good that is possessed. A perceived evil provokes repulsion or flight, and the corresponding emotion is *hate* [*odium*], or flight from an evil that is not yet present, and *sadness* [*tristitia* or *dolor*], for an evil that is present. These passions affect the soul as a whole—that is, both will and reason.

A similar situation is to be found with respect to the irascible appetitive power, or "spirited" faculty: this is not related to good or evil simply as such, but toward good and evil insofar as there is *effort* or some *difficulty* to overcome in the very acquiring or avoiding itself of the evil or good. The acts and corresponding emotions toward the good that is difficult to attain [*bonum arduum*] are hope and audacity [*spes, audacia*], and toward the evil that can only be avoided with effort are disappointment, fear, and anger [*desperatio, timor, ira*].

> We use, in part, the same names for analogous acts of the will, which nevertheless are different from the sense-drives and passions, which is also shown in the fact that contrary acts of this kind can simultaneously be present. Thus it is possible (e.g., at the dentist's) to welcome a pain with joy or hope on the level of will, for which we feel repulsion or a desire to flee at the level of sense, and we do this because we know that through suffering the pain we will attain a good, the grasp of which is in any case only possible for the reason.

But how are the passions to be understood, ordered, and evaluated within the context of human action, meaning in the perspective of morality? Are they influences that need to be neutralized as much as possible? Is the human being only then really capable of human action when emotions cease to play a definite role? A "stoic" ethics of "passionlessness" would more or less agree to this. But such an answer would be wrong: for passions are human phenomena. That level of human being from which they originate belongs to the reality

119. On this theme, cf. A. Malo, *Anthropologia dell' affettività* (Rome: Armando, 1999).

of the human person and its "I" (cf. below, 5.e). The passions play a positive role in human action and have to be integrated into it as principles of action. Human action, it is true, must be rational: it is determined and ordered by the reason. But the human being is not some kind of "reason in nature," not least because—as we will see later—reason, too, is "nature" in a certain way. Practical reasoning is the ordering principle of human striving. Before all rationality, the human being is a desiring, striving being. Without this appetitive dynamism of the human being, whose finite existence is really characterized in just this way, by "going after something," by desiring something, there would be no practical reasoning, nor would anyone rationally strive for anything.

Sense appetition (both desiring and spirited) belong to the phenomenon "human being." They are sense drives that orient the person in a specific way to human good, even though it is only through its integration into the order of reason that this good can provide practical orientation and be a drive for human actions. "Passions may well reveal values, but not their hierarchical order . . . [and] there is another point, too. Passions come and go, but values, often the very values revealed to us through passion, are of a lasting nature. If we act only out of passion, we will not be dealing fairly with reality. Feelings of anger may well evaporate, but it might still remain necessary to fight year after year against a particular injustice, by which time the passionate feeling of anger which first made us aware of the situation could well have turned into a calm, deep-seated sense of certainty. If we are only prepared to help people in need when actually feeling the emotion of sympathy, we will soon stop helping anyone at all."[120]

On the other hand, it is also possible to do good and right actions *without* passion and sympathy, even in spite of not having them, but simply because of a rational insight, a "consciousness of duty," and so on. But in this case an essential feature of the complete moral action is missing: the affective *connaturality* with the good, which consists in doing the good not only on the basis of a sense of duty and pure rationality, but rather with one's entire humanity. Whoever acts "dispassionately" runs the risk of acting without heart, and for just this reason misses doing the good in the concrete circumstance: perhaps by a lack of compassionate flexibility, or because it might take too much effort, or because he will not be willing to persist. Simply shutting off the emotions can lead to a stunted humanity.

Emotion is consequently a component of moral maturity. And it belongs to such maturity or fullness, Thomas says, "that man be moved to good not only in accordance with the will, but also in accordance with the sensitive appetite;

120. R. Spaemann, *Basic Moral Concepts*, trans. T. J. Armstrong, 31–32.

as it is written in Psalm 83: 'My heart and my flesh have exulted in the living God,' taking 'heart' to mean the intellective appetite (will) and 'flesh' to mean the sensitive appetite."[121]

Nevertheless, the emotions must be ordered in their appetitive dynamism by the reason. Only then can the entire human person be rational. And this is true in the light of a further consideration: through its integration into the order of reason, sensitive appetition becomes a source of practical knowing and orientation; it retains in this way a cognitive function *as affectivity* and becomes a principle of action. The emotion that has been integrated into the order of reason *shows* the good, indeed the *bonum rationis,* the good according to the reason. The human being as a whole then possesses that affective connaturality with the moral good that enables him or her to grasp and perform with passion what is reasonable, here and now, with ease and spontaneity, and a sure aim. *That* is moral virtue, and a truly human excellence.

Emotions also have a thoroughly positive influence on moral action—in fact, they are indispensable for virtuous action. To the extent that they are integrated into the order of reason they acquire a function that is at once cognitive and appetitive. But that also means that detached from reason and as it were absolutized in their *own* order, they interfere with reason and can exercise a disturbing influence upon the will, or reason-led appetition, whose natural identity consists in an inclination for the human good. Everyone knows this from personal experience.

But how, more precisely, do these interfering influences of the emotions on the reason and will come about? The influence on the will is of an indirect kind: it works by having an influence on rational judgment. Just as the ordered passion supports the judgment of reason, and actually shows it the way, the not-ordered passion can influence the reason's evaluation, can push it around, draw it to its own side. This leads to the so-called *error electionis* or *ignorantia electionis,* to an "error in the choice of action," or an "ignorance in choosing." This is what as a rule (but not entirely correctly) has been called "weakness of the will." What we have here is really not so much a weakness of the will as a subordination of the judgment of reason concerning the "good here and now" to the valuation made by the sense drive. The *consequence,* naturally, is that the act of will as it should have been carried out according to reason does not come into its fullness, and the will follows a judgment of reason that has been compromised by passion. The passion works only indirectly on the will, modifying its object for it through taking over the judgment of reason. This influence of the passions on the will has thus been called an influ-

---

ence *ex parte objecti* (from the object): it is really an influence on the judgment of the reason. Directly and immediately, the will—as a spiritual faculty—cannot be influenced by passion.

This *ignorantia electionis* is one of the great discoveries of Aristotelian ethics. Socrates, and Plato following him, held that virtue consisted in knowledge.[122] They said, roughly, that if someone has knowledge about what is good, he also does what is good. If someone does evil, this is simply caused by ignorance. Aristotle criticizes this position repeatedly, and he does so by distinguishing between two kinds of knowing: the knowledge, on the one hand, of right moral principles (universal kind of knowing) and, on the other hand, the knowledge that constitutes the concrete judgment of action that "p is good" or "p must be done." In this way someone can know that stealing is bad; nevertheless it is possible that, through the influence of desire, this universal knowledge would be cancelled at a certain moment, and the choice of carrying out an actual theft is judged as "good, here and now," so that the action succeeds in being carried out after all. This is a classic case of "incontinence" [*akrasia*],[123] and Aristotle compares the incontinent person with someone who is asleep: he possesses the right knowledge, but is not applying it.

Thomas Aquinas says, therefore, that the practical syllogism carried out by the incontinent person is not composed of three propositions as it normally does, but of four. The (normal) three-part process of the practical reason would work as follows (using an example invented by Aristotle): (1) "It is not good to eat sweets at an inappropriate time (and now is an 'inappropriate time'); (2) *this* is something sweet; (3) *this* is not to be eaten now (the choice of action, or the choice to not-perform the action of eating)." Here the sense perceptions and the desires that belong to them are subordinated to the judgment of reason (1), and this judgment determines, finally, the choice of action, (3). In the case of incontinence, there appears alongside the first premise (1), a second premise (1b), which is an evaluative act of the sense desire, which "says" that "all sweets are very delicious and to be eaten." (1b) can cancel out (1), render it ineffective, and the conclusion or choice of action (3), which is the underlying judgment of practical reasoning, will be determined by premise (1b), which leads in turn to the devouring of the sweet.[124]

---

122. Of course, the teaching was much more complex than this, and Plato's doctrine evolved rather subtly in this respect. The Aristotelian solution is really the final stage of this development. Cf. J. J. Walsh, *Aristotle's Conception of Moral Weakness* (New York and London: Columbia University Press, 1963).

123. Aristotle devotes nearly the entire book VII of the *Nicomachean Ethics* to the analysis of *akrasia*. For a full treatment of this, cf. M. Rhonheimer, *Praktische Vernunft und Vernünftigkeit der Praxis*, 441ff. See also T. Spitzley, *Handeln wider besseres Wissen. Eine DisKussion klassischer Positionen* (Berlin and New York: Walter de Gruyter, 1992).

124. Cf. In VII Ethic., lect. 3.

Whoever does what is evil is in fact ignorant. But this kind of ignorance is not one that has to do with principles, and what happens is not caused by a lack of knowing at this level. This ignorance can also not be warded off by the removal of the specific ignorance through instruction, but only through the ordering of the appetitions or passions, so that "staying awake" can be assured in particular cases. This ordering of the emotions nevertheless does not consist in canceling the emotions, but rather moderating them in such a way that not only the reason "says" (1): "it is not good to eat sweets at inappropriate times," but the sense desire itself also "says" the same. In this consists the moral virtue of moderation (temperance).

The emotions (or passions) do not work directly on the act of the will. On the other hand, the will can exercise an influence upon the passions in an immediate way: it can hold them back, and, in someone with an inclination to incontinence, can help the judgment of reason (1) be successful (and this is not yet virtue, but only "continence"). But the will can also ignore this and agree with ("consent to") the wrong choice of action (3). This is why even an action of incontinence through an ignorance in choice is a willing ignorance, for which one is more or less responsible.

But it is also possible that an emotion by its intensity exercises so much psychic energy and draws so much affective attention to itself that the will does not have any force as a rationally determined drive. In such a case, the question is only whether the emotional stimulation had itself been willed, that is, whether someone was responsible for it or not. If that were not the case, it would no longer be a question of a "human act" at all. In fact, the responsibility for an action can completely disappear through emotion overtaking the judgment of reason, as long as it is not willed: an example would be a sudden onrush of panic.

But this does not mean that an action "based on emotion," in which no judgment of reason but only passion is at work with respect to a concrete action, must be a nonmoral or amoral action. The criterion for the morality of an emotion is its correspondence to reason and not the degree of its intensity or the extent of its influence upon the determination of whether *this* or *that* is to be done. Married persons will normally carry out the act of conjugal union on the basis of sense drives (and that does not mean that they are acting without reason); and they do not do this *on the basis of* a judgment of reason: "it is good now ..." or "our duty is. ..." The question is whether passion (which can indeed also arise with respect to the spouse of one's neighbor) is *according to* reason. *If* it is, then the passion is purely and simply good, and in fact a very human way of doing what is good and according to reason. In the context of conjugal love, Thomas consequently speaks of "an apparent lack of continence," on the basis of which one "will be totally guided by a desire (concupiscence) that corresponds to the order of reason and is therefore good."[125] And *in* the act of conjugal union, for example, Thomas holds, the reason is completely canceled out "because of the intensity of the passion." What is decisive is not that one always acts *on the basis of* a judgment of reason, but that one acts according to the order of reason.[126]

> Nevertheless, Thomas thinks that this shutting off of the reason is flawed. Perfection would require that despite the intense passion the judgment of reason is still preserved, whereby in any event the enjoyment of the experience would be still more complete, namely, because it would be spiritually informed. This is why Thomas also maintains that in the state of original justice the *delectatio* ("enjoyment" or "delight") in the sexual act would had to have been richer and more intensive, not because of a "minus" of sense enjoyment, but because of a "plus" of spiritual content of the sensual actions and a correspondingly higher intensity of affective enjoyment.[127]

Our conclusion from what has been said about the criterion for the moral evaluation of emotion would be as follows: Emotions or passions are to be evaluated morally (1) only insofar as they are voluntary, that is, willed in some way. They are such whenever they are directly chosen and called forth by the will; or in the case when the will accedes to the passion in a spontaneous movement (subsequent consent). Emotions are evaluated (2) according to the object of action, that is, according to their object as they would be judged by the reason. To put it another way, an emotion (and the pleasure that results from it) is exactly as good or bad as the action that follows from it. Finally, emotion is also to be judged according to its intensity: even if the emotion according to its "object" is good, a too intensively heeded emotion can end up falling outside the order of reason. The human being is in a precarious equilibrium. This is why it can be good and necessary to practice self-denial at times, for example, in eating or sexuality, even though *in itself* abstinence is neither a virtue nor in accordance with reason. This would only be unnecessary if the equilibrium were perfectly stable. Thomas thus voices the shrewd and anthropologically deep insight that, in the original, unfallen state of mankind, sexual abstinence would not have been a praiseworthy act, but now it is to be praised, insofar as it exercises mastery over uncontrolled libido.[128]

---

125. II-II, Q. 156, a. 2: The act would not correspond to reason, if, for example, the married couple knew that they had serious reasons to avoid a conception. If the woman knew at the time that she was fertile, the action in accordance with reason would be to abstain.

126. Cf. In IV Sent., D. 26, Q. 1, a. 3 (= Supplementum Q. 41, a. 3, ad 2); and ibid., ad 6. See also In IV Sent., D. 31, Q. 2, a. 1, ad 3 (= Supplementum Q. 49, a. 4, ad 3).

127. Cf. I, Q. 98, a. 2, ad 3.

128. I, Q. 98, a. 2, ad 3.

The situation is similar with regard to anger: it can be "righteous." But whenever somebody always gives in to the feeling of anger, no matter how justified he might be, and does not pull himself back now and then—say, waiting until the feeling passes or "sleeping on it" overnight—such a person will soon be acting without respect toward other persons and will do them injury. But this is only necessary because the human being is never completely perfect, and the equilibrium between reason and emotion is always delicate. If it wasn't for this, it would be good to do anything that anger or the other passions drove us to do.

c) The Will and Its Freedom

The will is *appetitus in ratione,* "appetition in the reason." The will is not an appetitive (or "striving") faculty that is already rational by itself (no "striving" is already rational by itself); it is the appetitive faculty that pursues what the judgment of reason presents to it as "good." That there *is* such an appetition even in the rational "part of the soul" we know from our own inner experience: we are conscious of carrying out acts of striving that are not "determined to one thing only" but are open to many possibilities.

Now this does not mean that the will finds itself in an original indifference and moves with its own spontaneity toward its object. The will is not *pure* spontaneity. To think of the "will" and "freedom" as pure spontaneity in opposition to "nature" is the distinguishing characteristic of Kantian philosophy. As against this, we need to be very clear about something: the will is thoroughly determined by the reason and its judgments about the good; but reason itself possesses an openness to the many: it can have various conceptions of the good. And because the will is a reason-guided appetitive power, it also has the openness that belongs to the reason.[129]

But there is still a certain spontaneity or indetermination "left over" in the act of the will. Namely, the will, as already mentioned, is itself willingly related to its own act. We all necessarily want to be happy, because happiness is that good that the reason sets before the will as what is good in every respect. We cannot rationally will something else *in place of* what the reason has judged as good. But we can, for other reasons, not-will what the reason judges as good. That means that the will can, at times, not-will what it can only rationally strive for, for *other* reasons.

---

129. Cf., once again, the text I-II, Q. 17, a.1, ad 2 which has often been cited before; according to it, the reason is the "cause of freedom" [*causa libertatis*]: "It is because of this that the will can be freely directed to diverse things [*potest ad diversa fieri*]: because the reason can have diverse conceptions of the good [*diversas conceptiones boni*]."

Thus I can recognize that I need to undergo a certain operation in order to be healthy (which is something I want). And now I "will" to have this operation. But soon afterward I learn that the operation is bound up with certain side effects that I shrink from. This leads me *not* to want the operation any longer, although I cannot rationally pursue anything *in place of* the operation. And so although I want to be healthy again, I now, at the level of the means, no longer want to be healthy (because apart from this operation there is no other means available). This means that at the same time I want to be healthy and do not want to be healthy. Under the given circumstances, I do not will "to become healthy." If the will were fully determined by judgments, it would lead to a continuous tug-of-war between two rival acts of the will. But that is not what happens. The willing of health (which follows reason) is dominated by the act of the will "not to will the side effects of an operation" (which likewise follows the reason) and becomes ineffective for action. The will, then, can itself *not* will (at the level of the means) its own act, by which it was directing itself to a good according to a judgment of the reason: it has its power in its own hands, so to speak. The will has dominion over itself, or more precisely, man possesses in his will a mastery over his own willing.[130] Ultimately this freedom is grounded, in turn, in the fact that the will can only be determined by the reason, but reason reflects on its own judgments, and so itself becomes the object of an act of judgment. Thus "the root of all freedom consists in the reason": *totius libertatis radix est in ratione constituta.*[131]

Nevertheless, the above example, as has been noticed, is still an example that shows how the will is determined by the reason. For, according to the example, the will-to-become-healthy is no longer willed because "avoiding the side effects of the operation" is *preferred*. This preferential choice is founded in turn on a judgment of reason, which is what occurs in such a case, even though, as here, it can come into play on the basis of an emotion (e.g., fear). Where, then, is that leftover spontaneity of the will?

Let's assume I do want to become healthy, and, recognizing that the operation is a good, that is, that it is the only means, or the only way, to reach this goal, and nothing else prevents me, I would, insofar as I behave rationally, agree to have the operation. As stated before, there is nothing that I could rationally want to do *in place of* the operation. Nevertheless, I can, without any further "reasons," simply *not* want to do it. That would be irrational. But it is possible.

How can this be explained? To direct action according to what is rationally

---

130. Cf. also *De Malo*, Q. 6, a. unicus.
131. *De Veritate*, Q. 24, a. 2.

recognized as "good" means directing oneself according to recognized truth (and what is recognized as good is a form of truth indeed, even when it is good only under certain circumstances). To do what one has recognized as good and because one has recognized it as good—to act according to recognized truth—is the essence of that attitude that we call *humility*. Humility (which includes docility) is a kind of subordination to acknowledged truth. The will, whose act is nothing other than "love" (since every willing is a form of love), can prefer the "pure freedom of its own act" to subordinating itself to what it recognizes as good, and not on the basis of a judgment of reason, but on the basis of its spontaneity. This preference would be an act of pride or arrogance, the Augustinian *curvatio in seipsum* ["a bending-in-upon-oneself"], a kind of hidden self-centeredness. It is a case here of "I do not want," and this not-wanting is absolutely irrational. If, then, I do not even want to do something else *in place of* what reason recognizes as good, I can always simply not-will this recognized good. In order to bring the willing of what is rationally recognized as good effectively into action, the will must again "in pure freedom" agree to will that willing. This act of agreeing to will, as long as we act rationally, is usually not explicitly carried out. But the not-agreeing-to-will is explicit and conscious.

There are certain cases where the mere "I simply refuse" is apparent: in the case of children, for instance, or when some other person points out to us what is good to do and we fully recognize that the person is right, but we still refuse, simply *because* somebody else had to tell us (and we don't feel "free" anymore). It can also be the case that the will habitually prefers the pure spontaneity of its own act more than what the reason presents to it as good. The will would then pursue the good only under the condition that it did not come to it from "outside" itself as it were, that is, through reasoning. It would do what is good only under the stipulation: "p is good, *because I want to do it*," but is not ready to do it when "p is good, *because it is good*." This is arrogance or pride. In it purest form, an ethics in which freedom is identified with arrogance would be Sartre's "humanistic existentialism," according to which "freedom, in respect of concrete circumstance, can have no other end and aim but itself."[132] Kant's "autonomy of the will" is less unlike this than it may at first appear.

The will therefore possesses a double freedom: first, the "freedom of specification," which is identical with the openness of reason itself. In this sense, the will is exactly as free as the reason "is open to many things." With this kind of freedom we do not will what the reason necessarily recognizes as good, as,

132. J.-P. Sartre, "Existentialism and Humanism," trans. P. Mairet, 43.

for example, happiness; likewise we do not will "self-preservation" or "community life." This is because, rationally, the will cannot strive for anything *in place of* such goods. Secondly, the will possesses the "freedom of execution," to the extent that it has its own willing under its own control. And this is why we can say that the will pursues, with freedom, that which, at the same time, it pursues out of necessity, when seen from the point of view of the "what" specified for it by the reason. For nothing can compel the will to actually will and carry out what is recognized as good. Moreover, it can also at any time not-will, at the level of means, what it wills at the level of the goal/intention.[133]

> The spontaneity of the will's "freedom of execution" shows three things: (1) here is grounded the real cause of the freedom of every act of choice. (2) There is a certain primacy of the will: in order to do what the reason judges as "good," someone must finally *want* to do it. Reason *alone*, that is, rational arguments, are not capable of triggering any action. (3) The will can basically pursue more than only that which reason is able to reveal as good. This last point means that the appetitive dynamic of the will can be disposed through things like sympathy (connaturality with the appetition, feelings, sorrows, joys, etc., of *other* human beings): or through love, that is, attention given to another as the "good." Here is to be found, certainly, that possibility of openness of the will to be informed and dynamicized, which the Christian tradition calls *caritas* (supernatural love), and that makes possible the "wisdom of the heart" that reaches beyond the nature of the will. Of course in this way the reason is not in the least "shut off." Rather, it is, as it were, raised to another level, or affectively guided, *on the basis of the will's initiative.* It was, doubtless, Augustine's achievement to have overcome the one-sided emphasis of the Platonic-Aristotelian tradition on the role of the passions.[134]

Since the mere "I will not" is always *against* the reason, while the will by its nature is "appetition in reason," the act of "pure freedom" that consists in mere willing in independence of reason—Kant's "transcendental freedom"—is a failure to realize freedom as *rational.* It is an act of the free will, to be sure, but not a realization of freedom because to "realize freedom" means to will and to do *what is known to be good.* The will realizes freedom, then, when it consents to that appetition or striving that is determined through what is rec-

133. Cf. also *De Malo,* ibid.

134. A. MacIntyre recalls this quite rightly in *Whose Justice? Which Rationality?* chap. 9, 146–63. For a full treatment of this subject in Aquinas, see M. Sherwin, *By Knowledge and by Love: Charity and Knowledge in the Moral Theology of St. Thomas Aquinas* (Washington, D.C.: The Catholic University of America Press, 2005). Höffe's view, that a rehabilitation of Aristotelian ethics is only possible at the cost of giving up the concept of the will (cf. O. Höffe, *Categorical Principles of Law: A Counterpoint to Modernity* (University Park: Pennsylvania State University Press, 2002) is certainly due to his Kantian approach and may be countered by maintaining that the Kantian concept of the will is not the only one available.

ognized as good through the reason, that is, when it is humble. The scriptural verse "The truth shall make you free" (John 8:32) finds here its anthropological and ethical foundation. Willing what is acknowledged as good corresponds to the nature of the will. Thus Thomas can say that what the will pursues with necessity, because the reason necessarily judges it as good, the will pursues at the same time with freedom.[135]

Even the pure "I refuse" on the basis of a mere willing of independence and spontaneity in one's own act of willing is necessarily dependent on that striving that necessarily belongs to us all: the desire for happiness as a seeking of the satisfaction of the will through the good. The act of pride presupposes the necessity of the desire for happiness, and at the same time is the act that is most distantly removed from the fulfillment of this striving. For everything that we in any way conceive to be good on the basis of reason, no matter how distorted or blinded the judgment might be, possesses at least a glimmer of true happiness. It is only the act of pride, the willing of a pure spontaneity and independence of the will, that has no light of reason: it is the absolute and totally irrational, the "darkness" of mere fundamentally disordered self-love, as well as "evil" and "guilt." For evil is the lack of goodness, and "guilt" is the absence of due orientation of the will toward the good, which is of course the good recognized through the reason. In the act of pride, nevertheless, true freedom as self-determination toward what is known as good is replaced by a freedom that ultimately only recognizes self-determination as good. This is the kind of autonomy that finally must turn *against* reason.

d) Will, Reason, and Emotions

The will not only has dominion over itself: it also has dominion over all other powers of the soul. First, over the act of the intellect: *Intelligo enim quia volo:* "I understand, because I want to." This sentence does not come from Descartes, but from Thomas Aquinas.[136] And here we find another possibility for the will: on the basis of pure "not-willing" of what is known as good, to "control" the act of reason oneself, whether it be through mere neglect: *Was ich nicht weiß, macht mir nicht heiß* ["what I don't know, makes little difference to me"] and thereby lead oneself into a state of ignorance, or through a kind of instrumentalizing of reason. In this way, we make a judgment of the kind "p is good, because I want it to be," in which the reason, under the influence of the will, tries to find reasons to justify its own spontaneity. The reason here

---

135. Cf. *De Potentia* Q. 10, a. 2: *unde voluntas libere appetit felicitatem, licet necessario appetit illam.*
136. *De Malo*, Q. 6, a. unicus.

falls victim to the undertow of pride, which is thus revealed as a strategy for voluntary self-deception.

But the will has mastery also over the passions. It can "want" to perform the acts of the sensitive appetites. That is again a complicated process: the acts of the sensitive desires are not an object of the will as such. But the will can exercise an influence upon the judgment of reason, and in such a way that this judgment is "subjected" to the sense desire. The will dominates the passions by influencing the judgment of reason upon them. The incontinent action and the *ignorantia electionis* connected with it, as analyzed above, is a *willing* act. It does not involve an ignorance that excuses but a kind of ignorance that is itself a flaw and constitutes blameworthiness (see below, V.2.b).

The will can therefore directly choose a passion. It can even trigger it, by having recourse to the sense power of imagination (fantasy). We know about this sort of thing from our personal experience. And as has been said, the moral evaluation depends on the criteria that were mentioned. It can be very good to choose an emotion or to provoke one through imagination: the effort to imagine the actual sufferings of another person can bring compassion and stir up resolve, lending the necessary courage to do the right and appropriate thing. In this way reason can be turned to the truly good and the will can be directed accordingly. But ultimately, the judgment of reason is decisive; when it is missing, compassion and courage can lead to injustice.

Through the will, then, the striving human being has mastery over his urges and his actions. By its "nature," however, the will is an appetitive, striving power that follows reason. And *if* the will actually follows the reason, then it also *orders* all striving and doing according to the good provided through the reason, that is, the good in reality.

The will, in a certain way, is the soul of human action; when the will is good, action is good. The will governs action, guides it, *commands* it ("consent" is a kind of borderline case). The will exercises an influence over action that Thomas calls *imperium* (or "command").

But when, and why, is the will good? This is where everything depends on the reason. In this regard the reason emerges as the "commander" and as a *formal* element: as the authority that orders action by directing the will to the good. This "ordering" of the act of the will, and through it, the acts of the other powers all the way down to the bodily organs (as long as they are subject to the will) is likewise an *imperium:* a kind of (rational) ordering toward the good.

The command *(imperium)* of the (practical) reason is an act of the reason, but insofar as the reason is moved by the will.[137] It corresponds to the concept

---

137. Cf. I-II, Q. 17, a. 1.

we have analyzed above: the practical reason that is "embedded" in appetition, which both moves and orders further appetitions.

The command of the will as ordered by reason opens up the true perspective of praxis. The will moves us to intend something, to seek for means, to judge them, to find out the good, and finally to choose and do it. The will makes all these elements blend into a unity. It is the soul of action, and through it, the great variety of actions of a human being are accomplished in the unity of a lifetime.

Traditionally, the act of the will that the will carries out *as will*, which the will brings out of itself, so to speak, is called the *actus elicitus* the "elicited act" of the will: willing, loving, intending, choosing, hating, wishing, and so on. Acts of other powers or organs that are carried out through a command of the will and insofar as they are subject to such a command are known as the *actus imperati,* or "commanded acts" of the will.[138] In this respect, the movement of an arm in the context of a human action is likewise an act of the will. Even an act of knowing, too, insofar as it is subject to an act of the will, is an *actus imperatus* of the will, and consequently a "human action" capable of moral evaluation. This applies even to the making of a chair or the starting of an automobile engine: most voluntary actions that we carry out are such external actions ("external" for the will). The will is here the "form," the faculty or organ moved by the will is the "matter." But the intentional identity of the action, and its moral identity as well, depend on the reason. For the will is reason-guided striving.[139]

> With this understanding, the opposition between causal and intentional clarifications of action can once again be overcome. The two explanations each explain something *different*. Intentional explanations tell us something about the *content* (the "what") of an action, because they clarify actions by way of the reasons why they were carried out. But "reasons" do not *cause* any actions, no more so than mere reasoning can move someone to action. Causal explanations, on the other hand, try to explain how it comes about that someone does something. "Causalists" then designate as causal those very "reasons" to which the intentionalists rightly assign no causality, because they are in fact *components* of the action. Thus intentionalists are forced, in the tradition of Wittgenstein, to identify "doing and willing." Causalists, on the other hand, tend, on the basis of their understanding of causality, to materialistic or mechanistic positions. The classical doctrine about the interaction and mutual dependence of reason (formal reason of actions) and will (principle of movement) is revealed here to be essentially more differentiated and also make bet-

138. Cf. also S. Brock, *Action and Conduct,* 171ff.
139. This aspect appears to me to have been largely neglected by Brock (see note above).

ter sense of the phenomena, while staying free of the quandaries of analytical action theory.

What has just been pointed out applies not only to "actions" in the strict sense of the word (external actions) but also to acts of the intellect and sense desire, the passions. Insofar as the passions are subject to the imperium of the will (and the borderline case is again mere consent, which in a second phase can expand to a fully fledged imperium), the act of the emotion—the corresponding sense appetite as such—is an *actus imperatus* of the will. Human knowing, striving, and acting thereby attain in the will to that *unity* that must always be thought of whenever we think of the elements of action. The concrete formation of this unity is not given in nature (even if there are preliminary elements that are naturally conditioned, as we have seen). This formation is of course dependent on the reason, that is open to many things and possesses in itself unlimited possibilities of ordering one thing to another: emotional impulses; elements of matters of action; acts of corporal organs; means and ends; and so on.

It is useful to introduce the notion of the command or *imperium* of the will in order to know that we are always referring to an "organism" of virtues when we speak of the single virtues. "Prudence," "justice," "temperance," and "courage" are not a mere collection of various "rules of action," isolated basic attitudes or normative principles floating in a void, but are instead components of an acting-organism, of a life story or biography (whose soul is the reason-guided will), as well as definite kinds of practice in society.[140] The formation by reason decides concerning the "what" of action, its objective specification. The formation by will decides concerning whether or not, and to what extent, a "human action" is done at all. In order for the will to be "a good will," that is, in order for it to be really rational, the acting subject has need of virtues.

e) Human Nature and Ethics. The Concept of the Person

From the foregoing anthropology of moral action arises a methodological consequence, which it will be helpful to clarify; what is said about this now will be looked into more deeply at a later stage (V.1).

We saw, then, that philosophical ethics has its origin in the question about what is good for man, and that means the good that is the object of his action: the good, therefore, that he can realize *through* action. Now for every being, good is that which corresponds to its "nature." By "nature" one means the

---

140. This is exactly what A. MacIntyre was concerned with in his *After Virtue*.

essence of a being, insofar as this essence is the principle of a being's operation. "Nature as principle" here means the point of departure that endows the activity of a being, constituted according to a definite species, with its peculiar character: the classical formula for this idea is *agere sequitur esse:* "doing follows being" (or "doing reflects being").

Thomas tells us that the nature of a being is determined on the basis of its substantial form, and that in the case of the human being, this form is rational. Therefore, he concludes, the good for man is determined according to reason. To act according to nature, or to govern one's doing according to one's being, means, in the human being, nothing other than to act according to reason. And we act "against nature" insofar as we act in contradiction to the order of reason.[141]

But the essence of things as such is unknown to us: we recognize it on the basis of the faculties or powers that arise from this essence and from their acts, and by these, the basic underlying nature is revealed.[142] The way to the investigation of nature leads, consequently, by way of the analysis of the actions peculiar to the subject in question. And that means, in all cases of natural processes (except for the human being), identifying what is "normal"— what happens regularly and for the most part. And precisely what is "for the most part" what happens "as a rule" one way or another, is what is characteristic, what is according to nature and purposeful.[143] This is possible because natural processes are determined in general to the good that is peculiar to a definite kind of being.

Now the human being acts on the basis of reason, and reason is "open to many possibilities," making it possible to "have diverse conceptions of the good."[144] Exactly because of this, in the case of man "the normal situation" or the "regularly appearing" is not a compelling criterion for the determining of what is characteristic of man, or what is good or natural. It is the other way around: only the knowledge of what is good can allow us to conclude what is proper to man, what is normal for him, and what natural, and hence wherein lies the perfection that accords with human nature.

And really this is why there is such a thing as ethics. Ethics is not natural philosophy or natural science, even when someone treats it naturalistically.[145]

141. I-II, Q. 71, a. 2.

142. Cf. *De Veritate,* Q. 10, a. 1.

143. Aristotle, *Physics* II, 8. Also cf. R. Spaemann and R. Löw, *Die Frage Wozu? Geschichte und Wiederentdeckung des teleologischen Denkens* (Munich and Zürich: Piper, 1981); see also the article "Teleologie," likewise by R. Spaemann, in H. Seiffert and G. Radnitzky, eds., *Handlexikon zur Wissenschaftstheorie* (Munich: Ehrenwirth, 1989).

144. I-II, Q. 17, a. 1, ad 2: *ratio potest habere diversas conceptiones boni.*

145. Cf., e.g., the behavioristic ethics of John Dewey, *Human Nature and Conduct* (New York: Holt,

In the analysis of the activities of nonrational living things—to pass from the normal to what is proper and peculiar, to what is good for them (because purposeful) and thereby conclude about what is natural to such things—physics, chemistry, biology, behavioral psychology, and the like will suffice: a kind of *historia animalium*. We can come to a grasp of the nature of such beings through observation and description.

Ethics, however, is the science that emerges from this very rationality of the human being: his freedom. We cannot describe or observe it on the basis of "natural processes," but can only reconstruct it through reflection upon the activity of our own practical reasoning. This is the only way to ground what is good for man, and finally to determine by inference what is natural for him.

The concept of "human nature" is consequently not the concept of a mere naturally given or natural teleology, but rather includes the ordering-normative function of reason. "Human nature" is to be found only where the reason that belongs to this nature has ordered what is merely natural according to reason. Only the rational is natural here, and what is natural to the human being is precisely the rational. For this reason it is completely impossible to *derive* what is good and according to nature from the peculiar features of nature, because what is naturally proper to man—and thereby the human good and natural—is only what has been ordered through reason. It is only *virtue* or, at least, actions carried out *virtuously*.

As paradoxical as this may sound, we first must know "what is good for man" in order to know what "human nature" is at all, or to make an adequate interpretation of it. An understanding of human nature is one of the outcomes of ethics, not the starting point.

For the most part we have already been concerned in the course of our analysis with nothing but "human nature." And this shows how mistaken would be any attempt to present "human nature" as the "norm" or "measure" of moral good. Such attempts, like the attempts to show evil as what is "contrary to nature," would remain mere empty formulas unless we added that "human nature" is really that kind of nature in which the good that is according to nature is only determined and regulated by the *reason* that belongs to this nature. This is why ethics is neither natural science nor philosophy nor a metaphysics of good. It does not treat of an order that *is*, Thomas says, which human reason discovers and affirms, but rather an order which the reason *establishes* in the acts of the will.[146] This ordering is the ordering of moral virtue. If ethics is intended to be an instruction on what is good with respect to hu-

---

1922) 296: "Moral science is not something with a separate province. It is a physical, biological and historic knowledge placed in a human context where it will illuminate and guide the activities of man."

146. Cf. In I Ethic., lect. 1.

man nature, it can only be this as an instruction on moral virtue. That is, it can only be a *practical* philosophy in the sense of a reflection on human action and the practical reasoning that guides this action, and not a deduction of what ought to be from what is. The human nature and human existence that we call upon as decisive for establishing morality is always already an *interpreted* human nature.[147] That such recourse to an "ontological concept of perfection . . . has an unavoidable propensity to get involved in a circle and cannot avoid covertly presupposing the morality which it is supposed to explain"[148] was Kant's correct criticism of the academic philosophy of his time.

In connection with the question, for example, whether marriage is natural for the human being, Thomas Aquinas says, in contrast, that something is "natural" in two senses: first, what is caused by necessity through natural principles. Thus it is natural for fire to move "upward." Secondly, we can call "natural" "what nature tends toward, but which is only completed by free will; this is how the acts of the virtues are natural. And in this way, marriage is natural."[149] Free will is reason-guided striving; the good that is objectifiable to reason is by no means simply derivable from the inclination of nature. In order to establish the "naturalness" of marriage, Thomas has *arguments* that reconstruct the knowing-process of the reason (the "natural reason") that also belongs to human nature. Only in the light of these structures of reasoning can the inclination of "nature"—as what is according to nature for man—be *interpreted* as "human nature" (cf. below, V.1.e).

Recourse to human nature can never serve as an *argument* for establishing what is "according to nature" in the sense of what is good for man. Such recourse has another function altogether: it is an argument against ethical relativism and extrinsicism.[150] In other words, it points out that the good for man has to do with what man *is,* with the truth of his being *(agere sequitur esse)*—an ontological truth—and that therefore there are moral standards that are not simply to be instrumentalized and which have validity completely independently of human positing or of divine revelation. *What* this ontological standard contains, however, nobody can obtain through recourse to "human nature" or a mere "ontology"; what is needed instead is an investigation or hermeneutics of human nature in the light of the structures of reason.

Now this does not at all mean, that there is not also, besides what is ordered through the reason, something "natural" in human nature, in the sense

147. Cf. also M. Rhonheimer, *Natural Law and Practical Reason,* 16–22.
148. I. Kant, *Groundwork of the Metaphysics of Morals,* trans. M. Gregor, 49.
149. In IV Sent., Dist. 26, Q. 1, a. 1 (= Supplementum Q. 41, a. 1).
150. In another place I call this an "external recourse" to human nature, as distinct from an "internal recourse." See M. Rhonheimer, "Zur Begründung sittlicher Normen aus der Natur," in J. Bonelli, ed., *Der Mensch als Mitte und Maßstab der Medizin* (Vienna and New York: Springer Verlag, 1992), 39–94.

of natural presuppositions and natural givens, which along with special natural processes are ordered to a "good that comes from nature." Such would be, of course, a component of human good as a natural drive or inclination, but it is still not the specifically human good, and in this sense natural (cf. below, V.1.d).

It is a component, because the human being is not merely spirit in a body. Man is neither "spirit in the world" (K. Rahner), nor "reason in nature" (W. Korff). Man does not only *have* a body, drives, sense organs, but *is* all these. He does not belong to the *genus* of spirits, but rather to the genus of *animalia* [cf. Lat. *anima,* "be-souled things"]. The human being is a reason-endowed living thing (a mammal), an *animal rationale,* a spiritually ensouled body.[151] The human "I" can therefore be identified neither with soul nor spirit: *anima mea non est ego:* "My soul is not identical with my 'I.'"[152] The human being is a substantial unity of body and soul. We call this unity a *human person.* Within it, "nature" has a spiritual dimension and "soul" has a natural dimension, in complete contrast to the dualism current in modern thinking that starkly opposes "nature" to "spirit."[153]

It is certainly true that the specifically personal is the spiritual. Therefore, philosophically speaking, merely spiritual persons are also conceivable. Nevertheless, "being a *human* person" is not "being a spirit." The human being is a person *because of* his spirit, perhaps, but a "human person" is the *whole* human being as body-soul unity. Consequently, when we speak of the human being, we cannot speak of what is "natural" in man as "subpersonal" or as "standing beneath" him. What is "subpersonal" or "nonpersonal" is only that nature that we are *not,* that is, our nonhuman environment. "Person" is always the concrete individual: in the case of the human being it is the substantial unity of spiritual soul and body. These *together* constitute the human "I." Hence Thomas Aquinas held the view that the *anima separata,* the human soul as divided from its body at death, could not be called a person. It is only the soul of someone who was a person.[154]

Human reason as a standard is therefore always the reason of a human

151. Cf. D. Braine, *The Human Person: Animal or Spirit* (South Bend, Ind.: University of Notre Dame Press, 1992) and A. MacIntyre, *Dependent Rational Animals: Why Human Beings Need the Virtues* (Chicago and La Salle, Ind.: Open Court, 1999).

152. Thomas Aquinas, *Commentary on the First Letter to the Corinthians,* 15, lectio 2.

153. This idea was formulated by R. Spaemann, *Happiness and Benevolence,* 162. A thoughtful and fascinating attempt to think through, once again, the classical unity of animality and rationality can be found in J. McDowell, *Mind and World* (Cambridge, Mass.: Harvard University Press, 1994), esp. lectures IV and VI.

154. I, Q. 29, a. 1, ad 5. See also W. Kluxen, "Anima Separata und Personsein bei Thomas Von Aquin," in W. P. Eckert, ed., *Thomas von Aquino, Interpretation und Rezeption* (Mainz: Matthias Grünewald, 1974), 96–116.

person: of an entity constituted of body and soul. For the rational being that is man, therefore, bodiliness, senses, affects, drives, and the like are not the "environment," something "foreign," but rather are constitutive elements of his "I." They are not the field of subject matter for his actions, but the *principles* of his actions. Corporeal actions of a human being are consequently by their structure and teleological ordering always personal acts. This means that they are such as to be carried out in accordance with the body-soul unity of the human person, and as corporeal acts they are *at the same time* spiritual acts. The concept of moral virtue reflects this anthropological foundation. Moral virtue is the ultimate personal fulfillment of the body-soul unity, in which sense perception as well becomes a reason-shaped principle for action. The principles of practical reason, to be analyzed last, will once more reveal that the "nature" that man himself *is*, must likewise be a constitutive component and principle of the good for man, if reason and "spirit" are not going to operate in a vacuum.

IV

THE MORAL VIRTUES

1. The Concept of Moral Virtue

a) Preliminary Remarks on the Concept of Virtue

According to the classical/eudaimonistic approach, ethics is the doctrine about the good in which we can find our happiness as free, rational beings. But "happiness," we noted, is not simply subjective contentment, but rather the fulfillment of striving or appetition in accordance with rational standards. This means that in ethics we are concerned with analyzing the conditions for the "truth of subjectivity." Now a virtue ethics maintains that these conditions are to be found above all in the possession of virtue. According to the classical understanding, moral virtues are characteristic of the disposition of human persons, to whom what is really and rationally good also *seems* (subjectively) good. *Moral virtues are the affective condition for the rationality of acting subjects.* They guide the acting subject affectively toward the good and in this way empower the practical reason, especially its ability to recognize what is morally right concretely and in detail, and effectively to carry it out. This is how they have a double task, functioning anthropologically and cognitive/practically, and they do so (this is what needs to be shown) without making superfluous the concept of moral duty or a rational discourse about principles.

Moral virtues are a condition for the rationality of the acting subject in a twofold sense: on the level of universal principles, they provide an affective orientation toward what is rational, while on the level of concrete, particular action, they provide cognitive empowerment through the right motivational, affective disposition of the subject. In this way rationality (the cognitive aspect) and habitual affective disposition (the motivational aspect) are closely intertwined, in a classical, Aristotelian kind of circularity. Both aspects are right: moral virtue is a habitual disposition of the subject according to principles that are rationally transparent and accessible to an argumentative discourse (also intelligible as norms or rules, in a derived sense); at the same time, moral virtue is also itself an affective principle of knowing what is right in each case in the realm of immediate concrete actions. This is how what is virtuous in each case is also "what is obligatory," "what ought to be done," or the dutiful thing—not, however, understood as something in opposition to subjective desire, but rather, to the extent that the subject is virtuous, as "something obligatory," "what ought to be done," or "dutiful" that is adequate to this striving, feeling, and willing.[1]

"Virtue," however, is not only "moral virtue." In its most general meaning the word *virtue* [Ger. *Tugend*] refers to the perfect operation of some faculty. The relevant faculties are intellect (both speculative and practical), will, concupiscible appetitive power (sense desire), and irascible appetitive power. The German word *Tugend* does not express anything of the original Greek *aretē* or of the Latin *virtus*. *Aretē* means fittingness, thoroughness, what is highly valued. *Virtus* comes from the Latin word for man *(vir)* and originally meant manliness or courage, but then simply fittingness, excellence, moral perfection. *Arete* and *virtus* indicated the excellence of the human being as such. Somebody who was virtuous was not—in this classical sense—someone who lived a "blameless life," in the sense of not being blamed for anything, someone, perhaps, who was dear and beloved even if he hadn't done much with his life, but rather it was somebody who used his human ability for a good end, who did what was good with mastery, consistency, and joy, who was competent and had his wits about him, was knowledgeable and had the ability to size up situations quickly and correctly; in short, someone who realized what Aristotle called "the good life" and *eupraxia*. The good life is a life ordered by the demands of reason, and for this reason a life that was valued as fortunate—not fortunate because such a life is unconditionally the most successful, but because we think that it did succeed. Therefore, Aristotle explains in a seemingly paradoxical fashion, we can only really call someone happy with certainty after his life is over. That of course is the perspective of an observer. From the point of view of the first person we should add: the success of each person's own life can be known even during this life. It is revealed in the experience of meaningfulness.[2]

---

1. In most contemporary versions of virtue ethics, these two aspects seem rather to be left unreconciled; the conventional concept of virtue makes it difficult to understand them as a unity. Cf., e.g., the strict division between the "aretaic" aim, centered on motives and character traits, and the "deontological" aim, concentrating on rules of action, in N. J. H. Dent, *The Moral Psychology of the Virtues* (Cambridge: Cambridge University Press, 1984). For a critique of Dent, see K. Baier, "Radical Virtue Ethics," in French et al., eds., *Ethical Theory, Character and Virtue* (South Bend, Ind.: University of Notre Dame Press, 1988), 126–35, here 132ff. The set of problems is fully dealt with from the perspective of the contemporary "virtue ethics" school in M. Slote, *From Morality to Virtue* (Oxford: Oxford University Press, 1991).

2. That the question about the happiness or the good life under the empirical conditions of a life

b) The Difference between Dianoetic (Intellectual) and Moral (Ethical) Virtues

Virtues are perfections of those faculties that are dedicated to activity *(operatio)*. There are, to be sure, operative faculties that do not require such perfection because they naturally perform their activities perfectly. There is no virtue of seeing or tasting. Of course the activities of these powers may be more or less perfect, but this depends on the physiological state of the corporeal organ.

The sensitive appetitive powers likewise require in themselves no operational perfecting: they work with a natural spontaneity, and here too what is "better" and "worse" depends on physiological dispositions (which can be modified in various ways through habit). As faculties of a human person the sensitive appetitive powers nevertheless acquire their final perfection only through integration into the order of reason: through the orientation of their striving-dynamism toward what the reason had judged as good (the *bonum rationis*). For this they need virtue as a perfection that points beyond the nature of the power.

Something similar is true about the will: this power, by its nature, strives after the good of reason, but it does this with the constancy of a naturally given disposition only to the extent that there exists a relationship of fittingness or proportion between it (as the appetition of an individual) and the good that is sought. By nature there exists such a proportion between the act of the will and what is good only for the striving person as such. With constancy, then, the will only seeks one's own good, as self-preservation or recognition and assistance from others. But in order for the will to seek what is good for others as well, and with the same constancy—with a kind of natural constancy, even—it needs another perfection in addition: the virtue of justice (cf. below, IV.3.d).

The virtues of the appetitive powers (the sense powers of desire, the irascible power, and the will) are called *moral or ethical virtues* as in the Greek expression *aretē ethikē:* excellence of the *ethos,* or character, of affective dispositions or accustomed inclinations. Moral virtue is the excellence of what a human being customarily does, and to which he is inclined by his disposition. The Latin *virtus moralis* expresses something similar [*mos, moris:* "custom," "habit"]. Clearly the etymology is only of secondary relevance here.

Distinct from these are the so-called *intellectual virtues* (virtues of the understanding: called *dianoetic* by Aristotle): they are the corresponding operative excellence of the intelligence, not only theoretical but practical as well. The intellect possesses a natural orientation toward the knowledge of first

---

still being lived coincides essentially with the question of meaning has been correctly noted, in my opinion, by U. Wolf, *Die Philosophie und die Frage nach dem guten Leben,* 19f.

principles (both speculative and practical). It grasps these spontaneously in a way, and needs no further formation beyond that. But this does not hold for knowledge that is *on the basis of* such principles and by means of which further sense perceptions are disclosed, that is, for the actual inventive process of the reason as it draws conclusions (the *dianoia*).

The virtues of the theoretical intellect are called *wisdom (sophia/sapientia)* and *science (epistēmē/scientia)*. These virtues perfect the intellect in its grasping and processing of truth. In regard to knowledge of the ultimate and highest causes, we speak of the virtue of wisdom; it possesses an architectonic (i.e., ordering, judging) function in relation to all other knowledge. In regard to the knowledge of reality "from there down," the intellect is perfected through the various sciences, as numerous as the various categories of what is to be known. In this sense, for example, the knowledge and intellectual abilities that belong to the historian, the physicist, and so on are various kinds of intellectual virtues.

The practical intellect is perfected through the virtues of *art (technē/ars)* and *prudence (phronēsis/prudentia)*, whereby, in the case of art, one might better say *"poietic"* (or "making") intellect. The word *virtue* (and the German *Tugend* as well) is of course scarcely used anymore with respect to artistic practice (and "technique"); and the same might be said for wisdom and science. But our concern is not with words but with things and concepts: the virtue of an artist is the sense of fittingness or perfection of the intellect (and more precisely, the reason) with respect to "making" *(poiein/facere)*, or *recta ratio factibilium*, a mixture of knowing and skillfulness. Prudence, by contrast—likewise a much misused word—is fittingness or perfection of the reason with respect to "doing" *(prattein/agere)*, or the choice of good actions: *recta ratio agibilium*.

With the exception of the understanding of principles and prudence, we can leave the other intellectual virtues aside in the present context, where our concern is with philosophical ethics. Among the intellectual virtues, prudence has a special standing: while it is a perfection of reason, this perfection is nevertheless conditioned by affective dispositions (which does not apply to the other intellectual virtues). Prudence in its true sense is the virtue of practical reasoning, which, as we have seen, is embedded in the process of striving, the affective dynamic of appetition. But prudence is not only dependent on this power: as the virtue of the practical reason, it is also the perfection of the power that cognitively guides that appetition. This is why prudence is also numbered among the moral virtues. Indeed, it is the moral virtue par excellence, since a bad man cannot really be prudent. It is the "right reason of that which is to be done" *(recta ratio agibilium)*.

In any case, virtue is the perfection of an operative power, a perfection that is not already given in the nature of the power, and which brings it about that the power can execute the actions specific to that power in a more perfect manner. No matter how intelligent someone may be, without study, exercise, and experience, he cannot become an excellent mathematician, architect, or whatever. Without knowledge, exercise, and experience, nobody can become a good human being, either, and that means always—or at least for the most part—to judge what is good and right in *concrete action* and to do it. For a good person is not only someone who knows what is good to do in general, but who knows what to do here and now; and who not only knows it, but effectively *performs* it as well.

And what kind of perfection or "fulfillment" are we speaking of exactly, when we speak of virtue? It is a perfection that is something more than the power or faculty itself; and yet, it is still less than the "good act" of the power. The mathematician's perfection is something more than merely "being smart," and something less than the accomplishment of real actions of mathematical knowledge or calculation. For a mathematician is still a mathematician when he sleeps or plays tennis, or carries out actions that have nothing to do with mathematics. And the same goes for all other virtues, considering that acts of moral virtue play some kind of role in all human actions. Playing tennis, even apart from the athletic skill, is also a human action: you pursue the goal of playing the sport in order, for example, to earn your living or to get some refreshing exercise, or to cultivate friendship. And architects do not limit themselves only to the building of houses; they also seek something else by the means of "building houses" as well, that is not simply "building houses"; and this can be done justly or unjustly. But virtues are always perfections of a power or faculty, which make it possible to carry out well the acts that correspond to that power or faculty, but at the same time this virtue is not the same thing as the execution of those acts.

Such a perfection or fulfillment is known as a *habitus,* a kind of stable disposition or acquired tendency toward accomplishing a definite kind of actions, which makes it possible to carry out such actions with the perfection of that specific power, and with ease, spontaneity, and confidence of aim. Virtues are like a second, acquired nature on the level of the power itself, through which the act of that power (true knowing, producing beautiful things, shoemaking, doing just actions, etc.) can be carried out in the same way as mere nature can do with seeing, hearing, and so on. Virtue is thus a kind of *connaturality* with the actions that belong to the faculty, something like an acquired instinct.[3] Virtue is ability, virtuosity, brilliance, mastery, competence,

3. On the concept of connaturality, see R. T. Caldera, *Le jugement par inclination chez Saint Thomas d'Aquin* (Paris: J. Vrin, 1980); M. D' Avenia, *La conoscenza per connaturalità in S. Tommaso D'Aquino* (Bologna: Edizioni Studio Domenicano, 1992).

certainty of aim, and so on, in specific areas of knowing, making, and doing. It is the fulfillment of being human in the various realms of human activity, and it is therefore also the perfection and fulfillment of freedom.

To sum it all up, then, virtue in all its types is a habit for carrying out well the actions of a faculty: a *habitus operativus bonus*. But that only designates what is common to all virtue (as distinguished from vice). We also know, then, what constitutes vice: turning away from what the powers do, to really be powers. Vices are the deprivation of human being and the lack of what gives human freedom its ultimate meaning and value: orientation toward the truly good. A vice is not merely another possible way to use a power. False knowing is not simply another way of knowing, but rather a lack of knowing, and a turning away of one's knowing-power from the good that naturally belongs to it: the truth. Choosing what is bad and doing evil is not "another way" of realizing one's humanity, but rather a failure to realize one's humanity, a turning away from the natural good that belongs to man as man: virtue as an order of the reason. A human being who has a bad or unjust will is not someone who just looks at things "differently," but rather someone who increasingly does not see anything because he has distanced himself from reason. And it is reason that shows man what is good for man *qua* man. And yet vice is also a habit: in the will, it is pride and arrogance; in sense desire, it is indulgence or loss of feeling; in the irascible power, it is cowardliness or foolhardiness.

The label "good operative habit" *(habitus operativus bonus)* applies to *all* the virtues. But it is not specific enough for determining "moral virtue." What, then, is that, more precisely?

c) The Anthropological and Affective-Cognitive Dimension of Moral Virtue

Moral virtue is the perfection of appetition or striving (sense desire, irascibility, will; cf. III.5.b above), and through this, it is the perfection of definite actions according to the ordering of reason. Moral virtue is, in one way, the integration of the sensual/corporeal into the logic of the spiritual, and in another way, constancy in the will's openness toward the good of others, the "other" including fellow human beings as well as God.

As Aristotle said, reason governs the appetition of the senses not as a despot rules the body but with "a political and royal rule."[4] "Political rule" is rule over free persons. They are not simply in subjection, but act by their own initiatives and can even disagree. Sense desire can be in conflict with

---

4. *Politics,* trans. Jowett, I, 5 (1254b6); the contrast is between *archē despotikē* ("despotic rule"), on the one hand, and *archē politikē kai basilikē* ("political and royal rule"), on the other.

reason. What guarantees excellence of action is not the "despotic" rule over sense drives of a reason perfected in the knowledge of morality, but only the *participation* or *sharing* of sense desires in reason, so that the striving of the sense itself, thoroughly formed by reason, becomes a principle of human action.[5] This is how we can conceptualize the relationship between appetition and reason: every moral virtue is a participation in rationality of one of the several appetitive dynamisms, and is thereby a habit *(habitus)* of appetition in accordance with reason.

It is in accordance with reason that the senses desire what seems good according to reason's judgment; that one fears what the reason judges should be feared, and not merely the estimation of the senses, and acts accordingly (at times it is simply irrational to allow one's action to be determined by fear of pain or death, or to avoid things on that basis); it is likewise in accordance with reason to will for others the good that one strives for oneself.

Therefore, Thomas says, moral virtue is "a certain disposition, or form, that is stamped in the appetitive power through reason like some kind of seal,"[6] and that "moral virtue perfects the appetitive part of the soul, by ordering it to the good of the reason. The good of the reason is what is governed or ordered by the reason."[7] Moral virtue, consequently, does not only reside in the will. This is correct only for justice. *Every* appetitive power has its *own* virtue or virtues: sense desires have the perfection of temperance *(temperantia)*, and the irascible power has the perfection of fortitude or bravery *(fortitudo)*.

Virtue is not merely an "inner stance" or basic attitude. It is neither simply strength of will, nor simply rationality. Nor is it subjection to the categorical imperative, consciousness of duty, or a resolve for goodness.[8] Instead, it is the inner harmony of man and all his strivings with reason. The self-controlled person passionately desires in accordance with what is reasonable; the courageous person resists with passion all the dangers and obstacles that stand in the way of reaching what is reasonable (he is brave, consistent, and patient). And the just person not only does his duty toward others, but loves his fellow human being as himself and loves what is good for others as he loves what is good for himself. True justice is ultimately the most fundamental kind of good will. Prudence, however, is the habit of practical reason that chooses the means or the actions, and really is formed through the integration of this reasoning into the whole complex of the other moral virtues.

The subject or bearer of moral virtue is consequently in each case an appe-

5. I-II, Q. 58, a. 2.
6. *De virtutibus in communi*, a. 9.
7. I-II, Q. 59, a. 4.
8. Cf. also F. Ricken, "Kann die Moralphilosophie auf die Frage nach dem 'Ethischen' verzichten?" 172ff.

titive power. This is clear of course in the case of the will but even the sensitive appetites become in this way principles of action through which good action is urged, shaped, and as Aristotle emphasizes, even becomes pleasurable. "Virtuous acts are pleasant to the lover of virtue." And "the man who does not rejoice in noble actions is not even good; since no one would call a man just who did not enjoy acting justly, nor any man liberal who did not enjoy liberal actions."[9] Moral virtue is *affective connaturality* with the good; a connaturality, that is to say, of the *entire* human person and *all* his strivings.

The connection of the doctrine of virtue with the doctrine of pleasure lends a further action-theoretical meaning to the anthropological description of moral virtue, a meaning to which reference has already been made more than once. This is the *cognitive* function of moral virtue.

The good that we pursue in actions is in fact always an apparent good. As already remarked above (II.1.a), this "appearance" does not imply a "deception" but rather a "visibility," that is, the fact that the good is always objectified as good and thereby visible to the affectively bound evaluation of the striving subject of action. Virtuous action is an action based on an affective connaturality with the good: it is an action that meets the truly good in the concrete case, with spontaneity and certainty. The virtuous person is able as a rule to judge situations rightly just as they happen, and choose what is good. In this kind of action affectivity is suggestive: it directly guides the judgment of reason. And if, despite the fact that we know what is good in general, but in the concrete case choose badly, this is because the reason has been misguided by affectivity. This is the *ignorantia electionis* or the *error electionis* we have analyzed above, ignorance or error in choosing. The virtuous one nevertheless always chooses the good because what appears good to him is always what truly is good. He becomes himself a rule and measure for the truly good.[10] This is because his emotions, which are determinative for this "seeming," are oriented toward the good in accordance with reason.

Even the nonvirtuous or the only imperfectly virtuous can choose the good, not, however, on the basis of affective connaturality, but on the basis of knowing, mere "consciousness of duty," and also, for the most part, through the repression of affectivity that has not been ordered. For Kant, this is the unavoidable destiny of the human being, and identical with "virtue," which he thus calls "moral disposition *in conflict*."[11] It is therefore no wonder that Kant really reduces moral virtue to the virtue of courage, or *fortitudo*.[12] To act virtu-

9. *EN* I, 9 (1099a10–11; 17–20).

10. Cf. *EN* III, 6 (1113a24–b1).

11. I. Kant, *Critique of Practical Reason*, trans. M. Gregor, 72.

12. Cf., e.g., *Metaphysics of Morals*, trans. M. Gregor, 156: "Virtue is the strength of a human being's maxims in fulfilling his duty. Strength of any kind can be recognized only by the obstacles it can

ously therefore means to act by conquering and repressing one's inclinations, to act out of duty, with sheer obedience to the moral law. The motive of action is not the recognized good, but duty as attention to the moral law as it shows up in the categorical imperative. The Aristotelian notion, by contrast, without of course implying that the virtuous person has no consciousness of duty or sense of moral obligation, holds that duty is identical for the virtuous person with what seems good to him to do, where his feelings are tending and what he rejoices in[13] (cf. V.2.c). The virtuous person also has a *subjective interest* in what is truly good. The truly good, what is "in accordance with duty," is not simply "duty" or even a burden, but *his own interest*. Thus moral virtue is the highest empowering of freedom and practical reasoning, which precisely in this way becomes prudence.[14]

> Exactly this possibility—constitutive for classical ethics—of a unity of "moral ought" and subjective interest has been characterized by Hans Krämer as illusionary. For Krämer, then, there are two complementary, but never reconcilable, types of ethics: appetitive ethics (having to do with what is good-for-me because willed) and moral philosophy (having to do with what is good-for-others and therefore obliging).[15] Implied in an unreflective fashion here, in any case, is an understanding of being human according to which, in the realm of "what is good-for-me," there can be no "ought" (and thereby as well no wrong willing that is corrigible according to moral standards); and in the realm of "what is owed to others," no real willing, but only the *restriction* of my will which is in each case directed toward "what is good-for-me." The human being appears here as a radical egotist, and the moral ought as the channeling of this egotism toward the well-being of the other or for the purpose of facilitating human community life.

This is exactly why moral virtue is necessary for good action in the full sense of the word. Virtue is not simply a form of knowing, but rather an ordering of appetites in accordance with reason. Knowledge is only one part of virtue; as we shall see, it is the path to virtue, and in a way, as conscience, the "pilot" of virtue, which is incomplete and still "on the road."

That virtue includes a *knowing* about the good, and that, consequently, criteria of truthfulness must be recognized in its realm, was the original concern

---

overcome, and in the case of virtue these obstacles are the natural inclinations, which can come into conflict with moral resolution." Cf. also ibid., 164: "Virtue is therefore the moral strength of a human being's will . . . vices, the brood of dispositions opposing the law, are the monsters he has to fight. Accordingly, this moral strength as *courage (fortitudo moralis)* also constitutes the greatest and only true honor man can win in war."

13. *EN* IX, 8 (1169a 16–18).

14. Cf. G. Abbà, *Felicità, vita buona e virtù*, 251. This is a way to avoid playing emotions against reason, so typical of contemporary virtue ethics approaches.

15. Cf. H. Krämer, *Integrative Ethik*, 79 and 132.

of Socrates in the Platonic dialogue *Protagoras*. This work is concerned with clarification about what would need to be presupposed for virtue to be communicated through teaching. The unavoidable one-sidedness of this standpoint (ending in numerous contradictions), which arose above all as a counterposition to the Sophists, was only overcome by Aristotle, who nevertheless did not give up on the decisive point about knowledge: moral virtue *implies* knowledge and is a form of truth, which in any case, so goes Aristotle's correction, becomes *practical* as well only when that affectivity is aligned with this truth. The "practical," at any rate, consists here not only in the fact that practical knowing also leads to effective *action*, but also in that specific kind of knowledge that is only possible within the sphere of reason through the integration of the emotions: a knowledge that meets the right and the good in the *concrete* or the *particular*. Indeed, in itself, rational knowing is of a universal nature. But actions (or the particular "good," here and now) are always particular executions within concrete situations and in a context of definite persons. The acting person always stands in some relation to these persons: relationships that are, again, always embedded in a contingent life history. "Thus it is a knowledge of the particular situation that completes moral knowledge."[16] For sense-affects either *displace* one's view of what is good to do here and now, or else they actually *make it possible* to see it and do it. The same can be said for the will. "The Aristotelian concept of virtue not only requires that practical reason integrate the region of affectivity; Aristotle also maintains that moral knowledge is only possible on the condition of such integration."[17] This mutual relationship between affectivity and practical reason is in any case not only one of the most important insights of Aristotelian ethics; it forms one of its central problems. We shall return to this theme.

2. Moral Virtue as the Habit of Choosing Good Actions

a) The Aristotelian Definition of Moral Virtue

Thomas Aquinas bases his doctrine of virtues—against the trend of his time—not on the Augustinian definition but on the Aristotelian.[18] This definition is

16. H.-G. Gadamer, *Truth and Method*, trans. G. Barden and J. Cumming, 287.
17. F. Ricken, "Kann die Moralphilosophie auf die Frage nach dem 'Ethischen' verzichten?" (see note 8 above), 174.
18. The Augustinian definition (which Thomas presents at I-II, Q. 55, a. 4—taken, he says, mainly from Augustine's *De Libero Arbitrio* II, 19—but which he then sets aside) goes as follows: *virtus est bona qualitas mentis, qua recte vivitur et nullus male utitur, quam Deus in nobis sine nobis operatur* ("Virtue is a good quality of mind, by which we live rightly and no one can misuse, which God works in us without our cooperation"). This definition contains almost no relevant ethical or action-theoretical elements. Even though it is correct as such, it is too broad: it includes the infused virtues, and as a definition is

as follows: [*Moral*] *virtue is a habit of choosing, which keeps a mean in relation to ourselves according to the determination of reason, and in such a way as a wise man is accustomed to determine it.*[19]

The main elements of this definition are the following:

1) Moral virtue is a "habit of choosing" (Gr. *hexis prohairetikē;* Lat. *habitus electivus*).

2) This habit, and this choosing, is related to a "mean" (Gr. *mesotēs;* Lat. *medietas*).

3) This mean, or act of the habit (i.e., the choice of the mean) is determined by reason (Gr. *logos;* Lat. *ratio*).

4) The reasoning is that of a "wise man" (Gr. *phronimos;* Lat. *prudens* or *sapiens*), whereby "prudence" is identified as "practical wisdom."[20] The "norm" is not *any* reason, but rather prudence (Gr. *orthos logos;* Lat. *recta ratio agibilium*).

As a habit, moral virtue perfects the choice of actions, that is, the "choice of means" *(electio)*, and thereby actually produces good *actions*. Moral virtue in every instance, then, is a perfection of the choosing, and that means "action-triggering," act of the will, and it does this also when it actually and immediately brings about the fulfillment of a sense appetition. This is understandable when we recall the earlier discussion about the relationships among will, reason, and emotion and about the possibility for errors in choosing and ignorance. Moral virtue is precisely what keeps such errors from happening. And vice versa: moral virtue guarantees the rationality of the judgment that is involved in an act of choosing and determines it: the affectively guided, ultimate, immediately act-triggering judgment of the practical reason.

Secondly, according to the above definition, moral virtue consists in a "mean" or "middle"; this is a mean or middle "in relation to ourselves"; and it is determined by reason—by the reason, of course, that is called prudence.

b) Moral Virtue as a Mean

That "moral virtue consists in a mean" is perhaps one of the most frequently misunderstood sentences in Aristotle's works. The possibility for misunder-

---

only useful for theology. The rejection of this definition by Thomas seems unfortunately to have been overlooked by E. Schockenhoff in his otherwise so thorough study *Bonum hominis. Die anthropologischen und theologischen Grundlagen der Tugendethik von Thomas von Aquin,* 243. The Aristotelian definition from *EN* II, 6 (1106b36–1107a2), so decisive for Thomas, is not mentioned at all. For more detail on this point (and on all that follows in this section), see A. Rodríguez Luño, *La scelta etica. Il rapporto fra libertà e virtù* (Milan: Edizioni Ares, 1988), and M. Rhonheimer, *Praktische Vernunft und Vernünftigkeit der Praxis,* 62ff.

19. *EN* II, 6 (1106b36–1107a2).   20. Cf. In II Ethic, lectio 7.

standing lies in taking "virtue as mean" to imply a kind of balance, the attitude of not overdoing anything. This misunderstanding has a long tradition, going back at least as far as Hugo Grotius's *De jure belli et pacis* (1625).[21] For Bernard Williams, the doctrine of virtue as a mean is the most superfluous element of Aristotelian ethics, and deserves to be forgotten, as something that wavers between a useless analytical model and a lame exhortation to moderation.[22] But that virtue consists merely in a kind of moderation and balance is not what Aristotle is saying. For him, rather, the mean of moral virtue is finally nothing other than what is according to reason, and this is the right, the fitting or appropriate, the good as the "beautiful." As such, the mean in each case is the best *(ariston)* and an extreme *(akrōtēs)*.[23]

The "mean" first of all is related, as Aristotle emphasizes, to sense affects. Virtue lies in a mean between a "too much" and a "too little" in becoming influenced by an emotion. But this is still a pure description, not the designation of a criterion as such: "too much" does not mean the same as "much" and "too little" does not mean the same as "little." "Much anger" can in fact be not "too much" anger but rather just the "right amount" of anger—between "too much" and "too little." The question is whether anger, and this or that level of anger, is *fitting* or *appropriate* or *called for;* and that finally only the reason can determine. To "eat ten pounds" of meat is to eat a great deal, says Aristotle, and "to eat two pounds" is to eat a small amount. But that does not mean "eating six pounds" is the mean. For an athlete like Milo it would be too little, for a novice boxer it would be too much.[24] "Too much" and "too little" are really only names for a departure from what is "just right." The expression implies an evaluation. The middle stands by definition between a too much and a too little. The concept of mean as such does not say anything further. It only says that with regard to the virtues that have to do with the senses and their affects, there are in each case two opposing vices, characterized by being too much and too little, for which the virtue is the middle, that is, what is measured according to reason. This is the meaning of the sentence *stat in medio virtus* ("virtue stands in the middle").

This correctness—that is, the mean of the virtue—is determined, therefore, not according to a simple quantity of affect, but according to its appropriateness as judged by reason. The middle or mean is what is "reason-measured."

21. *De iure belli ac pacis libri tres (On the Law of War and Peace)*, trans. F. Kelsey (Oxford: Clarendon Press, 1925), prolegomena, sec. 43–45. For the impact on virtue ethics of Grotius's critique of the Aristotelian mean, see J. B. Schneewind, "The Misfortunes of Virtue," in R. Crisp and M. Slote, eds., *Virtue Ethics*, 178–200, here 182–83.

22. B. Williams, *Ethics and the Limits of Philosophy*, 36.

23. *EN* II, 6 (1107a8). Cf. also O. Höffe, *Aristoteles* (Munich: Beck, 1996), 223f., who also defends this Aristotelian doctrine of the mean against Kantian misunderstandings.

24. Cf. *EN* II, 5 (1106b1–7).

"That we must act according to the right reason *(kata ton orthon logon)* is a common principle and must be assumed."[25] Therefore Thomas calls the mean of virtue in general as "the mean of reason" *(medium rationis).*[26]

This middle of reason is determined, in the case of sense affects, "in relation to ourselves." "For instance, both fear and confidence and appetite and anger and pity and in general pleasure and pain may be felt both too much and too little, and in both cases not well; but to feel them at the right times, with reference to the right objects, towards the right people, with the right motive, and in the right way is what is both intermediate and best, and this is characteristic of virtue."[27] Virtue as a mean, therefore, is at once a best and highest degree, in what "should" or "ought" to be done. This "ought" expresses the good as determined by the reason.

It is determined "in relation to us." It depends upon who we are, to whom the emotion is directed, what the circumstances are. This is why, as Aristotle stresses over and over again, it can only be indicated "roughly" or "in outline" wherein virtue consists or the actions in accordance with virtue, and this is because human actions, emotions, and acts of choosing, the habit of which is moral virtue, have to do with what is concrete, contingent, bound up with situations, determined by a multiplicity of circumstances. The right and the good in action is "what can always be otherwise."

Nevertheless, Aristotle emphasizes that there are *boundaries* that cannot be crossed. Such boundaries also belong in a virtue ethics that must limit itself to showing things in outline, because it is a virtue ethics and not a "norm-ethics."[28] If there were no such boundaries, there would be nothing of which virtue is a fulfillment. To use an image: the virtues are like wide streets leading to a goal. The general, "in outline" features of the virtues are like the directing signs along the streets. But the streets do have edges to them, and at times guard rails for sleepy drivers. There could not otherwise be streets, nor would direction signs be of any assistance.

How much may one "desire" his own wife? Certainly not "too much"—but that does not make sense—he may desire her, indeed he should do so, and he may do it to a great degree. Here, "much" is certainly not "too much." But with respect to the wife of another man the same amount *would* be too much; indeed, *any* amount would be "too much." There is no mean here *at all.* Some-

---

25. *EN* II, 2 (1103b33).

26. I-II, Q. 64, a. 1 and a. 2.

27. *EN* II, 5 (1106b18–24). [Translator's note: In his (1981) revision of the (1925) Ross translation, Urmson uniformly replaced "virtue" as an English equivalent for Greek *aretē* with the English word "excellence." In quoting here from this (otherwise very serviceable) Ross-Urmson translation I have chosen to reverse Urmson on this point, and restore "excellence" to the more specific "virtue."]

28. See also A. MacIntyre, *After Virtue* (2nd ed.), 150.

times the excess or defect is indicated in the very word we use for the feeling or act. But Aristotle clearly points out that there are concretely describable ways of acting that are *always* bad, and thereby depart from the mean of virtue, and in fact have no mean at all.

> This striking passage should be cited here in full: "But not every action nor every passion admits of a mean; for some have names that already imply badness, e.g. spite, shamelessness, envy, and in the case of actions adultery, theft, murder; for all of these and suchlike things imply by their names that they are themselves bad, and not the excesses or deficiencies of them. It is not possible, then, ever to be right with regard to them; one must always be wrong. Nor does goodness or badness with regard to such things depend on committing adultery with the right woman, at the right time, and in the right way, but simply to do any of them is to go wrong."[29]

What Aristotle is saying here is not only that *unjust* killing (= murder) is always bad; or that whether an action is "adultery" depends on concrete circumstances, the number of times it was committed ("only once doesn't count"), or the intention of it. The problem of "intrinsically" evil actions, or actions that are bad "always and under all circumstances" I would like to postpone for the present. Nevertheless, such language is meaningful only in the framework of a virtue ethics, and not in an ethics that is essentially taken up with the establishment and justification of "norms" in the sense of *rules*.

> Such norms can be reformulated according to whim, so that if the formula permits it, they can be exceptionless or only valid in a few cases or in most cases. So-called absolute norms can only work when the formulation is so narrowed that the norm no longer applies to the majority of possible cases. It could then be said that the norm "it is always bad to kill a man" is only incompletely and therefore wrongly formulated. For it to be exceptionless, it would have to be narrowed as follows (using an example from B. Schüller): "To kill a man A only so that another man can be spared a small unpleasantness, is never morally justified."[30] The description of action such as "kill a man" in relation to which, as Aristotle says, "it is not possible . . . ever to be right . . . [but] always wrong," so that one could say "it is always wrong to do [such actions]," cannot be justified as a formulation of a rule for actions, starting from the concept of the norm (see below, V.3).

The "middle in relation to us" is thus a rationally determined middle, and a "best." This is part of the Aristotelian definition of virtue. But not every mean is one in relation to us. In the case of the virtue of justice, there is a different kind of "middle" or mean: it is the mean "in relation to the thing." Ar-

---

29. *EN* II, 6 (1107a9–18).
30. B. Schüller, *Die Begründung sittlicher Urteile*, 298.

istotle has sometimes been accused of inconsistently broadening his concept of virtue here, but the accusation is probably bound up with overlooking the essentially rational determination of the "mean with respect to us." The decisive characteristic of the virtuous mean is not the "middle" idea as such, but the rational determination of what is here being understood in various ways as the mean, that is to say, the mean as the *orthos logos*. And this is now to be applied to an area that is not so much that of affects and emotions but rather that of objects of external actions. When it is a question of the right division of goods or the finalizing of a contract, things and services and the rest must be assigned or distributed in right relation. The mean here is determinable as the "just," and this is a form of "equality" in the right proportion.[31] In this way, "just action is intermediate between acting unjustly and being unjustly treated."[32] But this "middle" or mean is likewise determined according to reason, and here again circumstances and concrete relationships are decisive for arriving at that mean. Accordingly, the reason that is determinative here is the reason that has been perfected through prudence. We will return to this point.

c) The Habitual Perfecting of the Choice of Action through Moral Virtue

Let us now take up the true core of the definition of virtue, that moral virtue is "a habit of choosing."[33] Choice must hit the mean, the mean of reason, and that signifies what is right according to reason. The choice of action is related to the "means to the end," that is, the concrete actions that are chosen for the sake of an end. Earlier (III.3) the connection between means and end, between choice of action and ultimate intention was analyzed. The action-theoretical insights that were then acquired are fundamental for understanding moral virtue as the habit of the right choice of actions.

Choosing the means is, of course, an act of the will. And this act of the will is good only when not only the chosen action, but also the intended goal is good (i.e., when both correspond to the ordering of reason). Moral virtue as habit of the "right" or "moral" choice must therefore in some way include both choice of means and intention of the end. Otherwise moral virtue would be nothing other than a kind of finesse or skill in finding an efficient route to any end whatsoever.

To go further: what we really ultimately want, when we choose something—so we noted above—is not the concrete action that we choose, but rath-

---

31. Cf. *EN* V, 6.

32. *EN* V, 9 (1133b31).

33. An extensive analysis of moral virtue as the *habitus* of the choice of action is found in A. Rodríguez Luño, *La scelta etica. Il rapporto fra libertà e virtù* (see note 18 above).

THE HABIT OF CHOOSING GOOD ACTIONS | 203

er the goal for the sake of which we choose it. For a choice of action to be good, it is not enough that the means is good. And in order for a concrete action (the means) to be good, depends first of all upon the intended goal. In choosing the means the end is always also willed. The content of the will is determined through the end and the means, which form a single object of the will in the act of willing. But a means is "good" when it is actually *suited* to lead to the end. This making-suitable is nevertheless a *moral* making-suitable (or "adaptation" of means to end): in order to reach a just goal, and therefore justice, the means considered *in itself* must correspond to justice.

> Only so-called consequentialism—as we must constantly recall—would say here: the adaptation of a means can only be determined by its ability, actually and foreseeably, to effect the existence of the state of affairs intended as a goal. In contrast, we say that the adaptation of means toward definite purposes must also be judged with a view to the means *in itself.* The controversy about the difference remains fruitless as long as one fails to grasp that consequentialism arises from a nonintentional and (consequently) questionable concept of action (cf. below, V.f).

Because both the reason-measured relationship to one's emotions and affects, and one's reason-measured actions consist in a mean, the intention of the end is revealed as the decisive element in this determination of the mean. Whether it is right in definite speech acts to say something or to be silent, as well as how to say it, if it is to be said, is determined by the end that one intends. It depends on whether it is an act of truthful saying or of untruthfulness, of cowardice or of prudence, of a lack of concern for or of love of neighbor. No concrete action can in general be said to be good or bad, except in the case of those in which the "boundaries" already mentioned would be crossed. And yet we still cannot go into this point any further as yet.

The term "moral virtue" thus acquires a certain ambiguity. The whole complex of ideas contains the following elements:

1) *The intentional orientation of the appetition of the end,* that is, of the emotions and will to that which is according to reason (*habitus* of the right appetition of the goal)

2) *The orientation of the reason that is means-determining or action-determining* toward ends that are according to reason (*habitus* of the right determination of means or actions = prudence)

3) The act of the *choice of action (prohairesis/electio)*

4) (External) *accomplishment of the action* (following immediately upon 3).

All these elements are necessary components of moral virtue, and each in a way *is* moral virtue in a certain sense, but only *as* an element of the whole complex. The whole complex is moral virtue as "habit of the right choice of actions." But we could also name the single elements "moral virtue" analogously: in this sense for Aristotle moral virtue (1) makes the end right, and prudence (2) makes the means right. Or alternatively: virtues are "choice or involve choice."[34] This corresponds to (3). Because if moral virtue is also a habit of the reason-measuredness of the feelings, it is in fact a habit that effectively leads to a choice of actions, for otherwise the ordering of the feelings would have no practical meaning. The real and specific *act* of moral virtue is then the reason-measured choice of action. The habit of moral virtue makes it possible to carry out this action in a complete way. And "complete" here means with ease and spontaneity, with steadiness, and with joy or delight.

When we speak here of "spontaneity" and of "habit," we do not mean to imply routine custom or some kind of instinctual "automatism," but rather an affective empowering of *practical reasoning*, that is, of the practical consideration of what is "good here and now."[35] The spontaneity in question is not one of being accustomed or a kind that would be possible *without* freedom and of a narrow instinct; it is rather "a freeing-up of the reason" for discernment of the good to which every action is heading. "What is to be done" is not for affectivity to determine: it is a matter of the judgment of reason. But this judgment is always *also guided* by affectivity, and consequently is carried out in a way that tends to be in agreement with it. The reason first judges everything *spontaneously* as "good" that corresponds to the affectivity, even if, as reason, it possesses the possibility of taking up a position counter to the feelings or of judging independently of them. This was clear to Kant as well, and that is why for him, as we saw before, virtue is equivalent to a kind of *askesis* or strenuous discipline of shutting off the feelings, and really nothing more than the virtue of courage. Aristotelian virtue is not "moral disposition in conflict" and yet it *is* "moral disposition" [Ger. *Gesinnung*]: for, if we reject the implicit anthropology of Kantian ethics, then we must not call a disposition or fundamental attitude "moral" simply because it comes into existence without the guidance of feelings, but rather insofar as it aims for what is truly *good*. In fact, if it seems pleasurable to someone to wish his neighbor well, so that he acts in a kindly fashion toward his neighbor, simply *because* it gives him this feeling, that would not be called a lack of "moral disposition," but the highest fulfillment of "moral disposition" (or "fundamental attitude," *Gesinnung*). This is not primarily because someone like that has it easier than someone who has to keep his moral disposition in "conflict," but simply because he is

---

34. *EN* II, 4 (1106a4).
35. Cf. G. Abbà, *Felicità, vita buona e virtù*, 216ff.

capable of *judging rightly* in concrete situations, because he is more capable in particular of meeting with the "good here and now" (cf. also below, V.2.c).

Thomas Aquinas therefore comments on Aristotle's statement that "the virtues are choice or involve choice" in the following way: "Moral virtue" can mean "the *act* of the virtue." And the most important act of a virtue is right choice of action; this is the *real* moral virtue, viewed in terms of the act. Moral virtue can, however, also be referred to as the external accomplishment of the action, or element (4), but only insofar as the external action results from an inner act of choosing, and is deliberate, free, willingly done. And to this extent someone can say: "moral virtue (as an external action) *involves* choice." Thirdly, we can treat moral virtue as the *habitus* of the rational ordering of the feelings, upon which in fact the virtuous choice of actions depends, and in this sense, too, moral virtue is not without choice, because every effect (choice of action) has its cause (the *habitus*).[36]

In every act of choosing, which is of course an act of the will, there is something double: the intention of the end (it is intentionally present) and the judgment about what is concretely to be done, that is, the judgment of the means.[37] In order for moral virtue to order the sense appetites and the will, it especially brings it about that the *appetition of the end* be carried out according to reason. Exactly in this way, the act of judging by the reason, which addresses itself to the means, is governed according to the goal of the virtue. It becomes an act of prudence. Someone whose will is habitually aimed to the good of another according to the requirements of reason will also choose the means that are right—even if he needs much further knowledge and competence and must deliberate about it, and when there are probably numerous possibilities of right ways of acting. He will at least not *willingly* cheat or slight someone. "To intend justice" does not only mean having good intentions, but also *really* to have directed one's will toward the good of others. And "really" here means as much as "according to the ordering of reason."

We will return to this theme again in connection with the virtue of prudence. But we can at least conclude the following for now: moral virtue makes the appetition of the end good, and operates to make the actions that we choose good actions. That may sound very oversimplified: but underneath this formula lies the doctrine (explained above) of the intrinsic infallibility of the reason. It cannot make sense otherwise. If the emotions are ordered according to the reason, the reason-that-determines-the-means meets the good infallibly, whereby, as mentioned before, this good does not have to be any-

36. Cf. In II Ethic., lect. 5.
37. Cf. I-II, Q. 56, a. 4, ad 4.

thing "universal" or accessible to a "norm." Every virtue has a multiplicity of possible good actions. It would require taking in all the circumstances of a situation to reduce this multiplicity to the one and only best way of acting here and now. And then there are situations where what is good is not necessarily "the ideal best," and many things appear equally good to do.

"Should I tell him, or not?" Neither alternative is really optimal, and yet one or the other has to be done, so long as "telling a lie" is being excluded. Whoever is truly a just person will do this or that for the sake of what is the best for the other person, and in any case with sensitivity and benevolence, because the just man seeks the well-being of the other. And he will certainly act rightly. He will definitely not say anything to degrade someone, injure him, or cause him loss. But to attempt to find a "norm" here, or to undertake a calculation of goods (in which, in principle, the possibility of telling a false statement would have to be included), in order to establish without any ambiguity which mode of acting would bring the optimum consequences for all concerned, or to formulate a "categorical imperative" in order to act so that the maxim of the action can also be thought of or willed as a universal law, seems to miss the most important thing: benevolence to the other as this concrete individual human being before me.

Kantian ethics has a real difficulty here. For it seems that for Kant, that person has a greater moral worth who does his duty (what is right) only out of duty, but not out of inclination (we will come back to this point again later). Philippa Foot has remarked that this is why something must be wrong with Kantian ethics. Whoever, for example, only does something for the sake of duty should not be undervalued, to be sure, but whoever does the same out of a real inclination, with pleasure, out of sympathy for other persons and because of love for them, is certainly a better human being than someone who does so only for a feeling of duty and by overcoming his own selfish inclinations.[38] As a matter of fact, Kant saw this lacuna, and discussed the issue in his (later) *Metaphysics of Morals*, in a chapter on the "Doctrine of Virtues" [*Tugendlehre*].[39] He says here, first, that doing something good to someone is duty, and that cannot be love, because love excludes duty (= what is necessary). One cannot love, or wish someone well, from duty. At first, the deed that demands beneficence *(amor benevolentiae)* is done out of duty, and by way of this, one *attains* to doing well to others out of human love. The decisive passage is this: "Beneficence is a duty. If someone practices it often and succeeds in realizing his beneficent intention, he eventually comes actually to love the person he has helped. So the saying 'you ought to love your neighbor as yourself' does not mean that

38. Cf. P. Foot, "Virtues and Vices," in Crisp and Slote, eds., *Virtue Ethics*, 163–77, here 173.
39. I. Kant, *The Metaphysics of Morals*, trans. M. Gregor, 145–69: "Introduction to the Doctrine of Virtue"; "Love of Human Beings" [*Menschenliebe*].

you ought immediately (first) love him and (afterwards) by means of this love do good to him. It means, rather, *do good* to your fellow human beings, and your beneficence (as an aptitude [or "perfection," *Fertigkeit*] of the inclination to beneficence in general) will produce love of them in you!"[40] Kant is attempting, then, to retrieve action that comes from inclination, benevolence *(amor benevolentiae)*, or good will. But he must neatly distinguish benevolence, as inclination, from the *deed* carried out by benevolence. Deed alone is the object of duty. Consequently this solution cannot appear completely satisfactory, because it is not clear how benevolence toward other people can arise from "acting from duty," that is, from the mere observance of the moral law (the "love of human beings" [*Menschenliebe*] of which Kant speaks here seems to be something rather abstract). This could only be possible, if "acting from duty" permitted to arise within us an *inclination* to act from duty (here, it is the benevolent deed and good will toward another in himself). But exactly to that extent we would no longer be acting from duty and therefore no longer acting morally. Kant's solution to the problem seems to lead to a contradiction of his own criterion of morality. But it also does not seem to be the case that Kant meant to say that beneficence would lead to loving the persons who need our benevolence. It would instead produce "love of human beings" in us, make us more generally inclined to do well to others, out of duty. But then *Menschenliebe* becomes reduced to love toward doing what is our duty. A virtue-oriented ethics of an Aristotelian kind would not be a victim of such circularity.

Moral virtue as the habit of right choosing implies something else, too: the choice of action, is, we have repeatedly emphasized, an act of the will. It is that act of appetition through which the acting subject, from the center of his person, moves to an action. It is not enough to act rightly. The expression "rightly" is used here deliberately. What is meant is that it is not enough to do the good as "technically correct." You have to do something because you *want* to, from rationally guided appetition. "If the acts that are in accordance with the virtues have themselves a certain character it does not follow that they are done justly or temperately. The agent must also be in a certain condition when he does them; in the first place he must have knowledge, secondly he must choose the acts and choose them for their own sakes, and thirdly his action must proceed from a firm and unchangeable character."[41]

In human actions it is not simply a question of carrying out "good works," but to be good oneself. We become "good" or "bad" on the basis of our acts of will, and that means, finally, on the basis of what we choose and willingly do. That is the difference between acting and producing, between moral virtue and art [*Kunst*]; in the realm of production or artistic activity—as such—it

40. Ibid., 162f.
41. *EN* II, 3 (1105a28–b1).

is a question of making a good product that is external to the maker. This is how blocks of marble or wood are "perfected": systems are made functional, houses are built, and so on. In the *life of a human being*—if this life is going to be successfully lived—that is not finally what matters. What matters is for someone to be good. And a man is good when his will is good. For it is peculiar to the will, and to everything connected to it, to make us similar to what we strive after, and that means to what we intend and choose. This is in fact the point of morality, and, as Kant saw in a way that cannot be surpassed, it is of service for nothing more than for this: to produce good willing in oneself. However, morality has a *telos* as its inner structural principle, and that is not—now *contra* Kant—freedom of the will from dependence on any experienced inclination, or the spontaneity and autonomy of the reason to the end of preserving this freedom, but rather freedom as orientation to the *good,* which alone stands open to the reason, because through the reason we open ourselves to reality, we live according to reality, we find ourselves. What we rationally strive for satisfies the will—even when everything goes wrong—and this satisfaction is known as happiness, even if it is incomplete. To become happy is what we all really always ultimately want. And happiness is the true privilege of the good will.

What is decisive therefore is not only *what* we do but *how* we do it. Acting on the basis of the categorical imperative or the weighing of goods neither makes us good nor satisfies our wills, nor makes us happy. Seeking pleasure as such produces nothing like that either. Of course, no one is claiming that the categorical imperative or the weighing of goods have the purpose of making us happy. According to Kant, the categorical imperative and action in accordance with it merely makes us *worthy* of happiness, and the weighing of goods, according to the thinking of utilitarian ethicists, while serving to make clear what is "right," still cannot make us "good" (to act with a good attitude).

But what is still puzzling for Kantian ethics and utilitarian ethics alike is how the human person can be changed by actions, becoming good or bad *thereby,* and how this comes about by the *choosing* of actions. This means that a habit of good intentions, for example, the habit of "intending justice," comes about directly through the constantly repeated choosing of just actions. Someone who acts in a Kantian way would never become a more just person, but only a more "duty-conscious" one (as discussed above), or only a person who is concerned with being "more deserving" of happiness, that is, a *Pharisee.* The utilitarian, on the other hand—if he really acted consistently as a utilitarian, as, fortunately, no one does—if he always looked for the optimization of consequences for all concerned, for the greatest happiness of the greatest number, or for the best state of affairs in the world—he would at best become a friend of humanity: he would "love" human well-being, the world, society, the totality of all persons affected, but no one individual person, not even himself. Any individual, including himself, would instead become a mere individual factor in his calculation of goods, which can only consider the well-being of the totality, of the world, of humanity, of society. Utilitarianism is self-defeating because it removes the foundation for finding out criteria for human good, according to which the well-being of the whole, of the world, of humanity or society could be judged (cf. V.4.f).

d) The Development of Moral Virtue into *Habitus* I: Problems of the Aristotelian Solution and Broadening of the Perspective

The concept of moral virtue as a habit *(habitus)* of good choosing opens a way to determining how such a habit can arise at all. It then becomes clear that virtue as habit is not simply a kind of customary behavior or conditioning, even though the "acquisition" of a virtue is in fact a special kind of "accustomization."

One acquires a moral virtue through repeating acts of the virtue in question. This means: through the repeated *choosing* of just, temperate, or courageous actions with the will to attain what is truly good through such actions. But, since one does not yet have the virtue, at least not completely, this also means effort, internal struggle, ability to conquer oneself, self-control, self-mastery, and so on—at times forgiving others, at times regretting what one has done. This is how an increasing commitment is formed, in the will and sense appetites, to what is according to reason. Similarly, this does not have anything to do with mere assimilation of behavior patterns or paradigms or with the internalization of rules and norms. The decisive thing here is not merely the "effort" but persistency in affective directedness toward that which reason presents.

That moral virtue is not a kind of "routine" may also shed some light on the fact that it really is a habit of *choosing*. It facilitates hitting the target of the good in one's choice of action. Now this good is always different: it is contingent and situational. There are nuances and shades of gray here that cannot be found through anything "routine" in nature. Whatever takes place merely routinely must have a characteristic of constant sameness, uniformity, the stereotypical. But that is precisely the opposite of moral virtue, whose business it is not to subsume the concrete case under the rigid paradigm of a universal, but rather to grasp the universality of the morally true and "beautiful" *in* the concrete instance. A virtue that was only a routine would not be able to achieve this. Here again, virtue can only be understood as an empowering of the reason, which will *judge* rightly in the case of the virtuous person. Acquisition of virtue, accordingly, always implies the exercise of deliberation and judgment. And there is a second, so to speak "aesthetic" element that enters the picture: the good, in its ultimate concretization as "means to an end" has, for the virtuous person, that quality of the "beautiful" that makes it "attractive." The beautiful speaks for itself, in a way: one does not ask "why" or "to what end." The virtuous person just "likes" it, it appeals to his taste. In this sense, as Gadamer rightly said, not only Aristotelian ethics but Greek ethics as a whole is in fact an "ethics of good taste."[42] This is an analogy of course. But it brings out something essential: just as in aesthetic matters "good taste" is not mere routine, but a rightly formed *judgment,* which allows one to grasp the universally beautiful in *this* concrete instance, to find it attractive and consent to it, so likewise is moral virtue.

It was said above that virtue is acquired through the steady orientation of the feelings toward that which reason offers. But what does reason offer? Just how does this "according to reason" we have so often been talking about actually become determined? This question, which is the really *normative* question, quite naturally presses to be answered. But we are not ready to discuss it yet. The Aristotelian doctrine of moral virtue will first make it possible for us rightly to take up the question and to propose it appropriately. What must first concern us is clarification about the *mode of perfection* of human actions, emerging as a result of the *anthropology* of human action. The question about moral norms is a *subordinate* question about the *cognitive conditions* of this perfection; a question, as we have already said, for which Aristotelian ethics, and classical ethics as a whole, supplies a rather insufficient answer.

Aristotelian ethics—and a brief historical digression appears to be appropriate at this stage for the sake of clarification—is concerned almost exclusively with the *mode* of virtuous action. That is its theme.[43] And here is where the infamous circularity of Aristotle's virtue ethics comes into play: Aristotle's ethics knows of two fundamental principles: (1) there is no *habitus* of the right judgment of actions (prudence) without moral virtue; (2) there is no moral virtue without prudence. The possibility of acquiring moral virtue appears to presuppose that it is already possessed.

Aristotle accepts this circularity as simply a fact that arises from the nature of moral virtue. But it is not a circularity at the level of justification or argument. Rather, we are confronted here with a circularity that comes into view within the structure or "organic operation" of virtuous action itself, and the demonstration of this point will compel us to make a deeper moral-philosophical analysis.

Aristotle's solution comes from the fact that his ethics reflects the life of

---

42. H.-G. Gadamer, *Truth and Method,* trans. G. Barden and J. Cumming, 38.
43. The thorough demonstration of this point is the thesis of my (already frequently cited) book *Praktische Vernunft und Vernünftigkeit der Praxis.*

the citizens of the ancient Greek polis. Now the solution is made up of four components: one must guide oneself after the example of the "best people" in the political entity, that is, those who are counted as the best by widespread opinion. In them one recognizes in what virtue consists, what are the true goals and values of human life. Secondly, insofar as he is committed to lead a life according to reason and has acquired a bit of experience in that, someone should really study ethics in order to acquire for himself, through reflection, the foundations of a life lived according to reason. Third, there is a concern to order the human society of the polis according to good laws that would lead the citizens to virtue. Fourth, and finally, education is decisive in the framework of the polis, both in the family and in social institutions. Consequently the *Nicomachean Ethics* has its conclusion really in the *Politics:* the doctrines of the polis, the making of laws and education.[44]

For Aristotle, then, the moral norm is a "polis-norm," which in turn is rationality. The "best people" in the state, such as the oft-mentioned Pericles, appear as the incarnation of moral reasoning. The polis itself makes it possible for men to "live in accordance with a sort of intellect and right order, provided this [i.e., order] has force."[45] The law in turn possesses "compulsive power, while it is at the same time a rule proceeding from a sort of practical wisdom and intellect."[46] Aristotle did not develop an analysis or even a theory of the moral/normative principles of practical reason through which an acting subject could find orientation, without having to belong to such a polis-ethos, even though such an analysis does have its place within Aristotelian ethics (see below, V.1.f). For Aristotle, too, virtuous action is neither a purely emotional event nor pure routine. Virtue has a rational structure, and that affects the specific goal-structure of the individual virtues: their principles necessarily have a cognitive structure. Consequently, in relation to them, it is fundamentally possible to have a discourse of justification, which Aristotle achieves in an exclusively dialectic way: as the presentation of the opinions about the good that can, admittedly, be considered as the opinions of the best representatives of the polis-ethos. The purely "hypoleptic" interpretation of Aristotelian ethics as a pure polis-hermeneutic, by contrast, comes from a neo-Hegelian reinterpretation (philosophy as "the times as captured in thought") and so-called neo-Aristotelianism.[47] To be more precise, it is a kind of "overinterpretation"

---

44. The transition is explicitly made in the last chapter of *EN* (X, 10).
45. *EN* X, 10 (1180a18).
46. Ibid., (1180a22).
47. Cf. the various and in their own way impressive contributions to Aristotle in J. Ritter, *Metaphysik und Politik* (Frankfurt am Main: Suhrkamp, 1969), esp. the 1967 essay "'Politik' und 'Ethik' in der praktischen Philosophie des Aristoteles," 106–32. In any case I agree with Apel's criticism of the Ritter school, that Aristotle could not have been a "neo-Aristotelian," because he was not only interested in

since Aristotelian ethics, as mentioned before, is in reality rather restricted in its themes, and does not require such interpretation. There is a reason for that limitation: Aristotle developed his ethics in a polemical fashion, and in conscious distinction from the virtue doctrine of the Platonic academy, according to which virtue consisted in universal knowledge of the good.

Aristotle disagreed: it is not about universal knowing of the good, but about having a right judgment—the judgment that leads to choice and is so closely bound up with emotions. And this needs the ordering of the emotions as well. "It is a question of bringing human beings to a point where *that which really is good is good in their view, too, that what is good in itself also seems to them to be a good for themselves.*"[48] It is exactly this problem of "realization" that forms the theme of Aristotelian ethics. Moral virtue is not simply "reason" but "action," and that always means appetition *along with* reason.[49]

In Plato's *Phaedo*, the opinion is expressed that the affects of the senses are nothing but an obstacle to virtue. The senses and in fact all human bodiliness hinders the understanding of truth. And true virtue consists in such understanding, which is here called simply *phronesis,* identified with the knowing that is relevant for action. Platonic "phronesis" is epistemic knowing, and this is the entirety of virtue. The question about the origin of virtue is here the question about the knowledge of truth. And the best way for that to happen, for Plato, would be if the soul were separated from the body. For the true philosopher, death is what is most to be wished for.[50]

The entire Aristotelian ethics is really an answer to this thesis, and its refutation. Virtue, for Aristotle, consists in an order established in the affections that is according to reason, and the habit of the right choice of actions includes, therefore, a habit of practical reason, which in turn presupposes this ordering of the affections. Consequently, phronesis is unsullied knowing of the good, not on the basis of metaphysical illumination, but on the basis of affective connaturality with the good, thanks to which the truly good also *seems* good to the person who acts.

All else is subordinated to this ultimate argument. The aforementioned circularity is not an argument against the Aristotelian position, but is really its point. The consequence? Aristotelian ethics leads necessarily to a theory of correct education. And Aristotle provided one, after his own fashion, in the *Politics.* The question remains, whether or not this solution still needs to be

---

the context of the polis, but also in a metaphysical and anthropological teleology that transcended that context in the dimension of principles and universals.

48. G. Bien, "Die menschlichen Meinungen und das Gute," in M. Riedel, ed., Rehabilitierung der praktischen Philosophie (Freiburg im Breisgau: Rombach, 1972), 1.363.

49. Cf. *EN* VI, 13 (1144b27–28).

50. Plato, *Phaedo* 63E–69E.

completed: a completion, through the analysis of the possibility of a practical knowledge of moral principles, which could guide the means-determining practical reason even independently of the possession of moral virtue, and which could thereby open the way to a theory of the cognitive conditions of moral virtue and a discourse of justification corresponding to that theory. We will return to this below, in the part entitled "Structures of Rationality" (V).

e) The Development of Moral Virtue into *Habitus* II: Training in Virtue. Authority and Freedom

The inner connection between virtue and politics—something that goes without saying for Aristotle—is no longer current today and appears rather dubious to us. This may be because in comparison with antiquity, the modern world has a much more limited conception of the political. A. MacIntyre has explained again how for Aristotle practical rationality needs moral virtue, and this in turn needs to be imbedded in the polis.[51] The polis is made up of the community institutions, especially the laws and the system of justice, the school, and especially the domestic community or family. Interpersonal relationships, as Aristotle emphasizes, are by nature oriented toward friendship and mutual well-being (cf. below, IV.4). "Between man and wife friendship seems to exist by nature; for man is naturally inclined to form couples—even more than to form cities, inasmuch as the household is earlier and more necessary than the city."[52] Even between parents and children there is a friendship that is based "on nature": "The friendship of children to parents, and of men to gods, is a relation to them as to something good and superior; for they have conferred the greatest benefits, since they are the causes of their being and of their nourishment, and of their education from their birth."[53]

This may provide the key for the possibility of training in virtue. The problem to be solved is: how can we know which *actions* we should carry out and, it being presupposed that virtue has not been formed, what motivation can there be to perform the actions of the virtue?[54] The answer is: through acknowledging the authority of others. But in order for such recognition of authority to really lead to *virtue*, that is, not merely to the (external) following of commands, but rather out of a *love* of justice, self-control, courage, and so on, such recognition of authority must not be mere subjection to the command of another; rather, it must have the characteristic of that kind of recognition that rests

51. Cf. A. MacIntyre, *Whose Justice? Which Rationality?* 103–45.
52. *EN* VIII, 12 (1162a17–19).
53. Ibid., 4–8.
54. Cf. A. MacIntyre, *Whose Justice? Which Rationality?* 113.

upon a consciousness of the goodwill of the one whose authority is recognized. When Aristotle says, in fact, that kings and parents are our benefactors "by nature"[55] ("by nature" here meaning that they are this way according to their very essence, even if they do not act that way), just so it is clear that there is "by nature" a recognition of authority that amounts to a recognition of the good intention of the person exercising the authority. Such acknowledgment is, again, a form of friendship, love, or what the Romans referred to as *pietas*.

And thus MacIntyre may be right when he says that training in virtue takes place when the first step to virtue consists in doing what is authoritatively commanded or held up for imitation in order to *please* the person who exercises the authority, "for the love of" someone.[56] Before there is the love of justice, there is the love of persons who exercise justice and show us what it is. The affective orientation to the good is therefore made possible through the recognition of the one who exercises authority as "good" and through the recognition of that person's life as a "good life."

If we start from the fact that man is destined to be educated, we must nevertheless add that the lack of instinctual direction of a free being such as man cannot be replaced by compulsion. Freedom demands education *in* freedom. If authority is to lead to virtue, it must not do away with freedom, but must form it through its exercise. Friendship, goodwill, and love are the only kinds of relationships that can communicate authority with freedom; love for the person who exercises authority is the only form of acknowledging authority that is fully in harmony with freedom. This is because love is an act of freedom (love itself cannot be commanded; only the act required by love can be commanded). Hence education cannot simply be equated with "socialization." At best, the latter is a (sociologically identifiable) *result* of education; at worst, it is a surrogate education: a mere "imposition" of models of behavior.[57]

And yet, this is only one side of the process. Since education in virtue is always also an education in having rational *insight,* the process of acquiring virtue also has an intellective aspect as well. Acquiring a virtue means having an increasing *insight* into the good. Growing in virtue is by no means an irrational process.[58] Recognition of authority on the basis of consciousness of the goodwill

---

55. *EN* VIII, 11 (1161a10 *ff.*).

56. MacIntyre, *Whose Justice? Which Rationality?* 114. MacIntyre's theory of the development and education of virtue can now be found more fully presented in his *Dependent Rational Animals,* 99ff.

57. Cf. also my treatment of this theme in "Sozialphilosophie und Familie. Gedanken zur humanen Grundfunktion der Familie," in B. Schnyder, ed., *Familie—Herausforderung der Zukunft.* Familiensymposium der Universität Freiburg/Schweiz, November, 1981 (Fribourg: Universitätsverlag, 1982), 113–40; and also *Familie und Selbstverwirklichung. Alternativen zur Emanzipation* (Cologne: Verlag Wissenschaft und Politik, 1979).

58. This was emphasized by R. Sorabji, "Aristotle on the Role of Intellect in Virtue," *Proceedings of the Aristotelian Society,* n.s., 74 (1973–1974): 107–29, esp. 124ff.

of the one who exercises that authority brings about the *affective* guidance that makes possible the empowering of the reason and frees the *individual's own* practical reasoning. What occurs in the process of all genuine training is a kind of "transfer" of virtue by way of the affective relationship between *persons*. But at the end, there is something more than the ordering of the feelings: the end of the process is the capacity to make one's own virtuous practical judgment.[59] And just for this reason, the initial, emotional bond with the exemplar-person that leads to virtue should not be mishandled. Education for freedom, without which no virtue is possible, also needs a process of separation and the formation of self-confidence and autonomy. In this way people can become "independent practical reasoners," i.e., autonomous, morally competent personalities.[60] Conflicts along the way cannot be avoided. They can be turned to productive results if the phase preceding the conflict allowed for the creation of mutual trust.

There are many virtues, and many possible ways of categorizing them and discussing them. What must be kept in mind is that they form a kind of interconnected, living, and dynamic organism. We will return to this idea; first we consider one by one the characteristics of the various virtues.

3. The Organism of the Moral Virtues: Cardinal Virtues and Single Virtues

a) The Concept of "Cardinal Virtue"

The word *cardinal* in the term "cardinal virtue" comes from the Latin *cardo,* meaning "door hinge," "pivotal point." The cardinal virtues are related to the particular virtues as the door hinges are related to the door: the particular virtues "hang" upon them, they rest on them and move on them. This is of course just an image used in order to characterize the main four classical virtues: *prudence, justice, temperance,* and *courage* (or *fortitude*). This systematization is not in Aristotle; its beginnings go back to Plato; with the Stoics[61] it became a firm component of the Roman tradition (Cicero, Seneca) and eventually of the Christian tradition as well with Ambrose of Milan's treatise *On the Sacraments* and Commentary on Luke. In what follows, our orientation is taken essentially from the presentation of Thomas Aquinas.

---

59. In fact a process of learning is implied here, which possesses an "inventive" structure. The "teacher" is not one who "implants" his convictions in the learner; rather, he actualizes the student's own ability to learn, so that "learning" always means reaching knowledge and wisdom oneself under the guidance of another. Cf. also Thomas Aquinas, *De Veritate*, Q. 11, a. 1, or the edition by G. Jüssen, G. Krieder, and H.-J. Scheider, *Thomas von Aquin. Über den Lehrer [De Magistro]* (Hamburg: Meiner, 1988). On *inventio*, see Rhonheimer, *Natural Law and Practical Reason*, 221ff.

60. A. MacIntyre, *Dependent Rational Animals*, 81.

61. Cf. Diogenes Laertius, *Lives and Teachings of the Famous Philosophers*, VII (on Zeno).

Looking more closely, we see that these virtues are "cardinal" in two different senses. First, they are cardinal in the sense that we treat them as *general* virtues containing all the others as subordinate species. In this sense they wouldn't really be virtues at all but only general terms for categories that are correlated to the various perfections of the various powers or faculties: "We call the virtue that produces the good of rational knowing, prudence; and every virtue that effects the good of what is appropriate and just in actions, justice; every virtue that measures and restrains the passions, temperance; every virtue that strengthens our courage in relation to any passion, courage."[62] To the extent that each moral virtue belongs to one of the four cardinal virtues, they exhaustively cover the entire range of the virtues.

Second, we can consider the cardinal virtues specifically in themselves, that is, as particular kinds of virtues or particular virtues. Then we use their names to designate the habit that perfects their most important and principal acts. Thus prudence is the virtue of the imperative, commanding act of the action-determining reason; justice is the virtue that rules one's actions appropriately among equals; temperance is the virtue that moderates the desires of the sense of touch and so on; courage is what strengthens one against the threat of death.

If we speak of the "parts" of the cardinal virtues, that is, of the particular virtues that belong to each, we are using the first definition, and we add the cardinal virtue (in the second meaning) to them, as the most important and ultimately decisive virtue in each case. "Part," however, can be understood in three ways:

1) as "part of the subject" *(pars subiectiva):* as the species "man" (alongside "lion," "hawk," etc.) is a part of the *genus* "living thing having sense perception," so there are "kinds," "species" of the *genera* "justice," "courage," and so on.

Hence there is a prudence in the area of individual actions, in the realm of certain social contexts (e.g., the family), or in the area of social organization, of the state or government (political prudence). Justice is related to the area of the relationships between human persons (so-called justice of exchange, or justice of contracts, known as *commutative* justice); to the area of the relationships of larger social institutions (the state or one's employer) toward individuals, with respect to the distribution of goods (*distributive* justice). Third, there is justice in an opposite way, in the relationship of individuals toward the competence, right-to-rule, lawmaking, and so on of the superior authority, especially the state, and this is known as *legal* justice. The virtue of temperance is

62. I-II, Q. 61, a. 3.

related most of all to eating, drinking and the sexual drive; the first does not seem to have a name, the second is called "sobriety," the third "chastity" (not to be confused with "continence").

2) as a "component part" *(pars integralis):* as a house is put together out of bricks, beams, window frames, panes of glass, doors, roof tiles, and the like, so there are part-virtues, whose acts in a way are components of the corresponding cardinal virtues and are all necessary within each realm, so that the act of the virtue in question can be carried out completely.

Hence to prudence belong insight and experience; to courage belong generosity, patience, and persistence; to temperance modesty, sense of shame, and decency.

3) as an "associated" or "conditional" virtue *(pars potentialis):* these particular virtues have something in common with the cardinal virtues, but are, as it were, conditions for their possibility, without fully characterizing the virtue in question.

To prudence are associated the virtue of good counsel *(euboulia),* the virtues of good judgment *(synesis* and *gnome);* to justice are associated, for example, religion, gratitude, truthfulness, affability or friendliness, magnanimity or liberality, as opposed to avarice), and fairness; to temperance, for example, abstinence and gentleness.

The classification, in any event, is not without ambiguities. And often the same names are used for a variety of things. There is the passion of anger that can lead to courage, but can be opposed to that virtue as well. "Anger" is also the name of a vice, such that it is opposed to the virtue of temperance, especially that of gentleness (irritability, violent temper). But our primary concern here is not with names as such, nor with providing a comprehensive, watertight system.[63]

This can be seen especially in the names of the vices. As such, every virtue is opposed to a vice, and one can recognize a vice on the basis of knowing the corresponding virtue, or the perfection to which the vice is opposed. The tradition developed a system of the so-called capital vices *(vitia capitalia)* that corresponds more to the reality as phenomenologically apparent than the system of the cardinal virtues ("capital" in the sense of Latin *caput,* "head," not in sense of "headings" but rather as each vice being a "head" from which others spring and function as members).

---

63. Thomas systematizes especially for didactic reasons, and his *Summa Theologiae* was intended, according to its prologue, as a "beginners" handbook. It was a matter of bringing a large amount of material into order, and that did not imply that there were not certain systematic contexts that came to expression. Still, it is not a "system" in the sense of German idealism.

The seven classical vices are reduced in turn to two main "heads," namely, pride *(superbia)* and covetousness *(coditia):* pride is the turning away of one's will from God, covetousness the inordinate desire for finite goods.

There are four main vices that arise from *pride:* they seek for happiness in disordered ways and seem especially opposed to the virtue of temperance:

—*Vanity* is unordered desire for goods of the soul, especially self-admiration

—*Gluttony* is unordered desire for goods of the body, or lust in the area of the drive for nourishment

—*Unchastity* is the same in the area of the sexual drive

—*Greed* (or covetousness in the narrower sense) is the unordered desire for external goods, really a kind of unordered self-sufficiency

Three other principal vices arise from covetousness (*coditia* in the broader sense). They have to do with passions related to courage (and are opposed to that cardinal virtue) and they correspond to reactions called forth when something *that one knows is "good"* is perceived as evil.

—*Sloth* or sluggishness of spirit (*acedia*) is sadness with respect to spiritual goods because of the effort required to attain them.

—*Envy* is sadness over the goods (successes, talents, etc.) that others possess, a sadness brought about by seeking to have one's own advantages be the only ones that matter.

—*Anger* is a conjunction of envy with a passion for revenge or "getting even" ("anger" here is understood as a vice, not as the passion that can be good at times).

This catalog of the principal vices reflects a differentiated but also realistic anthropology. The remedy for these leading depravities of the human being is the moral virtues. *All* the moral virtues will appear to be very relevant to interpersonal relationships. And in fact justice is more frequently injured by envy, greed, vanity, and all forms of lack of temperance than through injustice as such. But the will becomes unjust as soon as it begins to consent to these weaknesses, to justify them, so that they become real principles of acting that begin to lead the practical reason. Disordered striving toward finite goods and pride as a turning away from God's will (irreligiosity, which is not identical with atheism) are the ultimate roots of all injustice.

Nevertheless, this structure of injustice is not identical with the moral theological structure of sin as "turning away from God" *(aversio a Deo)* and an unordered "turning to creatures" *(conversio ad creaturas)*. It is only a part of this latter structure. The "turning from God" studied theologically is a turning away from God as a final end, a loss of the virtue of *caritas,* which is not of concern here. On the level accessible to philosophical reflection, a "turning from God" is simply a certain kind of injustice, an act against the virtue of *religio,* which will be discussed below.

b) The Objective Differentiation (Specification) of the Virtues

Single faculties, or powers, are characterized and differ from one another through their acts, and acts in turn by their objects. A habit *(habitus)* of a power is a disposition toward the completed accomplishment of the corresponding acts. Consequently, such habitual dispositions are differentiated through the objects of the acts whose accomplishment they perfect.

The question about the identifying the content of the virtues leads us back to the theme of the identity of human actions. Basically, particular kinds (species, types) of virtues can be correlated to certain types of basic intentional actions. But virtues are related not only to actions in the strict sense, but also to the ordering of the passions. But these too can lead to actions: acts of speech, movements of bodily members (such as striking something or someone), sexual acts, and so on.

In general, we could say that just as the intentional "why?" is constitutively related to a definite matter of actions, so the objective content of each moral virtue can be determined *formally* on the level of the intentional "why," but this is not possible on the level of the material content of the action, that is, the affective level. Thus Aristotle declares in connection with the virtue of courage that acceptance of suffering and defiance of dangers is not yet "courage" as such; to be sure, "suffering" and "defying dangers" is *matter* of courage. But what is courageous in the virtuous sense is not determined solely on the basis of the matter, but rather and more decisively by *why* the suffering is accepted and the dangers defied. "The man, then, who faces and who fears the right things and with the right aim, in the right way and at the right time, and who feels confidence under the corresponding conditions, is brave; for the brave man feels and acts according to the merits of the case and in whatever way reason directs. Now the end of every activity is conformity to the corresponding state. This is true, therefore, of the brave man as well as of others. But courage is noble. Therefore the end is also noble; for each thing is defined by its end. Therefore it is for a noble end that the brave man endures and acts as courage directs."[64]

Accordingly, it is possible "for courageous behavior to mean very differ-

---

64. *EN* III, 7 (1115b18–24).

ent things in different situations: sometimes it means staying put, at other times, running away; opening your mouth today about something, keeping it closed tomorrow; to give someone something today, to refuse it tomorrow, and so on. And then Aristotle tells us, that if we want to give a name to the common approach that is being realized in all these apparently disparate actions, you must recur to the description of the *habitus* (courage or fortitude) from which all these actions come. Because not only will you find no other description that fits this standing still *and* that running away *and* that refusal to sign something. . . . And furthermore, these various actions (in other situations) could come from another *habitus* (as, for example, 'cowardice', or 'generosity', and so on)."[65] This shows that by the name of any definite habit of moral virtue we refer to certain *species* (kinds or types) of intentional basic actions. Thus we can only describe virtues in their objective content—in a manner analogous to actions in general—in an intentional way, and not tie them firmly to this or that purely external or "physical" action or event. Discourse about virtues is therefore, as Aristotle emphasizes, always talking "in rough outline" [Gr. *en typōi*], a "typological" description.

Nevertheless, it is still possible to go beyond a pure phenomenology of virtue and describe the decisive formal element that specifies the objective-intentional content of the various virtues. While Aristotle limits himself largely to a phenomenology of virtue (and thereby, in the Socratic tradition, to historical examples and narrative expositions),[66] Thomas Aquinas offers an elaborated "criteriology" of moral virtues. This means that he determines the relevant *rational structure* of each virtue: the intentionally constitutive "why" of the accomplished actions and affective states. The objective differentiation of the virtues and their criteria does not need to be set forth in detail here.[67] A few hints should suffice in each case to bring out the essential connection between "moral virtue" and the concept of the object of intentional actions.

External actions as such—even those, in which any kind of emotion plays a role—are all regulated by the virtue of justice. Action based on the emotions is not to be associated merely to a virtue or a vice of the concupiscible or irascible appetitive powers, but also belongs to the region of "justice" or "injustice."

Actions always possess a relation "to another," whether this be a fellow human being or God. There is also required for them a "measurement toward the other" *(commensuratio ad alterum),* where there is in each case something "due" *(debitum)* or "not due" *(indebitum),* which are a kind of legal relation-

65. A. W. Müller, *Praktische und technische Teleologie*, 62.
66. Cf., e.g., *NE* III, 8.
67. Cf. I-II, Q. 60.

ship. This is the formal basis of "justice." But this is now specified according to the differentiation of the matter, that is, differently constituted realms of action. The realms form a *materia circa quam,* that is to say, a "matter concerning which" the action takes place, and the measuring of which through the reason constitutes the object of action (cf. above, III.4.b).

But the so-called *debitum,* that which is required in relation to others, is, again, going to be different according to differing matters of action. In this way *objectively* various relationships of justice arise between peers, inferiors, and superiors; or on the basis of contracts, promises, or grants. And thus there are objectively different virtues, such as religion, by which God is given his due; *pietas,* according to which parents and one's country are given what they should get; and gratitude, for benefactors. There is a justice in contractual relationships, loyalty, justice toward the possessions of another, relationships of justice in interpersonal communication (truthfulness), and so on.[68]

Actions such as "thievery," "adultery," "murder," or "lying," the objective identity of which was discussed earlier, therefore belong in each case to the area of a definite special virtue or corresponding vice. That concerns their *objective* content, but not necessarily the *mode* of their accomplishment. What this means is this: it is possible to commit an injustice "objectively," not out of injustice, but (for example) out of anger. The action is then not necessarily unjust in the sense of the vice, of a *habitus* that is, but is instead such only because of weakness, even though of course the action nevertheless remains an unjust action and belongs objectively to the realm of the vice.

> When someone is unfaithful to a spouse, he no doubt commits an injustice, and the action is bad, but he is probably not acting from injustice but from emotion. Contrition and regret can bring it about in this case that the will may even be strengthened in loyalty to the spouse, and the person who was responsible for the deed can actually become truer and more just. But this will not happen if he does not admit his mistake and is foolish enough to say it was "only a little slip-up" on his part, that he didn't mean or intend to do anything bad, and so on; then his will would in fact become a bad will. But weakness in conjunction with humility is really a way to virtue, when the other helps by being able to forgive. Forgiveness is one of the most important acts of goodwill toward another.

Moral virtues that have to do with the passions are differentiated and specified not in accordance with a measuring "in relation toward another," but with relation to the person himself, in terms of Aristotle's "mean in relation to ourselves." They are not specified according to their object *as* pas-

---

68. Cf. ibid., a. 3.

sions (this merely formulates the natural identity of the act), but rather with regard to the relationship of this object to the reason (which alone constitutes the moral identity of the object) because "in morality reason acquires a commanding and moving function."[69] And reason accordingly also constitutes the object of those virtues that are the perfections or completions of the sensitive appetites.

In this way, certain passions *as* passions operate contrarily to one another: for example, sadness and joy, fear and boldness. That does not mean that they correspond to two different virtues also. For in relation to the reason—that is, as regards their object or *bonum rationis*—they form an objective unity. The moral virtue will consist in the rationally measured *mean* of such affects: neither "too much" nor "too little" fear, boldness, sadness, joy, but just so much as is appropriate. *What* in each case is in fact the mean results not from the nature of the passions that happen to be involved, but from the judgment of the reason according to circumstances in which the acting subject finds himself.

> Someone who is always cheerful about everything, and incapable of feeling sad, does not have the *virtue* of cheerfulness. For one must also be ready to grieve in due measure over the presence of real evils when they happen, in order to resist such evils more easily[70] and to be able to console others not just with lovely words but through real "sym-pathy" [Gr. *syn*, "with," *path*-, "suffering"]. But with regard to what is good, the virtuous person cannot be sad (that would be the vices of *acedia* or envy), because the good is "connatural" to the virtuous person. *Virtus delectat in propriis* ["Virtue delights in what is its own"],[71] and that is of course the good.

It is also possible that the same virtue comes to be in relation to various passions, caused by an order of succession among them, which again will result from their relationship to reason. Thus the ordering of reason constitutes with respect to love (as the feeling of being seized by something desirable to the senses), the ensuing desire, and the resulting sensual delight, the same virtue as its opposite: dislike, flight or avoidance, and sadness. With the various virtues of courage this is not the case, because there is here no succession of distinct particular emotions. Thus, for example, courage is constituted (as a special virtue) with relation to the passions of fear and boldness; magnanimity with respect to hope and hesitation; gentleness with respect to anger (wherewith the most gentle of all gentle souls chased the money-changers out of the temple, because in this case it was *appropriate*).

This brief sketch should show how all the virtues are constituted through

---

69. Ibid., a. 1.
71. Ibid.

70. Cf. I-II, Q. 59, a. 3.

the ordering, measure-giving function of reason. The analysis of human actions and their objective identity corresponds therefore with the analysis of the objective identity of moral virtues. "Good" and "bad" in moral actions—as equivalent to what is according-to-reason or not—is always what is according-to-virtue or its opposite. And what corresponds to virtue is not only the good, but also the right. This explains why Thomas, in the prologue to his special treatise on virtue, calls it his program to understand a mistake in action on the basis of the virtue opposed to that mistake, so that the entire doctrine of morality could be reduced to an analysis of the virtues.[72] Moral error is always a willed missing of the good, a *lack* of the needed commitment of the will to what is good according to the reason, that is, a *privatio boni:* evil is not a being at all; as a lack, it is rather a "not-being." Only in the light of the knowledge of the good can we recognize such a nonbeing as lack and thereby evil; for one only recognizes a lack by knowing what it is a lack *of.*

c) Prudence

As already mentioned in passing, prudence is really an intellectual or dianoetic virtue—a virtue of the intellect—which on the basis of its dependence on appetition and its function of cognitively leading the choice of action, is also counted as one of the moral virtues. Traditionally it was called the *auriga virtutum,* the "charioteer of the virtues." Prudence is also known as the *forma virtutum,* the "form (or soul) of all the other virtues," since the matter of emotions or of actions that is specific to the other virtues is related to the act of prudence in the same way as matter *(circa quam)* is related to form. For understanding the relationship between the judgment of prudence and the matter of the other particular virtues, the same structural connections hold that were explained in the analysis of the object of actions.[73]

Prudence is the *habitus* of right or good judgment of actions, the judgment, that is, which informs the choice of actions (an act of will). We all naturally possess a certain knack or skill of the reason to find the way to an end. This skillfulness—Aristotle calls it *deinotēs*—which is a "natural virtue" or "natural disposition" of which some have more, some less, is nevertheless

---

72. Cf. II-II, prologue.

73. Höffe's formulation, that Aristotle's *phronesis* or prudence is the "necessary supplement of the virtues of character," must be seen as highly unfortunate (cf. O. Höffe, "Aristoteles' universalistische Tugendethik," in K. Rippe and P. Schaber, eds., *Tugendethik,* 59). Prudence does not "complete" the "virtues of character" justice, courage, and temperance, but rather makes it possible for these even to be *virtues* at all (and not just certain characteristics or dispositions which could also be misused). Secondly, as we shall see, prudence is itself a virtue of character, since it is inseparable from rightly disposed appetition.

not yet prudence (although Kant did identify it with prudence). It can also be cunning or mischievousness *(panourgia)*. There is an apparent prudence: for example, that of the skillful cheater on taxes; or one can be very "clever" in robbing a bank or some other kind of crime. This "prudence of the flesh" however, is no virtue, even if it is accompanied by a great deal of skillfulness. It is not prudence because it does not help one become a better human being; it is a counterfeit, bearing only the name of prudence.[74] True prudence, nevertheless, is always the "skillfulness" of reason for the good.

Here, too, a distinction must be made: a businessman or a ship's captain can possess that professional kind of prudence that makes it possible for them to be good in their professions. And in both cases, to want to become a good captain or a good businessman is again not a bad thing and *could* be part of a larger program of "realizing one's humanity." It could be said of a good businessman, "That was a prudent decision. Thanks to his decision, the company was saved." But that is not the prudence we are here concerned with.

The true virtue of prudence intends those goals that are meaningful for life *as a whole,* as *human life.* It is "wisdom in human affairs."[75] And this means the things that concern the common goal of human life, a goal that consists in directing all appetition according to reason. A "prudent" businessman can also be a very sly crook, even if he is not incompetent in any way *as* a businessman. Because he could still be unjust as a human being: if, for example, he conducts some unsavory political business with the profits he has earned in a perfectly innocent way. And the "prudent" ship's captain—who is blameless in the art of navigation and the management of his crew, an expert in his business—could still be a pirate.

Prudence, which has the task of determining the "means," that is, the concrete actions that lead toward an end, is not simply concerned with the means and efficiency. Or, to put it another way, in order for an action to be *morally* efficient as well, its goal must also be good (cf. III.3). The intended goal is intentionally present in the willing act of the choice of action. And just so, in the prudent act, an orientation toward good goals must be present. Otherwise, the concrete action is simply not good. Prudence, like action in general, always has a goal for its object, not insofar as to determine it, but insofar as it is directly dependent on it, and is always "for some goal," always judges for the sake of some goal. For the prudent person, the "why" is always on the right track.

Prudence constitutes the *practical truth* of action. "Practical truth" is what Aristotle calls the truth that is constituted through agreement with the right ap-

74. Cf. II-II, Q. 47, a. 13.
75. Cf. II-II, Q. 47, a. 2, ad 1.

petition of the goal.[76] This kind of truth is multiple by nature and, according to the contingency of the matter of actions and feelings, also something that is "always different." The decisive thing for the "practical truth" of a choice of action or of a willed action is (1) the rectitude or goodness of the striving, and (2) the agreement of action with this rectitude of striving. An objectively bad action (means) cannot be "healed" through a good purpose, because there cannot be any possibility of agreement between a bad will (act of choosing) and a good will (intention).

The habit of prudence is formed through directing the natural "skillfulness" of the reason toward the good. Three different actions are implied in this. The process of prudence moves through three phases: *consideration, judgment,* and *command* (to action). Consideration prepares the way for the act of judgment. Judgment as such, however, does not lead directly to action. There can frequently be right judgment, but then no action, when, for instance, fear intervenes. And this means that the person is not really prudent. For only he (or she) is prudent who also effectively *does* what is right and appropriate. The final act is decisive: the command to act, a genuine *imperium* or *praeceptum* of the practical reason.[77] (Aristotle accordingly calls prudence *epitaktikē,* "commanding" or "bidding.")[78] This final commanding act of the practical reason is nothing other than the cognitive aspect of the choosing-act of the will. Prudence is above all *imperium electionis* ("command of choosing"), the command of the practical reason to carry out action. Or, more precisely, *prudence is the virtue of the imperative act of the practical reason.*[79] This judgment of the practical reason is of the kind "p is good," "p must be done here and now," which immediately triggers action.

And once more we need to recall here that practical reason is reason that is embedded within the process of appetition (cf. above, III.3.a). "Human action" is an appetitive phenomenon. The process of practical reasoning is nothing other than a constant concretization of striving (or appetition), until the point of the choosing of a concrete action. The final judgment, which determines this appetition concretely to an action, is the judgment of prudence. All previous cognitive and appetitive elements are intentionally present in it. The commanding act of prudence comes into being because it is a judgment that is embedded in appetition. And that is why this striving must also be good, in order for the action which is embedded in it to be good. The prudent person is simply the good person, the virtuous person: the one who in action does not go astray in judging the good action and attains to what is according to

76. Cf. *EN* VI, 2 (1139a 30).   77. II-II, Q. 47, a. 8.
78. *EN* VI, 11 (1143a8).
79. Cf. also A. Rodriquez Luño, *La scelta ethica,* 83ff.

reason. Thus Aristotle says that prudence is "a true and reasoned state of capacity to act with regard to the things that are good or bad for man." The end here is "good action" itself.[80]

> This does not rule out that prudence must also possess specific competencies for the various particular fields of action. The action of a doctor, for example, also needs the technical competence that belongs to the area of medicine. The same goes for other fields. But in order for the action of a doctor to be prudent (in the sense of the virtue), it is not enough for him to be a skilled and competent doctor. One can perform unjust deeds with perfect medical competence in surgery (e.g., by doing an abortion), and thus the action is imprudent. On the other hand, to perform an operation (even one that is really called for and good to perform) without adequate special knowledge is not only medically incompetent but also morally wrong, that is, imprudent. We could call this being "irresponsible," and that would be a lack of prudence. In general, one should refer to what was said earlier about "good" and "right" (cf. also below, V.4.b).

To the extent that prudence is perfected, it is also known as the exclusion of the possibility of error *(error electionis)*. This does not mean that in every situation there is only *one* good concrete action possible. But in every case the action of the prudent person is good—and if it happens not to be, this occurs only through an inculpable ignorance of the circumstances, which does *not* arise from a lack of appetitive rectitude, or right striving. Prudence is consequently *recta ratio*, "right reason," in the genuine sense, not because reason here "applies" the right norm, but because "prudence" means practical reason under those conditions whereby reason itself can be a "norm," because it is truly *reason* here: on the basis of the right appetition of a goal and right emotional ordering, through the light of a knowing that is in no way distorted or distracted.

But now the question again arises: What happens when prudence is "imperfect," and how does one *acquire* prudence at all, since it presumes the possession of all moral virtues and these, in turn, can only come into being through the guidance of prudence? How can the practical reason engaged in a concrete choice of action meet with the good under the condition of an imperfect rightness of striving? How can prudence achieve this despite weakness and the real possibility of ignorance in choosing that goes with it?

These are questions that Aristotle solves by his "polis ethics," a solution that no longer seems adequate for us today. We need clarification about how the human being, independently in a certain way of the *habitus* of virtue, can recognize those principles that can guide his action-determining practical

---

80. *EN* VI, 5 (1140b5–7).

reason toward something that corresponds to virtue. According to Aristotelian action-theory, even this appetitive act that strives for a goal must somehow be guided by reason.[81] It cannot simply arise from conditioning. And *this* reason, which directs itself to the goals of virtue, that is, to its principles, would then be, in a way, the cognitive origin of all virtues, as a practical rationality capable of orienting action independently of virtue and prior to the possession of virtue (cf. V.1–3).

But we need a second thing in addition: a clarification of the judgment of action itself: how this judgment is, at least, implicit, that is, spontaneously present, even in the act of prudence. This is because, although every prudent judgment is an affective judgment, it is still a judgment of reason. Therefore there must be structures of reason in that act that can be separately analyzed (cf. V.4).

Now there are hints and starting points for this in Aristotle, perhaps in his doctrine of *euboulia* as the virtue of right deliberation, and in *synesis* and *gnomē* as virtues of right judgment. But this is still not enough to establish those basic structures of moral judgment insofar as they are not the *habitus* of prudence but mere practical reason that does indeed recognize what is in fact prudent—meaning, judges according to what is prudent and as the prudent person would judge—but nevertheless does this not on the basis of an affective connaturality with what is according to reason, but simply from mere rationality (how such a "mere" rationality is at all possible, being itself a problem). Such structures would reveal themselves, for example, in formal principles such as "the end does not justify the means" and "it is better to suffer injury than to do it." Such structures are related to questions like these: "Are we responsible for all the consequences of our actions?" "To what extent, and according to which criteria, must we include such consequences in our judgments of action?" "How are the circumstances of a choice of action to be weighed?" Or: "Are there actions that are always bad? How do we identify them?" A fourth kind of question is: "Should we always do what we recognize as good to do?" and "What degree of certainty is needed about the rectitude of an action in order to be able to do it?" Or, asked in another way: "Under what conditions is an action that turns out to be wrong still a good action, that is, when do we act with inculpable ignorance?" These are questions of conscience.

Such questions are actually questions that are related to prudence but

81. This is emphasized in the work of D.J.Allan that was so pioneering for more recent Aristotle interpretation: "Aristotle's Account of the Origin of Moral Principles" (1953), reprinted in J.Barnes, M.Schofield, and R.Sorabji, eds., *Articles on Aristotle*, vol. 2: *Ethics and Politics* (London: Duckworth, 1977), 72–78. Cf. also D.J.Allan, *The Philosophy of Aristotle* (Oxford: Oxford University Press, 1952; new ed. 1970).

not insofar as it is a habit, that is, a moral virtue.[82] They are not questions that prudence in the true sense of the word *poses* for itself or has to pose, but rather are questions *about* prudence. For someone who is a prudent person in the sense of having the virtue will not be in the situation of asking himself whether the end justifies the means, in order, on the basis of such a judgment, to leave off performing an act in certain circumstances, which he had been inclined to do, to begin with; or whether he should follow his conscience. *Insofar* as he possesses the virtue of prudence, he will never be inclined to a bad action and his spontaneous—even, affectively guided—judgment of action will always command a good action.

But who would be in that position? Or who would, at least, *always* be in that position? And must not even the prudent person come up against unfamiliar situations, in which he must reach back to structures of "mere rationality" (a classical example would be *in dubio pro reo:* "when in doubt, favor the accused")? Are not the circumstances of action and consequences often complex and always new, so that any *habitus* must really somehow lag "behind" the requirements of actual practical insight?

In fact, that is the case. Otherwise the basic moral questions about how to lead one's life would be no different than what they were two thousand years ago. In human life it is usually and most pressingly not a matter of highly complex decisions, but rather always those ever-familiar issues in the areas of relationships with oneself and one's fellow human beings: death and life, truthfulness, possession, loyalty, patience, persistence, moderation, and so on. Only when clarity reigns here can questions relating to acting in more complex contexts be satisfactorily answered: questions, that is, that concern society, humanity, the world as a whole. Even the solutions of these are measured, finally, by the answers to the basic questions.

In fact, Aristotle only treats the case of perfected prudence, the ideal case. He is aware, to be sure, of the imperfect human being and analyzes him: the vicious person, whom he holds to be incapable of improvement, and the incontinent person who does what is bad even though he really knows what is good. But as Julia Annas has maintained, ancient ethics posits the virtuous person in the complete sense, who possesses complete prudence, as an ideal that can then be effective as an ideal in a moral life understood as an evolutionary process.[83]

But just for this reason, the absence of an ethical theory of the "structures of rationality" is remarkable. Even Thomas Aquinas does not completely fill

---

82. This is how the doctrine of prudence is developed by P. Geach, *The Virtues*, 2nd ed. (Cambridge: Cambridge University Press, 1979), 88–109.

83. Cf. J. Annas, *The Morality of Happiness*, 83.

this gap. This is not surprising for a theologian, which Thomas ultimately is: there is a theological answer for the problem of incomplete prudence: the "healing of nature" through grace and the revelation of fundamental moral principles as divine law. This answer is of course the essentially and specifically theological answer. But it does not help philosophically, and theologically it is imperfect, as soon as one considers that revelation and grace always presuppose nature, and in a way "come to its aid." But they should do that also on the level of the judgment of actions. Then there would be a need of natural structures that would be susceptible to such assistance, in order to keep everything from falling into a revelatory positivism or what is—often unjustly—called "legalism." Thus there is a need not only for theological reasons but especially for philosophical reasons for a completion of classical ethics by an ethics of the judgment of actions and the practical principles that precede such judgment. That means there is a need for what is known in modern and contemporary parlance as "normative ethics" and "moral philosophy."

Such a need has been—and only very inadequately—supplied by the "deontologism" of Kantian ethics (its most genial critic being Hegel). No less unsatisfactory is the utilitarian theory of moral judgment that goes today by the name of "teleological ethics" (see V.4.f). But both Kantian and utilitarian moral philosophy, because they have left behind the classical doctrine of virtue ethics, have raised a real problem that must be treated in any virtue ethics today. But the solutions will now take on a very different coloring. On the other hand, the discourse-ethics that has been developed in the last three decades within the Kantian tradition once again leaves behind what is specific to virtue ethics, by allowing only an intersubjective discourse about norms to be the foundation for any possible claims of value, and thus from the outset is rather a kind of ethics of law and politics.

Classical moral theological handbooks, on the other hand, did develop such an ethics of the judgment of actions: in the form of a theory, for the most part incomplete, of conscience, and the classical doctrine of the *"fontes moralitatis,"*[84] the "double effect," and so on, mainly as guidance for enabling one to judge the actions of *others*. The reason for this peculiarity was the use of such handbooks in the preparation of priests for hearing confessions. The morality of the manuals reflected the classical wisdom of virtue ethics, but were in-

---

84. That this doctrine is really no part of a so-called normative ethics, but rather only presupposes the determination of (objective) "good" and "bad," has been shown rather fittingly, in my opinion, by B. Schüller, "Die Quellen der Moralität. Zur systematischen Ortung eines alten Lehrstückes der Moraltheologie," *Theologie und Philosophie* 59 (1984): 535–59. Cf. also G. Stanke, *Die Lehre von den "Quellen der Moralität." Darstellung und Diskussion der neoscholastischen Aussagen und neuerer Ansätze* (Regensburg: Pustet, 1984); G. Höver, *Sittlich handeln in Medium der Zeit. Ansätze zur handlungstheoretischen Neuorientierung der Moraltheologie* (Würzburg: Echter, 1988).

creasingly not understood in context. The new context was that of "law" and "conscience," which finally led to so-called moral positivism and legalism: a primarily casuistic treatment about "commands" and the conditions for when and how they were obliging, and how much had to be reserved for their claims as opposed to the freedom of the individual.[85] Contemporary criticism of legalistic morality nevertheless remains all too often dominated by the same fundamental categories. Thus someone, not seeing that a "command" is really a replacement sign for "virtue" and that it thus really points to the fulfillment of freedom, ends up trying to use moral norms to expand the "freedom" of the individual that has been (allegedly) thus constricted.

d) Justice I: Justice as Benevolence and Its Social Character

The virtue of justice is the perfecting of the will with regard to "seeking the good of others." It is the firm and constant will to give "each his own," to give each person what is due to each person, and to do this, of course, as already mentioned (IV.3.b) in the various fields of interpersonal relationships, which form, in turn, the various parts of the virtue of justice, as special virtues: commutative, distributive, and legal justice.

Why does the will need this at all—a habitual perfecting in its being directed toward the good of others? Thomas answers this question as follows:[86] The good of another person can only be an object of reason: the sense power cannot strive after and grasp a good for others, but only for oneself, the one who himself is striving.

In order, for example, for sexuality to really be a subject of human love and virtue, it must always be *more* than mere sexuality, since otherwise it would remain purely self-interested. In the same way, we have no drive to be nourished by food and drink that strives for the self-preservation of *others*. Only a rationally directed appetition would be capable of that. But the drive for nourishment as a sense-drive and self-interested drive, serves self-preservation, by its nature. Human sexuality, however, is by nature not at all self-interested, but rather a component of a relationship between two persons, and consequently it must *always* be directed toward the "good of the others" (and the good of the human species falls under the same category), which as *mere* sexuality, that is, as a mere drive, it could never do.

Since the reason has the good of another for its object, this good nevertheless transcends the "proportion" of the will. What the will naturally strives for *spontaneously* and *persistently*, that is, *habitually*, is only one's own good. The

---

85. For a presentation and criticism of this tradition, cf. S. Pinckaers, *The Sources of Christian Ethics* (Washington, D.C.: The Catholic University of America Press, 1985).
86. I-II, Q. 56, a. 6.

striving of the will must therefore also be directed according to reason. This is why it requires a *habitus* of justice in the will, namely, the virtue.

But this is not in the least meant to imply that the human being is an egotist by nature. There are principles of justice that are naturally reasonable, such as the golden rule: "Whatever you don't want others to do to you, don't do to them" or, put positively: "Do unto others as you would have them do unto you." Similar is also: "Love your neighbor as yourself." For such principles to be intelligible and to be able to strive to do what they command, reason and will do not need any virtue as such. Hence Aristotle can say that man feels toward man as a friend and belonging to a family.[87] There is a kind of natural solidarity among human beings that can only be destroyed by a habitual rejection of justice—by the vice of injustice. Thomas also speaks in a similar way about a "natural instinct" by which human beings help and support each other.[88]

The problem arises at the level of the *habitus*. Here, the will that *by nature* is directed to one's own good is stronger. It "naturally" possesses a habitual orientation to *one's own* good and is thus by nature *inclined* to favor the good of the self to the good of the other. It is only the *habitus* of justice that can lend the will that second nature of virtue that enables it to strive for the good of others with the same habitual firmness, constancy, and joy that it naturally has in seeking its own good. The just person is pleased about the good of the other to the same degree as he is pleased about his own good (and it is the same with sadness about the evil of others: the vices opposed to this virtuous joy and sorrow would be envy and delight in the misfortunes of others). It appears just as pleasant and attractive for the just man to seek the good of others as to seek his own. The other person becomes an *alter ipse* to him, "another self."[89] He has acquired that affective connaturality which he naturally has only with relation to what pertains or is owed to himself, but now also in relation to what pertains and is owed to others. He loves his neighbor "as himself." This is because "to love" in this context is only another word for "to will." Thus the virtue of justice is already a habit of "good willing" with respect to others, the first realization of that love that is called "the love [consisting in] friendship" *(amor amicitiae* or *amor benevolentiae).*

Justice, then, by its very essence has to do with the relationship with one's fellow human being: to the other as a person: to the life, physical integrity, material and spiritual goods that belong to him. Justice strives for a certain "equilibrium,"[90] an *aequalitas* that has the character of something owed to the

87. *EN* VIII, 1 (1155a21–22).
88. *Summa contra gentiles*, III, cap. 116.
89. *EN* IX, 4 (1166a 32); *Summa Theologiae* I-II, Q. 28, a. 1.
90. II-II, Q. 57, a. 1.

other person in each case. This is the "right" or "justice" of one's fellow man, *ius* or *iustum*, a datum that exists objectively for one who acts, and based on the actual state of things, on legal considerations and other limiting conditions.[91] This is precisely the object of the virtue of justice. For justice is nothing other than "a habit through which someone gives to each person what is just, with a constant and lasting will."[92]

Injustices, consequently, are all "injuries" [cf. Lat. *in + ius, iuris*] to what is just. They take respect away from the other person through denying what belongs to him. They destroy the balance between rights and duties. In saying this Thomas distinguishes between justice in general and special kinds of justice. The former refers to what we owe others as a whole, that is, to the common good. This priority of interest in the common good may be surprising, but it illustrates the fact that for Thomas the relation to fellow men is necessary and is always mediated through the shared structures of community living within society.[93] "Therefore the acts of all the virtues belong to justice, since they orient men to the common good."[94] Since it is the business of law to direct the actions of men to the common good, this general justice can also be called "legal justice." In this most universal sense, also: "All vices, insofar as they are opposed to the common good, have the characteristic of being unjust."[95] Whenever we do something bad we always—in this most general and unspecified sense—do something against justice.

And this must be distinguished from special justice, which is related in a direct and immediate way to the relationships with fellow human beings, whether in the distribution of goods *(iustitia distributiva)* or in transactions involving exchange *(iustitia commutativa).* Injustice is here an "imbalance in the relationship to others, to the extent that someone wants too many of the goods—such as wealth or honor—and too little of the evils—such as toil or loss."[96] Thus for each area of justice, there is a peculiar kind of injustice opposed to it. Special kinds of justice involve, as Thomas puts it, "co-ordination" with one's fellows when it comes to external actions and the things with which these actions are concerned. Justice cannot be separated from social coordination and cooperation. Justice always possesses a social character at its core. As such, it is the virtue through which man directs himself to the well-being of society and of all human beings quite independently of law. This is why it also

---

91. This concept of "right" should not be confused with "right" in the modern sense of a subjective "right" or claim on justice (a "right to" something).

92. II-II, Q. 58, a. 5.

93. Cf. also the chapter entitled "Individual and Social Justice" in T. Gilby, *Principality and Polity: Aquinas and the Rise of State Theory in the West* (London: Longmans, Green, 1958), 219–27.

94. II-II, Q. 58, a. 5.   95. Ibid., Q. 59, a. 1.

96. Ibid.

cannot be separated from *caritas,* or love, even though it remains different from love in its essence. Fundamentally—on the level of what is "owed" or duty—justice, for Thomas, is still just a basic form of that benevolence of which *caritas* represents the ultimate, grace-effected fulfillment. Precisely for this reason, every action that is opposed to justice is also opposed to love for human beings, because what corresponds to justice is always just what love also requires (the opposite is not the case: love requires many things that mere justice does not). Every injustice means in some way the injury of another, and every injury of another is in itself opposed to love which moves us to strive for the well-being of others.[97] Love and justice both find their common root in *meaning well,* in *benevolence* toward one's fellow man. Love is of course a higher form of this good-willing that completes and transcends it (as Aristotle had already said about friendship). But the shared structure of well-meaning reveals the nature and influence of injustice: it implies an antisocial, nonsolidarian relationship between human persons, and in the most varied ways. Thomas brings out this connection between justice and social relations more fully than Aristotle.[98]

For Thomas, then, in every act of injustice not only is the relationship to a concrete individual human being (who is injured) at risk, but also the relationship in which one stands to society as a whole, and thereby potentially every other human being as a member of that community. The well-known formulas of the principle of justice ("Give to each his own," "Harm no one," or the Golden Rule: "Do unto others as you would have them do unto you") may seem trivial, even empty formulas. But we must be careful to avoid the mistake of confusing the fundamental with the trivial. In fact what we see here are *principles,* and that means "starting points," for all further discussion about justice. There cannot be any discussion without the principles. Moreover, in such principles, which are themselves contents of judgments of the practical reasoning of the acting subject, the human person is constituted as a social being and as a subject of justice. We will return to this in chapter V.

But the good will or benevolence that we have been speaking of, which is the essential mark of justice, strictly speaking pertains only to the "justice" or "right" of another person. And "right" (what is "owed") can be taken in two senses:[99] that which is "naturally" or "by nature" just, and that which is

97. Ibid., a. 4. See for further details my "Sins Against Justice (IIa IIae, qq. 59–78)," in S. Pope, ed., *The Ethics of Aquinas* (Washington, D.C.: Georgetown University Press, 2002), 287–303.

98. Especially important in this connection is the virtue of truthfulness, which will be discussed below along with its opposed vice: lying (II-II, Q. 109 and 110, among the "potential parts" of the virtue of justice). We can call truthfulness (or sincerity) "justice in communication": indeed, the medium of language is the necessary precondition for, and most fundamental expression of, human social relations; misuse and violation of this medium is treated by Thomas as unjust in a fundamental way. We will return to this point.

99. Cf. II-II, Q. 57, a. 2.

just by human convention (positive justice). It is right by nature for a definite service performed to receive an equivalent compensation. An article for sale "naturally" has a price (but not a determined one). A gift "naturally" expects a "thanks" from the receiver. Something is just "on the basis of human convention," for example, when a contract is signed or something is done according to a regulation, or the like. This establishes relationships of justice. "Natural [justice is] that which everywhere has the same force and does not exist by people's thinking this or that; legal [justice is] that which is originally indifferent, but when it has been laid down is not indifferent, e.g. that a prisoner's ransom shall be a mina, or that a goat and not two sheep shall be sacrificed, and again all the laws that are passed for particular cases, e.g. that sacrifice shall be made in honor of Brasidas, and the provisions of decrees."[100]

e) Justice II: Human Rights and Political Ethics

"Human rights" are those rights that pertain to the human being "by nature": they are not attributed to man only on the basis of man-made legislation. But just as every man-made legal determination—in the realm of commercial contracts, for example—modifies and concretizes the justice that is already there by nature, just so human laws are always a modification of human rights. "Abstract" human rights that could be appealed to unconditionally as such are a figment of the imagination. This would be like "presenting a check for payment in a social order that lacked the institution of money."[101] "Human rights" and "natural rights" are always historically variable since they can only exist within concrete and ever shifting historical conditions. This is because human beings always live in particular historical conditions that change. But this does not mean that human rights themselves are only "historical" or "relative," or even, as MacIntyre himself maintains, "fictions."[102]

Consequently, human rights can also be injured. "Freedom of religion," for

---

100. *EN* V, 7 (1134b 19–24).

101. A. MacIntyre, *After Virtue*, 2nd ed., 67.

102. Ibid., 70. See also Rhonheimer, *Natural Law and Practical Reason*, 522–25, and E. Schockenhoff, *Natural Law and Human Dignity: Universal Ethics in an Historical World*, trans. B. McNeil (Washington, D.C.: The Catholic University of America Press, 2003), 30–41. MacIntyre is here arguing against the position of Gewirth,, *Reason and Morality* (Chicago: University of Chicago Press, 1978), 63, and his thesis (in MacIntyre's words) is that "every rational agent has to recognize a certain measure of freedom and well-being as prerequisites for his exercise of rational agency. Therefore each rational agent must will, if he is to will at all, that he possess that measure of goods" (*After Virtue*, 66). MacIntyre is correct to affirm in this connection that there is a difference between what someone needs and what someone has a right to, and in any event, Gewirth would scarcely deny this. But he also affirms that the above-mentioned principle expresses a claim on other persons, not to rob them of such basic presuppositions ("freedom and well-being") or to act against them (cf. *Reason and Morality*, 66). As soon, of course, as third persons are assumed, in suitable circumstances right-claims can be derived from needs that qualify.

example, means that everyone has a right to worship the God that he recognizes in his conscience as the true one. If other persons—for example, state authority—forbid a person from worshipping "his own" God, or compel him to practice a religion to which he does not, in conscience, subscribe, it is an injury to human rights. It can be the case, however, that such freedom can have a damaging effect on one's fellows, that it harms the community life or destabilizes the social order. If "human rights" were understood abstractly, even under these circumstances the public prohibition of such a religion would be considered an injury to religious freedom, and any legal prosecution of it would lead to an irresoluble conflict. Contemporary society is characterized by such conflicts that result from the appeal to rival, mutually exclusive, abstractly conceived "human rights" without taking the common good into consideration. No matter how fundamental it may be, every "human right" is always one component of the totality of the relationships of justice within a certain society and the assertion of that right must in turn be judged by moral criteria (even though that is often not possible through lack of consensus). The "others" always have "their" human rights, too, such, for instance, as the right to a peaceful and orderly society. Would we consider the prohibition of a religion that practiced human sacrifice as an infringement of human rights? Accordingly, human rights are not valid in unconditional abstractness, even if they are undeniable and inalienable in themselves.

The abstract idea of a "natural right" is a creation of the modern era, which contains many indispensable insights, but at the same time exudes the one-sided spirit of rationalism. A theory of natural rights would have to be completely recast in terms of the doctrine of justice as a virtue. Even apart from the fact that this is not the business of an introduction to the fundamentals of ethics, the problem of "human rights" is ultimately a theme of *political philosophy*, which according to classical understanding is the conclusion and crown of ethics, since it has for its theme the life of mankind in its totality.[103]

It would seem therefore to be both correct and illuminating to realize that, in view of the Aristotelian understanding of the human being as a *political* being (the *zoon politikon*, "political animal"), there really are no human rights that are, as it were, "prior" to politics: rights, in other words, of a human being considered as *outside* social, political, or civic existence, simply because there is no such thing as a nonsocial or nonpolitical human being; an approach like

103. Cf. Thomas Aquinas's "Proemium to the Commentary on Aristotle's *Politics*," where he states that "politics" is the first and most perfect of all the practical sciences; see Thomas Aquinas, *Commentary on Aristotle's Politics*, trans. R. Regan (Indianapolis, Ind.: Bobbs-Merrill, 2007). Cf. also for the medieval period in general G. de Lagarde, *La naissance de l'esprit Laïque au declin du Moyen Age*, 5 vols., 1 and 2 (Louvain and Paris: Ed. E. Nauwelaerts, 1956 and 1958).

that would completely miss the essence of the human being as a "political animal." In this sense, "the notion that certain rights are natural rights goes very far back in history. The impression easily arises that certain things like private property or the freedom to assemble could actually exist or have a meaning completely divorced from any kind of state. In reality, such things all assume a political order. It would make more sense to refer to these rights as political or social rights."[104]

Talk of "human rights" as "natural" or "prepolitical" rights provides a plausible, if easily misunderstood, interpretation of them as representing a kind of "ought" to be held against the actual "is" of a given social and political system that in certain ways despises such rights. Only for this reason can human rights even be realized at all within a historical process as an institutional and constitutional reality.[105]

Precisely this constitutional-institutional reality of human rights as *fundamentally actionable* civil rights that can be enforced through an independent administration of justice is nevertheless the political, and therefore the practical and real, content of human rights. There is no better illustration of this than the example of the freedom of religion: here it is not a question simply of tolerance practiced by the sovereign state on the basis of common insights into "human nature," but rather of an institutionally secured fundamental right that is intended to constitutionally *limit* sovereign power vis-à-vis individual freedom. This is also necessary because the interpretations of what constitutes human nature, true religion, and the like cannot be institutionally ascertained without eliminating the basic civil rights as individual liberty rights.[106]

> The intention of the Vatican II document *Dignitatis Humanae* on freedom of religion was to promote freedom of religion not as an "abstract" human right, but as *civil law (ius civile)*. It is not only the "true idea" that has a right to a social existence, but the *person*, the *citizen*, possesses rights. Of course this also means that, without removing the difference between error and truth, error may not be countered by political means, at least not *because* it is religious error, but only

104. C. J. Friedrich, *Der Verfassungsstaat der Neuzeit* (Berlin-Göttingen-Heidelberg: Springer, 1953), 182 (the original is *Constitutional Government and Democracy* [New York: Blaisdell, 1950]) Cf. also the ever indispensable standard work of G. De Ruggiero, *The History of European Liberalism* (1925; rpt., Boston: Beacon Press, 1959).

105. A good introduction can be found in M. Kriele, *Einführung in die Staatslehre. Die geschichtlichen Legitimitätsgrundlagen des demokratischen Verfassungsstaates,* 4th ed. (Opladen: Westdeutscher Verlag, 1990); cf. also N. Bobbio, *L'età dei diritti* (Turin: Einaudi, 1990).

106. For clarification of this, cf. also E.-W. Böckenförde, *Religionsfreiheit. Die Kirche in der modernen Welt* (Freiburg im Breisgau: Herder, 1990). See also my forthcoming *The Common Good of Constitutional Democracy: Essays in Political Philosophy and on Catholic Social Teaching* which collects a number of articles already published in different languages.

for political-legal reasons, that is, for reasons of the common good or injury done to a third party (cf. the previous example). Understood in this way, a declaration of religious freedom is also a declaration of political-institutional *pluralism* and of priority given to *personal freedom* of conscience (without necessarily including a declaration of religious pluralism, since there does not have to be such a thing; and still less does this mean excluding the possibility that only one religion is the true one. This would not be "fundamentalist" because fundamentalism means wanting to enforce such a claim with political means).

Thus it would be mistaken to understand a demand to "realize human rights" simply as a call for the sovereign state or existing power to act according to certain principles of natural right or to *preserve* certain rights and freedoms. Human rights are not "preserved" by higher political power, but rather are "anchored," "ascertained," "actioned for," and "established," "from below," *against* the sovereign power, for the limitation or restriction of its force (which also can happen with respect to the force of a sovereign people: "popular sovereignty" understood as a political absolute is incompatible, as is any unlimited sovereignty, with the idea of human rights).

The theme of "human rights" is consequently always the same as the theme "freedom of the individual" and "pluralism." A true *political ethics,* and there should be one, cannot limit itself to a pure virtue ethics: it must also become an *institutional* ethics. And that, despite all reservations, is the quintessence of modern political philosophy from Hobbes through Kant and Hegel to Rawls. MacIntyre's "antimodernism" and his "Return to Aristotle" fall short, and appear too one-sided. He also fails to see that modern political philosophy is not the cause of modern conflicts but is the attempt to bring them under control.[107] The problem is one of *mediation,* and of the balancing of virtue ethics with institutional ethics. In this mediation, a "moralistic fundamentalism" that is restricted to the pure pursuit of the goal of recovering the superhistorical "natural rights" postulates is overcome, while the conviction gains ground that political ethics as a truly *practical* philosophy must likewise operate, though not coercively, with the means of *institutionalizing* the reality of peace, freedom, and human dignity—and this is the basic aspiration of classical political liberalism. It does not make sense, therefore, to oppose a value-oriented "morality" to a purely "realistic" politics. This tearing asunder of means and end is not possible at all in the perspective of *praxis:* goals or ends can only take shape in action and become effective at the horizon of concrete means, and that is

107. Cf. also the remarks in the first chapter of my book *La filosofia politica di Thomas Hobbes.* The contradictions into which MacIntyre's critique of modern political philosophy falls are worked out—if not always with sufficient sensitivity for MacIntyre's justified intention—by S. Holmes, *The Anatomy of Liberalism* (Cambridge and London: Cambridge University Press, 1993), 88–121.

why every political morality that really wants to be morality is necessarily a statement about political realities, in the sense of the necessary institutional, legal, and economic demands that are made on political action in a concrete historical situation.[108]

But we do not need to enter into the details of political philosophy or political ethics in this context.[109] In the same way, here we are not treating the virtue of justice in various human relations as commutative, distributive, and legal justice, as a doctrine of government and social participation in "public business." Here, too, disciplines such as legal philosophy and social ethics, political and economic philosophy come into play. Even environmental ethics belongs here, since the environment is not only a component of the good life of individuals, but also of human community life. But it is not the environment that has rights; the human being has rights with relation to the environment: these are rights that ground claims and relations of justice toward those who would destroy it.

> Various aspects of justice will be spoken of below in the context of practical principles and action-judgments. Justice is founded upon practical principles and in the concrete instance it is formed by the structures of prudence.

f) Justice III: Religion

We still need to mention a virtue associated with justice, the virtue of *religion*. Religion is not only a fact, "something there," but also a human virtue that belongs to justice. Justice is giving every other person what is owed to that person. What does man owe God?

What man owes God, to be exact, is what cannot be paid back. If we remain at the merely natural level, we would want to set to one side the idea that man knows God as his *creator*. That is also possible on the basis of reason alone (but there are religions without the idea of God as creator). If God is recognized as the creator of all that is, man would be able to understand his life as a gift given by this known God, to whom he owes thanks. But even if he thinks of God only as the being that is above all other beings, he still can recognize that he owes something to this being, such as reverence.

---

108. This perspective is developed by B. Sutor, *Politische Ethik. Gesamtdarstellung auf der Basis der Christlichen Gesellschaftslehre* (Paderborn: Schöningh, 1991). Cf. also M. Rhonheimer, "Lo Stato costituzionale democratico e il bene commune," in E. Morandi and R. Panattoni, eds., *Ripensare lo spazio politico: Quale aristocrazia? Con-tratto—Rivista di filosofia tomista e contemporanea* 7 (1997): 57–122; republished in English in my forthcoming *The Common Good of Constitutional Democracy*.

109. For a few further reflections, cf. also Martin Rhonheimer, "Perché una filosofia politica? Elementi storici per una riposta," *Acta Philosophica* 1 (1992): 233–63; republished in *The Common Good of Constitutional Democracy*.

The identity of the various religions depends on the image of God at their basis. This is a question of the knowledge about God and the traditions in which man finds himself culturally. There are acts of religion that can be found in any form, everywhere. That this is the case is not in the least an argument for the relativity of all religions or against the view that there can be *one true religion.* Such a conclusion goes against all logic. The universality of the religious phenomenon (even where religion is officially prohibited) and the multiplicity of religions is in fact an argument that religion is a deeply human reality; that, in other words, to the extent that someone acknowledges the existence of God, the reason commands certain acts of justice toward this acknowledged God. And this is so despite its being always an imperfect justice, since perfect justice is only between equals.

The object of acts of religion is not God Himself. On the level of natural morality, "God" is never the object of an action, because He is not the goal of action here. The object is certain actions that are related to God, with which God's greatness is recognized and the debt of reverence that is owed Him is paid.

These actions are called *acts of cult.* Like all human actions, they are at once external and internal (acts of the will), and can be classified as a whole into three types: adoration, prayer, and sacrifice *(devotio, oratio, sacrificium).* All religions recognize these cult actions in some form or another.

The virtue of religion has an architectonic function in human life: it orders the will especially, and in a way all its own. Religion is the fundamental guarantee of justice as such, because it includes humility, which keeps a human being from seeking its own superiority in a disordered way. For this is also precisely what disturbs justice as between human persons.

> In any event: religion can also become fanatical. A sign of this is when, in the name of religion or a religious imperative, fundamental principles of human justice—for example, the prohibition of murder or respect for another person's conscience—are declared obsolete, or when there is a fundamental disregard for the rights of others, often bound up with an egocentric assurance of salvation (such as in the case of suicide bombers and the like).[110] As a rule, fanaticism is really not a religious phenomenon but a political one. This is a kind of politics that uses religious symbols but distorts and misuses their meaning.

Many actions that are not in themselves religious can have a religious dimension: scientific or academic knowledge can become worship of God. But even the demands of morality itself can be looked upon as "that which pleases God," or "what God commands." Kant thus defined religion as "the recogni-

---

110. On this, see esp. what follows concerning the virtue of courage.

tion of all duties as divine commands."[111] Of course, this is a reductive concept of religion—from which Fichte derived the conclusion that "the moral order is itself God"[112]—but it does emphasize all the same that moral action can also be religiously motivated, even though this motivation does not dispense us from the task of trying to figure out what our "duty" is in detail; something is good, not simply because God commands it; rather, because it is good, we recognize that God commands it (to the extent that it is not revealed).

But the human virtue of religion also implies the question whether this God has revealed Himself. The question about the *true* religion can therefore only be meaningful as the question where and when divine revelation is to be found: apart from revelation, a *true* religion that transcends the variety of cultures is unthinkable. The question about the existence of revelation is a reasonable question. It would be unreasonable to exclude the possibility of revelation from the outset as something irrational. That would contradict the reason of religion, that is, it would be irrationality in the area of the virtue of religion, and thereby, ultimately, injustice and lack of humility: a disordered striving for one's own superiority and freedom from limits. But if there were no such revelation, there would not be a *true* religion, but only better or worse religions. Actions of cult would (reasonably) only be those that human beings would judge as fitting according to the standards of reason and tradition and cultural precedent. But here, too, moral standards would exist. For there are religions that have immoral actions of cult, such as human sacrifice: they offend against interpersonal justice.

To sum up: injustice is the worst vice. Weaknesses with respect to the sense drives can always be countered through humility and goodwill. Even if the intemperate person often does unjust things, he does not have to be an "unjust person." But injustice is the perversion of the will itself. And since the will, again, has the act of reason in hand, and can exercise *imperium* [= command] over it, the unjust person is not only someone who is habitually inclined to do unjust things, but also judges what is unjust to be a good thing. Therefore we can call such an unjust will not only "bad" but "evil"—for injustice is something truly evil.

g) Fortitude (or Courage)

Fortitude is the virtue that perfects the acts or passions of the irascible appetitive power in a manner that is according to reason. Emotions of irascibility

---

111. I. Kant, *Critique of Practical Reason*, trans. M. Gregor, 108.

112. J. G. Fichte, *Über den Grund unseres Glaubens an eine göttliche Weltregierung* (*Werke*, ed. I. H. Fichte, vol. 5; rep., Berlin: 1971), 186.

arise on occasions of difficulties and dangers. The extremes that are opposed to the virtue are the fear of making an effort, which hinders the accomplishment of good (cowardice), and recklessness, which goes out against unnecessary and inappropriate risks. Fortitude especially enables one to conquer the fear of death, where such conquest is necessary to accomplish good or avoid evil. The classical case is martyrdom. The virtue of courage protects one against despair (*dis*-couragement) and allows hope; finally, it guards one from the vice of anger and leads to mildness.

More precisely, the virtue of fortitude perfects two aspects of the irascible appetite: what is to be done must be "stepped toward" boldly [cf. Lat. *aggredi,* "to advance toward"]. And resistance [Lat. *resistere*] is needed against difficulties, and for the persistent effort to bring what needs to be done to an end. To fortitude belong, in particular, *patience and persistence.*

Courage (or fortitude), for its part, is again only a condition for becoming prudent, just, and temperate. For whoever strives for what is good will always meet up with difficulties. And to be prudent is only to do what is good, effectively. The fearful or impatient person cannot acquire the virtue of prudence.

But the virtue of fortitude is not just any kind of courage, persistence, or boldness. Someone who does not shrink from wrongdoing does not on that account have the virtue of courage. He may be bold, persistent, fearless, and so on but that is not a virtue in this case. There are "heroes" who are really just crooks. Nothing is more dangerous than a heroic ethos that puts in brackets the question of right and wrong. For we do not praise someone for courage if we cannot *at the same time* praise him for being just. There are people who do not fear death, not for the love of good, but from a perverted love. This is a fearlessness that is "based upon a false appraisal and evaluation of reality."[113] Here "courage" becomes knavery and a functionalizing of the reality-disclosing reason, or fanaticism. In the truly courageous person, courage and justice are at one, and that also means that in order not to do what is wrong, one must be able to suffer wrong and *endure* it. The truly courageous person is, again, the prudent person.

The difficulties that stand in the way of doing good are internal and external. The internal ones are our own deficiencies. One who travels on the path to virtue experiences in himself the fact that the inclinations of his will and senses often rebel against his reason. In order to acquire the virtue of temperance some self-denial is necessary, more often than not, to repress the not-yet ordered inclinations. And self-denial is an act of courage. "It is by continence

---

113. J. Pieper, *The Four Cardinal Virtues* (New York: Harcourt, Brace and World, 1965), "Fortitude," trans. D. F. Coogan, 126.

that we are made as one and regain that unity of self which we lost by falling apart in the search for a variety of pleasures."[114]

External difficulties are frequently other people or structures of injustice in society. Fortitude is needed if you want to realize in action the Socratic maxim that "it is better to suffer wrong than to do it." Without courage there is no justice. The courageous person is marked by *serenity*. He is capable of giving others help and support. He learns to control his imagination, which sometimes counsels fear, in order to steel his nerves, and he overlooks trivialities in order not to be distracted from the essential. He does not act for praise or profit, but from a desire to do what is truly good.

h) Temperance

The virtue of temperance (or moderation) perfects the sense desire (concupiscible power), which is directed toward what appears attractive and pleasant [Ger. *lustvoll*] by the evaluation of the senses. There is pleasure or "lust" of seeing, hearing, smelling, and tasting, but at the basis of them all and the strongest is the sense of touch. This sense determines the desire for eating and drinking and the sexual drive, to which correspond just as many virtues.

The virtue of temperance contains the ordering of appetition in the complex of the personal body-soul unity of man. Without temperance there cannot be real love: neither love of the truth, nor love of another person. Sexuality that has been disintegrated or isolated from the body-soul unity, for example, makes a personal loving relationship between man and wife impossible.

Lack of temperance, the most dominant form of which is unchastity, has various consequences, depending on the situation: irrationality, hastiness in judgment, weakness of character, indolence, egocentricity, sentimentality, aggressiveness, and brutality. It destroys the inclination in a person toward being helpful to others and leads ultimately to a hatred of God.

> The hatred of God *(odium Dei)* is only the ultimate form of turning away from a love of truth. In one of the greatest passages of the *Confessions* Augustine asks himself: "But why does truth engender hatred?" The reason is that man strives by nature to delight in the truth. When he enjoys himself, he does not want to be deceived. Those who, through a lack of temperance, are trapped by sense pleasures would like *this* to correspond to reality. "Because they hate to be proved wrong, they will not allow themselves to be convinced that they are deceiving themselves. So they hate the real truth for the sake of what they take to

114. St. Augustine, *Confessions* X, 29, trans. R. S. Pine-Coffin, p. 102.

heart in its place. Men love the truth when it bathes them in its light; they hate the truth when it proves them wrong."[115] Truth is experienced here as a power that increasingly hides itself from the spirit, and at the same time as the greatest enemy of the fulfillment of one's own disordered striving for happiness.

The virtue of temperance, which is not a shutting off of passion, but its insertion into the ordering of the reason, is, as Aristotle remarks, the real "preserver of prudence" [Gr. *sōphrosynē* from *sōzein phronesin,* "save intelligence"].[116] The intemperate person cannot be prudent. Intemperance destroys most of all the right estimation of the goal and the good in concrete action. The intemperate person is principally misled in his affectivity and is subject to ignorance in choosing. The person who really has the vice of intemperance is, moreover, convinced that it is *in principle* good to follow the pure appearance of good. His reason is thus disassociated from good at the level of principles. In this way he is also unjust[117] (cf. also V.1.f).

And yet intemperance does not bring greater sensual enjoyment. The opposite happens. It destroys the "joy of pleasure" and leads to frustration. As mentioned before, the process can be characterized as an ever greater desire with an ever smaller satisfaction. This is because sense desire has a peculiar ability to grow infinitely. It can do this because it is the sense desire of a human being who possesses *reason.* The reason of the intemperate person is put entirely at the disposal of the sense desire, which can never be satisfied because the reason can keep going from "desire to desire."[118] Animals cannot be intemperate because they do not have reason. The object of this desire, nevertheless, is limited to what is sensed. It can never provide fulfillment, it is momentary and satisfaction here means also that the enjoyment is already gone. Only the integration of the sense power into the order of reason allows the pleasure to last for a long time and can fulfill the Faustian wish: "O moment, stay, thou art so beautiful!" But only in this way can pleasure contribute to the satisfaction of an entire human life. For what we all consider to be good are not moments of enjoyment, not a life full of pleasures, but rather a *life* that is rich in pleasure. But life as a whole can only be the object of reason. The intemperate person lives in a constant state of self-deception. He also becomes blind to what it is reasonable to hope for, and hopelessness is always waiting in the wings. The materialism of blind consumerism becomes a prelude to resignation and despair.

The intemperate person cannot have the virtue of courage, and he finally

---

115. Augustine, *Confessions* X, 23, trans. R. S. Pine-Coffin (with substitution of "they" for "he"), p. 101.
116. *EN* VI, 5 (1140b 10–22).   117. Cf. *EN* VII, 9.
118. Cf. Thomas Hobbes, *Leviathan,* chap. 11.

will do unjust things. And to the extent that doing injustices leads him to will to do unjust things, he becomes an unjust person. The temperate person, on the contrary, is one who does what is good with passion. His senses desire what is rationally good. He lives in harmony with himself. It makes him happy to do his duty. What is reasonable appears pleasurable to him, and he does it with spontaneity and firmness. The virtues work together: they form a kind of living and dynamic "organism."

i) The Inner Connection of the Moral Virtues

No moral virtue can be complete as long as the other ones are not also present. The foregoing summary presentation of the single cardinal virtues has shown that virtues are not perfections that are isolated from each other, but are "organized" into a living "organism" and ultimately form an indivisible whole for a lifetime.[119] Even when we speak of single virtues, these are only various aspects of a complex unity. Virtues, in fact, are not simply the perfections of distinct faculties or powers but are also always virtues of a human person. Now a person is a complex entity, of course, but this entity possesses an internal unity (see above, III.5.e). And likewise a "lived lifetime" forms a unity in the historical, narrative dimension, as the biography or life story of a human being. This is the classical doctrine of the *connexio virtutum*, the "conjunction" of the virtues.[120]

As we have already seen, then, prudence as the *habitus* of the correct determination of means, can only be perfected in one who possesses the other virtues. And vice versa, these virtues cannot reach their fulfillment if prudence is lacking. It is not injustice alone that causes unjust acts. This usually occurs through intemperance or a lack of courage, which does not in any way keep such acts from being unjust. They remain unjust acts.[121] But a lack of justice can also bring about cowardly and intemperate actions. When someone acts morally badly, he normally "offends" several virtues at once. And mor-

---

119. The thesis of the interconnection of the virtues is found in Aristotle, *EN* VI (13, 1144b36), but also in the Stoics; cf. J. Annas, *The Morality of Happiness*, 73ff.

120. This "narrative structure" of moral virtue, in contrast to an abstract norm ethics, is impressively developed by A. MacIntyre, *After Virtue* (esp. chap. 15, 204ff.) even if the result is still not completely satisfactory. The weakness of MacIntyre's book lies in its entire exclusion of an anthropology of virtue, and the lack of a theory of the practical reason, which appeared first in his 1988 book, *Whose Justice? Which Rationality?* Cf. also the continuing development by MacIntyre's student P. Hall, *Narrative and the Natural Law: An Interpretation of Thomistic Ethics* (South Bend, Ind., and London: University of Notre Dame Press, 1994).

121. Grotius, in *De jure belli ac pacis*, absurdly maintained that, according to this Aristotelian doctrine, one could no longer consider "adultery caused by lust, or killing caused by anger" as injustices. This is why Grotius considered the Aristotelian virtue doctrine to be destructive of human social order, since this order is based on the distinction between just and unjust.

ally good actions are always a joint effect of temperance, courage, and justice. Courage and boldness on behalf of what is unjust is not the virtue of fortitude. We would not praise such boldness. And prudence stands before all the virtues, guiding all human actions cognitively as the practical reason. The judgment of the action-determining practical reason is corrupted through injustice, lack of temperance, and fortitude.

The Thomistic doctrine of the interconnection of the virtues was criticized by Alisdair MacIntyre in his book *After Virtue*[122] as an intolerable exaggeration; MacIntyre used the term "unity of the virtues" in accordance with a longstanding (erroneous) convention, instead of the *connexio* of the virtues. But this expression "unity of the virtues" is easily misunderstood since it suggests that the doctrine is meant to say that there "really" is only one virtue.

MacIntyre bases his view on the following argument. Let's say there is a person whose ends and intentions are fundamentally bad, such as a Nazi who is intelligent and fully committed to his program, and very courageous and unflinching on behalf of his cause, but who then undergoes a "moral conversion." He becomes a just, modest, human being who respects the rights of others. He does not have to relearn all over again how "to avoid cowardice or intemperance in the face of dangers or suffering." He already had the virtue of courage when he was a fundamentally unjust, or evil, man. That the "bravery" of the fanatic Nazi was not really bravery or at least not some kind of virtue, MacIntyre does not allow, because, according to his view, this would imply that a moral convert would have to reacquire from scratch all his former unflinching courage, which is manifestly absurd.

MacIntyre's argument reveals a deeply entrenched misunderstanding of just what moral virtue is, or, at the least, an ignorance of what is really behind the classical doctrine of the "unity" or (better) the "interconnection" of the virtues.[123] The misunderstanding is identical with the equally erroneous but ever-recurring view that "virtues can be misused."[124] When we recall that

---

122. 2nd ed. (1984), 179–80.

123. This judgment, of course, is restricted to the concept of virtue as presented in *After Virtue*. I am not discussing here whether and to what extent MacIntyre has modified this position since the beginning of his "Thomistic" phase.

124. P. Foot has argued very well against this position in "Virtues and Vices" (available in R. Crisp and M. Slote, eds., *Virtue Ethics*, 163–77). MacIntyre, on the other hand, writes, "I do have to allow that courage sometimes sustains injustice, that loyalty has been known to strengthen a murderous aggressor and that generosity has sometimes weakened the capacity to do good" (*After Virtue*, 2nd ed., 200). The statement is at least ambiguous, since it is not clear whether MacIntyre means that even a virtuous person can "sometimes" make a *mistake* (say, in guessing the consequences of his action or concerning the concrete circumstances of an action), or whether he wants to say that, "sometimes," i.e., there are some people, who have the virtue of courage but are unjust at the same time, who have loyalty to a murderous aggressor as a true virtue, and whose generosity brings it about that their ability to do good is constantly weakened. The statement appears to be meant in the second sense, since MacIntyre is recalling here his argument for rejecting the Thomistic doctrine of the "unity of the virtues."

moral virtue includes in its very conception the rightness of the striven-for goal (of the will and intention), it is clear that there is a problem of misunderstanding here. MacIntyre is in fact interpreting virtue according to the logic of skills and special knowledge fields in order to reach the goods that inhere in certain types of practice. (MacIntyre's paradigm for such practice is the game of chess.) It is illuminating to notice that having such skills does not immediately imply that someone possesses the skill for other sorts of activities. But above all, MacIntyre confuses the virtue of fortitude with mere parts and components of this virtue which are, to be sure, necessary for having the virtue, but still do not make the virtue.[125] It is true: whoever is brave must have confidence, self-control, self-discipline, strength of will, an ability to conquer oneself, and fearlessness in the presence of pain. A crook can get a lot of training, which he would not have to acquire all over again after a "moral conversion" to a decent man. But the rest, which may appear courageous and confident, can simply be only the consequence of a fanatical attitude, which influences the judgment of reason such that certain dangers and difficulties are no longer taken as such (and that, of course, is a defect and would not belong to the virtue of courage). A "converted" fanatic would then, probably, suddenly not be quite so "unflinching" or prepared to take on danger. We can think, for example, of ex-kamikaze pilots or ex-terrorists.

A confident, fearless, self-controlled man is not yet someone who *has* the virtue of fortitude. If the doctrine of the interconnectedness of the virtues meant that someone who had no good intentions and was an unjust or evil person could not also be confident or self-controlled, or easily take risks, it would be a counterintuitive doctrine and not very difficult to refute. But the point is that the virtuous person is one whose strivings as a whole are oriented toward the good. Someone who has the virtue of fortitude, then, is someone who *on the basis of his affective orientation toward the good* is capable of overcoming contradictions and dangers and so on, because his love of the good brings it about that such dangers and obstacles cannot keep him from really doing what is required for the achievement of that good. The courageous person is not necessarily a fearless person, or someone who does not have any anxiety about anything, who does not even see dangers, or who has so much self-control that he can make himself do anything to reach his goal. People like that can be very dangerous. They can cause a lot of destruction when driving automobiles. The truly courageous person must perhaps really overcome his anxiety—according to the Gospels, Jesus sweat blood that night on the Mount of Olives: was he lacking in courage?—but this conquest is possible for such a

125. Cf. above, 3.a, on the "parts" of virtue.

one because his affections are anchored in the good: the good that he wants to reach is attractive to him. The judgment of his practical reason, or his prudence, will command him in a nondeceptive and really effective way, to carry out that good. It is certainly illuminating to see that a certain amount of self-control, fearlessness, and self-mastery are necessary, as acquired dispositions of character, even if they are not sufficient. And here, too, as mentioned before, there is a *too much:* it is not the one with the "most" courage and "self-mastery" who has the virtue of fortitude (it could be a case of the vices of recklessness or fanaticism), but the one who has these qualities in accordance with right reason (and consequently is also capable of yielding to the right things and to the right extent, and to have anxiety where it is appropriate to have it). MacIntyre's interpretation cannot be reconciled with the Aristotelian doctrine of the virtuous mean.

Peter Geach has also criticized the doctrine of the "unity of the virtues" in the context of his treatment of the virtue of fortitude (although he is incorrectly referred to by MacIntyre as a defender of the doctrine).[126] Geach attacks the thesis most of all because of the apparently intolerable implications it holds for prudence. According to the "unity thesis," says Geach, the lack of a virtue would lead to the corruption of prudence. It would mean that if someone ran afoul of one virtue he would have a corrupted prudence with regard to every other aspect, but that runs counter to all our experience, because many people are in fact praiseworthy in some respects, although we can fault the same persons for other reasons.[127] What I have said in reply to MacIntyre applies here as well. It must also be said that Geach incompletely reports the Thomistic doctrine of the "interconnection" (not "unity") of the virtues *(connexio virtutum).* As always, Thomas makes a distinction, and here it is between *virtus imperfecta* and *virtus perfecta.*[128] The first, incomplete sort is a quality of character, inborn or acquired through custom, such as moderation or courage, which makes someone inclined to actions of a corresponding kind. If we understood virtues in this way, Thomas says, they would not be joined to one another. And thus there are generous people who are also unchaste. But it is otherwise with complete virtue (and that is the real kind of virtue we are concerned with here). This kind can only be present when prudence is present; and this in turn presupposes the rectitude of the appetition of a goal. The real reason for the interconnectedness of the moral virtues is, then, the unity of

126. P. Geach, *The Virtues* (Cambridge: Cambridge University Press, 1977), 160ff.; cf. MacIntyre, *After Virtue,* 2nd ed., 179.
127. B. Williams also brings this objection into the fray against Aristotle (in *Ethics and the Limits of Philosophy,* 36).
128. I-II, Q. 65, a. 1.

the practical reason, or prudence.[129] Practical reason is the reason as embedded in appetition or striving and it cannot be perfected if the subject has a vice. In any event it must be conceded that even the complete or perfect virtues are present in a more or less imperfect way, since they must develop over the course of a lifetime. The completely virtuous person is an ideal.[130] What must be distinguished from the opinion that perfected virtues can coexist with vices is, of course, the (quite possible) coexistence of still incompletely developed virtues. Finally, the one who is virtuous in the full sense will still commit errors. The empirical fact that we can praise the same person in some respects and blame him in others can often be explained this way.

This is why the arguments of MacIntyre and Geach fail. It is not a question of the "unity" of the virtues, but of their interconnection, their inner juncture. And the foundation for this joining is the unity of the practical reason. All the realities of experience are adequately engaged, and the strange idea that continually reemerges but is so contra-intuitive—that a moral virtue can be used for bad ends, or misused—is swept off the table. It simply belongs to the concept of moral virtue, that it can only be "used" for a good end. The doctrine of the interconnection of the moral virtues reflects, again, the truth that virtues are not simply "knowing," nor are they only perfections of the will. All the powers of appetition that are engaged in action are perfected through the virtues, which is to say the human person as a whole as an essential body-soul unity, is perfected, and the practical reason along with that, on its way to becoming prudence.

4. The Social Character of the Virtues

a) The Primacy of the Person

Contemporary ethics is remarkable for being almost exclusively interested in questions of justice, or questions about interpersonal relationships. When it comes to the other virtues, which concern rather questions of how an individual conducts his own life, it appears impossible for such ethical theories to make any statements that would have general application. Apart from specifically political ethics, such limitation of the field is actually a dangerous reductionism. This reductionism is based on what was treated in the introduction as the typical modern conception of "moral philosophy." Morality is supposed to begin right where the pursuit of one's own interests is curtailed in favor of the

---

129. Cf. In VI Ethic., lect. 11, n. 1288: *Et ideo propter prudentiae unitatem omnes virtues morales sunt sibi connexae* ["And therefore, thanks to the unity of prudence, all the moral virtues are connected to each other"].

130. J. Annas, *The Morality of Happiness*, 83.

interests of others, or the community. No doubt there is another encouragement as well in the notion that an ethics that concerned itself with the "whole man," and not just with a man's relation to others, would be impossible, given that the metaphysical and anthropological foundations necessary for such an enterprise have been irretrievably lost. As a consequence, many—and this is most clearly the case with discourse-ethicists—have attempted the reduction of ethics to political ethics, which would operate completely within the medium of an intersubjective praxis of justification for competing claims of value. Habermas's contention that anyone who keeps to the classical/Aristotelian claim for the preference of certain ways of life over others does not take modern pluralism seriously,[131] is not very illuminating, since this is already a *political/ethical* or legal-justice argument, and secondly because it is merely an argument against the desirability of a recovery of the classical/Aristotelian unity of ethics and political philosophy, and not an argument against the possibility of an ethics that speaks for the moral excellence of certain ways of living; such an ethics, therefore, is not only a discourse about what could be acknowledged as validly "right" for a mass of persons living in a community of laws and public coercive authority, but is also a discourse about the truth about what is good and rationally to be pursued, in the orientation and praxis of a person's daily life.[132] Classical virtue ethics is indeed an ethics of the "first person." It places the acting person in the center, as a subject seeking the good and happiness. Classical ethics also thrives on the insight that the individual's own conduct of life and interpersonal morality stand in very close relationship with one another. This does not in any way imply a need to return to the Aristotelian paradigm of the relationship between politics and ethics. It is simply one of the irreversible achievements of the political culture of the modern democratic constitutional state that this relationship is no longer a kind of transposition of the one into the other, but has become instead a discontinuous relationship that takes into account the fact of pluralism and conflict and the demands of freedom and autonomy.[133] But it is nevertheless true,

131. J. Habermas, "Lawrence Kohlberg und der Neoaristotelismus," in Habermas, *Erläuterungen zur Diskursethik*, 89.

132. The idea that practical knowledge is solely qualified for determining the "right" and is at the same time disqualified from determining the "good," which latter is a matter of individual preference and cannot be subject to any universal standards, was very effectively decreed by J. Rawls, *A Theory of Justice* (Cambridge, Mass.: Belknap Press of Harvard University Press, 1971). A more qualified view can be seen in J. Rawls, *Political Liberalism* (New York: Columbia University Press, 1993), 173ff. See now also J. Rawls, *Collected Papers*, ed. S. Friedmann (Cambridge, Mass.: Harvard University Press, 1999), 449ff.; the most prominent critic of this dissociation is M. Sandel, *Liberalism and the Limits of Justice* (Cambridge, Mass.: Harvard University Press, 1982).

133. Cf. on this my articles already referred to, "Perché un filosofia politica?" and "Lo Stato costituzionale democratico e il bene commune," available in English in my forthcoming *The Common Good of Constitutional Democracy*.

assuming all this, that it is impossible to speak of the virtue of justice without considering it as a component of the total "organism" of the moral virtues.

And even if only the virtue of justice refers immediately to social relations, it should still have become clear that fortitude and temperance are no less important for them. It is simply a fact of life that justice and prudence, according to the doctrine of the interconnectedness of the virtues, are more frequently injured and destroyed by a lack of temperance and a failure of courage (or downright cowardliness) than by actual "injustice" or a general ignorance of the good. At any event, the opposite error must also be avoided, which is to be found among the proponents of the more recent *virtue ethics* school: the error, that is, of centering the ethical discourse so much on the emotional dispositions of the moral subject that the discourse about justice is practically omitted altogether. This leads to the curious result of a thoroughly subjective and relativistic virtue ethics.[134]

All of this admits of precise anthropological explanations. An ethics that is detached from anthropology, that leaves aside the primacy of the "human person," of the acting and striving subject, loses its object. This is perhaps the deepest wisdom we can learn again from classical virtue ethics.

b) Friendship: Political Virtues and Institutions

Justice, we have seen, is good willing in the area of what is owed to the "other person," what is the other's *right*. But good willing (or benevolence) is not exhausted in justice alone. The golden rule, or "love your neighbor as yourself," requires more. We not only want the other to respect our rights. We want their benevolence, too, even if we have no right to it, and even if they do not owe us anything. In fact we often take most interest in this. This "being interested" shows that there is an asymmetry on this level: in this way, we "owe" to the other a goodwill that goes beyond what is owed in legal terms, something that we would never demand as owed to us, but at the most can only anticipate as the benevolent attention of others: a benevolence that goes beyond justice but in a way completes it.

To have a good will for the other person in a way that goes beyond what is commanded by what is "just" is known as friendship. Friendship is based on

---

134. An example of this would be R. Hursthouse, "Virtue Theory and Abortion," in R. Crisp and M. Slote, eds., *Virtue Ethics*, 217–38. Hursthouse comes to her conclusions through a consistent bracketing-off of questions concerning justice. M. C. Nussbaum argues in general terms against a relativistic virtue ethics; see "Non-Relative Virtues: An Aristotelian Approach," in P. French, T. Uehling, and H. Wettstein, eds., *Ethical Theory: Character and Virtue*, 32–53, reprinted in somewhat expanded form in M. Nussbaum and A. Sen, *The Quality of Life* (New York and Oxford: Oxford University Press, 1993). In Nussbaum can be seen a correspondingly more prominent position given to questions of justice.

justice, indeed, but goes beyond it. Aristotle devotes all the eighth and part of the ninth book of his *Nicomachean Ethics* to the doctrine of friendship. We could say that the doctrine of friendship really forms the major part, the very core, of Aristotelian ethics.

Aristotle says that there is no need of justice among friends.[135] What he means by this is that among friends one does not ask what is the "just thing" for the other, but goes beyond this and simply thinks only of the friend's well-being. Such relationships of friendship, however, do not only arise between individual persons. Society as a whole is not based on this kind of friendship, since it has already left behind the question of legal relationship: that would be unrealistic and even dangerous. Society is always based first on relationships of justice. But this justice needs friendship as a "completion."[136] Where no justice exists, there can be no friendship either, which Aristotle characterizes as the bond that holds society together.

So is friendship a virtue? "Friendship," says Thomas Aquinas, "is not really a virtue, but rather a consequence of virtue. This is because if someone is virtuous it follows also that he loves those who are like himself."[137] This "love that is friendship" *(amor amicitiae, amor benevolentiae),* the first form of which is justice, consists, as already explained, in seeking the good for others, just as one seeks the good for oneself. The friend is "a second self,"[138] and this is true to the extent that the friend "wills the good for his friend as he does for himself."[139]

We all want that, to begin with, on the basis of a natural solidarity among human beings. "Man is a friend to man by nature"—that would be the antithetical formula to Hobbes's *homo homini lupus* ("man is like a wolf to man"). Hobbes's formula, which has put its stamp upon the entire modern tradition of social philosophy, does sound more realistic. In reality, the Aristotelian formula is no less realistic: the question is, which of the two is true?

The thesis that man is a friend to man by nature only means that the reason that brings about peace and justice among human beings does not command something *against* nature, as some kind of imperative of political reason that creates the coercive machinery of the state to bring about peace. But the Aristotelian view is not that peace and unity are already natural givens among men. They are rather the consequence of the *habitus* of virtue, ultimately, the virtue of justice, but since this requires the other virtues as well, it is the con-

---

135. Cf. *EN* VIII, 1 (1155a27).
136. Ibid., (1155a28).
137. Thomas Aquinas, *De Virtutibus,* Q. unica, a. 5, ad 5.
138. *EN* IX, 4 (1166a332).
139. I-II, Q. 28, a. 1.

sequence of *all* the virtues. The difference between Aristotle and Hobbes does not consist in the question whether peace and justice come about among men by nature or by reason, but rather whether they come about on the basis of the rationality of the moral virtue of individuals or on the basis of the rationality of the state—made possible through a rational political calculation of individual interests—and the state's coercive power and laws.[140]

The production of peace and justice through social organization *independently* of the virtue of individuals is the quintessence of Hobbes's political philosophy, and also of the philosophy of that secret Hobbesian, Rousseau;[141] it is present in Kant's famous dictum: "Establishing a state, as difficult as it may sound, is a problem that can be solved even for a nation of devils (if only they possess understanding) if only one could neutralize conflict between their hostile interests" through a system of compulsory laws under which they would cooperate through insight into the larger usefulness of the system for the individuals.[142] In Hegel's conception of "ethical substance" in which ethos as an organized reality of state and society becomes, as "second nature," an institution, and man is freed from the subjective compulsions of morality, "virtue in the strict sense of the word . . . actually appears only in exceptional circumstances or when one obligation clashes with another." Virtue as the foundational principle of formation is present only "when societies and communities are uncivilized."[143]

No one can dispute that there is not an element of truth being expressed here, namely, the necessity of a public legal order, of the institutionalization and sovereignty of decision making by public authorities. For it is in fact institutions or civic life under the conditions of the institutional resolution of conflicts and the consequent disburdening of the individual that *make* the good life *possible* in the first place, in the sense of training in the virtues, and especially those virtues that characterize the life of a citizen. This makes up the other side of the coin with regard to the Hobbesian (but not original with Hobbes) *homo homini lupus:* that there is also the truth that *homo homini Deus* ("man is like a god to man"),[144] the expectation, that is, that under the condi-

---

140. "By nature" (in the Aristotelian sense) there is not only friendship between human beings as such, but also in special ways between parents and children, husband and wife, rulers and the ruled. But the *habitus* of moral virtue must be presupposed in order for these natural arrangements to be really capable of determining action and interpersonal relationships.

141. Cf. *Du contrat social,* I, VII.

142. I. Kant, *Toward Perpetual Peace and Other Writings on Politics, Peace, and History,* ed. P. Kleingeld et al., trans. D. L. Colclasure (New Haven, Conn.: Yale University Press, 2006), 67–109, here 91.

143. G. W. F. Hegel, *Philosophy of Right,* sect. 150, trans. T. M. Knox (*Great Books of the Western World* 46), 56.

144. Cf. T. Hobbes, *De cive or The Citizen,* ed. S. Lamprecht (New York: Appleton-Century-Crofts, 1949). And also see F. Tricaud, "'*Homo homini Deus,*' 'homo homini lupus': Recherches des deux for-

tions of civil society as brought about through institutions of pacification and conflict resolution, that man will be a "god" to man, that is, will be benevolent.

Nevertheless, it is the tendency of modern political thought to hold that it is *alone* the publicly validated institutional regulations or laws that do this, and that all else belongs to the insignificant realm of "private conscience." It may be possible to get around this insignificance in the way B. Mandeville maintained, *contra* Hobbes, that private vices add up to common advantage.[145] But for the most part, the modern period has been concerned, again through very understandable reasons, to give priority to the rules for living together without conflicts in a legally ordered society, rather than reflection on the good life of the individual. This comes to expression most clearly in the doctrine of Pufendorf, going back to Grotius, on distinguishing perfect duties (the legal regulations essential to the existence and functioning of human society) from imperfect duties (the command to love one's neighbor, and virtue in general, i.e., the duties upon whose fulfillment the existence of society does not depend, and consequently are not relevant to any strictly legal claims).[146]

Of course, Aristotle was also well aware that peace and harmony can only be realized among men on the condition of "the rule of law," since law is "without emotion";[147] and he knew just as well that a civilized "quality of life" must be institutionally secured. But that is not enough, because laws sometimes miss what is right, and they should not be valid when that happens. To rule according to the letter of the law means to rule badly, and "where the law cannot decide or cannot decide well, should the decision be left to one, or to the best persons, or should it be left in the hands of everyone?"[148] Hobbes says, of course the decision should be put in the hands of one or of some sovereign body, but whether the ones who govern are the best persons or not plays no role; the point is, *they decide*.[149] Today the reality is: the decision ultimately lies in the hands of everyone, or of a few who are overseen by everyone, so it is the decision of majorities. This very much corresponds with Aristotle's view, which

---

mules de Hobbes," in R. Koselleck and R. Schnur, eds., *Hobbes-Forschungen* (Berlin: Duncker & Humblot, 1969), 61–70; M. Rhonheimer, *La filosofia politica di Thomas Hobbes*, 52.

145. For Mandeville, even this was only possible through "the clever management of an industrious politician," i.e., through governmental control. Mandeville was not a laissez-faire thinker; rather, his thought was mercantilistic; cf. B. Mandeville, *The Fable of the Bees; or, Private Vices, Public Advantage*, ed. F. Kaye (Oxford: Clarendon Press, 1924).

146. Cf. also J. Schneewind, "The Misfortunes of Virtue," in R. Crisp and M. Slote, eds., *Virtue Ethics*, 178–200; see also Schneewind, *The Invention of Autonomy*, 78ff. for Grotius, and 131ff. for Pufendorf.

147. Cf. *Politics*, III, 15 (1286a 19).

148. Ibid., 25–26.

149. For the background of this Hobbesian "decisionism," cf. M. Rhonheimer, "*Auctoritas non veritas facit legem*; Thomas Hobbes, Carl Schmitt und die Idee des Verfassungsstaates," *Archiv für Rechts- und Sozialphilosophie* 86 (2000): 484–498; available in English in my forthcoming *The Common Good of Constitutional Democracy*.

finally is very realistic. Only, he would add: this is exactly why it matters what kind of persons in the community are making the decisions.

The theme belongs to political philosophy and does not need to be treated further here.[150] What is decisive in this connection is that justice both as a virtue of individuals *and* as an institution can only exist when all the moral virtues are being lived, and that only in that way can that solidarity or friendship have existence among men, which is the fundamental condition for human society not to fall apart—even if it also needs a public legal system, institutional guarantees, and public decision-making authority for its existence, that is, elements that can guarantee justice and peace to a certain minimum extent even independently of the justice and peaceable behavior of individuals, or despite the absence of it altogether (and just this is one of the historical achievements of modern constitutionalism and of the state under the rule of law). But that this guarantee is a guarantee of *justice* has its foundation, again, in the fact that the production of such an institutional framework not only results from a calculation ultimately serving the private interests of individuals, but is also maintained by goodwill toward others: by justice and friendship, which are *always* virtues of individuals or the consequences of such virtues. A "population of devils" would certainly have only devilish laws.

c) Moral Virtue and the Happiness of This Life

Vicious men, according to Aristotle, "having nothing loveable in them . . . have no feeling of love to themselves."[151] The virtues of justice, fortitude, and temperance bring it about that the human being lives, as it were, in harmony with himself, that his appetition has the satisfaction and the joy that can only be found through the orientation to the good that his reason shows him. This is not an egotistical happiness, because it essentially consists in loving others

---

150. Cf. also M. Rhonheimer, *Politisierung und Legitimitätsentzug* (Freiburg and Munich: Alber, 1979), 313ff., as well as my article cited above: "Perché una filosofia politica?" The suggestions of D. L. Norton, *Democracy and Moral Development: A Politics of Virtue* (Berkeley-Los Angeles-Oxford: University of California Press, 1991) are interesting, if not convincing in all respects. Also relevant in this context is the debate in the United States between liberalism and "communitarianism," the details of which cannot now be treated. From the great abundance of literature on this can be cited at least the following: A. Honneth, *Grenzen des Liberalismus. Zur politisch-ethischen discussion um den Kommunitarismus, Philosophische Rundschau* 38 (1991), and Honneth, ed., *Kommunitarismus. Eine Debatte über die moralischen Grundlagen moderner Gesellschaften* (Frankfurt am Main: Suhrkamp, 1992); and finally, S. Mulhall and A. Swift, *Liberals and Communitarians* (Oxford and Cambridge, Mass.: Blackwell, 1992), which is an outstanding introduction. Finally, see also M. Rhonheimer, "L'immagine dell'uomo nel liberalismo e il concetto di autonomia: Al di là del dibattito fra liberali e communitaristi," in I. Yarza, ed., *Immagini dell' uomo. Percorsi antropologici nella filosofia moderna* (Rome: Armando, 1997), 95–133; available in English in *The Common Good of Constitutional Democracy.*

151. *EN* IX, 4 (1166b17).

as one loves oneself. This is how the earlier determination of the happiness of this life is redeemed: through the ordering of emotions or affects, of appetitions or strivings, and of actions according to reason.

The rational guidance of life, however, just because reason is in command, also opens us up to that opening of our will toward knowledge of the truth, which is the dominant goal of human existence. Moral virtue smoothes the path to "contemplation," to the "seeing" ownership of truth. Prudence itself, and thereby the fullness of moral virtue, is the "steward of wisdom."[152] As Aristotle has it, this is granted only to the few. And so it would have remained, if it had not been for the One Who is Himself all wisdom and truth, who came to tell the human being: "I no longer call you servants, but friends." Through the elevation of grace, God becomes friend to man and man becomes friend to God. And in this way those dimensions of *caritas* are opened which at once transcend and complete this delimited realm of philosophical ethics.[153]

152. The image appears in the almost certainly Aristotelian *Magna Moralia* I, 34 (1198b13). The doctrine is also in the *Eudemian Ethics*, VIII, 3. Cf. Thomas Aquinas, *De Virtutibus cardinalibus*, a. 1, ad 4.

153. Cf. also the remarks in the epilogue to this book.

V

STRUCTURES OF RATIONALITY

1. Principles of the Practical Reason

a) The Rational "by Nature"

It was established in the previous chapter that the intentional appetition for a goal belonging to each of the moral virtues is an affective principle for prudence or (in other words) for the judgment of actions. Moral virtue, however, is still not only an affective structure, but is also the *rectitude (rectitudo, orthotes)* of the appetition or striving. This assertion implies, again, that moral virtue is formed by the structures of reason. The coincidence of the judgment of actions with "right striving" Aristotle referred to as the "practical truth" of this judgment and of the subsequent actions. But what is the basis for this "rightness" of the striven-for goal, and ultimately what is the basis for the practical truth of the judgment of actions, of the choice of action, and of action itself?

In his comment on the passage of the *Nicomachean Ethics* where Aristotle introduces the concept of "practical truth," Thomas remarks that there seems to be some circular reasoning here: Aristotle maintains that the truth of the practical reason depends on the rectitude of the appetitive faculty, but that the rectitude of the appetitive faculty depends in turn on practical reasoning. Thomas solves the problem as follows: the practical reason, whose truth is secured by the agreement with right striving, is the reason that is directed toward the "means to the end." But the end itself is "determined by nature."[1] What this says is that the fundamental teleological structure of human action is not established through an act of freedom of choice, but rather lies, as a point of departure, "by nature," at the basis of every free choice and every rational consideration corresponding to choice. But what does that mean?

---

1. In VI Ethic., lect. 2 (1131).

Thomas refers to the third book of the *Nicomachean Ethics*. It says there, indeed, that ends are always something foundational and *given* for the choice of actions. And this is either "by nature" or as an acquired disposition. For the end of the virtuous person is "right," while the end of the vicious person is "perverse," and this is through one's own deserving (or one's own fault, as the case may be). What appears to us as good and right—that is to say, what we strive for as an ultimate, in order to make our life worthwhile as a whole— depends, in turn, on what we are as human beings or what kind of human beings we have made ourselves into. But since the goal, or the evaluation of what the goal is, does not come from our acquired dispositions, it is some- thing "given by nature."[2] This also holds for "happiness": we all strive for it "by nature."

Of course, this does not clarify what makes an end "right." But the circle is opened: we neither take counsel about nor choose the goals that give the fun- damental orientation to our action; otherwise, we would never act. We always deliberate and choose for the sake of an end. And this is *ultimately* precisely for the sake of those goals or ends that we strive for, whether "by nature" or on the basis of our acquired dispositions. What somebody takes to be good depends ultimately upon what kind of a human being he is, and that in turn depends on what he chooses and does. The "ends" or "goals" of which we are speaking here are irreducible starting points or *principles.*

> An *original* choice of end that does not already follow from a previous (and in this sense, "higher") end, that is, an absolutely primary, free positing of what we want, is unthinkable. A "pure choice of the end"—which is original and without any previous "for the sake of which"—would be a pure decision or positing *without reason.* For one can rationally *choose* only with regard to a previously existing end. In any case, this does not mean that the principles— that is, what is "first" in each case—are irrationally striven for. But they are not *chosen.* And that means that we are speaking about a level at which goals or goods are intellectively cognized *as such* and are consequently striven after without this coming from a positing in the sense of a (preferential) *choice.* In any case freedom is not thereby done away with, because one can always, at least to a degree, oppose oneself to the intelligibility of these ends and the ap- petitions that correspond to them: for example (to anticipate), even if "want- ing to live" is not something that we "rationally choose," but simply always will, we can set ourselves against this urge and "not want to live any more."

Nevertheless, Aristotle's contention that our conceptions of good depend in each case upon what kind of persons we are does not lead to the position

2. Cf. *EN* III, 7 (1114a32–b 25).

that everything is relative. Since the virtues that we do not possess "by nature" we likewise do not possess "against nature," we are so constructed "by nature" as to acquire them.[3] And Aristotle also speaks of a "natural virtue."[4] This kind of language emphasizes that for every *habitus* of moral virtue there are certain naturally given dispositions, which are variously pronounced in various men and women from birth, and forming a kind of core or template for moral virtues. But this alone would still not give us any cognitive orientation, since such virtue, which is purely potential, can suffer damage, too. Really "genuine" virtue, Aristotle says, is only there where prudence is also, where the natural disposition goes along with reason. But reason alone would likewise not be virtue. Reason needs the naturally implanted disposition or inclination. The *habitus* of prudence therefore perfects something that is naturally already present, but not as moral virtue. But this again does not help us get any farther. For to recognize "natural virtue" as natural *virtue*—as a disposition for the good—already implies that someone already knows what is good: it presupposes the experience of moral virtue as what is perfected and *thereby* in accordance with nature (cf. III.5.e). The concept of moral virtue is understood in terms of its perfecting, and only with reference to that is the natural disposition recognized as a disposition toward virtue. The problem of a cognitive principle for this perfection has not been resolved at this point.

The possibility for a solution depends on the answer to the following question: Are there ends, which we strive for by nature and can also *recognize* as "right" goals, independently of the possession of the *habitus* of virtue and the affective-cognitive service it renders? Happiness, or *eudaimonia*, would be just such an end. But happiness is not going to be sufficient for determining our choice-acts of actions (cf. III.1). Is there a good that we strive for by nature, but that can, at the same time, guide our action? If there is such a thing, it would in fact be a principle of action, such as we are looking for. It would be a "criterion" of the "rightness" of the goal we strive for.

And yet, one could also ask, why this would then be a criterion of *rectitude?* It would really be nothing other than a fact, but what is *right,* so one might object, can only be something that we arrive at through questioning its background, something that we agree with or deny. The objection sounds plausible at first. But there is an important reason to think it false.

First, if in case we actually do strive for something as good by nature, this would only make sense through one justification alone: because our *reason* (again, by nature) recognizes *as good* this sought-for object, and in the logical

3. *EN* II, 1.
4. Cf. *EN* VI, 13 (1144b2–17).

form of the structure of practical judgments of the kind: "p is good." Of course, the good to which the sense appetition is directed (on the natural-sensitive level) is not what is meant here. For such good is only a natural good, and not a good "of the reason" *(bonum rationis)*. But the will—the "appetition in the reason"—can direct itself to such goods that in their origin are merely sense goods, and can grasp them as a good of the reason, that is, within the ordering of reason (as "good for the reason"). And insofar as they are recognized as good and striven for in this natural ordering, they are in fact goods of human action sought after "by nature," and thus *principles* of the practical reason.

So where is the contradiction in the above objection? The contradiction goes like this: an appetition or striving that is directed toward that which the *reason* "by nature" recognizes as good is necessarily also "right." The freedom that would recognize such a striving only as a mere fact, in order to then question it for its rectitude, would in this way be annihilated as reason-guided freedom. It would be asking, that is to say, whether the rational is rational, when otherwise the question about rightness has been the same as the question about rationality. But that this is the case has already been shown: "good" and "bad," "right" and "wrong" in human actions are determined according to reason. And so, in case the reason recognizes something as by nature good or evil, there is a corresponding seeking of good or avoidance of bad that is *necessarily*—and indeed, by definition—also right. For what is right is precisely what is according to reason, and not the reverse. And what is "by nature rational" and "naturally reasonable" is also what is "by nature" right or good. To pose the question whether that appetition is right that seeks for what we grasp by nature as right, means wanting to call into question rationality on the basis of rational criteria. And yet here also it is true that "One cannot hear reasons for why someone should listen to reasons."[5] The question goes on endlessly, as does a freedom that would seek to make problematic what is grasped by the reason as good by nature.

A "fact of reason" of this kind that is underivable and which can also not be derived from "the consciousness of freedom," but lies at the basis of it, was recognized by Kant as well,[6] except that, for Kant, this "fact" is really not something that is of an original rationality that has "good" for its object, but is instead the pure givenness of the consciousness of a *will*, which for just this reason, according to Kant, needs the self-legislation of reason, because this is the only kind of determination that allows the will to be independent of empirical conditions and (consequently) to be left in its autonomy. Kant circumscribes this consciousness *voluntaristically* with the slogan *"sic volo, sic iubeo"*

5. R. Spaemann, *Happiness and Benevolence* (South Bend, Ind.: University of Notre Dame Press, 2000), viii. A similar idea is found in K. Baier, *The Moral Point of View*, 317ff.
6. Cf. *Critique of Practical Reason*, trans. M. Gregor, 27.

(thus I wish, so I command).[7] For Kant, then, previous to all rationality is the autonomy of the will (transcendental freedom), whose rationality, however, is threatened by just such an autonomy that is not limited by reason. For reason is legitimated in his system not through its task of effecting the orientation of the will toward the good, but rather through ensuring the freedom and autonomy of the will; but this turns the relationship between the reason and will (freedom) on its head. This is why Kantian ethics in its deepest structure is not an ethics of the autonomy of the reason, but an ethics of the autonomy of the will.[8] At any event this was anticipated by Kant in his response to Rousseau ("Rousseau made me see it right": *Rousseau hat mich zurecht gebracht*) and in the specification (grounded in the Kantian reception of Rousseau) of the "moral feeling" as a feeling of enjoyment in the exercise of one's own freedom.[9] Kant wrote as follows in the years 1764–1765: "The will is perfect, insofar as, according to the laws of freedom it is the greatest reason for good as such. The moral feeling is the feeling of the fulfillment of the will."[10] And further: "We have *contentment* [*Vergnügen*] in certain of our perfections, but much more so, when we ourselves are their cause, and most of all, *when we are the freely operating cause.* For free will to subordinate everything to itself, is the greatest perfection. And the perfection of free will as a cause of possibility is far greater than all other causes of good, even if they were to bring about real effects immediately . . . the feeling [*Gefühl*] of pleasure and displeasure is either concerned with that against which we suffer, or is *concerned with us ourselves, as an active principle, through freedom, before good and evil. The latter is moral feeling* [*moralisches Gefühl*]."[11]

To determine the "rational by nature," Aristotle bequeathed us with no theory, but Thomas Aquinas did. This is his doctrine of the "natural law," the *lex naturalis.* A few remarks are necessary in regard to this term, in order to ward off possible misunderstandings.[12]

7. Ibid., 29.

8. For this reason, the view of A. Anzenbacher, *Einführung in die Ethik* (Düsseldorf: Patmos Verlag,1992), 97ff., that between Thomas Aquinas and Kant there is no difference in the "central fundamental-ethical conception," appears to me as an inappropriate harmonization and mollification of a deep-seated difference. Ch. Schröer, *Praktische Vernunft bei Thomas von Aquin* (Stuttgart-Berlin-Cologne: Kohlhammer, 1995), 205, note 14, is also critical of Anzenbacher's harmonizing of Kant and Thomas.

9. Cf. J. B. Sala, "Das Gesetz oder das Gute? Zum Ursprung und Sinn des Formalismus in der Ethik Kants," *Gregorianum* 71 (1990): 67–95, 315–52, and esp. 87. Sala's article also brought to my attention the other passages referred to here.

10. Immanuel Kant, *Bemerkungen zu den Beobachtungen über das Gefühl des Schönen und Erhabenen*, Akademie Ausgabe, 20.136 (here, trans. Malsbary).

11. Ibid., 144f. For the connection between this position and Kant's further development, see J. B. Sala (note 9 above), 88–95 and 315ff. For the historical background of the genesis of Kant's concept of autonomy, cf. J. Schneewind, *The Invention of Autonomy.*

12. A thorough presentation of the Thomistic doctrine on the natural law can be found in my book *Natural Law and Practical Reason: A Thomist View of Moral Autonomy.* For an analysis of the connection between the doctrine of the *lex naturalis* and the Aristotelian doctrine of virtues, see in *Praktische Vernunft und Vernünftigkeit der Praxis.* Further details are in both of these works.

b) On the Concept of the Natural Law (Lex Naturalis)

Lex naturalis, or "natural law," is an extremely confusing expression. The context that surrounds it whenever it is used is of utmost importance. In the Scholastic doctrine of the lex naturalis there are at least two traditions that flow together: the ancient Roman tradition of the jurists and their ius naturale, especially Ulpian,[13] as well as the Christian theology of "law" which is in part biblical, and in part based on the Augustinian doctrine of the lex aeterna. This latter Judeo-Christian tradition is decisive for the lex naturalis terminology.[14]

In the Summa Theologiae Thomas turns his attention to the specifically theological question about the law only after he has already treated human actions, their specification, and moral qualification through the reason: only after he has treated "good" and "evil" in human actions, the emotions (or "passions"), and the moral virtues, using Aristotelian categories as much as possible to say everything essential on the subject. When taking up this theological question he begins with his reception of the Augustinian concept of the eternal law: the ratio of the divine mind, the plan according to which all created being is ordered to its end. Here the theme is the "divine law" (lex divina): the revelation of the ordering of creatures to their supernatural end as it exists in the divine mind, which is also positive (although not human) law. Here again the law of the Old Testament (lex vetus) must be distinguished from that of the New (lex nova or lex evangelica), which exists above all in the grace of the Holy Spirit and is only secondarily written law (lex scripta). Then there is a discussion of human positive law. These are all understood as participations in the eternal law: the plan that is identified with the ratio of the divine mind, according to which creatures are ordered to their end. Seen in this light, all nature as nature—that is, the natural order, both human and nonhuman—is a "participation in the eternal law," since it is "ruled" by this law. "Law" is itself here defined as the ordering of the divine ratio to the good (ordinatio rationis divinae).

> "Law" in general is more precisely defined by Thomas as "a rule and measure, according to which someone is led to action or is kept from acting"; it "obliges to action"; it is "the measure of human actions"; "first principle of human actions"; something that "pertains to reason"; something that "is constituted through an act of the reason"; laws are "universal propositions of the practical reason pertaining to actions"—the reason that is meant here is the reason that

---

13. How little, in fact, Thomas's concept of the natural law was influenced by Ulpian's ius naturale or (to put it another way) how much Thomas's teaching transformed Ulpian's, is shown by W. E. May, "The Meaning and Nature of the Natural Law in Thomas Aquinas," American Journal of Jurisprudence 22 (1977): 168–89.

14. Cf. for the evolution of the Thomistic concept of the lex naturalis from its specification through the Augustinian lex aeterna to the Aristotelian doctrine of virtue, G. Abbà, Lex et virtus. Studi sull' evoluzione della dottrina morale di san Tommaso d'Aquino (Rome: LAS, 1983).

moves, because it itself is moved by the will, that is, is embedded in appetition. The concept of the law thus satisfies all the essential requirements of an ordering established by practical reason and is defined, finally, as an *ordinatio rationis*.[15]

As human beings we find ourselves, first of all, living fixed within a "natural order." But this order, while it is a participation in the eternal law, is not itself a law because "law" is only present where there is practical reason; every law, in fact, is an *ordinatio rationis*. The sense appetites of the human being, on the other hand, as well as all nonhuman entities in the world, seek the good that is proper to them *not* on the basis of reason; and thus they do not set up a "law."

> Of course, as created beings, they are subject to the eternal law. And insofar as they participate in that, they can be called a "law," but this is only in a derived ("participated") sense, and not in the proper sense of the word.[16] This kind of "lawfulness" is nevertheless not of interest at all in the present context: if there is going to be a "natural law" that is relevant at all for moral action and ethics, it must be a reality that corresponds to the inner structure of human action as free, reason-guided, and willing action.

Second, human beings encounter a revealed guidance toward the good (as the divine law). But this does not come from *man's* reason: it is only recognized and accepted by man. Third, and finally, human life is bound up within the guidance of human laws. And now the question arises: Is there not also an *ordinatio rationis*, an ordering or guidance by reason toward the good, that is "natural" to man—that belongs to him "by nature"—and in this sense can be called a *natural* law? This means: Is there a practical reasoning that comes to be by nature in the human being, which can show the way to the good, independently of the divine or human legislative positing of law? Such a "law" would then be neither a divine nor a human positive law, but also not "nature" (since this as such does not constitute an *ordinatio rationis*); it would not be a "law *of* nature" nor a "natural regulation." Instead, it would be something that "by nature" has the character of a law, that is, of an ordering of reason toward the good. Yes, says Thomas, there is such a thing: it is nothing other than an ordering that the practical reason of the acting subject "by nature" establishes in human inclinations and actions through its own *preceptive* (i.e., guiding) acts.

As soon as it has been said that the "natural law" is the practical reasoning of the human being establishing order within human inclinations and

---

15. All these definitions of law in general can be found in I-II, Q. 90, a. 1, *corpus*, as well as ad 2 and ad 3.

16. I-II, Q. 90, a. 1, ad 1.

actions it starts to become clear that in the context of a purely philosophical ethics, the term "law," at least in this connection, is redundant when understood precisely. The category of the *lex naturalis* really involves nothing new that would need to be added to the doctrine of the standard-giving role of reason; rather, it leads, for Thomas, back to the doctrine of the practical reason, to the doctrine of human actions, and of the determination of good and bad through reason; to the anthropology of reason, will, and sense appetition, and to the doctrine of moral virtue.[17] The only thing that is new here is just the integration of this doctrine into the context of a Christian theology of law—an integration that Thomas can establish biblically in other passages[18]—and the referring of human reason to the divine reason, as proposed within the framework of a philosophy of the eternal law and as providing witness to the theonomic (or divinely instituted) origin and the theonomic foundation of practical reason (cf. below, V.2.c).

"Lex naturalis," then, means nothing other than the principles of the practical reason, on the basis of which the appetitive goal seeking of moral virtue is cognitively guided. The "natural law" is a "law" of practical reason, and that means *it is a law in relation to human appetitions and actions and to the difference between "good" and "bad," as measured and governed through the practical reason of the human being,* and thereby through the entire ensemble of the cognitive principles of moral virtue. Consequently, from this point forward, it will be enough to speak of the practical principles or of the natural principles of the moral virtues instead of "the natural law."

It is just here, when someone forgets this original context of a "theology of law," that the concept of "natural law" becomes problematic, captious, and simply misleading. Starting from what was originally a purely *theologically* understood integration of the doctrine of the practical reason and human personal autonomy into the biblical context of the "Law," there rises a self-standing philosophical category in which the perspective of "nature" comes into the foreground *instead of* reason. This is reinforced by the modern natural scientific concept of "natural laws" and its combination with the modern natural law tradition *(iusnaturalism)*. The *ius naturale,* what is "right by nature," is really not yet "natural law" but is only grasped through the practical, ordering act of the *reason* as such a "right by nature." When Thomas speaks, therefore, of a "natural law" that is ordained prior to human-positive law, he compares this again to the first principles of the practical reason, under the guidance of which human law "finds in addition" *(adinvenit)* its particular concretions.[19]

17. This was very well pointed out by J. Tonneau, *Absolu et obligation morale* (Montréal and Paris: Librarie J. Vrin, 1965), 89f.

18. Cf. Thomas's *Commentary on the Letter of the Romans,* II, lectio 3.

19. Cf. I-II, Q. 91, a. 3.

In this way we can begin to understand the real meaning of Thomas's statement referred to earlier, that the goals of the virtues are "determined by nature": these goals are not really natural teleologies or an order of nature, recognized by the reason in the light of its divinely instituted or theonomic origin, as an obligatory "ought" correspondingly to be adopted or followed. Rather, these goals or ends are a *naturaliter cognitum,* something that the human reason grasps in a natural way, and independently of the knowledge of a creator God standing behind the natural order. But this natural way of reasoning, although "rational," does not correspond to that rationality with which we deliberate about the "means to an end," but is rather a kind of reasoning that is itself "natural": but "natural" means that which is *determinatum ad unum* ("determined to a single thing"). It is a question here of an act that is peculiar to the principle-grasping intellect, through which everything that forms the starting point and foundation for all further practical knowing is understood with a natural spontaneity or immediacy. We are now uncovering, so to say, the practical reason insofar as it is "nature," or the *natural reason (ratio naturalis),* and also a will that corresponds with it "as nature" *(voluntas ut natura).*[20]

If there were no "reason as nature" or "natural reason," nothing "rational by nature," there could likewise be nothing in reason and rationality that would be determined by nature to preordain and be the foundation for all subsequent rationality; there would be no reason at all, but only blind striving, appetition, affective conditioning, social conventions, internalized social compulsions, the right of the stronger, the power of the experts; there would be no authority that would not also be a threat to freedom; there would be no practical truth. There would be no difference between "good" and "bad" except the difference made by the one who holds the power to enforce it. A reason without "nature" would be a groundless reason without any orientation. It would be a mere tool for any purpose whatsoever. We all naturally know that reason is not this and cannot be allowed to be this.

> Proponents of discourse-ethics would raise objections, of course, since discourse-ethics not only claims to be an adequate reconstruction of moral reasoning, but also proceeds from the assumption that no kind of ascertained, naturally given moral insights of individual subjects could ever create a foundation for the acknowledgment of moral obligations. We lack, they say, the conceptual means for doing this in the postmetaphysical, value-pluralistic, rationally skeptical era we live in. Moral norms can only be grounded through a process of intersubjective understanding, and insofar as the morally relevant presuppositions that are always at the basis of all discourses (or of all consensus-oriented

20. Cf. I-II, Q. 10, a. 1.

action) are analyzed, and thus raised to the level of being conditions for the possibility of normative value claims. Discourse-ethicists attempt in this way to recover moral reason as consensual and communicative reason. But the problem with discourse-ethics consists in the fact that the discourse-participants must already be moral subjects if they are going to fulfill the conditions that would make them competent or acceptable participants in the discourse. And according as this moral competence of the individual agents and discourse-participants is conceived, and as corresponding value-preferences become effective, the discourse will end up for the most part becoming what discourse-ethicists call a "discourse of application."[21] Through the discourse as such, in any case, the agents do not become moral subjects because if they were not already such in the discourse-ethical sense, they would be excluded from the conversation. This is why all discourse-ethics already presupposes what a theory of the "rational by nature," or of the principles of practical reason, really tries to show: the answer to the question about the origin of the moral competence of the acting subject. If such an answer is possible, the claim of the discourse-ethical program is clearly deflated.

c) The First Principle of Practical Reason

A "principle" (Gr. *archē*, Lat. *principium*) is a starting point for everything that follows it. A principle of knowledge is the starting point for acts of knowing. And a principle of *practical* reason is the starting point for practical rationality. Since practical reason is reason that is embedded in striving (appetition), its principles always have the character of an *imperium* or *praeceptum* ("command" or "instruction"). They are "order," "command," "prescription," that is to say, a cognitive act that *moves* to action. A "first principle" of the practical reason is something from which this imperative or preceptive action-guiding process of the practical reason takes its original starting point, and is itself the principle of other, more specific principles. It must also do this "by nature" (and not on the basis of deliberation and choice), and it must be a "principle by nature," that can be shown, but not really justified (which is true of all principles).

21. Cf. the contribution of A. Matheis, "Ethik und Euthanasie. Diskursethische Kritik von Peter Singers Konzept Praktischer Ethik," in K. O. Apel and M. Kettner, eds., *Zur Anwendung der Diskursethik in Politik, Recht, und Wissenschaft* (Frankfurt am Main: Suhrkamp, 1992), 232–59, where life-and-death decisions are given a privileged attention (251, 253), and where there is discussion about the "nonnegotiability of existential borderline situations," which correspond to natural preferences, something that is *not* shared by the Singerian position criticized by Matheis. The decisive discourse-ethical argument that handicapped persons must represent their own interests in the dialogue appears to go into a vacuum here, because those handicapped persons, whose life Singer claims is lacking a certain quality, are the very ones who could not participate in the discourse (as, e.g., an anencephalic infant or a patient who has been in a long-lasting coma, a "permanent vegetative state" [PVS]).

One could, of course, object that there really are no practical *principles*. At the beginning there is the theoretical knowledge of that which "is," and then practical applications can be explicated from that. Someone must first understand what the human being is, and only then can he say something about the ordering of the human being's actions. Practical "principles" are always derived propositions, which can only be established through metaphysics, anthropology, or empirical humanistic or scientific knowledge.

> Critics of a virtue ethics in the Aristotelian or classically based tradition usually presuppose that the position formulated in the above objection constitutes the only authentic and possible position of such an ethics, that is, that practical principles do not possess any self-standing status, but are in some way derived from hard metaphysical or theoretical premises.[22] Since such critics are convinced that such premises are not (or no longer) justifiable, they consider any kind of "neo-Aristotelian" project foredoomed to failure.

But, to the above objection that practical principles are only propositions derived from metaphysical or otherwise already acquired truths about the nature of man, one must respond as follows: How can we ever know "What is man?" In order to know what man is, it is not enough to know what people actually do, what they actually strive for and consider good, or under what natural and social conditions as catalogued by the natural and social sciences their actions unfold. In order to know what man is, we must know what is good for man, or what one can alone rationally seek as good (see above, III.5.e). But we can only know that when we know that man in fact seeks for what is *rationally* known by nature as "good." Consequently, a purely theoretical, external study of the human being cannot tell us any more that we could know about him independently of the acts of his practical reason: such that he belongs to the class of mammals or that he is very weak in instincts. One theory that is really consistent in this respect is behaviorism, which belongs to the class of naturalistic theories. It begins by determining "What man is" in order to derive something normative from that.

Even the fact that we know we are "*rational* mammals" only comes from the experience that we have of our own rationality. And that we are mammals who are always seeking what we understand as good on the basis of reason, again, we only know because we have our own experience of our acts of practical reasoning. And we know these acts because we know their content (their object). And this object is, in general, the good. A derivation of the principles of praxis from the knowledge of "what man is" would be circular reasoning.

---

22. Cf., e.g., E. Tugendhat, "Retraktationen," in Tugendhat, *Probleme der Ethik*, 146; J. Habermas, "Lawrence Kohlberg und der Neoaristotelismus," in Habermas, *Erläuterungen zur Diskursethik*, 81.

In reality, every nonnaturalistic or nonreductionistic anthropology already assumes the self-experience of every spiritual act, which we cannot simply observe, except as within or in regard to ourselves. Practical reason is one of these spiritual acts. It becomes clear in this way that an ethics that represents a substantial theory of the good with a universally binding claim upon us cannot be founded on metaphysics. It is the other way around.

It also corresponds to our experience that the acts of the practical reason have their *own* starting point, and are not "derivations" or "applications" of theoretical judgments about "what man is." Earlier (III.3.a) we saw that from the knowledge that we are beings that need to be nourished by food to survive, we could not derive that "it is now 'good' to nourish oneself" (i.e., in the sense of a judgment "p is good," "p should be done," which *moves* to action). Because we could only do this to the extent that we knew that it is "good" to survive. And further: that "it is good *for me*" to survive. But how do we know that? And how could we establish that? We know it, ultimately, only because and insofar as we actually *do* seek (or strive for) survival as good for us, and not on the basis of some deliberation whether it is good now to do it, or whether we should choose to do it, but simply "by nature." And therefore the reason grasps this striving as "good" and it will be striven for by the will as a good in the order of reason *(bonum rationis)*. But that is not a *justification* of the goodness of surviving. Its goodness is rather the very first thing that is grasped by the reason in this case and—as something "rational by nature"—it is therefore the basis of all further justification.

Only a thoroughgoing "naturalist" would mistake attention to the fact of appetition as part of a "justification": such a "naturalist" position would say that we necessarily follow our drives, and whatever the drive directs us to do we call "good." But if that was alone the criterion of "good," there would be no morality, but only the natural sciences and various scientific techniques for the optimal direction of drives. From the moral standpoint, it can be a very bad thing to follow one's drives! The natural fact as such—insofar as it is not also a fact of reason—is no criterion for the moral good. Only a judgment of the reason, "p is good," in relation to this fact can constitute the "good for man." We must have already grasped the good as good objectified to the reason in order to be in a position to assess the natural fact or given according to criteria of "good" and "bad." And that means: we must already know "what is good for man" in order to be able to rightly interpret ourselves and to understand "what man is." If the "ought" is also to be grounded in what "is" every attempt at an *original* derivation of "ought" from "is" will end in a cul-de-sac. The original grasp of appetitions as "good" is an accomplishment of the practical reason. It constitutes the "ought" that makes it possible for us to understand the human being adequately without a naturalistic fallacy. *The naturally conditioned state of practical knowledge of the good and the ought must not be confused with the derivation of practical knowledge from (theoretical) knowledge about nature.* The latter is a route that is closed to ethics (cf. also III.5.e): the assertion that practical reason and morality as a whole finds its starting point in something "naturally rational" has nothing whatever to do with the idea that universal moral norms or values can be originally derived from a metaphysics of "human nature." This would only be possible if one understood by such a metaphysics a philosophical view of man that already presupposed and included the original *practical* experience of the "naturally rational."

> In this context, it is extremely important to distinguish metaphysical (ontological) questions from epistemological ones. Metaphysically speaking, we may affirm that the order of morality is grounded in being and in human nature. But ethics fundamentally and specifically deals with another question: the question about *how we come to know the good,* how the relationship between being/human nature, on one hand, and the good as an object of our practical knowledge and acting, on the other hand, takes shape. The fact that the practical knowledge of the good has its roots in human nature and is an expression of this nature does not imply that *originally* this knowledge is also *cognitively derived* from some kind of theoretical insight, or even from metaphysics or some sort of "ontology." It is rather the other way round: the analysis of the natural conditioning of practical knowledge, as proposed here, leads to a fuller understanding of human nature and in this sense it is itself part of, and necessary condition for, an adequate metaphysical understanding of human nature. In other words, what we are dealing with here is not the question of the ontological, but of the *cognitive,* grounding of the moral good. To be sure, the moral epistemology presented here already presupposes certain metaphysical insights into the structure of being, namely, what we earlier called the "metaphysics of action." It also presupposes that moral knowledge is both an expression of human nature and is grounded in the ontological structure of that nature, bringing it fully into light. The following is therefore nothing other than part of an analysis of human nature, leading as such to a deeper metaphysical understanding.

The practical judgment "p is good" is a judgment in the context of an appetition. And since practical reason is reason embedded in striving, it must also possess its own starting point that is not to be reduced to any other judgments.[23] What is this starting point?

---

23. One should recall here the earlier exposition (III.3.a) about "what is practical in practical reason." Aristotle's doctrine of practical principles is closely connected with his doctrine of motion developed in *De anima* III and *De motu animalium*.

It is something different from a theoretical judgment of the kind: "A is B." There is a first principle for the theoretical reason: "Something cannot be and not be in the same respect." This principle is based on the structure of being as such *(ratio entis)*. If it did not exist as a principle, a judgment of the kind "A is B" would immediately have to be completed by the judgment "A is not B"—which means it could not be valid. Hegelian dialectic is a theory that maintains that both of these judgments can stand together, on the ground that there is no such thing as the principle of noncontradiction. But this theory is based, in turn, on the contention that pure being is identical with pure nothingness.[24] Now this is itself a first principle: not one that establishes anything, but rather one that "removes and annihilates" [or "supersedes and suppresses," German *aufhebt*] every object in order to construct the "true object." Hegel was the philosopher who most consistently followed to its conclusion the modern notion that experience is not "given" but is a construction. But what is leftover afterward is no object at all, but only the experience-constructing subject of modern idealism.

But we could never act on the basis of judgments that are valid about the structure of being. The practical reason must therefore have its own starting point. Its first principle is not based on the structure of being, but on that of the good.[25] This *ratio boni* is as follows: "The good is that for which all things strive."[26] Practical reason is constituted through striving. The first thing that any reason that is practical grasps is something "seek-able." And this is objectified as a "good." The concept of the good is indeed nothing other than the concept of what correlates to a striving or seeking and insofar as it is such a correlate.

And likewise there is something that is opposed to the striving, which flees from something, to which the striving relates by way of aversion, avoidance, or flight. We call this evil (or bad). On the basis of this foundational structure of "good" and "evil" is formulated the first principle of the practical reason (which Thomas in his context, of course, calls the "first command" [*praeceptum*] of the natural law): "Good is to be done and pursued, and evil to be avoided" *(bonum est faciendum et persequendum, et malum vitandum)*.[27]

This may appear obvious or trivial. It would be a triviality if we understood

---

24. G. W. F. Hegel, *Science of Logic*, trans. W. H. Johnston and L. G. Struthers (London: Allen & Unwin, 1929; rpt. 1966).

25. For the following, cf. I-II, Q. 94, a. 2. See also G. Grisez, "The First Principle of Practical Reason: A Commentary on the Summa Theologiae I-II, q. 94, a. 2," *Natural Law Forum* 10 (1965): 168–201. A somewhat abbreviated version is available in A. Kenny, ed., *Aquinas: A Collection of Critical Essays* (South Bend, Ind.: University of Notre Dame Press, 1976), 340–82.

26. Cf. *EN* I, 1 (1094a 3).

27. I-II, Q. 94, a. 2.

it as a mere "statement," as a judgment of the theoretical reason. It would only be a tautology, a mere explication of the meaning of the words "good" and "evil." The point is, rather, that such a theoretically explicative statement—that we call "good" what is to be done or pursued, and "evil" what is to be avoided—already presupposes the experience of this principle as *practical.* The theoretical statement arises from a reflection *upon* this principle and is not the origin of the principle (in order to act, we do not say to ourselves first, "the good is to be done, . . ."). It has its origin as a principle of action already right in the *practical* reason, in the reason embedded in striving. The reflective theoretical judgment would not be possible independently of this fact.

> This does not signify that the good sought after and understood by practical reason is not grounded in being or not even a form of being. However, as Aquinas explains in article 5 of Question 21 of his *De Veritate,* the practical or the moral good is not constitutive of man's essential or substantial being, but rather accidental being, in a way added to its substantial being. It is a *perfection* of human nature, and as perfective being, it belongs to man as a being only *secundum quid* ("in a certain sense"); as "good" however, the moral good is precisely *bonum simpliciter* (or *absolute*), the good in the proper sense. This is why it is metaphysically impossible to identify "nature" with the moral good or to simply want to derive the latter from the former. Nature and substance, or the proper *esse* of every being, is what is properly perfected by operations and moral actions through which an additional, accidental being is generated, *according* to nature. Goodness in the proper sense, that is, moral goodness, belongs to this accidental, perfective being. And this goodness is always something more than nature and something more than what can be analyzed on the level of mere nature or substantial being. Moral epistemology, as a part of ethics, shows us how to understand the nexus between nature and the moral good and its cognitive genesis. A natural law theory is precisely such a moral epistemology. It cannot be reduced to "ontology" or an analysis of nature and its teleological structure. The teleologies inherent in nature cannot be known independently from the good toward which they tend because nature relates to this perfective good as potency to act; and yet the potencies, and that also means the teleological structures of nature, are known through the corresponding acts and goods. Therefore any normative ethics that would refer to natural teleology in order to establish moral norms would either *already* presuppose the kind of epistemological analysis and theory of the moral good as presented in these pages or else be caught in a vicious circle (see also the previous discussion at III.5.e).

As a judgment of the *practical,* in-striving-embedded reason the principle is also no tautology. Tautologies only belong to the realm of theoretical judgments, that is, mere statements "about" something. The willing of a concrete action 'p' has the same content as the carrying out of this concrete action 'p.' If it were not the same, one could never do what one wants, could never actually accomplish the willed action 'p.' But nevertheless, "willing p" and "doing p" are again not the same. It is not a matter of indifference between wanting to do something and actually doing it. That is why we would also not say, that action is a mere tautology, in this case a reiteration of 'p,' a mere saying of 'p' again. What is decisive about willing 'p' is that it *leads to* doing 'p,' and that "doing p" is in fact something *more* than "willing p." And it is the same way with the first principle of practical reason. Namely, it leads us to do good at all, or to avoid evil. It is the fundamental *action-grounding* judgment as such. It constitutes the practical difference that is already the moral difference. The first principle of practical reason *moves* to action. It is an *imperium* or *praeceptum*. This is because action only comes to be under the difference of "good" and "evil," and also, insofar as this difference belongs to the process of appetition. The first principle of the practical reason lies implicitly at the foundation of every subsequent judgment of the kind "p is good," "p is to be done" (or "p is bad," "p is not to be done"): *it is, in the truest sense, the principle of praxis.*

Now, looking more closely: that the first principle of practical reason, as all subsequent principles, is the principle of praxis and not of ethics, means that it is the principle of action of a concrete acting subject, and not the principle of discourse *about* praxis, for example, of a discourse about norms conducted by philosophers of ethics. It is the principle that lies at the basis of all rational human action and forms its inner intelligible dynamism. Practical principles are not principles of reflection or thought, but are moving principles and principles of action.[28]

28. In critizing John Finnis's claim that practical reason has its own starting point, Ralph McInerny commits the mistake of confusing the original grasp of practical principles, on the one hand, with ethical reflection (or "practical arguments"), that is, normative ethical discourse, on the other hand. McInerny writes as follows (emphasis added): "Finnis, it seems, wishes to maintain that the end, the good, *that guides ethical reflection* is known in what he earlier called purely practical knowledge. It is not preceded by, is independent of, any and all theoretical knowledge—knowledge, for example, of such brute facts as that man alone speaks and is spoken to. The good(s) are grasped in practical knowledge; this is the beginning point of practical thinking. After that, all kinds of theoretical knowledge can enter into the picture. *Practical arguments* are often mixtures of practical and theoretical considerations—of 'ought' and 'is' judgments—*but what must be avoided like sin is any suggestion that our first and primary practical knowledge is dependent on theoretical knowledge of nature.* That is Finnis's fundamental point" (R. McInerny, *Aquinas on Human Action: A Theory of Practice* [Washington, D.C.: The Catholic University of America Press, 1992], 188). I agree with McInerny in his critique of Finnis's rejection of the Aristotelian *ergon* argument (I have myself criticized Finnis for this in my *Praktische Vernunft und Vernünftigkeit der Praxis*, 53–59), though the ergon argument does not in fact belong to the basis of moral knowledge, but already to the stage of reflective-metaphysical analysis of basic practical experience. Yet the rest of McInerny's critique is rather the expression of what Aristotle called an *ignoratio elenchi* ("ignorance of what is to be refuted," i.e., a refutation of something that is not at issue, a kind of "red herring"): neither Finnis nor I have ever maintained that practical principles are prin-

Practical reason and its principles are, first of all, not "ethics" or a "discourse about norms," but rather the reasoned insights of the acting subject, him- or herself. This goes as well for practical principles in general or the *lex naturalis:* here, too, it is not a question of statements about praxis in the mode of reflection, but rather the immediately action-causing practical judgments of a universal kind that constitute the human being as a moral subject who in his acting is beholden to the difference between good and evil. Practical principles are consequently not really "norms" to which practical knowledge must attend, but genuine achievements of practical knowing by the acting subject, which then subsequently can become the foundation and standard for "moral norms" (see below, V.3).

---

ciples that guide *ethical reflection;* the point of contending that practical reason has its own starting point and thus its own principles—which, being *principles,* cannot be derived from previous theoretical knowledge—is that they properly are the basis of *practical* and *moral* knowledge (which is not "ethical reflection"). "Ethical reflection" comes in later, and already *presupposes* the knowledge of these principles and uses them. Ethical reflection, to be precise, reflects theoretically on them (a reflection which, being reflection on practical issues, in turn becomes practical). Interestingly, McInerny refers to human language and linguistic communication as a "brute fact" which, as he assumes, is originally known by theoretical reason; yet he completely overlooks how theoretical reason could ever grasp language and communication as such a "brute fact," and even less as a human good, distinguishing it from animal forms of "communication" and uttering "linguistic signals" (which are not "language" in the human sense) without a previous *inner* and *practical* experience of the linguistic and communicative acts of human beings. And here can be seen McInerny's second error: he overlooks how the grasp of practical principles in fact *leads* to a deeper and more complete knowledge precisely of *human nature.* Whether this knowledge originally is theoretical or practical does not matter so long as it is *knowledge* by the human intellect, a faculty which is single in the human being and which in all its acts is essentially orientated toward knowing the truth of being. Are not the natural inclinations of the human person (in which the intellect grasps these goods and becomes practical just because they are *inclinations*) not also a part of human *being?* Even if my position is not identical with Finnis's, I share with him the fundamental idea that the practical grasp of human goods or practical principles *is* a kind of knowledge of human nature which is properly indispensable for the knowledge of *human* nature. For this nature is (also) spiritual and thus cannot be understood by simply theoretical observation and description (see also above, III.5.e). This is why an ethical doctrine of practical principles is, as Finnis contends, "an indispensable preliminary to a full and soundly based knowledge of human nature" (J. M. Finnis, *Fundamentals of Ethics* [Washington, D.C.: Georgetown University Press, 1983], 21). And this is why he, in my view, rightly asks, "why suppose that our techniques for developing a description of *human* nature are limited to those available for describing beings whose nature we do not share?" (ibid., 20). I think Finnis's fundamentally anti-Humean account of the origin of the knowledge of human nature through practical reason—the human intellect embedded in the dynamics of the natural inclinations—is not only fundamentally Aristotelian, but also Thomistic. Apart from the famous and already quoted I-II, Q. 94, a. 2, see, e.g., the *Quaestio disputata de virtutibus in communi,* Q. un., a. 8, where Aquinas affirms that there are not only principles of speculative but also of practical reason. He then asserts of both theoretical and practical principles: *Haec autem naturaliter nota sunt principia totius cognitionis sequentis, quae per studium acquiritur; sive sit practica, sive sit speculativa* ("But these naturally known things are principles of all subsequent thought that is acquired by study, whether it be practical or theoretical"). Now, if practical principles, exactly like theoretical principles, are *naturaliter nota,* they cannot be possibly derived from judgments of the theoretical intellect! This is what Aquinas very explicitly explains in I-II, Q. 94, a. 2. There undeniably exists for Aquinas a parallelism of theoretical and practical knowledge, each having its own starting point and specific principles, all of which contribute to our understanding of human nature.

This is exactly why it must appear as "short-shrift" to regard the first principle of practical reason as merely the "structure of practical reasoning in general" which "maintains the formal noncontradiction of what is recognized as good."[29] According to this understanding, practical truth would only be understood as the coherence of thought about praxis, and the Aristotelian idea of practical truth as the agreement with *right appetition* would be taken as merely the agreement with "any given, comprehensive goal."[30] No less unsatisfying appears the characterization of the first principle of the practical reason as "the principle of practical *noncontradiction*."[31] In this way of thinking about it, the purely logical side dominates the dynamic/practical, action-psychological aspect, which to my way of thinking is decisive. The fundamental difference of "true/false" or "yes/no," proper to the theoretical reason, does not have its extension for Thomas in a difference of "good/bad" that would then be the practical reason's "mode of statement." The practical extension for the theoretical declaration "true/false" or "yes/no," is, as we saw, the *persequi* or *facere/vitare* or *fugere* ("pursuing" or "doing"/"fleeing" or "avoiding").[32] These are not "statements about something" (nor expressions of a theoretical kind) but are rather acts of rationally informed appetition that bring it about that the acting subject does something or not. In distinction from theoretical affirmations and denials, the practical "affirmation" is a "pursuing" and a "doing," and the corresponding "denial" is an "avoiding," a "fleeing from," and a corresponding "not-doing." This is precisely the logic of the first principle of practical reason: it *moves* to rationally guided action.

d) The Constitution of Specific Principles of Action

On the basis of the first principle of practical reason alone, nothing is done yet. It is fully unspecific. As already mentioned, this does not mean that it is tautological or empty of content.[33] On the contrary, it has a very abundant

29. L. Honnefelder, "Wahrheit und Sittlichkeit. Zur Bedeutung der Wahrheit in der Ethik," in E. Coreth, ed., *Wahrheit und Einheit in Vielheit* (Düsseldorf: Patmos, 1987), 147–69, esp. 156 and 167.

30. Ibid., 167 and 151.

31. L. Honnefelder, "Absolute Forderungen in der Ethik. In welchem Sinne ist eine sittliche Verpflichtung 'absolut'?" in W. Kerber, ed., *Das Absolute in der Ethik* (Munich: Kindt Verlag, 1991), 13–33, esp. 25f. Cf. also Honnefelder, "Praktische Vernunft und Gewissen," in A. Hertz, W. Korff, T. Rendtdorff, and H. Ringeling, eds., *Handbuch der christlichen Ethik* (Freiburg: Herder, 1982), 3.19–43.

32. This follows quite clearly from I-II, Q. 94, a. 2; cf. also a thorough treatment in M. Rhonheimer, "Practical Reason and the 'Naturally Rational': On the Doctrine of the Natural Law as a Principle of Praxis in Thomas Aquinas," in W. Murphy, ed., *The Perspective of the Acting Person: Essays in the Renewal of Thomistic Moral Philosophy* (Washington, D.C.: The Catholic University of America Press, 2007), 95–128.

33. As L. Honnefelder maintains; see "Die ethische Rationalität des mittelalterlichen Naturrechts. Max Webers und Ernst Troeltschs Deutung des mittelalterlichen Naturrechts und die Bedeutung der Lehre vom natürlichen Gesetz bei Thomas von Aquin," in W. Schluchter, ed., *Max Webers Sicht des okzidentalen Christentums* (Frankfurt am Main: Suhrkamp, 1988), 254–75, at 260f. A brief critical exchange

content, since it drives the subject to the good as such and as it were brings the nature of the good as that which is striven for to expression. The question is only, how does this principle become further subdivided into specific areas of action? For only in that way can it become a functioning principle of praxis, since actions always have a specific good for their content, never the "good in general" or the totality of goodness. But this "subdividing" is not to be understood as "deduction." Nothing can be "deduced" from the first principle. Instead, it "shows itself" *in* the various specific principles and develops in them its foundational-practical effectiveness, not only as a principle of thinking, but as a *principle of movement.*[34]

The relationship of the practical reason to "good" and "evil," we have seen, is a relationship that is naturally given. It belongs to the realm of reason as nature. If there were still something else that the reason grasps as good "by nature," this would also have the character of a principle. Therefore, Thomas goes on to say, all other commands of the natural law are grounded in this principle (i.e., all the other principles of the practical reason), so that "everything that is to be done or avoided belongs to the commands of the natural law [= the naturally given principles of practical reason], *which the practical reason naturally grasps as good."*[35]

What, then, can practical reason naturally grasp as "good for man"? Everything to which man has a "natural inclination" *(naturalis inclinatio):* "The reason comprehends naturally as a good everything to which the human being has a natural inclination and is consequently to be pursued through action, and what is opposed to that, it grasps as evil and to be avoided. Therefore the order of the commands of the natural law [= the principles of the practical reason as given by nature] goes according to the order of the natural inclinations."[36]

It appears that we have once again returned to "nature." In a certain sense that is correct, and we would never want to leave nature out of the picture. In fact, we have arrived at nature, but we didn't start out from nature. Or, bet-

with Honnefelder is available in Ch. Schroer, *Praktische Vernunft bei Thomas von Aquin* (see note 8 above), 205ff., and more fully in M. Rhonheimer, "Practical Reason and the 'Naturally Rational'" (see note 31 above).

34. Of course, thinking is implicit in this movement and also the possibility of self-reflexivity, that is to say, the possibility of taking up a position toward one's own striving at every phase of the striving, to make it an object of judgment and willing (or not willing) and thereby in every act of appetition not only to grasp "something" as a good, "but in grasping the good in each case, always to grasp oneself as a being determining itself through reason in freedom, in order to be this kind of being" (L. Honnefelder, "Absolute Forderungen in der Ethik," 30). Cf. also the previous exposition (III.3.a) of the "practical syllogism."

35. I-II, Q. 94, a. 2.

36. Ibid.

ter: we started out from the nature that reason is. This reason is not just any free-floating reason, but the reason of a human person. And the human being is a body-soul unity and fundamentally a striving being that is oriented toward good and the reality of being. If practical reason is reason embedded in appetition, it is fundamentally a reason that is embedded in the structure of those inclinations and appetitions that constitute the I-structure of the human person (cf. above: III.5.e). The human being is not simply reason or freedom. The human being is an *animal rationale,* a physical being with sense perception that realizes its animality in a spiritual, rational way and which also has inclinations that arise from the reason-guided appetition, to which belongs as well—in relation to all the other inclinations—an architectonic or ordering function. The reason of man is not only concerned with what is around him, what he deals with, and to which he relates himself. There is also the "nature" (bodiliness, sense perceptions) that constitutes his personal "I," that he himself *is.* And this nature possesses, in its multiple aspects and levels, a dynamic of appetition. This nature is oriented toward what corresponds to the various sensitive faculties and the will (the good of the reason), for also in the will there is a "natural inclination." The reflexivity of reason and will (as the rational striving) opens up the possibility of distancing oneself from nature, to not only be one's nature but also to have it (and in this sense the human being not only *is* his body, but *has* it too). In any case the practical reason does not do this as contentless reason, but always as a reason that finds itself as practical reason already embedded in the appetitive, "striving dynamic" toward what is by nature good for man. The practical reason cannot remove itself from this dynamic: it cannot be "pure rationality as such" that stands over against a nature to be ruled by "pure rationality."

The various natural inclinations are therefore also natural objects of practical reasoning. And insofar as the practical reasoning of a human being grasps the inclinations peculiar to his human nature, it grasps them naturally as good for the human being. But that is, again, obvious. But it is crucial here, again, not to banish or overlook what is obvious: on the basis of the understanding of the natural inclinations as "human goods," the very *identity* of the human person is fundamentally constituted. The principles of the practical reason accordingly constitute the consciousness of "who" or "what" we really are.

> The fundamental structure of the human goods as marked out by the various natural inclinations does not in itself cause any problem. There is a wide consensus on this point. The question concerns the interpretation of these goods: Are they merely "nonmoral" goods that one can make use of or toss into a balance to weigh? Or are they the irreducible principles of all practical reasoning

and thereby the conditions under which the practical reason operates in the framework of human identity? We are here concerned to show that the latter is the case. For, as the correlates of appetitions, these goods constitute in a fundamental way the intentional framework of relations and the object-content of all human action and thereby of moral good. Treating "goods" as correlatives of appetitions means treating them in a practical perspective, and "morality" cannot be ignored in thinking from the perspective of action. "In contrast to the analysis of the human being as a mere natural entity, the action of the human being as a human being always moves on the horizon of morality."[37]

This human identity is constituted in the grasping of the natural inclinations *through reason*. And this is the real point to be made about why we have not simply returned to mere nature. Exactly as "natural virtue" (as a mere, natural nonrational disposition) is to be distinguished from "real" rationally guided virtue, just so the natural inclinations (as natural dispositions) are to be distinguished from the "good for man." This is valid, says Thomas, for all parts of human nature, for the "irascible" and the "concupisciple" faculties.[38] We have arrived again at the theme of the moral virtues. The practical principles—constituted on the basis of grasping the natural inclinations as human goods—converge with the ends of the moral virtues.

The connection becomes even clearer when Thomas says: "Just as reason dominates in man and commands the other faculties, so must all the natural inclinations be ordered according to reason."[39] The natural inclination that commands all these other ones is the inclination to follow reason, and this inclines the human being "to act according to reason. And that means nothing other than acting according to virtue. Consequently all the acts of the virtues belong to the natural law [= belong to the practical principles]: because every person's reason commands him to act virtuously."[40]

The naturalistic thesis would run as follows: a natural appetition is a human good, simply because, and insofar as, it is natural. What we are saying, however, is that a human appetition, because it is natural, is also naturally recognized by the reason as a human good. But only insofar as it is recognized by the *reason* as "good"—that is, as a "good of the reason"—and not just because it is "natural," does it disclose its identity as a "human good."

---

37. O. Höffe, "Philosophische Handlungstheorie als Ethik," in H. Poser, ed., *Philosophische Probleme der Handlungstheorie* (Freiburg and Munich: Alber, 1982), 233. One would also have to agree with the following statement: "Since philosophical action theory explicates the conditions for all human action, it takes over a large part of the role of justification in ethics." Cf. also O. Höffe, "Sittlichkeit als Horizont menschlichen Handelns," in O. Höffe, *Sittlich-Politische Diskurse* (Frankfurt am Main: Suhrkamp, 1981), 23–51.

38. I-II, Q. 94, a. 2, ad 2.　　　　　　　　39. I-II, Q. 94, a. 4, ad 3.

40. Ibid., a. 3.

"Interpreting an appetite does not occur by itself. The interpretation does not belong to nature. Rather, it is what we call the rational. Only in the light of reason does nature *as* nature appear."[41] And that also means: "as *human* nature." The comprehension and interpretation by reason already implies a standard-giving governance through the reason. Human goods are always *intelligible* goods, that is, they are correlates of human inclinations on the level of their intelligibility as functioning elements of the concrete, essential unity of the "human person."

In contrast to this, according to W. Korff (a revisionist moral theologian), the natural inclinations remain on the level of mere nature. They are, to be sure, not just any formable matter, but are already "metanorms," that is, "factors, open to structuring, that bring about dispositions" [*dispositive entwurfsoffene Größen*], which bring their own teleology with them, but not "action-guiding rules": "If what is intended by nature is to be arrived at with them, they need normative correction. But that is the task of the practical reason as 'prudence,' which has to make known the proper way and means, and ultimately formulate the goal in each case in a more precise form. The world of norms that concretely regulate human action is not simply pregiven in man, but rather open to shaping by way of the 'natural law' that works in him."[42] On closer inspection one discovers that with this interpretation there is really no *lex naturalis* left, that is, no *universal principles of the practical reason* that precede the act of prudence. The only universal for Korff is the metanorm "natural inclination," but this is still mere "nature." The rational, by contrast, is to be found only on the level of concretion, in the act of prudence (which always has the particular for its object).[43] Norms are only "shaped" afterward. What falls by the wayside, nevertheless, is the "universal of the *reason*" that is presupposed by prudence, that is, the (natural) *principles* of practical reason; these are exactly what we mean by the *lex naturalis*. The nature/reason distinction—for Korff, whose anthropology is dualistic—turns into a disjunction of parallel, heterogeneous factors. At the same time, it remains unclear just where the normative significance of the "metanorm" comes from, how its "being" implies an "ought."[44] Natural inclination, for Korff, remains firmly on

41. R. Spaemann, *Happiness and Benevolence*, 166.
42. W. Korff, "Der Rückgriff auf die Natur. Eine Rekonstruktion der thomanischen Lehre vom natürlichem Gesetz," *Philosophisches Jahrbuch* 94 (1987): 285–96, here 289; see also Korff, *Norm und Sittlichkeit. Untersuchung zur Logik der normativen Vernunft*, 2nd ed. (Freiburg and Munich: Alber, 1985). A. Anzenbacher also depends on Korff for his presentation of this point: *Einführung in die Ethik*, 132f.; cf. also p. 87ff. for an exposition of the *lex naturalis* doctrine that broadly agrees with what is offered here, but at the same time leaves still unclarified the decisive question of the relationship between natural inclination and reason.
43. On the responsibility of prudence, according to Korff, for "more precise formulations of the goals" (the *praestitutio finis*), see my exposition in *Praktische Vernunft und Vernünftigkeit der Praxis*, 362ff. and 583ff.
44. Cf. Ch. Schroer, *Praktische Vernunft bei Thomas von Aquin*, 120, esp. note 179.

the level of reasonless nature, at the level of a merely naturally given drive. He only avoids a crude naturalism by understanding moral normativity as a work of "shaping prudence." Such a shaping prudence, then, is practical reason, but without any principles of reason! By contrast, the position I am developing here holds that the natural inclination as an *intelligible* inclination has already come into the order proper to it through the reason, thereby coming to itself as (human) "nature," and consequently as a practical principle of reason, and then as a principle of prudence and a principle for the consequent discourse about norms. This does not mean that such principles—for example, that of individual survival—are already capable of guiding action; but there is still up for debate the question to be handled below—at least in an ethics that tries to connect morality with rationality—concerning the possibility that the *limits of what is morally possible* are not subject to disposal.[45]

In the comprehension and interpretation of natural inclination through reason, we find once again the distinction between natural and moral identity, of matter and form. A natural inclination grasped by the reason as "good" is more than the mere naturalness of this inclination. It is already *formed* by the reason, and—since the principle of this forming, reason, is itself the "nature" of man—it reveals only in this way its true naturalness as something that is "according to nature" for a human person. In the case of the inclinations that arise from reason-guided appetition, or will, natural and moral identity are at one.

Thomas is working here with one of his most overlooked distinctions. It is the distinction between the "proper act and proper end" (actus et finis *proprius*) of an inclination from its "right (what-'ought'-to-be) act and end" (actus et finis *debitus*). Only the inclination that originates from the reason is an inclination to the *debitum*. Or: what is "proper" *(proprium)* to the reason is really the inclination to the ought.[46] All that is originally "proper" to the nonrational inclinations is only brought into the order of the *debitum* through being grasped by the reason. And that means: through the reason it passes from the *genus naturae* into the *genus moris*. The moral difference is therefore constituted in every case by the reason, and not through the fact of "naturalness." On the other hand,

---

45. This incoherence of Korff's position is not mentioned by E. Schockenhoff, *Natural Law and Human Dignity* (see above, IV.3.e, note 102), 138–40, nor by F. Bormann, *Natur als Horizont sittlicher Praxis. Zur Handlungstheoretischen Interpretation der Lehre vom natürlichen Sittengestz bei Thomas von Aquin* (Stuttgart-Berlin-Cologne: W. Kohlhammer, 1999), 230ff. A critique of my own interpretation has been offered especially by G. Wieland—continuing the work of L. Honnefelder—in "Secundum naturam vivere. Über das Verhältnis von Natur und Sittlichkeit," in B. Fraling, and G. Wieland, *Natur im ethischen Argument,* Studien zur theologischen Ethik 31 (Freiburg: Herder, 1990), 13–31, esp. 21–26. My own fully developed answer to this criticism is found in the "Postscript" to the English edition (2000) of my *Natur als Grundlage der Moral* (1987): *Natural Law and Practical Reason,* 562ff., and in "Practical Reason and the 'Naturally Rational'" (see note 32 above).

46. Cf., e.g., I-II, Q. 91, a. 2.

without the natural inclination and what is proper to it, the reason would have no object. Nor could the reason provide any practical orientation.[47]

Practical principles that are constituted through the intellective grasp of the natural inclinations as "good" are thus not identical with natural inclination: rather, they are—as principles of the reason—rules, standards, order *in* these inclinations. Without natural inclination there would neither be practical principles nor actions. But the principles themselves are not these inclinations as natural, but rather as practical, universal judgments of the kind "p is good" *with relation to* these inclinations. Every practical principle, and that means, again, every precept of the "natural law," is an ordering of the reason *in relation to* or *in* the natural inclinations.

e) Practical Principles, Virtues, and Intentional Basic Actions

Gradually, a complete picture is forming: the picture that began with the analysis of human actions and was developed with the concept of the object of action as the content of intentional basic action was filled in, finally, by the moral virtues. But at this point we need to ask: What are the fundamental natural inclinations, on the comprehension of which the practical principles are constituted?

The following can be mentioned as the most important: first, the drive for self-preservation: keeping one's own life and existence. Dependent on this are the drives to be nourished, to maintain and to defend oneself. Going further,

---

47. This is why the notion that we must choose between seeing the reason as a reason that "reads off" (or only "discerns") or as a reason that "shapes" (or "constitutes") is not very helpful; cf. L. Honnefelder, "Natur als Handlungsprinzip. Die Relevanz der Natur für die Ethik," in L. Honnefelder, ed., *Natur als Gegenstand der Wissenschaften* (Freiburg and Munich: Alber, 1992), 151–90, at 178. The choice is misleading, since, without reason, there cannot even be a "natural inclination" in man as an appetition relevant for praxis. The stated choice would presuppose the possibility of a reason that simply "stands over against" the natural inclination *as pure nature*, to then "configure" or "shape" it. But to this the following must be objected: when the human being—in the mode of reflection—puts himself with his reason in relation to himself as a striving, appetitive being, he is not related to his natural inclinations as to something that is purely nature and not yet formed through reason, but rather as to a striving or appetition already formed by reason, or to human goods that are already *intelligible* as object to this appetition. Honnefelder (as also G. Wieland, "Secundum naturam vivere," 25) proceeds from something that in my view seems impossible: from an original self-relation of practical reason to one's own appetitions as "pure nature," which "only in this way can become meaningful for the context of action" (Wieland, ibid.); cf. my own criticism in the "Postscript" to the English edition of my *Natur als Grundlage der Moral* (1987): *Natural Law and Practical Reason*, 562ff., and in M. Rhonheimer, "Practical Reason and the 'Naturally Rational.'" A reason that as pure form, and not yet in relation to the objectivity of any inclination, lays claim to being the principle of reason-guided praxis, is really not reason at all; for reason, and even practical reason, is a cognitive power, but without an object there cannot be any cognition. The reason discussed by Honnefelder and Wieland rather appears to be the original experience of the autonomy of the will, what Kant called "transcendental freedom." On the mixture of Kant and Thomas, see, again, Ch. Schroer, *Praktische Vernunft bei Thomas v. Aquin*, 205ff.

there is the inclination to connect oneself with the opposite sex: the sex drive. Finally, there are inclinations that arise from the reason: to live together in a community with one's own kind of beings (to this belongs such things as communication, goodwill toward others, friendship, and the avoidance of what goes against these); knowledge of the truth (or avoidance of ignorance); reverence for God. The inclination to play, to make artistic products, and to enjoy aesthetic experiences as well as "practical reasonableness" itself could also be included here:[48] nobody would think it good to pursue one of the other goods unless it was on the basis of insight, one's own willing and self-mastery, and not, as it were, only passively. The goodness of each good would disappear.

> This is why pleasure, enjoyment, and contentment *as such* are not human goods. A condition of complete contentment in which we do nothing—having, as it were, reward without labor, or joy without an object *over which* we feel joy, or a feeling of satisfaction without reality or some activity that satisfies— we would not consider as "good" but as something undignified. Pleasure and contentment are human goods only as "pleasure *in* the good" or "joy *about* the good," or "contentment *with* the good" (cf. above, II.2.b).

We strive for self-preservation insofar as we "exist" and "live." The connection with the opposite sex is a natural inclination which, as Thomas says, quoting the Roman jurist Ulpian: "nature has taught all animals *(animalia)*."[49] But does this mean that we strive for self-preservation at all costs? Or that every sexual inclination is equally good? Of course not. For these natural inclinations constitute human goods and practical principles to the extent that they are pursued within the order of reason; insofar, that is, as the *will* seeks after them in accordance with the order of reason, as "goods of reason." Even self-preservation and sexuality—as human goods and not merely as natural inclinations—are always the *will* to survive and the *willing* (or loving) of another person. The comprehending of these inclinations through the reason orders these same inclinations according to the demands of reason, and only so are they the object of the will and a principle of human actions.

In this way, self-preservation and sexuality are also ordered in the context of the other inclinations. As human goods, both have something to do with social life, communication, goodwill, friendship, and so on (which also reveals why it does not go against the human good of "survival" to offer one's own life in behalf of a friend). Only in this integration into the *whole* of what the human being is do the single goods that correspond to the natural inclinations of the human being become visible as "goods for man." Only in this way

---

48. Cf. J. M. Finnis, *Natural Law and Natural Rights* (Oxford: Clarendon Press, 1980), 87ff.
49. Cf. I-II, Q. 94, a. 2.

do they form their proper, *intelligible,* human identity. This forming of natural inclinations into their identity as human goods—that is, into their identity as "good for the reason," or as "good objectified to the reason"—arises from an inventive process of the natural reason,[50] which, still operating within the realm of principles and thus not in a way that would be accessible to a proper justification, can nevertheless be reconstructed in argument. In this way we can succeed in identifying action-specific principles that are nothing other than the goals of the single virtues. Action-specific principles have for their content not only "good is to be done and pursued, bad to be avoided," but also "P, Q, . . . R, is to be done and pursued, S, T, . . . U, is to be avoided," whereby P, Q, . . . R are understood as "good" kinds of actions and S, T, . . . U as "bad" or "evil" ones. The first principle of practical reason is here merely being specified, but still implicitly present as the cause of the disjunction of the moral difference.

It is important at this point to emphasize something: on the one hand, the single natural inclinations must be *distinguished* from one another, as they are not derivable one from the other, but are each fundamental in their specificity. A specific origin can be pinpointed for each inclination (a person inclines to self-preservation because he "lives" or "is"; sexuality is rooted in the bodily/animal level of the human being: i.e., it is something that "nature has taught all animals"; the remaining inclinations are *specifically* human, meaning that they are only possible through reason and arise from the "logic of the spirit"). On the other hand, none of these inclinations is understandable as *human* in itself or by itself alone. The horizon for understanding each single inclination—its intelligibility—is always the *whole human being* as a body-soul, personal *supposit.* Even when, for example, "the inclination to the joining of male and female" is something "that nature has taught all animals," just so, nature has not taught all living things the way she has taught man, that is, in the sense of an inclination whose object is integrated as a human good into the order of reason. The individual inclinations mutually interpenetrate one another, and only in this interpenetration—and thus in each case as the "component" of a higher, complex whole, only as objectified to the reason—do they form what makes for the corresponding "human good" in each of these inclinations. It is—now on the level of principles—this very *standard-giving* and *ordering* task of the reason that was already encountered in the constitution of the objects of action.

For the above reasons, none of the human goods just mentioned can be treated in isolation; they form in their totality a mutual interrelatedness that has

---

50. On the process of the *inventio* of the natural reason, cf. *Natural Law and Practical Reason,* 267–74. See also section f.

been referred to as "integral human fulfillment."[51] Nevertheless these goods form a hierarchically structured unity of order (see also above: II.3.b); this is not because they can be derived one from another, which they cannot, but because it is really *in* the mutual relatedness of what is originally underived that relationships can be verified, stemming from their common foundation and dependence. So, for example, the good of interhuman communication is both correlated and subordinated to the good of human social life; and "truthfulness" is not *derived from* "sociability," but as a human good is immediately intelligible as "good."

Let us now illustrate these connections in several aspects by a reconstruction or "phenomenology" of the cognitive genesis of such practical principles, which are, at the same time, fundamental human goods.

1. *The genesis of the principle of "justice":* Every human being strives by nature for self-preservation, "to be" and "to live." Needs arise from this: you must nourish yourself, clothe yourself (as protection from cold, but also by a feeling of shame, since shame pertains in a certain way to self-maintenance and has a protective function). One seeks one's own space to live in, which again serves the cause of protection and self-maintenance. One works, in order to take care of these needs. To ensure the continuing satisfaction of needs one acquires things like tools, a workplace, capital (which can all be lost again), and so on. Thus possessions come into being.

Man does all this on the basis of reason. These are already human actions. The animal kingdom, of course, has functionally equivalent structures of self-preservation and the meeting of needs. The rational way that the human being carries this out also includes what is already *specifically* human such as "working" and the "acquisition of goods." Likewise, maintaining oneself with respect to other living creatures, especially one's own kind, is to be found among animals. But with human beings this acquires in addition the characteristic of "law" or "legal right" [*Recht*]. As a free, responsible, rational being, man understands the meeting of his needs and the relationships and states of affairs that emerge from them as "lawful" or "just" vis-à-vis the claims of others doing the same. Possession becomes "rightful ownership."

But it also pertains to reason to recognize "others" as being *of one's own kind*. The recognition of another as "like me" cannot be rationally argued. One can reject such recognition in practice, but someone cannot give reasons why

---

51. Cf. above all, G. Grisez, J. Boyle, and J. Finnis, "Practical Principles, Moral Truth, and Ultimate Ends," *American Journal of Jurisprudence* 32 (1987): 99–151. For an opposing position (with objections that are justified in part, with which I agree), see R. Hittinger, *A Critique of the New Natural Law Theory* (South Bend, Ind.: University of Notre Dame Press, 1987); and further R. McInerny, *Ethica Thomistica: The Moral Philosophy of Thomas Aquinas* (Washington, D.C.: The Catholic University of America Press, 1982), esp. 48ff.

he *recognizes* another human being as "his equal." That is the very essence of this kind of recognition.

Hegel's attempt to reconstruct this in his *Phenomenology of the Spirit*[52] actually implies the rejection of such fundamental recognition and makes it dependent instead on the "work" and "achievements" of the other, through which this other is emancipated to become a subject worthy of being recognized. Equality is here only the *result* of recognition. This shows an inhuman slant. The fundamental recognition of the other as "my equal" can also be hindered by confusion about what an other is (as in the famous question, "Who is my neighbor?"). Hence the phenomenon of discrimination, whereby someone of another race, or an unborn child, is not recognized as an "other" or as "like me." One does not feel oneself as connected with such through the bond of justice, or at least some other standard of justice is applied. It seems clear that this is not the case of a failing principle so much as it is the case of a false opinion about reality corrupting the principle. Discrimination (e.g., racism, abrogation of the right to live for unborn human beings, slavery) arises (in an analogy with moral standards based on ethnic origins) strictly speaking not from a different moral logic or structure of thinking, but from different conceptions of what constitutes a human being, one "who is like me" (which then leads to a different morality). On the basis of Hegelian recognition-theory, someone becomes a recognition-deserving human subject through "work," that is, a certain form of achievement. That too is a kind of discrimination.[53]

Through the recognition of the other as "like me," interaction patterns arise, and to the extent that a human being needs fellow human beings for meeting his own needs (e.g., their work, the products of their work, their ability to protect, their knowledge, etc.) communities arise for the sharing of labor. "Society" is already in existence in the sense of the "procreative community" (to be discussed shortly, below). The human being by nature needs a community with others of his own kind. Reason makes possible a transference of self-preservation to others, as "responsibility for others," for aid and support, and so on. Societies (the forming of communities) come into being because they

52. In the famous chapter on "Lordship and Bondage." Cf. G. W. F. Hegel, *Phenomenology of the Spirit*, trans. A. V. Miller (Oxford: Clarendon Press, 1977), 111–19.

53. In continuity with the Hegelian theory of recognition, discourse-ethics also appears to make recognition dependent on a certain "ability to achieve" in the sense of performance competency: on the ability, namely, to be a participant in the ethical discourse. Contractualistic theories also have a certain tendency to exclude groups that are not qualified to be partners in the contract, such as the seriously handicapped, etc. Cf. O. Höffe, *Politische Gerechtigkeit. Grundlegung einer kritischen Philosophie von Recht und Stadt* (Frankfurt am Main: Suhrkamp, 1987), 427. Höffe, at all events, is aware of this problem and thus opts for a fulfillment of justice through solidarity with those in relation to whom no rights of freedom can be established (as in the case of the seriously handicapped). By contrast, consider the unconditioned recognition of human beings as persons in R. Spaemann, *Persons: The Difference between 'Someone' and 'Something,'* trans. O. O'Donovan (Oxford: Oxford University Press, 2006), 180ff., 236ff.

are needed, and to the extent that they are necessary. And they are not only a necessity because it is more rational to maintain oneself and meet one's own needs through cooperation in the context of a society of one's peers, but also because things like cooperation, taking responsibility for others, giving and receiving assistance and care, associating with others, communicating with others, and the like are all themselves naturally grasped as good things. To maintain the opposite would be counterintuitive, to say the least. "Society" is therefore a *natural* need of the human being.

"Work" also acquires a new dimension in the context of reason: it turns into a social interpersonal process: cooperation in work, sharing of labor, division of labor, work as service, work in general—as the bearing of responsibility for others and for society as a whole. But most important, however, is this: insofar as the other is recognized and known as my equal, there arises that natural friendship or solidarity that is the origin and bond of all social and community life. Even if man had no need to preserve himself, he would still have a need to live with others. It would be a human good, as in the biblical account of creation: "It is not good for man to be alone" (Gen. 2.8). To be a human is not only to be concerned with mere bare-bones survival, since "the really important thing is not to live but to live well."[54] Community with one's own kind of beings is part of the good life.

> This is not only reflected in the classical political doctrine of man as a social animal (Gr. *politikon zoon,* Lat. *animal sociale*), but also, and very much so, in modern contractual theory. Here false oppositions have often been constructed. In fact, it was the view not only of John Locke, but also of the radical individualist Thomas Hobbes, that man strives through a natural compulsion for a life of peace and cooperation with his fellows. For Hobbes, nonnatural sociability is brought in only because nature is considered helpless and incapable of bringing about such a state of affairs by herself; only the artificial product of the "state"—political institutions—can guarantee peace, security, and thereby community and cooperation in civil society.

But as soon as the other is known and acknowledged as "one like me," the basic principle of "justice" arises that has found an expression to be met with in practically all cultures: the so-called *golden rule.* "Do not unto others, what you would not have them do unto you," or as positively formulated: "Do unto others as you would have them do unto you." This "principle of justice" is thus nothing other than the principle of the symmetry of legal rights on the basis of the acknowledgment of one's fellow man as "one like me," and thus an equal: the rights that I have are also the rights that the other has. And:

54. Plato, *Crito* 48b, trans. Tredennick.

what I can expect from another with regards to my own rights, so the other can expect from me with regards to his, even if he cannot articulate this expectation, as in the case of a seriously handicapped person or an unborn child or an infant, or someone unable to speak through illness or old age.

It follows from this that someone *owes* something to another: human actions thus always acquire as well a *proportio ad alterum*, a "proportion to another." The golden rule as such is not at all a standard for what is owed to the other; as a rule, it is really no standard at all for the good.[55] Its value rather consists in transforming what is "good for me" into something that could be a good owed to others as well, changing it into the fundamental structure of human fellowship. For we know, of course, what we do not want others to do toward us, and also what we want others to do toward us. We want others to respect our life, our dignity, our good reputation, our possessions; that they mean what they say when they say something to us, that is, that they tell the truth and do not lie; that they help us when we are in need; that they perform what they have promised; and so on. The golden rule as an expression of the acknowledgment of the other as "one like me" transforms what we all want as "good for us" into principles for what we owe others. And we know, not only in reference to ourselves, but also in the area of community life with others, what the good is that we are to do and pursue, and what the evil we are to avoid. Not to do the good that is required, or choosing the evil and doing it, always means betraying oneself as a human being, to act against reason, and not to strive for what man can alone rationally strive for, but it also means attacking the foundations of community living with one's fellow man. Ultimately, every act of injustice is implicitly an act of *not acknowledging* the other as "one like me" and, in this fundamental sense, as an equal. This is the "badness of the will" that was already treated before, in the context of the virtue of justice.

Now it could of course be objected that this only means that we would have to call it "just" for someone to do to another what corresponds to the acting person's notion of "good" (and thus to the interest of the same), but does not correspond to the other's interest. "[F]or then a masochistic person would be morally bound to let others suffer injury, i.e. become sadistic and torture them, or a proud person who never lets himself receive assistance would not be permitted to help others."[56] The objection does hold in the case of someone, as I mentioned, who improperly took the golden rule as the *standard* of

55. Cf. also O. Höffe, "Die Frage nach dem Moralprinzip," in O. Höffe, *Sittlich-politische Diskurse*, 66 (this article is an interesting and at the same time doubtful attempt to combine utilitarianism with transcendental formalism).

56. O. Höffe, "Die Frage nach dem Moralprinzip," 66.

just and unjust ("what is just is what is done according to the golden rule"). But it does not attain to the formal structure of the principle of justice. Whoever has false ideas of good and bad and applies the golden rule will not perform just actions, but unjust ones. On the basis of the golden rule, we cannot establish *what* good and evil are, let alone what is just and unjust. And since it is a question here only of principles, we cannot have any kind of deductive discourse for the establishment of norms. But even so, it is not necessary that on the basis of false ideas of good and bad and the golden rule that a masochist would become a sadist: it is more likely that such a person wouldn't even apply the golden rule; and when someone is so proud "on principle" as not to let himself be helped, will not "not-help" others on the basis of the golden rule; rather, he will "not-help" them simply because he is proud (and in fact he will even be inclined to help them all the more, for the sake, perhaps, of getting a good reputation or to feel satisfaction in being superior to someone, etc., but *not* because of justice, that is, because he feels he *owes* it to him).

The principle of justice constitutes, then, various types (species) of actions in an area that includes a number of action-relations (life, possession, communication, etc), and then, according to the various realms of action or matters of action, all the way down to the lowest threshold of intentional basic actions. In the same way, in this principle and its action-specific development, the goals of the moral virtues are cognitively given. It does not seem necessary in the present context to explain this in detail, since the essential point has already been made above (III.4 and IV.3.b).

This is why the tradition spoke of the principles of the natural law, or the natural inclinations, as the *semina virtutum,* "seeds of the virtues." All moral virtues are in fact already contained in these principles in germ, in all their cognitive teleological structure and affective intentionality, and thus order human action in such a way that those affective dispositions come into being that we call "'moral virtues" to the extent that they guide our choices of actions.

In this way also, the traditional distinction between "first" (or "common") precepts of the natural law and *praecepta secundaria* or "secondary precepts" can be clarified.[57] The first *(communia* or *communissima)* are such as the golden rule, which reaches too widely for single actions. The "secondary" principles, are then the action-specific principles. To the first group belong, for example, "Give to each his own"; to the second: "one should return what was owed," "one should keep contracts," and so on; the first form the overarching goal of virtues (at the level of the cardinal virtues); the second form the specific goals of the single virtues, which Thomas also calls the *finis proximus* of

57. Cf. also R. A. Armstrong, *Primary and Secondary Precepts in Thomistic Natural Law Teaching* (The Hague: Martinus Nijhoff, 1966).

an action, and this, again, is identical with the object of an action. Each basic intentional action defines the object of a specific virtue.

Something further needs to be added: the concrete shaping of the principle of justice is closely connected with the concrete shaping of a society and its ethos, and what is defined as right through its positive legislation. If it is unjust to disregard traffic rules because it puts the lives of others at risk, or because one's own convenience is attained at the cost of another's, the possibility of such injustice naturally depends, in turn, only on the existence of the traffic rules. And consequently it is good to drive on the right side of the road in most countries, but to do so in Great Britain would be grossly irresponsible, where it is good to drive on the left. The example is obvious but should suffice for the present.

Justice as the principle of "giving to each his due," or what each has a right to, is specified all the way to the level of specific action-types or basic intentional actions such as "respect another's possessions" or "respect another person's life" or "tell the truth," or alternatively, *not* to steal, murder, or lie. The question, whether there are "exceptions" here, is really not meaningful. To steal—by the very word—is always bad and an offense against justice. If there were an exception, it would be saying that stealing is not stealing. Something unjust cannot by exception be something just. And in reverse: the violation of a traffic rule is always the violation of a traffic rule. But perhaps this is not necessarily an injury of justice. The question *when* a concrete action is "just" or "unjust" is not yet answered through principles alone. For this, we need the formulation of principles that are related to descriptions of action, so that certain ways of acting can be identified as falling under a certain principle. This is also a question of the concrete judgment of actions (cf. V.3 and 4). "Justice" defines an "ethical context," and only in relation to this context can intentional actions be adequately described and define the corresponding moral norms.

2. *A second example of "natural inclination" is sexuality* or the inclination of the human being to connect with the opposite sex, an inclination that has its origin in the sex drive. This drive is naturally oriented toward "another" and also has a naturally given function: the transmission of human life, procreation, survival of the species.

All this is what "nature has taught all animals." But what is human sexuality, or the sexual inclination as a human good grasped by the reason? Is *human* sexuality something that "nature has taught all animals"? Clearly not.

Human sexuality, or its truth and identity as a human good, is *conjugium*, that is, "a spousal (or nuptial) community," or married love. With animals, sexuality is instinctively guided to acts of copulation, and to partnerships that are more or less stable and lasting, and often entirely absent. The procreative consequences of animal sexuality even have certain social effects, although rather limited ones. In human beings, sexuality is a matter of drives, but not simply instinctually guided ones. The guidance operates through reason and will (to the extent that sexuality is not removed from this context). The relationships that arise between man and woman on the basis of the sexual drive (and thus, social effects of sexuality), as well as the attitude toward the procreative consequences of sexual copulation, are such that they are constituted through the guidance of reason and reason-led will. They are relationships that we can call love, the self-giving of *one* person to *one* other, fidelity, procreative responsibility, permanence of the bond.

All these things are not goods that come in addition to sexuality: they already *are* sexuality as a human good, that is to say, they are the sexual drive of a human person in its meaning through the reason of this person whose drive it is. The natural inclination is here taken up into the order of reason, which brings into realization the nuptial character of human sexuality. Procreation is here not carried out in the way nature has taught all animals: instead, it is a way of responsibility. *Reasons* can be given for having more or fewer children, and the human being can modify his sexual behavior according to these reasons. Between parents and their children, social connections are constituted for the purpose of caregiving: connections that have the character of justice relationships, and are spread out into a structure that handles the most varied needs. Thus the child has a right to being fed and clothed and cared for (help in surviving) and for upbringing (help in acquiring virtues, knowledge, education, skills). The child also has a right to grow up in a family (divorce is, among other things, an attack on justice toward the child), and so on.

Something similar is true for the relationship between husband and wife themselves. Sexuality creates a couple. And not only are two bodies involved in this, joining with each other as directed by their drives, but also two human persons. The relationship with the other constitutes, in turn, relationships of justice and friendship: equality, fidelity, a shared life. A friendship that is marked by sexual relationship and at the same time transcends itself and fulfills itself in the task of transmitting life possesses the character of mutual giving, with regard to a work being carried out in common. It has an affective depth and totality which must measure up to that personal bond if the specifically personal (freedom, communication, etc.) is not to be subordinated to the merely sensitive drive. Friendship between man and woman therefore becomes a love that is known as *married* or *conjugal* love: a community of living of two persons in an exclusive and *nonterminable* fidelity, whose affective fulfillment is really the act of that drive from which this love arises, and which acquires in addition a task with respect to which this love is defined as a *specific* form of love: corporeal unity, from which a new life can come. Human reproduction is then recognizable as that kind of procreation that arises from the love between two persons, just as this love is essentially formed by serving the transmission of human life. This explains the indivisible essential unity of human sexuality through two meanings: procreation of life and community of love: human sexuality is personal love that serves the transmission of life.[58]

It is not a question here of a comprehensive treatment, but only to show how the natural inclination "sexuality" is constituted as a human good and thereby formulates principles of action which come into existence through the integration of the sense inclination into the order of reason. The corresponding basic intentional actions and moral virtues are thus formulated: mastery of one's sexual drive in the service of personal love and the responsible transmission of life (chastity as part of the virtue of temperance, and to this belongs, as one component, that virtue we can call "procreative responsibility"):[59] conjugal fidelity. Action species like upbringing, caring for the elderly, but also friendship between parents and children, which is not a symmetrical friendship: seen from the child's perspective, it is the virtue of *pietas;* seen from the parents' perspective, this friendship is parental authority, trust, and care. Here too, what is concrete—that is, an action species like "upbringing"—is by no means provided in the principles.

f) The Genesis and Application of Practical Principles: The Role of Experience and Prudence

On the basis of the above examples that I have sketched out as a reconstruction of the cognitive genesis of practical principles, it should be clear that I am not arguing for a kind of deductive ethics of principles. The practical principles that operate as a kind of natural moral law are neither simply and immediately present to the moral consciousness, standing "ready" for application, nor do they immediately allow the determination and guidance of concrete

---

58. Cf. also M. Rhonheimer, "Sozialphilosophie und Familie. Gedanken zur humanen Grundfunktion der Familie," in B. Schnyder, ed., *Familie—Herausforderung der Zukunft* (Freiburg and Ue: Universitätsverlag, 1982), 113–40; *Familie und Selbstverwirklichung* (Cologne: Verlag Wissenschaft und Politik, 1979); *Sexualität und Verantwortung. Empfängnisverhütung als ethisches Problem*, IMABE Studies No. 3 (Vienna: Institut für medizinische Anthropologie und Bioethik, 1995). An English version is now available as chapters 2 and 3 of *Ethics of Procreation and the Defense of Human Life* (Washington, D.C.: The Catholic University of America Press, 2010).

59. See also my remarks in *Sexualität und Verantwortung;* a briefer version is available in "Contraception, Sexual Behavior, and Natural Law: Philosophical Foundation of the Norm of *Humanae vitae*," *Linacre Quarterly* 56, no. 2 (1989): 20–57. See the longer version in my *Ethics of Procreation* (see note 58 above).

actions. For both of these things—the explication of principles as well as the concrete carrying out of actions—there is need *both* for situationally mediated and narratively structured experience that is integrated into concrete social contexts *and* the reasoning that has the particular thing to be done here and now for its object, whose perfecting is the virtue of prudence.

At all events, the universality of such principles needs to be emphasized in opposition to the communitarian tendency to reduce moral principles to the context of traditions and communities. A. MacIntyre's thesis about the tradition-bound nature of practical reason and conceptions of justice does not, however, necessarily imply that there are "no universally valid foundations of justice,"[60] but only that it is always in connection with distinct social contexts that practical reason and conceptions of justice are formed that reflect these traditions. The question whether there is a discourse of justice that can transcend this contextuality and can decide between rationality and the "moral rectitude" of traditions has not yet been answered.[61] MacIntyre does not mean that there cannot be a neutral standpoint outside of definite traditions or certain culturally specific givens, and that whoever, accordingly, tries to operate in a vacuum has no rational resources at his disposal for deciding in a rational manner which tradition is to be followed. MacIntyre's intention is outspokenly directed against relativism and "perspectivism." In his view, the necessarily context-bound nature of the practical reason is really the foundation for the discourse about the moral rectitude or preferability of a definite tradition.[62]

It is not unusual to hear it maintained that there is an unbridgeable abyss between (on one side) an ethics based upon a system of principles and corresponding moral rules, and (on the other side) a prudence-based ethics that puts into the foreground the particularity and uniqueness of situations and persons.[63] There would be such an abyss indeed if we were to begin with the

---

60. This is how Höffe rather idiosyncratically interprets MacIntyre's *Whose Justice? Which Rationality?* (cf. O. Höffe, *Aristoteles' universalistische Tugendethik*, 58).

61. Habermas argues in a similar way, though with a different purpose in mind, against Rorty's contextualism; cf. J. Habermas, "Wahrheit und Rechtfertigung. Zu Richard Rorty's pragmatischer Wende," in Habermas, *Wahrheit und Rechtfertigung*, 230ff.

62. Cf. A. MacIntyre, *Whose Justice? Which Rationality?* 367. On the very different, i.e., relativistic and pragmatic, contextualism of Rorty, see R. Rorty, "Solidarity or Objectivity" and "The Priority of Democracy over Philosophy," in *Objectivity, Relativism, and Truth: Philosophical Papers, Vol. 1* (Cambridge: Cambridge University Press, 1991), 21–34, 175–96; also Rorty, *Contingency, Irony, and Solidarity* (Cambridge: Cambridge University Press, 1989), e.g., 68: "I want . . . increasing willingness to live with plurality and to stop asking for universal validity . . . when we abandon the notion that 'reason' names a healing, reconciling, unifying power—the source of human solidarity . . . the idea of truth as correspondence to reality might gradually be replaced by the idea of truth as what comes to be believed in the course of free and open encounter."

63. So M. C. Nussbaum, *Aristotle's De Motu Animalium. Text with Translation, Commentary, and Interpretive Essays* (Princeton, N.J.: Princeton University Press, 1978), Essay 4: "Practical Syllogisms and Practical Science," 165–220, and "The Discernment of Perception: An Aristotelian Conception of

assumption that concrete actions are not basically susceptible of being judged in the light of universal principles, or that the level of the particular and the universal are simply incommensurable; that only the practical reason that deals with the singular, that is, prudence, can have for its object what is right or obligatory at each moment, which fundamentally eludes any application of norms by way of universal rules.[64]

If someone does not agree with such an outlook, it does not in any way require that the knowledge and determination of particulars must be seen as exclusively resulting from the mere application or derivation of universals, or that it is only necessary to subsume concrete situations and cases under the appropriate rule, in order to arrive at what is right and obligatory in concrete actions. Instead, one can maintain that the particular—the concrete action to be done here and now—is in fact a "concretizing" of the principle, a kind of exemplification in a concrete case, an exemplification that the principle as such does not accomplish, but is an additional, genuine accomplishment of the practical reason directed to the particular—that is, prudence; and this is carried out under the cognitive direction of practical principles, whose meaning and importance are clarified for the unique situation and thereby become practical in the fullest sense.

Of course, several difficulties are raised at the same time here, which will have to be treated below in due time. For the moment, we will have to concentrate on the two points mentioned in the title of this section: the genesis and application of practical principles.

Private and Public Rationality," in Nussbaum, *Love's Knowledge: Essays on Philosophy and Literature* (New York and Oxford: Oxford University Press, 1990), 54–105; D. M. Nelson, *The Priority of Prudence: Virtue and Natural Law in Thomas Aquinas and the Implications for Modern Ethics* (University Park: Pennsylvania State University Press, 1992). The connection between the *lex naturalis* and prudence is, by contrast—and critical of the position of Nussbaum and Nelson—well developed by P. M. Hall, *Narrative and the Natural Law*. Cf. also D. Westberg, *Right Practical Reason: Aristotle, Action, and Prudence in Aquinas* (Oxford: Oxford University Press, 1994). For a better understanding of the importance of a narrative account of natural law I am indebted to R. A. Gahl; see also his "From the Virtue of a Fragile Good to a Narrative Account of Natural Law," *International Philosophical Quarterly* 37, no. 4 (1997): 459–74.

64. As P. M. Hall shows, *Narrative and the Natural Law*, 109f., M. C. Nussbaum's insistence on an incompatibility between principle-ethics and prudence-ethics is founded on the assumption of an underlying fragmentation and confusion of human and environmental relationships that does not permit any ethical universals at all. On such a foundation as this it is naturally impossible to order any concrete actions to general principles or ends of "man as such" or "for the human good." Pamela Hall rightly remarks that Thomas proceeds from a brokenness and confusion not of the world, but of man himself. The meaning of morality and the conditions for the success of life is then no longer the self-assertion of the human being in a broken and confused world, but rather the deconfusing of man himself, the pointing him in the direction of the good, so that human striving can develop according to the order of the good that originally inheres both in man and in his environment, as the creation of God. That for Thomas this can ultimately be solved only by a Christian-theological completion of ethics is indisputable, but this does not compromise the validity of the purely philosophical content of his moral theory. See the epilogue.

On the first point: as the *lex naturalis,* practical principles order our action toward the goals and goods which the reason grasps as specifically "good for man" on the basis of the natural inclinations. This grasping or comprehending is a process that takes place over time and in concrete social contexts (family, neighborhood, school, society, cultural context, the dominant ethos, etc.). Such contexts can support this learning process but can also hinder it or at least partially mislead it. As modern developmental psychology (e.g., in the work of Jean Piaget or William Damon) has also ascertained by empirical studies, principles of justice are formed in our early childhood through interaction with the surrounding world. The awareness of these principles of action is refined and grasped ever more deeply through application in concrete situations, and not least through experiences of our own weakness, failure, and culpability. In order for the real content of the specific principles to become formed—recalling our reconstruction of the principle of justice—there is a need, alongside the growing consciousness of one's own complex of needs, affectivity, and so on, for the experience of interactions with other persons in concrete human relationships.[65] This is how the human reason is able, in the above- mentioned process of *inventio,* to grasp something more specific, in between the world of experience and the most general principles such as the golden rule or the principle "one must give to each his own." This more specific something does have the characteristic of a "conclusion," of something "concluded" from universals. But this does not mean that it is won from the mere "deduction" of a "superordinated" universal; nothing at all can be derived from the principle "one must give to each his own." To the contrary, it is a question of grasping the principle *in* the concrete and particular and thereby attaining to a deeper and more nuanced grasp of the principle itself, on the basis of the experience of the particular. And prudence is also needed, which by this means, as Thomas expressly teaches, in a certain way participates in the formation of the goals of the single virtues, and with that, in the formation of practical principles.[66]

Practical principles—or the *lex naturalis*—are discovered in particulars, through experience. This is necessarily the case because in the human world there simply do not exist any universal persons, relationships, things, or actions. Real universal contents are always the content of subsequent knowl-

65. Cf. the various researches of J. Piaget, *Judgment and Reasoning in the Child,* trans. M. Warden (Totowa, N.J.: Littlefield, Adams, 1976); W. Damon, *The Moral Child: Nurturing Children's Natural Moral Growth* (New York: Free Press, 1988), and also Damon, *The Social World of the Child* (San Francisco: Jossey-Bass, 1977); G. Nunner-Winkler, "Zum Verständnis von Moral—Entwicklungen in der Kindheit," in F. E. Weinert, ed., *Entwicklung im Kindesalter* (Weinheim: Beltz, 1998), 136–57.
66. On the doctrine of the *praestitutio finis* through prudence, cf. M. Rhonheimer, *Praktische Vernunft und Vernünftigkeit der Praxis,* 362ff. and 583ff.

edge, in the light of which the concrete individual is more deeply grasped, that is, understood as belonging to a universal: the concrete action as a particular practical requirement "here and now" can be understood as the concretization of the "good life," of the "good for man." Concrete ways of acting become transparent as a path to that good that is the goal of human strivings and virtues, and is, in turn, the content of practical principles. Or, looking at it from the opposite perspective, we see definite ways of acting becoming intelligible in their contradiction to moral commandments and goods.

In fact all universal principles—even those of a theoretical character, such as that the whole is greater than the part—which are naturally formed in a spontaneous way, require the initial grasp of a singular instance *in which* the universal can be understood. There is, consequently, an inner cognitive connection between the universal so discovered—the principle—and the particular. In a reconstruction, the one can subsequently be represented as a conclusion from the other—such as, for example, the prohibition of murder as a conclusion from the more universal principle of "to give to each his due"—without this implying that the specific or the particular can be directly and immediately derived *without* experience from the universal. It is really not a deductive process at all, but a reflective one, a constant, reflective deepening of one's own practical understanding of one's own actions and judgments, which does not take place in a linear-deductive fashion, but rather, to use an image, takes place in an *inventive* (or "discovering") manner, in a kind of circular or spiral motion.

Martha Nussbaum asks herself, in the course of her Aristotle interpretation, whether principles are mere rules-of-thumb that result from the (always provisional) generalization of individual cases, whereby the individual case always remains the ultimate authority and can correct the principle in the circumstances; or whether, alternatively, principles are the "final authorities," on the basis of which the correctness of particular decisions can be judged, so that the latter would be as it were deduced from the former.[67] Nussbaum rightly sympathizes, of course, with the first alternative, because she rightly affirms that principles are unable "to capture the fine detail of the particular, which is the subject matter of ethical choice" (300). But in any case, Nussbaum is not distinguishing here between principles and *rules* (or norms), which in my opinion is an important distinction to make. She mentions the decisive point only at the end of her account (306), namely, that the particular would be "surd and unintelligible" without the guiding and differentiating power of the universal. Precisely so: and therefore, *pace* Nussbaum, this is really the function of moral principles: they lend the particular decision or concrete action its *moral* identi-

---

67. M. C. Nussbaum, *The Fragility of Goodness*, 299ff.

ty, that is, their character of being "cases" of definite virtues or "ways" to deter-minate moral goals (which cannot be the function of rules or norms, since these are related, by their moral identity, to already defined action-types; cf. below, V.3). This really shows once again how closely interwoven universal principles and prudence are in their genesis as well as in their application.

Already in their basic structure, then, practical principles or the *lex natu-ralis* are by no means opposed to prudence. Without the reasoning that is di-rected to the particular, the excellence of which is the virtue of prudence, and which makes the principles comprehensible in their specific determinateness in a process enriched by experience, it would be impossible to have knowl-edge of a universal that would be relevant for praxis. And this is not circular reasoning, for what is being said does not contradict the fact that principles are principles, that is, they logically precede what is determined on their ba-sis. For, as mentioned before, the formation of the principles and their interac-tion with situational experience is a process with all the marks of a narrative structure. The human being *evolves* as a moral subject in time. He is not sim-ply already like that or born that way. It is not to be doubted, of course, that certain foundational principles, especially fairness, justice, and here in par-ticular, justice in communication and ownership (i.e., the areas of lying and stealing) develop quickly and clearly in children. Nevertheless a person needs a differentiated experience, and often a rather long experience to be able to understand properly the content of practical principles. For these principles really carry out the task of ordering concrete actions to the fundamental goals, to the fundamental structure of the good that is built into our natural incli-nations. They ought to produce practical truth in actions, its agreement with right appetition. And this requires not only general knowledge of principles, but also experience and prudence. This is why, again, the assistance and in-fluence of role models and authorities, and the social and cultural context, are of crucial importance for a suitable cognitive development. The concrete ethos in which the subject is bound up is decisive for certain concrete specifications of the morally obliging, but can be questioned in the light of practical prin-ciples and can be recognized as being in need of correction. Both the concrete ethos and the emotional distortion of the reason can hinder the process of dis-covery of principles; for it is the "property of vice, to destroy the principle."[68] Therefore there is not, as Thomas emphasizes, "the same justice for all." And this is so, not only because here and there a concrete circumstance would bring it about that the application of a principle of justice would bring about injustice (as when one would not give back a borrowed weapon to the owner if

---

68. Aristotle, *EN* VI, 5 (1140b20). Cf. also below, under subsection h, "Knowledge of Principles and Affective Dispositions."

the owner has suddenly become insane), but also because vicious individual and social habits, and at times even pathological natural dispositions, can destroy moral judgment.[69] In fact, the *lex naturalis* cannot be a guide for action without its expansion into an ethos (to which pertains also the legal order of positive human laws as well as culture in all its dimensions).[70] All the same, the natural law is necessarily more than a mere "structure of principles that is open to configurations" (at the level of the most common principles, *principia communia*), which would then be completed and fulfilled through the "positive human laws as well as the divine positive laws and the determination in history of this structure."[71] The *lex naturalis* contains, at least in the Thomistic understanding of reason, action-specific principles of a material kind that are fundamentally accessible, and that are not only capable of being the standard for the legitimation of an ethos, but are also substantial enough to ground the framework of a specific moral ideal that corresponds to a specific understanding of the human being and the anthropological truth that goes with it.

The second point, which is the role of prudence in the application of principles, is immediately connected with the first point. Practical principles, or the commands of the natural law, cannot as such exercise the function of the concrete regulation of actions. That can only be accomplished by reason, directed to the concrete situation.[72] Without prudence, practical principles cannot guide action concretely. Someone who not only wants to understand what respect for another's property or truthfulness toward other human beings means in theory but to *act* accordingly in concrete situations, needs a differentiated understanding of property rights and communicative situations in order to grasp just what the principle means and requires here and now.[73] This is exactly why prudence developed in this way leads to a deeper understanding of the principle.

On the other hand, the practical reasoning oriented toward concrete actions could never become prudence—that is, practical reasoning that directs human action toward what is truly "good for man"—without its cognitive recourse to the universal as grasped in the principles. The particular action to be done here and now is always complex, contingent, and less certain than the principles. If the latter have only very little immediate power to determine

---

69. Cf. I-II, Q. 94, a. 4. We shall return to this point.

70. W. Kluxen, "Menschliche Natur und Ethos," *Münchener Theologische Zeitschrift* 23 (1972): 1–17; *Ethik des Ethos* (Freiburg and Munich: Alber, 1974).

71. Cf. L. Honnefelder, "Die ethische Rationalität des mittelalterlichen Naturrechts. Max Webers und Ernst Troeltschs Deutung des mittelalterlichen Naturrechts und die Bedeutung der Lehre vom natürlichen Gesetz bei Thomas von Aquin," in W. Schluchter, ed., *Max Webers Sicht des okzidentalen Christentums* (Frankfurt am Main: Suhrkamp, 1988), 254–75, here 267.

72. Cf. Rhonheimer, *Natural Law and Practical Reason*, 275 and 322.

73. Cf. also P. M. Hall, *Narrative and the Natural Law*, 38–43; and also below, 3.d and e.

action,[74] even so the particular is only intelligible through being subsumed under the universality of a principle as a concrete instance of the "good for man," and thus as morally required. In this sense these principles really *regulate* concrete action because in a sense they determine the place of, or the necessary tracks for, the actions that are part of the program of a "life that turns out well." Just for this reason, practical principles, despite their fundamentally positive character of ordering action to the "good for man," are often formulated in a negative, prohibitive form.

As C. Schröer has rightly maintained, "practical principles and the material requirements that are ever being brought out of them . . . have the meaning of limiting conditions for the more concrete levels of action in each case, under which conditions alone a certain action can be a rationally determined action. It is a consequence of this schema of justification that the concrete level of action reached in each situation never completely matches or replaces the principles that preceded it, and that, inversely, each particular level of action remains liable to a reexamination."[75] That this is precisely, in the case of a negatively formulated principle or prohibitive norm, what can lead to an exceptionless practical rule will be discussed later. But even in that case it is a question of the connection of particular action with the principles, which formulate nothing other than the goals of virtues, the "good for man."

In any event, misunderstandings are possible here, above all the misconception that I am advocating a moral theory according to which it would be possible for the practical reason to simply derive concrete ways of acting from universal principles, so that the concrete judgment of action is a kind of prolongation of the principle to the particular case. E. Schockenhoff in particular has taken up a critique of just such an interpretation of the view presented here,[76] and takes issue above all with the basis of my thesis on the "unity of

---

74. Insofar as it is not a question of negative principles or prohibitive norms; cf. below, 3.d.

75. Ch. Schröer, *Praktische Vernunft bei Thomas von Aquin*, 202. This is why, as Schröer also rightly says, Thomistic ethics is at once a principle ethics, a virtue ethics, a duty ethics, and a law ethics.

76. Cf. E. Schockenhoff, *Natural Law and Human Dignity*, 154f., and "*Compte Rendu* on Rhonheimer, *Praktische Vernunft und Vernünftigkeit der Praxis*," *Studia Moralia* 34 (1996): 133–47. For my debate with Schockenhoff, see the "Postscript" to M. Rhonheimer, *Natural Law and Practical Reason*, 574ff., and M. Rhonheimer, "Praktische Prinzipien, Naturgesetz und konkrete Handlungsurteile. Zur Diskussion über praktische Vernunft und *lex naturalis* bei Thomas von Aquin," *Studia Moralia* 39 (2001): 113–58. The English version of Schockenhoff's book *Naturrecht und Menschenwürde* (*Natural Law and Human Dignity* [Washington, D.C.: The Catholic University of America Press, 2003]) contains some significant changes in the presentation of my position, as do his subsequent books. As he explicitly and generously declares in *Natural Law and Human Dignity* (140, note 19), some of his former presentations of my position were due to misunderstandings of it. I nevertheless have let the original discussion stand in the present English translation of this book because disagreements still remain and, as Schockenhoff's earlier misunderstandings are still represented in the writings of some other authors, my arguments against them are still of some interest. I would, however, like to take advantage of the occasion to ex-

the practical reason and its fulfillment in prudence,"[77] as well as my recalling of the Aristotelian doctrine (belonging to the same context) of the inerrancy of the prudent man.

But the thesis merely says that the practical judgment of action by the prudent man is a judgment of the *same* practical reason that has the principles for its object, and their actual fulfillment. This is not intended to say that the concrete judgment is derived from the principles and provides only a "prolongation" [*Verlängerung*] of them. What the thesis says, rather, is that the universal practical reason is insufficient for ordering concrete action, but that practical reason is only complete when it is in a position to regulate the particular and concrete. And it can do this only by prudence. This is the practical reason at its highest stage of perfection because only in this stage is it capable of doing what practical reason is really meant for: action.

> This has been explained as follows: "Both—i.e., both the principle-discerning intellect and prudence—are acts of the *same* practical reason. And more: they are *the same* act of the practical reason in each different 'stage' of its explication and *extensio ad opus* ['extension to a task']. If we maintain that 'prudence' is directed toward the 'operative concretizing' of the universal principles, we are naming it for exactly what it has *before* the intellection of the principles; that means: we are calling it, with regard to the intellection of the principles, not a restriction or something 'less,' but something '*more.*' Prudence—insofar as we are considering it as a distinct 'stage' of the process of practical reason— is not thereby '*limited* to the middle,' but it is described the other way around: through prudence, practical reason acquires a greater share of perfection than it does as the intellection of principles. It is, namely, that perfection which the practical reason *as practical* really most of all needs: the right understanding of the particular and the contingent. For the goal of the practical reason is to figure out what is *to do,* and that doing is always of a particular and contingent nature."[78]

In the act of prudence, however, the principles—that is, the goals of the virtues—are intentionally present, and that is to say, that prudence determines the particular as the "means" to the goals of the virtues (as an action that "leads to the end"). The prudent person is virtuous in the proper sense of the word because he does in the concrete situation what corresponds with the goal of the virtue, and because he really *does* it. The emphasis lies on showing that prudence is the perfection of the practical reason directed to the concrete doing

---

press my grateful appreciation of Schockenhoff's intellectual integrity in making these corrections in the English version of his book.

77. See *Praktische Vernunft und Vernünftigkeit der Praxis*, 558ff.

78. M. Rhonheimer, *Praktische Vernunft und Vernünftigkeit der Praxis*, 561.

that leads to a goal—the "means"—and that its character of being this means-determining reason in no way compromises its dignity, because it is always one and the same single practical reason in the various stages of its complete action and fulfillment. R. A. Gauthier treated Aristotelian prudence in contrast to this as the faculty of the right setting of the goal, and called Thomas to task for changing the Aristotelian doctrine by degrading prudence to a mere means-determining reason.[79] But the specific achievement of Thomas appears to have consisted in his blending of the doctrine of the *lex naturalis* as a doctrine of practical principles with the Aristotelian doctrine of prudence, and having in this way adequately understood the unity of the practical reason and its fulfillment in prudence.[80] This makes prudence recognizable as the habitus in which "all the threads twine together": the habit of the means-determining practical reason, which chooses actions that effectively realize the goals of the single virtues. This is how the *habitus* of prudence is itself a perfection and fulfillment of the same faculty of practical reasoning that has for its object the goals that are principles of action (in the sense of the *lex naturalis*).

The perfecting of the practical reason is revealed, as I have said, in the "operative concretizing" of the goals of the virtues because practical reason is oriented toward action, and action is always concrete. This concretizing is not a "deducing" or "deriving," but a genuine knowledge of the particular, wherein contact with the principles is always preserved and in such a way as to ensure that reasoning about concrete actions is also *moral* reasoning.[81] The concretizing practical reason is therefore a genuine actualization and fulfillment of the practical principle, of the goal of moral virtue. Prudence is not simply the reason that determines the means; it is also the reason that chooses the morally unobjectionable means. Making the principle concrete implies, for example, that the concrete action whatever its content is a *justified* action. It is a question here of the "morality of the means." This is precisely the theme of ethics: not only the material question, "What is the right thing to do here and now?," but rather "What is right here and now, because it (for example) accords with justice?" or "What is the *just* thing to do?" which is the question about the moral meaning of "right."

The distance between the general and the particular of praxis is not infinite: the universal and the particular do not belong to two different worlds. As the universal is not ascertained independently of its single instance, so also

---

79. Aristote, *L'Éthique à Nicomaque. Introduction, Traduction, et Commentaire* par René Antoine Gauthier et Jean Yves Jolif, 2nd ed. (Louvain and Paris: Publications universitaires, 1970), 1.273–83.

80. M. Rhonheimer, *Praktische Vernunft und Vernünftigkeit der Praxis*, 558ff.

81. Cf. also the "concession" of M. C. Nussbaum (in *The Fragility of Goodness*, 306), mentioned above: "Still, it is now time to say that the particular case would be surd and unintelligible without the guiding and sorting power of the universal."

every particular instance is related to the universal and actualizes it.[82] For just this reason, the particular can also contradict the universal, and thereby, *on the basis of the principle* can be disclosed as morally wrong.[83] The relationship between the judgment of prudence and the practical principles is nevertheless not a relationship of deduction, but an intentional guidance of the particular judgment of action through practical principles. "The fundamental design of a rationally willed action proceeds, as it becomes increasingly concrete, from the most general principles, through particular stipulations and increasingly specified dispositions, until it finally reaches the application of its consideration of action to the concrete situation where the action takes place."[84] This concretizing, since it is not a "deducing" from principles, is the peculiar achievement—the "negotiation"—of the reasoning of prudence that really is prudence, and not mere slyness or cleverness, because it is intentionally related to the goals of the moral virtues formulated through the practical principles.

For it is precisely here that the originally Aristotelian doctrine of the "inerrancy" of the prudent person finds its relevance. For Aristotle, prudence is "a true *(alēthē)* and reasoned state of capacity (Gr. *hexis*, Lat. *habitus*) to act with regard to the things that are good or bad for man."[85] This "un-deceived" *(a-lēthē)* habitus, as I have often pointed out, determines the "practical truth" in the concrete judgment of action. Thomas consistently takes this teaching further. Of course: it should not be misunderstood as maintaining prudence brings about a "factual freedom from error" in the concrete judgment of action, which would be an epistemological or technical misinterpretation of practical reason, because it is simply a question of "practical truth," that is, the moral rectitude of this judgment, its agreement with the goals of the virtues. The statement that prudence guarantees an inerrancy of the reason should not be taken to mean that prudence would be able to deduce from the universal principles of the *lex naturalis* what would be "right in itself" for the concrete situation, and translate that into action. It is not primarily a question here of material rectitude. What concerns us here rather is the "moral rectitude" or the moral goodness of the action, which in turn will coincide with the practical truth just referred to. Still less is it being maintained that there is only one single morally correct action possible for the practical reason in each situation. In a given situation various material possibilities of "rectitude," though not all equally optimal, will fall under the same moral rectitude, that is to say,

82. Cf. R. Elm, *Klugheit und Erfahrung bei Aristoteles* (Paderborn: F. Schöningh, 1996), 279.

83. As L. Honnefelder also maintains; see *Absolute Forderungen in der Ethik*, 13–33, 28.

84. C. Schröer, *Praktische Vernunft bei Thomas von Aquin*, 201. Likewise M. Rhonheimer, *Praktische Vernunft und Vernünftigkeit der Praxis*, 369.

85. *EN* VI, 5 (1140b5–6).

in their variety they can all agree with the corresponding goals of virtue. Concrete action "is never unambiguously determined by this end, since the matter of actions is contingent. Various possibilities of action—although not just *any* possibilities whatever—are capable of the same rectitude of end."[86] The "infallibility" of prudence means in fact that the prudent person unerringly chooses what is "good," what is *morally* right, that is, what agrees with the goals of the virtues. In itself the action may not be unconditionally the best (it may be only "the best thing for me," in completely personal circumstances). This moral inerrancy can also—especially in complex and unfamiliar situations—go together with uncertainty, wavering, or ignorance on the part of the subject. But the action of the prudent person will always be such as to coincide with the goal of virtue: he will not do anything unjust, will not act precipitously or intemperately. In the realm of the virtues of temperance and courage his well-ordered emotions will keep his head clear, and allow him to see what is right. He will not incline to injustice through cowardice, love of comfort, resentment, or the like, or become "partial"; he will not make an "A" into a "B." He has a sense for the right of the other, and he loves the truth, even if it causes him some discomfort. He is capable of being loyal, ready to make a sacrifice, and act in solidarity, that is, he is inclined toward the well-being of others, he has a right interest in it (according to the "golden rule"), and thus his judgments of action will be *just* judgments.

And even if the emotions and will of the prudent person are so ordered that his reason has the right *affective* guidance, and he acquires this moral "inerrancy," this does not mean that a prudent person cannot make a mistake (which could happen, e.g., because of a certain piece of missing information he was not aware of, or because of the complexity of a problem, or because there was insufficient time) or that all uncertainty would simply disappear. Rather, the prudent man is capable of acting, when action is required, despite uncertainty (since he will not be a scrupulous or nervous person), but will also be able to restrain himself, to wait and seek the counsel of others when the uncertainty is too great or the risk too high. Indeed, someone who is prudent knows when uncertainty forbids swift action because he does not act hastily when the matter requires seeking someone's advice. He will also be inclined to listen to the advice of others, even if it means putting his own opinions and himself in doubt; for the prudent man is interested in "doing what is good in truth," and not only "what *appears* good to himself." The very one who in certain cases feels called to "assert the freedom of his own conscience" shows, just in that, a lack of prudence.

86. Rhonheimer, *Natural Law and Practical Reason*, 322.

What is at issue here is how that human good that the intellect knows at the universal level of the principles and that constitutes a practical command can be transferred to concrete action, so that this action in fact *agrees* with this good (this being the practical truth of the judgment of action), that is to say, leads the human person to this good and in this way allows him to become a "good person." We want to be human beings who are just; but we cannot *practically* realize justice simply by striving for it; we must *do* what is just and keep ourselves from doing injustice. The prudent person is the one who, whatever he may choose, chooses what is in agreement with the goal of justice, in order to fulfill this goal and its corresponding principle. That is his "infallibility"— which does *not* imply that there is only a kind of one-to-one correspondence between the "principle of justice" and the action that his prudence determines. And still less does this mean that anything can be *deduced* or *concluded* for concrete action from universal principles of justice. And yet the concrete, just action is in fact the realization and fulfillment of the principle of justice, and thereby of rationality, through which the acting person becomes a just person—even if here and there he makes a mistake, or acts "less than optimally." This moral "infallibility" of prudence does not, accordingly, dispense anyone from the task of an ethical/normative discourse. This was already mentioned in the section on the virtue of prudence. But in the following section, another aspect of the theme will be treated: the question about the certainty of concrete judgments of action.

g) *Excursus:* The Multiple Stages of Practical Reason and the "Law of Decreasing Certainty"

In the German-speaking world especially, interpreters of Thomas Aquinas frequently point out that, according to Thomas, the "certainty" of practical knowledge decreases, the more concrete it becomes. Now the assertion of the existence of such a law of the decreasing certainty of increasing concreteness appears quite questionable, one could say, because such a law holds only for the theoretical reason, which cannot say anything certain at all about the particular case and does not have it for its object. Theoretical reason has certainty only at the universal level. It is the other way around for the practical reason: the closer a judgment is to the action, the closer the practical reason is to its goal and the more certain will be its knowledge about what is to be done. If it were the reverse, an action could never even be chosen. In any event we must allow for the fact that with an increase of concreteness the possibilities of making a mistake increase, but that is trivial, since that is true for theoretical reason, too: the further along a process of knowing goes, the sources of error only accumulate (whereby it is often the case that a question becomes increasingly clear through the progress of knowing, and thus with the increase of concreteness the certainty actually increases). It is likewise true that universal/necessary (epistemic) statements cannot determine anything for the concrete action. In this sense, from the perspective of the general principle, the concrete thing to be done is still "uncertain," that is, it cannot be seen on the basis of the principle, nor can anything be derived from that principle.

This is why the fundamental law of the decrease of certainty with the increase of concreteness of practical judgments—so often emphasized not only by authors like E. Schockenhoff and L. Honnefelder, but also by C. Schröer—is trivial. With respect to Aristotle and Thomas, it can only mean what has been already sufficiently emphasized, namely, that the uniformity of the universal rule is not capable of reaching the particular in all its singularity. The particular is always something less than universal, but it is at the same time something "more" in its particular determinateness, and in this sense it is richer and closer to reality. That I should act justly, that I should give to each what is due to each, is a general rule, whose certainty consists in its ability to include all the cases of concrete actions and thereby always find application. But on its basis I cannot know what is fitting for this particular person. The certainty of the general rule corresponds to a great multiplicity and with that, to a great contingency of application as well. The particular escapes the grasp of an epistemic and universal/necessary knowledge. For it is, as Aristotle would say, "always otherwise."

It would mean something else, again, to maintain—and exactly this is explicitly held by the authors above mentioned—that as the concreteness increases, the uncertainty of the judgment of action also increases, as if the acting person could never attain to any certainty with regard to what is concretely to be done; could never reach certainty about having acted morally, that is, in fulfillment of the principle; and consequently practical judgments would be less binding than those general rules that are necessarily valid and without exception. This is the direction taken by certain statements of L. Honnefelder[87] and F. J. Bormann.[88] Schockenhoff, on the other hand, expresses

---

87. Cf. L. Honnefelder, *Absolute Forderungen in der Ethik*, 26: "while Thomas proceeds from the fact that only the most universal rules bind without exception and necessarily, and in the process of the concretizing determination the general rules lose their power to bind along with their universality, and not because the concretizing as such reduces its demand, but because it permits the certainty of knowing what is demanded to decrease."

88. So Bormann, *Natur als Horizont sittlicher Praxis*, 293, says that the practical reason proceeds "through a complicated, many-stage process all the way to the insight (only to be won by a discursive path) into what is the right action alternative to be taken here and now . . . *in that the certainty of the rectitude of each judgment steadily decreases as the concreteness increases* [my italics]." Even if the universality of the judgment obviously decreases, surely the "certainty of the rectitude" of judgment does

himself unclearly and ambiguously on this matter: "This is why it is not possible for a truth or a practical correctness shared by all persons to exist on the level of the concrete inferences drawn by the practical reason: individual actions in their singularity and contingency cannot be known by means of universal and necessary concepts."[89] To say that the singular withdraws itself "in its singularity and contingency" from the universal concept is of course trivial and merely tautological.[90] But what is it supposed to mean to say that "on the level of the concrete conclusions of practical reason, there can no longer be any truth or practical rectitude that is common to all"? This could not be maintained from an Aristotelian point of view. What Aristotle means when he refers to "*practical* truth" is what is common to all the various practical concrete judgments: their agreement with "right striving," that is, with the goals of the moral virtues. Just *this* kind of truth and universality is the way in which the singular, the contingent, the *operabile* in its concreteness, can be called "true"; a genuinely practical type of truth, which does not remove the *operabile* in its singularity and contextuality, but orders it intentionally at the same time to a practical principle that formulated the goal of a moral virtue, so that it can, according to circumstances, be called a "just" or "temperate" or "courageous" action. The "truth" of the concrete finally consists in its being justified through the principle that is there to be realized, and in this sense can be "derived" from it: its falseness would lie in contradiction to this principle, in its "underivability" from it. Precisely in this sense is praxis—which only consists in the final concreteness of the individual case—also accessible to knowledge through universal concepts, and that there can even be such a thing as practical science.[91]

It is likewise trivial to point out that concrete judgments of action leave the acting person in uncertainty or even perplexity because of the complex nature of the matter of actions or the circumstances. This is, again, not caused by the concreteness of the judgment as such, but by the complexity of the matter and the circumstances. Looking at the question from the perspective of action theory and the acting person, it must be emphasized, to the contrary, that the concrete judgment of action must actually show a higher degree of certainty than the general principle. Actually, the universality of principles,

---

not. This would not make sense because it would mean that someone would either never, or always, act with a bad conscience or fear that he had acted wrongly.

89. E. Schockenhoff, *Naturrecht und Menschenwürde*, 176; English ed., *Natural Law and Human Dignity* (see note 76 above), 168.

90. Nor does the situation improve when Schockenhoff goes on to say: "In its concrete judgments practical reason confirms, however, the law of decreasing certainty, which is why on this level from the outset we have to take account of a wider field of results."

91. Cf. W. Kluxen, *Philosophische Ethik bei Thomas von Aquin*, 222.

thanks to their practical indeterminacy, does not authorize any concrete actions—and action is always concrete—and thus leaves someone called upon to act in a condition of uncertainty and inconclusiveness, and this lasts until he reaches the concreteness of what, for example, is the "just thing to do" here and now: what is appropriate or owed to his fellow man. Action comes into being just when that degree of certainty is reached that alone makes possible the concretizing of the principle, through the judgment of prudence. The one who acts will then perceive the final, action-triggering statement of his practical reason *(iudicium electionis)* as the most binding of all its judgments and will then feel "obliged" to do what reason bids him do. To maintain, as Honnefelder does, that "the certainty of knowledge of what is demanded" decreases "in the process of concretizing determination," would mean that as the concreteness of the practical reason increased, the acting subject would be ever more removed from the decision to act, only to end up at the judgment of the particular action, finding himself in a condition of maximum uncertainty with regard to what he is morally obliged to do. What *does* decrease is the *capacity to universalize* what the concrete situation demands: the possibility that the rectitude of *this* concrete action is also right for *other* cases or for *all* cases. But again, that too is trivial.

At times serious misuse has been made, in fact, of this "law of decreasing certainty" and the interpretation of the multistage practical reason that is bound up with it. Texts of Thomas are cited in its support which on closer inspection say something entirely different.[92] Schockenhoff cites for support here the famous passage about the "mutability of human nature";[93] Honnefelder, for his part, calls upon the principle that "there is not the same rectitude for all" *(non est eadem rectitudo apud omnes)*,[94] which according to Thomas is valid for practical knowing, which, unlike speculative/theoretical knowing, has for its object the particular and contingent rather than the necessary. In fact, Thomas is explaining in this passage that in the realm of the most universal principles, the practical reason too has the same rectitude for all people; but that this does not hold for the specific principles or commandments that are in relation to certain determinate types of actions such as murder, theft, or the obligation to restore borrowed property. But does this variation in "rectitude" formulate a "law of decreasing certainty and power to bind" of the practical reason? In the article cited here, it would be very difficult to find any support for this thesis. Thomas is only showing here that, first of all, certain specific principles (or better: norms and rules), such as that

92. For a fuller account of this, cf. *Natural Law and Practical Reason*, 495ff.
93. E. Schockenhoff, *Naturrecht und Menschenwürde*, 176.
94. I-II, Q. 94, a. 4.

one must return what has been borrowed, do not work in some cases and do not correspond with justice (which can be recognized in a particular case, depending on the circumstances, more certainly and unambiguously). Thomas is speaking here of an *impedimentum particulare*, a "concrete hindrance" to the possible following of such a rule in a concrete case, when following it would lead to a perversion of its meaning, and would change a principle of justice into a principle of injustice (as when someone would return a borrowed weapon even though the owner has suddenly gone mad).[95] Secondly, Thomas is maintaining here—although this is not mentioned by those who like to cite this passage for support—that the rectitude changes or is disturbed with the increasing concreteness "because some people, through emotion, bad customs or a (pathological) deficiency of nature have lost their reason."[96] The Aristotelian perspective of the prudent person or the *spoudaios* fits in with this: an incorrect knowledge of the specific principle of action is based on the loss of rational understanding through certain emotional or culturally specific disorientations that are conditioned by socialization, if not through some pathological cause.

Thomas is more precise than Aristotle in his observation of the conditioning of moral insight through culture and ethos. This is not something that should be overlooked, as I have mentioned before. But he also understands that such conditioning does not compromise the universal validity of moral principles. Only what is concretely to be done, or what, in a sense is *within* these principles or upon their basis, cannot be said in a universal way. The range of human possibilities and situational contingency is too great, let alone the legitimate multiplicity and diversity of cultures. In general, concrete action can only be "normed" in an immediately practical way through *negatively* formulated principles, because these formulate the boundaries within which practical truth, that is, agreement of concrete action with the goals of moral virtues, is to be found. Single actions can no doubt be justified through principles, but never derived necessarily from them. It is different with prohibitions (or prohibitive norms): they can, in certain circumstances, be derived necessarily from the principle, since the knowledge of the contradiction to a principle includes all actions of which the contradiction is true, without exception.

95. Cf. also A. M. González, "*Depositus gladius non debet restitui furioso:* Precepts, Synderesis, and Virtues in Saint Thomas Aquinas," *The Thomist* 63, no. 2 (1999): 217–40. It is not a question here of an "exception" (as if the principle were not always valid), but rather that an individual case cannot be subsumed under a certain principle. The difference—it goes back ultimately to whether or not one is using an intentional concept of action—is important in connection with the attempt to derive the legitimacy of a teleological (or consequentialist or proportionalist) ethics from the assertion of "justified exceptions" (cf. below, V.3 and 4).

96. I-II, Q. 94, a. 4.

h) Knowledge of Principles and Emotional (Affective) Dispositions

The convergence between principles of action and the goals of the moral virtues, as well as the role of prudence in the genesis and application of practical principles, as presented above, establishes a characteristic that is very significant for practical reason and has been mentioned several times before. It has a key significance for a virtue ethics: this is the importance of the affective (emotional) dispositions both for the knowledge of these principles and for the degree of their effectiveness. This brings us back to the theme of moral virtue and its affective/cognitive achievement that consists in producing a "connaturality with the good."

For, as Aristotle emphasizes, "vice destroys the principle." And yet not all judgment is "destroyed and distorted through pleasure and pain." And so the "judgment on the question, whether the angles of a triangle are equal to two right angles" is not endangered by anyone's emotion; it is a purely theoretical question. What *is* at risk are the judgments that are emotionally connected, such as those of the practical reason, judgments about "what is to be done. For the principles of the things that are done consist in that for the sake of which they are to be done; but the man who has been ruined by pleasure or pain forthwith fails to see any such principle—to see that for the sake of this or because of this he ought to choose and do whatever he chooses and does; for vice is destructive of the principle."[97]

Affectively acquired dispositions, that is, virtues and vices, have an influence upon the knowledge of principles as well as upon their efficiency in guiding action. The virtuous person does the good on the basis of emotional connaturality with the good. The intentional striving for a goal that belongs to his affective disposition brings it about that he does what fits with the principles with ease, consistency, and joy. Virtue "either natural or produced by habituation is what teaches right opinion about the first principles."[98] This is how prudence becomes possible, "a reasoned and true state of capacity to act with regard to human goods."[99]

The incontinent individual, on the other hand, knows, of course, what is good, but he makes erroneous choices: his practical judgment is emotionally led astray. But "the best thing in him, the principle, is preserved."[100] In this case, there will typically be insight after the fact, and regrets.[101] The truly vicious person has some *other* principle instead of the principles, namely, that which corresponds to his emotional dispositions. Aristotle contrasts the merely incontinent or morally weak person to "a city which passes all the right de-

---

97. *EN* VI, 5 (1140b 13–21).
99. Ibid., VI, 5 (1140b 21).
101. Ibid., VII, 8 (1150b 31).

98. Ibid., VII, 8 (1151a 19).
100. Ibid., VII, 8 (1151a 26).

crees and has good laws, but makes no use of them," but the vicious man "is like a city that uses its laws, but has bad laws to use."[102]

But this makes ethics a dangerous business. At the very beginning of the *Nicomachean Ethics*, Aristotle states clearly that someone who "tends to follow his passions" and not his reason is "not a proper hearer" of lectures on ethical subjects. This is, of course, an overstatement, but it does hit upon the truth, even if we would have to qualify it to say that nobody is a proper hearer of ethical discourses who doesn't have the *intention*, or is not at least in some way motivated, to act in accordance with his reason. For this is exactly the person who does not want to hear any reasons, who is not ready to question his own preferences and priorities and, when appropriate, to adjust them. For that is truly the business of ethics.

As Aristotle says in the first book of the *Nicomachean Ethics*, the ethical philosopher must presuppose the principle as being something "evident." "Hence anyone who is to listen intelligently to lectures about what is noble and just and, generally, about the subjects of political science must have been brought up in good habits. For the fact (the *hoti*) is a starting point, and if this is sufficiently plain to him, he will not need the reason (the *dihoti*) as well; and the man who has been well brought up has or can easily get starting points. And for him who neither has nor can get them, let him hear the words of Hesiod: *Far best is he who knows all things himself; / . . . / Good, he that hearkens when men counsel right; / But he who neither knows, nor lays to heart / Another's wisdom, is a useless wight [Works and Days, ll. 293–97]."[103]

Now it is quite possible to connect the Aristotelian doctrine on the principles of practical reason with his doctrine on the inductive knowledge of principles, as Aristotle himself did in his *Posterior Analytics* in the case of theoretical knowledge, and to which he alludes in the *Nicomachean Ethics*.[104] But Aristotle never did develop an ethical doctrine of principles. But it can be found—even if only as a by-product—in the work of Thomas Aquinas, and it can be looked upon as a happy satisfaction for something that was lack-

---

102. Ibid., VII, 10 (1152a 20–24). In his first work on Aristotle (*Praktische Philosophie. Das Modell des Aristoteles* [Munich and Salzburg: Pustet, 1971; rpt. 1996]), 141, O. Höffe made this important difference between the vicious and the merely incontinent seem to disappear, with his assertion that according to Aristotle, the vicious one is distinguished by "not having any principle at all," while the virtuous one is characterized by "following the principle of striving for the good." But this removes the difference, which is very important for Aristotle, between the truly good and the only apparently good, and sets up a formalistic concept of virtue "to act on the basis of principles" that is indeterminate in contents. In reality, according to Aristotle, the vicious one also acts on the basis of principles, just bad or false ones. Only the incontinent one does not act on the basis of principle but out of a momentary weakness. Cf. my brief critique of Höffe in *Praktische Vernunft und Vernünftigkeit der Praxis*, 435, note 48.

103. *EN* I, 2 (1095b 4–11).

104. *EN* I, 7 (1098b 3).

ing, the filling of a certain "gap" in Aristotelian ethics.[105] The Christian philosopher grants the human person a higher degree of cognitive autonomy and rationality than the pagan. This has its ultimate cause in the Christian conviction of "man being made in the image of God."

This is why, as Thomas points out, there are principles that as universals are in no way "destructible" through affective dispositions *(nullo modo potest e cordibus humanis deleri)*, but can be rendered inoperable in particulars *(deletur tamen in particulari operabili)*.[106] This would mean, for example, the golden rule, and, of course, the first principle of practical reason. For without the reality of this principle not even the vicious man could do anything; for he only acts by pursuing what seems good to him and avoiding what he perceives as evil. In this sense, even this principle stands, in a way, "beyond good and evil," because this difference founds all human action as such and thereby the moral difference. Thomas also recognizes a "destruction" of the principles through the customs of society (one might think here of the practice of polygamy), which form the context of an ethos, which under some circumstances nobody has the occasion to question without being considered a "bad" person for doing so. Thomas speaks of the ancient Germani, who believed that thievery was permissable.[107] A custom can become so much a part of the assumed ethos that it disguises the principle so that those who live in the culture do not ascribe something to the vice of injustice, even when injustice is done.

The cognitive stability and indelibility of the very first principle, on the other hand, not only permits the possibility of an argumentative reconstruction and justification of the principles specific for action on their basis; it also permits the possibility of an ethical discourse, which does not—as Aristotle did—exclude from the outset those whose dispositions are not in harmony with the principles, and which, finally, always offers the possibility for questioning an ethos as to its rationality. Even so, ethics remains *practical* philosophy: it is practiced by subjects who are already engaged in action, and it directs praxis. And because it does speak about praxis, personal interest and knowledge are more intensely interwoven with each other than in any other discipline. It can never be treated from the nonparticipatory position of the "third person," of the mere observer. In philosophical ethics, "scientific objectivity" always implies a challenge to reflect upon one's own life, to examine it and attempt to improve it.

---

105. This in fact is the central thesis that I attempted to present in my *Praktische Vernunft und Vernünftigkeit der Praxis.*

106. Cf. I-II, Q. 94, a. 6. This statement also is related, of course, to the natural law *(lex naturalis)*.

107. I-II, Q. 94, a. 4.

2. Moral Knowledge and Conscience

a) The *Habitus* of Moral Knowledge

Knowledge of the principles is an act of the practical reason, a reason that is embedded in appetition. Principles guide human action all the way to the concrete choice of action: by this is meant the final, action-triggering concretizing of appetition, and in this way, the practical reason that had its point of departure in the principles has its intentional fulfillment. For the just person does justice for the sake of justice—otherwise, although he may perform just actions, he would not be just.

But the reason—as a spiritual faculty—has the ability to reflect upon its own act. This reflection is carried out spontaneously: only the degree of attention that we pay to this reflection can be governed by the will. In this reflection, the subject knows its own practical knowing—whether on the level of principles or on the level of the concrete judgment of action—as *content and subject matter.* In this form, reflection builds up a habitual moral knowledge *(scientia moralis),* whose application to action is known as moral conscience.[108]

"Conscience" is always a form of "knowing-with" *(con + scientia).* Knowing in fact *whether* one did something and *what* one did is "conscience" in the most general sense. And so we act, "conscious" or "unconscious" of *what* we do or even *that* we have done something at all. Sense-consciousness comes from the (nonreflective) feeling of feeling, whereas spiritual or intellectual consciousness comes from recognizing or knowing feelings and inclinations, but also from "knowing about knowing." Spiritual consciousness is realized in the mode of reflection.

This is how all the inclination to good or fleeing from evil that constitutes practical reason is grasped in reflection as content and subject matter, and is formulable as a statement: "the good is to be done and pursued, the evil to be avoided." The golden rule can also be reflectively formulated: "One should never do to another, what one does not want done to oneself." The "ought" as a mode of statement appears right here, at the level of moral consciousness.

Through this, reflection makes possible the objectification of the ensemble of our practical judgments as *practical experience,* and to formulate this in reflection—a formulation that is always of a linguistic nature. Such formulations of practical experience in reflection are *normative statements,* that is, statements in the mode of the "ought": they are statements about objectifiable imperatives or preceptive acts of the practical reason. This is why they are statements about the human good, whether on the level of principles or concrete

108. Cf. *De Veritate,* Q. 17, a. 1.

judgments of action. This makes sense of how the experience formed on the level of concrete action becomes, in turn, a part of prudence.

Normative statements, that is, statements in the mode of the "ought," do not really correspond to the fundamental structure of the practical reason, but arise from reflection upon its original act. As the reflective contents of a practical kind, they still belong to practical reason and are capable of guiding it. Possibilities of reflection and reflective processes are not subject to any limitations. The contents of reflection can become the subject of new reflection, or they can become immediately the subject of an imperative act of the practical reason: as when, for some reason or because of some emotion, someone flees or avoids some bit of practical "knowing," in the form of saying: "It is not good to carry out this just deed" (or "this just deed is not to be carried out"), for fear, say of one's own loss—in other words, when someone knows what he should do (content of reflection, moral knowing), but decides it is not good, here and now, to do it, that is, that it must "be avoided," out of fear of the consequences, and the like. It is only over the consent of the intellect to the first principles—that is, over its fundamental relationship to truth—that the will possesses no command.[109]

The contents of reflection form a cognitive habit: moral knowledge *(scientia moralis)*. In this *habitus,* the contents of practical rationality are brought forward and become "useable." On this level of knowing is formed, on the level of the first principles, the *habitus of the first practical principles,* as Thomas reinterpreted in an Aristotelian sense what was known in tradition (based on a chance etymology) as *synderesis.*[110]

Thomas calls this habitus a "natural habit." It is not inborn, but it takes shape with a natural spontaneity, and this is the same spontaneity that is also at work in the realm of the theoretical reason, where the principle that "the whole is greater than the part" is known habitually. The habitus of the first principles is, in a way, the "law of our intellect," and it contains the "precepts of the natural law, which are the first principles of human actions."[111] The function of this most fundamental habit of the practical reason consists in "urging to the good and dissuading against evil, to the extent that we proceed on the basis of the first principles to discover what is to be done and to judge what we discover."[112] This is how the habit of the first principles becomes a "preamble to the virtuous act."[113]

109. Cf. I-II, Q. 17, a. 6.
110. Cf. M. B. Crowe, *The Changing Profile of the Natural Law* (The Hague: Martinus Nijhoff, 1977), 136ff., and O. Lottin, "Syndérèse et conscience aux XIIe et XIIIe siècles," in O. Lottin, *Psychologie et morale aux XIIe et XIIIe siècles* (Louvain and Gembloux: J. Duculot, 1948), 2.103–350.
111. I-II, Q. 94, a. 1, ad 2.
112. I, Q. 79, a. 12. On "synderesis," cf. also *De Veritate,* Q. 16.
113. *De Veritate,* Q. 16, a. 2, ad 5.

It is another question just how the habit of moral knowledge actually comes into being in a given person's life. Other factors also come into play, such as the recognition of authority (parental authorities, religious authorities), instruction of various kinds, influences of the social environment, initiation into a certain ethos, and so on. As long as we do not understand all these simply as externally imposed conditioning, socialization, or superego formation, they do not replace the cognitive process of grasping principles, but at the most stimulate it, support it, or even hinder it. And further, moral knowledge contains, of course, not only that which belongs to the realm of principles but also all that is a consequence of personal life history. And we must also add to this the cognitive dispositions that convey an ethos, the dispositions that make someone part of a concrete historical and social context and which, therefore, despite the unity of the principles, make possible the plurality of their historical, social, and individual concretions.

Accordingly, when we speak of the principles of practical reason or of the *lex naturalis* or "natural law," we really mean one or the other of two different things. This could be, first, the principles as the cognitive content of those judgments of the practical reason which are embedded in our striving and "unfold" from the very first principle all the way down to the concretion of the judgment of action. This is the same as saying that we speak of the *lex naturalis* as the original *ordinatio rationis,* in which the practical principles are *constituted* (this was the theme of the foregoing section). Alternatively, we can speak of the principles as they are given in the mode of reflection as the content of the ordering of reason. Here is revealed the ensemble of the principles as consciousness of human identity or "human nature," as they are constituted through the regulation of the natural inclinations through the reason as the *ordo rationis,* or order of reason. In this way—as the formulated ensemble of normative statements—we often speak about the (moral) "natural law," which nevertheless should not lead us astray into any doubt that its origin is to be seen precisely in the ordering-imperative act of the practical reason of the acting subject.

This is what we mean by "human nature," to the extent that we treat it as that being to which action must correspond if the action is going to be good human action. This human nature is not "mere nature" (what is naturally given, "order of nature"), but in fact is already the "ordering of the reason." As already said above (III.5.e), the "human nature" to which we refer in ethical discourse is already that which we have *interpreted* as such in the light of moral knowledge. It presupposes one's own experience of practical reasonableness and includes this as a hermeneutic key to self-understanding. Just for this reason there cannot be an original theoretical-metaphysical derivation of the "good for man" from mere "nature." Starting from reflection upon its own acts, "human nature" is recognized through a "complete return" *(reditio completa)* to the cause that underlies it: this is how (through reflection upon the acts of our spiritual faculty, as shaped by various objects or content) we recognize the nature of the faculty, and thereby the nature of the act that makes a human being human: the soul. This is the way we can adequately understand the "nature" that we ourselves are.[114]

Further reflection upon the reflective content of practical rationality, and in fact the mode of reflection itself, is accordingly not really practical reason but theoretical (observing) reason: here the reason observes something that "is," and not really immediately for the sake of action (in order to know "what to do"), but rather to *understand*. The interest here is primarily an interest in "the truth of being." But this knowledge contains as its object nothing other than the dynamic of appetition, ordered to the "good for man," and consequently from such knowledge something further can be deduced that has practical-normative validity. No longer do we have the problem, here, of the impossibility of making a conclusion about what ought to be done from what is. An anthropology and metaphysics that stems from such knowledge remains normatively relevant as well.

b) The Conscience

"Conscience" belongs to the phenomenon of "consciousness," and thus means a "knowing with" *(con + scientia)*. The moral conscience is a phenomenon of consciousness and nothing other than the "becoming practical" *(Praktischwerden)* of this consciousness, that is, the application of moral consciousness or moral knowledge to concrete judgments of action or to actions already accomplished, an application that influences the process of practical reasoning in a cognitive manner, on the level of praxis.[115] But this takes place, nevertheless, in a way peculiar to the act of conscience.[116]

The conscience is neither a special faculty nor a "disposition." Of course, it could be shown to be such in a purely phenomenological way. But what is phenomenologically given would not be capable of revealing the complex underlying structure of conscience. This would only be possible through a metaphysics of action. The real truth of the matter is that the conscience is an *act* of the habitus of "moral knowing," and that means a *judgment*. And it is the kind of judgment in which moral knowing is *applied* to concrete consid-

114. Cf. *De Veritate*, Q. 10, a. 9.
115. Cf. I, Q. 79, a. 13; *De Veritate*, Q. 17.
116. Cf. for the following as well the chapter entitled "Conscience" in R. Spaemann, *Persons* (see note 53 above).

erations and judgments or to actions already done, in order to examine these actions in the light of this knowledge, and if necessary, to make a corrective intervention. Conscience makes it possible for the human being to question his judgments of actions that are always so bound up with the emotions, and to examine them again, cognitively, with respect to their goodness.[117]

Conscience can also be called simply "the action-guiding reason in relation to itself."[118] Through this relation-to-itself—the reflection of the reason upon itself with the possibility of agreeing or denying—it follows that: "To have a conscience is not simply to grasp an objectifiable good and thereby become moral, but rather by grasping what is good in each case, to grasp oneself above all as a being that determines oneself in freedom through reason, and in order to be this being."[119] This is to pinpoint an essential aspect of practical reason and human praxis: the human person can only grasp the good in "the self-determination of will through reason"; the good for man is always to be *secundum rationem* ("according to reason").[120] As we have already seen from the beginning in our treatment of the concept of "human action" (II.1.b) and in the section on freedom of the will (III.5.c), the "whole origin of the freedom of the one who acts" lies in the "reflective relationship to oneself, made possible" by the act of reflective reason.[121] This very broadly conceived concept of the conscience has the disadvantage, nevertheless, of no longer permitting a distinction between the reflectivity of reason that is necessarily included in all practical knowing (on the one hand) and the act in which moral knowledge is applied to the action-guiding judgment of the practical reason or to already accomplished actions (on the other hand). Here we do not designate the general self-relatedness of the practical reason as "conscience," but only a certain kind of such self-relatedness; we have already considered the reflective content of practical reasoning that, as moral consciousness, leads to the habit of moral knowing. It is only the application of this knowledge to concrete action—or the

---

117. E. Schockenhoff, *Das umstrittene Gewissen* (Mainz: Matthias Grünewald, 1990), identifies the concrete action-determining practical reason with the conscience (without differentiating the latter from prudence), and thereby misses the distinction that is so central here between the judgment of conscience and the judgment of action *(iudicium electionis)*, since it is the latter which is concerned with the concretizing of action in the manifold particularity of what is to be done here and now, the virtue of which is prudence. In his subsequent book on conscience *Wie gewiss ist das Gewissen? Eine ethische Orientierung* (Freiburg im Breisgau: Herder, 2003), he clearly and rightly distinguishes judgments of prudence (which are the judgments of actions) and judgments of conscience (see 107). In *Grundlegung der Ethik. Ein theologischer Entwurf* (Freiburg im Breisgau: Herder, 2007) Schockenhoff proposes a coherent and impressive virtue ethical approach in which the confusion between judgments of conscience and judgments of prudence is entirely overcome.

118. L. Honnefelder, *Praktische Vernunft und Gewissen*, 26.

119. Ibid., 28.

120. Ibid.

121. Ibid.; Honnefelder also refers here to *De Veritate*, Q. 24, a. 2: "Only the reason that reflects upon its own act . . . can judge its own act of judgment: therefore all freedom is rooted in the reason *(unde totius libertatis radix est in ratione constituta)*."

confirmatory, retrospective relation of concrete action to this knowledge—that shall be referred to here as "conscience" or "the act of conscience."

Accordingly, the conscience "warns," "advises," "urges," or "prohibits." And with regard to an already accomplished action, it "praises" or "blames." The latter is the "pang of conscience" [German *Gewissensbiss;* cf. Middle English *agenbyte of inwit*]. In this way, the judgment of the conscience can in its reflection examine a judgment of action, intervene, stop its accomplishment, or bring it about that the matter is weighed in the light of higher principles, regulations of prudence, or the awareness of actual legal realities, so that the course of action is influenced thereby, as if by "still looking through the principles" *(quasi adhuc speculando per principia),* "someone once again judges [what he intended to do] with recourse to principles."[122] The conscience is the way that moral knowledge becomes immediately practical again.

> In this way the process of practical reasoning embedded in appetition, that is, the affectively guided judgment, can incline to a judgment that "p is good" and "p is to be done." But the conscience can intervene and declare that "p" is unjust (e.g., theft) and that one should not do such a thing, or that a legitimate public law is in existence that prohibits "p," and that it pertains to justice to obey laws. This is how the conscience can prohibit an action or at least put off the actual carrying-out of "p is good." If "p" is carried out after all, this takes place against the conscience. The consequence is then the "pang" of the "guilty conscience" after the fact, when it accuses and blames. This can, in turn, lead to a desire to silence conscience (since will does have command over the intellect), or (alternatively) to regret: "I shouldn't have done p" or "it was bad to do p."

A peculiar characteristic of the judgment of conscience is here revealed: it is not affectively conditioned to the same degree as practical judgments in the proper, more limited sense (the judgments that determine the free will to action-triggering choices). "Because the judgment of conscience consists in pure knowing, but the judgment of the free will consists in an application of knowing to affectivity: this judgment is the choosing judgment."[123]

Even the conscience can in its turn be guided affectively before, during, and after its judgment. For someone can even *will* moral ignorance, by not informing oneself, that is, by not informing the conscience, by "looking the other way" or (after the fact) by trying to silence it through self-justification. But *in itself* the judgment of conscience is a judgment that is not affectively bound. It represents a reflective content and habitual moral knowledge, and reflection

---

122. *De Veritate,* Q. 17, a. 1, ad 4.
123. *De Veritate,* Q. 17, a. 1, ad 4.

itself is a spontaneous act of the intellect that is not affectively caused; and the habitus of moral knowledge is not eliminated by affects that are contrary to it.

This is why we also experience the "voice of conscience" as a voice that competes with the voice of our emotions, with what we are inclined to do. It is something "objective," in opposition to the "subjectivity" of the affections. It can be misleading to speak of "objective" and "subjective": in reality, we are concerned with two forms of subjectivity. But we experience the subjectivity of conscience as the claim of truth, that is, as the *truth of subjectivity,* and in this sense as something "objective."

> To say that something is "objectively" good or right, as distinct from a merely "subjective" impression, pertains to the phenomenology of the act of con-science. But the term "objective" cannot be taken to mean that "the truly good" is something that is a given (law, norm, nature, order of being) independent of the acting subject or something to be *distinguished* from that subject, to which then the free subject is related through "recognizing" or "obeying." The oppos-ing of "subject" ("freedom," or the acting, judging person) to "objective norm" comes from the subject-object dualism of modern legalistic morality (which is still fundamental for Kant). The question of objectivity is a question of the truth of subjectivity. The subjectivity of the acting person, the "I," also belongs to the "objective world," to "nature," or to the "order of being." The objectivity of what is normative really only comes about through reason, as the human being's *standard-giving subjectivity.* The distinction between "merely subjec-tive good" and "objective good" is accordingly a distinction *within* the subjec-tivity of the acting person; it is the Aristotelian distinction between what only "appears good" and what is "truly good," as something that transcends the former. Consequently, it is also risky to speak of the conscience as a "subjec-tive norm" as distinct from an "objective norm," because doing so excludes the whole question of truth: in fact, the conscience can only be "norm" insofar as it can be "true," that is to say, because it is capable of being "objective" *in* its subjectivity.

In fact, the conscience is always *my* conscience. All practical, action-guiding knowledge is always "my" knowledge and "my" reason.[124] The con-science also arises from the cognitive, personal autonomy of man as acting subject. But it reveals itself—on the basis of its detachment from affectivity—as the voice of the *truth* of this subjectivity. This is why the deepest and most ultimate failure of a human being consists in not following one's conscience, and the greatest degradation of another human being consists in suppressing,

---

124. Cf. T. Styczen, "Das Gewissen—Quelle der Freiheit oder der Knechtung?" *Archiv für Religions-psychologie* 17 (1986): 130–47.

through force, the freedom of that person's conscience and action in accordance with the conscience. For this is really the denial of the human being, or the self-denial of oneself as a *human* acting subject. That which is done in contradiction to one's own judgment of conscience is irrational in the most fundamental sense, it is "not according to reason," it is in contradiction to human identity, and therefore a moral evil.

> The obligation to follow one's own conscience follows from the reality that human action is action on the basis of reason. Not to act according to what is recognized as good would be the denial of oneself as a moral subject of actions. But "to follow my own conscience" does not simply mean doing what "appears good" to me, but doing what I am certain is "the truly good." When I am mistaken about this, I will have an erroneous conscience, but will still follow my conscience precisely because I am convinced that my conscience is showing me the truth. And insofar as I am convinced of the "truth" of my judgment of conscience, I am still obligated. In this case, the conscience binds *per accidens*, that is, because it is taken to be true. But if I believe that my conscience is not bound up with truth, but only establishes something "good for me," I really am throwing away the indispensable claim of the conscience to bind: I am removing from the conscience the authority to obligate *at all*. To the extent that someone thinks that "freedom of conscience" is an "autonomy" of conscience unconnected with truth, he destroys both the authority *and* the autonomy of the conscience, that is, its *obligating* character, and thereby the foundation for the fact that freedom of conscience is a human good.

Freedom of conscience, therefore, means freedom of the *act of conscience*. This cannot mean that the conscience is the source or origin of the truth about what is good for man. The source of that are the acts of the practical reason, as analyzed in the foregoing section, and here there is something that is "naturally right." The moral knowledge that is applied by the judgment of conscience is something received, something that has its origin in what the practical reason understands as naturally good for man: "conscience" is in fact related to the moral knowledge originally formed through reflection upon practical experience, which in the judgment of conscience is, in turn, merely applied to action. The conscience is consequently a kind of *regula regulata*, a "normed norm," and can accordingly find itself in *error*.[125] To separate the conscience from this connection to truth would be tantamount to destroying the cognitive autonomy of man; that is to say, it would mean replacing a rationally acting subject with one of a different kind: one that only pursues what "seems" good to him, without troubling himself about whether this appearance has anything to do with the truth. As Spaemann has rightly emphasized,

125. *De Veritate*, Q. 17, a. 2, ad 7.

the "absolute claim of conscience" should not be confused with "an objective entitlement demanding recognition."[126]

A comparison with Kant in this matter is instructive. For Kant, "an erring conscience is an absurdity."[127] To be sure, he acknowledges that "I can indeed be mistaken at times in my objective judgment as to whether something is a duty or not."[128] But for Kant the role of conscience is not to ascertain a harmony between that which I judge as good in a practically reasoned, subjective way, and that which is objectively my duty; instead, it is only that inner voice or "moral predisposition" that ensures that I actually carry out in fact what my subjective-practical reasoning judges as being in accordance with duty.[129] If I do that, I am acting according to conscience and morally well, independently of whether what I recognize as according to duty is also "objectively" good. In the latter case, one can make a mistake, but this is irrelevant to the question of whether or not one has acted well and according to conscience. Therefore, according to Kant, there can be no defect (or error) at all in conscience; it is only possible for there to be an "un-conscientiousness," that is, "the propensity to pay no heed to its judgment."[130] Despite the differentiation of practical reason (which prescribes the rule) and conscience as a "court of justice" with regard to subjective-practical judgments, this leads, in fact, to the removal of the "two-stage nature" of affectively bound practical reason—completed in the act of choice—plus (subsequent) cognitive-inspecting conscience, so that every really practical judgment, to the extent that one actually carries it out, is to be treated as a judgment of conscience and the latter, in turn, is *de facto* identified with the act of choice, or *iudicium electionis*.

The highest moral imperative, then—so seems to be the outcome of Kant's theory of conscience—means following one's own conscience, that is, doing what, in each case, one judges subjectively as good or as one's duty (and this, of course, in Kant's understanding, happens according to the examining process of the categorical imperative, which does not really determine duty, but only ascertains the correlation of our subjective maxims with a will that autonomously expresses what is according to duty, in the sense of being free from heteronomous influences and self-serving motives). Now this is not at all a problem with respect to the requirement that someone must follow his own conscience, as such. The problem has to do with the fact that this command is understood to be absolute and not to be questioned, which means that it leads

126. R. Spaemann, *Persons*, 173.
127. *The Metaphysics of Morals*, trans. M. Gregor, 161.
128. Ibid.
129. Cf. also *Metaphysics of Morals*, "Doctrine of the Elements of Ethics," sec. 13.
130. *Metaphysics of Morals*, 161.

to the conception of conscience that holds that it is morally good to follow it *entirely without regard to what specific kind of subjective-practical judgment is commanding such a conscience to be followed.* It leads to the notion of conscience that itself cannot, and need not, be called into question regarding its contents, since the single command that it can allow to be issued is precisely to follow it.[131] This fits in precisely with the Kantian primacy of the autonomy of the will—or pure subjectivity—with respect to the reason: for Kant, indeed, "reason" itself is *in service* to the autonomy of the will; in truth, however, any correctly understood autonomy of the will is based on rationality, and it is only through recourse to rationality that autonomy can be justified as a human good at all. On this point, Hegel's dictum against the pure "subjectivity of conviction" is valid: "Really, my being convinced *is* something supremely trivial if I cannot *know* the truth."[132] In Kant's defense it could of course be added here that in a certain sense, the universalizing function of the categorical imperative ("Act on a maxim that can also hold as a universal law")[133] really does assure—through the importation of the moral point of view—the "moral truth" of action, and thereby rectitude of conscience.[134] But this remains such a "weak" concept of truth and rectitude (detached as it is from all conceptions of the "good life"), that Hegel's criticism still appears justified.

> Now, it is not at all in contradiction with the cognitive autonomy of the human being to allow the moral conscience to be formed by such authorities as are *reasonable* for it to recognize. Mere subordination to authority is not a rational action, but reasonable believing would be (whether in the interpersonal or the religious area) because it presupposes a rational insight into the credibility of an authority (such credibility being the basis of all educational processes). Even when what is thus accepted through authority is not immediately intelligible, still, its reception by way of an act of faith and trust in the authority *does* correspond to the dignity of the conscience and the cognitive autonomy of the human person (cf. above, III.3.c).

131. In any case, I suspect that the Kantian concept of conscience involves circular reasoning; it appears to be defined by itself in the sense of "being bound by conscience," but only tautologically, as "following one's own conscience" can be described. In exactly the same way, for Kant, "the duty here is only to cultivate one's conscience," which means "to sharpen one's attentiveness to the voice of the inner judge, and use every means . . . to obtain a hearing for it" (*Metaphysics of Morals*, trans. M. Gregor, 161), but not to put effort into making sure that the conscience is directed at what is truly good, that is, not involved in any error.

132. G. W. F. Hegel, *The Philosophy of Right*, section 140, trans. T. M. Knox (*Great Books of the Western World* 46), 53.

133. I. Kant, *Metaphysics of Morals*, trans. M. Gregor, 17–18.

134. This is how Habermas defends not only Kant but also discourse ethics from the objection: by arguing that the universal command of the categorical imperative not only requires formal consistency, but is also the "application of a substantial, content-rich moral perspective"; see J. Habermas, "Treffen Hegels Einwände gegen Kant auch auf die Diskursethik zu?" in Habermas, *Erläuterungen zur Diskursethik*, 9ff., 21.

We can sum it up as follows: to act against one's conscience is a moral evil, and constitutes guilt, even when the conscience is in error. But does this mean, then, that on the other hand, when someone *follows* a conscience that is found to be in error—in the subjective conviction of doing the right thing—that that person is not only free from blame, but also acting well, and through such action becoming a better human being?[135] Does the loyalty to one's own conscience and the consequent spontaneity and authenticity guarantee the goodness of the action and of the one who acts? One would not answer this question lightly. On the basis of a virtue ethics approach it must be said that when someone follows a conscience that is erroneous through that person's own fault, that person is all the more to blame. Sticking to an erroneous conscience *without blame* is unthinkable, at least in the case of fundamental moral principles and norms. We do not think it credible that, say, a Nazi like Adolf Eichmann acted well and was really a good human being when he defended himself before the court through his subjective conviction, his conscience, and his consciousness of duty, just because he always followed this conviction and his conscience and always did what he thought was his duty. "To be a good person" is not the same as "following one's conscience." Rather, we believe that subjectively convinced Nazis would be especially despicable human beings *because of* their malformed consciences, that this malformed conscience was blameworthy, and that the actions that followed upon this conscience were not only not right, but also made them into evil persons and drove them ever more deeply into guilt. Of course, not all cases are quite so dramatic. Nevertheless, a virtue ethics must proceed on the understanding that a conscience that is found to be erroneous about what is good is at least *partly* responsible for having acquired this error through previous blameworthy action—or has remained attached to the error though one's own participation in it—and the erroneous actions that follow from that conscience can in no way contribute to making the actor into a better human being. *To the extent that we are responsible for the formation of our conscience, the following of a conscience of this kind (i.e., an erroneous one) only confirms us more deeply in the guilt in question, even if we are subjectively convinced that we are doing what is right.* In other words, we bear the responsibility for having the conscience that we have. And in no small way is the dignity of the human being demonstrated by the free will being essentially determined by the reason. Even in cases of minimal responsibility, following an erring conscience will make it harder for the acting person to have insight into the human good. A true error of conscience is not simply an intellectual defect, but a moral one as well.[136]

135. Cf. above, III.3.c.
136. Cf. also the presentation in V.1.h above on the "knowledge of principles and affective disposi-

This is why Thomas Aquinas holds that whoever acts against his conscience always sins, even in the case of an erring conscience; on the other hand, whoever follows an erring conscience does not thereby have a good will.[137] It is often objected to this that someone who is in error is in fact subjectively convinced that he is doing the right thing *objectively;* accordingly he would not be able to recognize error as such, which would have the consequence that his action is satisfying the requirement for being good action, which consists in "acting according to reason" *(agere secundum rationem).* Therefore someone could maintain the opposite from Thomas's point of view.[138] In fact, however, Thomas also holds that someone who has a culpably erring conscience must here and now—presupposing this conscience—be convinced of the rightness of what is wrong.[139] But Thomas still firmly maintains that such a person fundamentally has the possibility of recognizing the error for what it is and rejecting it. This is also why he does not find himself in a situation of utter perplexity.[140] For Thomas, apparently—except for cases of *ignorantia facti*—it is not a question of an alternative of "knowing" and "not knowing" or "being convinced" and "not being convinced," from which there is no escape. For him, the alternative is rather "virtue" and "vice": the erring conscience, which is of interest here, is really always basically correctible on the basis of reason and its principles (only Aristotle doubted the possibility of "conversion" from a condition of unseeing vice). The erring conscience also finds itself incomplete and unsatisfied when in error, and can call itself into question. So, also, someone who has mistakenly entered a freeway going the wrong direction, despite his firm conviction that everyone other than he is going in the wrong direction, might be able to recognize that *he* may in fact be mistaken about it, and not everyone else. This is possible because one's own convictions can be experienced as being in need of correction, which is

---

tions," as well as R. Spaemann, *Persons,* 173ff.—Kant in his earlier writings still recognized this clearly; cf. I. Kant, *Eine Vorlesung über Ethik,* ed. G. Gerhardt (Frankfurt am Main: Suhrkamp, 1990]), 146: "It is a bad thing, to excuse oneself with an erroneous conscience; many things can be excused by it, yet one is also responsible for one's errors" (trans. here Malsbary).

137. Cf. I-II, Q. 19, a. 5–6; *De Veritate,* Q. 17, a. 4–5.

138. Cf. E. Schockenhoff, *Das umstrittene Gewissen,* 88ff. Schockenhoff also cites on this point the passage from *Quodlibetum* 3, q. 12, a. 2, according to which human action is considered virtuous or vicious on the basis of the conceived good as such, to which the will stands in relation, *and not on the basis of the material object of the act.* In any event Schockenhoff appears to miss the point that Thomas is saying this only in the case of an *ignorantia facti* (someone mistakes his father for a deer while hunting; that does not make him guilty of the murder of his father). In the case of an *ignorantia iuris,* ignorance about the moral justification of an action (with respect to a "moral norm," that is), such an excuse is not valid, *except in the case of the insane and feeble-minded (Quodlibetum* 3, q. 12, ad 2). Clearly Thomas has great trust in reason.

139. Cf. I-II, Q. 19, a. 6, ad 3.

140. Ibid., and cf. also *Quodlibetum* 3 (note 137 above). "Perplexity" of the conscience is present when all alternatives of action (or nonaction) appear immoral, or when there is no longer in sight any "way out" to the good, and one can no longer recognize the immoral as such or feels forced to be content with it.

due—for example—to the relationship these convictions must have with one's surroundings. And therefore for Thomas in the realm of the "moral norm" (except for someone who is ill) there can never be a totally blameless erring conscience, even when one's fault is small and the fault of to others is yet greater (in the case of the Nazi war criminal, on the other hand, we would say that the individual's guilt is very great). The way to the goodness of the acting person does not mean simply "following one's own conscience," but rather in getting rid of the error, in the turning of one's attention to the good for man, and this of course needs enough humility to call oneself into question, listening to others, and the formation of conscience.[141]

If the moral knowledge is incomplete or in error, without this incompleteness or error originating in the *will,* then to that extent one is *blameless* and consequently finds oneself in a position of invincible ignorance, and such a conscience always excuses someone from a bad or wrong deed. But this is exactly the reverse of the situation of an error in choice or ignorance in choice: here, the error and ignorance *constitute* and increase the guilt, for these errors are caused in fact by affective dispositions, and to the extent that such dispositions distort the judgment of action, it is always "willing" in various degrees. Ignorance in this case is in fact a moral fault.[142]

It is also entirely possible, to do something which someone is convinced—on the level of the judgment of actions—is "good," and yet not follow one's conscience in doing it. People who emphatically call on their conscience in such situations can in reality—through affective compulsion—act fully against their conscience, or with a bad conscience. Calling on one's conscience emphatically and aggressively is often really a sign that someone has a bad conscience. And this very thing can become the road that leads ultimately to a deformed conscience.

But insofar as emotions shut out the will, that is, make it impossible for a judgment of action to even come into play, then such action is not to be understood as "human action" and it cannot be counted as earning praise or blame; that is to say, it stands outside the moral difference.

Emotional or affective dispositions of this kind (as *habitus* or states) can, in any event, also be one's own fault: in this case, a moral assignment of responsibility (of praise or blame) is possible even for actions that in themselves

---

141. Cf. also below, at V.4.g. Of course we must also consider here the influences and compulsive force of the sociocultural context, which often considerably reduces the degree of individual responsibility. Fundamental for this theme in Thomas Aquinas is R. Schenk, "*Perplexus supposito quodam.* Notizen zu einem vergessenen Schlüsselbegriff thomanischer Gewissenslehre," *Recherches de Theologie ancienne et medievale* 57 (1990): 62–95; see also T. G. Belmans, "Le paradoxe de la conscience erronée d'Abelard à Karl Rahner," *Revue thomiste* 90 (1990): 570–86.

142. Cf. *De virtutibus in communi,* Q. un., a. 6, ad 3.

are not free. When someone voluntarily gets drunk, he no longer has control over many things that he does in his drunken condition. But insofar as he willingly put himself into this condition—and only insofar—will he also bear responsibility for what he does in that condition. It is ascribable to him as "voluntary in virtue of its cause" *(voluntarium in causa)*. If someone falls into deep water by a mishap or by being forcibly pushed, no one would blame him for his condition and would sympathize with his plight if he has difficulties trying to get himself out. If he fell in because he ignored all the relevant warnings, we would rather be inclined to blame him for his situation and chuckle at his efforts to get out. But even in this latter case we would of course still help him if we could.

The knowledge that is cancelled or rendered ineffective in the concrete, erroneous act of choosing is really the habitual moral knowledge applied in the act of the conscience. Thus there is a double requirement for moral action: first, the formation of the conscience, and second, the acquisition of moral virtue, that is, those affective dispositions that make it possible for a human being to realize his cognitive autonomy and personal dignity in concrete action as well. A completely virtuous or prudent man, Aristotle said, is someone who can live at peace with himself: he possesses that freedom or inner calm that results from the harmony of conscience with judgment about actions and with the accomplishment of actions. The more human action is formed by moral virtue, the more the conscience plays the role of an observer who approves of what has been done.

c) Moral Obligation, Duty, and Virtue

According to Kant, a person acts from "duty" [*Pflicht*] when he acts on the basis of a pure command of the reason, and not by an inclination. But it is not merely the person who acts in accordance with duty who acts morally, but only the person who acts *out of* duty, that is, one who acts with attention to the moral law. For example, someone who visits a sick friend would only be acting morally if duty commanded him to do so. If someone visits a friend only because he is inclined to do so for friendship's sake and the action makes him happy, such a person is not really acting morally but hedonistically, that is to say, for the sake of his own benefit, even though he is doing the right thing, or what is in accordance with duty. But duty is not the motive for his action and consequently the action is not "moral."[143]

---

143. A similar example can be found in the essay (now become classic) by M. Stocker, "The Schizophrenia of Modern Ethical Theories" (originally appearing in *Journal of Philosophy* 73 [1976]: 453–66), available also in R. Crisp and M. Slote, eds., *Virtue Ethics* [Oxford: Oxford University Press, 1997], 66–78).

This conception does not seem to harmonize very well with our moral intuitions, although we would concede that it certainly can happen that someone does the right thing (what is according to duty) for selfish motives. But we are all inclined to rank as morally superior someone who visits a sick friend—who does the right thing just because he is a friend, and is by inclination is glad to visit, because he loves his friend—than someone who only does this because he thinks he is obliged to do so, on the ground that the maxim that underlies his action can be raised to a universal law. Kant himself, of course, realized this, too, and tried to soften such consequences of his moral theory in the "doctrine of virtue" [Tugendlehre] of his later work The Metaphysics of Morals.[144] But the dichotomy between duty and inclination still remains. Kant's "doctrine of virtue" cannot properly address the point of all virtue ethics, namely, that the virtuous person who visits his friend just out of friendship does the right thing exactly because he means his friend well, loves him, and therefore feels obliged in duty to visit him. The duty-conscious Kantian subject, by contrast, does what is right (or dutiful) because the categorical imperative commands him to do it as a kind of action that can become a universal law; only someone who has acted in this way, that is, out of duty, can afterward go so far as to love those whom he benefits, such love representing "the aptitude [Fertigkeit] of the inclination towards doing well."[145]

But the definition of human love as an "aptitude of the inclination toward beneficence" does not meet the essential characteristic of moral virtue. If I understand Kant correctly, by "inclination to beneficence" he means the inclination to carry out in each case what corresponds to duty. It involves, consequently, an inclination to do what is right in each case—but this right thing is not determined by inclination or virtue (i.e., by love or friendship), but through the moral law which is expressed in the categorical imperative. The inclination itself contributes nothing to the moral knowledge, to knowledge, that is to say, of what is right; it merely makes the subject be inclined to also do what in each case the subject judges as right (and perhaps also to do it with joy, because he enjoys "doing good," which seems in any event to come close to the self-satisfied attitude of the Pharisee, which Scheler criticized). But in the Aristotelian sense, virtue is not simply an "inclination to do the

144. Cf. Metaphysics of Morals, trans. M. Gregor, "Introduction to the Doctrine of Virtue," 145–69, and "Love of Human Beings," 161–62; see also above IV.2.c.

145. Cf. again Metaphysics of Morals, trans. M. Gregor, 162: "Beneficence is a duty. If someone practices it often and succeeds in realizing his beneficent intention, he eventually comes actually to love the person he has helped. So the saying 'You ought to love your neighbor as yourself' does not mean that you ought immediately (first) to love him and (afterwards) by means of this love do good to him. It means, rather, do good to your fellow human beings, and your beneficence will produce love of them in you (as an aptitude [Fertigkeit] of the inclination to beneficence in general)."

right thing" (whereby it remains open *how* the right thing is to be determined); this would then correspond to the trivial understanding of virtue as a disposition to act in a morally positive way. In a nontrivial sense, virtue is not the inclination to do what is right in each case, but rather the disposition "to do what is right by inclination," that is, to arrive at what is good just because of one's inclination. The emotional maturity of the virtuous subject enables him to grasp what is right to do here and now, and also to do it because it "appears good to him" to do it. He knows what is right, what to do, his "duty," *through* his inclination, through his emotional refinement, which permits him to have an undistorted view of what is good to do here and now as "something good for him" (which, as I trust I have sufficiently emphasized, is no irrational process, but rather a process in which practical reason is affectively guided and empowered).

In contrast to this, then, Kant represents, as we saw above,[146] the viewpoint that virtue or moral action is realized precisely from pure duty only when the acting person is conscious of having pushed aside his inclination for the sake of following duty. For Kant, the conflict between inclination and moral reason, or consciousness of duty, is constitutive of what he means by "virtue." Aristotle, on the other hand, holds the position that this dualism is really removed through moral virtue. Kant also thinks, so far in agreement with Aristotle, that for the bad man, "what he does clashes with what he ought to do, but what the good man ought to do, he does; for reason in each of its possessors chooses what is best for itself, and the good man obeys his reason."[147] For Aristotle, however, quite otherwise than for Kant, the virtuous person is the one who does what he is affectively inclined to do, because his inclination in fact corresponds to reason. Virtue is the unity and harmony of inclination and reason, of inclination and duty, of "subjective" motives and "objective" moral reasons for acting.[148] For Aristotle, intermediate between the bad man and the virtuous man is to be found the person who does not have the virtuous inclination, but nevertheless does what is good, for example, through self-mastery—that is, he fulfills his "duty," but does so against his inclination. For Kant it is just this latter type—the self-ruled, self-restrained, strong person who can hold out against bad inclinations—this is the moral, virtuous one, since "even the most hardened scoundrel, if only he is otherwise accustomed to using his reason"

146. Cf. above IV.1.b.
147. *EN* IX, 8 (1169 a 16–18). (Note: Urmson's revision of the Ross translation has systematically replaced the word "reason" with "intellect"; the present quotation reverses that replacement.)
148. Cf. also M. Stocker, "The Schizophrenia of Modern Ethical Theories" (see note 142 above) where the divorce of motives from reasons for acting is indicated to be the decisive defect, the "schizophrenia," in fact, of modern moral philosophy.

can have a good will through submitting to the "moral ought."[149] The good will, then, appears to be capable of being united with otherwise bad inclinations. The critique does not mention that this is not possible. An intemperate man can surely have a will that is good, that is, a will to be free of his vices, before he actually succeeds in becoming a temperate man. This is not virtue, but only the first step on the road to virtue. But it does not appear that this distinction means anything to Kant, or at least that it plays any role in his ethical theory. Seen in Kantian perspective, the will to set oneself against bad inclinations is enough for "virtue." Kantian ethics is therefore not a virtue ethics, even if it contains a "doctrine of virtue" as a kind of appendix. A mere ethics of duty and the imperatives of reason, an ethics that consists in the taming, through reason, of a bad and egoistical nature, is a doctrine that from the perspective of virtue ethics necessarily leaves out something essential to morality.

> Something should be added here. Kantian ethics, of course, attempts to be a virtue ethics *also,* and to consider virtue as a renewal of the inner man. But this "attempt" seems to me to come too late, and remains ambivalent. This becomes very clear in Kant's work on religion belonging to the same later period of his writings as the *Metaphysics of Morals,* where Kant speaks of the revolution of the inner man, of the "change of heart" that is necessary to reach true moral perfection.[150] This cannot only consist in doing that which is in accordance with virtue for "empirical reasons," or "in conformity with the precious principle of happiness," that is, pursuing "temperance for the sake of health" or avoiding injustice "for the sake of peace or profit." For someone to be morally good—that is, to become virtuous "in its intelligible character"—"requires no incentive other than the representation of duty itself."[151] This rising from the level of the merely empirical-egoistic-hedonistic to the level of the intelligibly moral could be taken to be fully Aristotelian, but then it would mean that someone does what is just (for example) for the sake of justice, for the love of justice (and not, that is to say, according to the "precious principle of happiness," for the sake of any personal advantage of one's own). So, one should visit a friend because it is "just" or "corresponds to friendship," or really, because it is "good" and "right" (and does not bring us any future advantage). But now we have reached the point of saying that someone acts morally who visits his friend out of friendship, that is, out of an inclination to the good. According to Kant, the "concept of duty" cannot be the same as acting according to the (Aristotelian) meaning, that is, to attain to the good that is peculiar to the virtue in question, for this would mean moral action is action carried out

---

149. I. Kant, *Groundwork of the Metaphysics of Morals,* trans. M. Gregor, 59.

150. *Religion within the Limits of Reason Alone,* trans. T. Greene and H. Hudson (New York: Harper & Row, 1934; rpt. 1960), 40–49.

151. Ibid., 42–43.

by an inclination to the good. For Kant, acting from duty can only mean acting in obedience to the categorical imperative, which commands us to act in each case that the maxim that underlies this action can become a universal law. The reason for moral action (the "concept of duty") is not the good specific to each virtue, but rather the transcendental formalism of the universalization that is peculiar to the categorical imperative.[152] The ambivalence of the Kantian concept of virtue is also revealed by his statement that someone can acquire virtues *previous* to the "revolution of the heart" through "long practice," without "change of heart," and through the "mere change of practices [*Sitten*]."[153] Acting *from duty* (virtue of an intelligible character) only comes in afterward, as a mode of motivation to be distinguished from mere (empirically motivated) virtue, and the former alone grounds morality. But this, again, is only the formalism of the "concept of duty" (the actual goods that are specific to the single virtues appear, on the other hand, to belong only to the not-yet-moral level of mere "practices" [*Sitten*]). Thus Kant concludes consistently that the "moral growth" of a man does not come "from the improvement of his practices but rather in the transforming his cast of mind and in the grounding of character."[154] This would all be in harmony with Aristotle, if it were not based on the dichotomy between inclination and consciousness of duty, and the reduction of morality to acting from duty, and if it did not thereby involve a completely non-Aristotelian concept of virtue: virtue as "mere practice" at the level of custom [*Sitte*], and not as *hexis prohairetike* or *habitus electivus*, that is, as the habit of making the right choice of action, whereby the will, the "sensibility," the "heart" of the person is oriented toward the truly good in accordance with the goals of the single virtues.

Aristotle and Kant are nevertheless agreed on one point: "duty" has something to do with a "command of the reason." Kant, of course, would say that the Aristotelian commands of reason are not categorical imperatives (meaning commands that express what ought to be done, completely independently of our wishes and expectations, and thereby holding their power to bind within themselves, and not in their "efficiency" for reaching some preset goal), but

---

152. This is exactly why F. Ricken's objection (in *Aristoteles und die moderne Tugendethik*, 397) to M. Stocker—that the opposition between "doing something for friendship's sake" and "doing something because of duty" has simply been misconstrued—is not a valid objection, and misses Stocker's point. Ricken holds that if someone visits someone out of friendship, that he has recognized this as his duty ("Smith has the duty to visit his friend, because he is his friend"); consequently the opposition between reason for acting and motivation would disappear. That would make sense under Aristotelian assumptions, whereby in each case what is according to duty is the virtuously good and right. But this is not the case with Kant or in general with what Stocker calls "modern ethical theories": Smith does not have the duty to visit his friend *because he is his friend*. The good of friendship is not permitted to be both reason and motive; "duty" alone—as distinguished from the motivation of friendship—allows the visit to become a moral action. On this theme, and the comparison of Aristotle and Kant, cf. R. Audi, "Acting from Virtue," *Mind* 104 (1995): 449ff.

153. *Religion within the Limits of Reason Alone*, trans. Greene and Hudson, 42.

154. Ibid., 43.

are rather merely hypothetical imperatives, that is, imperatives that have the form of "if-then" conditional sentences and are concerned with what is useful for realizing our wishes and intentions, and particularly the goal of happiness. If someone visits a friend out of an inclination to friendship, this would occur, in case he follows a hypothetical imperative, because he is choosing to visit a friend as a means to the end of satisfying his own desire for happiness. This is the classical argument against eudaimonism, also propounded by Max Scheler and the "ethics of values" he originated.[155] But it misses the classical position as represented by Aristotle: when someone visits a friend out of an inclination to friendship, he does this simply because he recognizes this as "good" and his will has the habit of benevolence, so that he wants a good for his friend that is appropriate in this context: a visit. (The "hypothetical" context that lies at the basis of this action would be something like this: he visits his friend, in order to visit him; "visiting him" is the "good for the sake of which" the action is being accomplished; and the action *is* the visiting.) In other words, he loves his friend, and because he wishes him well, it makes him happy to visit him. What he strives for is to "wish well," and the satisfaction of that striving is happiness, and causes joy.

But where is the "duty" here? It appears to have vanished, but perhaps it is still present. But it shows itself as "pure duty" only to the degree that what is reasonable separates from the inclination. Or it can be the case that our man has some urgent, rival obligation to take care of (conflict of duty), and he is in a "divided" state of mind. Finally, however, the judgment wins out that "my friend simply needs a visit; I cannot leave him in the lurch, and the other matter can wait, even if it means further difficulties will arise, etc. This means: 'It is my duty to visit him.'" Reason intercedes, and if our fellow obeys it, he does it from the *habitus* of friendship, out of benevolence toward his friend and not just to be happy or because he promises to get greater satisfaction from that course of action. The reverse is also possible: the visit should be postponed because of some other serious obligation, and this can be explained to the friend by way of a phone call, so that the visit may have to take place in less convenient circumstances, which might still better express the value of the friendship. Friends normally understand each other in such situations and judge the motives of the other rightly and with a good will. Of course there is not a question here of the "collision" of various virtues. On the contrary: conflicts of duties are resolved though virtues in such a way, that in most cases, possible contradictions between colliding duties are removed

155. Cf. Max Scheler, *Formalism in Ethics and Non-formal Ethics of Values* [1916], trans. M. S. Springs and R. L. Funk (Evanston, Ill.: Northwestern University Press, 1973), esp. part II, chap. 5: 239–369, where cf. esp. 345: "All practical eudaemonism has its roots in the wretchedness of man."

(a certain amount of "tragic residue" can never be completely eliminated). In any case, if we look upon virtues from the perspective of duties or of abstract moral obligations, without taking into account their narrative and contextual character, one can arrive at the strange notion that virtues can conflict with one another. If someone speaks about the collision of various *virtues*, he has lost sight of one of the essential aspects of what virtue really is.

A virtue ethics can establish that the judgment "p is my duty" is nothing other than the judgment of reason that "p is truly *good*." The mechanism of the Kantian categorical imperative is instead an auxiliary technique for providing a criterion for the determination of what is good to the practical reason, once such reason has been distilled out of the context of all (hedonistically interpreted) affective inclinations. So if I can think of, or will, the maxim, "one should visit sick friends" as a universal law, then I am also "duty-bound" to follow it. In doing this, the last thing I would think of would be wishing my sick friend well.

Now the doctrine of the categorical imperative is by no means the last word of Kantian ethics, which, as mentioned before, is essentially a maxim-ethics. The categorical imperative is a method of examination for determining the moral compatibility of our subjective maxims (for Kant, these are the hypothetical imperatives related to our intentions and wishes). To the extent that the categorical imperative is connected to such maxims and clarifies them as reconcilable with a universal legislating, it not only has the function of a (formal) condition of the possibility of morality, but also that of a (material) determination of *what* in each case is the right thing to do. In this respect it can compete with the utilitarian calculus of the "weighing of goods," although not with the best results. This explains why many Kantians are also utilitarians and why Kant himself sometimes takes refuge in utilitarian arguments.[156]

d) The Theonomous Justification of Moral Obligation: God and the Eternal Law

In the context of a virtue ethics, as sketched out so far here, the phenomenon of obligation is not something that "has to be added." The reason that grasps the good is itself the basis for anything that obligates or "binds." Conscious-

---

156. This is seen, e.g., in the "political organization of a nation of devils" mentioned above (IV.4.b) or in his essay entitled: "On a Supposed Right to Lie Because of Philanthropic Concerns" (available in English as a "Supplement" to I. Kant, *Grounding for the Metaphysics of Morals*, trans. J. W. Ellington [Indianapolis, Ind., and Cambridge, Mass: Hackett, 1981], 63–67). Generally speaking, the universalizing criterion of the categorical imperative has a great affinity with certain forms of the rule-utilitarian calculus. Cf. also, e.g., O. Höffe, *Sittlich-politische Diskurse*, 52ff. For similar reasons, G. Patzig, *Ethik ohne Metaphysik* (Göttingen: Vandenhoeck, 1971), 60, holds that the categorical imperative needs to be completed through the utilitarian evaluation of consequences.

ness of duty is nothing other than the grasp of the intelligibility of the good. Thomas, for whom every "law" is essentially an ordering of reason, traces the binding character of law back to the reason: "law" is a rule of action that binds the one who acts. The rule and measure of human action is the reason, whose task is to set in order to the goal, and the good.[157] The acting subject is bound by what the reason discerns as good in its judgment of action; this judgment of reason concerning the good actually possesses, as Thomas says, a "compelling power" *(vis coactiva)*.[158] This can be explained by the fact that practical reason is reason embedded in striving or appetition: what reason recognizes as good is that to which the striving power necessarily directs itself. Obligation is nothing other than the willing of what is recognized as good through the reason. Duty is inclination in accordance with reason, as articulated in the formula "p is good," "p is to be done" (which can in its turn be further shaped through a judgment of conscience). Thus the highest form of consciousness-of-duty is that of the virtuous person, who will act as little in fact as possible from duty, and mostly from enjoyment in the good.[159] This is why Thomas can write as follows: "[t]he reason, which is the principle in moral matters, has the same status within man with regard to things that concern him, as a prince or judge has within the state."[160]

Nevertheless, Kant still needs the postulate of God's existence for the ultimate intelligibility of moral obligation, since God is the one who will in fact bestow happiness or blessedness [*Glückseligkeit*] on a human being who has proven himself worthy of such blessedness through moral actions. "We ourselves make" the idea of God, "for the purpose of serving as the incentive in our conduct": "to have religion is a duty of the human being to himself."[161] But what happens to God in a virtue ethics? Does He become superfluous?

In fact, God is much less necessary here than in Kantian ethics.[162] Virtue ethics never needs to ascertain moral obligation by recourse to God. In the methodical development of a virtue ethics, God only appears after moral obligation has been successfully established through a theory of the good. Of course, the experience of moral obligation through rational insight into the good leads to questions concerning the ground of this phenomenon. The question about the origin of moral obligation appears here in exactly the same way as

---

157. Cf. I-II, Q. 90, a. 1.

158. *De Veritate*, Q. 17, a. 3, ad 2.

159. A thorough reconstruction of the classical "symbiosis" of duty and virtue can be found in G. Abbà, *Felicità, vita buona e virtù.*

160. I-II, Q. 104, a. 1, ad 3: "ratio, quae est principium moralium, se habet in homine respectu eorum quae ad ipsum pertinent, sicut princeps vel iudex in civitate."

161. I. Kant, *Metaphysics of Morals,* trans. M. Gregor, 193.

162. Cf. also the earlier discussion at I.4 above.

the question about God generally appears both in ordinary human experience and in metaphysics: the question, What is the *source* of that which exists? For the phenomena of "morality," of "moral experience," of "conscience," of "moral obligation" all in fact *exist*. Consequently, we ask ourselves, *Why* do they exist? *Where* do they come from?

The answer to this question actually sheds new light on the nature of human reason and the moral obligation that springs from it.

> It is important to emphasize the difference between this concept and another one, according to which what is "natural" is recognized by reason (as a natural order and natural teleologies), and then this in turn as "created by God" and only *from this* is then derived the moral obligation to follow this order. The obligating character of the judgments of practical reason would then only arise as a consequence of knowing that such judgments bring to expression an order created by God, which is then recognized as normative. This is exactly the position—ascribable to F. Suárez (1548–1617)—that became dominant in Neo-scholasticism. But according to the position developed here, the process works in a different way: at the beginning there is the imperative-ordering act of the practical reason toward the good; this already includes *as reason* the element of "moral obligation." And only *afterward* is this ordering, when seen in its "obligatory character," referred to God as to its origin.[163]

The question about origins leads to God. It has always led to God. There has never been a philosopher who maintained the opposite: the only thing that is maintained is that such "leading" is a *deception*. Kant is the last person who would deny the inevitability of such an inference. His view is that the reason *can really do nothing else* but rise to the idea of God as the origin of everything that is. But Kant also says that this natural disposition of the reason unfortunately leads to a mere "dialectical appearance," toward which we are oriented, to be sure, as the regulative idea for natural knowledge and as the motive force for our practical conduct, but which we are not permitted to treat as certain knowledge. Because we need God for morality, Kant says, we must postulate Him: He must be "made by us."

---

163. F. Bormann, *Natur als Horizont sittlicher Praxis*, 199f., maintains that my position is that recourse to God as legislator is necessary for the establishment of the "binding power" of practical knowing. Bormann reached this mistaken impression of my position through an erroneous reading of my earlier book, *Natur als Grundlage der Moral* (= *Natural Law and Practical Reason*), esp. on p. 70 (= 64–65), which he read without reference to 63–69 (= 58–64). Bormann likewise seems to have overlooked my discussion in *Praktische Vernunft und Vernünftigkeit der Praxis*, 531ff., as well as the argument of the present work, which appeared earlier in Italian. In one case, strangely enough, my arguments have been read in a totally opposite way, as the demand for an "ethics without God"; cf. F. Di Blasi, *Dio e la legge naturale. Una rilettura di Tommaso d'Aquino* (Pisa: ETS, 1999), 83ff. (also available in English translation as *God and the Natural Law* [South Bend, Ind.: St. Augustine's Press, 2006]). These two diametrically opposed readings might suggest that I in fact hold a middle position between them.

Now the existence of God, here, is not being denied; Kant is precisely for-
mulating, rather, the peculiar manner in which we can be sure of His existence. We cannot know God's existence, we can only postulate it and believe
it. What remains, then, is the certainty of a "rational belief." No philosopher
has tried until now to *prove* that God doesn't exist. They have only said that
He either cannot be known or that what we know as God is not "God" but
only ourselves. The most significant step in this direction was probably taken
by Fichte: "The moral order is itself God: we do not need any other God and
cannot comprehend any other God. There is no basis in reason to depart from
that moral world-order, and by some logical process move from conclusions
to principles and arrive at some special entity, to be understood as the cause
of it." To those who still attempt it, Fichte replies, "You have not been thinking about God, as you would like to think, but only yourselves, magnified in
thought."[164] With this we have essentially already reached Feuerbach, for
whom the knowledge of God is nothing other than a (confused) knowledge of
human nature. Marx does not even discuss the question, and only disposes of
it by requiring that one must first put oneself at the standpoint of "atheistic
socialism."[165] And Sartre maintains that "even if God existed that would make
no difference from the point of view [of existentialist philosophy]," since, in
order to maintain human freedom, one must disregard God anyway.[166]

Whoever maintains, then, that knowledge of *what is* leads to questioning
about the *origin* of what is, namely, to questions about God, only maintains
what everybody really acknowledges anyway, even if their acknowledgment
only amounts to a rejection of the answer as deception, mere appearance, or
simply irrelevant. But whoever does in fact maintain that God's existence is
knowable has a different understanding of the human capacity to know, or
about the attractiveness of the truth of God's existence. But this discussion
is not part of ethics. What stands beyond any doubt is that the experience of
moral obligation and of a "moral order" leads to a question about its origin,
and that means it leads to the question about God as the origin of this order of
the practical good.

This is why Thomas Aquinas developed his doctrine of the natural law as
the "participation of the eternal law in the rational creature."[167] This presupposes, again, a creation metaphysics: it is the most developed form of answer

164. J.G. Fichte, "Über den Grund unseres Glaubens an eine göttliche Weltregierung," *Werke*,
5.186, 187.

165. Cf. K. Marx, *Pariser Manuskripte von 1844*, in Karl Marx, *Die Frühschriften*, ed. S. Landshut
(Stuttgart: 1968), 246–48.

166. J.-P. Sartre, "Existentialism and Humanism," in *Basic Writings*, ed. S. Priest, trans. P. Mairet, 46.

167. Cf. I-II, Q. 91, a. 2.

to the question about the origin. According to the Thomistic doctrine, the reason that "by nature" orders us to the good is nothing other than participation in the divine reason, through which all creatures are ordered to their end. This is also how the natural law is a part of divine providence. Indeed, through the rational knowledge of the good, man takes part in an active/cognitive way in God's *providentia* [Lat. *pro* + *videre*, "fore-seeing"].[168] As a personal act of the human being, this human "fore-seeing" *belongs to* the providence of God.[169]

Man participates in the eternal law in a twofold manner: passively, in his natural inclinations; active-cognitively, by his reason. The natural inclinations are, to be sure, a participation in the "eternal law," but they are not yet "natural law," which is the ordering of reason for good action, or the moral order. "Natural law," rather, is the ordering of reason established *within* these inclinations, through which alone natural inclinations can be ordered to the moral "ought"—as "human goods." It is not the "natural" in the natural inclinations that are the natural moral law, but the principles of the practical reason, formulated with respect to these inclinations. Once the natural law is understood as participation in the eternal law, these principles can themselves be understood as the manifestation of the divine will to man, so that a "recognition of all duties as divine commands"[170] is possible. But in order for moral obligation to become a practical "incentive" [*Triebfeder,* in Kant's usage], religious reinforcement is not at all necessary in Thomas's view. The "incentive" here is just the (practical) insight into the good. This is, in any case, nothing other than participation in the practical reason of God, that is to say, in the "eternal law." Thomas also loves to cite in this connection verse six of Psalm 4: *Multi dicunt, Quis ostendit nobis bona?* ("Many say, who shows us good things?"), to which the answer is, *Signatum est super nos lumen vultus tui, Domine* ("The light of thy countenance, O Lord, is signed upon us"), and Thomas provides his interpretation: "this means, the light of the natural reason, by which we distinguish what is good from what is bad—and that is the function of the natural law—is nothing other than the seal of the divine light upon us."[171]

> Every law requires a promulgation, and so does the natural law. It is constituted in the fact that God grants the human mind the ability "'to know it naturally.'"[172] On the basis of this "light of the reason that has been given us by

168. Cf. also *De Veritate*, Q. 5.
169. *Summa contra Gentiles* III, c. 112.
170. I. Kant, *Critique of Practical Reason*, trans. M. Gregor, 108.
171. I-II, Q. 91, a. 2. (The text of the Psalm passage is that of the Vulgate Psalter used by Thomas, cited here in the Douay-Rheims translation.)
172. I-II, Q. 90, a. 4, ad 1.

God," one can say that "God speaks within us."[173] For just this reason, Thomas does *not* call the natural law a *lex divina* or a "divine law": the divine law is that which God reveals *in addition,* through which He speaks to man by way of positive legislation.

In this perspective of having recourse to the origin, it can make sense to characterize the order of practical principles as natural *law.* But one should likewise grant that the reverse is possible, and perhaps even more plausible: namely, that speaking of "eternal law" and of "divine laws" itself originates from a (very understandable) anthropomorphism. What this means is that an authentic and original human experience of human-positive legislation lies at the basis of such expressions, and it is in the context of this experience that both moral obligation and the ordering toward the good can be interpreted as corresponding to the divine wisdom. In any event, whether we speak of "law" or "moral order," "practical principles," or "human nature," what is always meant is what alone can meaningfully lie at the basis of such words: the ordering of moral virtue, which is an ordering of the reason toward the good for man and thereby also "concerns above all the ordering to happiness."[174] This is why Thomas can also say that we only offend God when we act against our own well-being.[175]

But the reference, so understood, of our morality to its origin in God is able to give us—apart from revelation—no further conclusions about what we are to do here and now: about what is "good," and what makes for our well-being. For we know the "will of God"—insofar as revelation is not at issue—only through our rational knowledge of that which is "good." This is precisely the point of the insight that the human being actually *shares* in divine providence through his participation in the eternal law. This means that human foresight is really itself an active, cooperative component of divine *providentia.*

The doctrine of the natural law as participation in the eternal law is a philosophical, creation-metaphysical *reductio* ["leading-back"] of the givenness of a materially specified rational ordering toward the good. Consequently it is not possible to understand "theonomy" as the permission granted to man to enter into the obligation to "design creative norms" (theonomous autonomy). Philosophically we can only speak of God as the origin of that which is. But the

---

173. *De Veritate,* Q. 11, a. 1, ad 13.

174. I-II, Q. 90, a. 2. This is how the problem mentioned by A. MacIntyre in the postscript of his book *After Virtue* (2nd ed. [1986], 278) should really be solved. His reference there to H. Jaffa's *Thomism and Aristotelianism* (Chicago: University of Chicago Press, 1952) must be considered unfortunate, because Jaffa's very influential misinterpretation of Thomistic moral justification arises from an ignorance and superficiality that McIntyre himself overcame in his sequel, *Whose Justice? Which Rationality?* (1988).

175. *Summa contra Gentiles,* III, cap. 122.

theoreticians of "creative reason" and "theonomous autonomy" are making a statement *about* this created reality *from the viewpoint of God*, even though this concept of God already presupposes a knowledge of this (created) reality as being that is to be referred back to its origin, and is a concept that was originally derived from such knowledge. The whole idea stands revealed as circular argument, as an illegitimate mixture of philosophical and theological methods.[176]

Understanding the theonomy of moral obligation provides the judgment of conscience with a further source of motivation. What is recognized as good can in addition be commanded by way of the conscience as something that corresponds to "the will of God." Of course, this has nothing to do with "legalism." For there is always presupposed an insight into the goodness of what is understood, for just this reason, as being the will of God. In terms of motivation, this viewpoint that makes its presence known in the conscience can then become the stimulus for doing the good for which one would, in certain circumstances, feel no natural inclination whatsoever to do. In any case, in every act of theonomous motivation there is present an element of the acknowledgment of God, which lends to the act which is thus motivated the characteristic of being an act of religion.

In his retrieval of the original concept of Thomistic natural law in the encyclical *Libertas praestantissimum,* Leo XIII rightly underlined the double character of human reason as being both autonomous in its function of distinguishing good from evil and dependent (for having such authority proper to law) on its origin in God's eternal law. So Leo XIII famously wrote that the natural law "is written and engraved in the heart of each and every man, since it is none other than human reason itself which commands us to do good and counsels us not to sin." Then, he adds: "But this prescription of human reason could not have the force of law unless it were the voice and the interpreter of some higher reason to which our spirit and our freedom must be subject." The question which arises from this text is whether human reason—in order to have the authority of an effective, morally commanding, and binding force—requires an explicit recognition by the acting subject of its divine origin in each of its prescriptive acts. On the basis of what has been expounded so far this cannot be the case because practical reason has precisely the function of *prescriptively ordering* man's acts to the good and making him avoid evil. But this is precisely the function of a law. Leo states explicitly that it is properly the "prescription

---

176. So F. Böckle, *Fundamentalmoral* (Munich: Kösel, 1977); K.-W. Merks, *Theologische Grundlegung der sittlichen Autonomie. Strukturmomente eines "autonomen" Normbegründverständnisses in lex-Traktat der Summa Theologiae des Thomas von Aquin* (Düsseldorf: Patmos, 1978). On the criticism of the concept of "theonomous autonomy," as used by German revisionist moral theologians (namely F. Böckle), cf. also M. Rhonheimer, *Natural Law and Practical Reason,* 195–256. I suggest there that a more suitable category could be "participated autonomy," which as the mediation of theonomy is also a "participated theonomy."

of human reason" that has "the force of law." So, this force cannot come from concomitantly and explicitly recognizing the ordering acts of reason as being grounded in a kind of divine command. And yet the question can still be asked whether it is possible for reason to have this property of law, which commands and requires obedience, from itself alone. Precisely the existence of this question is the reason why the experience of the presence of a moral law in us (and the subsequent "voice of conscience") has always been considered to be *a path to* acknowledging the existence of God. If the prescriptive role of reason already *presupposed* in each of its acts the explicit recognition of its origin in a higher reason (which is the eternal law existing in God's mind), then moral experience could not be also a *way to* God (because it would already presuppose the knowledge of His existence). So, what Leo XIII asserts cannot be that the effective authority of human reason's prescriptive role needs an explicit and concomitant recognition of its being the voice of divine authority, but only that the morally binding force of human reason as a law to which we properly owe obedience can be ultimately (i.e., metaphysically) *explained* only by recognizing it as the voice of another, higher authority, which is God. This shows that morality is ultimately grounded in God, without therefore losing its cognitively autonomous grounding in the ordering acts of human reason. The reference to eternal law is, thus, not "practical" in the sense of being required for reason to accomplish its task of ordering man's acts to the good; the reference to eternal law springs, rather, from the metaphysical grounding of reason's preceptive role in its ultimate cause. As such, and applying this metaphysical knowledge as habitually possessed in a human person's moral knowledge, the recognition of the theonomous grounding of reason's authority can then, as was said above, develop a supplementary motivational function.

At this point the question arises: Is morality or moral behavior possible without God? Can the "atheist" be just as moral as one who recognizes the existence of God? The first question, of course, is just what is an atheist? And to what extent do there really exist atheists who are convinced of the nonexistence of God? But that question does not need to be addressed here. The following remarks may suffice: the structure of rationality that leads to knowledge of the practical principles and their translation into concrete action, as well as the consciousness of moral obligation on the basis of rational insight into the good, and with that, the possibility of moral virtue: all this cannot depend on knowledge of God's existence. To this extent, then, there is also an "atheistic morality," that is, to the extent that knowledge of the existence of God is not necessary for it. But the atheist must necessarily be convinced that man himself—or, what would be even more doubtful, some other kind of this-worldly reality—would be the highest thing that exists. This would not be a practical principle, but only an assumption about reality that is not irrelevant or inconsequential for human action, that is to say, for the realization of practical principles in action. If "the human race" is proclaimed to be the highest entity (as it was by Marx and Feuerbach), this would have consequences for the area of human affairs that concerns the virtue of justice: the well-being of the individual is subordinated to the well-being of the race. Or alternatively if—which appears to be less dangerous at first sight—the subjectivity of the individual or the autonomy of the will becomes the highest good, then this would no less effectively distort the reality of human behavior, in a different way. The result would be the understanding of rationality itself as a threat to the autonomy of the subject, and thereby lack of interest in "truth," the "lack of interest in the way things are according to their essence"—identified as the fundamental principle of the culture of the Enlightenment.[177]

Aristotle said long ago that the human being is not the best thing there is in the universe. Consequently, practical knowledge, which has to do with human things, is also not the highest form of knowing. *Wisdom* is higher than that.[178] Love of wisdom as love of the truth can only be assured where the human being is not recognized as the highest entity. For this is where the principle of justice itself is endangered, through the natural propensity of the human being to favor his own good, and ultimately the "autonomy of subjectivity" over the good of the "other," or to put reason itself at risk through seeking after autonomy of the will. What is problematic is not the autonomy of the *reason,* but the autonomy of the *will.* It was already influential at the epistemological level in the *cogito* of Descartes and was elevated by Kant to a principle of ethics. Autonomy of the reason leads to the recognition of God as supportive ground; autonomy of the will already contains within itself the germ of the denial of God, as a disturbance.

3. Moral Norms

a) Formulating Principles as Norms

"Norms" are standards or measures, according to which something *ought* to be done or not done, and they lay claim to validity, an expectation of compliance. Norms are concerned in each case with a class of actions, a kind of action: they are universals by nature.[179] *Moral* norms are standards relating to the accomplishment of human actions, according to which accomplishable types of ac-

---

177. Cf. H. Lübbe, "Philosophie als Aufklärung," in H. Lübbe, *Praxis der Philosophie, Praktische Philosophie, Geschichtstheorie* (Stuttgart: Reclam, 1978), 5–34.

178. *EN* VI, 21*ff.*

179. It seems inappropriate to understand requests, orders, permissions, and empowerments as being norms as well—that is, all linguistic formulations in which expressions such as "must," "ought," "may," "right," "good" and "bad" occur; cf. N. Hoerster's article, "Norm," in H. Seiffert and G. Radnitzky, eds., *Handlexikon zur Wissenschaftstheorie* (Munich: Ehrenwirth, 1989), 231.

tions are identified as "good" or "bad," as morally right or wrong. In a certain sense, practical reason is itself a norm, because it is a measure. And practical principles are equally such. But when we are speaking about moral norms we are nevertheless placing ourselves within the point of view of the observer: we are looking at human actions from "outside" as it were. This means that a discussion about moral norms is really a discussion *about* the making of moral norms—or "norming" [Ger. *Normierung*]—for human actions by way of practical principles, a perspective that is not identical with the perspective of "norming" the morality of an action in the perspective of actually carrying it out.

> We should recall that the practical principles that we identify as the *lex naturalis* are true *principles* of praxis (cf. V.1.c). Practical principles are cognitive principles of movement—since praxis is a kind of movement—which are not only inward, but actually constitute this subject as an acting subject. That is, without practical principles we wouldn't act at all. Practical principles in this sense form a component of the "organism" of the practical reason. "Norms," by contrast, arise from discourse *about* practical reason. Norms of action or moral norms, consequently, are not really principles of praxis, but only principles of discourse about action, principles of judgment concerning the governing of praxis. In this sense they are *principles of ethics*. As principles of the normative discourse about praxis they then become practical principles themselves, once recognized by the practical reason as norms and habitually possessed in the form of moral knowledge.

The concept of the "norm" was originally taken from the terminology of ancient architecture [Lat. *norma*, "plumbline," "T-square"], and was introduced into legal language by Cicero.[180] The word took up definitive residence within the realm of ethics thanks to the Enlightenment preference for juristic concepts. The word is here to stay in ethical philosophical discourse, and at any rate the problem is not in the word but in the interpretation of the concept. Discourse about *moral* norms takes its point of departure on the level we characterize as "moral knowledge": the level of reflection upon action. The "normative proposition" belongs to this level, and that means propositions in the mode of "ought." Such propositions, we have already explained, always have a linguistic structure. They are the reflective-linguistic formulations of principles.

Consequently the norm has a dual nature: rooted in practical principles, it reflects them, and gives them linguistic expression. With norms we can speak about human actions from a "third-person" perspective. Even though moral norms are a linguistic phenomenon, they possess a natural transparency both to the practical principle that lies at their foundation and to the virtues that

---

180. Cf. the article on "Norm," in the *Historisches Wörterbuch der Philosophie* (Basel: Schwabe, 1984), vol. 6, col. 906ff.

correspond to that principle—they are an expression of "the good for man"— and only on the basis of this transparency can the norms themselves be understood and interpreted. This is because moral norms and practical principles are not fundamentally different: what differs is the point of view from which the same structure of reason is being considered.

Moral norms as an expression of "the truly good for man" formulate the "rules of the game" for success in human life; they are also the linguistic medium through which human beings make sense of these rules. This is true, despite the fact that social, historical, cultural, and even individual contexts— the current ethos—also opens up the possibility for a certain plurality of concrete norm making.[181]

> It is quite possible that, in various cognitive contexts—each one being culturally mediated and provided with a corresponding ethos—the identical practical principles can lead to different socially recognized norms of behavior. A typical example would be certain norms that govern the respect and love that children have for their parents, that can lead to practices that would appear shocking to us.[182] In fact, the morality of specific ethnicities and groups can provide examples of how identical moral principles such as the golden rule, the prohibition of murder, formation of solidarity between generations, respect for property, and the like can find an expression at the level of the concrete ethos that vary and in part contradict each other. This is not to equate morality with culturally conditioned relativism, as if, for instance, the Indian caste system could embody the principle of justice no less than a society of Western type based on freedom and equality.[183] Differing forms of *ethos* in no way have to be valued equally, or considered as if they were all to the same degree in accordance with human dignity, and in this sense as equally true in their praxis. Likewise it is not necessary to maintain that they are all equally suited for realizing moral principles that are in themselves identical, since an *ethos* often realizes certain moral principles at the cost of others.[184] Various cultures or configurations of *ethos* in their variety as such demonstrate, rather, the universality and astounding transcultural invariance of moral principles, which is expressed in a concrete way in each *ethos*.

181. On this theme, cf. also W. Kluxen, *Ethik des Ethos* (see above, note 69).

182. Cf. the interesting chapter on "Cultural Relativism" in H. Arkes, *First Things: An Inquiry into the First Principles of Morals and Justice* (Princeton, N.J.: Princeton University Press, 1986), esp. 148ff.

183. This is the view of M. Walzer, *Spheres of Justice: A Defence of Pluralism and Equality* (Oxford: Oxford University Press, 1983), 313–15. M. C. Nussbaum also argues against the relativizing of ethical standards as occurs, for instance, in communitarianism and contemporary "virtue ethics"; see "Non-Relative Virtues: An Aristotelian Approach," in P. French, T. Wehling, and H. Wettstein, eds., *Ethical Theory: Character and Virtue,* Midwest Studies in Philosophy 13 (South Bend, Ind.: University of Notre Dame Press, 1988), 32–53, and also in a slightly expanded form in M. Nussbaum and A. Sen, *The Quality of Life* (Oxford: Clarendon Press, 1993).

184. In Muslim countries, the practice of polygamy originally had the function of providing a form

b) Legal Norms, Rules of Behavior, and Moral Norms

The logic that characterizes human action and practical reason is logic of the recognition of principles and of virtues with their intentional structure, articulated through principles. "Normative formulations" can have a different meaning, depending on whether they are the linguistic expression of the order of moral virtue, or whether they are the positive-law rules of rational behavior. The latter are familiar to us as traffic laws, tax laws, codes of behavior, rules of procedure, the criminal code, examination rules, and so on. In general, one can say that the expansion of the modern state and bureaucracy has molded the concept of "norm" into "legal regulation," in terms of which we are inclined to interpret the phenomenon of moral norm as well, and thereby miss the meaning of this other reality and distort it.[185]

What is the logic of a regulation of positive law? Let's take the case of a norm of justice in the area of tax regulation: the rightness or appropriateness of an action falling under this norm is measured on the basis of its agreement with the norm and the purpose (distributive justice), for the sake of which the norm was established. This means that the norm itself here *constitutes* or *establishes* the justice or reasonableness of certain actions to be carried out in accordance with justice. In this sense the norm "makes a norm for," or "norms" [*normiert*] actions. This is most clearly seen in traffic regulations: what is right and reasonable is action that corresponds to the norm or the regulation, and is so *because* and to the extent that it thus corresponds to the norm. And this is the case because the norm itself is justified by a certain purpose or utility. If the norm did not exist, there would be no universally valid standard for the corresponding rightness of the action.

It can happen, however, that a concrete action, falling under a norm by being subsumed under that norm, contradicts the very purpose for which the norm was established. In this case *epikeia* is needed, that is, one makes an "exception" by acting against the rule literally, in order to reach the purpose

---

of solidarity to isolated individuals, especially women who were widowed as a result of war. The polygamous family is thus a very significant social welfare system. But this is achieved at the cost of other moral principles relating to the community formed by married couples, and not least the principle of the equality of man and woman (as an example, one need only think of resulting institutionalized dependence of women on men).

185. Such a distortion is also present in the concept of moral norm as a certain form of social norm, which in turn is understood as a sanctioned social claim; this is approximately what Tugendhat maintains, in "Drei Vorlesungen über Probleme der Ethik," in Tugendhat, *Problem der Ethik*, 57ff. In criticism of Tugendhat, Ursula Wolf has attempted to bring back the point of view of the good life, in the tradition of "Enlightenment morality"; cf. U. Wolf, *Das Probleme des moralischen Sollens* (Berlin: de Gruyter, 1984). Cf. also Tugendhat's "Retraktationen," in *Probleme der Ethik*, 132ff. On Tugendhat from a discourse-ethical or "cognitive" perspective, see J. Habermas, "Diskursethik—Notizen zu einem Begründungsprogramm," in Habermas, *Moralbewusstsein und kommunikatives Handeln*, 78ff.

and the meaning of the rule.[186] The application of the rule, in other words, is suspended for reasons of being faithful to its purpose, and exactly the purpose for which the norm was set up in the first place, so that the norm is fulfilled not to the letter but in spirit.

This is the logic of legal norms and codes of conduct. It should not be forgotten that many positive-law norms formulate immediately moral norms, and this just because of a public interest in their maintenance. But there are ethical theories that apply the above-described logic of positive-law norms or rules in a fundamental way to the phenomenon of the moral norm—for example, so-called rule utilitarianism.[187] In utilitarian theories, moral norms in principle only have the function of placing a certain action under a rule, because behavior according to rule is considered to be the behavior that on the whole leads to the best results. Norms are not looked at here as an expression of the good, but as right or wrong, rational or irrational, according to whether the outcome of following the norm is desirable or not. For utilitarians who are consistent, the action of "saying 'thank you'" is not an act of retributive justice, but a means to encourage people to do good in the future, and the appropriate norm for this would have to do with making sure this purpose is accomplished. By utilitarian logic, it is wrong to sacrifice innocent persons to appease an angry mob not because it would be an act of injustice in itself, but because it would undermine the ability of the penal system to function—and only for that reason.[188] Norm-utiliarianism provides a fundamentally inadequate interpretation of the phenomenon of the moral norm.

Modern utilitarianism, as founded by J. Bentham, also originates from an interest in an efficient legislation for the social order. A fundamental norm-utilitarianism is represented by the position of Thomas Hobbes, which has become so decisive for the modern philosophy of society. The distinction between "just" and "unjust" is only based on normative differences in positive laws, that is, only to the extent that there is a coercive power to legislate.[189] Actions

---

186. Cf. II-II, Q. 120, a. 1.

187. For a typical example, cf. R. Brandt, "Einige Vorzüge einer bestimmtten Form von Regelutilitarismus," in O. Höffe, ed., *Einführung in die utilitaristische Ethik. Klassische und zeitgenössische Texte* (Munich: Beck, 1975), 133–62. Also cf. J. Rawls, "Two Concepts of Rules," *Philosophical Review* 64 (1955): 3–32, reprinted as chap. 2 in Rawls, *Collected Papers*, ed. Samuel Freeman (Cambridge, Mass.: Harvard University Press, 1999), 20–46. Both authors have since significantly changed their positions, but that makes no difference to the present context.

188. Cf. B. Schüller, *Die Begründung sittlicher Urteile*, 290ff. For criticism of the position, cf. M. Rhonheimer, *Natural Law and Practical Reason*, 396–97; also, "Menschliches Handeln und seine Moralität. Zur Begründung sittlicher Normen," in M. Rhonheimer, A. Laun, T. Goritschewa, and W. Mixa, *Ethos und Menschenbild. Zur Überwindung der Krise der Moral* (St. Ottilien: EOS Verlag, 1989), 76ff. There are also rule-utilitarians like J. J. C. Smart who are quite ready to justify judicial murder; cf. his article, "An Outline of a System of Utilitarian Ethics," in J. J. C. Smart and B. Williams, *Utilitarianism For and Against* (Cambridge: Cambridge University Press, 1973), 3–74, esp. 69ff.

189. Cf. T. Hobbes, *Leviathan*, chap. 15.

are judged just or unjust according to their agreement with the legal norm. But the legal norm in turn is only legitimized through its efficiency in guaranteeing peace. The real heart of Hobbes's theory is a working out of the logic of the normativity of positive legislation, and the governmental monopoly of power needed for it. At the same time, however, Hobbes also (and mistakenly), subordinated the logic of all moral normativity in the sphere of justice to this.[190]

Ethicists who understand moral normativity according to the model of legal normativity are either extreme legalists and conventionalists, or—going to the other extreme—they treat moral norms merely as "artifacts,"[191] as a kind of exonerative institution or device,[192] as rules of thumb that can be completely overruled. The opposite position, on this basis of understanding norms, is then branded as legalism—whereby a legalistic understanding of norms is more often to be met with on the side of such revisionist "antilegalism."[193] Of course, according to these thinkers norms are not simply arbitrary: for they emphasize that human action is subject to natural and social conditioning and factual constraints, in the midst of which the arbitrariness of human action is to be rationally governed by norms (in any case no further norms can be formulated to limit the arbitrariness involved in changing such constraints). But this rationality is nevertheless such that it treats norms as *constitutive rules* for rationality or for the moral rectitude of actions. Norms are rational here only because and to the extent that we attain something good with them. And morality—as the following of such rules or norms—then possesses no other purpose but to reach this goal. "Moral conduct" here must itself once again be justified as useful.

But moral norms and their rationality are really not constitutive rules at all. The constitutive rule for the rectitude of human actions is rather practical reason, insofar as it—primarily "by nature"—reveals what is good for the human being and what are the corresponding types of intentional action. Moral norms are then merely subsequent linguistic formulations of the principles of practical reason, that is, the order of moral virtue, which is an order and structure of rationality, which in turn is related to types of intentional action and continually brings human identity to expression.

So, then, moral norms, as distinct from legal norms, lay claim to satisfaction because they express how a certain kind of behavior belongs to a virtue or is opposed to a virtue—and thereby opposed to human nature. When we "follow" a moral norm, we do not follow a purposeful rule; instead, we carry out

190. On this cf. M. Rhonheimer, "'Auctoritas non veritas facit legem': Thomas Hobbes, Carl Schmitt and die Idee des Verfassungstaates," *Archiv für Rechts- und Sozialphilosophie* 86 (2000): 484–98.

191. The term comes from W. Korff, *Norm und Sittlichkeit* (see note 41 above), 9.

192. Thus F. Furger, *Einführung in die Moraltheologie* (Darmstadt: Wissenschaftlich Buchgesellschaft, 1988), 97ff.

193. E.g., W. Korff, *Wie kann der Mensch glücken? Perspektiven der Ethik* (Munich: Piper, 1985), 13f.

the act of a virtue, that is, we *intend* and *choose* a particular aspect of what is good for man, of what is appropriate for myself or others, of what is just, and the like. The expression "to follow a norm" is only a way of speaking about this: in reality, we do not speak about norms, we only speak in a normative way about virtues; in reality (if we are fairly typical human beings), we do not follow rules or norms, but choose and carry out good or bad actions.

> When someone finds a wallet on the street—filled with money, say—and returns it to the owner or takes it to the "lost and found," he does this, not in order to follow the rule, "one should return lost valuables to their owners or bring them to the lost and found," but rather to return property to its owner, or help to get it back to its owner. Even when the finder is tempted to pocket the contents of the wallet and his conscience reminds him of the rule, "you should return a person's property when you find it or take it to the lost and found," even then he will not follow this rule for the purpose of following the rule ("for reasons x, . . . y, . . ."), but rather, in order to do what is expressed by the rule as being "good" and "right." A rule-utilitarian, by contrast, must do what the rule commands with the intention of fulfilling the rule because he is convinced that the rule brings to expression the fact that through its being carried out, certain desirable consequences can be effected, which in fact establish why the rule is valid and also a moral norm. Therefore one follows the rule with the intention of following the rule, and this in turn is done with the further intention of bringing about the consequences that result from the rule's being followed (following the rule is thus the means for reaching that for which the rule was really set up in the first place). That this kind of practical consideration does not correspond very closely to our normal moral intuitions, is not evidence against the description of rule-utilitarianism offered here, but points, rather, to the fact that rule-utilitarianism is not capable of an adequate reconstruction of our moral intuitions and "common sense."[194]

Likewise, when it comes to "obeying moral norms," rule-based behavior (behavior that agrees with the norm) is not capable of establishing the goodness or rightness of an action; "good" or "right" can rightly be attributed only to the accomplishment (or nonaccomplishment) of those single actions that come under the norm, and concerning whose goodness or badness the norm only makes a statement. A moral norm thus *contains* the practical good (the carrying out of the acts of the single virtues or the omission of actions that are opposed to them); a moral norm is not a rule that ascertains that a certain rule-based behavior is right because (by experience or anticipation) certain desir-

---

194. This is true, as already pointed out, despite the fact that there really are rules that are established and obeyed just for their desirable consequences (e.g., traffic regulations, rules of procedure, etc.). But these are not moral norms, even though the following of such rules can be subsumed under a moral norm (i.e., not to follow the rules of traffic or procedure is unjust, irresponsible, unfair, lazy, etc).

able conditions, states of affairs, or events would be thereby brought about.

For this reason also, there cannot be a phenomenon here of *epikeia* or the "exception."[195] "One should honor contracts," as a moral norm, is the expression of an act of justice. We do not mean to say that honoring contracts is right because following the norm "one should honor contracts" is useful—for the reason, say, that only in this way could the practice of "contract making" exist as a social institution (why such practice is desirable at all would then have to be established)—what we mean, rather, is that the honoring of contracts is right just because it is an act of *justice*. It could be objected that the rule-utilitarian justification described above is really a justification for *why* keeping a contract *is* an act of justice at all, as opposed to a justification for why someone should *do* a just action, such as honoring a contract; the objection then goes on to say that it goes without saying that someone should do a just action; the distinction is therefore irrelevant. Now, before we can answer this objection (in the following section), we must make the following clear: the idea that one should be faithful to contracts can be formulated as a norm of justice because keeping a contract is an *act* of justice; this means that the justice of an action of honoring a contract lies *in the action itself*, and not in following the rule under which the act is subsumed. For there can be cases in which it is not an act of justice to honor a contract (or a promise). But this cannot be interpreted as an exception to the norm: the norm itself is only related to acts of justice, so that an "exception" would mean not being just, as an exception. If it is ever in accordance with justice *not* to honor a contract or a promise, this cannot be because following the norm does not correspond to the purpose of the norm, but rather because the action in question does not fall under this norm. To subsume it under the norm here would simply be to call something what it is not: a wrong correlation of word to thing.

Overlooking this fundamental difference between practical principles (the teleological structure of the virtues) and the formulation of moral norms as speech *about* these principles (and the virtues that correspond to them) is what causes apparent problems and difficulties to arise, as, for example, the so-called conflict of duties, which then leads to a kind of "borderline-case ethics." This is the dominant tendency not to look at ethics as a doctrine about the good and happy life, but as a theory for solving and deciding "moral problems," "perplexities," "puzzling cases" and so on.[196] So-called conflicts of du-

195. The opposite view is maintained by G. Virt, *Epikie—verantwortlicher Umgang mit Normen. Eine historisch-systematische Untersuchung zu Aristoteles, Thomas von Aquin und Suarez* (Mainz: Matthias Grünewald Verlag, 1983). Of course, Virt's position presupposes a thorough-going norm-ethical approach to ethics.

196. A just and stimulating criticism of this can be found (along with some dissatisfying sugges-

ties are often, if not always, merely a result of the way we *speak* about our duties.[197] This must be investigated more closely.

c) The Description of Norms and Actions: Norm Utilitarianism and Virtue Ethics

The distinctions I have developed in the foregoing section may at first have the appearance of oversubtle refinements. In fact, what I have just presented reflects two alternative conceptions of human action and morality. These alternatives can be described as follows.

1) The first is that of *norm ethics*, or a utilitarian understanding of norms (in the sense of rule utilitarianism). According to this idea, norms (as rules) are correlated to certain "externally" describable actions. These actions are identified (a) on the basis of a certain structure of events (e.g., linguistic expressions, bodily movements), that is to say, on the basis of the events and states of affairs that are *present in* the accomplishment of the actions; and (b) on the basis of certain conditions *resulting from* the accomplishment of such actions. The moral "rightness" of the single actions described in this way is determined by their being subsumed under a rule, whereby it can be ascertained that the accomplishment of the action in question leads directly, on condition that it preserves the rule, to the optimal balance of good and bad consequences as a whole. In this sense, the rule constitutes a moral norm.

This means that it is only the *norm*—under which *single* actions are subsumed—that lends these actions their moral identity as morally "right" and rational ways of acting. Thus a "promise" is a certain form of linguistic expression, by means of which the speaker of the promise puts the other person into a state of certainty that what has been said by the one who promises will in fact be done (a description of action). In relation to the carrying out of this action, then, a norm can be formulated: "One should keep promises," and this, of course, is because it seems very good on the whole for human society that people be certain that their fellow human beings always do what they promise. "One should keep promises," then, is a rational norm according to this conception, because keeping to it would have salutary effects for the practice of "promise making." The rightness of *single* acts of "keeping promises" (as an act of justice) would be grounded here only by the norm (and its useful-

tions) in E. L. Pincoffs, *Quandaries and Virtues: Against Reductivism in Ethics* (Lawrence: University Press of Kansas, 1986), esp. chap. 2: "Quandary Ethics."

197. Cf. the article entitled "Pflichtenkollision" by M. Forschner in O. Höffe, ed., *Lexikon der Ethik*, 3rd ed. (Munich: Beck, 1986), 192–93. Collisions of duties are here presented as "conflicts of norms," and this leads automatically to the understanding of classical virtue ethics as a system of the "hierarchical ranking of goods and duties."

ness: there would be no reason to consider a *single* act of "keeping a promise" as being good or just "in itself," i.e., as an act of justice and benevolence toward an actual person). But *if* it should be the case that the evil consequences of keeping a promise would be foreseen to predominate, then it would be just as right *not* to keep to the norm (since keeping it would no longer have any purpose). This means that it would then be right to make an exception to the norm. There are, to be sure, rule utilitarians who treat such exceptions as illegitimate in principle, because they think that the consequences of keeping to a rule without any exceptions are better on the whole, even if keeping the rule in a particular case might lead to undesirable consequences. In this way, rule utilitarianism leads to an extreme "conventionalism" which has been named (by Smart, for instance) as "rule-fetishism." Such extreme rule utilitarians represent the view that norms are *established* in a utilitarian way, but that the concrete choices of actions by agents, by contrast, actually must *not* be utilitarian: what is required is rather to *follow* the useful norm.

The peculiarity of norm ethics, then, consists in the fact that it correlates norms to actions that can be described in their physical process of accomplishment, in their purely natural event structure, *but not to actions in their moral-intentional identity.* It is rather the norms themselves that constitute this identity; in the case of an exception to the norm, the corresponding consequentialist judgment of action (calculation of consequences, and usually a "weighing of goods") is what provides the identity. But norms here are only grounded consequentially. And this is why a norm can suffer an exception, when the consequences of following it in a concrete case turn out to be bad. Therefore, in principle, every kind of action can be morally justified on the basis of circumstances, even those that are regularly excluded through a norm. This conception, in other words, rests upon the transfer of the logic of positive-law norm making into the area of the norm making of moral actions, and it is suited to the same model of actions we have encountered earlier (III.3.c): a model that splits actions into an observable event component and an intentional component.

In this respect, the picture sketched here of an understanding of the objective identity of actions does not differ essentially from what was commonly held in earlier Neoscholasticism. In the once widely known handbook of D. Prümmer,[198] for example, we find the following statement: the action "killing a man" consists of two components: first, of its *esse physicum* ("includit et vires physicas, quae causaverunt occisionem, et ipsum effectum physicum occisio-

---

198. D.M.Prümmer, *Manuale Theologiae Moralis secundum principia S.Thomae Aquinatis* (1915), 15th ed. (Freiburg im Breisgau: Herder, 1961), I, no. 99: "De natura et divisione moralitatis," p. 67f.

nis," a physical event, distinct bodily movements, and their fatal effect); and second, of its *esse morale*, which is the characteristic through which the action (i.e., the complete physical event together with its effect) is either good in the moral sense (permitted) or bad (not permitted). This latter characteristic, according to Prümmer, arises from a *transcendentalis relatio humani actus ad normam moralitatis* ["transcendental relationship of the human act to the moral norm"]. What is peculiar, significant, and decisive here is that the *human act* is described as something carried out exclusively on the "physical" plane; the relation to the plane of morality is merely added by the action theory as a relationship to a norm, and appears to have nothing to do with the act as such. The morality of the action—as constituted in the relationship to the *norma moralitatis*—remains fully external to the action itself. The morality is only constituted *through* the norm (and it is quite understandable that the concept of the "moral law" as norm comes into the foreground, and ultimately as well the concept of God as Lawgiver, and in such a way that all morality and normativity sink into nothingness apart from that conceptual anchorage). Prümmer asserts that all authorities are agreed on this, and that disunity reigns only over the question in what precisely this *norma moralitatis* consists. Today's "teleological ethics" or consequentialism is essentially a kind of further position taken in this old discussion. It differs from its predecessors in its use of a utilitarian concept of norm, which, it could be argued, works more efficiently in the framework of a norm ethics.

2) The other alternative is the concept of an ethics of *virtue* or *principles* ("principles" being understood as the goals of the virtues). According to this idea, norms, as explained, are simply formulations of the *objective* moral rightness or wrongness, of the rationality or irrationality of ways of acting. This means that they are related not to the physical process or event structure of carried-out actions, but rather to *intentional basic actions* (see III.2.a). With this, the actions to which norms relate must be described as intentional actions. *Moral norms are normative statements about intentional actions*, that is to say, expressions in the mode of the "ought" ("one ought/ought not to do 'p'"; "one ought never do 'p'"; which can in turn be formulated as "'p' is good/ bad," "'p' is always bad," or "'p' is intrinsically bad," etc.). And this means also: *only those actions for which an intentional description is possible, on the basis of which the norm would be formulated, could also fall under the appropriate norm;* in other words, only in this case is the norm also an adequate normative expression regarding this action. But if a concrete action falls under a norm, then its objective-intentional identity cannot be changed through any further circumstances or consequences. The norm, in other words, *is valid.*

For example: we have just described a promise as "a distinct form of linguistic utterance, by means of which the speaker places someone else into a condition of being certain that what was contained in the spoken utterance of the former will in fact be done." But "I promise you that I will kill you to-morrow," is a statement that would cause a certain expectation on the part of the person addressed; but all the same it is not a promise but a threat, or a communication of someone's intention. On the other hand, "I will arrive by train in the morning" also "puts someone into a condition of . . .," but this is only a communication. "Placing someone else into a condition of being certain that . . ." is consequently not at all the description of a promise, but only the description of the cause of a (psychic) state of affairs through a speech act. In any case one could also say, "You can depend on it, that I will. . . ." The causation of this state of affairs can be subject to a great variety of intentional descriptions; that is, very different things can be *meant* by it.

> In the terminology of the modern theory of speech acts as developed by J. L. Austin and J. R. Searle—the theory shows how in speaking we not only make utterances about states of affairs, but also *do* something—there is a distinction between the propositional content of a speech act (e.g., the fact that I will arrive by train tomorrow) and its "illocutionary" role, which does not consist in what was just said, but in what is done with what is said, for example, an act of warning or promise. "This dog bites" can be a warning or (in the case of someone trying to sell the dog to a customer) an item of information that promises something (because the customer wants to buy a good watchdog). But the sentence can be either a simple statement about a state of affairs or it can convey an expectation. Using the expression discussed above, completely different things can be meant by saying "You can count on it, that . . . ," and that means that there are various illocutionary roles for such a sentence.

"You can depend on it, that tomorrow I will arrive on the train at nine," *could* be a promise, but it could also be a threat. What is decisive is, what does it mean to say "*I promise you,* I will arrive on the train tomorrow at nine"? It means to put the other person *in a very definite way* "into the condition of being certain that . . . ," namely, by providing him with a *claim,* or a *right,* to it. The "certainty" here is based on the expectation that the speaker will correspond to justice within an assumable context. That alone is the intentional identity of the action "to promise something," and the norm that "one should keep promises" is related to it.

If person A promises person B that he will do x, the intentional "why" of this action consists in establishing a *relationship of justice* between A and B with respect to A's performance of x. Keeping the promise "to do x" is thus an act of justice. No person A can give a person B a right to "count on" A doing an act of injustice. This is because no person can have a *right* to another person's doing something unjust.

Consequently, a promise to accomplish knowingly an unjust action is already an unjust action and is by that very fact opposed to the virtue of justice. The not keeping of such a promise—if, for example, the person sees his mistake—is consequently the omission of an act of injustice, that is, an act of the virtue of justice. This is why it is also not unjust *not* to keep such a promise.

In case someone *mistakenly* promises to do something unjust and realizes it in time, the person realizes in effect that he had *not* done what he really wanted to do, which was to perform a just action in relation to another person. But to keep the promise despite this realization would naturally be an act of injustice, to which the other person can lay no claim; depending on the circumstances, at most he would have a claim to compensation for some losses.

In neither of these cases is the not keeping of a promise an exception from the norm, nor does it do any damage to the institution of "promise keeping." On the contrary, it strengthens it.

But it is different when what is promised only becomes an injustice afterward, through a change of circumstances. If I promise my friend to return a hunting rifle to him tomorrow, but he in the meantime has lost his wits so that giving him the rifle would very likely lead to a blood bath, the return of the rifle would amount to assisting in the commission of murder. In this case, it is as if two norms are at issue: "one should return borrowed things," and "one should keep promises." Both are norms of justice: their intentional identity consists in giving the other what is due (his right). But the return of the rifle would no longer be an act of justice: it falls outside of this intentional identity, so to speak. But not returning it does not collide with either of the norms because both are concerned with acts of justice, and here not returning the rifle is really rather an act of justice (properly speaking, of course, it is an act of prudence, which precisely excludes any violation of justice).

> One could object here that what is "just" is simply arrived at by the foreseeing of consequences. That is not incorrect, but still the objection does not have force. The injustice of returning the gun is founded on *one* consequence and not on (all) the anticipated consequences. This one consequence gives the act its objective-intentional identity, that is to say, it removes the rightful claim of the other. It shows that the action of returning the rifle is an action of "putting a weapon in the hands of a potential murderer," as if the weapon did not belong to him at all. Paying attention to a consequence here does not amount to a calculation of consequences, but only to a judgment about whether the person in question still has a right to the return of his gun. Of course, this assumes a nonconsequentialist understanding of the norm "one should return borrowed things."[199]

199. On this see also M. González, "*Depositus gladius non debet restitui furioso:* Precepts, Synderesis, and Virtues in Saint Thomas Aquinas," *The Thomist,* 63, no. 2 (1999): 217–40.

The two examples presented above are of course unproblematic, and one could arrive in practice at the same result by using norm-utilitarian argumentation (because it would presumably treat the same consequence as the *only* decisive one). The difference only becomes really clear in the question whether there exist kinds of actions which despite evil consequences are to be *avoided in all circumstances*. In a norm-utilitarian way, indeed, one could never establish that one could *in principle, never* condemn an innocent person, independently of any other considerations. This is because that approach to ethics does not ask whether such an action is bad in itself, but only whether the consequences are better for keeping or for not keeping the norm "one should not condemn innocents." But when someone nevertheless arrives at the conclusion (e.g., Bruno Schüller) that one should not condemn an innocent because to do so would endanger the stability of the institution of "criminal law," then the argument against the condemnation of an innocent person, here, is not the fact that the kind of action is unjust in itself, but rather that the calculus is alone decisive, which reveals the best overall balance of consequences. But what happens, when it is not *expected* to be so, or when a kind of criminal law practice is instituted that is resistant to such dangers?[200]

According to a virtue ethics, on the other hand, one can establish that the removal of another's possession is not theft (i.e., not an injustice), if the "remover" is in a situation of extreme emergency about his survival and has no other possibility of a way out (stealing for hunger), and this is because in such a case no one has a *right* to his possession. Objective-intentionally, it is not a question of a theft, but only an act of survival.[201] Seen from the point of view of the owner, it would be simply unjust to insist on property rights, which would be seen not to exist to the degree that they collide with the sheer survival of the "thief."[202] A norm-utilitarian ethics, on the other hand, would fundamentally (on the level of the physical carrying out of actions and events, i.e., nonintentionally) describe theft as "taking away what belongs to another," and must maintain that theft-for-hunger is only an exception from the norm "one must not steal" because the consequences of keeping the norm are, on the whole, worse than not keeping it (this illustrates a weighing of goods in a conflict of duties or norms). The outcome is doubtless the same, but the sec-

200. Cf. H. G. McCloskey, "A Note on Utilitarian Punishment," *Mind* 72 (1963): 599.
201. Cf. II-II, Q. 66, a. 7.
202. In the fact that the word 'thief' must still be used (even if in quotation marks), can be seen the limitations of our speech—its frequent inability to provide accurate accounts of moral phenomena. This leads to our eagerness to use words like 'exceptions' when talking about moral phenomena. On closer inspection the 'exception' quality lies only on the level of language. Thus we would imply that such a 'theft' would 'in this concrete case' or 'exceptionally' not be a theft at all. Unfortunately, no less misuse is made of this phenomenon of linguistic insufficiency by moral theologians when they maintain that there cannot be any exceptionless moral norms.

ond way of arguing is problematic in structure and leads one to defend the position that stealing can be justified in general, provided that the consequences of the stealing are on the whole better than the consequences of respecting ownership (i.e., that concrete choices of actions would always imply a weighing of goods; that norms also come into being through such a process, i.e., they formulate a "weighing" that *as a rule* is correct; and only in the case of a collision would a new weighing need to be made). In this way, even norms that were permanent and valid for all circumstances finally only remain tautological formulations of the kind "one should never unjustly—that is, without a justified reason—steal, kill, make a false statement . . . etc."

Of course: there are many decisions that we have to make on the basis of a weighing of consequences, and perhaps most of them. This is especially true for decisions made in a larger social context (i.e., social, economic, academic, and public research contexts). But the possibilities of action that correspond to these are *limited* for moral reasons, namely, on the condition that they harmonize on the level of the concrete action with the fundamental "rectitude of appetition" (cf. also below, 4.f and g). Here, accordingly, there are negative responsibilities, which we are accustomed to formulate as so-called *absolute prohibitions*. Weighing of goods and calculation of consequences are simply excluded here.

d) Absolute Prohibitions: Murder and Lying

Norm-utilitarian ethics and virtue ethics are founded, as explained above, on two profoundly different understandings of the nature of human and moral action. We will return to this below (cf. V.4.c and f). In the context of founding norms for action, however, this distinction is often not visible, because—despite their different argumentative structures—frequently the result may be the same. It was already mentioned in passing that there are cases where the difference comes out clearly: namely, in the case of the absolute prohibitions, or negative norms that are valid without exception.

> In terms of the logic of action, negative norms have different characteristics from norms that command to do something positively. For example, let two norms be considered that are basically identical, but depending on whether they are positively or negatively formulated, reveal the difference in the logic of normification: "One should always speak the truth!" does not mean that omitting the action "speaking the truth" is already a violation of the norm; the norm only says that *if* you say something, it should correspond to the truth. But you could also just not say anything. The norm does not prescribe carrying out always and under any circumstances the action that it commands; one could

also simply not do it. Positively formulated normification, therefore is not "absolute," that is, it is not applicable to all cases. As a universal positive, it is still not capable of norming action in a conclusive way. But a negatively formulated norm, or prohibition, such as "you should not lie" (i.e., "One should never say something that is not the truth") gives an absolute norm. To not do what this norm prescribes, that is, to *not* omit the prohibited action (i.e., lying)—which is to perform the action that it prohibits—is in every case to violate the norm. Thus the universal negative can conclusively normify praxis in its situation-bound particularity, that is to say, it has exceptionless validity.

By an absolute prohibition of action, then, we understand more exactly a norm that states that a concrete way of acting, describable as an intentional action—that is, a definite type of intentional basic-action—is always (under all circumstances) to be avoided, which can also be formulated in the expression that all such actions are "evil *in themselves.*" Another name in common use for these is "intrinsically evil" *(intrinsece malum).* This rather ambiguous terminology has the disadvantage that "intrinsically evil" ("evil from the inside") stands in contrast to "extrinsically evil" ("evil from the outside"). Looked at in this way, the concept of the "intrinsically evil" would be identical with the evil of an action that is bad not because it is prohibited, but prohibited because it is bad. In this sense, however, every *morally* evil action would also be *intrinsically* evil, that is, evil on the basis of its own immoral essence, and not—like "driving on the left side of the road" or "eating meat on Fridays"—evil because of the respective civil or ecclesiastical rules. If the expression "intrinsically evil actions" were understood in this way, it would be of little help in ethical analysis and in fact superfluous.

A more meaningful use of the term "actions evil in themselves" would be to use it to characterize an action that we call bad *independently of any additional factors or intentions.* This would be distinguished from an action such as (to use a classical instance) almsgiving, which is good ("in itself," in this sense) but which, when it is practiced only for the sake of making a good appearance, becomes bad through that additional factor. In this sense, one would say that to kill an innocent person is an action that is bad "in itself," *independently* of any further or additional intentions, even praise-worthy ones.

It would be misleading to think that the expression "intrinsically evil action" meant that the action was evil "in itself" in the sense of being evil "independently of the will of the doer." This is because "intrinsic evil" does not define an area of objectivity completely independent of the subject, an objectivity, that is, which would be set opposite to a subjective willing or intending (in the sense, say, of the Neoscholastic distinction between the *finis operantis* and the *finis operis,* or "purpose of the actor" and "purpose of the action"). A human act cannot even be described without the intention of the will as formed through the reason. To talk about the "intrinsic evil of an action" means that the action is already bad on the level of its basic intentionality, *independently* of any further intentions added to that.

But why is this so important? It is important because it means that it is possible to describe at least *some* actions or ways of acting definitively, in such a way that they cannot be redefined or redescribed through further intentions. In such cases, then, the object of action is, as it were, resistant to further, added-on purposes or evaluation of consequences and the expectations related to those consequences. This corresponds to the Common Sense-Intuition described by G. Patzig, "that we operate over large areas in life in full harmony with utilitarian doctrine. We consider what probably would result from a certain way of acting, and if it seems dissatisfying or threatening, we consider such a way of behaving as immoral. . . . *Nevertheless, we are convinced that certain actions are morally bad even without considering any of their consequences.*"[203] But we can make sense of this only when we accept that there are choices of actions that remain resistant to any redefining and a corresponding redescription of their moral identity through *further,* added, praiseworthy intentions, or through the foreseeing of certain undesirable consequences.

In his detailing of some of the "vices of virtue ethics," Robert Louden also points out the inability of virtue ethics "to identify certain types of action" that are absolutely prohibited, that is, virtue ethics cannot establish prohibitions that "mark off clear boundaries in such areas as the taking of innocent life, sexual relations, and the administration of justice according to local laws and customs." Here we must think of actions "which produce harms of such magnitude that they destroy the bonds of community and render (at least temporarily) the achievement of moral goods impossible." It is not a question here simply of "bad" actions, but of "intolerable" ones.[204] It may be the case that certain forms of today's virtue ethics cannot establish absolute prohibitions, since they attempt to determine the rectitude of actions in a one-sided way, from the perspective of the motivation structure of the agent, and not on the basis of the characterization of the action itself. But this is not the case in classical virtue ethics. Aristotle speaks explicitly of actions that are evil in themselves, independent of circumstances.[205] In response to Louden's point

---

203. G. Patzig, *Ethik ohne Metaphysik* (see above, note 155), 60 (italics not in the original).

204. R. B. Louden, "On Some Vices of Virtue Ethics," *American Philosophical Quarterly* 21 (1984): 227–36; also available in R. Crisp and M. Slote, eds., *Virtue Ethics* (Oxford: Oxford University Press, 1997), 201–16, here, 207–8.

205. *EN* II, 6 (1107a 9–18). The passage has already been cited more fully above (at IV.2.b).

it must be said (cf. also IV.2.b above) that a virtue ethics in the classical tradition *is* capable of establishing the existence of such absolute prohibitions,
while a norm or rule-utilitarian ethics can at best succeed only in the sense
of founding a *prima facie* validity of such prohibitions. For moral norms are
verbally formulated universals: they are related to types of actions, to classes
of actions with the same characteristics. In an ethics built upon the phenomenon of the "norm," a prohibitive norm must be related, just as all norms are,
merely to *typical* cases. Circumstances and consequences that are not covered
in the formulation of the norm can subsequently relativize the absoluteness
of a prohibition when it comes to discourse on the application of the norm.[206]
For a prohibition of action to be really "absolute" and resistant to any relativ-
ization in its application, such a prohibition or universally prohibiting norm
must be conceived as related to moral principles which in turn refer back to
"what is rational by nature"; that is to say, they are to be understood as an expression of a contradiction or incompatibility with the goals of certain virtues
which in each case define a specific "ethical context," and not, as in a norm-
ethics, simply as in contradiction to a class of actions as defined by certain
characteristics.[207] Incompatibility of a concrete way of acting with the moral
principles expressed in the teleological structure of a virtue, and thereby, with
a specific ethical context, establishes that the way of acting in question is not
only *prima facie* to be avoided but in all cases, because any "subsequent"
points of view, circumstances, or evaluation of consequences cannot change
this intentional incompatibility with the goal of one or more virtues. The only
thing that can change through "subsequently" added points of view is not the
validity of the prohibition, but only what the changed situation requires doing
in place of the action to be avoided.

Now there are two possibilities of speaking of actions that are always to be
avoided (actions that are "*intrinsically* or *per se* evil"):

1) "Always to be avoided" is the choice and accomplishment of an action
that is objectively bad, that is, unjust. To choose an *objectively* bad action
implies, indeed, an intentional relationship to what is opposed to the goal of
a certain virtue: for example, overlooking what is another's right or what is
owed to him. This is why one must always return what has been borrowed,
insofar as the "return" of the thing is objectively an act of justice. But it will be
just on the basis of the contingency, or changeableness, of the matter of ac-

206. Cf. J. Habermas, "Richtigkeit versus Wahrheit. Zum Sinn der Sollgeltung moralischer Urteile und Normen," in Habermas, *Wahrheit und Rechtfertigung*, 281f.
207. For the concept of the "ethical context," cf. my earlier treatment in *Natural Law and Practical Reason*, 475ff.

tions only in most cases, and not always. Norms of this kind are an adequate normative expression about an action only *ut in pluribus* ("for the most part"). This means: the *physical* action of "returning borrowed property" does not always, or in all cases, or under all circumstances possess the *intentional* identity of an act of justice (to give someone his own, what pertains to him, his right), and consequently does not fall under the (intentional) description of a way of acting on the basis of which the norm "return what is borrowed" was formulated. Something analogous holds for theft and the keeping of promises and contracts.

> This "failure" of a norm in individual cases results from the imperfection of the normative *formulation,* as explained in the preceding section. In a norm an externally performed action must also be formulated, but this formulation cannot forsee that on the basis of a circumstance, this concrete externally performed action could contain an intentional identity different from the one that underlies the formulation of the norm, since the latter has to do with an *intentional* action (cf. below, 4.d).

2) "Always bad" or "intrinsically evil" can mean that a concretely describable way of acting *keeps* its intentional identity under all circumstances: that a norm can be formulated with respect to it not only "for the most part" *(ut in pluribus),* but in *every* conceivable case, because the performance of the action that pertains to it *can* never fall under another intentional description as the consequence of some circumstance. Such norms in the area of justice, for example, are "not killing" and "not lying." These norms belong to the ones we can call prohibitions in the absolute sense. At the same time, this label does not prevent us from considering murder, carrying out the death penalty, killing in war or the "murder of tyrants" as other types (or "species") of intentional actions, because their *genus moris,* their moral identity, is different in each case. Consequently they fall under *different* norms.

This certainly deserves to be further explained. We can begin with an analysis of the intentional and therefore objective identity of the action "to kill a man (x)." "To kill x" means the same thing as "take the life from x." There is physical action that corresponds to this (or it could be the permitting of something to happen that one could have willingly prevented, but chose not to). But the physical act or the event alone does not make the action "killing x." Otherwise, one would have to say that an earthquake or a pistol "kills x" in *exactly the same way.* An earthquake can cause the death of x, but one could not say that this cause is identical with the human action "killing x."

The intentional act "killing x" (which is something neither a pistol nor an earthquake can do) implies at least a willing *(intentio)* that is directed against the life of the victim, of his physical existence or presence within human society.[208] Seen in this way, "killing x" would mean:

1) according to the first alternative, to "get x out of the way," that is, to consider his existence an evil. And this evil might either be considered in itself, that is, the ultimate intention of the killing action is simply that x "not be around anymore" (that would be rare); or as the means for some other goal: in order to obtain some advantage (e.g., an inheritance); in order to marry the dead person's spouse; in order to protect one's own life; in order to save other persons (e.g., in a crisis situation). In all these cases, the choice of the action involves a judgment that "p is good," whereby "p" stands for "causing the (physical and social) nonexistence of x." Whether at the level of means or ends, there is always implied here a judgment on the nondesirability of the existence of a particular human life, such that this life is contingent on the decision of the will following upon that judgment.

Assuming we hold the recognition of another as my equal to be the foundation of all justice, that the other has a right to life that is exactly equal to the right to life that I have, then it is clear that the intentional act of killing x is an act of fundamental injustice; in some circumstances, it can be an explicit act of nonrecognition of the other as equal to myself, insofar, namely, as I not only *undervalue* his right to life, but do not even *grant* him one to begin with (e.g., in the case of abortion). In any case, for x, "life" is "what is good for x" in the most fundamental sense. Intentionally, the action is immediately directed against that which we owe to others in the most basic way; the acting person obtains an advantage through this violation of justice at another's expense (the action is "unfair") and the action of killing is likewise an attack on society, which is in fact constituted upon the mutual recognition of equal rights. At the same time, it represents a threat to those who are living. The prohibition of murder is therefore defined relatively to the ethical context of "justice." It is not the destruction of a certain good (the good of life)—a good which, even though of the highest value, would nevertheless still not be a moral but only a physical good—but the removal of the recognition of the other as my equal, and thus fundamentally an injustice. Murder is bad because it is someone relating, in a fundamentally unjust way, toward a

---

208. The position of J. Fuchs and R. A. McCormick and others that I criticized in my above-mentioned article, "Intentional Actions and the Meaning of Object: A Reply to Richard McCormick," neglects the fact that "killing" as an act performed by a human being—it is no mere event—cannot be described without such a basic intentionality. Otherwise, we would understand "action" as only the "willing causation of events" (here, a "death-event"), whereby in fact, only the *purpose* for the sake of which the event was caused would be morally qualified; the act of "killing" as such would remain below this threshold.

concrete living human person through the willing destruction of that person's life. What is violated here is not "the good of life" but a claim, "rational by nature," that is founded in the natural inclination to self-preservation, that is to say, the right of a human person, and thus that person as such. *The moral evil of murder lies in its injustice.* It does not lie in the physical destruction of a human life, but in the unjust relationship between one human being and the life of another human being. And conversely: insofar as killing is unjust in this fundamental way we have described, so is it not only a physical evil but a moral evil as well.

> This argument does not work for the case of active euthanasia carried out at the request of x. The intentional identity of such an action of "killing x" is rather assistance in self-killing, or rather, co-perpetration of murder. The action gets its identity in this case from the action "suicide." This is itself an act of "injustice" against oneself, even though one can only say that in a metaphorical sense. Quite apart from creation-metaphysical arguments (life as a "gift of God") in this way the suicide eliminates himself as a moral subject. If there is no life after death, this action would have no consequence at all for the subject, since he no longer exists. Otherwise it can be established that suicide as a morally (immanent) action, the irreparable moral self-destruction of a human acting subject *that will continue to exist,* the total alienation from oneself. This is also expressed when a suicide fails and the perpetrator survives his own attempted murder. Assistance or co-perpetration of suicide is consequently a serious injustice. The only just thing to do is to attempt to keep a person from this action.

2) A second kind of "killing x" would be to do it as an act of passion. Here the will is not primarily directed against the life of another, since the action is the result of emotions. Precisely to the extent that the emotion is willed emotion, the case can be referred to the first kind: the action would then be unjust, but in the sense of not originating *in* injustice, but in emotion. If the free will is completely shut off through passion, there is no humanly accountable action.

3) A third kind of killing can be considered, as retribution or *punishment.*[209] In general, punishment is an act of compensation: "through punishment the balance of justice is restored."[210] Punishments are enacted in various realms by parents, teachers, supervisors, and finally by civil government. When there is no punishment for misdeeds, we spontaneously perceive the injustice. Someone who performs an injustice gets a personal advantage at the cost of others. Punishment has the purpose of restoring and preserving

209. On what follows here, see also the discussion by J. M. Finnis, *Fundamentals of Ethics,* 127ff. Cf. also Agnes Heller, *Beyond Justice* (Oxford: Blackwell, 1987), 156 ff.

210. II-II, Q. 108, a. 4. On the Thomistic theory of punishment, see also J. Finnis, *Aquinas: Moral, Political and Legal Theory* (Oxford: Oxford University Press, 1998), 210ff.

justice: where someone can get away with doing unjust acts, the basis of human community life, based on justice, is destroyed.

"To punish" means to apply some evil to someone who has done an injustice, against that person's will, which compensates ("retributes") the advantage that was willingly but unfairly gained, thereby restoring justice. Punishment is not directed toward the injury of the guilty person (that would be revenge, not punishment) but toward the restoration of damaged justice. A punishment always presupposes blame: one can only be punished for what one is responsible for; otherwise there would be no reason to restore damaged justice, because a (factual) injustice without blame, or a danger based on the mere existence of a person, is not any compromise of justice.

An act of punishment is intentionally related to the "restoration of justice." It is *objectively* an action of justice. It does not damage the right of another, but only takes away the advantage that he acquired at others' expense. It restores what the guilty person willingly took away from the balance of justice. But additionally punishments are also carried out for a certain specific purpose: for example, to improve the guilty person, to protect others, or to defend the integrity of the social order. Yet, this presupposes that the act in question is already justified as an act of punishment (restoration of the balance of justice).

If someone who has committed a grave injustice is able to escape from justice but then suffers some injury through a mishap or natural accident, it would not be considered "restoration of justice." The human instinct for justice does not require the injury or some evil for the sinner (to intend that would not be intentionally an act of justice). What is required is the punishment, that is, a *judgment to punish* on the part of the specific person responsible for the preservation of justice (hence mercy and amnesty in appropriate circumstances are felt as just). An indication that this is true is that—in the above-mentioned case—men are inclined to interpret injury by accident or natural causes as "God's just punishment." This interpretation is fully permissible in the light of the concept of divine providence, and it also keeps human beings from the temptation to rejoice over the *injuries* of others. What we alone licitly rejoice in is the restoration of justice.

It is very important to distinguish the real *object* of the act of punishment from the *goal* that it may have in addition. A punishment that really "accomplishes" nothing other than retribution, we would not consider *meaningful;* nevertheless, it could be a *just* punishment (as in the case of *Michael Kohlhaas,* the hero of Heinrich von Kleist's famous novella, who—after having suffered grave injustice by being deprived of his horse and thereby of the possibility of earning a living—because of his excessive sense of justice, seeks justice on his own and tragically becomes a seditious person and a murderer; after a tribunal has recognized the initial injustice and restored his horse, the rehabilitated Kohlhaas is condemned to capital punishment and executed).

Punishments always have a purpose: in any event the restoration of justice is such a purpose. It is meant for the preservation of just relations between human beings. Other purposes are always subordinate or ordered to this: rehabilitation, deterrence, defense, security. It depends on whether the punished person is *culpable* and that he is punished *to the extent that* he is such, that is, that he possesses a will that is directed against the rights of others equal to him, and consequently injures the community of subjects who are related to him as equals with mutual recognition of rights. Only in this way can the further goals of rehabilitation or security be justified. But consequently any further purpose of punishment is itself never the *sufficient* reason for punishing, or the only reason why the act of punishment is an act of justice. This would be a utilitarian theory of punishment, according to which punishment is in essence a means for bringing about an optimal state of affairs in society. Using this argument, one could in principle grant the possibility of "punishing" even an innocent person, if doing so would promise a better outcome for the society as a whole or for all concerned parties. Since ethicists who argue in a utilitarian fashion think in this way, they hold the position that the traditional norm "one may never kill an innocent person" simply rests upon a weighing of goods: a culprit is simply anyone whose existence or life poses a threat to the common good *in any way whatsoever.*[211] But this is not the case: the traditional norm intends that a blameworthy person is someone who is culpable for a threat to the common good, that is, bears culpability for it because he has done harm to justice.

It is also revealing to note that an injustice that injures the "common good" can only be punished by an authority or person who has the competence for taking care of this public well-being. Punishments such as monetary fines, restriction of travel, removal of citizen privileges, expulsion, prison, exile, or the death penalty can only be acts of the society as a whole, or legitimate public authority (just as the imposition of taxes under the threat of punishment is an act of distributive justice; as an act of a private persons, this would be extortion and theft). The death penalty means exclusion from the social order by eliminating the physical existence of a person. As an act of retribution (restoration and preservation of justice) this can only be carried out by those who have the corresponding competence to do so. But this is true of all punish-

211. Cf. R. A. McCormick, *Notes on Moral Theology 1965 through 1980* (Washington, D.C.: The Catholic University Press of America, 1981), 453. For the contrary position, see J. Finnis, *Fundamentals of Ethics,* 127ff.

ment: retribution without competence is unjust. Parents do not permit their children to punish each other, nor are such actions acceptable between fellow students, employees of a firm, or soldiers. Competence to punish (which is competence for restoring justice) presupposes responsibility for the whole, in relation to which the justice must be restored (in the case of the abdication of authority, communities form an *ad hoc* authority by themselves).

Whoever acts, then, with relation to the whole, acts in a different ethical context than someone who acts as a private person. An act of retribution without competence *cannot be* a restoration of justice. When someone "punishes" an injustice as a private person, he only compensates injustice with injustice. He does not *intend* the restoration of justice, but only the *evil* of the other as retribution for the evil that the other had first given him (vengeance). Of course, he can do this because he believes that justice must be restored. But because he has no competence to do it, the *objective* content of the intentional basic action "killing x" cannot be an act of justice (the classical description of this is found in Kleist's *Michael Kohlhaas* who tries to do precisely this: restore justice by himself, illicitly).

Therefore, since a private person—that is, a person who is simply a member of that community in relation to which justice is to be restored—cannot in principle "punish" at all, such a person is likewise (and *a fortiori*) incapable of "punishing" with the death penalty. Consequently, there is no conceivable case where "killing x" would be a justified action for a private person. It is unjust always and under any circumstances.

But it does not follow from this that the death penalty *has* to exist—that is, that its actual exercise is justified always—or under any circumstances. Such a position is not established on the basis of these considerations. In fact, on the basis of what has been said thus far, it is possible even to maintain the opposite. What has been shown is only the following: *Insofar* and *if* "use of capital punishment" is an action of *"punishing"* (restoration of justice), then the implicit choice of the action "causing the death of x" or of the action "killing x" has an *intentional identity* different from any conceivable killing action carried out by a private person. It is a question of an *objectively* different action in the *genus moris:* the implicit "why" is different. If punishment through killing can be justified, the legitimately executed death penalty is an act of justice and not an "exception" to the absolute prohibition "thou shalt not kill."[212] And therefore, to these different types of action, different norms pertain.[213]

This is the solution to the problem here at issue. The question whether cap-

---

212. This formulation from the Decalogue is a command addressed to a private person, as its context makes clear. The Decalogue is part of the Mosaic Law, in which capital punishment was permitted.
213. Cf. once again the citation from I-II, Q. 1, a. 3, ad 3, referred to above (at III.4.c, note 90).

ital punishment, in fact, and under such and such circumstances, corresponds with justice must be distinguished from the question whether *the only possible justification* of the death penalty is to think of it as an exception to the norm "thou shalt not kill," which would involve ceasing to consider this norm as an absolute prohibition. The second question—and that alone is what concerns us here—must be answered in the negative.[214]

Capital punishment is no more an exception than the power to levy taxes or fines is an exception to the obligation not to take away someone else's possessions or personal freedom. If someone should maintain that the death penalty cannot be justified *as every other kind of penalty* is, as an act of justice, that person is saying, implicitly, that even "to punish" is in principle to make an exception to generally valid norms. But then one may regret to find oneself very close to a theory of punishment that considers punishments in general not as acts of retributive justice, but as "useful" measures to be taken, regardless of the actual culpability of the punished.[215]

In order for a concrete act of punishment to be justified, it must be *appropriate*. This is true for fines, incarceration, and death—that is, equally for all punishments. The appropriateness of the death penalty is measured by the *necessity* of the death of the perpetrator for the restoration and preservation of justice (i.e., the community life of men, lived according to the standards of justice). This in turn is largely dependent on the circumstances and on the possibility of actually carrying out the punishment. In general, we can say: In order to justify the death penalty as an appropriate punishment, one would have to show that it is *necessary* for the restoration of justice, and that in turn means: preserving human society as a community of justice. An unnecessary punishment is therefore an inappropriate one. Raising the threshhold of this necessity is closely connected with the possibilities of the modern penal system, and can thus be characterized as progress of civilization.[216] For it first of

214. For a few unclear points in Thomas Aquinas's justification of capital punishment, cf. M. Rhonheimer, "Sins Against Justice," in S. J. Pope, ed., *The Ethics of Aquinas* (Washington, D.C.: Georgetown University Press, 2002).

215. Cf. J.-C. Wolf, *Verhütung oder Vergeltung? Einführung in ethische Straftheorien* (Freiburg and Munich: Alber, 1992), 39, where, at any event, the utilitarian theory of punishment is presented as superior. Wolf is arguing against placing retributive theory in the context of "justice," since he thinks that maintaining a conceptual connection between "punishment" and "retribution" (restoration of justice) is to make an illegitimate "fusion of definitions" [*Definitionssperre,* "locking-together of definitions"], 53.

216. Cf. H. Hattenhauer, *Europäische Rechtsgeschichte* (Heidelberg: C. F. Müller, 1992), 319, who writes as follows concerning so-called painful punishments in the High and Late Middle Ages: "There was still no secular incarceration punishment. Simple solutions were sought. The gravest of these solutions was to kill the guilty party. Another one consisted in his being made a public spectacle. And in addition to this, there was permanent or temporary banishment." The idea that killing in certain cases is in itself a requirement of retributive justice ("an eye for an eye . . . a life for a life") would rather be of more recent and rationalistic origin, in the sense of an *ex post facto* legitimization of a system of punishment that could no longer be justified, as in earlier times, as a "simple solution."

all seems more just to provide the evildoer with the possibility of being rein-
tegrated into the social order, so that incarceration would itself appear as an
appropriate punishment. There are also strong arguments against the death
penalty, such as the irreversibility of a judicial error.[217]

Consequently, on the basis of the argument that the death penalty—like
any penalty—is in principle an act of retributive justice, nothing further has
been decided whether or not it is an *appropriate* act of retributive justice. This
can also depend on the circumstances; and it is also possible to understand
it as *in principle* inappropriate. It is characteristic of many traditional arguments for capital punishment (but also common in utilitarian arguments) *not*
to distinguish these two questions.[218] Therefore, let me repeat: acts of self-
preservation on the part of society can only be justified, because, and to the
extent that, they are *in themselves* acts of justice, and such acts can only concern those who are culpable.[219] We could not, then, say, in a utilitarian way,
that capital punishment is to be avoided by considerations of utility, and *at
the same time* that it can in principle be discussed whether, in a particular
instance, the death penalty could in fact be levied against an innocent person
because it would serve a purpose. Even if, as a rule, utilitarians find reasons to
show that this too would not lead to the optimal balance of consequences, it
gives one pause that they even consider this seriously.

Analogous arguments would hold for killing in war and the assassination of
tyrants, but they need not be gone into here. It has been noted that ideologi-
cal pacifism, which maintains that any killing whatsoever for collective self-
defense is immoral, leads to the situation that—in case anyone has to defend
his life at all—then simply *everything* is permitted, and the differences between
war, murder, and massacre become insignificant.[220]

217. We must not confuse the idea of retribution with the idea of atonement. That a crime must be
"atoned for" is actually a misuse of the word *atonement,* since what is meant is, rather, "vengeance."
Atonement is an action or process of the culpable person himself, and doubtless also an act of compensation and inner purification, which would more likely take place under the circumstances of a long
or indefinite imprisonment, as long as this was carried out in a humane fashion, than by the planned
physical liquidation of the person.

218. This is admirably done, however, by Agnes Heller, *Beyond Justice* (see note 209 above). To
this extent, and for the same reason, one can agree with the rehabilitation by Otfried Höffe of Kant's
idea of retribution as a partial but still fundamental legitimization of punishment in *Kategorische Rechtsprinzipien. Ein Kontrapunkt der Moderne* (Frankfurt am Main: Suhrkamp, 1990), 228f. But the thesis
of J.-C. Wolf, *Verhütung oder Vergeltung?* mentioned above (note 214) is hardly equal to the two-stage
nature of retributive theories.

219. So also, with respect to justice in general, see Michael Walzer, *Spheres of Justice* (see note 183
above), 268–71.

220. On this question, cf. G. E. M. Anscombe, "War and Murder," in *The Collected Philosophical Pa-
pers of G. E. M. Anscombe* (Oxford: Blackwell, 1981), 3.51–61; T. Nagel, "War and Massacre," in T. Nagel,
Mortal Questions (Cambridge: Cambridge University Press, 1979), 53–74; J. Finnis, J. Boyle, and G. Grisez,
Nuclear Deterrence, Morality, and Realism (Oxford: Clarendon Press, 1987).

There are some conclusions to be drawn, then, from this interpretation of normative formulations: the norm "One may never kill an innocent person" is a norm that is related to the ethical context of the assigning of penalties through ministers of justice who represent public coercive authority. For this reason it cannot be applied, for example, in order to justify abortion in a situation where the fetus in a woman's womb threatens the life of the mother. An abortion could never be an act of restoring justice. The fetus is not an aggressor: it bears no culpability and consequently does not injure justice in any way.

One could try to justify abortion as an act of self-defense. But that too is impossible. For that would mean that it is right to kill someone, provided you have a good purpose. The action chosen as a means is unjust: it possesses the intentional identity of an act of killing. Not even in the case of an aggressor is it permissible to justify the death of the aggressor as a means to saving one's own life.[221] We are not considering here the case of a legitimate self-defense that results in death for the aggressor. That is a question to which we will return a little later (V.4.e).

> Owing to its origin within the context of legal practices (and from similar determinations of the Mosaic Law), there is an alternative formulation of the commandment against murder, whereby it is morally prohibited to kill an *innocent*. In current Catholic moral theology this is the standard expression for the prohibition of murder.[222] It has the advantage, of course, that it is clear and intelligible to the popular understanding. But while it is not in conflict with the foregoing analysis, it still entails a few obscurities. In this particular formulation, the norm only prohibits (1) unjustly sentencing someone to the death penalty (i.e., legal murder or conviction without proof) and (2) killing outside of any legal process (ordinary murder, private retribution, vengeance, abortion). The disadvantage is that with this formulation of the prohibition of murder, killing of the aggressor *in legitimate self-defense* as well as *killing in (just) war* (= legitimate collective self-defense) is permissible only under the presumption that the aggressor is considered guilty. In that case, only self-defense against an *unjust aggressor* would be considered legitimate, which finally ends up to be the same as saying that only "justified self-defense" is legitimate, and that is tautological. It is really the category of the "innocent" that causes confusion here, since

---

221. Cf. II-II, Q. 64, a. 7.

222. And in addition the precision is usually added, "the *direct* killing of an innocent is immoral." Cf. the encyclical *Evangelium vitae* (March 25, 1995), no. 57. And certainly here there are also other formulations that replace the expression "direct" with the intentionality that is present in the act, e.g.: "The willing decision to take away a human being's life is always shameful from a moral point of view and can never be permitted, either as an end or as a means to an end" (ibid.). Cf. also M. Schlag, *Das moralische Gesetz in "Evangelium vitae"* (Frankfurt am Main: Suhrkamp, 2000), 124ff. The topic is more extensively treated in my *Vital Conflicts: A Virtue Ethics Approach to Craniotomy and Tubal Pregnancies* (Washington, D.C.: The Catholic University of America Press, 2009).

it is a category that has its origin in a different context. Troops in combat are not personally guilty of the aggression against which the other side's troops may be justly fighting. In some cases of legitimate self-defense, the aggressor, for example, can be a highly dangerous mentally ill person, who bears no guilt. Nevertheless, his being killed in self-defense (see below, at V.4.e) would not be considered a violation of the prohibition, even though someone kills an "innocent." But if we broaden the concept of the "guilty" to include such cases, the category loses all its precision, and the norm that one should never kill an innocent becomes completely tautological: it would merely define a noninnocent person as one whose killing is morally permissible. In the concrete case, that would mean that someone would have to clarify whether the one to be killed is innocent or not. Since this would have to be determined, on the above model, independently of the question about *personal* culpability, the moral category of the culpable would be immediately replaced by the pragmatic category of the "threatening" or "harmful." This would allow the (consequentialist) justification of judicial murder (for the purpose of avoiding worse consequences) or the killing of a person who has contracted a virus that may be fatal to others, and more besides. The determination of who is "not innocent" or "threatening," or "harmful" would take place consequentially from case to case. In this way, then, the norm "one may never kill an innocent" would be totally undermined. For this reason, we are here attempting to define the prohibition of murder in a way that is completely independent of the concept of the "innocent," and only on the basis of the analysis of the intentional basic action, "to kill." This is also why the case of legitimate self-defense has not yet been treated, since it has a completely different intentional structure. These remarks do not alter in the least the validity of the formulations that the killing of an innocent can never be morally justified; it is to be hoped that we have clarified why the formula is somewhat imprecise for analysis. As long as one sets aside the case of legitimate self-defense and legitimate collective self-defense (just war), and keeps the above difficulties in mind, in practice this formulation of the norm is still the most useful.

A second instance of an absolute prohibition is the one against *lying*. Lying is a deceptive communicative behavior. That means it is an attack on that (potential) part of the virtue of justice known as *sincerity* or *truthfulness*. We could call the virtue of truthfulness "communicative justice."

Truthfulness is the kind of justice that builds the communicative foundation of human social life. A lie is a willingly false statement within a communicative context. A communicative context is characterized by a social community that exists in virtue of linguistic communication, in which speech has the function of being a sign of the thoughts, feelings, intentions, and so on of the one who uses the sign. Misuse of speech through false statements are acts of communicative deception.

We can distinguish "lies" from "misstatements" *(falsiloquium)*. A misstatement is a speech act in which the sign (the word) does not agree with the thoughts of the one who speaks. This can happen, for example, when someone does not have a proper command of the language or through mistaken speech. A lie is a *willing* misstatement, in which the lack of agreement is *willed*.

On the basis of its intentional identity—that is, *objectively*—a lie is linguistic action that is directed against the order of human community life, as well as against the "good of another": against someone's right to have the words that he hears correspond to what the one speaking is thinking. A person has this right "not to be deceived" because he has the "right to live in the social order" and the right to equality of recognition by others as being a member of that society. At the same time, he has the right to have the relevant institutions functioning properly that accompany this social order, which presupposes truthfulness. Lying is consequently opposed to benevolence toward others and a denial of the recognition of the other as my equal.

This objective identity of willingly false statements within a community of communication comes to be independently of the further purposes with which one perpetrates a lie: to hurt someone; to produce an advantage or avoid a disadvantage for oneself or even for the person lied to; or as a practical joke. Finally, a misstatement is to be treated as an injustice, whenever the other person can reasonably expect that the other will be telling the truth ("reasonably" does not mean "foreseeably," but rather "justly"; this is because someone who is a known habitual liar and whom nobody believes anyway is still acting unjustly).

Accordingly, we can think of contexts where a willing misstatement is not an injustice. In a game, for example, the point of which is to bluff the opponents, no one will expect someone to tell the truth, since false statements belong to the rules of the game, and the same can be said of an experimental subject who is employed for testing a lie detector. The communicative context is modified in accordance with the rules of the game. False statements here in no way injure the communicative basis of the human social order.

Another case would be the deceptive reports and misleading signals given in wartime situations (such as misleading the enemy about planned operations or the whereabouts of troops, answers to be given under interrogation, false documents, etc.). One would not treat such actions as injuries to the communicative community since such a community does not even exist here. When military operations such as pretended retreats, camouflage, and the like are used, there is no reason not to use speech acts to the same end.

Nevertheless, one must be precise: just *to the extent that* there is no sharing in community life between hostile parties in wartime, so there is no possibility of an injury to the communicative basis of such a shared life. But warriors fighting each other are still in a fundamental sense "fellow human beings." War is an exceptional situation and the corresponding actions of war are only justified—presuming that the war itself can be morally justified—until the normal situation of "peace" can be restored. Such persons are potentially partners of a shared social order, and thereby as well potential members of a communicative community. Thus in war there are also actions that serve to restore the community of communication, for example, offers of peace through a white flag, and so on; to use these as means of deception is an especially grievous violation of communicative justice and is equivalent to lying. This would apply to the misuse of all other actions or communicative measures in a similar way. The boundaries here are fluid and there can be "shades of grey."

Fichte is responsible for the saying, "You must not lie, even if the world should fall apart as a result of the truth."[223] His meaning, doubtless, was that it should be clear to a moral subject "that in the plan of its [the world's] survival, there is no accounting for a lie." But the statement is really questionable because a situation in which refraining from a lie would shatter the world would *at the least* be equivalent to a wartime situation. Before one discusses such subtleties, it would make sense to begin with a concrete example.

Hegel once made an amusing reference to Fichte's "System of Ethics" in his 1819–1820 lectures on the Philosophy of Right (it appears to have originated with Benjamin Constant and was already treated by Kant).[224] This is the case: "A man holding a dagger bursts into a room in search of someone he wants to murder, who is hiding there. The question is whether someone else who is in the room, and knows where the person is hiding, is obliged to tell the truth." Hegel provides an elegant solution: in this case, "Speaking is not merely speaking but an action, and in fact, such an action as would be equivalent to handing someone a dagger who wants to kill someone and doesn't have a dagger."[225]

That is certainly correct. But Hegel actually avoids the issue. Because what do you do if the intruder will not *let* you simply keep silent, but demands an answer? It is not a problem not to say anything. But can you say something false? It appears that the following position can be held: Just as telling the truth would be equivalent to "handing the man a dagger," a false statement would also be a purely defensive action of "taking the dagger away from him."

223. *Du darfst nicht lügen, und wenn die Welt darüber in Trümmer zerfallen sollte;* J. G. Fichte, "Über den Grund unseres Glaubens an eine göttliche Weltregierung," in I. H. Fichte, ed., *Fichtes Werke* (Berlin: Walter de Gruyter, 1971), 5.185f.

224. Cf. the already mentioned essay "On a Supposed Right to Lie Because of Philanthropic Concerns" (note 155 above).

225. G. W. F. Hegel, *Philosophie des Rechts. Die Vorlesungen von 1819/20 in einer Nachschrift,* ed. D. Heinrich (Frankfurt am Main: Suhrkamp, 1983), 118–19 (trans. here G. Malsbary).

There is no question here of a communicative context. The intruder cannot reasonably expect the truth to be told him in this situation. And if he was only in a passionate rage to kill the man, he would probably, after getting control over himself, even *thank* the man who prevented him from doing something foolish by being a "liar." It is really meaningless to discuss such cases in a casuistic manner. In reality, according to each situation, there is a multiplicity of possibilities. One should and must try to stop the intruder, disarm him, push him away, or at least flee. . . .

As long as a communicative context or communicative community exists, so long is the norm prohibiting lying an absolutely valid norm: lying is an attack on the virtue of truthfulness and therefore on the virtue of justice. The communicative context is precisely that context in relation to which the virtue of truthfulness constitutes itself and lends to the action "false statement" the intentional identity of an "injustice" (though not in the sense of a violation of legal justice). The intentional action "lying" is directed against the "good for man": against the good, that is, of existing as a member of a community of human beings; it also goes against this good as a "good for others," that is, for the other person as "my equal" existing along with me in a community of shared life. This is especially clear even in the case of the most harmless form of lying, just "kidding" for fun, when this is systematically practiced on someone without apology, which can deny another person respect and can disturb the community between persons. But insofar as no communicative context exists, these goods cannot be injured, and we cannot really speak of an injustice.

But it is a different matter in case a lie is—according to utilitarian or consequentialist standards—merely seen as an *unjustified* false statement, and it is assumed that a false statement is only a premoral evil and the action of "making a false statement" is merely the causing of such nonmoral evil, so that one could allow only *one possible* formulation of the norm: "One may not, without justification, that is, without a proportionate reason, make a false statement." This implies, in fact, that "communication" in general is being considered as a premoral good that permits of being damaged for a "good enough" reason. But this leads to the position that it is right in certain circumstances to injure the communicative basis of human community, if it can be foreseen that a greater number of good consequences can result. And thus it becomes a subject of discussion whether it is right for a witness in a trial to say something untrue in order to protect a defendant (even a repentant one), who is known to be guilty, but whose acquittal would be foreseen to have better consequences than his conviction. Since justice, according to a theory like this, is not bound up with intentional actions, but rather, for each case, the totality of foreseeable consequences for all those concerned must be taken into account to assess the "justice" of the action—then this would be a "justified" false statement, and not properly a lie, and not unjust. In this case, of course, one could also set up the norm in a rule-utilitarian way, and say that it is best for the well-being of society always to tell the truth in a court of law (in order not to undermine the institution), but such a rule would only be reasonably followed as long as it was expected that the lie could in fact become apparent. And then, considering the situation in a utilitarian way, the lie would have to be abandoned anyway. Consequently, the utilitarian can only pose the question, whether he should "risk" telling the lie at all—unless he is not a "rule fetishist" (i.e., one who, in J.J.C. Smart's terminology mentioned above, *on principle* and therefore *in all cases* abides by the rules).

Now it is not at all incorrect to formulate the norm "thou shalt not lie" as "one should not make unjustified false statements" because a lie (a willing misstatement) is just for this reason a bad action because it injures justice; and it injures that part of justice that is governed by the virtue of truthfulness: the communicative basis of human community. *Inside* this ethical context "not to lie" can be formulated as an absolute prohibition, that is, as a negative norm within the sphere of the virtue of justice, which—as all such norms—permits no exceptions. The justification of an "exception" would here be equivalent to justifying the principle "The end justifies the means."

If the prohibition of lying means "One should not make false statements," the reason for the injustice cannot be indicated by a bad intention or by a preponderance of bad consequences, but only by the context of an existing communicative community, *a context that exists, or does not exist, quite independently of intentions and further consequences.* Within this ethical context there is accordingly no contingency of the matter of actions; it is the context itself that is contingent—which is to say, it does not always exist. And an absolute prohibition, like any moral norm and any intentional action, can only be defined with relation to an ethical context.

> Kant takes objection with good reason against the maxim, "It is a duty to tell the truth, but only to those who have the right to the truth." He sensibly restricts this to the case when someone "cannot get away without a yes or no answer." The maxim is in fact false, insofar as it means that *within* an ethical context the one who speaks ought, in each case, to ask himself whether or not another has a "right" to the truth of what he is saying in that case. Kant rejects this and we must agree with him. But we could also understand the above maxim to mean that the existence of such a right depends upon the existence of a communicative context (which as such a context generates the right). Then Kant's objection would *not* hold. Instead, he has to establish the prohibition of lying in a rule-utilitarian way, which in any case leads him to say, consistently, that "one

never in fact harms anyone through a certain lie"; one only harms the principle of all justice, and thereby humanity, "which is much worse than committing an injustice against any one person."[226] Ironically, Kant hereby justifies the logic of rule-utilitarian consequentialism.[227]

Insofar, then, as a communicative context is present—the context of human society—a willingly false statement or "lie" is unjust, intrinsically and always. But because norms must always be formulated in relation to ethically relevant contexts and the corresponding intentional actions, we speak of "exceptions" in cases of noncommunicative contexts. Strictly speaking, however, the exception does not pertain to the norm, but to the ethical context to which the norm relates. Just as with the prohibition of murder, as long as we keep in view the limitation of all norm formulations, and their reference to practical principles, virtues, and intentional actions, the prohibition of lying admits of no exception.

Evasive answers such as "I don't know" (as an answer to someone asking who has no right to the information in question), or "He isn't here" (as a strategy to "protect" someone from an unwanted telephone call) *can* in some circumstances constitute an injury to communicative justice and therefore to the virtue of truthfulness. This would occur when the person asking can reasonably assume that the other (i.e., the one who has been asked and who answers that he doesn't know) really does not know, or that the person being called is not really "there" when the telephone rings, and someone else answers. In this case, false information is being reported, and there can be deliberate deception.[228] But there are contexts in which, by convention, such answers are nothing other than recognized methods of handling certain situations, which serve to say in a courteous, and not blunt way, that someone cannot, may not, or would not like to, answer such a question, or that the person being called to the phone would not like to come to the phone right now and would like his privacy respected. For the latter case, other solutions are conceivable that are still less "blunt."

226. Cf. I. Kant, "On a Supposed Right to Lie Because of Philanthropic Concerns" (note 156 above), 64: "Thus [by telling an untruth] as far as in me lies, I bring it about that statements in general find no credence, and hence also that all rights based on contracts become void and lose their force, and this is a wrong done to mankind in general."

227. In his ethics lectures Kant argues in a more traditional fashion and hence more flexibly. He still uses arguments that are influenced by a thoroughly virtue ethics approach in *Vorlesungen über Ethik* (see note above), 244: "To the extent that I were to be forced by some coercion that is being exercised against me, to provide a statement of my position, and if unjust use were being made of what I say, and I cannot escape by being silent, then a lie is a defensive weapon." What is meant here naturally is that it is really not a lie at all, but simply a *falsiloquium* and, morally considered, is objectively an act of self-defense. Here there would no longer be any "communicative justice" of an ethical context. Kant's polemic against the *reservatio mentalis* is likewise consistent, because it too can injure the justice of communication, since a "mental reservation" does not in any way presuppose the breakdown of the corresponding ethical context.

228. Kant argues in exactly the same way in his ethics lectures (see note 226), 245.

Since the lie is a willingly false statement, and only *as such* is an attack on communicative justice, it loses its injustice and evil to the extent that the will of the speaker is subject to influence by fear of the impending evil (and then it is less of a "lie"). Aquinas says that the greater the good to be attained by the lie, the less is the *culpability* of the liar.[229] This is why we are inclined to excuse lying in certain situations. But that has nothing to do with its normative justification. One should, of course, excuse an unavoidable lie, but this can only be the case when someone is not saying that it is a "justified false statement," that someone has acted "rightly" by doing so. For in that case, one shouldn't need to be "excused," but praised. In fact, unavoidable lies are signs of weakness, of cowardice ("a liar is a coward"),[230] and often the (subjective) "unavoidability" is the consequence of unintelligent behavior.

The examples of norms that we have been considering so far all have their origin in the area of the virtue of justice. Similar statements would hold in the case of the virtues of self-control and courage, *mutatis mutandis*. Here for the most part only very formal criteria can be given, since the "mean" of these virtues is always only a "mean with respect to ourselves." In the area of these virtues, which establish the rational ordering of the sensitive appetites, what is "bad" is not really definite actions, but rather the relationship of the will to the emotions. An emotion—so far as the will is involved—is bad when it incapacitates the mastery of reason over sensitive desires, or disturbs the judgment of reason about the good. Enough has been said already in reference to the moral importance of these virtues. In this connection it is not so much norms of action that can be formulated, but rather criteria for making moral judgments.

But there are, even so, actions in the sphere of these virtues, in relation to which norms can be formulated, because such actions establish or bring to expression a certain relationship of the reason and will to the structure of one's own drives. "To get drunk" (willingly) is an action by which the mastery of reason is cancelled out. An absolute norm can be formulated in this case, at least in relation to the virtue of self-control (and thereby to an ethical context): the prohibition of the act is valid for all acts of abandoning self-control, but not (for example) for persons who place themselves into a state of drunkenness for a scientific experiment or for anesthesis in the case of an emergency operation.

There are, then, two kinds of action to consider: (1) a way of acting that hinders or makes impossible the responsible modification of the dynamism of the sensitive appetites (the modification, that is, achieved through reason

229. II-II, Q. 110, a. 2.
230. Kant, "Lectures on Ethics," 245.

and will)—so that the reason is suspended from its mastery over the structure of sensitive drives—or (2) an action that has for its goal to make such responsible modification *superfluous,* in that, for reasons of avoiding responsibility, the consequences of acts of this drive are hindered, so that, in order to avoid these consequences the drive no longer needs to be governed by reason and will, and can be left to its own inconsequential dynamism. These are actions that in themselves work against the virtue through which the corresponding appetition is perfected.[231]

e) Prohibitive Norms: Borderline Conditions for the Preservation of Human Identity

The foregoing discussions show that prohibitive norms are nothing other than the formulation of the *boundaries* of human actions. They can further be treated as the minimal requirements for human action to take place within the bounds of human identity, of "the good for man." This is why they are so important, although they do not in themselves constitute the core of morality. In a purely normative ethics, absolute prohibitions cannot be stringently justified because there the norm can always be formulated in such a way as to be valid absolutely or nonabsolutely. Insight into the existence of absolute prohibitions of action only arises in the context of a virtue ethics. This is where it emerged for the first time: in Aristotle's *Nicomachean Ethics* (see above, IV.2.b).

> "Absolute prohibitions of actions" must not be confused with absolute values or goods. Such things are not to be found *within* the created world. Absolute prohibitions of action are normative statements that are always valid. They refer to human actions. Despite the contingency and relativity of all this-worldly goods, there can be *intentional actions* whose moral quality have a "morally absolute" character. That means that in them, the very "being-human" of the person as a whole is at risk. For man as subject of actions, his "being human" (human identity) is an absolute, not-to-be-relativized good.

We have been speaking thus far about "absolute" prohibitions of actions. Strictly speaking, however, the word "absolute" is superfluous. A prohibitive norm, as the traditional expression has it, prohibits *semper et pro semper*

---

231. The latter, I would maintain, applies to the action of "contracepting," in respect of which, therefore, an absolutely prohibiting norm of action can be formulated. For a description of the object of this action see above, III.4.c; for the justification of the norm, cf. M. Rhonheimer, "Contraception, Sexual Behavior, and Natural Law: Philosophical Foundation of the Norm of 'Humanae Vitae,'" *Linacre Quarterly* 56, no. 2 (1989): 20–57; more extensively in M. Rhonheimer, *Ethics of Procreation and the Defense of Human Life* (see note 58 above), chapters 2 and 3.

("always and in every case"). It formulates a boundary that cannot be transgressed, if someone does not want to abandon the region where potentially virtuous action resides. "Killing" and "lying" are actions that strike against the fundamental conditions of justice because by them the will of the acting person completely turns aside from the goal of "justice" or "doing what is just." Such actions are simply incapable of being united with any possible action of the "just" kind. To want to make exceptions to an absolutely prohibitive norm would mean wanting to justify that someone "by an exception" does not need to pursue what is good for the human being, or act well; that here and there a little dose of immorality, when seen as part of the total picture, is finally better (utilitarianism certainly does not *intend* to say this; such a criticism can only be established from the viewpoint of a virtue ethics). The concept of "absolute" prohibitions of actions is nevertheless justified because there are also prohibitive norms that do not only relate to a stable ethical context, but also, and at the same time, to a contingent matter of actions (e.g., stealing, keeping of contracts or promises, return of borrowed items). The condition by which the norm is valid must also be included in its formulation (in the example of stealing, the ownership of the stolen thing must be justified: consequently, stealing is the taking of something *rightly* possessed by another). With so-called *absolute* prohibitions this would not be necessary. Simply knowing the ethical context is sufficient.

> It may be useful to repeat here that the expression "intrinsically evil actions" or an "action evil in itself" does not indicate an "inner" evil of an action that would be, as it were, *in rerum natura*, and independent of the will of the acting person. What it means, rather, is that there exist certain describable actions that are immoral in all cases *independently* of any further, added intentions. This does not compromise the fact that even the "intrinsically evil" actions in question can never be thought of without a basic intentionality; "intrinsically evil actions" are always intentional actions, to whose description belongs the reason-guided willing of an agent.

A positively formulated norm, by contrast, which asks us to do something and which we could thus call an *exhortative* norm, does not formulate boundaries, but rather the virtues that operate within the boundaries. The prohibition of action is the shoulder of the road and the guard rail, the exhortative norm (the virtue) is the road itself and the destination. They are the real theme of ethics. Nobody would say that the shoulder of the road and the guard rail are the most important things about a highway: what is most important is the road itself and where it leads. Similarly, the "problem of norms" is not the principal theme of ethics. Nor could it be said that the concept of virtue has only a "parainetic" (i.e., "advisory") function, that is to say, that it only serves as a kind of encouragement to do what is right with the best intentions, with a good attitude, with confidence; in a "normative ethics," it really contributes nothing to speak about virtues and in general about what makes human purposes and intentions morally good.

Of course, exhortative norms are also valid without exception. Insofar as they are norms for goals of virtues ("one should act rightly"), they are equally valid in every single case. But that is not very relevant for the discursive justification of norms. Exhortative norms of action, by contrast, that are norms for concrete actions, are always valid, but not in every case. "To tell the truth" is a good action *considered in itself* (objectively). But with respect to the circumstances or even the intention, "to tell the truth" can be a bad action. One can be called to be silent in some circumstances, which is not the same as saying something false. On the other hand, "to keep a promise" is "in itself" a good action. But it can be bad if the situation changes such that keeping the promise obliges someone to do something that was not at all foreseen when the promise was made. This is a case of the change of the matter of actions, similar to "stealing" or "robbery for reasons of hunger." "To get married" is in itself a good action, but not for everyone, or in every situation. For what is concretely always *bad* and therefore not to be done, actual norms of action can be formulated. They are in fact the starting point and boundary for every prudent action. But what is *good* to do concretely and in each case, here and now, must only be figured out through prudence—there cannot be moral norms.

4. Ethics of the Judgment of Actions (Structures of Prudence)

a) The Unity of the Practical Reason and the Perspective of Morality: Recapitulation and Deeper Justification of the Fundamental Points

We will now make a summarizing overview of what has been developed so far, while taking the opportunity to remark on some matters more closely: the process of all activity of the practical reason has its starting point in practical principles, which at the same time formulate the teleological structure of the human virtues. The practical reason unfolds itself more and more concretely down to the final practical judgment, which establishes what should be done, here and now, in a way that "triggers" action. On the basis of the habitual direction of human appetites and affects, this concrete action-determining reason is formed into the virtue of prudence.

This is not to imply that every practical consideration leads *from* the principles in a discursive path all the way down *to* the concrete judgment of action. The principles, as "starting points," are the final foundation of all the intelligibility of the concrete good: they ground the intelligibility of "what is good for man," in reference to which every concrete judgment is fulfilled and toward which every concrete judgment aims in its cognitive structure. Without a grasp of the fundamental structure of justice on the level of principles it would be impossible to recognize particular actions as right ways of acting. What is "just" in the concrete must be subsumable under the principle of "justice," and must be capable of being chosen and carried out as a just act. And this does not mean—once again, in order to ward off any possible misunderstanding—that the concretely just can be *derived* from principles of justice. It is, rather, the object of a genuine practical knowledge that is oriented toward the particular. But only in the light of the principles can a concrete action be understood and chosen as an action that corresponds with justice.[232] The principles, then, show the way to human action, but they also—as shown in the immediately preceding section—perform the function of laying down clear boundaries.

If we distinguish the reason that grasps principles from the reason that carries out concrete judgments of action and develops into the virtue of prudence, this must not allow us to forget the fundamental unity of the practical reason. The activity of the practical reason is *one single activity* that orders and guides appetition, a knowing focus upon "what is good for man" that concretizes itself toward the concrete action. We need to observe here not only the unity of the intellective faculty but also the *intentional* unity of the acts of the practical reason. "The consideration of means, too [= the concrete actions to be chosen for the sake of a goal], insofar as these means are an object of consideration in view of a goal, is still the same act of thinking as the act that has the goal for its object."[233] Means and end are related to each other just as matter and form and they form an essential, objective unity. This applies to appetition as well as to knowing involved in it.

The reason that determines the concrete means is accordingly the ultimate *perfection* of the practical reason that has for its object the ends, as both foundation and point of departure. The more concrete and closer to action practical reason becomes, the greater the perfection that it gains; for acts of the practical reason are in fact carried out for the sake of action; and actions are always a particular concretion of the good. But practical reason in the fulfillment of its ultimate concretization is nevertheless still the *same* reason that has the principles for its object. In every concrete judgment of action the prin-

232. Cf. above, V.1.f: "The genesis and application of practical principles: the role of experience and prudence."
233. In II Sent., d. 38, q. 1, a. 4, ad 3: "cogitatio de eo quod est ad finem, prout consideratur in ordine ad finem, est eadem cum cogitatione finis."

ciples are intentionally present, but with the particularity needed for what is to be done here and now.[234]

The same can be said for the reason-guided will. This is why the one who acts is always, in every concrete act of choosing and acting, also related intentionally to "what is good for man" on the universal level of principles, and thus his will is either good or bad. When this action-determining reason has the virtue of prudence, the fulfillment is twofold: not only is the immediately action-guiding concretion of the practical reason present, but also the *affective* connaturality with the human good on the part of the rational acting subject. The "rational by nature" that is objectified for the practical reason by way of the natural inclinations possesses thereby the function of ensuring the truth of knowledge of "what is good for man," and is the ultimate grounding for the original rectitude of appetition. There is, then, no transcendental function that accrues to the "rational by nature" (since it is not an *a priori*, but rather an empirical given that has been integrated into the reason); as a condition for the possibility of practical truth, however, it is functionally equivalent to a transcendental principle. The practical truth of concrete judgments of action, finally, is not the agreement of these judgments with any states of affairs, but rather their agreement with right striving, which has its ultimate ground, as we have said, in the "rational by nature," and in the practical principles that form themselves on that horizon.

The action-determining reason, which is developed into prudence—into the *recta ratio* of action, and with that, in fact, to a "habit of practical truth"—forms the affective/emotional striving toward ends. This, moral virtue's own rationally measured goal seeking, is acquired by the acting subject through actions in accordance with virtue. For "natural virtue" is only given through the natural grasp of the principles. True moral virtue is formed through the constantly repeated choosing and doing of what is concretely good. In this sense, one can say that the action-determining practical reason that develops into prudence is really the *cause* of moral virtue. As prudence, this is the actual rule and adequate measure of human action. Moral virtue, however, is a special kind of "rule": not uniform but malleable, and open to multiple options. This is because it must govern "what is always otherwise." Nevertheless, it is a rule that in fact brings this "always otherwise" into agreement with right appetition. The principles themselves, or that which is "given by nature," are not enough for this; concretizing is needed in order to do the principle justice *within* the multiplicity of the practical. And that precisely is the achievement of the reason known as prudence.

234. Cf. (also for what follows): *De virtutibus in communi*, q. un., a. 6 and 7.

We can conceive of utilitarian ethics (of whatever kind) as theories of how one reaches the "right" decision in a given situation *completely without reference to whether the will of the acting person is good or not*; Kantian ethics, on the other hand, can be understood as the opposite, namely, a theory of under what conditions one's will is good or not, *completely without reference to what is the right decision in a given situation.* Kantian ethics is a (transcendental) theory of the conditions for the possibility of a good will; utilitarianism is a theory of right action. Each operates at a different level, and it should not be surprising that they are complementary to one another: as a utilitarian, one can also be a Kantian and as a Kantian, one can also be a utilitarian. Kant himself, as we have seen, proceeds at first in a rule-utilitarian way when dealing with the prohibition against lying, only to exalt unconditional obedience to the norm thus arrived at as the irreducible condition for the morality of the will (a level with which utilitarians do not concern themselves at all).

These are, then, theories about the *goodness of the will* and about the *rectitude of actions,* respectively. Modern moral philosophy requires at least *two* different theories that are disparate in themselves, which then must be combined in order to get an understanding of the whole picture (contemporary *virtue ethics* concentrates on one of the two sides, namely, the former). *The distinguishing mark of classical virtue ethics, by contrast, is to bring together in one embrace both goodness of will and rectitude of action.* This comes, to be sure, at the price of not being able to offer unequivocal solutions for concrete dilemmas.[235] It remains a "science in outline." The very concept of moral virtue requires that it be in relation to "that which is always otherwise." If a critic of modern virtue ethics complains that "consequently we cannot expect it to be of great use in applied ethics and casuistry,"[236] this applies to virtue ethics in the classical tradition only to a limited extent. If someone expects from casuistry such things as final solutions for dilemmas and an unambiguous guide for actions, then any form of virtue ethics is going to be a poor assistant. But that does not mean that there cannot be a casuistry specific to virtue ethics or a discourse about applications. These would of course not have the same priority as in a normative or rule-ethics.

This is because virtue ethics at the same time connects this "always otherwise" to the truth, namely, *practical* truth, which Aristotle defined as the agreement of choice and action with *right appetition.* Virtue ethics is interest-

---

235. This is the emphasis taken up in the excellent discussion by E. D. Pellegrino, "Der tugendhafte Arzt und die Ethik der Medizin," in H.-M. Sass, ed., *Medizin und Ethik* (Stuttgart: Philipp Reclam, 1989), 40–68; the same can be said for the works of Hans Jonas (see, e.g., his "Humanexperimente" in the same volume, 232–53).

236. R. Louden, "Some Vices of Virtue Ethics," in R. Crisp and M. Slote, eds., *Virtue Ethics,* 206.

ed in the fundamental rectitude of the intentional orientation of the acting subject toward the good. And here, again, the interest is not so much in the rationality of the decision-making process as success in living. But perhaps it is just this interest, that life as a whole be "right," that ultimately makes for rationality in concrete decisions; and this is, of course, a *moral* rationality. To show this will be the object of the critique of consequentialist ethics in section (f) below.

This proves that practical principles are likewise not merely propositional principles—that is, linguistically formulated rules of a rational discourse. They are not merely principles of a reason that "speaks about actions" and not merely principles of the academic discipline "Ethics," or a normative sociopolitical discourse. If this is all they were, then all moral reflection would ultimately only be a "morality of the experts" that would leave out of consideration the moral competence of the ordinary person, of the moral subject as such, and push it aside as meaningless. And certainly we do not need "to listen regularly to the pronouncements of academic moral philosophers before we can constitute ourselves as moral subjects and remain such."[237]

Practical principles, rather, are the principles of the reason of a subject that strives for the success of its life. As such they are not principles of discourse about praxis, but principles of praxis itself, which constitute the human being as the subject of action and reveal themselves at the same time as the fundamental principles of the rectitude of striving, since they underlie the acting subject, the subject's own willing, and the practical judgments distinguishing between good and evil that are embedded in that willing. Someone who acts against these principles is not one who thinks wrongly and ends up making a mistake in his decisions. Rather, he is someone who *because* his striving has missed what is right, has a will that is "not right," that is, a bad will. Here there is an essential difference from all types of utilitarian rationality (seen from Kant's perspective, the last statement is completely beside the point): utilitarian rationality, that is to say, grasps practical principles as orientating rules for decision-making processes. But these rules—and this is essential—are themselves, again, only products of a certain "decision-making theory"; they are nothing other than generalizations that arise from the same decision-rationality, which they then are supposed to regulate. They have no origin of their own, are neither subordinated to, nor superior to, decision-rationality as such, and finally are also unable to limit this rationality in a fundamental way, that is, *by principle*. For these principles or rules can—or

237. H. Lübbe, "Moral und Philosophie der Moral," in *Der Mensch und die Wissenschaften vom Menschen*, Die Beiträge des XII. Deutschen Kongresses für Philosophie in Innsbruck vom 29 Sept. bis 3. Okt. 1981 (Innsbruck: Solaris-Verlag, 1983), 545–55, at 545.

indeed, must—be ever again adapted and newly formed, according to the logic of decision-making that they regulate. Thus all principles as a formulation of "duties" have only a *prima facie* validity, that is, they are provisional in kind.[238]

But practical principles as here understood—as the goals of the moral virtues—possess a status previous to, and superior to, all concrete processes of decision making and their logic. They do not arise from this logic itself, but form a self-standing moral measure for concrete processes of decision making. This is why it is possible to see how concrete decisions can be untrue in *praxis*, when they do *not* agree with right striving. Such principles cannot be undermined by the logic of decision, but formulate a direction and boundaries for moral rationality and legitimacy. Within these boundaries there is a multiplicity of decision-logics possible, even including the balancing of goods and weighing of consequences. And this will depend on what type of decision is needed, or what kind of matter is of concern. The theme of "decision-making logic" as such is not really the theme of ethics: it belongs to the various areas of specialized competence (economics, sociopolitics, education, scientific research, technology, etc). To understand ethics as a special kind of "decision-making logic" is either to reduce it or to confuse it with such forms of specialized knowledge, or it tends to identify moral knowledge as *one* of these special competencies, which would mean giving up on ethics altogether. Ethics originates, in fact, from a question that, transcending all specific logics of decision making, asks about the compatibility of *any* decision with the rectitude of striving, that is, with practical truth, the truth of *praxis*. It is right here that "absolute" untransgressible boundaries become visible, as well as the fact that, for example, there can never be a determination concerning the fundamental rectitude of our actions by means of the weighing of goods.

That there are conditions for the fundamental rectitude of our actions, which are bound up with the foundational structures of "right striving," so that one can describe concrete actions and behaviors whose very *choice* always involves a wrong appetition, is one of the most important foundational teachings of classical virtue ethics. This would never appear within the purview of an ethics that understands itself, on the level of a normative ethics, as a rational discourse about the establishment of *norms*. Norm-ethics are "objective" in a way that prohibits them from including within reflection the subject of action and the subject's willing stance in relation to the "good" and "evil" implied in that subject's acts of choice for certain ways of acting. And this means they are likewise unable to pose the question about the "rectitude

238. The concept of *"prima facie* validity" comes from W. D. Ross, *The Right and the Good.*

of striving" or the "truth of subjectivity" at the level of concrete action choices *independently* of the consideration of *further* intentions with respect to the state of affairs, or without balancing the consequences foreseen to result from doing or not doing the action.

Now it is correct, as it has been suggested,[239] that the traditional doctrine of the "sources of morality" alone does not solve any problems of normative ethics, but already presupposes their solution: everything would depend on what someone means by the "object" of an action. Nevertheless, this classical doctrine contains a truth that cannot be circumvented: namely, that quite *independently* of *further* intentions, there must be a *distinction* between an "object" that morally specifies the action (i.e., the will of the acting person) and these further intentions (for more on this, cf. sections c, d, and e below); that there are certain actions that can be carried out which despite the best intentions are bad, because the *choice* of the concrete action *through which* such praiseworthy goals are obtained, is already morally bad.[240] Such a doctrine could never be made intelligible on the basis of an ethics that understands itself as a discourse about norms. And this is because in such discourse the *distinction* between "object" and "further" intention falls out of the picture. The only things that an argumentative norm-ethics can show in terms of action theory are certain "events" (actions), on the one hand, and certain consequences that result from them, on the other. If someone *intends* the best consequences, in each case these are what must be described as the "object" of the action.

In reality, we follow neither norms nor rules, nor do we determine our action exclusively on the basis of the consequences foreseen from the action for all concerned. Instead, our action takes place, rather, within the framework of certain "moral relationships": the relationships between persons (friends, spouses, parents/children, employer/employee, partners in contracts, persons with whom we communicate regularly, etc.).[241] What always matters here is

---

239. Cf. B. Schüller, *Die Quellen der Moralität.*

240. Cf. on this also the following formulation from the encyclical *Veritatis Splendor* (August 6, 1993), no. 79: "Therefore the position typical for teleological and proportionalist ethical theories is to be rejected: that it is impossible to judge as morally evil the conscious choice of some ways of acting, or of concrete actions, by their species or 'object,' without taking into account the intention with which the choice was made, or the totality of foreseen consequences of the action for all concerned." Cf. also M. Rhonheimer, "'Intrinsically Evil Acts' and the Moral Viewpoint: Clarifying a Central Teaching of *Veritatis Splendor,*" *The Thomist* 58, no. 1 (1994): 1–39 (reprinted in J. A. Di Noia and R. Cessario, eds., "*Veritatis Splendor" and the Renewal of Moral Theology* [Princeton, N.J.-Huntington-Chicago: Scepter/Our Sunday Visitor/Midwest Theological Forum, 1999], 161ff., and in *The Perspective of the Acting Person.*

241. The category of the "personal relationship" and the responsibilities that are built upon it have been worked out very well by R. Spaemann, "Wer hat wofür Verantwortung? Zum Streit um deontologische oder teleologische Ethik," *Herder Korrespondenz* 36 (1982): 345–50, and 403–8. The critical responses by A. Elsässer, F. Furger, and P. Müller-Goldkuhle that follow (ibid., 509ff., 603ff., 606ff.) unfortunately do not engage with the fundamentals of Spaemann's argument, as Spaemann himself had to

what we owe to others, the justice and goodwill we must exercise in relation to our neighbor, the particular relationships of responsibility we have to our fellow human beings. Such relationships hold a privileged place (in comparison with other circumstances) for the determination of our willing. A wife is not obliged to turn in her husband to the public authorities for a crime he has committed, even when she recognizes that it is necessary for the health of the community for wrongdoers to suffer penalties.[242] Both the wife and the police fulfill their duty, and both are just from their own perspectives, which is to say, their action is good and therefore also right.

The fundamental difference between a virtue ethics and a norm-ethics consists, accordingly, in this: that in the former, the morally right, as the rightness of appetition toward "what is good for man," is always *also* determined on the level of concrete actions with relation to one's fellow human beings—to those with whom the acting person (whether by natural relationship or by relationships set up by promises, contracts, etc.) stands in a morally qualified relationship (and the acting person also stands in a relationship to himself). This is why there can be talk of actions that are "intrinsically" or "always" evil. But a norm-ethics of a utilitarian kind, that is to say, a norm-ethics that is finally an ethics that operates through arguments, has no room to concede a privileged status to such relationships: they must, consequently, separate the category of the "rectitude of actions" from the category of the "goodness of the will." They cannot comprehend how the intentional relationship of the will to "justice"—that is, right willing—is at risk in every particular choice of action.

The peculiarity of human action that has been placed in the foreground time and again in the course of this exposition of a rational virtue ethics—that it is intentional action (it is crucial never to lose sight of this) and that there is an essentially intentional structuring of the objects of action—both grounds and reflects the perspective that is distinctive of all morality: moral actions are immanent acts which, apart from their effects upon other acting subjects, always change the acting person himself. Through action as an intentional accomplishment the human being acquires, as a being, that increased fullness of being—perfection, completeness—which we have in mind when we speak of a "good person." "Intentional actions" are fulfillments through which the acting subject in his reasoning-and-striving *aims at* something and changes himself as well through this "aiming at something" (the good). Consequently

clarify in his reply (*Herder Korrespondenz* 37 [1983]: 79–84). Cf. also E. Schockenhoff, *Natural Law and Human Dignity*, 202f., who depends on A. Gewirth, "Are There Any Absolute Rights?" in Gewirth, *Human Rights: Essays on Justification and Application* (Chicago: University of Chicago Press, 1982), 218–33; Gewirth's article is also available in J. Waldron, ed., *Theories of Rights* (Oxford: Oxford University Press, 1984), 91–109.

242. Cf. this example in I-II, Q. 19, a. 10.

we become "good" or "bad" human beings through intentional actions, and that means that we reach the only thing one can reasonably seek for its own sake, through which our appetition experiences that satisfaction we are all looking for in our desire to be happy. The question about morality is never simply, "What should I do? What action is the right one here and now?" These questions are doubtless questions of ethics and morality, but they are all subordinated to the first and decisive question: "What kind of a person do I become, when I do this or that—that is, when I freely *choose* to do it? Where am I going? Where is my life heading as a whole, if I do, or do not, carry out this or that action?"

Moral goodness is something "more" than mere goodness, due to the fact of being a human: metaphysically speaking, it is accidental (additional) being—even a morally depraved person does not lose thereby his or her ontological dignity as a human being—but in the perspective of the good, it is the only real goodness on the basis of which we can say about a human being that he or she is a good human being. As moral subjects, we become, or we are, what we strive for, and what we do on the basis of our striving. It would do the human being no good if he could make the whole world better, but not become or be a good human being himself. It would not really make the world better, because a world without persons of good will—without "good human beings"—is not a good world.

Now, this may sound a bit as if we were only playing with words. One could say—and utilitarian ethicists do in fact say it—that ultimately, one is a better human being just by trying to make the world better. But this objection really misses the main point: we can strive for, pursue, and work together to produce the good for the world, for society—in short, for our fellow human beings—only to the extent that we are ourselves seeking for the "good for man." But we can only do that by first asking the question, "What is truly good for me?" It is impossible to wish the good of others when we don't know what belongs to our *own* good. For we relate to others most deeply—and also cognitively—not simply as *others* but as others *who are the same as I am,* and thereby, too, as "another self." The commandment to "love your neighbor as yourself," the Golden Rule—these are not trivialities. Rather, they constitute— quite apart from their parainetical function—the cognitive structural law of practical reason.

The development of moral virtue through the action-determining practical reason *within* this perspective of morality encourages us to formulate some fundamental structural principles of an "ethics of the judgment of actions," and to refine it through criticism of the opposing position of utilitarianism. Such an ethics of the judgment of actions reflects the moral logic of the reason that determines action concretely, that is, the logic whose observance is the very condition for this reason to make judgments according to the structure of prudence, and finally makes possible the acquisition of the habit of prudence.

b) Prudence and Competence

Alasdair MacIntyre takes to task Kant's "distinction between the good will, the possession of which alone is necessary and sufficient for moral worth, and what he took to be a quite distinct natural gift, that of knowing how to apply general rules to particular cases, a gift the lack of which is called stupidity. So for Kant one can be both good and stupid; but for Aristotle stupidity of a certain kind precludes goodness."[243]

Such stupidity would be incompetence, and to the extent that one is responsible for having it in any form, it is scarcely reconcilable with a good will. Kant would certainly not deny that, but it is not a theme of his ethics, and to this extent MacIntyre may be correct. Incompetence means here the lack of those skills and knowledges that are indispensable in all the realms of human activity for rational achievement. Special competence (of a medical doctor, of a mechanic or a housewife/homemaker, of teachers, taxidrivers, journalists, bakers, lawyers, computer specialists, pilots, nurses, engineers, etc.) is the kind of competence needed for realizing what is good for man in concrete actions. But specialist competence can be misused, and therefore it is not moral competence nor is it moral virtue. Moral virtue is precisely that kind of *habitus* that cannot be misused. Virtue is thus the condition for the right use of all special competencies, but without special competence virtue itself would be the sort of thing MacIntyre points at with the saying, "Be good, sweet maid, and let who will be clever."

Special competence, or the ability to do what is right in special areas of human activity, forms a unity with moral virtue and with prudence. The prudent person, first and foremost, is one who endeavors to acquire the appropriate special competence, knowledge and skills needed for his field of activity, who consequently also possesses the ability to estimate consequences of his actions, and to assess how much responsibility he bears for these consequences.[244] It should be sufficient just to mention this, but such mention is also necessary, in order not to distort the profile of the virtue of prudence. The prudent person is competent, that is, he strives for the greatest of all competencies, and at the same time understands how to put this competence into

---

243. *After Virtue* (2nd ed.), 154.
244. On the theme "consequences of actions," cf. also R. Spaemann, *Happiness and Benevolence,* 145ff.

service for the good of man. And exactly for this reason he will know that the best purpose can never justify a bad means.[245]

c) Does the End Justify the Means?

It is fundamentally valid for every purposeful reasoning toward a goal, that carrying out a particular action is only going to be justified through being aimed at a good purpose. This is because the means, or the concrete action performed, really serves to reach the end in view. And precisely *insofar* as it serves to do this, the end, and only the end, justifies the means. Hegel, who always treats action-theoretical issues very subtly, makes a similar observation: "The phrase, 'if the end is right, so is the means' is a tautology, since the means is precisely that which is nothing in itself but is for the sake of something else, and therein, i.e., in the end, has its purpose and worth—*provided, of course, it be truly a means.*"[246]

But, as Hegel goes on to say, "when someone says 'the end justifies the means,' his purport is not confined to this bare tautology; he understands by the words something more specific, namely that to use as means to a good end something which in itself is simply not a means at all, to violate something in itself sacrosanct, in short to commit a crime as a means to a good end, is permissible and even one's bounden duty."[247] But what is here referred to as a "crime" is not "a general maxim, left vague and still subject to dialectic; on the contrary, its specific character is already objectively fixed." Understood in this way, the principle becomes an expression of the view that "the subjective conviction, and it alone, decides the ethical character of an action," so that if someone agrees with this principle, he neglects that "certain actions are inherently and actually misdeeds, vices, and crimes."[248]

In this is also to be found the shocking content of the "Machiavellian principle." But Machiavelli himself did not vouch for the principle in this form, but only in the first, weaker sense, which is both trivial and correct. For it is simply *impossible* to establish the principle at all in the stronger, second form criticized by Hegel. When Machiavelli says, "it is necessary for a prince, if he wishes to maintain himself, to learn how not to be good, and to use this knowledge or not use it, according to the necessity of the case,"[249] what he means is

---

245. Cf. on this, and also for what follows, M. Rhonheimer, "Gut und böse oder richtig und falsch—was unterscheidet das sittliche?" or the expanded version called "Ethik—Handeln—Sittlichkeit. Zur sittlichen Dimension menschlichen Tuns," in J. Bonelli, ed., *Der Mensch als Mitte und Massstab der Medizin.*

246. *Philosophy of Right,* section 140.d (trans. T. M. Knox; italics added), 51.

247. Ibid.

248. Ibid., section 140.e (trans. Knox), 52.

249. N. Machiavelli, *The Prince,* XV (trans. L. Ricci), 56.

that the good as it is determined according to current criteria of "being good" can in certain circumstances be opposed to the necessity of maintaining oneself in power, and just to this extent such "moral laws" fail in their function of determining what is "good." For Machiavelli, the "end" in no way justifies an "evil" means, but rather determines under what conditions the normal criteria for "being good" can specify what "a *good* means" really is. For him, the current moral criteria finally only formulate the means for reaching a good; and one of these goods is the maintenance of power by the prince. Consequently, Machiavelli only uses the principle in the first, trivial sense of the word.

So, then, Machiavelli's position is not even "Machiavellian," but only a typical, albeit paradoxically and quite forcefully expressed, formulation of norm utilitarianism. Modern utilitarianism has developed the refined art of saying the same thing in less shocking style. The principle of "the end justifies the means" is the maxim of amoralism: as such, it is not even capable of being discussed and nobody who claims to be engaged in ethics would want to take the position. In fact, every respectable utilitarian will rightly steer clear of it.[250] No ethical position, not even Machiavelli's, is an amoral position in this sense (even if it is perceived as such).[251] The utilitarian principle, by contrast, is a principle intended to ground a definite kind of *morality*. But there are reasons for considering that principle to be wrong.

When we ask ourselves the question, whether the "good end" does not, perhaps, justify an action that we would consider "intrinsically evil," we mean that *in this case* this action could not really be evil. We do not mean to say that the good purpose justifies the (bad) means, but rather, that *in this case,* this means is no longer evil. This is because everyone knows that a good purpose can never be attained by an evil means.

As a loose maxim for action, then, this position cannot be justified, and the terms "good" and "bad"/"evil" suddenly contain a suspicious ambiguity. But the utilitarian calculus as sketched above is quite capable of being justified (and utilitarians are not loose but rigorous): for, according to utilitarians of all stripes, actions considered in themselves have no moral (objective) identity independently of the consequences they give rise to. They are considered physical events, caused by human agents, consciously provoked processes, which effect certain circumstances and states of affairs. These developments

---

250. Cf., e.g., B. Schüller, "Der gute Zweck und die schlechten Mittel," in B. Schüller, *Der menschliche Mensch. Aufsätze zur Metaethik und zur Sprache der Moral* (Düsseldorf: Patmos, 1982), 148–55.

251. In contrast to *Il Principe*, a work written for a certain occasion, Machiavelli's truly major work *Discorsi sopra la prima deca di Tito Livio* (= *Discourses on the First Ten Books of Livy*) provides a more qualified point of view, esp. Book I, chaps. 9 and 26. Cf. also H. Münkler, *Machiavelli. Die Begründung des politischen Denkens der Neuzeit aus der Krise der Republik Florenz,* 2 vols. (Frankfurt am Main: Suhrkamp, 1982 and 1984).

obtain their moral identity through the balancing of the consequences they give rise to, which then can lead through a normal balancing to the establishment of a utilitarian rule. And for Machiavelli, too, the moral criteria for goodness are just such rules. Therefore utilitarians do not operate according to the fundamental expression "the end justifies the means." Instead, they make this expression simply empty of content, because for them *only* ends determine (i.e., the optimal balance of consequences) what can be good or bad anyway. According to utilitarian logic, nobody *can* do what the principle "the end justifies the means" forbids, because what someone does for the sake of a good (or to be more exact, an "optimal") end is, by definition the *right thing* (to pursue which, by principle, in one's action, is considered the mark of the moral goodness of the action).

Nevertheless, assuming that this logic is wrong, and that actions possess a moral identity as intentional basic actions independently of further purposes and consequences, it stands to reason (from the point of view of virtue ethics), that even when utilitarians do not *intend* to argue according to the basic principle of the "end justifies the means," they cannot evade the reproach of extolling this very principle. This is because the utilitarian denial of this fact cannot change the reality that the means—the concrete actions—that we choose are always already intentional actions on the basis of which we become "good" or "bad," "just" or "unjust" human beings—independently of any further intentions. An *objectively* bad, unjust action is, in fact—and here we can cite Hegel again—*in reality not a means at all* for reaching something good or just—no more than stones can be a means of nourishing oneself, which is the case, even if someone is erroneously convinced that he *can* get nourishment that way.

Essential, then, for the morality of the judgment of action is the question, "Is what *I want to do* also objectively (i.e., in itself) a 'good' action?" Or can doing-x be a means? Is doing-x *in itself* a choosable action by moral criteria? Is not this or that action rather something to avoid under any circumstances? Do I have to ask myself about the consequences of an intentional killing of an innocent person, or should I not rather restrain myself and say, "I may not do this—at all." Utilitarians cannot even *ask* such questions because they are meaningless for them, or else because the categorical "NO!" is always something provisional for them, something that can be relativized again by another calculation of consequences—for this reason they have reasonably acquired the reputation of representing the view that "the end justifies the means." To be sure, this reflection on the objective meaning of what one wants to do is not always something clear-cut. And it is no more clear-cut what our will is really aiming for when we choose a concrete action and what kind of person we become through doing it: a person aims for what his reason proposes to him as "good." Now, one could say that it is only important in each case to *think* that what reason takes to be good, that is also what really *is* good for man. And then the will would also have to be good. But apart from the fact that probably no one would seriously be satisfied with a life based only on what one *thought* to be the case, someone who committed himself to the easy-going proposition of "What I don't know, doesn't concern me" [*was ich nicht weiß, macht mir nicht heiß*], would already have missed out on "what is good for man" in the most fundamental sense, namely, the good, which consists in living according to reason. This good is an essential component of what we call human dignity.[252]

To be able to identify in each case what we *objectively* do, independently of further intentions, and what our will is actually aiming at, when we choose it, the circumstances *and* the consequences play a role: that is, they play a role in the clarification of the objective content of what one intends to do. The utilitarian would probably object at this point—but, as we have seen, he would be wrong to do so—that he poses just such questions as these. He is likewise concerned about nothing other than the "objective" meaning of his action, but which can only be determined, he maintains, through the consequences it brings about.[253] What are circumstances and consequences?

d) Circumstances and Consequences: Principles for the Moral Evaluation of the Consequences of Action

The objective content of every intentional (basic) action, is, we observed, an object of *reason*. The reason is what puts together the various elements of an action (behavioral patterns, circumstances, the "why?," the ethical context) into an objectified unity and which it then—with respect to the principles (virtues)—is able to identify as good or bad: *species moralium actuum constituuntur ex formis prout sunt a ratione conceptae,* "The types of moral actions are constituted out of forms, according as they are grasped by reason."[254]

If we treat an action in its natural identity (its *genus naturae*) as a purely physical process of action, there will be, of course, a multitude of circumstances and consequences or effects of this process, whose assessment by rea-

---

252. Cf. on this R. Spaemann, "Über den Begriff der Menschenwürde," in R. Spaemann, *Das Natürliche und das Vernünftige. Aufsätze zur Anthropologie* (Munich: Piper, 1987), 77–106.

253. Cf., e.g., S. Ernst, "Hat die autonome und teleologische Ethik die Objectivität sittlichen Handeln vergessen?" Marginalien zu M. Rhonheimers Buch "Natur als Grundlage der Moral," *Theologie und Glaube* 78 (1988); and my reply, "'Natur als Grundlage der Moral': Nichts als Spiegelfechterei?" ibid., 79 (1989): 69–83. What follows here can be taken as a reply to Ernst's final objections (ibid., 84–87).

254. I-II, Q. 18, a. 10.

son is what alone provides this action with its moral identity *(genus moris)* as an intentional act. For a theft to be a theft, the thing that has been taken away has to be rightly possessed by the person from whom it was taken. With regard to the physical action process of "taking something away from someone," this is merely a "circumstance" (it is part of what "stands around," Lat. *circumstantia*). For the reason, however, this becomes again a constitutive element of the moral identity of this action: the will directs itself here *against* the right of the other. The injury (i.e., the damage done to "what pertains to another," to "what is owed to another," to "what belongs to another") is the special objective effect of this way of acting, as it is objectified to the reason; since only the reason is able to judge of justice in accordance with the principle that comes from the reason itself. The action is accordingly an act of the species "injustice." While only a circumstance on the level of the natural identity of the act, it must be given another name on the level of the moral identity of the act as intentional action: it must be called an "objective condition" that constitutes an opposition to the order of reason *(principalis conditio obiecti rationi repugnans*, "principal condition of the object that is repugnant to reason")[255] or an "essential objective difference" *(differentia essentialis obiecti).*[256] At the level of the *genus naturae*, even the intentional "why?" the purpose of "taking something for oneself" is only a circumstance; for the reason, however, this belongs to the formal essence of the action. Whether the theft takes place in the morning or the afternoon, whether two or only one horse is being stolen, whether it takes place in the city or the country, changes nothing about the fact that it is a theft. These various givens are only circumstantial in relation to the moral identity of the action. For the reason they form at best a quantitative element (a more or less serious theft).

In case the victim of the robbery has to use his horse for business reasons and as a consequence of the theft suffers an economic loss in addition, this is a circumstance—or a consequence—(with respect to the objective identity of the "theft") that lends the action a *further* objective dimension as an additional injury (even when this was not a further goal aimed at by the thief). Or: When A sets fire to B's house, this is objectively a material injury done to B. Whether B is in the house or not when it is burned, is merely a circumstance with respect to the natural identity of the action, but not with respect to its moral identity: if B, as a *consequence* dies in the burning, in relation to

255. I-II, Q. 18, a. 10.
256. I-II, Q. 18, a. 5, ad 4. This is why sometimes the object is identified simply with just this "differential" aspect which makes the action different from other species of actions, though in reality the "object" is the entire *materia circa quam* as objectified by reason and chosen by the will (see above III.4 and also the extremely useful book by J. Pilsner, *The Specification of Human Actions in St. Thomas Aquinas* [Oxford: Oxford University Press, 2006], esp. 86–91).

the moral identity of the action this is either an unintended result (because A thought the house was empty), for which A nevertheless is fully responsible; or alternatively, A burned B's house because he wanted to murder B. In that case the action is objectively murder (even though with respect to the natural identity of the accomplished action "burning B's house," "B's being there at the time" is no more than a circumstance; morally considered, however—for the reason, that is—this constitutes an objective condition). Now it is conceivable that B is a dangerous terrorist, and that his death has the consequence that an assassination he was planning for the next day will not happen. In this way, perhaps many people's lives were spared by A's action. *This* consequence is again only a circumstance—certainly an important one—of the moral identity of A's action, but it changes nothing about its objective identity. A carried out an injustice against B (murder), even if it was done with an intention that was good in itself. A's action of "killing B" is neither justified nor made "better" thereby, even though the *entire* complex of action (i.e., with the further intention included) is certainly less bad than it would have been, if the intention had been bad.

For the practical reason there are, accordingly, two kinds of circumstances and consequences: (1) those that are mere circumstances *with respect to the act considered as physical or natural,* since they do not belong to the natural reality of the act, but are constitutive for the object, and hence objectively condition its moral identity; and (2) those that are only circumstances *with respect to the moral identity,* but do not change this identity. And here we must add that such circumstances of the second kind can, again, with relation to the natural act, *not* be circumstances at all, but its necessary consequence: if a child is conceived through an adulterous sexual act, the conception is a "direct, essential consequence" and not a mere circumstance; but it is a circumstance with respect to the moral identity of the action "committing adultery": the action is adultery (an injury to marital fidelity) completely regardless of whether or not a child is conceived.[257] On the basis of this intentional analysis of actions we can formulate a few principles for judging our actions on the basis of consequences:

1) Those consequences that are objective conditions mold the objective content of what we choose. The reason judges whether or not a consequence is an objective condition with respect to the goal of the virtues. If "taking away a horse from A that he rightfully owns" has *as a consequence* that the

---

257. T. Nisters, *Akzidentien der Praxis. Thomas von Aquins Lehre von den Umständen menschlichen Handelns* (Freiburg and Munich: Alber, 1992) shows analogues to the juridical problems of defining actions and assigning of culpability. This study points emphatically to the plasticity of act definition which is, again, a characteristic of virtue ethics (cf. esp. 189).

horse suddenly doubles itself into two horses, so that now both A *and* B possessed a horse, there would be no injustice here. But the consequence, in fact, is that A *no longer* has a horse to which he has a right of ownership. Consequently the action is *objectively* unjust.

2) For the good consequences of our good actions we can take credit and win praise. And this is the case even if we did not foresee the consequences.

3) For the bad consequences of our bad actions we also take responsibility, even when these consequences actually had not been foreseen, provided these consequences are in some way intrinsically connected with the freely performed action and precisely to this extent *could* have been foreseen in their kind (there is a guilt of negligence). For example, someone who sets fire to his house in order to commit an insurance fraud and thereby kills a child playing in the immediate neighborhood, or who provokes the explosion of a gas pipe causing severe damage, is of course responsible for these consequences, because there is an intrinsic and generally foreseeable connection between the evil act and *this kind of consequences.* If, on the other hand, someone steals a fruit container in a port which unfortunately contains a bomb, placed there by some terrorists, and this bomb later explodes right in front of a school, killing many children and teachers, one would not say that the thief is morally responsible for the disastrous effects of the bomb, because there is no intrinsic or in any way foreseeable connection between stealing fruit containers and bomb explosions (though the disaster would not have happened if he had abstained from stealing). In contrast to the incendiary insurance fraud, we would say that this was bad luck, and that the ones who are really responsible for the children's and the teachers' deaths are the terrorists who put the bomb into the container.

4) Good consequences of bad actions cannot be credited to the one who does the bad actions. This is because the *real* action to be "credited" is the *bad* consequence, that is, the effect that the bad action has caused to be so, and this is the consequence that constitutes the intentional identity of the action (e.g., the violation of a right). What may come out good *in addition to this* is then to be considered as a side effect of the intentional action (circumstance), according to the reasons given above, and this will be the case even if the deed was done for the purpose of obtaining this side effect.

5) For the *unforeseeable* bad consequences of our good actions, we are not responsible. They are merely unintentional, provided that we really *could* not have foreseen them. (If what was said under the third principle is the case—i.e., if there is an intrinsic connection between the action and the bad consequence, a consequence of a type that can in principle be foreseen—then we have what is considered under the seventh principle, below.)

6) The *foreseeable* bad consequences of *omitting* to do an action cannot be ascribed to our culpability as long as the accomplishment of the omitted action would have been objectively evil (= the end does not justify the means). Otherwise, principle (4) is valid.

7) The *foreseeable* bad consequences of objectively good actions cannot be attributed to the agent's culpability, provided, (a) the action was not done only to bring about this consequence (that is to say, there is a reason to do the action independently of the foreseeable occurrence of the consequences);(b) the reason for doing the action despite the evil consequences is sufficiently serious in comparison with the consequence; and (c) one has done everything in his power to avoid the occurrence of the consequence. The evil consequence in this case is also nonintentional, that is, it is a nonintentional *side effect.*

This last principle is the most controversial. It is known as the principle of "indirect action," or better, perhaps: "the principle of the indirect voluntary" *(voluntarium indirectum),* often formulated as the "principle of double effect." More precisely, the dispute concerns how relevant the difference is between principles (6) and (7).

e) Actions with Nonintentional Side Effects

According to what has been presented so far concerning the intentional determination of the objective content of human actions, we can distinguish two kinds of consequences of an action: those that constitute the *object* of an action (e.g., damage of someone's ownership rights, communicative deception as an injury to the communicative community between human beings; restoration of justice, etc.), and those consequences that exist in relation to this object as circumstances, as something added. Utilitarian (or consequentialist) theories reject such a distinction as meaningless. For them, the *objective* content of every action, and thereby the "rectitude" of every action, is solely characterized by its success in bringing about the optimal balance of *all* foreseeable consequences. The human being is therefore "responsible for all foreseeable consequences of his actions,"[258] and the distinction between principles (6) and (7) listed above is meaningless: if someone bears responsibility for all foreseeable consequences and it is only these consequences (or the intentional relationship of the agent to them) that forms the objective content of a particular way of acting—an "expanded object" (R. A. McCormick), as it were, or a "total object" [*Gesamtobjekt*]—then someone would have to feel himself

258. B. Schüller, *Die Begründung sittlicher Urteile,* 290.

responsible for the consequences of *every* omitted action, and vice versa, one could never say, as one must for principle (7), that he bears *no* responsibility at all, under some circumstances, for foreseeable bad consequences.

In this context, it is interesting to observe how the French Nazi collaborator Paul Touvier defended himself in his trial of March 1994. When Touvier (along with Victor de Bourmont, the Lyons chief of police) ordered the execution of seven Jews on June 28, 1944, he prevented, so Touvier claimed in his defense, the carrying out of the threatened execution of one hundred Jews by Werner Knab, the head of the Gestapo in Lyons, in punishment for an attack made by the French Resistance. In reality, Touvier claimed, he did not kill seven innocent persons, he rescued ninety three. The action, according to the argument, should not be defined in terms of the "limited object" of "killing seven innocent persons"; for had Touvier not done what he did, he would have been responsible, it was implied, for the unavoidable deaths of one hundred innocent persons. This consequence is then relevant for the definition of the action that was accomplished. In view of this expanded object of their action, Touvier and his accomplices in fact carried out the "rescue" of ninety-three persons. The killing of seven innocent persons thereby simply disappears from view.[259]

This point of view can only be justified when someone begins with a "physicalist" concept of action, that is, when it is denied that there is such a thing as a basic *intentional* action—here, the killing of an innocent person—that we can qualify as good or bad in itself, and independently of further intentions. The physicalist concept of action assumes—as has been shown—that action is the cause of events or states of affairs through bodily movements or other kinds of physical effects. It is exclusively the events, states of affairs, or conditions brought about by these movements that are subject to moral assessment; the moral judgment on the rectitude of an action rests exclusively on the actual capacity of that action to bring about such effects. As already shown at length, this concept of action embraced by utilitarians (for the most part unreflectively) is untenable.

If we start with an intentional concept of action, we understand what is meant by an "unintentional side effect": it is the consequence of an action of which the intentional-objective content is good (or at least not bad) and the accomplishment of which, under some circumstances, is commanded by the reason. This means that not to do the action would be bad (e.g., an injustice),

---

259. Of course, by arguing in a consequentialist way, one could "expand" the argument still more and make the claim that the collaboration implicit in the "rescue operation" performed by Touvier contributed to the support of the Nazi regime in France and to the weakening of the Resistance, which, the longer it lasted, took its toll in the loss of life of many more Jews. Cf. on this my critique of R. A. McCormick's concept of the "expanded object" in Rhonheimer, "Intentional Actions and the Meaning of Object," 291ff., and also R. Spaemann, "Einzelhandlungen," *Zeitschrift für philosophische Forschung* 54 (2000): 514–31.

which is to say, it would be appropriate to do the action even in case the bad consequence would not be realized (or not foreseen) *and*, in view of the bad consequence, there is a proportion between the good effect of the action itself and that consequence. If the action were not appropriate in the case when the bad consequence were not present or if it were in any case not proportionate, it would mean that bringing about the bad consequence is in reality the object of the action, which becomes a means to an end.

A classical example used in the clarification of this is the case of the pregnant woman with cancer of the uterus whose life can only be saved through removal of the uterus (hysterectomy). Of course, considered physically, this operation necessarily and directly causes the death of the unborn child. But the action considered intentionally is an act of the rescue of the mother's life, that is, a life-saving therapeutic intervention. The proof of this is that the hysterectomy would obviously be appropriate to carry out if the woman were not pregnant. It would without any doubt be the indicated therapy.

Since it is objectively good, then, to rescue the life of the woman through the operation, the consequence of the death of the conceived child falls, as it were, out of the intentional object structure of the action: it is a case of an unintentional side effect. The killing of the fetus here is certainly not a means (because it is the effect of the action of "removal of the uterus" which is in itself a good action), and also not the purpose of the action (which would have been carried out had the woman not been pregnant). The action is also proportionate: the life of the woman is at stake. Consequently, the action *can* be carried out without it having to be characterized by the consequence "killing of the fetus." The death of the unborn child here is to be seen as a natural event (which someone could have prevented, but for which there was a proportionate reason not to).

> In case someone were to object that the death of the fetus is here chosen as a means—since its death is a necessary condition for the success of the operation—then the answer would be that the only "means" that is chosen is the removal of the uterus. This alone is what is intended (willed). The death of the fetus is a mere consequence of that. It has no positive influence on the choice of the action "removal of the uterus," but if anything tends to steer away from it. An opposite example is the justification for use of the atomic bomb for ending the war against Japan: here, the killing of the civilian population was in no respect the nonintentional side effect of an otherwise justified act of war. To reach the goal of "ending the war," the killing of hundreds of thousands was chosen: it was the actual, chosen means for forcing the surrender: it was the "object" of the chosen act of war.[260]

260. A fuller discussion of this example can be found in M. Rhonheimer, *Natural Law and Practical Reason*, 458ff.

Now we could also consider another example of an action-process that is physically identical but which is, with respect to intentionality, quite differently structured. Let us say that the pregnant woman's cancer has not yet progressed so far as to be life-threatening for her; the child could be born and the hysterectomy carried out afterward, although this would also involve some unpleasantness and a certain amount of risk. In this case, to carry out the removal of the uterus and thereby kill the fetus, in order to avoid this pain, would be *disproportionate*. Considered intentionally, this would mean: one *could have* prevented the death of the child, but did not. The circumstance of the improperly justified timing of the operation becomes the objective condition of the action. In terms of intention, this means that the death of the fetus is still a side effect, but a side effect that could have been avoided without giving up on the action that was good in itself (rescuing the mother's life). And thus one could not say that the death of the fetus had nothing to do with the will of the acting person, who in such a case would be responsible for its death.

Finally, if a pregnant woman were to have her uterus removed without having cancer at all, and then were to say that this is only an "indirect" killing of the fetus, we are confusing the physically "indirect" with the intentionally "indirect." The sign of this would be that if the woman were not pregnant, she would not have wanted the operation, nor would it have been indicated. The killing of the fetus is therefore the real "why" of this action, or its "object." Physically considered, all these actions are identical. Intentionally considered, they are three different actions: the first is "saving a life"; the second is "avoiding pain and discomfort (at the cost of a human life)"; the third is "killing a human being" (an abortion).

In this way as well becomes clear the difference from an abortion as a medically indicated procedure (i.e., the case that scarcely occurs anymore, when a pregnancy or birth has fatal consequences for the mother, while the child survives). In this case to abort the child means to kill someone as a direct means to an end. Intentionally, the action is "killing a human being."

> Furthermore, to the extent that an embryo and fetus are living beings belonging to the category of "human"—and according to today's knowledge nobody would reasonably deny it—there is *in itself* no fundamental difference between the killing of a fully grown-up person and the killing of an embryo/fetus. Because the latter means killing the grown-up individual that the embryo or fetus would have become, had he or she not been killed. The killing of an unborn child is the elimination of the entire life history of an individual. One should not in this try to prove that the embryo is already a *person*, although this is possible; it is enough to show that the person is a living thing of the kind "hu-

man being," and therefore *will* at least become one. Consider: If today I keep A from doing x tomorrow, I cannot say tomorrow that I would *not* be responsible tomorrow for A not being able to do x, because A could not do x at the time I hindered him. Women who have had abortions say afterward that they have not merely killed an "embryo" or "fetus" but a human being who would *now* be alive, had it not been aborted.[261]

Often the even more seldom borderline case is cited that in case a fetus is allowed to live, both mother *and* child would die.[262] But one must be cautious when it comes to arguments about borderline cases because one cannot assume that for all cases there will be a solution that can be justified in a normative way. Nor can one derive from such cases any conclusions about the exceptionless validity of norms.[263]

But an answer should be given, nevertheless, for the situation we are discussing. The basic problem here lies in the fact that a decision to let both mother and child die, when one could at least have saved the mother, and the child would have died *in any event,* is a decision that cannot be rationally carried out, especially from the doctor's perspective. We can reconstruct the thinking of someone in a position like this as follows: the norm that prohibits killing another human being seems simply meaningless and pointless in this situation. Its meaning is to keep someone from doing an injustice. But it is not clear in this situation how one would be disregarding the child's right to life. A life story, when it is certain that it will not take place, is not something one can "prevent" from happening. The argument that a person may not dispose of human life and not calculate its worth or its significance against other life, appears not to be relevant here, since nature herself has already spoken her

261. Nevertheless, human fetuses should not be treated only as *potential* persons, but as persons; cf. R. Spaemann, "Sind alle Menschen Personen? Über neue philosophische Rechtfertigungen der Lebensvernichtung," in J.-P. Stüssel, ed., *Tüchtig oder tot. Die Entsorgung des Leidens* (Freiburg im Breisgau: Herder, 1991), 133–47 (slightly edited under the title "Person ist der Mensch selbst, nicht ein bestimmter Zustand der Menschen," in H. Thomas, ed., *Menschlichkeit der Medizin* [Herford: Busse-Seewald, 1993], 261–76), as well as Spaemann, *Personen* (see above), 252ff.; G. Pöltner, "Achtung der Würde und Schutz von Interessen," in J. Bonelli, ed., *Der Mensch aks Mitte und Maßstab der Medezin;* L. Honnefelder, "Der Streit um die Person in der Ethik," *Philosophisches Jahrbuch* 100 (1993): 246–65; M. Rhonheimer, "Human Fetuses, Persons and the Right to Abortion: Toward an Absolute Power of the Born," in Rhonheimer, *Ethics of Procreation and the Defense of Human Life,* ed. W. Murphy (Washington, D.C.: The Catholic University of America Press, 2010); S. Schwarz, *The Moral Question of Abortion* (Chicago: Loyola University Press, 1992).

262. Other examples of possible borderline situations are ectopic pregnancy (pregnancy in the fallopian tube) or the occurrence of hemorrhaging in the uterus during the last stage of pregnancy. Here, too, there are life-saving alternatives available for the child *and* for both mother and child. See my *Vital Conflict* (Washington, D.C.: The Catholic University of America Press, 2009), chap. 6.

263. On borderline cases, cf. *Natural Law and Practical Reason,* 469ff., and also B. Williams, "A Critique of Utilitarianism," in J. J. C. Smart and B. Williams, *Utilitarianism: For and Against* (Cambridge: Cambridge University Press, 1973), 75–150.

judgment. Only the life of the mother is still subject to a human's power to intervene. With respect to the fetus, this is no longer the case in the sense of a decision between "killing or allowing to live." The only thing that can still be chosen and really will be chosen is whether or not to rescue the mother. Regarding the life or death of the fetus or embryo, nothing more can be decided and chosen here. And only *this* alternative, "kill or allow to live?," is morally relevant. The only thing still left to decide in this situation is the alternative for the mother, "to let her die or rescue her?" It is clear that such an alternative is not one of "right or wrong." Only in the ethical context "justice" can an action of killing be described as an unjust action and here there is really no context in which damage done to human rights can be meaningfully spoken of.[264] Everything that marks the killing of an innocent person as wrong, a crime, an injustice—which would make it something for us to avoid or even something to condemn—is lacking. At the most, all that could be objected to such an action with its consequence of death for the embryo or fetus, is that the killing here is direct, that is, *physically* direct. But that alone is still not a morally relevant viewpoint.

For this reason, it seems, in this case a killing of the fetus does not consist in choosing the death of a human being as a means for rescuing the life of the mother. *Intentionally* (objectively), we could describe the case simply as "rescuing the life of the mother." The death of the fetus could then only be chosen as a means if it were otherwise to survive. Nobody *wants* the death of the fetus *in order* to rescue the mother. With respect to the death of the fetus there is no longer any willing needed: it will die in any event. The killing of the fetus falls back into the mere *genus naturae* of the moral (intentional) action of "rescuing the life of the mother."

Therefore, too, it would also be erroneous to treat such a case as an "exception" to the prohibition of murder; here we have nothing to do with the intentional action "killing an innocent human being," to which the prohibition is directed. Cases that follow this pattern cannot be subsumed at all under a norm, and can thus not be normatively justified, not even as "exceptions." But it is not necessary to do so: for in addition to the pressure of having to be decided quickly, such cases also possess the peculiarity that when they occur there are not two rationally supportable alternatives. Only the rescue of the mother's life can be rationally justified here. The physical action of killing (e.g., through craniotomy and extirpation of the fetus or through inducing

---

264. This does not imply that the embryo or fetus had lost its right to live in such a situation. That would not be apparent. But no more is it apparent why this right should be *infringed* through the way of acting that is in question here. We are not concerned here with the *existence* of the right to life, but with the *violation* of its right to life. I have treated this question systematically in my *Vital Conflicts: A Virtue Ethics Approach to Craniotomy and Tubal Pregnancies*.

premature birth) is intentionally characterized only by the will to rescue the mother's life. The action does not require any *normative* justification: it is only the nonintentionality of killing the fetus that needs to be justified. This appears possible through attending to the disappearance of the ethical context of "justice" that is a given in this situation, and consequently the killing of the fetus is just as little to be ascribed to the fault of the agent as if its death occurred through the agent's doing nothing at all: it remains a merely natural event despite the intervention.

The absolute prohibition of murder, therefore, says that one may never *choose* the death of a human being as the *means* to an end. That is to say, the death of a human being may never be *intended* as the object (the "why") of an action: not even when there is an intention to save someone's life can it be justified to *choose* between the death and the life of another person. And this also holds for a final case which has not yet been mentioned: the case of self-defense. Thomas Aquinas says categorically: "It is not permissible for a human being to intend the death of another human being, in order to defend oneself."[265] The *intentio* here referred to is the choice of means-to-an-end for the purpose of self-defense.

Even though Thomas maintains that it is not allowable to want to kill someone in order to save one's own life, he had shown previously that it is very "permissible" to want to defend oneself with an action that has the death of the attacker as a *consequence.* Of course, "physically," both actions are identical. Thomas argues that moral actions obtain their species through what someone intends, not through what falls outside of the intention. As long as someone intends to preserve his own life by an action, the accomplished action is objectively an action of self-defense and not the action "killing a man" with the intention of defending oneself. The question is only, is that in fact the case? It is the case, when one uses no more force than is necessary to ward off the life-threatening aggression. The (physical) act of self-defense must be *proportionate* (Lat. *proportionatus*) to the action of "defending oneself"; otherwise the action would be intentional and that means it would objectively not be an action of self-defense, but rather the intentional action "killing the aggressor" for the *purpose* of "saving one's own life."

This "proportion" between the force and the self-defending intention is accordingly not a criterion for whether one "may" kill someone (choice of means) *in order to* save one's own life (choice of goal). Rather, it is only a criterion for whether the killing of the aggressor is nonintentional, that is, whether or not it can be treated as a nonintended side effect.

265. II-II, Q. 64, a. 7.

Consequently it cannot be justified, for example, to kill an assailant when one could have fled the aggression, nor can all cases be justified of a planned killing action based on the consideration that thereby one could forestall the aggression of the other (of course, this does not apply to wartime situations). But a casuistic discussion of "cases" does not really solve the problem here. The nonintentionality of killing the aggressor comes to the fore, generally speaking, in the reactive quality of the self-defensive action, which is characterized less by reason and calculation than by fear and the reflex to escape an evil. The excessive use of force is no more than an external criterion of judgment. The decisive thing is what occurs in the heart of man.

But now, it may be objected that an abortion to save the life of the mother would be violence "proportionate" to saving one's own life. In this way, the action of "abortion" could be interpreted as self-defense, with a nonintended consequence of "death of the fetus." But the argument does not hold: the question of proportionate violence is not a criterion in this case for judging the nonintentionality of the action. For an instance of self-defense implies that *not doing it* would result in death, that an "omission" of the action would be equivalent to "permitting the aggressor's commission" of the act of killing. The use of force is directed, in fact, against an "act of murder" (aggression) by another, not against the aggressor's life. This is not the case with a fetus. Abortion is not an *act* of self-defense, but simply the intentional action of "killing someone" (as a means) *with* the intention of staying alive oneself. The life-threatening fetus is not in any way an aggressor, and consequently no act of preventing aggression is conceivable here.

This also shows how risky it is to use the language of "unjust aggressor" in the context of private self-defense. Such language only makes sense in connection with public justice (or wartime actions), where there is punishment for someone's *fault*. In the foregoing context there is simply no difference between "just" and "unjust" aggression. Every person is obliged in every situation to defend himself and to consider the death of an assailant as a possibility. This is so even in the case of someone sentenced to death who has escaped the day before his execution.

It seems appropriate to recall once again here the purpose for these seemingly all-too-subtle analyses of the intentional identity of actions: it has to do with the question—basic to all morality—about the quality of the acting person's will. The analytical logic of the above discussion should not lead us to forget that it only reflects what goes on "within the heart" of the person who acts. "It is from the heart that evil thoughts come: death, divorce, lust, theft, false witnessing and slander. That is what makes a man unclean" (Matt. 15:19f.). If, as the utilitarians say, it is only a matter of the conditions we bring about as the consequences of our actions, and if we were to measure the "purity of the heart" exclusively with regard to *which* conditions we want to bring about, the above considerations would indeed be nothing but irrelevant hairsplitting. But somehow we know that it is not just hairsplitting. And this is simply because we already feel it as unjust even to *will* something unjust, even when someone decides *not* to do it—in view of the foreseeable evil consequences—and the willing remains without consequence. In the perspective represented here, such wishes are not at all inconsequential: they have serious consequences for the person who has such wishes and *thereby* have serious consequences for the "state of the world." Here another passage could be cited: "A good man draws good things from his store [Gr. *thesauros,* or "treasury"] of goodness; a bad man draws bad things from his store of badness" (Matt. 12:35, Jerusalem Bible trans.).

My intention here is not to appeal to the Gospel as a way to justify my argument, but simply to show that the position developed here is the same as the one in the Gospels. What is it? It is the "perspective of morality" as presented from the beginning: namely, that in all the concrete actions that we choose on the basis of a judgment of reason, our whole humanity is at stake: our orientation toward "what is good for man"; that our human identity as rationally striving subjects is really at stake in the choice of what we willingly do; and that living a life does not consist in good intentions, but in good actions actually carried out. Good intentions are useless where there are not also *actions* that correspond to them. Only in this way can a coherently lived life take shape that can be characterized by certain kinds of attitudes, values, and commitments. And this means, above all, that all human actions carried out must be understood not as physical events but as the *intentional* accomplishments of persons.

If we look at matters this way, it becomes clear that a utilitarian position can no longer be opposed by the argument that "utilitarianism" is only a theory about how we can *determine* what concrete actions correspond to such good intentions (and thus determine their rightness). Such an argument is pointless, because in every utilitarian ethics the judgment of *what* someone does and *what someone wants with respect to his own actions* is "bracketed," that is, made superfluous or secondary. This must now be explained.

f) The Weighing of Goods and Balancing of Consequences
("Teleological Ethics" or Consequentialism)

"Utilitarianism" is not intended here as a pejorative label, but as the designation for a position that its adherents themselves accept. Today utilitarianism is presented under the name of "consequentialism," "proportionalism," or "teleological ethics." (The last of the three names is an unfortunate use of terminology, if not a completely mistaken term).[266] All three concern an ethics according to which the rectitude of our actions is measured exclusively on the basis of their foreseeable consequences (cf. above, III.3.c). That action is always the right one whose consequence consists in a maximum of non-moral goods or a minimum of nonmoral evils, and with respect to all those concerned in the action. A "weighing of goods," then, underlies any such consequentialistic "balancing."[267]

In this way "actions" become—as has already been repeatedly said—understood as physicalistic or "eventistic," as causes of the states of affairs of the world[268] (by "world" is meant here only the part of the world that is "relevant," or accessible to the awareness of the agent). Only states of affairs have meaning, not the actions that bring them into being. "Consequentialism is basically indifferent to whether a state of affairs consists in what I do or is produced by what I do . . . all that consequentialism is interested in is the idea of these doings being *consequences* of what I do."[269] It is also a matter of indifference whether something occurs as the consequence of an action or as the consequence of refraining from doing something, and whether "I" or "someone else" does it; for consequentialism, "all causal connexions are on

266. The distinction between the "teleological" and the "nonteleological" characteristics of ethical argument derives from C. D. Broad, "Some of the Main Problems of Ethics," *Philosophy* 21 (1946), but more recently reprinted as C. D. Broad, *Broad's Critical Essays in Moral Philosophy*, ed. D. R. Cheney (London and New York: Allen & Unwin, 1971), 223–46. For Broad, it simply appears that any ethics that grounds "duty" in the "good" is consequentialist; cf. also his earlier book, *Five Types of Ethical Theory* (London: Routledge & Kegan Paul, 1930), 278.

The name "consequentialism" originates from G. E. M. Anscombe, "Modern Moral Philosophy," *Philosophy* 33 (1958) and also available in R. Crisp and M. Slote, eds., *Virtue Ethics*, 26–44.

The term "proportionalism" designates a type of consequentialist ethics, which has an argument structure that proceeds essentially as follows: one may in acting directly cause "physical evils" (e.g., the amputation of a leg or the death of a person), as long as the cause of this evil is not the purpose of the action as such and if the action appears justified by a *proportionate* reason in the whole context of the action (or of all its conceivable consequences); as with consequentialism in general, the method is the weighing of goods. In the case of a leg amputation, such a mode of arguing is quite to the point; in the case of killing a human being, the matter becomes more problematic.

267. For the differentiation among the names "utilitarianism," "consequentialism," "proportionalism," and "teleological ethics," cf. J. M. Finnis, *Fundamentals of Ethics*, 81–86. For an exact decision-theoretical definition of consequentialism, see also J. Nida-Rümelin, *Kritik des Konsequentialismus*, 2nd ed. (Munich: R. Oldenbourg, 1995).

268. The concept "eventistic" is taken from A. W. Müller, "Radical Subjectivity: Morality versus Utilitarianism," *Ratio* 19 (1977): 115–32. The view that "eventism" is merely "a new name for the position commonly known as "Erfolgsethik" [result ethics] (W. Wolbert, *Vom Nutzen der Gerechtigkeit* [Freiburg, Switzerland: Universitätsverlag and Freiburg-im-Breisgau: Herder, 1992], 81), does not seem adequate to me, since the "result ethical" perspective is not one of action-judgments, but of judgments *about* actions (after the fact).

269. B. Williams, "A Critique of Utilitarianism," in J. J. C. Smart and B. Williams, *Utilitarianism: For and Against*, 75–150, here 93–94.

the same level," so that it "makes no difference . . . whether the causation of a given state of affairs lies through another agent, or not."[270] So then, if in consequence of my not doing something, someone else does what I do not do, I am just as responsible for it as if I had done it; in such a case I might as well do it myself—and in fact I am obliged to do so, if I could foreseeably do it in a less bad way or could ward off some other evil by doing it.[271]

This principle of "negative responsibility" really designates the decisive point of the consequentialist concept of action.[272] In fact, what lies behind it is a very specific theory of action inherent in consequentialism, but silently presupposed and not subjected to reflection. The question, for whom and for what we really bear responsibility when doing something or refraining from it, is central for the theory, and one cannot afford to assume or bracket this question in a debate with teleological ethics. To criticize consequentialism with the argument that we are not responsible in the same way for the consequences of what we actually do as for what happens (or is done by others) when we refrain from doing it would be begging the question: the ultimate issue is whether in fact this is the case, and why, if so. Only in dealing with this question does it become clear what we understand by an "action" as distinct from a mere omission and what distinguishes "one's own action" from an "action by another." Only when this has been clarified can it be shown that the consequentialist mode of argument is not simply another style of ethical argument, but rather

270. Ibid., 94. Cf. also J. Nida-Rümelin, *Kritik des Konsequentialismus*, 57, and his diagnosis that in utilitarianism, "persons are looked on in a certain sense as unessential for ethical judgment."

271. Thus J. Nida-Rümelin, ibid., 92, concludes that "strictly consequentialist-motivated behavior reduces the person to an instrument of (impersonal) value-maximization and is thereby irreconcilable, under virtually all empirical conditions, with the integrity of the person."

272. Williams's analysis of *negative responsibility* as the distinguishing feature of consequentialism has remained controversial in the English-speaking world and has naturally been rejected by consequentialist ethicists, who have time and again attempted to prove the identity, in principle, of doing and not-doing something, especially with reference to the bioethical problem of the difference (for consequentialists, the nondifference) between "killing" and "letting die." Representative for many other contributions to the discussion are J. Harris, "Williams on Negative Responsibility and Integrity," *Philosophical Quarterly* 24 (1974): 265–73; J. Glover and M. Scott-Taggart, "It Makes No Difference Whether or Not I Do It," *Proceedings of the Aristotelian Society*, suppl., 49 (1975): 171–209; N. Davis, "Utilitarismus und Verantwortlichkeit," *Ratio* 22 (1980): 18–37. A useful bibliography on the debate can be found in S. Scheffler, ed., *Consequentialism and Its Critics* (Oxford: Oxford University Press, 1988). Cf. also B. Steinbock and A. Norcross, eds., *Killing and Letting Die*, 2nd ed. (New York: Fordham University Press, 1994); the contribution by J. Rachels, "Active and Passive Euthanasia," 112–19 (1994 ed.) is particularly instructive: here, as in J.-C. Wolf, "Active und passive Euthanasie," *Archiv für Rechts- und Sozialphilosophie* 79 (1993): 393–415, it can be seen how exponents of consequentialism employ an eventistic concept of action instead of an intentional one.—The critics of Williams's thesis usually trivialize his position by reading into it a denial that there can be omissions whose consequences must be judged as if they were one's own actions. But that is not what Williams is saying: he certainly allows for omissions that are really actions (e.g., if someone neglects to prevent a child from playing with an electric appliance: here someone is responsible for the consequences of another's actions). According to Williams, the consequentialist view generally levels out the difference between doing and not doing or between one's own and another's action and then carries out an analysis of action on that basis.

(in cases where it is held to be the fundamental and definitive explanation of ethical or normative questions) fundamentally misconceives the whole phenomenon of the ethical, and the perspective of morality.[273]

Consequentialists see their position as opposed to what they call "deontological ethics"—which is just as serious a terminological mistake. According to them, an ethics like that maintains that certain ways of acting are intrinsically bad and can never be carried out, *regardless of their consequences*.

But such a characterization must appear unsuitable for two reasons: first, because it implies that a nonteleologist has the view that carrying out an intrinsically bad action has no consequence at all. But if someone speaks of intrinsically bad actions, he doubtless means that doing them involves at least *one* bad consequence—namely, the one by which it possesses its intentional identity—and that this action should not be chosen precisely on account of this consequence. If the position of the so-called deontologist consisted in maintaining that carrying out an action evil "in itself" had *no* bad consequence and that such a consequence was not the reason why it should not be carried out, he would be maintaining an impossible position.

A "genuine" deontological formulation would be something like the following: "One may never do X . . . because X is against the will of God," or "because this is bad in itself" . . . or "because I have no right to . . ."—"despite all consequences." But these are not normative formulations of *why* one may not do it, or *why* it is against the will of God, why it is bad in itself, or why one has no right, etc. The "deontological" here is only an application of judgments about the goodness of actions or the application of normative expressions to concrete modes of action. The deontological element is a typical characteristic of a *judgment of conscience* with relation to a concrete action X: "One may never do X, because it is intrinsically evil." But *why* it is intrinsically bad or wrong (the establishment of a norm) is not a judgment of conscience and cannot be formulated in a deontological way. If someone were to do X anyway, it would not be because someone had a mistaken idea about the goodness of the action, but because the person was acting against his or her conscience. The opposing of a "deontological" concept of norm *justification* to a teleological one results from a confusion of two different categories of practical judgments.[274]

In reality, the so-called deontologist is only saying that certain actions are characterized by evil consequences that cannot be outweighed by any other

273. The weakness mentioned here can be found, in my opinion, in the otherwise illuminating and helpful critique of teleological ethics by E. Schockenhoff, *Natural Law and Human Dignity*, 214–19. The author largely argues on the basis of a thesis, highly disputed by consequentialists, that we are responsible only for our own actions and not for those of others which they (e.g., in an emergency) carry out as a consequence of our nonactions.

274. This confusion is clearly present in C. D. Broad's thinking; cf. "Some of the Main Problems of Ethics" (see note 265), 230ff.

evil consequences that foreseeably result from not doing the action, and thus are fundamentally incapable of becoming part of a balancing of goods. An action that is intrinsically unjust, such as an act of killing a human being carried out by a private person as a means to some end, is what we call an injustice. The action has two evil consequences: the injury of another's rights, and the intending of this injury existing in the agent's act of choice, whose will has departed from what he owes to his fellow human being, and is thus a bad will. These are true *consequences* of the action. At the same time, they are consequences that constitute the action itself as an intentional action, and as a *bad* action. An act of lying (deception, injury done to the communicative community with one's neighbor) is similarly not *without consequence*. Precisely because the will of the one who acts, if he chooses to carry out such a false statement, is directed "intrinsically" and thus "always" (the communicative community with one's neighbor being presupposed) toward deception and injury to the communicative community, this intentional action is also "intrinsically" and "always" bad. Again, the consequence is what gives the action its identity.

The point of consequentialist or "teleological" ethics consists, in fact, and only consists, in leaving out exactly this aspect of human actions, and in systematically excluding it from any consideration. It does not place its balancing of goods on the level of intentional actions, but *only* on the level of the total context of external circumstances caused by these actions. In reality, then, consequentialism is merely a *restricted* or *one-sidedly* teleological ethical position. It is, moreover, inconsistent: once an action is determined to be the "right" one on the basis of a balancing of consequences (or is considered as a "wrong" one and its not-doing as morally obligatory), the consequentialist judgment becomes itself deontological: "I should do (not do) x, because x is right (wrong)—*independently* of all further consequences." For, according to a completed balancing of consequences and determination of the right way to act, often only *some* bad consequences remain to be accepted (one can hardly imagine, and nobody acts in such a way, that a consequentialist calculation means that one only considers those actions as right that bring about *exclusively* good consequences). For one who practices teleological ethics, it is necessary that he determine a way of acting as *the* right one (or wrong one) *in concreto, independently* of further consequences of its accomplishment (or nonaccomplishment).

And this is what follows: once the way of acting has been determined, consequentialism can no longer say that we are responsible for *all* the consequences of our actions. But this contradicts the basic principle of this kind of ethics, namely, that we bear the responsibility in each case for *all* the foreseeable consequences (a principle that nonteleological ethics denies). If someone were to maintain that we also bear responsibility for the *evil* consequences that we *must* accept on the basis of a "balancing" comparison of consequences, it would be simply unbearable. The only rational interpretation consists in understanding consequentialism—just as any "nonteleological" ethics—as a theory about which consequences we bear responsibility for and which ones we do not. This means that even for this theory, certain actions are right or wrong *independently* of their consequences. Its distinction from "deontological" ethics at the outset only serves as a disguise of this fact; it distracts from the real difference between the two positions. In reality, the difference consists only in the *criteria* according to which the rightness of actions is determined independently of further consequences.

Therefore, the real difference from so-called deontologists is not at all what consequentialists suppose it to be. It is to be found elsewhere: first, a consequentialist will never say of an action that it is *good* or *bad (evil);* he can only speak of "right" and "wrong" actions; second, he will only determine the "rightness" or "wrongness" of actions with respect to the entire, complex state of affairs that can be foreseen to be caused for all those concerned ("states of the world"). These two aspects are closely interrelated.

The first results from the second. Complexes of possible and foreseeable consequences are contingent structures without stable identities. The *acting person* appears in their midst as only one element out of many. The person is "objectified." Consequentialism is an ethics of the "third person." The judgment of action is carried out from the perspective of an impartial observer of a structure of events, a perspective that must first decide on the identity of concrete actions. This lends utilitarian ethics all the plausibility and attractiveness we associate with objectivity, fairness, and impartiality. But on closer inspection one sees immediately that such an ethics excludes precisely that which is the very point of morality: the identity of the acting subject as a being that strives toward the good and that transforms itself toward good or bad in its actions and corresponding acts of choosing, as well as the identity, founded upon that, of basic intentional actions as good or *bad* actions, independently of the total structure of all foreseeable consequences; an identity of actions that is constituted, rather, in the context of "the good for man," *toward which the human being is intentionally related in every choice of actions.* This identity of actions in their intentional relation to the "good for man" is also what is "good for me" in each case and "what is good for the other as my equal," that is to say, that other person, to whom my actions are immediately related in each case. For a virtue ethics grounded in the concept of intentional action, what is always constitutive for the goodness of actions, is the *immedi-*

ate relationship *toward other individual persons* whose recognition as "another self" can never, no more than one's own self, be reduced to being only one element in an ensemble or complex of states of affairs, and thus subordinated to the optimization of that same ensemble or complex. This principle of human dignity, championed by Kant, is eliminated in consequentialism.[275] It is expressed in the generally accepted principle that utilitarians do not dispute that not even for the good of humanity should you "sell your own grandmother." Consequentialism will always try in vain to ascertain and justify the logic implied in this saying, because it can only establish it as a rule of action to the extent that its adoption by someone would forseeably lead to the best consequences. But then you have already departed from the rule, which says in fact, that precisely such calculation is immoral.

I would like to emphasize here that neither this nor subsequent statements I make about utilitarianism are meant as statements about the intentions or the moral status of those who support utilitarian ethics. It is solely and exclusively a question of the analysis and criticism of a certain structure of thinking and justification. Utilitarianism tries, like every ethics, to reconstruct and justify the phenomenon of "morality," and to improve moral praxis. The single question of interest here is whether utilitarianism succeeds in this. All the arguments I am bringing forward with the goal of revealing the immoral and self-contradictory implications of a consequentialist ethics are not intended to suggest that the proponents of utilitarianism are immoral subjects; rather, the arguments arise out of the expectation that a utilitarian could also be convinced by these arguments, if they are in fact correct, and such an expectation implies that utilitarians are *not* in fact immoral subjects.

C. D. Broad held the peculiar viewpoint, that the expression "moral phenomenon" relates to *all* facts—and only to such facts—"in the describing which we have to use such words as 'ought,' 'right and wrong,' 'good and evil,' or any others which are merely verbal translations of these."[276] If this were correct, all actions, even such as recommended in cooking recipes or user manuals, would be considered moral phenomena. But Broad has clearly indicated here an important presupposition of consequentialist ethics. The clarification shows that consequentialism is a form of ethics that looks at everything but what is specifically moral in moral phenomena. For the question of morality is not simply the question how we "ought" to do something, or how we can do something "rightly" or "wrongly," how we are "good" or "bad" in whatever re-

---

275. Cf. the full exposition of this in M. Rhonheimer, "Menschliches Handeln und seine Moralität," 83; and also R. Spaemann, "Über den Begriff der Menschenwürde."

276. C. D. Broad, "Some of the Main Problems of Ethics," in D. R. Cheney, ed., *Broad's Critical Essays in Moral Philosophy*, 223.

spect (because in cooking or building houses one "ought" to do certain things, one can do things "rightly" or "wrongly," and be a "good" or "bad" cook or architect); rather, it is the question whether there is a specifically *moral* kind of "ought," or of "right" and "wrong," "good" and "evil," that is not related to the coming into being of "good food" or "good houses," but rather to the quality of our free, willing actions, with which we do something in relation to our own humanity and in relation to the humanity of our fellow human beings. Only then does the following statement become meaningful: the moral question does not consist in asking which condition of the world we should aim for as the best—there is no small agreement on this—rather, on how we should *act,* in order to reach the best conditions. This is no longer a question of recipes or rules but is really about *good or bad kinds of actions.* A virtue ethics holds the view that "morality" means that what human beings *do* are specific elements of the goodness of the state of the world. Consequentialists, by contrast, are persuaded that what someone does only has its meaning with respect to the changes that the action brings about for the resulting state of affairs. By the term "morality," therefore, they designate the rules in accordance with which someone's action can lead to the optimization of the consequent state of affairs (such rules are thus "right or wrong," according to them one "ought" or "ought not" to do such and such, and accordingly one can also say about someone that he is a good or bad person). Thus ethical thinkers who are consequentialists discuss seriously even today the question first formulated by the idealist English philosopher F. H. Bradley (d. 1924): "Why be moral?" "Why should I be moral?" The answer must then be established—how else?— in a consequentialist way. When someone like J. J. C. Smart poses the question, "What is the purpose of morality?"[277] the theme of "morality" is already lost to view (from the viewpoint of virtue ethics, the question cannot even be posed, because it has been answered already by the understanding of what morality is). Of course, the utilitarian finds an answer to his question: the usefulness of morality is ultimately the optimization of the consequences of actions and the best possible condition of the world. But as an answer to the question "Why be moral?," it is not a definition of morality, but only the definition of what morality is good for. And many of those who say that there is no such thing as "morality" also want the best possible condition of the world.

277. Cf. J. J. C. Smart, "An Outline of a System of Utilitarian Ethics," in J. J. C. Smart and B. Willliams, *Utilitarianism: For and Against,* 3–74, here 68. But the question is not only posed by utilitarians. It is also typical for any moral philosophy that sees the "moral" in opposition to what is in our own interest and what is "useful" for ourselves. A nuanced discussion of the question, "Why Should I Be Moral," can be found in B. Gert, *Morality: Its Nature and Justification* (New York and Oxford: Oxford University Press, 1998), 338ff.

It is important, nevertheless, to stress that the question "What is morality good for?" only refers to the question "What is the usefulness of human beings *behaving* morally?" It is aimed, then, at the justification of those characteristics, standards, or rules of human behavior that we refer to as "morality." If someone answers that this usefulness consists in optimizing the state of the world, then we can always further ask, why we want that. Then there are various answers: for example, the social eudaimonist answer (the greatest happiness of the greatest number), and that in turn can be hedonistic or nonhedonistic. One can also give a theological answer to the question (and that is the answer of moral theologians who subscribe to utilitarianism): one can conceive the optimization of the world as the basic Christian project (which, after all, is not completely incorrect). But none of this changes the fact that "morality" itself— that is, the standards for whether our actions are worthy of praise or blame— must be "useful" for the optimization of the world. Even the theologian must pose the question whether what he understands by morality is really an *adequate* conception of morality: mere reference to the theological dimension of the ultimate goal of all action (love of God and neighbor, following Christ, etc.) is little use to him here.

The difference between a consequentialist ethics and one that consequentialists call "deontological" consists therefore in the bracketing off of the identity of the acting human subject as a subject that changes himself through his relation to "good" and "evil," a relationship that is decided in concrete actions, insofar as the subject intentionally directs himself to the good for himself and the good for others. Such an ethics—a virtue ethics—is of course quite misleadingly labeled "deontological." Rather, it is radically and in the fullest sense of the word *teleological*. Consequentialism is only another kind of "teleological" ethics: namely, one that does not have in view the goodness of acting subjects and their actions, but only weighs out the optimal condition of the world; consequently here too there are obviously no longer any "good" or "bad" actions, but only "right" and "wrong" ones. And happiness is describable by consequentialists only as the optimization of nonmoral states of affairs, rather than as the only morally relevant condition of good action.

The fundamental axiom that underlies consequentialism, then, is the distinction between "morally *good*" attitudes, and approaches and "morally *right*" (or wrong) actions, or, according to Broad's terminology, the distinction between the "right-making properties" and the "good-making properties" of actions. This distinction is therefore doubtful in principle because we must always describe actions as objects of *choice acts* and thus as intentional. And in this perspective the goodness of the will is first of all connected to the goodness of the choice of actions; and these choices are themselves describable as definite forms of *rightness*—namely, rightness of striving. In case a human action is actually "wrong" in the *moral* sense (and not merely in the "technical" sense), this implies a wrongness of the will, and that means it is a *bad* action in the moral sense. Consequentialism is plausible because it is coherent: it draws the correct consequences from its presuppositions. As has been shown, however, these presuppositions of the theory, that is to say, its concept of action, are wrong. The coherence does not help. Moreover, the distinction asserted above leads to serious contradictions and eventually to the self-destruction of consequentialist ethics.

Once again, as was explained in III, we should recall here that an "intentional action" is not simply the "causation of a physical event + the intention with which someone causes this event." Rather, the cause of the physical event is already "intentional" and no mere "event," but always also an action (at least a basic intentional action), that includes a willing stance on the part of the subject toward good or evil in the moral sense. But short of the threshold of basic intentional action, it is no longer possible to speak of a "human action"; here there are only bodily movements, happenings, and so on. Only on the basis of such a concept of intentional action, I would say, can the ethically relevant difference between "doing" and "refraining from doing" be adequately understood (since both are expressions that in the first place refer to the physical characteristics of actions, especially bodily movements). Whether, for example, "letting someone die" is murder in the moral sense or a mere refusal to prolong life any longer cannot be decided on the basis of what is "done" or "not done," but only insofar as one considers what is *chosen* here (i.e., "willed"). The "active" turning off of a heart-lung machine or an oxygen supply (a "doing") can be either a murder or a legitimate decision not to prolong life. If someone chooses to end a human life with his physical action, he kills. But one who chooses this type of action under the description of "abstaining from prolonging life," is not killing, because he is not choosing the killing of a human being. Of course the linguistic expressions here are always ambivalent, since they are not capable of adequately expressing the intentional content of the doing or refraining from doing. The difference between "killing" and "not prolonging life" can in any event not be described in physical-behavioristic categories like "doing" and "refraining from doing." If "letting someone die"— in the sense of "not taking life-prolonging measures," which is itself a mere physical-behavioristic description—is chosen under the description, "declining to prolong life," it becomes clear that the death of a human being is not being willed, only that someone is merely choosing to cease taking life-prolonging actions. The real difference between the decision to kill someone through a not-doing or through the shutting-off of an oxygen supply (a "doing"), or to abstain from prolonging life, cannot, as I have said, find any adequate or unequivocal linguistic expression. The difference arises from the difference of intentional structuring which in turn depends upon situational elements, but especially upon the judgment that "letting someone die" is nothing other than to abstain from any longer wanting to hold back (in the case of old age or the progress of a disease) the natural and irreversible process of dying that is in its last stage and/or the necessary means of life support have become disproportionate. Such a difference can only with difficulty be reflected in unambiguous descriptions of action or linguistic categories.[278]

The contradictions and tendentious self-destructiveness of consequentialist ethics can be illustrated by an example. Even a virtue ethicist could have agreed with the consequentialist calculation, "In order to bring about as quickly as possible a surrender of Japan, and cause the smallest possible number of deaths, the 'right' action is the use of atom bombs to destroy the civilian population *en masse*." If President Truman had foreseen the long-term damage to the health of the population and the effect the action would have on the arms race, he might not have considered this action the "right" one. It makes sense, but it seems that the determination of "rightness" here leaves something out: the willingness to kill innocent persons, which is an act of injustice. The consequentialist can only object as follows: "Provided that this measure was the right one for optimizing the consequences that were foreseen *at the time*, it *could not* have been an unjust action. Its justice depends on the fact that *not doing it* would have brought worse consequences, according to what was known at the time. Therefore, it would be quite irrelevant to point out that the victims were 'innocent.' Guilt or innocence, in fact, plays no role here at all." Such an objection, which expresses consequentialist logic, shows that the category of "rightness," when set against the category of the goodness of an action, cannot serve to concretize "good intentions" or (moral) "attitudes" *(Gesinnung)* behind an action, so that here, "action" and "attitude" belong to two totally disparate realms, so that fundamentally *every* way of acting with a "good" attitude can be carried out—as long as someone does what is "right."

This shows the error of the above calculation, which in its very point of

---

278. These difficulties are also considered by D. Birnbacher, *Tun und Unterlassen* (Stuttgart: Reclam, 1995), but he draws the opposite conclusions. He consistently refuses to adopt an intentional concept of action and attempts to understand "omission" as unambiguously contrasted to "acting" (cf. 24ff.). On the same problem, see also W. Lübbe, *Verantwortung in komplexen Prozessen* (Freiburg: Universitätsverlag, 1998), chap. 3, and on the question of letting die in connection with euthanasia, see J. Keown, ed., *Euthanasia Examined: Ethical, Clinical and Legal Perspectives* (Cambridge: Cambridge University Press, 1995), especially the discussion between John Harris and John Finnis on 6–71. See instead the correct intentional definition of (active) euthanasia in John Paul II's encyclical *Evangelium Vitae*, no. 65 (referring also to an earlier text of the Congregation for the Doctrine of the Faith on this subject): "Euthanasia in the strict sense is understood to be an action or omission which of itself and by intention causes death, with the purpose of eliminating all suffering. 'Euthanasia's terms of reference, therefore, are to be found in the intention of the will and in the methods used' (*Declaration on Euthanasia Iura et Bona, 5 May 1980).*"

departure already misses the perspective of morality. Of course, dropping the atom bombs on Japan was the "right" thing to do—the "right" thing, that is, for bringing about the speediest surrender possible. But the calculation simply excluded *from the outset* the question about the justice of such a choice of action. This would have also been the case had President Truman considered the question of the damaged health of the survivors as well as all the psychological and social damages, and had come to the conclusion that the evil of such consequences outweighed the good of a speedy surrender, and so had decided not to drop the bombs after all. As I said, perhaps we could have understood why someone would have made that decision. But the only *morally* right and also good decision capable of being justified would have been: one may not massacre innocent persons even to achieve a good end. This kind of rightness also shapes the "attitude." Today we know that such a way of acting, just because it would have been just, would probably also have had better consequences. At the time perhaps no one could have known. But we are responsible for the evil consequences of our bad actions even if we could not have foreseen them (provided they are, as was explained earlier, in a way intrinsically connected with the bad action, which is certainly the case here).

So we could say, then, that "right" in the moral perspective is really the good for man, and vice versa. Actions are the operative concretizings of an intentional orientation toward the good. *And this orientation toward what is good for man is at stake in every single action.* Choice of action, and the carrying out of that action, shape the attitude, stance, or basic disposition of a human being. They determine the "heart" of the person.

In his judgments of action the consequentialist intends to create the best possible world, so long as this is *foreseeable* to him on the basis of the *foreseeable* consequences of his actions. He maintains that we bear the responsibility for what we are able to foresee. This sounds quite reasonable. And certainly it does not mean that consequentialists want to claim that in fact they will be able to optimize the state of the world through their actions. They introduce the "optimizing of foreseeable consequences of actions" as a rational criterion for rightness.[279]

Can such a thing really work? This is precisely the claim that is to be con-

---

279. In his response to R. Spaemann's critique of consequentialism, B. Schüller appears to have overlooked that Spaemann's criticism of the concept "optimizing of the total world situation" is intended as a criticism of the consequentialist criterion for the "rightness" of actions, not as a criticism of any presumption and expectation on the part of "universal teleologists" that they *in fact* do optimize the total world situation. As Schüller puts it, "Who can really be confident that through his action he is optimizing the 'total world situation'? In any case, this could be made into an explanation for why there is scarcely an ethicist alive who could seriously think he could have control over such a doubtful matter." Cf. B. Schüller, "Das Muster einer schlagenden Widerlegung des Utilitarismus," in B. Schüller, *Pluralismus in der Ethik* (Münster: Aschendorff, 1988), 55.

tested here: The "optimization of consequences" can certainly be a criterion for the rationality of certain public decision processes, especially in the areas of economics and financial policies. But *moral* rationality cannot be limited to this kind of rationality. Accordingly, it is rather dubious to describe, as the "inventor" of proportionalism in Catholic moral theology has proposed, the "basic formula" for a moral decision making as follows: "Basically, we are concerned with an economic calculation, but not only to maximize profit in particular, so that by a certain time period there would be the maximum differential between income and expenditure; rather, we are also concerned with optimizing profit. *To the extent that one keeps to a point of view that takes in 'the big picture'—for the long run and the entire situation—the calculation becomes properly ethical.*"[280] But this must appear implausible already for the simple reason that in this way every calculation would become an ethical one simply by a point of view "for the long run and with the entire situation in mind." Inspected closely, moral rationality is here simply abandoned, and replaced with another kind of reasoning, which can be quite legitimate in its own place, but which must always be subordinated to an ethical judgment and in certain cases be relativized to such judgment and brought into its framework.

The position of a virtue ethics, on the other hand, can be characterized by the requirement that in concrete actions one does not seek at all for "a state of the world," not even the best possible one. And this is simply because before we have reached it, we cannot know what it possibly might be, and we likewise would not know whether the one we have already reached is in fact the best possible one. Rather, and much more logically, one would say, that world is the best possible one that results as a *consequence* of the virtues of human beings, that is, from their just action. For if someone acts this way, he also acts *rightly.*

Now, this cannot mean, of course, that virtue is ultimately the better way to attain the optimization of the total world state, or that we consider this world the "best world" that results from the virtue of human beings. Because this would mean virtue itself is being justified by a calculation of consequences. In reality, virtue often leads not to the best in *this* sense—even if we introduce the perspective of divine providence, since "for those who love God, all things are directed to good."[281] But this does nothing to change the condition of the world, but only the condition of those who do good. Consequently the

280. The words are those of P. Knauer, "Fundamentalethik: Teleologische als deontologische Normenbegründung," *Theologie und Philosophie* 55 (1980): 333: *"Dadurch, daß man den Gesichtspunkt 'auf die Dauer und im ganzen' einführt, wird der Kalkül zu einem eigentlichen ethischen."*
281. Cf. Letter to the Romans, 8:28.

above statement can only mean that at each time that situation of the world is best, that is marked by the existence of just human beings. For a state of the world in which a benefit to the whole is purchased as the consequence of injustice against a few is not a good state of the world. Such a world, for instance, would be one in which cancer could be conquered, but at the cost of using people for involuntary medical experimentation.[282]

As mentioned briefly in the introduction, consequentialists sweep such virtue ethics arguments off the table by presupposing a trivial concept of virtue, maintaining that virtues are merely dispositions to action that are deemed morally positive. For this reason they cannot serve to determine what is morally right in each case, since the reverse is what is really occurring, that is, a morally positive disposition, or virtue, is determined by the morally right (this determination having already been carried out in a consequentialist way). Virtues could then never emerge as real moral standards that would be capable of unmasking the immorality of the consequentialist calculation.[283] Criticism of this type is a *petitio principii* ("begging the question"), since it presupposes a consequentialist, trivializing concept of virtue. The point of the virtue ethics argument of Philippa Foot really consists in making the criticism that in the consequentialist understanding of a best world situation that results from a particular action, the actor or agent *as such* is excluded, so that it *can no longer even be thought* that a best world situation—describable in nonmoral terms—could also be attained even through an unjust action (because, viewed in a consequentialist way, such an action would in fact be "right," according to the definition, and therefore also just). But such an action would be "wrong" according to the virtue ethics perspective because it can already be described as unjust, even without any reference to the sum total of the effects that it is foreseen to cause. And this is possible because an action must not necessarily be judged with respect to all the consequences it has for all concerned before the verdict that it is *unjust* can be reached. In case this judgment is in fact reached, it is also possible to play off the moral integrity of the agent against other possible beneficial consequences of an action already judged as unjust. In such a move, the requirement of moral integrity on the part of the doer is discernible

---

282. Cf. Philippa Foot, "Morality, Action, and Outcome," in T. Honderich, ed., *Morality and Objectivity: A Tribute to J. L. Mackie* (London: Routledge & Kegan Paul, 1985), 332. For the problem of the adequate guarantee of individual rights in consequentialism, cf. J. Nida-Rümelin, *Kritik des Konsequentialismus* (note 266 above), 95ff.

283. This is P. Schaber's argument in *Moralischer Realismus* (Freiburg and Munich: Alber, 1997), 309ff., against Philippa Foot's article, "Utilitarianism and the Virtues," in S. Scheffler, ed., *Consequentialism and Its Critics* (note 271 above), 224–42. The denial that the concept of virtue contributes to normative ethics is also typical for adherents of the so-called New Natural Law Theory, as, for example, John Finnis; I have argued against this in a response to Finnis, published as "Ethics of Norms and the Lost Virtues: Searching the Roots of the Crisis of Ethical Reasoning," *Anthropotes* 9, no. 2 (1993): 231–43; reprinted in an enlarged version under the title "Norm-Ethics, Moral Rationality, and the Virtues: What's Wrong with Consequentialism?" as chap. 2 of my *The Perspective of the Acting Person*.

as one *component* of what we could call the "best world situation." This state of affairs would then no longer be conceived of as an amoral, but rather as a thoroughly moral one.[284] This is precisely the structure of a possible virtue ethics argument that presupposes, to be sure, a nonconsequentialist (and a nontrivializing) concept of virtue. If a consequentialist does not want to argue in a circle, he needs first to find arguments against the action-theoretical assumptions implied in this concept of virtue.

If there ever was someone who opted for the best state of the world as a consequence of virtue, it was Socrates as depicted in Plato's *Apology*.[285] When the tyrannical oligarchy of the "Thirty" gave him and his companions the assignment to sentence the innocent Leon of Salamis to death, he did not engage in a calculation of goods, but simply refused to carry out an action that he judged to be unjust in itself, knowing that such disobedience would mean his own death (which did not in fact happen, only because the Thirty were deposed before they could kill him, something he could not have known beforehand).[286]

Socrates acted according to the maxim (ascribed to Democritus), "It is better to suffer injustice than to do it."[287] We all agree to this without hesitation. The sad thing for the consequentialist is that he is unable to justify it.[288] This maxim presupposes the concept of intentional action, and the perspective of the acting subject, the morality of the first person: "to suffer injustice," in other words, for one who decides in this situation, is a nonmoral evil, a mere "state of affairs," a condition that makes him neither a good nor an evil per-

284. This is exactly the heart of Foot's argument, 237ff.: "there indeed is a place *within* morality for the idea of better and worse state of affairs. . . . It is not that in the guise of 'the outcome' it (the idea of maximum welfare) stands *outside* morality as its foundation and arbiter, but rather that it appears *within* morality as the end of one of the virtues." It is just this part of Foot's argument that S. Scheffler seems to have missed in his (nonconsequentialist) critique of her article; cf. S. Scheffler, "Agent-Centered Restrictions, Rationality, and the Virtues," in Scheffler, ed., *Consequentialism and Its Critics*, 243–60.
285. 32c–e.
286. Cf. the reverse model in the afore-mentioned case of the Nazi collaborator Paul Touvier, who, to keep ninety-three Jews from being shot, ordered seven others to be shot, and defended this as an act of "rescuing" the ninety-three.
287. Fragment B 45 in Diels/Kranz, *Die Fragmente der Vorsokratiker*, 2.156.
288. Cf. for more detail my discussion in "Gut und Böse oder richtig und falsch—was unterscheidet das Sittliche?" in Hans Thomas, ed., *Ethik der Leistung* (Herford: Busse Seewald, 1988), 47–75. There I point out that Democritus's maxim is "groundless and ultimately meaningless" for consequentialism, in the sense that it can no longer be *justified*. At any event my view does not appear to contradict the fact that the maxim also rests upon an ultimately unproven foundation, but that in a consequentialist ethics it can no longer get any traction *on the level of concrete action* (i.e., it falls out of the picture, so to speak), namely, the assertion "*Doing no injustice* is better than doing an injustice." This sentence is self-evident, but not at all trivial. I think, however, that every consequentialist would reply that this sentence is tautological insofar as it could not play a role on the level of the choice of action. This would be my reply to Werner Wolbert's objection that I am "nonconsistent" [*"nicht konsequent"*—note the German word play] in my criticism of consequentialism (cf. W. Wolbert, *Vom Nutzen der Gerechtigkeit* [see above, note 267], 72, note 13; cf. also ibid., 84.)

son. "Doing injustice," however, *is* a moral evil (even for the consequential-ist), through which one becomes a bad human being. Therefore the meaning of the sentence is clear: "I prefer to be put into a bad *condition* rather than to *do* something bad (because then I would become a bad person)." This corre-sponds to the literal translation of Democritus's maxim: "He who does injus-tice is more unfortunate than he to whom it happens."[289]

The problem for the consequentialist, then, consists in the fact that his theory does not *permit* him to carry out such a choice. An *action* is only "un-just" for him insofar as it is "wrong." And to determine this wrongness (or rightness), he must weigh all foreseeable consequences for all those involved, and he must do this not only for what he might do, but also for what he might refrain from. A consequentialist Socrates would have had to ask himself: (a) What are the foreseeable consequences of incriminating Leon of Salamis and his resulting execution? (b) What are the foreseeable consequences of my re-fusal to incriminate him, and my own resulting death? He would have had to balance his own death against that of Leon's. Thus consequence structure (a) stands over against consequence structure (b). We then see immediately that the question whether or not to *do* an injustice is no longer meaningful. The question is only: Which "event" brings about the better outcome? And then the *right* action (doing or nondoing) would be the one that produces that out-come.

The question "Is it better to suffer injustice or to do injustice?" is recast by consequentialism into a different question: "What is better: that I bring about an evil consequence for myself through omitting to do an action, or that I cause an evil consequence for someone else by doing it?" In this way, the "radical subjectivity of the moral"[290] is bracketed: the fact that *I* am the one who is act-ing. One's own action is treated as a mere "event" that sets off certain conse-quences. The judgment of action then becomes a matter of determining which consequence is more desirable. For example, one could ask, "Which is better: that a hundred be killed by an earthquake or only fifty?" Naturally everyone would agree that the former earthquake would be worse than the latter one. But an earthquake is only a natural event, unlike human actions.

Socrates could have come to the conclusion that the consequences of his own death would have been worse than Leon's (and no doubt he would have had good reasons to think so; but today we know that Socrates' nonconse-quentialist convictions had the best consequences, because otherwise, had Socrates not been Socrates, there would never have been a Plato, etc.). But

289. The sentence is also found in this sense in the Platonic dialogue *Gorgias* (470b–c) in Socrates' famous conversation with the young Polus.
290. A. W. Müller, "Radical Subjectivity: Morality versus Utilitarianism" (see note 268).

applying the utilitarian calculation to the case of Socrates shows, really, that by transforming all moral actions into a mere "causing of states of affairs and world conditions," and by balancing such alternatives, such calculation makes superfluous the question of what someone actually *does* and what kind of person he makes himself by willingly doing this or that.[291]

But this very thing has devastating consequences because human nature itself takes vengeance. Each utilitarian calculation stands or falls with the possibility of judging and weighing consequences according to the criteria of "desirable" or "undesirable." Where do these criteria come from? Consequentialists insist that they apply obvious criteria such as justice, fairness, benevolence toward fellow human beings, and so on.[292] But how do criteria and ideals such as "justice," "fairness," and "benevolence" serve as a standard for the balancing of goods? The answer is unambiguous: they arise from practical judgments on the justice, fairness, and degree of benevolence of *types of action* in the sense of basic intentional actions. The first principles cannot be enough, since they only tell us we should give to each person what is his due, and to not do what we would not have him do to us, and so on. But the utilitarian ethicist says that what is "due" to the other, that is, the "just" thing, is what is "right"; but *this* only can come out of an optimal balance of consequences. What we cannot reasonably want someone else to do to us can only be what is "not-right." Even a utilitarian Socrates could not have wanted the foreseeable consequence of "his-own-death-by-refusing-to-incriminate-Leon" except under the supposition that such an incrimination was not "right," that is, that Leon's death would have had worse consequences than his own. The recourse to principles always either presupposes the utilitarian calculation of consequences, or needs to make one. It is a perfectly circular argument, just hanging in the air: a calculation without a *standard*.

The "revenge" of human nature I mentioned consists precisely in the fact that the one who acts in a utilitarian way loses sight of the criteria according to which he must weigh his consequences, because he has no way to establish such principles.[293] They remain mere empty formulas without relation to any categories of action. The analysis of value (moral principles) is completely sundered from the analysis of actions. The consequentialist practical reason cancels itself out; it becomes blind toward the good, the just, fairness, and so on. Not only can it not provide any criteria for why consequence x, y, . . . z is

291. Cf. G. E. M. Anscombe, "Modern Moral Philosophy," in R. Crisp and M. Slote, eds., *Virtue Ethics*, 43.

292. So, e.g., B. Schüller, *Die Begründung sittlicher Urteile*, 285. On the failure of this attempt, see *Natural Law and Practical Reason*, 391ff.

293. Cf. also L. Honnefelder, "Natur als Handlungsprinzip" (note 46 above), 173f.

"good" or "bad" at all, and for why some consequences are worse than others, it cannot even establish by any *moral* criteria why it is good even to bring about better consequences. This is why utilitarianism has had to be reduced to a position like that of Hobbes: it is better, simply for reasons of survival. Theologians who think in utilitarian modes must have recourse to faith, love, and the like,[294] and such recourse operates in this case as a kind of emergency anchor for an ethics that is itself essentially devoid of moral content.

In any event, consequentialism does not solve the problem about the good, but only makes it more seriously problematic. If utilitarians are thoroughly coherent, they reach an understanding that everyone must answer the question for himself. But wasn't the question about what is good the very starting point for ethics and its true meaning? As Norbert Hoerster claims, utilitarianism needs to be supplemented, since it always takes seriously the ones who are "benefited" as "independent persons, insofar as it gives them the possibility to decide for themselves where they see a 'benefit.'" Therefore: "One could say that it solves its original problem, in that it refuses to give any answer for the benefit of the individual in question." The only thing that is to be excluded on principle is the orientation of actions "whose content consists in nothing but frustrating the satisfaction of others' interests or pleasure."[295]

This is how utilitarians make a virtue out of necessity, which always arises when they are faced with the problem of determining what should be considered a consequence. For "to choose an action" means in this case to choose the *consequences* of a certain action, and the decisive point of interest is the foreseeing of the consequences. But then there arise some insoluble problems: Am I, in each instance, responsible for the consequences that I *actually* foresee? If that is the case, does the adulterer bear no responsibility for the suicide of his depressed wife or the destruction of his family, since he had no idea these things would happen? One could also say that the less responsibly someone behaves (i.e., the less conscious someone is of the evil consequences of his deeds), the less responsible he is for those consequences. Since this is absurd, the quality of an action cannot only depend on the *actual* foreseeing of consequences.

A further possibility would be to say that we only bear responsibility for the consequences that we *can* foresee, or *could have* foreseen. Now, we can hardly provide universal criteria for this *"could have"*; on the other hand, if we

---

294. The quite extreme position of J. F. Keenan has been mentioned ("Die erworbenen Tugenden als richtige [nicht gute] Lebensführung"; see III.3, note 69, above) where the moral good (as distinct from the merely "right") only appears on the (supernatural) level of love.

295. N. Hoerster, *Utilitaristische Ethik und Verallgemeinerung*, 2nd ed. (Freiburg and Munich: Alber, 1977), 15.

insist that the criteria be suited to each individual, we have landed back at the position we just started with: for a definite individual *can* foresee (at a certain point of time, i.e., the moment of choice) exactly and only that which he actually *does* foresee. A third variant would be to hold that someone is responsible only for what in actuality *will* result as a consequence; but then we depart from the principle of "foreseeing," or we must maintain that a human being is capable of predicting every single result of any event (which, again, is absurd and could never be empirically verified, and in fact is easily falsified). What is left over, then, is only the possibility that the responsibility is connected only with those consequences that the agent *should* have foreseen. But in order to establish this *"should,"* the consequentialist would have to violate his own principle for grounding the moral rectitude of actions, since this principle means that the rightness of an act ("what one *should* do") depends upon the *foreseeable* consequences. A consistent consequentialist, therefore, cannot in any way establish a connection between the "foreseeing of consequences" and "responsibility," even though this is the very cornerstone of his argument.

But even if this were possible, such an ethics would no longer be something that could be expected of an individual person. It leads to the paradoxical outcome that experts and specialists would have more chances for determining what is right than those who have less of a command over complex chains of events. The ideal form of moral reasoning would be the intelligence of the expert.[296] But if this were the ideal, then the normal type of moral judgment would be a deficient mode of practical reasoning. Normal human beings would not be moral subjects in the full sense of the word: they would have to have recourse to experts for any right and responsible action. Alternatively, we would have to arrive at the conclusion—and it would be paradoxical for a utilitarian—that the "right" could not be determined at all in a normal judgment of action; it would then be the most reasonable course of action for everyone to do what he *took* to be the right thing to do. R. M. Hare actually drew such a conclusion: the perfect utilitarian, Hare says, would have to be an "archangel," an ideal observer of all things. As agents, we are always mere "proles" who have to stick with the principles that were inculcated by our educators, and we should heed the emotional repugnance we feel in opposing them. But for cases where a conflict appears, and when selecting the principles we want to inculcate in the next generation, we must then take on the role of an archangel who can impartially compare his own principles with those of others and choose what appears to be the most useful for all concerned; utilitarian-

296. Cf. R. Spaemann, *Basic Moral Concepts*, 52–53; see also the chapter "Consequentialism" in Spaemann, *Happiness and Benevolence*, 119–30.

ism then becomes a training program for the *well-educated man.* But as for what is *right* in each case, Hare contends that we simply do not know at the moment of the choice of action.[297] And this means that what is right is not in fact what is reasonable at all, but rather an adherence to the rules we were brought up to follow.

This is one possible way to get along as a utilitarian, to be sure, but it does not make the doctrine more commendable. But apart from adopting this possibility, we can also ask ourselves what it would mean for interpersonal relationships if all human beings were consequentialists and if everybody knew it. For it is the worst thing for a consequentialist to have someone else know that he is one. Thus there are consequentialists who debate the question whether it is right for precisely utilitarian reasons openly to urge the adoption of the doctrine because a consequentialist cannot even function in a society composed only of consequentialists.[298]

For in fact it would be very strange always to know that someone who thanks me for a favor only does this because he would like to encourage me to show favors to him in the future, or because he is of the opinion that in this way he follows a rule that ensures that human beings in general are ready to do good to their fellows. Or that my fellow human beings keep promises just because in this way they feel obligated to do so through a generally recognized practice, and since they are convinced that the survival of this practice has consequences preferable to its extinction. The relationship of one person to another is endangered, everything being functionalized into an indirect intention *(intentio obliqua).* But because there will always be conflicts between such principles, we unfortunately do not know what rule someone is actually following. And thus we could not know what he really is doing. If he thanks us for something, it could be that he does not actually want to encourage us to do good in the future, but only because he is busy following the rule that one should only act toward one's fellow man in such a way that the other person does not have the impression that he has a bad opinion of him.

In reality, thanking someone is an act of recognizing someone's benevolence toward us and an answer to it as well: it is an act, that is, of retributive justice. Benevolence and thankfulness lead to friendship among human beings. But it can never get that far on utilitarian grounds. If someone wanted to draw these consequences of benevolence and thankfulness into a consequentialist calculus, this is what would happen: "thanking" would not simply

---

297. Cf. R. M. Hare, "Ethical Theory and Utilitarianism," in A. Sen and B. Williams, eds., *Utilitarianism and Beyond* (Cambridge: Cambridge University Press, 1982), 23–38; also R. M. Hare, *Moral Thinking: Its Levels, Methods and Point* (Oxford: Oxford University Press, 1981), esp. 44ff.
298. Cf. H. Sidgwick, *The Methods of Ethics* (1874; repr. of 7th [1907] ed., with a foreword by John

be something owed, that is, an act of justice, but only a means of obtaining friendship. But as soon as I know that someone is only thanking me in order to become my friend, I cannot become his friend. This is because friendship results from the revelation of my benevolence toward another. But thanking as a means to acquire friendship is not a revelation of any benevolence on my part. It is not thankfulness at all, but only some "talk" used to get something. And vice versa: ingratitude is not bad because it prohibits the development of friendship—although in fact that is the effect—but because it is an injustice.

Now of course, this does not mean to say that consequentialists maintain that we *should* behave according to the above model. Rather, what is meant to say is that, if the consequentialist theory really reflected adequately the structure of moral action, then we would *have* to act that way. But we all know that we don't structure our actions like this. And this is what the foregoing considerations have tried to show: utilitarianism cannot in any way come to terms with the simplest moral givens and with the intuitions of common sense. It is really the concept of moral virtue that is adequate to these givens and these intuitions. It is a concept that brings to expression what every form of utilitarianism denies: that we are always intentionally related to the "good for us" and the "the good for the other" in every concrete action we choose; this relation forms the "heart" of the person who acts and makes him into a good or bad human being.

g) Prudence and Conscience

It would be silly, of course, to say that consequences have no meaning at all for our actions. Once again, let Hegel be cited: "The maxim, 'Ignore the consequences of action' and the other, 'Judge actions by their consequences, and make these the criterion of right and good' are both alike maxims of the abstract Understanding."[299] There are "consequences [that] are the outward form whose *inner soul* is the *aim* of the action"; these consequences, as "the shape proper to the action and *immanent* within it, exhibit nothing but its nature and are simply the action itself."[300] This somewhat intuitively grasped characterization by Hegel appears to be justified in the concept of the basic intentional action.

Rawls [Indianapolis, Ind., and Cambridge, Mass.: Hackett, 1982]), 489f. Utilitarianism is not necessarily refuted by pointing out that a society composed solely of consequentialists is undesirable, since it is something even consequentialists concede (cf. J. Nida-Rümelin, *Kritik des Konsequentialismus* [see note 266 above], 140ff.); nevertheless, the argument shows that utilitarianism cannot be an adequate moral theory. If we were all brought up to be utilitarians in the sense of espousing utilitarianism as a moral ideal, society could not function.

299. G. W. F. Hegel, *The Philosophy of Right*, section 118 (transl. Knox; italics added), 43.
300. Ibid.

A weighing of goods can accordingly only take place where the objective moral content of concrete ways of acting—that is, the object of the basic intentional actions—has already been clarified. We make use of the weighing of goods in many situations. If I know that doing x is good in itself, it can always happen that doing x has the consequence y, and to omit (doing x) has the consequence z. So then y and z must be weighed against one another in order to decide whether to do or not do x.

Or: I come to the conclusion that not doing x is bad in *any case,* and that I should do x without reservation. But it can also be true that x done in one manner (manner "a") has the consequence y, while x done in another manner (manner "b") has the consequence z. And so, in order to decide between doing x in manner "a" or "b," I must weigh the consequences y and z against one another.

If no one bears responsibility for the evil consequences of not doing an action that is bad in itself, there is still a responsibility under some circumstances for solving the problems that arise in the event of such consequences. If someone declines to help a friend get out of a dilemma by the use of deception, so that the friend gets into even worse problems, he would still feel some responsibility to help him solve these other problems. I could say, for example, "I'm not to blame for your problems" because I *should not* get him out of difficulties by immoral means. But I will not say "I don't feel any responsibility for the solution of these problems" because, after all, I am his friend.

As long as we are not consequentialists, a morally responsible practical judgment will always take its starting point from asking whether the way of acting x, y, or z is *objectively* a good way to act, or at least a way that is not intrinsically evil. This is how the complexities of human action take shape—not through the extrapolation of possible alternative ways of acting onto the best possible world conditions or by the balancing of consequences—by reasoning as it were "from top to bottom"—but the reverse: we begin with what we owe in certain situations to ourselves and to others and we ask ourselves, in the light of "what is good for man" (i.e., the principles), just what this good would have to look like, here and now; then we exclude at the outset certain possibilities of action that stand in contradiction to "what is good for man." This is how a complex of actions is formed "from bottom to top" as it were; what emerges in each case is the best state of affairs that could have been attained. The action-complex is formed "from bottom to top" because we really do not decide on the basis of some extrapolation of future world states, that is, we do not decide which of these situations we want to bring about through a certain action now to be taken, but instead, independently of such extrapolations we do what we are now called to do as good (i.e., just) and omit what appears disallowed to us, as bad (i.e., unjust). The consequences—foreseen and subsequently—that result from this give further shape to the context of our action, and this is how a meaningful and coherent "life story" comes into existence, consisting both of intentional actions (directed to the goals of the virtues) and of the consequences of those actions to which we responsibly relate in the subsequent actions we accomplish. Never, therefore, will someone be able to say, "I have no responsibility *for this* because I didn't foresee it."

Only in such contexts do *further* virtues come into the picture—virtues such as patience, consistency, loyalty, the *moral value* of "suffering for the sake of justice," the value of self-denial, and so on. What concerns us here is what we could call the "accomplishment value" of actions, as opposed to their "effect value": the point of loyalty, gratitude, persistence, or self-denial does not consist in "causing some effect," *even if* something is often in fact effected; but this is not the reason for choosing certain actions. What is decisive is the *willing* that is incarnate in such actions. And this "willing" decides what sort of a human being each of us ultimately becomes.

Certainly, there are some complexes of actions that really are concerned with striving for certain conditions of the world. These are actions that in their origin are related not only to certain persons but (for example) to an entire society. These would also be the case with decisions in the areas of politics, law, business, the military, education, research programs, and so on. But here too it still holds that, depending on the means available for reaching certain goals, under some circumstances we will have to decide *not* to will to reach certain ends. Even when we know, by all we can foresee, that the goal is highly desirable and reachable, this still would not justify the means of reaching it. We can recall here the example of finding a cure for cancer at the price of using people in involuntary experiments; or killing human embryos for (allegedly) very promising therapeutic stem cell research. In the realm of gene technology such questions are currently being debated. Here the principle of justice with regard to the individual human person is unmistakably present. Thus even in these cases where certain world conditions are being intended, we can see the formation of action-complexes "from bottom to top."

The habit of prudence consists, finally, in affective connaturality with the good, and that is to say with an affective inclination to do the good and avoid the evil in the concrete. It is a question not merely of felt preferences resulting from one's upbringing, but of an affectivity that is structured by reason and by the habitual benevolence of the will. The habit of prudence is formed in the course of a coherent life history under the guidance of the conscience. But we must not forget that the conscience does not only speak to prohibit some action. Its genuine and most important function is to encourage us, and yes, even to command us, to remember to do what is good. The way to prudence lies in acting according to one's own conscience, and not only to follow what appears good here and now for merely emotional reasons.

It is precisely here that we can see the inadequacy of the Kantian categorical imperative and its universalizing logic. These imperatives are very enlightening, of course. But, as Kant himself said, they can only tell us what is "permitted" and what is "forbidden."[301] The categorical imperative cannot supply the most important thing: the determination of what is to be done here and now, that is, the forming of the concrete choice of action, "p is good," "p is to be done." The categorical imperative is only a "testing device" for ascertaining whether a subjective maxim does not stand in contradiction to its assumed role as a universal law. If someone wanted to determine by means of this universalization what is really the good thing to do here and now, only a tautology would result: because what is good for someone to do here and now is good for everybody to do here and now, provided he finds himself in the *same exact* situation. To think of a concrete action that takes place in a concrete situation as a universal law makes no sense.[302]

Admittedly, this is not what Kant wants to say, either. As we saw earlier, Kant's categorical imperative does not have the function of determining *what* we should do here and now. Its task is rather to examine whether what we already want to do on the basis of a subjective maxim is in concordance with the autonomy of the will. The categorical imperative is thus self-examination for the possibly selfish motives of our conduct. If the examination is "passed" (i.e., if the action is "permitted"), or if it "does not pass" (i.e., it is "forbidden"), then we must follow our maxim or not follow it, respectively. Whether the choice itself is moral only depends on whether it is permissible—according to the criterion of the autonomy of the will vis-à-vis self-interested motives—to go ahead with it. The categorical imperative can therefore never determine the goodness or rightness of a concrete action, only the fundamental permissibility or morality of a maxim. An action that follows a maxim that has "passed" the examination of the categorical imperative is *moral*, but still not necessarily the right action. It could also be a stupid act. For the fact that it is universalizable is not enough to make clear what should be done, here and now. What is to be done here and now cannot be thought of as a universal law, unless in a way that does not add anything to the idea of the concrete action, that is, in a tautological way. This is why in Kantian ethics—just as in utilitarianism—the conditions for morality (good will, good disposition) are formed independently of what we actually do in the concrete.

After this excursus we can return to our principal theme: our conscience is

---

301. I. Kant, *Groundwork of the Metaphysics of Morals*, trans. M. Gregor, 46.
302. Cf. on this also M. Rhonheimer, "Menschliches Handeln und Seine Moralität," 103, note 11.

formed through judgment upon the objective meaning of our actions. In this way the conscience becomes, as it were, the "ultimate" and immediate norm of our action. It is the highest norm, we could say—but not because the conscience is the origin and source of the difference between "good" and "bad," but because it provides that *final* normative orientation that simply cannot be gotten around. If the conscience tells us "*x* should be done," there is simply no other power or authority to be thought of that could question this judgment any further—not even a God who reveals Himself with normative instructions. Because when we give our trust to the God who reveals and do what He tells us, we do this on the basis of a judgment of conscience: "I should obey God." Even if something other than what God commands us to do seems better to us, and provided we happen to follow our own viewpoint on that, we would not, actually, be following our conscience, but only "what seems good to us."

The judgment of conscience cannot be gotten around. This is why prudence must also lend an ear to the conscience. If someone has a *positive doubt* about the goodness of an action, he acts against his conscience if he carries out the act before his doubt is removed. If someone is *uncertain* whether the judgment he is making truly reflects his conscience, he has to consider that his conscience might be erroneous. But if in such a situation and because of the uncertainty he simply *omits doing* what his possibly erroneous conscience commands him *to do* (or if he *does* what that same possibly erroneous conscience commands him *not to do*), he acts against his conscience. But he should likewise not do (or omit to do) what it judges that he should do or omit to do, just because the conscience is possibly in error and because he would be responsible for such error. It is important to try hard to reach certainty before one acts.[303]

The problem, here, is that my conscience can find itself in error without my being able to know if it is or not. This possibility grounds the duty to form my conscience. It is clear that the best formation of conscience consists in the acquisition of moral virtues. The path to it is readiness to admit one's errors, taking of counsel, when it can reasonably be had, and informing oneself adequately on each situation. An ethics of virtue is founded on the fact that the enemy of our orientation toward "what is good for man" is disorder of the affections and the will. But this "good for man" is the only thing that we can rationally seek for its own sake, which makes life meaningful as a whole and, in this sense, happy. A virtue ethics, accordingly, requires from an individual that he begin with himself, in order to make his own life a moral success and in order to contribute to the morally successful lives of his fellow human beings. The consequence of this—to the extent we are responsible—is without a doubt also the best possible state of the world.

303. On the erroneous conscience, cf. V.2.b above.

FROM THE PHILOSOPHICAL TO THE
CHRISTIAN PERSPECTIVE OF MORALITY

"The best possible state of the world"—this is the vista attained by our analysis of the "perspective of morality". And what should be immediately added is that this "best possible state of the world" of course includes, for those of us who have such a state in view, our *own* happiness, the success of our *own* lives.

But is this "successful life," this happiness, really that much of a success? Is it really the happiness we are all striving for? Isn't it rather the case, as many have said, that happiness in this life is always two-edged, partial, doubtful, incomplete . . . and very brief?

In fact, we made the point earlier on that what philosophical ethics has to say about the possibilities of human life and its success—about happiness, that is to say—is something incomplete, a kind of "torso" without the head: the human desire for happiness drives the human being beyond his naturally given possibilities. The last word would seem to indicate modesty, and a wise resignation: it would be a shame to create false hopes for ourselves.

Aristotelian ethics is thoroughly conscious of this incomplete character of human existence. And what is worse, the human being appears to be an unfinished, even self-contradictory being; still more questionable is what Aristotle tells us about happiness: really genuine happiness is only possible for the few, and even for them it is only possible through the favor of destiny. You need luck—good fortune *(tyche)*. This means that someone has to be lucky to be counted among the fortunate few who have been granted the chance to devote themselves to the leisured contemplation of truth. The majority must be content with a second-rate happiness, which is not really true happiness. Someone who only can share in this second-rank kind of happiness of the practical life is in fact an unfortunate person. And this is without even mentioning the still greater number of noncitizens and slaves, whose lot is not even worth discussing. And then, the truly happy sort (who devote themselves to theoretical truth) could not even exist so happily as they do if it weren't for the rest, who work for them.

But we are still only looking at the surface of the matter. For now a deeper problem presents itself: according to a purely "philosophical" perspective, it is the case that the happiest person is the one who is lucky enough not to have misfortune! Happiness, which seemed so dependent on the responsible use of our freedom, our own self-determination, our own moral actions, turns out to be a matter of destiny, of determination by something outside ourselves. Are we really the ones who fabricate our happiness? The more "morally" we live, the more we risk not having a successful life at all. Once again, the last word seems over and over again to be: only he can truly be happy who is lucky.

This leads to the question "Why be moral, anyway?"—the question posed by ethicists over and over again. Morality is its own justification, and probably because the good is its own justification. To be moral means to strive for the good and to do it, to be good. We don't need to ask "why?" beyond that.

So the question is really a different one: namely, Why should those who have good luck be happier, all else being equal, than those who don't? From the perspective of this question, there is an inner contradiction in the "perspective of morality." For it is simply inconceivable how the blows of fortune, bad luck, or more precisely sickness, injustice, lack of inborn gifts or other disadvantageous conditions, bad environment, victimization by other human beings, and so on could contribute to happiness or to success in life. To be sure, someone could be happy *despite* such factors and demonstrate moral excellence in that way (here is where the Stoics would agree, while Aristotle would balk). But it is still the case, at least if we think in Aristotelian terms, that *really* to be happy requires good fortune, and that is only given to a few— and yet how often it happens that the ones who have such good fortune are not in fact happy because they are not *doing* what is good. In order to be happy, it is not enough to have good fortune.

So the paradox remains: the more complete the happiness, the "thinner" it seems to be spread, and of course, who can be blamed for this? It is only to be expected. What someone can in fact realistically hope to expect is not happiness and a successful life, but only a dim version of it, a life constantly marked by futility, chance, irrereversible events and above all transitoriness. Whoever rebels against such contingency of human existence—and it is a sign of Aristotle's greatness that he does not rebel—turns either to ideologies or (alternatively) simply "gives up" on being human, reducing everything to libido, existential destiny, being-unto-death, genetic programs, natural selection, maximization of pleasure, and all the rest.

As we said earlier: faith stands as a corrective against both false ideologies and resignation. All religion has this function of correction and, in this sense, is the practice of coping with contingency. This functional determination is, of course, inadequate, and becomes simply false once the question of the truth of the religion is posed. This is no merely theoretical question, but rather an eminently meaningful one for praxis. Only that religious belief can be *true* that in fact brings practical reason to its completion, while a faith that is only *useful* or "functional" would not do so. Otherwise, religion would be only a placebo. That would be useful, of course, but if it is correct that only *true* faith can bring reason to its fulfillment—and that appears to be the case: for reason itself is oriented toward the truth—so only *true* faith can help lead someone to *true* happiness. If someone considers the question of the truth of a religion as unanswerable and contents himself with a "placebo," he is assuming the truth-function of the human mind to be obsolete.

So what is the situation for Christian faith, or to be exact, for Christian morality? A few lines of the pencil should be enough to show in this epilogue why Christian morality is neither a threat to reason nor a dispensation from it, but rather a completion—in fact, it "rescues" the ethics we have been presenting on the basis of mere philosophical reason. In the Christian perspective, death is not only turned into resurrection, but failure into victory, and suffering becomes a source of meaning and joy. The cornerstone of Christian ethics is the cross—not merely the ancient Roman instrument of punishment, but the cross that the God-Man Jesus Christ carried *for us,* and which, since the actions of God are not limited by time, He continues to carry for us. But this cross is only the focal point of the further contents of faith: the revelation that the situation of human beings in the world is the consequence of an original fall into sin, which is a rebellion against God; that God, the Trinity, sent His own Son, who became a man, in order to reconcile us with God; that He take upon himself *our* sins and weaknesses, and all the tedium of human life, in order to suffer and die *for us;* that He rise again from death, so that *we too could rise again* from death; that He sent us His Spirit, in whom we can trustingly call God "Our Father."

The commandments of morality as already confirmed through revelation in the Decalogue of the Old Testament receive their definitive confirmation and completion in Christ, in the perspective of the cross and resurrection: "Blessed are those who mourn . . . ," "Blessed are those who hunger and thirst for righteousness," "Blessed are those who are persecuted for righteousness' sake . . . ," "Blessed are you when you are scorned and persecuted, and people abuse you and use all manner of calumny against you on my account. Rejoice and be glad: for your reward in heaven will be great." This is a totally new perspective: "foolishness to the pagans."

Nevertheless, this is the perspective of morality, the perspective of happiness. Here the real issue is success in life, in the true sense of the word. And we see that no longer can only those few who may have good fortune share in happiness. *Paradoxically, it is only in the Christian perspective that we actually become the creators of our own happiness,* only here does everything really depend upon us, as long as we are ready to let God do what *cannot* depend on ourselves: the ones who want to be happy, the "men of goodwill," can have happiness *whether or not they have good fortune.* This is because we *all* have the good fortune that God loves us. And this does not depend on chance *(tyche)* anymore, but on God's *providentia,* which, in an unprejudiced and gratuitous way, is *love for all,* a love that through grace makes our own abilities flourish. And thus it is the case that *"for those who love God, all things work together for good"* (*diligentibus Deum omnia cooperantur in bonum;* Romans 8:28). The Christian anticipation of happiness depends on the initiative taken by the mercy of God: "For love does not consist in the fact that *we* have loved God, but that *he* has loved us, and sent his own son as reconciliation for our sins" (1 John 4:10).

Is this supposed to mean, then, trust in the next world? That would be missing the mark. The happiness that Christian faith promises is by no means simply trust in the next world. That would be only a caricature, and in fact the opposite is true, even if Christian hope only finds its last fulfillment after death. Christian faith, in fact, discloses the one truly realistic perspective on happiness in *this* life. It is not a matter of *beatitudo perfecta* in all its completeness, but then again neither is it a second-rate, imperfect "happiness in this life," but rather the beginning *(inchoatio)* of the *beatitudo perfecta,* which reaches its fulfillment in the eternal life—to be more precise, it is the beginning of that same eternal life. The imperfect happiness of life in this world in the Christian perspective is by no means simply the happiness that divides itself into the *duplex felicitas* we spoke of earlier, but rather the ultimate happiness itself, in an embryonic stage. It is characterized by the so-called theological virtues faith, hope, and love: faith already "knows" what transcends the reason, in hope it is already present in its blessings, while love draws us "upward" to fulfillment. This is how the hiatus between contemplation and practical life is overcome: right here *in* practical life, a loving glimpse of God is constantly present. Contemplation does not here mean the abandonment of action, but rather *living* and *acting* in consciousness of the fact that we are led by the loving hand of God, and responding to this fact with the love with which Christ loved the cross as the means of salvation. This is not a contemplation for the few "fortunate ones," but for everyman, to the extent anyone opens himself to God's love.

The core teaching of the Gospel or Good News is a genuine call to happiness for *this life* and not merely trust in the world to come: "Anyone who has left behind houses or brothers or sisters, father or mother or children or land for the sake of my name, will win in return a hundredfold and eternal life" (Matt. 19:29), and that hundredfold is in *this life* (cf. Mark 10:30 and Luke 18:30). "So do not have anxieties and do not ask, 'What shall we eat? What shall we drink? What clothes shall we have?' for the pagans ask for all these things. Your Father in heaven knows that you need all these things. Seek first the Kingdom of God and his justice, and all these things will be given to you in addition" (Matt. 6:31–33). And finally, "Come to me all you who labor and have heavy burdens to bear, and I will give you rest. Take my yoke upon you and learn from me . . . and *you will find rest for your souls* [*in this life also*], *for my yoke is gentle and my burden light*" (Matt. 11:28–30).

Nevertheless, this does not provide any escape from the "emptying" *(kenosis)* of the cross. The verses just quoted are not cheap promises made to maximize pleasure. Christian morality is not, finally, just a more beneficial "calculation of utility." The "hundredfold" and "what is given in addition" are often not what we would have dreamt of for ourselves, not at least if we go by human standards. The cross remains. No human efforts can ever drive it from the world. The decisive question here is: Will it remain only *our own* cross, or will it become a cross that Christ carries along with us, so that it finally becomes that "light burden"? Christian faith does not merely proclaim the cross—it is not sadism, intended only to load something upon us—rather, it takes some of the weight off. Christian faith does not simply proclaim the cross and the need to weep in this "vale of tears"; instead, it proclaims the *liberating power* of the cross: the cross as root and source of meaning, joy, and happiness right here *in* this vale of tears. Christian faith, in other words, is not just the diagnosis—it is also the therapy. Jesus of Nazareth was not the first to be crucified by the Romans, and we would not count any of his predecessors in that experience to have been "happy" or as having lived a successful life. Jesus did not invent the cross (the Romans get the credit for that), but he did transform it into a means of resurrection, into a path to victory and life. The life of Christ succeeded as no other life has ever succeeded. That—and the following of Christ that it demands—is the core of Christian ethics, which, like the classical doctrine of the philosophers, is a eudaimonistic ethics, a teaching about the happy life. It neither distorts nor relativizes reason, but completes and "rescues" it. Only in the Christian perspective does it become possible to keep to the truth of human reason and to "sit firmly in the saddle" philosophically speaking: resistant both to resignation, on the one hand, and to the deceptive glimmer of ideologies promising earthly paradise, on the other.

In any event, Christian ethics is virtue ethics because it is eudaimonistic, a doctrine of happiness and, in specifically Christian terms, a doctrine of beatitude. And thus we can repeat the final words of the last chapter—but this time in a new key: virtue ethics requires from each person that he begin with himself if he wants to make his life a success and if he wants to contribute to the lives of others. What results from *that*—at least to the extent we are responsible—is without any doubt the best possible state of the world.

Bibliography

I. Frequently Cited Sources (in historical order)

Plato

Hamilton, Edith, and Huntington Cairns, eds. *The Collected Dialogues of Plato.* Princeton, N.J.: Princeton University Press, 1961.

Aristotle

Barnes, Jonathan, ed. *The Complete Works of Aristotle: The Revised Oxford Translation.* Vols. 1 and 2. Princeton, N.J.: Princeton University Press, 1984.

Thomas Aquinas

a) Commentaries

In Ethic. (Commentary on Aristotle's *Nicomachean Ethics*): *In Decem libros Ethicorum Aristotelis ad Nichomachum expositio,* edited by R. M. Spiazzi. 3rd ed. Turin: Marietti, 1964 (Cited as follows: In I Ethic., lect. 1, n. 1 = Commentary on the First Book, lectio 1, number 1). The text of this edition must occasionally be compared with the later critical edition by R. A. Gauthier (part of the *Editio Leonina*): Sancti Thomas de Aquino Sententia libri ethicorum, in *Opera Omnia,* vol. 48. Rome: Apud Sedem Commissionis Leoninae, 1969.

In de Anima (Commentary on Aristotle's *De Anima*): *In Aristotelis librum de Anima commentarium,* edited by A. M. Pirotta. 5th ed. Turin: Marietti, 1959.

In Sent. (Commentary on the *Sentences* of Petrus Lombardus): *In quattuor libros sententiarum Petri Lombardi.* "Index Thomisticus" edition: S. Thomae Aquinatis *Opera omnia,* vol. 1. Edited by R. Busa. Stuttgart: 1980 (Cited as follows: In II Sent., d. 35, q. 1, a. 1 = Book II, Distinctio 35, Quaestio 1, a. 1).

In De Div. Nom. (Commentary on the *De Divinis Nominibus* of Pseudo-Dionysios the Areopagite): In Librum Beati Dionysii De Divinis Nominibus Expositio. Edited by C. Pera. Turin: Marietti, 1950.

b) Summae

C.G.: = *Summa contra Gentiles.*
Edited by C. Pera, P. Marc, and P. Caramello. Turin: Marietti, 1961.

I = *Summa Theologiae: Prima pars*
I-II = *Summa Theologiae: Prima secundae*
II-II = *Summa Theologiae: Secunda secundae*

III = *Summa Theologiae: Tertia pars*
Edited by P. Caramello. Turin: Marietti, 1952.

c) Disputed Questions

De Veritate: *Quaestiones disputatae de Veritate.* In Quaestiones disputate [= QD], vol. 1. Edited by R. Spiazzi. 10th ed. Turin: Marietti, 1964.
De Malo: *Quaestiones disputatae de Malo.* In QD [see immediately above], vol. 2. Edited by P. Baazzi, M. Calcaterra, T. S. Centi, E. Odetto, and P. M. Pession. 10th ed. Turin: Marietti, 1965.
De Potentia: *Quaestiones disputatae de Potentia.* In QD, vol. 2.
De Virtutibus in communi: *Quaestiones disputatae de Virtutibus in communi.* In QD, vol. 2.
De Virtutibus cardinalibus: *Quaestiones disputatae de Virtutibus cardinalibus.* In QD, vol. 2.
De Caritate: *Quaestiones disputatae de Caritate.* In QD, vol. 2.

(*Note:* all quotations from Thomas Aquinas in *The Perspective of Morality* have been translated for this edition by Gerald Malsbary.)

Immanuel Kant

a) Principal Moral Treatises

Groundwork of the Metaphysics of Morals. Translated by Mary Gregor. New York: Cambridge University Press, 1998. (Original German ed. 1785)
Critique of Practical Reason. Translated by Mary Gregor. New York: Cambridge University Press, 1997. (Original German ed. 1788)
The Metaphysics of Morals. Translated by Mary Gregor. New York: Cambridge University Press, 1996. (Original German ed. 1797)

b) Other Works of Kant, unless specially indicated, are quoted from

Hutchins, Robert M., editor-in-chief, *Great Books of the Western World* 42: *Kant.* Chicago: Encyclopedia Britannica, 1952.

II. Other Sources

Abbà, Giuseppe. *Lex et virtus. Studi sull'evoluzione della dottrina morale di San Tommaso d'Aquino.* Rome: LAS, 1983.
———. *Felicità, vita buona e virtù. Saggio di filosofia morale.* Rome: LAS, 1989.
Ackrill, J. L. "Aristotle on Eudaimonia." In *Essays on Aristotle's Ethics,* edited by A. O. Rorty, 15–34. Berkeley-Los Angeles-London: University of California Press, 1980.
Albert, Hans. *Traktat über kritische Vernunft.* 5th, enlarged ed. Tübingen: Mohr, 1991.
Allan, David J. *The Philosophy of Aristotle.* 2nd ed. Oxford: Oxford University Press, 1970.
———. "Aristotle's Account of the Origin of Moral Principles" (1953). In *Articles on Aristotle,* vol. 2: *Ethics and Politics,* edited by J. Barnes, M. Schofield, and R. Sorabji, 72–78. London: Duckworth, 1977.
Annas, J. *The Morality of Happiness.* Oxford: Oxford University Press, 1993.

Anscombe, G. E. M. *Intention.* 2nd ed. Oxford: Basil Blackwell, 1963.

———. "Modern Moral Philosophy." *Philosophy* 33, no. 124 (1958): 1–19; also available in Crisp, Roger, and Michael Slote, *Virtue Ethics* (see below), 26–44, and in *The Collected Papers of G. E. M. Anscombe,* 3.26–42. Oxford: Oxford University Press, 1981.

———. "Thought and Action in Aristotle." In *Articles on Aristotle,* vol. 2: *Ethics and Politics,* edited by Jonathan Barnes, M. Schofield, and R. Sorabji, 61–71. London: Duckworth, 1977.

———. "War and Murder." In *The Collected Philosophical Papers of G. E. M. Anscombe,* vol. 3. Oxford: Basil Blackwell, 1981.

Anzenbacher, Arno. *Einführung in die Ethik.* Düsseldorf: Patmos, 1992.

Apel, Karl-Otto. "Das Apriori der Kommunikationsgemeinschaft und die Grundlagen der Ethik. Zum Problem einer rationalen Begründung der Ethik im Zeitalter der Wissenschaft." In *Transformation der Philosophie,* vol. 2: *Das Apriori der Kommunikationsgemeinschaft.* Frankfurt am Main: Suhrkamp, 1976.

———. *Diskurs und Verantwortung. Das Problem des Übergangs zur postkonventionellen Moral.* Frankfurt am Main: Suhrkamp, 1990.

———. *Auseinandersetzungen in Erprobung des transzendentalpragmatischen Ansatzes.* Frankfurt am Main: Suhrkamp, 1998.

———, and M. Kettner. *Zur Anwendung der Diskursethik in Politik, Recht und Wissenschaft.* Frankfurt am Main: Suhrkamp, 1992.

Arkes, Hadley. *First Things: An Inquiry into the First Principles of Morals and Justice.* Princeton, N.J.: Princeton University Press, 1986.

Armstrong, R. A. *Primary and Secondary Precepts in Thomistic Natural Law Teaching.* The Hague: Martinus Nijhoff, 1966.

Ashley, Benedict M. "What Is the End of the Human Person? The Vision of God and Integral Human Fulfillment." In *Moral Truth and Moral Tradition: Essays in Honour of Peter and Elizabeth Geach,* edited by L. Gormally, 68–96. Dublin: Four Courts Press, 1994.

Audi, Robert. "Acting from Virtue." *Mind* 104 (1995): 449–71.

Augustinus, Aurelius. *Confessions.* Translated by R. S. Pine-Coffin. In *Great Books of the Western World* 16. 2nd ed. Chicago: Encyclopedia Britannica, 1990.

———. *Homilies on the Gospel of John.* Translated by John Gibb and James Innes. In *The Nicene and Post-Nicene Fathers,* Series 1, vol. 7, 19–25. Edited by Philip Schaff. Peabody, Mass.: Hendrickson, 1995 [1888].

Austin, John L. "A Plea for Excuses." *Proceedings of the Aristotelian Society* 57 (1956–1957): 1–30.

Baier, Kurt. *The Moral Point of View: A Rational Basis of Ethics.* Ithaca, N.Y., and London: Cornell University Press, 1958.

Beckermann, A., ed. *Analytische Handlungstheorie.* 2 vols. Frankfurt am Main: Suhrkamp, 1985.

Belmans, Theo G. "Le paradoxe de la conscience erronée d'Abelard à Karl Rahner." *Revue thomiste* 90 (1990): 570–86.

Bien, G. "Die menschlichen Meinungen und das Gute: Die Lösung des Normproblems in der aristotelischen Ethik." In *Rehabilitierung der praktischen Philosophie,* vol. 1. edited by M. Riedel. Freiburg: Verlag Rombach, 1972.

Birnbacher, Dieter. *Tun und Unterlassen.* Stuttgart: Reclam, 1995.

Bobbio, Norberto. *L'età dei diritti*. Turin: Einaudi, 1990.

Böckenförde, Ernst-Wolfgang. *Religionsfreiheit. Die Kirche in der modernen Welt. Schriften zu Staat-Gesellschaft-Kirche*. Vol. 3. Freiburg im Breisgau: Herder, 1990.

Boethius, Anicius Manlius Severinus. *The Consolation of Philosophy*. Translated by Victor Watts. Revised ed. London: Penguin Books, 1999.

Bonelli, Johannes, ed. *Der Mensch als Mitte und Massstab der Medizin*. Vienna and New York: Springer-Verlag, 1992.

Bormann, F. J. *Natur als Horizont sittlicher Praxis. Zur handlungstheoretischen Interpretation der Lehre vom natürlichen Sittengesetz bei Thomas von Aquin*. Münchner philosophische Studien, Neue Folge, Band 14. Stuttgart-Berlin-Cologne: Verlag W. Kohlhammer, 1999.

Bradley, D. J. M. *Aquinas on the Twofold Human Good: Reason and Human Happiness in Aquinas' Moral Science*. Washington, D.C.: The Catholic University of America Press, 1997.

Braine, D. *The Human Person: Animal and Spirit*. South Bend, Ind.: University of Notre Dame Press, 1992.

Bretone, M. *Geschichte des römischen Rechts: Von den Anfängen bis zu Justinian*. 2nd ed. Munich: C. H. Beck, 1998.

Broad, C. D. *Five Types of Ethical Theory*. London: Routledge & Kegan Paul, 1930.

———. "Some of the Main Problems of Ethics." *Philosophy* 21 (1946). Reprinted in *Broad's Critical Essays in Moral Philosophy*, edited by D. R. Cheney. London: Allen & Unwin; New York: Humanities Press, 1971.

Brock, Stephen L. *Action and Conduct: Thomas Aquinas and the Theory of Action*. Edinburgh: T & T Clark, 1998.

———. "*Veritas splendor* §78, St. Thomas, and (Not Merely) Physical Objects of Moral Acts." *Nova et Vetera* (English ed.) 6, no. 1 (2008): 1–62

Bubner, Rüdiger. *Handlung, Sprache und Vernunft*. 2nd ed. Frankfurt am Main: Suhrkamp, 1982.

Caldera, Rafael T. *Le jugement par inclination chez Saint Thomas d'Aquin*. Paris: J. Vrin, 1980.

Cessario, Romanus. *The Moral Virtues and Theological Ethics*. 2nd ed. South Bend, Ind.: University of Notre Dame Press, 2008.

Crisp, Roger, and Michael Slote, eds. *Virtue Ethics*. Oxford: Oxford University Press, 1997.

Crowe, Michael B. *The Changing Profile of the Natural Law*. The Hague: Martinus Nijhoff, 1977.

Damon, William. *The Moral Child: Nurturing Children's Natural Moral Growth*. New York: Free Press, 1988.

———. *The Social World of the Child*. San Francisco: Jossey-Bass, 1977.

Danto, A. C. "Basic Actions." *American Philosophical Quarterly* 2 (1965): 141–48.

D' Avenia, M. *La conoscenza per connaturalità in S. Tommaso D'Aquino*. Bologna: Edizioni Studio Domenicano, 1992.

Davidson, Donald. *Essays on Action and Events*. Oxford: Clarendon Press, 1980.

Dent, N. J. H. *The Moral Psychology of the Virtues*. Cambridge: Cambridge University Press, 1984.

Dewan, Lawrence, O.P. "St. Thomas, Rhonheimer, and the Object of the Human Act." *Nova et Vetera* (English ed.) 6, no. 1 (2008): 63–112.

Dewey, John. *Human Nature and Conduct*. New York: Holt, 1922.

Di Blasi, Fulvio. *Dio e la legge naturale. Una rilettura di Tommaso d'Aquino*. Pisa: ETS, 1999.

Diogenes Laertius. *Lives of Eminent Philosophers*. Translated by R. D. Hicks. London: Heinemann, 1950.

Donagan, Alan. *The Theory of Morality*. Chicago and London: University of Chicago Press, 1977.

Elders, Leo J., and Klaus Hedwig, eds. *The Ethics of Thomas Aquinas*. Vatican City: Libreria Editrice Vaticana, 1984.

———. *Lex et Libertas: Freedom and Law According to St. Thomas Aquinas*. Vatican City: Libreria Editrice Vaticana, 1987.

Elm, Ralf. *Klugheit und Erfahrung bei Aristoteles*. Paderborn: F. Schoningh, 1996.

Engberg-Pedersen, Troels. *Aristotle's Theory of Moral Insight*. Oxford: Oxford University Press, 1983.

Ernst, Stephan. "Hat die autonome und teleologische Ethik die Objektivität sittlichen Handeln vergessen? Marginalien zu M. Rhonheimers Buch 'Natur als Grundlage der Moral.'" *Theologie und Glaube* 78 (1988): 80–89.

———. "Erwiderung auf die Replik von M. Rhonheimer zu meiner Rezension seines Buches 'Natur als Grundlage der Moral.'" *Theologie und Glaube* 79 (1989): 84–87 [for the reply, see under Rhonheimer].

Fichte, Johann Gottlieb. "*Werke*." In *Werke*, edited by I. H. Fichte, 5.175–89. Reprint, Berlin: Walter De Gruyter, 1971.

———. *Appellation an das Publikum gegen die Anklage des Atheismus* (1799). In *Werke*, edited by I. H. Fichte, 5.191–238. Reprint, Berlin: Walter De Gruyter, 1971.

Finnis, John, Joseph Boyle, and Germain Grisez. *Nuclear Deterrence, Morality and Realism*. Oxford: Clarendon Press, 1987.

Finnis, John. *Natural Law and Natural Rights*. Oxford: Clarendon Press, 1980.

———. *Fundamentals of Ethics*. Washington, D.C.: Georgetown University Press, 1984.

———. "Practical Reasoning, Human Goods and the End of Man." *New Blackfriars* 66 (1985): 438–51.

———. "Object and Intention in Moral Judgments According to Aquinas." *The Thomist* 55 (1991): 1–27.

———. *Moral Absolutes: Tradition, Revision, and Truth*. Washington, D.C.: The Catholic University of America Press, 1991.

———. *Aquinas: Moral, Political, and Legal Theory*. Oxford: Oxford University Press, 1998.

Flannery, Kevin L., S.J. *Acts Amid Precepts: The Aristotelian Logical Structure of Thomas Aquinas's Moral Theory*. Washington, D.C.: The Catholic University of America Press, 2001.

———. "Review of Martin Rhonheimer, *Die Perspektive der Moral*." *Gregoranum* 83 (2002): 591–94.

Foot, Philippa, ed. *Theories of Ethics*. London: Oxford University Press, 1967.

———. *Virtues and Vices and Other Essays in Moral Philosophy*. Oxford: Basil Blackwell, 1978.

———. "Morality, Action and Outcome." In *Morality and Objectivity: A Tribute to J. L. Mackie*, edited by T. Honderich. London: Routledge & Kegan Paul, 1985.

———. "Utilitarianism and the Virtues." In *Consequentialism and Its Critics*, edited by Samuel Scheffler. Oxford: Oxford University Press, 1988.

———. *Die Wirklichkeit des Guten. Moralphilosophische Aufsätze*. Edited by Ursul Wolf and Anton Leist. Frankfurt am Main: Suhrkamp, 1997.

Forschner, M. *Die stoische Ethik: Über den Zusammenhang von Natur-, Sprach- und Moralphilosphie im altstoischen System*. Stuttgart: Klett-Cotta, 1981.

Frankena, William K. *Ethics*. Englewood Cliffs, N.J.: Prentice-Hall, 1963.

Frankfurt, Harry. "Freedom of the Will and the Concept of a Person." *Journal of Philosophy* 67 (1971): 5–20.

Frankl, Viktor. *On the Theory and Therapy of Mental Disorders: An Introduction to Logotherapy and Existential Analysis*. New York: Brunner-Routledge, 2004 [1956].

French, P. A., T. E. Uehling, and H. K. Wettstein, eds. *Ethical Theory: Character and Virtue*. South Bend, Ind.: University of Notre Dame Press, 1988.

Friedrich, Carl J. *Constitutional Government and Democracy*. New York: Blaisdell, 1950.

Fuchs, Josef. "The Absoluteness of Moral Terms." *Gregorianum* 52 (1971). Reprinted in *Readings in Moral Theology, No. 1: Moral Norms and Catholic Tradition*, edited by Charles E. Curran and Richard McCormick. New York: Paulist Press, 1979.

Furger, Franz. *Einführung in die Moraltheologie*. Darmstadt: Wissenschaftliche Buchgesellschaft, 1988.

Gadamer, Hans-Georg. *Truth and Method*. Translated by Garrett Barden and John Cumming. New York: Seabury Press, 1975.

Gahl, Robert A. "From the Virtue of a Fragile Good to a Narrative Account of Natural Law." *International Philosophical Quarterly* 37, no. 4 (1997): 459–74.

Gallagher, David M. "Thomas Aquinas on Self-Love as the Basis for Love of Others." *Acta Philosophica* 8 (1999): 23–44.

Ganter, Martin. *Mittel und Ziel in der praktischen Philosophie des Aristoteles*. Freiburg and Munich: Alber, 1974.

Geach, Peter. "Good and Evil." *Analysis* 17 (1956): 33–42. Republished in *Theories of Ethics*, edited by Philippa Foot. Oxford: Oxford University Press, 1967.

———. *The Virtues*. 2nd ed. Cambridge: Cambridge University Press, 1979.

Gert, Bernard. *Morality: Its Nature and Justification*. New York and Oxford: Oxford University Press, 1998 (= third edition of Gert, *The Moral Rules: A New Rational Foundation for Morality*, 1970).

Gewirth, Alan. *Reason and Morality*. Chicago: University of Chicago Press, 1978.

———. *Human Rights: Essays on Justification and Application*. Chicago: University of Chicago Press, 1982.

Gilby, Thomas. *Principality and Polity: Aquinas and the Rise of State Theory in the West*. London: Longmans, Green, 1958.

González, Ana Marta. *Moral, razón y naturaleza. Una investigación sobre Tomás de Aquino*. Pamplona: Ediciones Universidad de Navarra, 1998.

———. "*Depositus gladius non debet restitui furioso:* Precepts, Synderesis, and Virtues in Saint Thomas Aquinas." *The Thomist* 63, no. 2 (1999): 217–40.

Grewendorf, Günther, and Georg Meggle. *Seminar: Sprache und Ethik. Zur Entwicklung der Metaethik*. Frankfurt am Main: Suhrkamp, 1974.

Grisez, Germain. "The First Principle of Practical Reasoning: A Commentary on the *Summa Theologiae*, 1–2, Question 94, article 2." *Natural Law Forum* 10 (1965):

168–201. A slightly abridged version is available in *Aquinas: A Collection of Critical Essays*, edited by A. Kenny. Garden City, N.Y.: Anchor Books, 1969.

Grisez, Germain, Joseph Boyle, and John Finnis. "Practical Principles, Moral Truth, and Ultimate Ends." *American Journal of Jurisprudence* 32 (1987): 99–151.

Habermas, Jürgen. *Moralbewusstsein und kommunikatives Handeln*. Frankfurt am Main: Suhrkamp, 1983.

———. *Erläuterungen zur Diskursethik*. Frankfurt am Main: Suhrkamp, 1991.

———. *Faktizität und Geltung. Beiträge zur Diskurstheorie des Rechts und des demokratischen Rechtsstaats*. Frankfurt am Main: Suhrkamp, 1992.

———. *Wahrheit und Rechtfertigung. Philosophische Aufsätze*. Frankfurt am Main: Suhrkamp, 1999.

———. "Richtigkeit versus Wahrheit. Zum Sinn der Sollgeltung moralischer Urteile und Normen." In Habermas, *Wahrheit und Rechtfertigung* (see above), 271–318.

Hall, P. M. *Narrative and the Natural Law: An Interpretation of Thomistic Ethics*. London and South Bend, Ind.: University of Notre Dame Press, 1994.

Hare, R. M. *Moral Thinking: Its Levels, Methods and Point*. Oxford: Clarendon Press, 1981.

———. "Ethical Theory and Utilitarianism." In *Utilitarianism and Beyond*, edited by A. Sen and B. Williams. Cambridge: Cambridge University Press, 1982.

Hedwig, Klaus. "Über die Theorie der Praxis bei Thomas von Aquin." *Philosophisches Jahrbuch* 99 (1992): 245–61.

Hegel, Georg Wilhelm Friedrich. *Phenomenology of the Spirit*. Translated by A. V. Miller. Oxford: Clarendon Press, 1977.

———. *Philosophie des Rechts. Die Vorlesungen von 1819/20 in einer Nachschrift*. Edited by D. Heinrich. Frankfurt am Main: Suhrkamp, 1983.

———. *The Philosophy of Right*. Translated by T. M. Knox. In *Great Books of the Western World* 46. Chicago: Encyclopedia Britannica, 1952.

———. *Science of Logic*. Translated by W. H. Johnston and L. G. Struthers. London: Allen & Unwin, 1929.

Heidegger, Martin. *Einführung in die Metaphysik*. 3rd ed. Tübingen: M. Niemayer, 1966.

Heller, Agnes. *Beyond Justice*. Oxford: Basil Blackwell, 1987.

Hertz, A., W. Korff, T. Rendtdorff, and H. Ringeling, eds. *Handbuch der christlichen Ethik*, vol. 1. Freiburg im Breisgau: Herder, 1978.

Hittinger, Russell. *A Critique of the New Natural Law Theory*. South Bend, Ind.: University of Notre Dame Press, 1987.

Hobbes, Thomas. *De cive or The Citizen*. Edited by S. Lamprecht. New York: Appleton-Century-Crofts, 1949.

———. *Leviathan*. Edited by C. B. MacPherson. Harmondsworth, U.K.: Penguin Books, 1986.

Hoerster, Norbert. *Utilitaristische Ethik und Verallgemeinerung*. 2nd ed. Freiburg and Munich: Alber, 1977.

Höffe, Otfried, ed. *Praktische Philosophie. Das Modell des Aristoteles*. 2nd ed. Berlin: Akademie, 1996 [1971].

———. *Einführung in die utilitaristische Ethik. Klassische und zeitgenössische Texte*. 2nd ed. Tübingen: Francke, 1992 [1975].

———. "Kategorie Streben." In *Ethik und Politik. Grundmodelle und -probleme der praktischen Philosophie*. Frankfurt am Main: Suhrkamp, 1979.

————. "Sittlichkeit als Horizont menschlichen Handelns." In *Sittlich-politische Diskurse*. Frankfurt am Main: Suhrkampt, 1981.

————. "Philosophische Handlungstheorie als Ethik." In *Philosophische Probleme der Handlungstheorie*, edited by H. Poser. Freiburg and Munich: Alber, 1982.

————. *Immanuel Kant*. Munich: C. H. Beck, 1983.

————, ed. *Lexikon der Ethik*. 3rd ed. Munich: C. H. Beck, 1986.

————. *Politische Gerechtigkeit. Grundlegung einer kritischen Philosophie von Recht und Staat*. Frankfurt am Main: Suhrkamp, 1987.

————. *Kategorische Rechtsprinzipien. Ein Kontrapunkt der Moderne*. Frankfurt am Main: Suhrkamp, 1990.

————. *Aristoteles*. Munich: C. H. Beck, 1996.

————. "Aristoteles' universalistische Tugendethik." In *Tugendethik*, edited by K. P. Rippe and P. Schaber. Stuttgart: Reclam, 1998.

Hoffmann, Tobias. "Moral Action as Human Action: End and Object in Aquinas in Comparison with Abelard, Lombard, Albert, and Duns Scotus." *The Thomist* 67 (2003): 73–94.

Honnefelder, L. "Praktische Vernunft und Gewissen." In *Handbuch der Christlichen Ethik*, 3rd ed., edited by A. Hertz, W. Korff, T. Rendtorff, and H. Ringeling. Freiburg-Basel-Vienna: Herder, 1982.

————. "Die Begründbarkeit des Ethischen und die Einheit der Menschheit." In *Die Welt für morgen. Ethische Herausforderungen im Anspruch der Zukunft*, edited by G. W. Hunold and W. Korff. Munich: Kösel, 1986.

————. "Wahrheit und Sittlichkeit. Zur Bedeutung der Wahrheit in der Ethik." In *Wahrheit und Einheit in der Vielheit*, edited by E. Coreth. Düsseldorf: Patmos-Verlag, 1987.

————. "Die ethische Rationalität des mittelalterlichen Naturrechts. Max Webers und Ernst Troeltschs Deutung des mittelalterlichen Naturrechts und die Bedeutung der Lehre vom natürlichen Gesetz bei Thomas von Aquin." In *Max Webers Sicht des okzidentalen Christentums*, edited by W. Schluchter. Frankfurt am Main: Suhrkamp, 1988.

————. "Absolute Forderungen in der Ethik. Im welchem Sinn ist eine sittliche Verpflichtung absolut?" In *Das absolute in der Ethik*, edited by W. Kerber. Munich: Kindt Verlag, 1991.

————. "Natur als Handlungsprinzip. Die Relevanz der Natur für die Ethik." In *Natur als Gegenstand der Wissenschaften*, edited by L. Honnefelder. Freiburg and Munich: K. Alber, 1992.

Honneth, Axel. "Grenzen des Liberalismus. Zur politisch-ethischen Diskussion um den Kommunitarismus." *Philosophische Rundschau* 38 (1991).

————. *Kommunitarismus. Eine Debatte über die moralischen Grundlagen moderner Gesellschaften*. Frankfurt am Main and New York: Campus, 1992.

Hösle, Vittorio. *Die Krise der Gegenwart und die Verantwortung der Philosophie. Transzendendentalpragmatik, Letztbegründung, Ethik*. 3rd ed. Munich: C. H. Beck, 1997 [1990].

Höver, Gerhard. *Sittlich handeln im Medium der Zeit. Ansätze zur handlungstheoretischen Neuorientierung der Moraltheologie*. Würzburg: Echter Verlag, 1988.

Hume, David. *A Treatise on Human Nature*. Edited by D. F. Norton and M. J. Norton. Oxford: Clarendon Press, 2000.

Irwin, Terence. *Aristotle's First Principles.* Oxford: Clarendon Press, 1988.

Jaffa, Harry. *Thomism and Aristotelianism: A Study of the Commentary by Thomas Aquinas on the Nicomachean Ethics.* Chicago: University of Chicago Press, 1952.

Jensen, Steven S. "A Long Discussion Regarding Steven A. Long's *Interpretation of the Moral Species.*" *The Thomast* 67 (2003): 623–43.

———. *Good and Evil Actions: A Journey through St. Thomas Aquinas.* Washington, D.C.: The Catholic University of America Press, 2010.

Jonas, Hans. *Das Prinzip Verantwortung. Versuch einer Ethik für die technische Zivilisation.* Frankfurt am Main: Suhrkamp, 1984 [1979].

———. *Technik, Medizin und Ethik. Zur Praxis des Prinzips Verantwortung.* Frankfurt am Main: Suhrkamp, 1987 [1985].

Kant, Immanuel. (see also "Frequently Cited Sources," for items not listed here).

———. *Religion within the Limits of Reason Alone,* translated by T. Greene and H. Hudson, 40–49. New York: Harper & Row, 1934 [rpt. 1960].

———. "Bemerkungen zu den Beobachtungen über das Gefühl des Schönen und Erhabenen." In *Werke,* Prussian Academy ed., vol. 20. Berlin: Walter de Gruyter, 1968 [1902].

———. "On a Supposed Right to Lie Because of Philanthropic Concerns." Published as "Supplement" to *Grounding for the Metaphysics of Morals,* translated by J. W. Ellington. Indianapolis, Ind., and Cambridge, Mass.: Hackett, 1981.

———. "Eine Vorlesung über Ethik." Edited by G. Gerhardt and Paul Menzer. Frankfurt am Main: Fischer Taschenbuch, 1990.

———. *Toward Perpetual Peace and Other Writings on Politics, Peace, and History.* Edited by P. Kleingeld et al. Translated by D. L. Colclasure. New Haven, Conn.: Yale University Press, 2006.

Keenan, J. F. "Die erworbenen Tugenden als richtige (nicht gute) Lebensführung: Ein genauerer Ausdruck ethischer Beschreibung." In *Ethische Theorie praktisch. Festschrift K. Demmer,* edited by F. Furger. Münster: Aschendorff, 1991.

———. *Goodness and Rightness in Thomas Aquinas's "Summa Theologiae."* Washington, D.C.: Georgetown University Press, 1992.

Kenny, Anthony. *Action, Emotion and Will.* 5th ed. London: Routledge & Kegan Paul, 1976.

———. "Happiness." *Proceedings of the Aristotelian Society* 66 (1965–1966): 93–102.

———. *Will, Freedom and Power.* Oxford: Basil Blackwell, 1975.

———. "Thomas von Aquin über den Willen." Translated into German by J. Beckmann. In *Thomas von Aquin im philosophischen Gespräch,* edited by W. Kluxen. Freiburg and Munich: Alber, 1975.

Kleber, Hermann. *Glück als Lebensziel. Untersuchungen zur Philosophie des Glücks bei Thomas von Aquin.* Münster: Aschendorff, 1988.

Kluxen, W. *Philosophische Ethik bei Thomas von Aquin.* Hamburg: Felix Meiner, 1964.

———. "Menschliche Natur und Ethos." *Münchener Theologische Zeitschrift* 23 (1972): 1–17.

———. *Ethik des Ethos.* Munich: K. Alber, 1974.

———. "*Anima separata* und Personsein bei Thomas von Aquin." In *Thomas von Aquino. Interpretation und Rezeption,* edited by W. P. Eckert. Mainz: Matthias-Grünewald, 1974.

———. "Glück und Glücksteilhabe. Zur Rezeption der aristotelischen Glückslehre bei Thomas von Aquin." In *Die Frage nach dem Glück,* edited by G. Bien. Stuttgart and Bad Canstatt: Frommann-Holzboog, 1978.

———. "Thomas von Aquin: Zum Gutsein des Handelns." *Philosophisches Jahrbuch* 87 (1980): 327–39.

———. *Moral-Vernunft-Natur. Beiträge zur Ethik.* Edited by W. Korff and P. Mikat. Paderborn: Schöningh, 1997.

Knauer, Peter. "Fundamentalethik: Teleologische als deontologische Normenbegründung." *Theologie und Philosophie* 55 (1980): 321–60.

Korff, Wilhelm. *Norm und Sittlichkeit. Untersuchungen zur Logik der normativen Vernunft.* 2nd ed. Freiburg and Munich: Alber, 1985 [1973].

———. *Wie kann der Mensch glücken? Perspektiven der Ethik.* Munich: Alber, 1985.

Korff, W. "Der Rückgriff auf die Natur. Eine Rekonstruktion der thomanischen Lehre vom natürlichen Gesetz." *Philosophisches Jahrbuch* 94 (1987): 285–98.

Krämer, Hans. *Integrative Ethik.* Frankfurt am Main: Suhrkamp, 1992.

Kriele, Martin. *Einführung in die Staatslehre. Die geschichtlichen Legitimitätsgrundlagen des demokratischen Verfassungsstaates.* 4th ed. Opladen: Westdeutscher Verlag, 1990.

Léonard, André. *Le fondement de la morale. Essai d'éthique philosophique.* Paris: Editions du Cerf, 1991.

Leist, Anton. *Die gute Handlung. Eine Einführung in die Ethik.* Berlin: Akademie, 2000.

Lisska, Anthony J. *Aquinas' Theory of Natural Law: An Analytic Reconstruction.* Oxford: Oxford University Press, 1996.

Long, Steven A. "A Brief Disquisition Regarding the Nature of the Object of the Moral Act According to St. Thomas Aquinas." *The Thomist* 67 (2003): 45–71.

———. *The Teleological Grammar of the Moral Act.* Naples, Fla.: Sapientia Press, 2007.

Lottin, Odon. "Syndérèse et conscience aux XIIe et XIIIe siècles." In *Psychologie et morale aux XII et XIIIe siècles,* vol. 2. Louvain and Gembloux: Abbaye de Mont César, 1948.

Louden, Robert B. "On Some Vices of Virtue Ethics." *American Philosophical Quarterly* 21 (1984): 227–36. Reprinted in Crisp, Roger, and Michael Slote, *Virtue Ethics* (see above).

Lübbe, Hermann. *Praxis der Philosophie, Praktische Philosophie, Geschichtstheorie.* Stuttgart: Reclam, 1978.

———. "Moral und Philosophie der Moral." In *Der Mensch und die Wissenschaften vom Menschen.* Die Beiträge des XII. Deutschen Kongresses für Philosophie in Innsbruck vom 29. September bis 3. Oktober 1981. Innsbruck: Solaris Verlag, 1983.

Lübbe, Weyma. *Verantwortung in komplexen kulturellen Prozessen.* Freiburg: Alber, 1998.

Machiavelli, Niccolò. *The Prince.* Translated by L. Ricci. In *The Prince and The Discourses.* New York: Modern Library, 1950.

———. *Discourses on the First Ten Books of Titus Livius.* Translated by C. Detmold. In *The Prince and The Discourses.* New York: Modern Library, 1950.

MacIntyre, Alasdair. "Was dem Handeln vorhergeht." In *Analytische Handlungstheorie,* vol. 2: *Handlungserklärungen,* edited by A. Beckermann. Frankfurt am Main: Suhrkamp, 1977.

———. *After Virtue*. 2nd ed. South Bend, Ind.: University of Notre Dame Press, 1984.

———. *Whose Justice? Whose Rationality?* South Bend, Ind.: University of Notre Dame Press, 1988.

———. *Three Rival Versions of Moral Enquiry*. South Bend, Ind.: University of Notre Dame Press, 1990.

———. *Dependent Rational Animals: Why Human Beings Need the Virtues*. Chicago and La Salle, Ill.: Open Court, 1999.

Malo, Antonio. *Antropologia dell'affettività*. Rome: Armando, 1999.

Marx, Karl. *Pariser Manuskripte von 1844*. In *Die Frühschriften*, edited by S. Landshut. Stuttgart: Kröner, 1953.

May, William E. "The Meaning and Nature of the Natural Law in Thomas Aquinas." *American Journal of Jurisprudence* 22 (1977): 168–89.

———. *Moral Absolutes: Catholic Tradition, Current Trends, and the Truth*. Milwaukee, Wis.: Marquette University Press, 1989.

McCloskey, H. J. "A Note on Utilitarian Punishment." *Mind* 72 (1963): 599.

McCormick, Richard A. *Notes on Moral Theology 1965 through 1980*. Lanham, M.D., and London: University Press of America, 1981.

McDowell, John. *Mind and World*. Cambridge, Mass., and London: Harvard University Press, 1994.

McInerny, Ralph. "The Principles of Natural Law." *American Journal of Jurisprudence* 25 (1980): 1–15.

———. *Ethica Thomistica: The Moral Philosophy of Thomas Aquinas*. Washington, D.C.: The Catholic University of America Press, 1982.

———. *Aquinas on Human Action: A Theory of Practice*. Washington, D.C.: The Catholic University of America Press, 1992.

———. *The Question of Christian Ethics*. The 1990 Michael J. McGivney Lecture. Washington, D.C.: The Catholic University of America Press, 1993.

Merks, K.-W. *Theologische Grundlegung der sittlichen Autonomie. Strukturmomente eines "autonomen" Normbegründungsverständnisses im lex-Traktat der Summa Theologiae des Thomas von Aquin*. Düsseldorf: Patmos-Verlag, 1978.

Melden, Abraham. *Free Action*. London: Routledge & Kegan Paul, 1961.

Melina, Livio. *La conoscenza morale. Linee di riflessione sistematica sul commento di S. Tommaso all'Etica Nicomachea*. Rome: Città nuova editrice, 1988.

Mill, John Stuart. *Utilitarianism*. In *Great Books of the Western World* 40. Chicago: Encyclopedia Britannica, 1952.

Moore, George Edward. *Principia Ethica*. Cambridge: Cambridge University Press, 1903.

Mulhall, Stephen, and Adam Swift. *Liberals and Communitarians*. Oxford and Cambridge, Mass.: Basil Blackwell, 1992.

Messner, J. *Das Naturrecht*. Innsbruck and Vienna: Tyrolia Verlag, 1966.

Müller, Anselm W. "Radical Subjectivity: Morality versus Utilitarianism." *Ratio* 19 (1977): 115–32.

———. "Praktische und technische Teleologie. Ein aristotelischer Beitrag zur Handlungstheorie." In *Philosophische Probleme der Handlungstheorie*, edited by H. Poser. Freiburg and Munich: Alber, 1982.

———. *Praktisches Folgern und Selbstgestaltung nach Aristoteles*. Freiburg and Munich: Alber, 1982.

————. *Was taugt die Tugend? Elemente einer Ethik des guten Lebens.* Stuttgart: W. Kohlhammer, 1998.

Müller-Goldkuhle, P. Response to "Wer hat wofür Verantwortung? Zum Streit um deontologische oder teleologische Ethik," by Robert Spaemann. *Herder Korrespondenz* 36 (1982): 606ff.

Murphy, William F. "Martin Rhonheimer's *Natural Law and Practical Reason.*" *Sapientia* 56, no. 210 (2001): 517–48.

————. "Aquinas on the Object and Evaluation of the Moral Act: Rhonheimer's Approach and Some Recent Interlocutors." *Josephinum Journal of Theology* 15, no. 2 (2008): 205–42.

Nagel, Thomas. "War and Massacre." In *Mortal Questions.* Cambridge: Cambridge University Press, 1979.

————. *The View from Nowhere.* Oxford: Oxford University Press, 1986.

Nelson, D. M. *The Priority of Prudence: Virtue and Natural Law in Thomas Aquinas and the Implications for Modern Ethics.* University Park: Pennsylvania State University Press, 1992.

Nida-Rümelin, J. *Kritik des Konsequentialismus.* 2nd ed. Munich: Oldenbourg, 1995.

Nisters, Thomas. *Akzidentien der Praxis. Thomas von Aquins Lehre von den Umständen menschlichen Handelns.* Freiburg and Munich: Alber, 1992.

Nunner-Winkler, Gertrud. "Zum Verständnis von Moral—Entwicklungen in der Kindheit." In *Entwicklung im Kindesalter,* edited by Franz E. Weinert. Weinheim: Beltz, 1998.

Nussbaum, Martha C. "Practical Syllogisms and Practical Science." In *Aristotle's De Motu Animalium. Text with Translation, Commentary, and Interpretive Essays.* Princeton, N.J.: Princeton University Press, 1978.

————. *The Fragility of Goodness: Luck and Ethics in Greek Tragedy and Philosophy.* Cambridge, Mass. and New York: Harvard University Press, 1986.

————. "The Discernment of Perception: An Aristotelian Conception of Private and Public Rationality." In *Love's Knowledge: Essays on Philosophy and Literature.* New York and Oxford: Oxford University Press, 1990.

————. "Non-Relative Virtues: An Aristotelian Approach." In *Ethical Theory: Character and Virtue,* edited by P. French, T. Uehling, and H. Wettstein. South Bend, Ind.: University of Notre Dame Press, 1988. Slightly expanded version available in *The Quality of Life,* by M. Nussbaum and A. Sen. Oxford: Oxford University Press, 1993.

Patzig. Günther. *Ethik ohne Metaphysik.* Göttingen: Vandenhoek u. Ruprecht, 1971.

Pellegrino, Edmund D. "Der tugendhafte Arzt und die Ethik der Medizin." In *Medizin und Ethik,* edited by H.-M. Sass. Stuttgart: Reclam, 1989.

Piaget, Jean. *Judgment and Reasoning in the Child.* Translated by M. Warden. Totowa, N.J.: Littlefield, Adams, 1976.

Pieper, Annemarie. *Ethik und Moral. Eine Einführung in die praktische Philosophie.* Munich: C. H. Beck, 1985.

Pieper, Josef. "Fortitude." Translated by D. F. Coogan. In *The Four Cardinal Virtues.* New York: Harcourt, Brace and World, 1965.

————. *Happiness and Contemplation.* Translated by R. Winston and C. Winston. Chicago: Henry Regnery, 1966.

————. *In Defense of Philosophy.* Translated by L. Krauth. San Francisco: Ignatius Press, 1992.

———. "Schriften zur Philosophischen Anthropologie und Ethik: Das Menschenbild der Tugendlehre." In *Werke in Acht Bänden*, edited by Berthold Wald, vol. 4. Hamburg: Meiner, 1996.

Pilsner, Joseph. *The Specification of Human Actions in St. Thomas Aquinas*. Oxford: Oxford University Press, 2006.

Pinckaers, Servais. *The Sources of Christian Ethics*. Washington, D.C.: The Catholic University of America Press, 1985.

———. *Ce qu'on ne peut jamais faire. La question des actes intrinsèquement mauvais. Histoire et discussion*. Fribourg: Éditions Universitaires de Fribourg; Paris: Éditions du Cerf, 1986.

Pincoffs, Edmund L. *Quandaries and Virtues: Against Reductivism in Ethics*. Lawrence: University of Kansas Press, 1986.

Pöltner, Günther. "Achtung der Würde und Schutz von Interessen." In *Der Mensch als Mitte und Maßstab der Medizin*, edited by J. Bonelli. Vienna and New York: Springer, 1992.

Rahner, Karl. "Über das Verhältnis von Natur und Gnade." In *Schriften zur Theologie*, vol. 1. Einsiedeln: Benziger, 1956.

Rawls, John. "Two Concepts of Rules." *Philosophical Review* 64 (1955): 3–32. Reprinted in *Collected Papers*, edited by Samuel Freeman. Cambridge, Mass.: Harvard University Press, 1999.

———. *A Theory of Justice*. Cambridge, Mass.: Belknap Press of Harvard University Press, 1971.

———. *Political Liberalism*. New York: Columbia University Press, 1993.

Raz, Joseph. *The Morality of Freedom*. Oxford: Clarendon Press, 1986.

Rhonheimer, Martin. *Politisierung und Legitimitätsentzug*. Freiburg and Munich: Alber, 1979.

———. *Familie und Selbstverwirklichung. Alternativen zur Emanzipation*. Cologne: Verlag Wissenshcaft und Politik, 1979.

———. "Sozialphilosophie und Familie. Gedanken zur humanen Grundfunktion der Familie." In *Familie—Herausforderung der Zukunft*, edited by B. Schnyder. Freiburg: Universitätsverlag, 1982.

———. *Natural Law and Practical Reason: A Thomist View of Moral Autonomy*. Translated by Gerald Malsbary. New York: Fordham University Press, 2000 [orig. *Natur als Grundlage der Moral: Eine Auseinandersetzung mit autonomischer un teleologischer Ethik*. Innsbruck and Vienna: Tyrolia, 1986].

———. "Natur als Grundlage der Moral: Nichts als Spiegelfechterei?" [A reply to S. Ernst, "Hat die autonome und teleologische Ethik . . ."]. *Theologie und Glaube* 79 (1989): 69–83.

———. "Gut und Böse oder richtig und falsch—was unterscheidet das Sittliche?" In *Ethik der Leistung*, edited by Hans Thomas. Herford: Busse Seewald, 1988.

———. "Menschliches Handeln und seine Moralität. Zur Begründung sittlicher Normen." In *Ethos und Menschenbild. Zur Überwindung der Krise der Moral*, edited by M. Rhonheimer, A. Laun, T. Goritschewa, and W. Mixa. St. Ottilien: EOS Verlag, 1989.

———. "Contraception, Sexual Behavior, and Natural Law: Philosophical Foundation of the Norm of *Humanae Vitae*." *Linacre Quarterly* 56, no. 2 (1989): 20–57.

————. "Ethik—Handeln—Sittlichkeit. Zur sittlichen Dimension menschlichen Tuns." In *Der Mensch als Mitte und Maßstab der Medizin*, edited by Johannes Bonelli. Vienna and New York: Springer, 1992. (Slightly edited and expanded version of "Gut und Böse oder richtig und falsch . . . ," above.)

————. "Zur Begründung sittlicher Normen aus der Natur. Grundsätzlich Erwägungen und Exemplifizierung am Beispiel der I.v.F." In *Der Mensch als Mitte und Maßstab der Medizin*, edited by J. Bonelli. Vienna and New York: Springer, 1992.

————. "Perché una filosofia politica? Elementi storici per una risposta." *Acta Philosophica* 1 (1992): 233–63.

————. "Die Instrumentalisierung menschlichen Lebens. Ethische Erwägungen zur In-Vitro-Fertilisierung." In *Fortpflanzungsmedizin und Lebensschutz*, edited by F. Bydlinski and Theo Mayer-Maly. Innsbruck and Vienna: Tyrolia, 1993.

————. "'Ethics of Norms' and the Lost Virtues: Searching the Roots of the Crisis of Ethical Reasoning." *Anthropotes* 9 (1993): 231–43.

————. *Praktische Vernunft und Vernünftigkeit der Praxis. Handlungstheorie bei Thomas von Aquin in ihrer Entstehung aus dem Problemkontext der aristotelischen Ethik*. Berlin: Akademie Verlag, 1994.

————. "'Intrinsically Evil Acts' and the Moral Viewpoint: Clarifying a Central Teaching of *Veritatis splendor*." *The Thomist* 58 (1994): 1–39. Reprinted in "*Veritatis Splendor" and the Renewal of Moral Theology*, edited by J. A. Di Noia and R. Cessario. Princeton, N.J.-Huntington-Chicago: Scepter, 1999, and in *The Perspective of the Acting Person*, chapter 3.

————. "Empfängnisverhütung, Sexualverhalten und Menschenbild." *Imago Hominis* 2 (1995): 145–52.

————. "Sexualität und Verantwortung. Empfängnisverhütung als ethisches Problem." IMABE-Studie Nr. 3. Vienna: IMABE—Institut für medizinische Anthropologie und Bioethik, 1995. Translated by Joseph T. Papa for *The Ethics of Procreation and the Defense of Human Life*, chapters 2, 3, and 4.

————. "Human Fetuses, Persons, and the Right to Abortion: Toward an Absolute Power of the Born." In *Ethics of Procreation and the Defense of Human Life*, edited by W. Murphy. Washington, D.C.: The Catholic University of America Press, 2010.

————. "Intentional Actions and the Meaning of Object: A Reply to Richard McCormick." *The Thomist* 59 (1995): 279–311. Reprinted in "*Veritatis Splendor" and the Renewal of Moral Theology*, edited by J. A. Di Noia and R. Cessario. Princeton, N.J.-Huntington-Chicago: Scepter, 1999, and in *The Perspective of the Acting Person*, chapter 4.

————. *La filosofia politica di Thomas Hobbes. Coerenza e contraddizioni di un paradigma*. Rome: Armando, 1996.

————. "Ethik als Aufklärung über die Frage nach dem Guten und die Aristotelische 'Perversion des ethischen Themas.' Anmerkungen zu W. Pannenbergs Aristoteleskritik." *Anthropotes* 13 (1997): 211–23.

————. "Lo stato costituzionale democratico e il bene comune." In *Ripensare lo spazio politico: Quale aristocrazia?* edited by E. Morandi and R. Panattoni. Special issue: *Con-tratto—Rivista di filosofia tomista e contemporanea* 7 (1997). Padua: Il Poligrafo, 1998.

———. "Fundamental Rights, Moral Law, and the Legal Defense of Life in a Constitutional Democracy: A Constitutionalist Approach to the Encyclical *Evangelium Vitae.*" *American Journal of Jurisprudence* 43 (1998): 135–83. Translated by P. Carozza for *Ethics of Procreation and the Defense of Human Life*, chapter 7.

———. "Contrattualismo, individualismo e solidarietà: Per rileggere la tradizione liberale." *Per la filosofia* 16, no. 46 (1999): 30–40.

———. Author's Postscript (1995). In *Natural Law and Practical Reason: A Thomist View of Moral Autonomy*. New York: Fordham University Press, 2000 (pp. 555–92 of English translation of *Natur als Grundlage der Moral;* see above [1986]).

———. *Etica della procreazione. Contraccezione—Fecondazione artificiale—Aborto.* Rome: Pontificia Universita Lateranense and Milan-Mursia: Edizioni PUL, 2000.

———. "*Auctoritas non veritas facit legem:* Thomas Hobbes, Carl Schmitt and the Idea of the Constitutional State." [German orig. 2000] Translated by Gerald Malsbary. Forthcoming in *Essays in Political Philosophy and Catholic Social Teaching.* Washington, D.C.: The Catholic University of America Press, 2010.

———. "Practical Reason and the 'Naturally Rational': On the Doctrine of the Natural Law as a Principle of Praxis in Thomas Aquinas." [German orig. 2000] Translated by Gerald Malsbary for *The Perspective of the Acting Person*, chapter 5.

———. "Praktische Prinzipien, Naturgesetz und konkrete Handlungsurteile in tugendethischer Perspektive. Zur Diskussion über praktische Vernunft und lex naturalis bei Thomas von Aquin." *Studia Moralia* 39 (2001): 113–58.

———. "Sins against Justice (I–IIae, qq. 59–78)." In *The Ethics of Aquinas*, edited by Stephen J. Pope. Washington, D.C.: Georgetown University Press, 2002.

———. "The Cognitive Structure of the Natural Law and the Truth of Subjectivity." *The Thomist* 67, no. 1 (2003): 1–44. Reprinted in *The Perspective of the Acting Person*, chapter 7.

———. "The Moral Significance of Pre-Rational Nature in Aquinas: A Reply to Jean Porter (and Stanley Hauerwas)." *American Journal of Jurisprudence* 48 (2003): 253–80. Reprinted in *The Perspective of the Acting Person*, chapter 6.

———. *Abtreibung und Lebensschutz. Tötungsverbot und Recht auf Leben in der politischen und medizinischen Ethik.* Paderborn: Verlag Ferdinand Schöningh, 2003.

———. "The Perspective of the Acting Person and the Nature of Practical Reason: The 'Object of the Human Act' in Thomistic Anthropology of Action." [Italian orig. 2003] Translated by Joseph T. Papa in *Nova et Vetera* 2, no. 2 (2004): 461–516. Reprinted in *The Perspective of the Acting Person*, chapter 8.

———. "Practical Reason and the Truth of Subjectivity: The Self-Experience of the Moral Subject at the Roots of Metaphysics and Anthropology." [Italian orig. 2004] Translated by Gerald Malsbary for *The Perspective of the Acting Person*, chapter 9.

———. *The Perspective of the Acting Person: Essays in the Renewal of Thomistic Moral Philosophy.* Edited by William F. Murphy. Washington, D.C.: The Catholic University of America Press.

———. *Cristianismo y laicidad. Historia y actualidad de una relación compleja.* Madrid: Rialp, 2009. Originally published in Italian as "Cristianesimo e laicità: Storia ed attualità di un rapporto complesso, in *Laicità: La ricerca dell'universale nella differenza,* edited by Pierpaolo Donati (Bologna: Il Mulino, 2008), 27–138. English translation "Christianity and Secularity" in my forthcoming *The Common Good of Constitutional Democracy: Essays in Political Philosophy and on Catholic Social Teaching.*

———. *Vital Conflicts in Medical Ethics: A Virtue Approach to Craniotomy and Tubal Pregnancies.* Washington, D.C.: The Catholic University of America, 2009.

———. *Ethics of Procreation and the Defense of Human Life: Contraception, Artificial Fertilization, and Abortion.* Washington, D.C.: The Catholic University of America, 2010.

Ricken, Friedo. *Der Lustbegriff in der Nikomachischen Ethik des Aristoteles.* Göttingen: Vandenhoek u. Ruptrecht, 1976.

———. *Allgemeine Ethik.* Stuttgart: W. Kohlhammer, 1983.

———. "Kann die Moralphilosophie auf die Frage nach dem 'Ethischen' verzichten?" *Theologie und Philosophie* 59 (1984): 161–77.

———. "Die Rationalität der Religion in der analytischen Philosophie: Swinburne, Mackie, Wittgenstein." *Philosophisches Jahrbuch* 99 (1992): 287–306.

———. "Aristoteles und die moderne Tugendethik." *Theologie und Philosophie* 74 (1999): 391–404.

Riedel, Manfred. "Handlungstheorie als ethische Grunddisziplin." In *Handlungstheorien interdisziplinär,* edited by H. Lenk. Vol. 2, I. Munich: W. Fink, 1978.

Rippe, Klaus Peter, and Peter Schaber. *Tugendethik.* Stuttgart: Reclam, 1998.

Ritter, Joachim. *Metaphysik und Politik. Studien zu Aristoteles und Hegel.* Frankfurt am Main: Suhrkamp, 1969.

Rodríguez-Luño, Angel. *La scelta etica: Il rapporto fra libertà e virtù.* Milan: Edizioni Ares, 1988.

———. *Etica.* Florence: Le Monnier, 1992.

Rorty, Richard. *Solidarität oder Objektivität? Drei philosophische Essays.* Translated by J. Sculte. Stuttgart: Reclam, 1988.

———. *Contingency, Irony, and Solidarity.* Cambridge: Cambridge University Press, 1989.

Ross, W. D. *The Right and the Good.* Reprint. Oxford: Clarendon Press, 1965.

Rotenstreich, Nathan. *Practice and Realization: Studies in Kant's Moral Philosophy.* The Hague-Boston-London: Martinus Nijhoff, 1979.

Rousseau, Jean-Jacques. *Du contrat social,* in *Oeuvres complètes,* edited by B. Gagnebin and M. Raymond, vol. 3. Paris: Gallimard, 1964.

Sala, Johannes B. "Das Gesetz oder das Gute? Zum Ursprung und Sinn des Formalismus in der Ethik Kants." *Gregorianum* 71 (1990): 67–95, 315–52.

Sandel, Michael. *Liberalism and the Limits of Justice.* Cambridge: Cambridge University Press, 1982.

Sartre, Jean-Paul. "Existentialism and Humanism." Translated by P. Mairet. In *Basic Writings,* edited by S. Priest. New York: Routledge, 2000.

Schaber, Peter. *Moralischer Realismus.* Freiburg and Munich: Alber, 1997.

Scheffler, Samuel, ed. *Consequentialism and Its Critics.* Oxford: Oxford University Press, 1988.

Scheler, Max. *Formalism in Ethics and Non-Formal Ethics of Values.* Translated by M. S. Springs and R. L. Funk. Evanston, Ill.: Northwestern University Press, 1973 [1916].

Schenk, Richard. *Die Gnade vollendeter Endlichkeit. Zur transzendentaltheologischen*

Auslegung der thomanischen Anthropologie. Freiburger Theologische Studien 135. Freiburg im Breisgau-Basel-Vienna: Herder, 1989.

———. *Perplexus supposito quodam.* "Notizen zu einem vergessenen Schlüsselbegriff thomanischer Gewissenslehre." *Recherches de Theologie ancienne et medievale* 57 (1990): 62–95.

Schlag, Martin. *Das moralische Gesetz in Evangelium Vitae.* Frankfurt am Main: Suhrkamp, 2000.

Schnädelbach, Herbert. "Was ist Neoaristotelismus?" In *Moralität und Sittlichkeit. Das Problem Hegels und die Diskursethik,* edited by W. Kuhlmann. Frankfurt am Main: Suhrkamp, 1986.

Schneewind, Jerome B. "The Misfortunes of Virtue." In *Virtue Ethics,* edited by Roger Crisp and Michael Slote (see above under "Crisp").

———. *The Invention of Autonomy: A History of Modern Moral Philosophy.* Cambridge: Cambridge University Press, 1998.

Schockenhoff, Eberhard. *Bonum hominis. Die anthropologischen und theologischen Grundlagen der Tugendethik des Thomas von Aquin.* Mainz: Matthias-Grünewald, 1987.

———. *Das umstrittene Gewissen. Eine theologische Grundlegung.* Mainz: Matthias-Grünewald, 1990.

———. *Natural Law and Human Dignity: Universal Ethics in an Historical World.* Translated by Brian McNeil. Washington, D.C.: The Catholic University of America Press, 2003 [orig. *Naturrecht und Menschenwürde. Universalethik in einer geschichtlichen Welt.* Mainz: Matthias-Grunewald, 1996].

———. *Wie gewiss ist das Gewissen? Eine ethische Orientierung.* Freiburg im Breisgau.: Herder, 2003.

———. *Grundlegung der Ethik. Ein theologischer Entwurf.* Freiburg im Breisgau.: Herder, 2007.

Schröer, C. *Praktische Vernunft bei Thomas von Aquin,* Münchener philosophische Studien. Neue Folge 10. Stuttgart-Berlin-Cologne: W. Kohlhammer, 1995.

Schüller, Bruno. *Die Begründung sittlicher Urteile. Typen ethischer Argumentation in der Moraltheologie.* 2nd ed. Düsseldorf: Patmos, 1980.

———. "Der gute Zweck und die schlechten Mittel." In *Der menschliche Mensch. Aufsätze zur Metaethik und zur Sprache der Moral.* Düsseldorf: Patmos, 1982.

———. "Die Quellen der Moralität. Zur systematischen Ortung eines alten Lehrstückes der Moraltheologie." *Theologie und Philosophie* 59 (1984): 535–59.

———. "Das Muster einer schlagenden Widerlegung des Utilitarismus." In *Pluralismus in der Ethik. Zum Stil wissenschaftlicher Kontroversen.* Münster: Aschendorff, 1988.

Schuster, J. *Moralisches Können. Studien zur Tugendethik.* Würzburg: Echter, 1997.

Schwarz, Stephan. *The Moral Question of Abortion.* Chicago: Loyola University Press, 1990.

Seidl, Horst. *Sittengesetz und Freiheit. Erörterungen zur Allgemeinen Ethik.* Weilheim and Bierbronnen: Gustav-Siewerth-Akademie, 1992.

Sherwin, Michael. *By Knowledge and by Love: Charity and Knowledge in the Moral Theology of St. Thomas Aquinas.* Washington, D.C.: The Catholic University of America Press, 2005.

Sidgwick, Henry. *The Methods of Ethics.* Reprint of the 7th ed. [1907; orig. 1874] with a preface by John Rawls. Indianapolis, Ind., and Cambridge, Mass.: Hackett, 1982.

Slote, Michael. *From Morality to Virtue*. New York and Oxford: Oxford University Press, 1992.

Smart, J.J.C. "An Outline of a System of Utilitarian Ethics." In *Utilitarianism For and Against*. Edited by J.J.C. Smart and B. Williams. Cambridge: Cambridge University Press, 1973.

Sorabji, Richard. "Aristotle on the Rôle of Intellect in Virtue." *Proceedings of the Aristotelian Society*, n.s., 74 (1973–1974): 107–29.

Sousa-Lara, Duarte. "Aquinas on the Object of the Human Act: A Reading in Light of the Texts and Commentators." *Josephinum Journal of Theology* 15, no. 2 (2008): 243–76.

———. "Aquinas on Interior and Exterior Acts: Clarifying a Key Aspect of His Action Theory." *Josephinum Journal of Theology* 15, no. 2 (2008): 277–316.

Spaemann, Robert. "Wer hat wofür Verantwortung? Zum Streit um deontologische oder teleologische Ethik." *Herder Korrespondenz* 36 (1982).

———. "Die kontroverse Natur der Philosophie." In *Philosophische Essays*. Stuttgart: P. Reclam, 1983.

———. "Nochmals: Deontologische oder teleologische Moralbegründung?" *Herder Korrespondenz* 37 (1983): 79–84.

———. "Über den Begriff der Menschenwürde." In *Das Natürliche und das Vernünftige, Aufsätze zur Anthropologie*. Munich: Piper, 1987.

———. *Basic Moral Concepts*. Translated by T.J. Armstrong. London and New York: Routledge, 1989 [orig. 1982].

———. *Happiness and Benevolence*. Translated by J. Alberg, S.J. South Bend, Ill., and London: University of Notre Dame Press, 2000 [orig. 1989].

———. *Persons: The Difference between "Someone" and "Something."* Translated by O. O'Donovan. Oxford: Oxford University Press, 2006 [orig. 1996].

———. "Teleologie." In *Handlexikon zur Wissenschaftstheorie*, edited by H. Seiffert and G. Radnitzky. Munich: Deutshcer Taschenbuch, 1989.

———. "Sind alle Menschen Personen? Über neue philosophische Rechtfertigungen der Lebensvernichtung." In *Tüchtig oder tot. Die Entsorgung des Leidens*, edited by J.-P. Stüssel. Freiburg im Breisgau: Herder, 1991. (For a slightly altered version, see "Person ist der Mensch selbst, nicht ein bestimmter Zustand des Menschen," in *Menschlichkeit der Medizin*, edited by H. Thomas. Herford: Busse-Seewald, 1993.)

——— and Reinhard Löw. *Die Frage Wozu? Geschichte und Wiederentdeckung des teleologischen Denkens*. Munich: Piper, 1981.

Spitzley, Thomas. *Handeln wider besseres Wissen. Eine Diskussion klassischer Positionen*. Berlin and New York: Walter de Gruyter, 1992.

Stanke, Gerhard. *Die Lehre von den "Quellen der Moralität." Darstellung und Diskussion der neuscholastischen Aussagen und neuerer Ansätze*. Regensburg: Pustet, 1984.

Steinvorth, Ulrich. *Klassische und moderne Ethik. Grundlinien einer materialen Moraltheorie*. Reinbek bie Hamburg: Rowohlt, 1990.

Stocker, Michael. "The Schizophrenia of Modern Ethical Theories." *Journal of Philosophy* 73 (1976): 453–66. Also in Roger Crisp and M. Slote, eds., *Virtue Ethics* (see Crisp above).

Styczen, Tadeusz. "Das Gewissen—Quelle der Freiheit oder der Knechtung?" *Archiv für Religionspsychologie* 17 (1986): 130–47.

Sutor, Bernhard. *Politische Ethik. Gesamtdarstellung auf der Basis der Christlichen Gesellschaftslehre*. Paderborn: Schöningh, 1991.

Taylor, Charles. "What Is Human Agency?" In *Human Agency and Language: Philosophical Papers*, vol. 1. Cambridge: Cambridge University Press, 1985.

———. "What's Wrong with Negative Liberty?" In *Philosophy and the Human Sciences: Philosophical Papers*, vol. 2. Cambridge: Cambridge University Press, 1985.

———. *Sources of the Self: The Making of the Modern Identity*. Cambridge, Mass.: Harvard University Press, 1989.

———. *The Ethics of Authenticity*. Cambridge, Mass. and London: Harvard University Press, 1991. Also available as *The Malaise of Modernity*. Concord, Ontario: Anansi, 1991.

Tonneau, J. *Absolu et obligation en morale*. Montréal: Institute d'études médiévales; Paris: J. Vrin, 1965.

Tugendhat, Ernst. *Probleme der Ethik*. Stuttgart: Reclam, 1984.

Veatch, Henry B. *Rational Man: A Modern Interpretation of Aristotelian Ethics*. Bloomington and London: Indiana University Press, 1962.

———. *Human Rights: Fact or Fancy?* Baton Rouge: Louisiana State University Press, 1985.

———. *Swimming against the Current in Contemporary Philosophy*. Washington, D.C.: The Catholic University of America Press, 1990.

Virt, Gunter. *Epikie—verantwortlicher Umgang mit Normen. Eine historisch-systematische Untersuchung zu Aristoteles, Thomas von Aquin und Franz Suarez*. Mainz: Matthias-Grünewald-Verlag, 1983.

Von Wright, Georg Henrik. *The Varieties of Goodness*. Bristol, U.K.: Thoemmes Press, 1993 [1963].

———. "Das menschliche Handeln im Lichte seiner Ursachen und Gründe." In *Handlungstheorien interdisziplinär*, edited by H. Lenk, vol. 2, II. Munich: Fink, 1979.

Vossenkuhl, Wilhelm. "Freiheit zu handeln. Analytische und transzendentale Argumente für eine kausale Handlungstheorie." In *Prinzip Freiheit*, edited by H. M. Baumgartner and K. O. Apel. Freiburg and Munich: Alber, 1979.

Wald, Berthold. "Moralische Verbindlichkeit und menschliches Richtigsein. Zur Rehabilitierung der Tugend." *Theologie und Philosophie* 72 (1997): 553–64.

Waldron, Jeremy, ed. *Theories of Rights*. Oxford: Oxford University Press, 1984.

Walsh, James. *Aristotle's Conception of Moral Weakness*. New York: Columbia University Press, 1963.

Walzer, Michael. *Spheres of Justice: A Defence of Pluralism and Equality*. Oxford: Oxford University Press, 1985.

Weinreb, Lloyd. *Natural Law and Justice*. Cambridge, Mass.: Harvard University Press, 1987.

Wellmer, Albrecht. *Ethik und Dialog. Elemente des moralischen Urteils bei Kant und in der Diskursethik*. Frankfurt am Main: Suhrkamp, 1986.

Westberg, Daniel. *Right Practical Reason: Aristotle, Action, and Prudence in Aquinas*. Oxford: Clarendon Press, 1994.

Wieland, G. "Secundum naturam vivere. Über das Verhältnis von Natur und Sittlichkeit." In *Natur im ethischen Argument*, Studien zur theologischen Ethik 31, edited by B. Fraling. Freiburg: Herder, 1990.

Williams, Bernard. *Morality: An Introduction to Ethics*. New York: Harper & Row, 1972.

———. "A Critique of Utilitarianism." In *Utilitarianism: For and Against*, by J. J. C. Smart and Bernard Williams. Cambridge: Cambridge University Press, 1973.

———. *Ethics and the Limits of Philosophy*. Cambridge, Mass.: Harvard University Press, 1985.

Wittgenstein, Ludwig. *Philosophical Investigations*. Translated by G. E. M. Anscombe. Edited by G. E. M. Anscombe and R. Rhees. Oxford: Basil Blackwell, 1958.

Wittmann, Michael. *Die Ethik des Hl. Thomas von Aquin*. Munich: M. Hueber Verlag, 1933.

Wolbert, Werner. *Vom Nutzen der Gerechtigkeit. Zur Diskussion um Utilitarismus und teleologische Theorie*. Freiburg, Switzerland-Freiburg im Breisgau: Universitätsverlag, 1992.

Wolf, Jean-Claude. *Verhütung oder Vergeltung? Einführung in ethische Straftheorien*. Freiburg and Munich: Alber, 1992.

———. "Der intendierte Tod." In *Das medizinisch assistierte Sterben. Zur Sterbehilfe aus medizinischer, ethischer, juristischer und theologischer Sicht*, edited by A. Holderegger. Freiburg, Switzerland-Freiburg im Breisgau-Vienna: Herder, 1999.

——— and Peter Schaber. *Analytische Moralphilosophie*. Freiburg and Munich: K. Alber, 1998.

Wolf, Ursula. *Das Problem des moralischen Sollens*. Berlin and New York: Walter de Gruyter, 1984.

———. *Die Philosophie und die Frage nach dem guten Leben*. Reinbek bei Hamburg: Rowohlt, 1999.

Wolter, Hans., ed. *Testimonium Veritati*. Frankfurt am Main: J. Knecht, 1971.

Index

Rendtdorff, Trutz, 29n68, 273n31
res aliena, 150–51
"return to Aristotle" (MacIntyre), 237
revelation, 25–26, 29–30, 81–83, 85, 89–90,
229, 240, 261, 424; morality considered independently of revelation, 147, 185, 333; of
(human) benevolence, 417. *See also* faith;
God; revelation
Rhonheimer, Martin, 39n4, 91n117, 91n120,
104n15, 109n19, 111n26, 116, 124n51,
131n62, 154n98, 156n100, 158n101, 160n103,
185n147, 197n18, 236n106, 252n144,
254n150, 273n32, 273n33, 277n43, 289n58,
295n72, 297, 298n80, 299n84, 300n86,
304n92, 334n176, 340n188, 341n190,
360n214, 362n222, 370n231, 378n240,
390n259, 391n260, 393, 403n275, 420n302
Ricken, Friedoc, 7n12, 16n43, 42n9, 49n7,
194n8, 197n17
Riedel, Manfred, 47n2, 137, 212n48
right reason. *See* reason; *recta ratio*
right/wrong, as distinct from good/bad, 127,
131–33, 249n132, 401, 405. *See also* moral
rights. *See* human rights; natural
Ringeling, Hermann, 29n68, 273n31
Rippe, Klaus, 14n38, 74n68, 223n73
Rodriguez-Luño, Angel, 197n18, 202n33,
225n79
Rorty, Amély O., 70n56
Rorty, Richard, 290
Ross, W. D., 131n64, 133n67, 377n238
Rousseau, Jean J., 266
routine and moral virtue, 204, 209–11
Ruggiero, Guido de, 236n104
Ryle, Gilbert, 56

Sala, Johannes B., 260
Sandel, Michael, 249n132
sapientia / sophia, 191
Sartre, Jean-Paul, 2, 24, 42, 177, 331
Sass, Hans-Martin, 375n235
Schaber, Peter, 9n21, 11n25, 14n38, 17n46,
74n68, 223n73, 410n283
Scheffler, Samuel, 399n272, 410n283,
411n284
Scheler, Max, 20, 95, 323, 327
Schenk, Richard, 321n141
science(s). *See* theoretical and practical
sciences
Schlag, Martin, 362n222
Schluchter, Wolfgang, 273n33, 295n71
Schnädelbach, Herbert, 9n19

Schneewind, Jerome B., 19n53, 199n21,
253n146, 260n11
Schnur, Roman, 252n144
Schnyder, Hans-Josef, 214n57, 289n58
Schockenhoff, Eberhard, 66n47, 77n87,
197n18, 234n102, 278n45, 296n76, 302,
303, 304, 313n117, 320n138, 379n241,
400n273
Schofield, Malcolm, 109n19, 227n81
Schröer, Christian, 260n8, 273n33, 277n44,
279n47, 295, 299n84, 302
Schüller, Bruno, 127n54, 201n30, 229n84,
340n188, 349, 378n239, 383n250, 408n279,
413n292
Schuster, Joseph, 14n38, 19n52
Schwarz, Stephan, 393n261
scientia / epistēmē, 191
Scott-Taggart, M., 399n272
Searle, John R., 347
self-defense, 156, 362–63, 368n227, 395–96.
See also killing
self-denial, 28, 174, 241, 316, 419
self-experience, 40, 267. *See also* experience;
reflectivity
self-interest, 5–6, 9, 13, 230, 420
self-preservation, 52, 57, 75, 120, 123–24, 126,
141, 178, 190, 230, 279–82, 356. *See also*
natural inclination
self-realization, 59–60
semper et pro semper, 370. *See also ut in
pluribus*
Sen, Amartya, 22n58, 250n134, 338n183
Seneca, Lucius Annaeus, 215
sense perception, 51–52, 57n25, 77, 80, 116,
121, 163–69, 172, 187, 191, 216, 275
sense pleasure. *See* pleasure
sensitive appetites. *See* concupisciple appetitive power; irascible appetitive power
sexuality, 26, 107, 153, 156, 164, 174, 217–19,
230, 242, 280–81, 287–89, 370n231, 387. *See
also* adultery; chastity; conjugal union;
natural inclination; temperance
"should." *See* ought
Sidgwick, Henry, 416n298
sin, 166n116, 320, 424–25. *See also* vice(s)
Singer, Peter, 265n21
Slote, Michael, 14n38, 32n71, 159n102, 189n1,
199n21, 206n38, 245n124, 250n134, 253n146,
322n143, 352n204, 375n236, 398n266,
413n291
Smart, J. J., 340n188, 345, 367, 393n263,
398n269, 404

The Perspective of Morality: Philosophical Foundations of Thomistic Virtue Ethics was designed and typeset in Meta Serif with Meta Sans display type by Kachergis Book Design of Pittsboro, North Carolina. It was printed on 60-pound House Natural Smooth, and bound by Sheridan Books of Ann Arbor, Michigan.